Reformation and Early Modern Europe

a guide to research

Edited by

DAVID M. WHITFORD

Sixteenth Century Essays & Studies 79
Truman State University Press

Cover art: Hans Holbein the Younger, The Ambassadors, 1533. Oil on canvas, National Gallery, London. Photo reproduced by permission of Erich Lessing / Art Resource, NY.

Cover design: Shaun Hoffeditz
Type: MinionPro is a registered copyright of Adobe Systems Inc.
Printed by: Thomson-Shore, Dexter, Michigan USA

Library of Congress Cataloging-in-Publication Data
Reformation and early modern Europe : a guide to research / edited by David M. Whitford.
    p. cm. — (Sixteenth century essays & studies ; v. 79.)
Includes bibliographical references and index.
ISBN 978-1-931112-72-7 (cloth bound : alk. paper)
1. Reformation—Europe. 2. Europe—Church history—16th century. 3. Europe—Church history—17th century. I. Whitford, David M. (David Mark)
BR305.3.R42 2007
274'.06072—dc22
                                                                        2007046362

Contents

Preface
New Schools, New Tools,
and New Texts

In 1982, Steven Ozment began his preface to *Reformation Europe: A Guide to Research* by stating, "There is no field of historical study today that is more alive with change and fresh ideas than that of Reformation Europe." This remains very true today, but for very different reasons than when Ozment edited that first guide to research, or even in 1992 when William Maltby edited the second.[1] These reasons are new schools, new tools, and new texts. I have used the phrase "new schools, new tools, and new texts" for some time in my first lecture on the European Reformations; it is catchy enough for students to remember easily and encompassing enough to be useful. Many students already know that the Reformation was born out of a newly established school, the University of Wittenberg, and they also know that new tools such as the printing press spread the message of the Reformers and their opponents far and wide, pouring out new texts at great speeds. But there are other new schools, tools, and texts of which they might never have heard: new schools of thought in areas as diverse as painting, or music, or philosophy; new tools that made possible advances in mapmaking, navigation, philology, and painting; and new texts that were born to new audiences and presented in new and exciting ways.

The explosion of these new texts and new tools enabled fifteenth- and sixteenth-century humanists and scholars to look at themselves and their

---

[1]Maltby's research guide, titled *Reformation Europe: A Guide to Research II*, was also published by the Center for Reformation Research. Another volume, *Catholicism in Early Modern History: A Guide to Research* (by John W. O'Malley), was published in 1987.

world differently. Similarly, twentieth- and twenty-first-century developments in information technology have given scholars of early modern Europe access to methods and approaches to practicing history, a sort of contemporary version of "new schools, new tools, and new texts." When Ozment's Reformation research guide went to press, IBM was rolling out the first IBM PC, which ran an 8088 processor at 4.77 megahertz and had 16 kilobytes of memory. When Maltby edited the second Reformation research guide in 1992, the Internet did not exist. I managed to make it through my entire higher education journey without ever emailing a professor, and when I went to Germany to do dissertation research, I handwrote letters and licked stamps to mail them home. I did use disk-based databases for bibliographic research and as a work-study student even helped transfer a card catalog to a computer catalog, but throughout my educational experience one still had to double-check the card catalog and the paper indexes. Today card catalogs are gone from nearly all libraries and most indexes are not even put on disk anymore, let alone paper.

As I write this preface, I am sitting in my home office, which is linked to my office at the university. A four-gigabyte thumb drive on my key chain automatically syncs to my hard drive; it is roughly 62,000 times the size of the 8088 PC on which I wrote my senior thesis, my master's thesis, and at least half of my dissertation. Advances in information technology have transformed early modern historiography in dramatic and exciting ways. Traveling for archival research is becoming less and less essential, because often primary documents can come to you. It is now possible to sit in an office in the United States, and access the British Archives, search for a sea captain, and download a PDF copy of his last will and testament executed in March 1584. These texts also become part of a personal digital library of hundreds of thousands of pages of early modern texts. The ability to search full-text editions of sixteenth-century texts, such as Early English Books Online or the online edition of *Luthers Werke,* has only become available since 2000, and the implications of research that uses this technology to its fullest extent have barely been felt. These new tools have radically democratized the availability of scholarship.

There are still, of course, the haves and the have-nots; however, the gap is shrinking. Even as recently as ten to fifteen years ago, a scholar at a small teaching-intensive college with no chance for a sabbatical had very little opportunity to research archive-intensive projects. This is no longer true—archives and libraries across the globe are digitizing their collections;

the Google Books Library Project has massive numbers of books digitized and ready for download. While some must still make periodic treks to a research university to get access to subscription-based websites, many primary resources are freely available. In these ways, the new tools of Internet and online research have vastly increased the number of new schools at which one can do serious and sustained primary-source research.

These new tools have opened a wealth of new texts to scholarly investigation, making early modern historians resemble early humanists exclaiming with joy over a newly found classical text. Of all historians, Reformation scholars have perhaps the most to gain from the texts these new tools make available. For historians of the classical and medieval eras, the dependence upon hand copying limited the number and volume of potential texts to be found and examined. While unknown classical or medieval texts do crop up in old libraries and secluded monasteries, these are rare and even more rarely earthshaking. For modern historians, personal papers, memoranda, and the like remain hidden away in archives, but printed works are widely disseminated, easily found, and freely available through interlibrary loan. The early modern historian of earlier generations, in contrast, had to deal with exponentially exploding numbers of texts that are rare, valuable, and never loaned. Certainly many important texts were available in critical editions, but the editors of critical editions often distorted these texts by impressing their own perspectives on them. Today, because of the Internet, PDF versions of early modern editions make it possible to see what people read in the sixteenth and seventeenth centuries without editorial lenses getting in the way. Certainly, in earlier eras, texts were microfilmed or microfiched, but these copies, too, were often difficult to track down and do not nearly approach the width and breadth of texts currently available online. The availability to find, download, and analyze these newly available texts is transforming our understanding of the early modern era.

The previous research guides helped a generation of young scholars orient themselves to the field of sixteenth-century European history. These previous guides continue to have great value in that they track where the scholarly community was ten and twenty years ago, but like maps that must be updated with new roads and name changes, the guides must be updated to be of any practical use. This new research guide has eighteen chapters of varying lengths. There has been no attempt to duplicate information on the previous research guides; instead, we have worked to update what needs to be revised and pointed out the ways in which the fields are continuing to evolve. Some topics are completely new and are therefore longer.

As in previous research guides, three questions have guided this volume: What is the present state of research in the field, especially the trendsetting new studies that are challenging (or perhaps trying to reassert) traditional views? What are the key issues scholars in the field are struggling with and trying to resolve? And what are the fundamental works in the field and where are the strategic collections or centers of research? In other words, where are we now, where are we going, and how do we get from here to there? Many of the essays include a discussion of the Internet's role in the field; even where the Internet and its new tools and new texts may not touch scholarship today, they will soon. The students who read this volume today will no doubt help write that story.

While the articles are organized thematically and geographically, there are places of overlap among many of the articles. This is a conscious choice—one cannot study sixteenth-century art without understanding sixteenth-century religious and political realities. This volume is designed so that one may read just one article; however, the authors hope that reading one article will raise enough questions and spark enough interest that readers will want to look at others as well.

Acknowledgments

I would like to thank a few persons who helped make this project possible. Daria Schaffnit, a divinity student at United Theological Seminary, helped me convert diverse author styles into a consistent presentation. I also thank the authors in this volume who realized the importance of issuing a new research guide and who have kept before them the mission of helping new students acclimate themselves to the field of early modern studies. Members of the Society for Reformation Research stepped into the gap to take ownership of the idea behind the research guides when the Center for Reformation Research ceased to exist. Merry Wiesner-Hanks, then president of SRR, encouraged me to undertake the task when I raised it as an idea. My wife, Laurel, and daughter, Abby, who remind me of the importance of the twenty-first century even while patiently listening to me rattle on about the sixteenth. Finally, in a volume dedicated to helping students, I would like to thank two historians who taught me to love history. First and foremost, I thank my father Charles. Though he left the ranks of professional historians to become a Methodist pastor, he has remained a historian by avocation. He worked his way through graduate school as a researcher for the Minuteman National Park Project (now the Minuteman National Historic Park) in Concord, Massachusetts. When we were growing up near Concord, my dad would take my brother and me to the Old North Bridge and tell us stories of the men who fought and died there. I still remember hiding behind a stone wall with him and my brother to get a feel for what the patriots did. My childhood was a running history lesson, and he is more responsible for my love of history than any other person. I also thank Professor Karlfried Froehlich of Princeton Seminary, who was the first to introduce me to the life of the professional historian. His simple joy in teaching and depth of scholarship inspired me to continue my studies. I cannot thank him enough for his encouragement. He will no doubt recognize in this preface echoes of a lecture on Scholasticism from many years ago.

Reformation and Early Modern Europe

a guide to research

PART 1
Confessional Trends

1
Contributors to the Lutheran Tradition

David M. Whitford

In the previous two research guides, Martin Luther was treated alone and his life and theology were separated for individual articles. A very positive developing trend has been to expand the focus beyond Luther exclusively and to examine the ways in which others contributed to the formation of Lutheran tradition. Luther still demands the lion's share of attention from the scholarly community, but events like the 1997 five hundredth anniversary of Philip Melanchthon's birth have provided important opportunities to look beyond Luther. In what follows, we shall briefly examine some of the current trends in the study of Luther and those who chose to follow him. Along the way, we will cast our gaze beyond the theologians to see how others contributed to the success or failure of the Lutheran Reformation.

Martin Luther

In 1982, when Ozment's *Reformation Europe: A Guide to Research* was published, the best and most exhaustive biography of Luther remained Julius Köstlin's 1875 *The Life of Martin Luther*. Today Köstlin, who can still be helpful, has been replaced by Martin Brecht's *Martin Luther*. This three-volume biography, both exhaustive and encyclopedic, will remain the authoritative examination of Luther's life for the foreseeable future. Numerous other (and shorter) biographies continue to pour out of popular and academic presses. The most important of these is Heiko Oberman's *Luther: Man Between God and the Devil* (1990). The sentimental favorite will remain Roland Bainton's 1950 *Here I Stand*; though it is certainly dated in both its approach and research, it remains unsurpassed as pure narrative. Richard Marius's *Martin Luther* should be approached with caution and should not be read without also consulting Oberman's review of it.[1] The 2002 *Luther's Lives* (underwritten by the Sohmer-Hall Foundation) provides side-by-side translations of two contemporary biographies of Luther (one by Melanchthon and the other by his foe Johannes Cochlaeus).

Theology continues to be a focus in Luther scholarship where exciting (and controversial) new trends have recently emerged. Bernhard Lohse's *Martin Luther* and *Martin Luther's Theology* provide excellent introductions to Luther's thought. Other authors that offer a broad introduction to Luther's theology and life include Alister McGrath (*Reformation Thought*), David Bagchi and David Steinmetz (*Cambridge Companion to Reformation Theology*), Donald McKim (*Cambridge Companion to Martin Luther*), Carter Lindberg (*Reformation Theologians*), Timothy George (*Theology of the Reformers*), Jaroslav Pelikan (*Christian Tradition*), Heiko Oberman (*Luther: Man Between God and the Devil*), Oswald Bayer (*Martin Luthers Theologie*), and Thomas Kaufmann (*Martin Luther*). For introductions into the theological world from which Luther emerged, one should consult G. R. Evans (*The Medieval Theologians*), Oberman (*The Harvest of Medieval Theology*), and Ozment (*The Age of Reform*). For more general introductions to the historical and theological context of the Reformation, one should consult Lindberg (*The European Reformations*) and Euan Cameron (*The European Reformation*). Helpful works on particular loci in Luther have also been recently published. Robert Kolb (*Bound Choice, Election, and Wittenberg Theological Method*) explains clearly and comprehensively the historical dimensions of the debate over the will in Luther and Erasmus, while Gerhard Forde (*The Captivation of the Will*) plumbs the theological depths of the issue. At the end of his career, Gerhard Forde poured out a number of important works on Luther's theology including his doctrines of the Word, the theology of the cross, eschatology, atonement, and the Incarnation.[2] In *The Assurance of Faith*, Randall Zachman examines the conscience and the doctrine of assurance in both Luther and Calvin. Oswald Bayer's *Martin Luthers Theologie* offers a thorough presentation of both justification and sanctification.

---

[1] Oberman, Review of *Martin Luther*.
[2] Forde, *Theology Is for Proclamation*; *On Being a Theologian of the Cross*; and *Captivation of the Will*.

The most significant development in the study of Luther's theology has been the withering of two twentieth-century trends and the emergence of the so-called Finnish interpretation of Luther. Twentieth-century scholars have spent considerable energy trying to determine precisely when Luther made his turn to Evangelical theology. Key to this issue was the significance of Luther's "tower experience" in 1517. This preoccupation with when and to what degree Luther suddenly embraced an Evangelical theology has given way to the idea that Luther's theology was evolving and changing from as early as 1516 through at least 1522. Marxist interpretations of Luther and the Reformation have also largely disappeared since the 1989 collapse of East Germany and the Eastern Bloc.

The Finnish interpretation of Luther or the so-called Finnish school is centered on the work of Tuomo Mannermaa and his students. In 1979, Mannermaa (at the time a professor of church history at the University of Helsinki) published *In ipsa fide Christus adest: Luterilaisen ja ortodoksisen kritinuskonkäsityksen leikkauspiste* [In Faith Itself Is Christ Really Present: The Point of Intersection Between Lutheran and Orthodox Theology].[3] The heart of Lutheran theology has always been his doctrine of justification; Luther himself noted that it is the doctrine upon which the church either stands or falls.[4] The traditional line of interpretation has been that during the 1510s, or perhaps as late as the early 1520s, Luther's understanding of justification underwent a process of significant change.[5] He began to understand justification forensically, viewing righteousness as something imputed to the sinner rather than God's distributive justice that judges the sinner. Mannermaa argues that the focus on forensic (or passive) justification overshadows an equally important aspect of Luther's understanding. Mannermaa believes that Luther paid at least as much attention to the idea that justification is a real indwelling of Christ in the sinner that transforms the believer through a process of *theosis* or deification. Thus, there is no distinction between Christ *for* us and Christ *in* us. According to Kirsi Stjerna (a former Mannermaa student and the editor and translator of the English edition), Mannermaa offers a deeper appreciation of Luther as a

---

[3]It was translated into German in 1989 and into English in 2005 as *Christ Present in Faith: Luther's View of Justification*. The delay in translation meant that the impact of the Finnish school was not truly felt until the 1990s.

[4]"quia isto articulo stante stat Ecclesia, ruente ruit Ecclesia." WA 40/3:352.

[5]The exact date of the "Reformation breakthrough" is much debated. For a discussion of the debate, see Lohse, *Martin Luther's Theology*, 85–88; and Brecht, *Martin Luther*, 2:221–37.

spiritual and mystical theologian.[6] As such, Mannermaa's interpretation is seen as a rejection of nearly two centuries of Luther scholarship held "under the spell of neo-Kantian presuppositions,"[7] in which the spiritual, the mystical, and the ontological were sublimated by a focus on justification as an external act of God.[8]

While originally this new understanding of Luther was undertaken in an attempt to provide a bridge between Finnish Lutherans in conversation with their Orthodox brethren, the focus on theosis, mysticism, and ontology have proved equally useful to theologians in dialogue with Roman Catholics. The Finnish school has developed a significant following among American theologians, especially Carl Braaten, Robert Jenson, and David Yeago, and the Finns have also garnered their fair share of critics. While the supporters tend to come from the ranks of systematic theologians, the critics are almost entirely made up of historians. For the historians, the Finnish reading of Luther is not "new nor, in the final analysis, [is it] germane to the heart of Luther's theology."[9] For the historians, the Finns ignore Luther's historical context and disregard the debates surrounding justification in the sixteenth century in an attempt to find a more "ecumenical" Luther.[10] What they discover may in fact be an ecumenical Luther, but what they have most definitely not found, according to the historians, is the Luther who lived, wrote, and disputed in the sixteenth century.[11] This debate over Luther and justification is by no means settled. It played a major role in the 1997 and 2002 Luther Congresses and in the discussions surrounding the Lutheran-Catholic *Joint Declaration on Justification*. Those wishing to be conversant in Lutheran theology in the early twenty-first century will need to be aware of and understand the contributions and limitations of the Finnish school.[12]

---

[6]Stjerna, "Editor's Introduction," in Mannermaa, *Christ Present in Faith*.

[7]Bratten and Jenson, *Union with Christ*, viii.

[8]The central culprit in this play is Hermann Lotze, the nineteenth-century German philosopher. Risto Saarinen, a Mannermaa student and disciple, argues that Lotze takes from Kant the idea that a thing cannot be known in itself but only in its effect upon us. Thus, justification is understood as something that happens to us rather than something that happens in us. This warps and distorts Luther, for whom justification is as much about ontology as it is about soteriology.

[9]Wengert, Review of *Union with Christ*, 433.

[10]Specifically, the debate over Osiander's theology, which bears a striking resemblance to their own position but which, unfortunately for the Finnish interpretation, was soundly rejected by Luther himself.

[11]Whitford, Review of *One with God*.

[12]A full bibliography of the Finnish school (updated often) can be found at www.helsinki.fi/~risaarin/luther.html.

The reception of Luther's theology also remains an important avenue of investigation. In 1978, Gerald Strauss examined parish visitation records from 1527 to the beginning of the Thirty Years' War. He argued in *Luther's House of Learning* that the reception of Luther's theology remained tenuous at best and that the common people remained largely ignorant of evangelical tenets. Mark Edwards, in *Luther's Last Battles,* noted the challenge this posed to the study of Luther and called for greater attention to the reception and institutionalization of the Reformation. Confessionalization studies have emerged as a significant avenue of investigation into the lasting effects of Luther's Reformation.[13]

Luther's involvement in political and social affairs also remains important. Studies into Luther's relationship to Islam and the Turks—given a new relevance since September 11, 2001—are an especially interesting and long-neglected area of inquiry. Adam Francisco's *Martin Luther and Islam* and Gregory Miller's "Luther on the Turks and Islam" provides an excellent introduction to the field, but there is much that remains to be unearthed. The impact of Luther's theology on early modern understandings of poverty and the poor also remains a dynamic field of inquiry with much that can still be learned. For an introduction to Luther's theology of the poor, see Carter Lindberg's *Beyond Charity.* For a more broad-based examination of early modern poor relief, see the many works by Thomas Max Safley, especially his excellent *The Reformation of Charity.*

Luther was a prodigious exegete throughout his career, and much has recently been gleaned by looking at his place in the history of exegetical writing. *The Bible in the Sixteenth Century,* edited by David Steinmetz, provides an excellent introduction to this field of inquiry. His 1986 *Luther in Context* is also, largely, a republication of articles on Luther the exegete. Heinrich Bornkamm's *Luther and the Old Testament* is now almost forty years old, yet still very helpful. More recently, Mickey Mattox (*Defender of the Most Holy Matriarchs*) has examined Luther's exegetical method by looking at key women in the Old Testament. This book has an added bonus of contributing to the dearth of information on Luther's views on women. In *Luther on Women,* Susan Karant-Nunn and Merry Wiesner-Hanks have brought together a wonderful collection of Luther's writings on women, gleaned from his exegetical, theological, and personal writings. Jonathan Trigg's *Baptism in the Theology of Martin Luther* is largely derived

---

[13]For a full explanation of the confessionalization thesis, please see chapter six in this volume.

from the Genesis Lectures. For Luther's hermeneutical framework, one should consult Kenneth Hagen's more recent work on the subject as well as Gerhard Ebeling's 1942 classic.[14]

By looking at Luther the exegete, we may also put him into dialogue with his own more theological and even social writings. Kristen Kvam and Bergit Stolt have both looked at the ways in which Luther's marriage affected his exegetical understandings of Adam and Eve and the first household.[15] David Whitford used Luther's Genesis lectures to assess whether Luther abandoned his "two kingdoms" doctrine later in life.[16] As with many other avenues of Luther scholarship, the digitization of Luther's writings opens up many exciting avenues to scholars interested in tracking Luther's exegetical views on specific topics and issues. Finally, no less than Luther, others such as Melanchthon are also in need of further exegetical investigation.

Primary Sources for Research on Luther

The standard version of Luther's writings is *D. Martin Luthers Werke. Kritische Gesamtausgabe*, commonly referred to as the Weimar Ausgabe (because it was published in the city of Weimar). Publication began in 1883, and revisions and republications continue to this day. The Weimar Ausgabe is broken into three sections. The first, *Shriften*, contains Luther's German and Latin writings and treatises. It is commonly abbreviated WA and has sixty-one volumes. Some of these volumes are themselves broken into subvolumes, thus WA 10/1 or WA 10/2. In older works, the Weimar Ausgabe is often cited by volume, then page, then the specific line upon which the quote falls: WA 10/1:357, 7–9. This format has largely dropped out of fashion. In its place, authors now refer to the volume and page only (e.g., WA 10/1:357).

The second section of the Weimar Ausgabe is the *Briefwechsel* (Letters), abbreviated WABr. It is made up of eighteen volumes and contains letters and correspondence both from and to Luther. The third section is the *Tischreden* (Table Talks), abbreviated WATR or WATr, consisting of six volumes. As Luther became more famous and influential, students began to jot down his discussions with students over meals and in other informal

---

[14]Hagen, *Luther's Approach to Scripture*; and Ebeling, *Evangelische Evangelienauslegung*.

[15]Kvam, "Luther, Eve, and Theological Anthropology"; and Stolt, *Martin Luther, mannisckohjärtat och Bibeln*.

[16]Whitford, *"Cura Religionis* or Two Kingdoms."

settings. Some of the *Tischreden* are more reliable than others and should thus be consulted with due caution. The final section of the WA, the *Deutsche Bibel*, abbreviated WADB, is twelve volumes and contains Luther's translations of the biblical texts. A more affordable (and more compact) edition of Luther's works in Latin and German can be found in the *Luthers Werke in Auswahl, Studienausgabe*. Often referred to simply as the Studienausgabe, this eight-volume set contains the most significant works by Luther, helpfully cross-referenced to the Weimar Ausgabe.[17] Another option is the eleven-volume *Die Werke Martin Luthers in neuer Auswahl für die Gegenwart*.

For decades, the Institut für Spätmittelalter und Reformation in Tübingen has been compiling a comprehensive (though not exhaustive) index of the Weimar Ausgabe. Though the volumes are now being published, literally generations of work have been nullified by the release of two electronic versions of Luther's writings. The first is an electronic edition of the entire Weimar Ausgabe released in 2000 (the Chadwyck version), access to which is limited to academic libraries that have purchased it.[18] Using the Chadwyck version, one may search Luther's *Werke* by word or root-word (in German, Latin, Hebrew, and Greek) using either key word or Boolean logic. The ability to search by the root of a word (in fact, one may even search by just using the first couple of letters of a word) allows one to find all of the references to a word even if Luther spelled them slightly differently. One may search within a specific volume, a specific treatise, a specified time frame, or the entire Weimar Ausgabe. The second electronic option is offered by Alexander Street Press (www.alexanderstreetpress.com). Like the Chadwyck electronic Weimar Ausgabe, the Alexander Street Press version is available at academic libraries by subscription; it is far more affordable than Chadwyck's electronic version of the Weimar Ausgabe and is priced with even small academic libraries in mind. While the Chadwyck version is based on the nineteenth- and twentieth-century scholarly edition of the Weimar Ausgabe, Alexander Street Press has moved in a different direction, offering the Latin edition of Luther's writings published in Wittenberg by Hans Lufft (who also published many of Luther's other works) between 1550 and 1558. The choice of a sixteenth-

---

[17]Studienausgabe is still in print and can be picked up for about 150 euros from Walter De Gruyter. The eleven-volume *Die Werke Martin Luthers* is a bit larger and about 100 euros more expensive; it is available from Vandenhoeck & Ruprecht.

[18]An overview of the project can be found at luther.chadwyck.com.

century text over the more recent text reflects a developing trend in early modern scholarship that values editions published at the time over later scholarly editions.[19] Like Chadwyk's version, the Alexander Street Press version has a fully developed search capability. In addition, this version has two significant advantages. First, it provides not only an electronic version of the text but also an image of each page from which the text was taken, allowing one to look at textual marginalia and so forth. Second, Luther's writings are a very small part of the complete Alexander Street Press library. There are literally hundreds of early modern authors in the Alexander Street Press Digital Library of Classic Protestant Texts and its companion, the Digitial Library of the Catholic Reformation. The advantage to the scholar is obvious: one can compare a keyword, exegetical point, or doctrinal loci across many theological perspectives with the simple click of a mouse-button. Alexander Street Press continues to add new content all the time; the true impact of these new research tools has barely been felt.

For those without access to an academic library or whose library cannot afford either of the electronic versions already discussed, there is another new option. In 2006, Vandenhoeck & Ruprecht released a CD-ROM version of their eleven-volume collection (at a cost of about 45 euros). The search apparatus is less sophisticated than the other electronic versions; on the other hand, the price is affordable on almost any budget.[20]

The standard English version (often called the American Edition) is *Luther's Works* (abbreviated *LW*). *Luther's Works* was published between 1955 and 1986 by Concordia Publishing House and Augsburg Fortress. In fifty-four volumes plus one index volume, many of the most important of Luther's treatises, letters, and table talks are translated and introduced. A CD-ROM version of *Luther's Works* was released in 2001 (it also contains the full King James Version of the Bible and the Tappert edition of the *Book of Concord*).[21] This version also has full-text searching, but like the Vandenhoeck & Ruprecht CD, the search engine is not very sophisticated. In 2007, Concordia announced that, beginning in 2008, it will publish twenty new volumes of previously untranslated works by Luther. The first three volumes will contain material from Luther's sermons and a new comprehensive index to all volumes will be compiled.

---

[19]Richard Muller (*The Unaccommodated Calvin*, 1–17) has argued that scholarly apparati can, at times, distort rather than enhance our understanding of sixteenth-century texts.

[20]The CD-ROM set is available at http://www.theologische-buchhandlung.de/luther-deutsche-inhaltsverzeichnis.htm.

[21]This CD-ROM of *Luther's Works* can be purchased for approximately $250.

Research Aids

Each year, the *Lutherjahrbuch*, the *Archiv für Reformationsgeschichte, Literaturbericht*, and *Luther Digest* (since 1993) publish bibliographies and summaries of Reformation research, including Luther research. These are indispensable aids for finding and locating current research on Luther. Also helpful are searches in the online ATLA Religion Index and OCLC's World-Cat FirstSearch. Both of these indices are widely available at academic and seminary libraries and support key word and Boolean logic searches. The previous research guides include comprehensive lists of Luther research review articles; those since 1990 are included in this bibliography.

Other important aids to Luther research include Kurt Aland's *Luther Deutsch* (commonly called *Lutherlexicon*), which provides German definitions of some key Luther terminology. A more exhaustive dictionary is Philipp Dietz's *Wörterbuch zu Dr. Martin Luthers deutschen Schriften*. Heinrich Vogel's *Cross Reference and Index to the Contents of Luther's Works* provides cross-references between the Weimar Ausgabe, *Luther's Works*, and older American and German editions of Luther's writings. Georg Buchwald's *Luther Kalendarium* (1929) is very dated and can be inaccurate at times, but also provides a snapshot of what Luther was working on at a given time. Sachiko Kusukawa's *Wittenberg University Library Catalogue of 1536* gives a shelf list of the university library available to Luther and Melanchthon and provides, therefore, a wealth of information about not only what texts were available but what may not have been, what was valued and what may have been ignored. For example, John Calvin's *Institutes of the Christian Religion* was there, even though they were only published earlier in 1536. What was missing? Erasmus' *De libero arbitrio diatribe sive collatio*, for one The shelf list provides only shorthand references to works, but Kusukawa has helpfully added the full title with publication city and date in an adjacent column. Beutel's *Luther Handbuch* provides a very up-to-date summary of Luther research in Germany. *Hilfsbuch zum Lutherstudium* presents a comprehensive list of Luther's writings, first compiled and edited by Kurt Aland. The most recent (1996) updated edition is broken into five parts:

- An alphabetical list of Luther's writings, postils, sermons, and letters. This alone takes up nearly four hundred pages!
- Keys to the nineteenth- and twentieth-century editions of Luther's works, including a complete key to *Luther's Works* (*Luther's Works* was not yet complete at the time of the 1970 edition).

- Keys to the major editions of Luther's works published from the sixteenth to the eighteenth century.
- A chronological list of Luther's writings.
- A cross-reference key to Josef Benzing's *Lutherbibliographie*.

Josef Benzing's *Lutherbibliographie* is a complete list of all publication runs for Luther's works by various printers up to 1546. Benzing is most useful when one is trying to determine how quickly or widely a particular treatise was published. For a sense of the full bibliographic importance of a work, one should also consult *Das Verzeichnis der im deutschen Sprachbereich ershienenen Druckschriften des XVI. Jahrhunderts,* usually called VD16. This resource exists in book form (currently twenty-five volumes), as well as on CD-ROM and online (www.vd16.de). The bibliographic information in VD16 was assembled by looking at the existing catalogs of German libraries. In 2006, it was also incorporated into the much larger Hand Press Book Database (HPBD), now part of OCLC. The HPBD contains searchable bibliographic information on works published in Europe during the handpress era (ca. 1455–1830). Searchable by author, title, imprint, or key word, it is constantly being updated, and currently consists of fifty databases from around the world.[22] The VD16 is helpful in determining bibliographic information for Luther or Melanchthon within the Holy Roman Empire; the HPBD allows one to look at all of Europe. Both online sources allow the user to email selected records; HPBD allows the user to download records directly into bibliographic software like Endnote. Finally, for an excellent examination of the role of printing in the spread of Luther's ideas, see Mark Edwards's *Printing, Propaganda, and Martin Luther.*

Philipp Melanchthon

Philipp Melanchthon was one of Luther's closest colleagues at the University of Wittenberg and the most important of his followers. Born in Bretten in 1497 as Philipp Schwartzerdt, he changed his name (following a humanist practice) to the Hellenized equivalent, Melanchthon (meaning "black earth"). Melanchthon received a university education first at Heidelberg (1509–12) and then Tübingen (1512–18). In 1518, a recommendation from the famous humanist Johannes Reuchlin, his relative by marriage, led

---

[22]For examples, HPBD contains not only the VD16 and VD17, but also the British Library Incunabula Short-Title Catalogue, and holdings lists for the Oxford University Library, and the Slovenian Library. For a full list, consult OCLC's FirstSearch.

to a teaching position in Greek at the University of Wittenberg. Thus he arrived at the very time Luther was launched onto the world stage. Melanchthon and Luther would come to be close theological allies. Though they did not agree always, Melanchthon can be counted as the systematizer and synthesizer of Luther's thought. When the imperial ban of 1521 prevented Luther from attending the Diet of Augsburg in 1530, Melanchthon was entrusted with writing the statement of faith on behalf of the Evangelicals. He was the chief drafter for both the Latin and German versions of the Augsburg Confession and in 1531 was the author of its defense, *The Apology of the Augsburg Confession.*[23]

Following the death of Luther in 1546 and the defeat of the Schmalkaldic League in 1547, Melanchthon was among the first to attack the Augsburg Interim. However, he also sought to mitigate its severity through negotiation with the newly appointed Roman bishop. This attempt at mitigation, though it prevented the dissolution of the University of Wittenberg and the revocation of Luther's reforms in total, won him few friends and a number of enemies (many drawn from his former students). Despite the fact that the political future of the Evangelical churches was assured after Princes' Rebellion of 1552 and the Peace of Augsburg in 1555, Melanchthon continued to be embroiled in theological controversy throughout the 1550s. He died in 1560 and is buried next to Martin Luther in the Castle Church in Wittenberg.

Melanchthon's most important work is the *Loci communes rerum theologicarum* (The Commonplaces of Theological Matters). This systematic presentation of Lutheran theology is based on the Epistle to the Romans and was written as a guide to scripture. The *loci* format was a popular early modern device for theological explication and biblical explanation. Melanchthon first published his *Loci* in 1521, but continued to work, shape, and revise the *Loci* in editions of 1535 and 1543. In 1555, he published a German edition. In his revisions, Melanchthon added and subtracted text and sections to match and respond to the wider theological context of the developing Reformation.

Although Melanchthon was an important theologian of the Reformation, he was first and foremost a biblical scholar. Important work has been done in the last three decades on Melanchthon the exegete; Timothy Wengert's scholarship does more to advance our understanding of Melanchthon

---

[23]Both the *Augsburg Confession* and the *Apology* were retranslated and introduced in English in the 2000 *Book of Concord,* edited by Robert Kolb and Timothy Wengert.

14 David M. Whitford

than does anyone else's. The bibliography for this chapter lists six works written or edited by Wengert that are essential reading for those who hope to understand Melanchthon and his contribution to the Lutheran tradition. Other key authors include Heinz Scheible, Günter Frank, Karin Maag, John Schofield, John Schneider, William Hammer, and James Estes.

The works of Melanchthon are collected in the *Corpus Reformatorum: Philippi Melanchthonis opera quae supersunt omnia*. Eighteen of the most important works by Melanchthon (including a complete edition of the 1546 *Loci* published in Basel) are available in ASP's Digital Library of Classic Protestant Texts discussed above, and a smaller collection of essential texts is available in *Melanchthons Werke in Auswahl* (*Studienausgabe*), edited by Robert Stupperich. Melanchthon's correspondence is being published under the editorship of Heinz Scheible, *Melanchthons Briefwechsel: Kritische und kommentierte Gesamtausgabe*; eighteen volumes are in print with the final editing of the letters expected by 2030. The most comprehensive list of sixteenth-century publications of Melanchthon's works is available in the VD16. As with Luther, one should also consult the HPBD.

Music

When Martin Luther published the first Evangelical hymnal in 1524, the Reformation was already being carried across the countryside by music. Robert Scribner helped launch a revolution in the understanding of the Reformation through his attention to the ways in which the Reformation affected the common people. Until Scribner, it can be safely argued, the history of Lutheran music focused on elite representations of music, and the scholars of such music were almost exclusively musicologists. But what of the music sung by the common person? What contributions can music make to our understanding of history? Rebecca Wagner Oettinger notes that singing was ubiquitous among the common folk during the early modern era and that songs were used to advance social and political agendas (she has a disturbing account of anti-Jewish songs used to support the expulsion of Jews).[24] What made the Reformation important was that ecclesiastical music started serving a different purpose. It became not merely devotional but persuasive, a tool for conversion rather than a tool solely for prayer. Christopher Boyd Brown argues convincingly that music can be a very helpful tool in the assessment of the Reformation's impact.[25]

[24]Scribner, *For the Sake of Simple Folk*; and Oettinger, *Music as Propaganda*, 22.
[25]Brown, *Singing the Gospel*.

Alexander Fisher offers just such an appraisal in *Music and Religious Identity in Counter-Reformation Augsburg*. Fisher's work has the added benefit of looking at music's influence in a multiconfessional context. The study of music as an entrée into historical inquiry, rather than the "history of music," is a field that has barely begun to be fully explored. Thus, Oettinger has looked at music's role in the Schmalkaldic War and Brown at the influence of hymnal publication, while Fisher offers a detailed examination of its influence upon one city. Many other detailed studies of cities, the use of hymns within other communities of faith and expression, and the role of music in the propaganda campaigns of the sixteenth century will help provide a more fully rounded understanding of this important but understudied aspect of the Reformation.

The Evangelical Princes

Philip the Magnanimous, landgrave of Hesse, was present at every major diet of the Holy Roman Empire from the Diet of Worms to the 1555 Diet of Augsburg. He was a major force in the advancement of the Reformation, the Schmalkaldic League and War, and the Peace of Augsburg. To date, however, there is not a single major scholarly biography of Philip in any language.[26] Perhaps Philip is an exception to the norm? Most people assume that the Evangelical princes who protected and helped spread the Reformation have already been studied in detail, but the contrary is actually true. While brief details of all the major princes are well known, the intricacies of their lives and engagements with the Reformation remain a dark alley of early modern scholarship. A major debate among scholars is the degree to which the princes advanced the Reformation out of political or religious ends; this question cannot be answered without a thorough review of the correspondence and records of the individual princes. Biographies are sometimes not considered important or sufficiently impressive, but they are necessary and they need to be well written by those who know the field the best. Perhaps the time has come to take biographies seriously.

Despite the devastation of far too many wars, the archives and even scholarly editions of the writings and correspondence of many of the princes survive. Scholarly editions can be found in many major university libraries. Archival materials are found in the state archives of the individual German states and in some cases the cities that were the seats of the

---

[26]Richard Andrew Cahill (*Philipp of Hesse and the Reformation*) deals only with Philip's life up to the 1526 Diet of Speyer.

princes before later consolidation. These archives can yield enormously rich material. For example, Ocker's study of church property confiscations (*Church Robbers and Reformers*) is an excellent new addition to this field and depends on just such archival research.

Bibliography

Electronic Resources

Corpus Reformatorum, Melanchthon volumes (Google Books has digitized most of these volumes; they can be downloaded). A link to the individual volumes is available at: http://en.wikipedia.org/wiki/Corpus_Reformatorum

Die Bibel, Martin Luther translation (full-text edition): http://quod.lib.umich.edu/l/luther/

The Digital Library of Classic Protestant Texts (digitized editions of Protestant texts with full text searching): http://solomon.tcpt.alexanderstreet.com/

Herzog August Bibliothek (contains a vast collection of Reformation-era primary sources): http://www.hab.de

Kessler Reformation Collection, Emory University (vast collection of sixteenth-century imprints; a definite focus on the Lutheran Reformation): http://www.pitts.emory.edu/SpecColl/kesslercoll.html

Luther Center, Wittenberg (digitized primary source documents on and by Luther): http://www.luther-zentrum.de/

Luther's *Gesammelte Werke*, CD-ROM (may be purchased at http://www.theologische-buchhandlung.de/luther-deutsch-inhaltsverzeichnis.htm)

Luthers Werke Online (full-text searchable edition of the Weimar Ausgabe): http://luther.chadwyck.co.uk/

Luther's Works, American Edition, CD-ROM (may be purchased at http://www.logos.com/products/details/1663)

Thrivent Reformation Library, Luther Seminary (huge collection of microfiched Reformation era imprints): http://staupitz.luthersem.edu/?m=60

Verzeichnis der im deutschen Sprachbereich erschienenen Drucke des 16. Jahrhunderts (VD16) (bibliography of materials published in Germany in the 16th century; the "Digital VD16" catalogs those works in the VD16 that are available, free of charge, in digital format): http://www.vd16.de

Printed Sources

Aland, Kurt. *Hilfsbuch zum Lutherstudium*, 4th ed. Bielefeld: Luther-Verlag, 1996.

———. *Luther Deutsch: Die Werke Martin Luthers in neuer Auswahl für die Gegenwart.* Stuttgart: Ehrenfried Klotz Verlag, 1957 (commonly called *Lutherlexicon*).

Althaus, Paul. *The Ethics of Martin Luther*. Translated by Robert C. Schultz. Philadelphia: Fortress Press, 1972. Originally published as *Ethik Martin Luthers* (Gütersloh: Mohn, 1965).

———. *The Theology of Martin Luther*, trans. Robert C. Schultz. Philadelphia: Fortress Press, 1966. Originally published as *Theologie Martin Luthers* (Gütersloh: Mohn, 1962).

Arand, Charles. P. *That I May Be His Own: An Overview of Luther's Catechisms*. St. Louis, MO: Concordia, 2000.

Aulén, Gustav. *Christus Victor*. Translated by A. G. Hebert. London: SPCK, 1945.

Bagchi, David. *Luther's Earliest Opponents: Catholic Controversialists, 1518–1525*. Minneapolis, MN: Fortress Press, 1991.

Bagchi, David, and David Steinmetz, eds. *Cambridge Companion to Reformation Theology*. Cambridge, MA: Cambridge University Press, 2004.

Bainton, Roland H. *Here I Stand*. New York: Abingdon, 1950.

Bayer, Oswald. *Living by Faith: Justification and Sanctification*. Grand Rapids, MI: Eerdmans, 2003.

———. *Martin Luthers Theologie: Eine Vergegenwärtigung*. Tübingen: Mohr Siebeck, 2003.

———. *Promissio: Geschichte der reformatorischen Wende in Luthers Theologie*. Göttingen: Vandenhoeck & Ruprecht, 1971.

Bell, Theo. *Divus Bernhardus: Bernhard von Clairvaux in Martin Luthers Schriften*. Mainz: Zabern, 1993.

Benzing, Josef. *Lutherbibliographie: Verzeichnis der Gedruckten Schriften Martin Luthers bis zu dessen Tod*. Baden-Baden: Heitz, 1966.

Beutel, Albrecht. *Martin Luther: Eine Einführung in Leben, Werk und Wirkung*. Leipzig: Evangelische Verlags, 2005

———, ed. *Luther Handbuch*. Tübingen: Mohr Siebeck, 2005.

Bizer, Ernst. *Fides ex auditu: Eine Untersuchung über die Entdeckung der Gerechtigkeit Gottes durch Martin Luther*. Neukirchen: Erziehungsverein, 1958.

Bornkamm, Heinrich. *Luther and the Old Testament*. Philadelphia: Fortress Press, 1969.

Brady, Thomas. "Luther and the State: The Reformer's Teaching in Its Social Setting." In *Luther and the Modern State in Germany*, edited by James D. Tracy, 31–44. Kirksville, MO: Sixteenth Century Journal Publishers, 1986.

Bratten, Carl, and Robert Jenson, eds. *Union with Christ: The New Finnish Interpretation of Luther*. Grand Rapids, MI: Eerdmans, 1998.

Brecht, Martin. *Martin Luther*. Translated by James L. Schaaf. 3 vols. Philadelphia: Fortress Press, 1985–93. Originally published as *Martin Luther* (Stuttgart: Institut für Auslandbeziehungen, 1981–87).

Brown, Christopher. *Singing the Gospel*. Cambridge, MA: Harvard University Press, 2005.

Buchwald, Georg, and Gustav Kawerau. *Luther-Kalendarium*. Leipzig: M. Heinsius Nachfolger, Eger & Sievers, 1929.

Cahill, Richard Andrew. *Philipp of Hesse and the Reformation*. Mainz: Zabern, 2001.

Cameron, Euan. *The European Reformation*. Oxford: Clarendon Press, 1991.

Cranz, F. Edward. *An Essay on the Development of Luther's Thought on Justice, Law and Society*. Cambridge, MA: Harvard University Press, 1959.

Die Bekenntnisschriften der evangelisch-lutherischen Kirche, 11th ed. Göttingen: Vandenhoeck & Ruprecht, 1992. Translated by Robert Kolb and Timothy J. Wengert as *The Book of Concord* (Minneapolis, MN: Fortress Press, 2000).

Dietz, Philipp. *Wörterbuch zu Dr. Martin Luthers deutschen Schriften*. Hildesheim: G. Olm, 1870, 1961.

Dingel, Irena. *Concordia controversa: Die öffentlichen Diskussionen um das lutherische Konkordienwerk am Ende des 16. Jahrhunderts*. Gütersloh: Gütersloher, 1996.

Dost, Timothy. *Renaissance Humanism in Support of the Gospel in Luther's Early Correspondence: Taking All Things Captive*. Burlington, VT: Ashgate, 2001.

Duchrow, Ulrich. *Christenheit und Weltverantwortung: Traditionsgeschichte und systematische Struktur der Zweireichelehre*. Stuttgart: Klett, 1970.

Dykema, Peter, and Heiko Oberman. *Anticlericalism in Late Medieval and Early Modern Europe*. Leiden: Brill, 1993.

Ebeling, Gerhard. *Evangelische Evangelienauslegung, eine Untersuchung zu Luthers Herme-neutik.* Munich: Lempp, 1942.

————. *Luther: An Introduction to His Thought.* Translated by R. A. Wilson. Philadelphia: Fortress Press, 1970. Originally published as *Luther: Einführung in sein Denken* (Tübingen: Mohr, 1964).

Edwards, Mark. U., Jr. *Luther and the False Brethren.* Stanford, CA: Stanford University Press, 1975.

————. *Luther's Last Battles: Politics and Polemics, 1531–1546.* Ithaca, NY: Cornell University Press, 1983.

————. *Printing, Propaganda, and Martin Luther.* Berkeley: University of California Press, 1994.

Estes, James. *Peace, Order, and the Glory of God: Secular Authority and the Church in the Thought of Luther and Melanchthon, 1518–1559.* Leiden: Brill, 2005.

Evans, G. R., ed. *The Medieval Theologians.* Oxford: Blackwell, 2001.

Fisher, Alexander. *Music and Religious Identity in Counter-Reformation Augsburg.* Burlington, VT: Ashgate, 2004.

Flogaus, Reinhard. *Theosis bei Palamas und Luther.* Göttingen: Vandenhoeck & Ruprecht, 1997.

Forde, Gerhard O. *The Captivation of the Will: Luther Vs. Erasmus on Freedom and Bondage.* Grand Rapids, MI: Eerdmans, 2005.

————. *Justification by Faith: A Matter of Death and Life.* Philadelphia: Fortress Press, 1982.

————. *A More Radical Gospel: Essays on Eschatology, Authority, Atonement, and Ecumenism.* Grand Rapids, MI: Eerdmans, 2004.

————. *On Being a Theologian of the Cross: Reflections on Luther's Heidelberg Disputation, 1518.* Grand Rapids, MI: Eerdmans, 1997.

————. *The Preached God: Proclamation in Word and Sacrament.* Grand Rapids, MI: Eerdmans, 2007.

————. *Theology Is for Proclamation.* Minneapolis, MN: Fortress, 1990.

Francisco, Adam S. *Martin Luther and Islam: A Study in Sixteenth-Century Polemics and Apologetics.* Leiden: Brill, 2007.

Frank, Günter, ed., *Der Theologe Melanchthon.* Sigmaringen: Thorbecke, 2000.

————, and Martin Treu. *Melanchthon und Europa.* Melanchthon-Schriften der Stadt Bretten 6/1. Stuttgart: J. Thorbecke, 2001.

————, and Kees Meerhoff. *Melanchthon und Europa.* Vol. 2, *Westeuropa.* Melanchthon-Schriften der Stadt Bretten 6/2. Stuttgart: J. Thorbecke, 2002.

George, Timothy. *Theology of the Reformers.* Nashville, TN: Broadman, 1988.

Gesammelte Aufsätze zur Kirchengeschichte. Vol. 1, *Luther.* Tübingen: Mohr/Siebeck, 1921.

Grane, Lief. *Martinus Noster: Luther in the German Reform Movement, 1518–1521.* Mainz: Zabern, 1994.

Haile, H. G. *Luther: An Experiment in Biography.* Garden City, NY: Doubleday, 1980. Reprint, Princeton, NJ: Princeton University Press, 1983.

Hagen, Kenneth. *Luther's Approach to Scripture as Seen in His "Commentaries" on Galatians 1519–1538.* Tübingen: Mohr/Siebeck, 1993.

Hamm, Berndt, Bernd Moeller, and Dorothea Wendebourg. *Reformationstheorien: Ein kirchenhistoricher Disput über Einheit und Vielfalt der Reformation.* Göttingen: Vandenhoeck & Ruprecht, 1995.

Hammer, William. *Die Melanchthonforschung im Wandel der Jahrhunderte. Ein beschreibendes Verzeichnis.* Gütersloh: Gütersloher Verlagshaus, 1967.

Harnack, Th. *Luthers Theologie.* 2 vols. Erlangen: Blaesing, 1862, 1886.

Hendrix, Scott. "American Luther Research in the Twentieth Century." *Lutheran Quarterly* 15 (2001): 1–23.

———. *Luther and the Papacy: Stages in a Reformation Conflict.* Philadelphia: Fortress Press, 1981.

———. "Luther's Impact on the Sixteenth Century." *Sixteenth Century Journal* 16 (1985): 3–14.

———. "Martin Luther und die Lutherischen Bekenntnisschriften in der englischsprachigen Forschung seit 1983." *Lutherjahrbuch* 68 (2001): 115–36.

Hoepfl, Harro, ed. and trans. *Luther and Calvin on Secular Authority.* Cambridge, UK: Cambridge University Press, 1992.

Holl, Karl. "Die Rechtfertigungslehre in Luthers Vorlesung über den Römerbrief." *Zeitschrift für Theologie und Kirche* 4 (1910): 245–91.

Holm, Bo Kristian. *Gabe und Geben bei Luther: Das Verhältnis zwischen Reziprozität und reformatorischer Rechtfertigungslehre.* Berlin: De Gruyter, 2006.

Hsia, R. Po-chia, ed. *The German People and the Reformation.* Ithaca, NY: Cornell University Press, 1988.

Janz, Denis. *Luther on Thomas Aquinas.* Stuttgart: Steiner, 1989.

Junghans, Helmar. *Der junge Luther und die Humanisten.* Göttingen: Vandenhoeck & Ruprecht, 1985.

———, ed., *Leben und Werk Martin Luthers von 1526 bis 1546.* 2 vols. Göttingen: Vandenhoeck & Ruprecht, 1983.

Kailus, Jörg. *Gesetz und Evangelium in Luthers Grossem Galaterkommentar sowie bei Werner Elert und Paul Althaus: Darstellung in Grundzügen und Vergleich.* Münster: Lit Verlag, 2004.

Karant-Nunn, Susan. *Luther's Pastors: The Reformation in the Ernstine Countryside.* Philadelphia: American Philosophical Society, 1979.

Karant-Nunn, Susan, and Merry Wiesner-Hanks, *Luther on Women: A Sourcebook.* Cambridge, UK: Cambridge University Press, 2003.

Kärkkäinen, Pekka. *Luthers trinitarische Theologie des Heiligen Geistes.* Mainz: Zabern, 2005.

Kärkkäinen, Veli-Matti. *One with God: Salvation as Deification and Justification.* Collegeville, MN: Liturgical Press 2004.

Kaufmann, Thomas. *Luthers "Judenschriften" in ihren historischen Kontexten.* Göttingen: Vandenhoeck & Ruprecht, 2005.

———. *Martin Luther.* Munich: Beck, 2006.

Keen, Ralph. *Divine and Human Authority in Reformation Thought: German Theologians on Political Order, 1520–1555.* Nieuwkoop, Netherlands: Graaf, 1997.

———, ed., *A Checklist of Melanchthon Imprints through 1560.* St. Louis, MO: Center for Reformation Research, 1988.

Kittelson, James. *Martin Luther: The Story of the Man and His Career.* Minneapolis, MN: Fortress Press, 1986.

———. "Successes and Failures in the German Reformation: The Report from Strasbourg." *Archiv für Reformationsgeschichte* 73 (1982): 153–75.

Köhler, Walter. *Zwingli und Luther: Ihr Streit über das Abendmahl nach seinen politischen und religiösen Beziehungen.* 2 vols. Leipzig: Heinsius, 1924, 1953.

Kohnle, Armin. *Reichstag und Reformation: Kaiserliche und ständische Religionspolitik von den Anfängen der Causa Lutheri bis zum Nürnberger Religionsfrieden.* Gütersloh: Gütersloher Verlagshaus, 2001.

Kolb, Robert. *Bound Choice, Election, and Wittenberg Theological Method: From Martin Luther to the Formula of Concord.* Lutheran Quarterly Books. Grand Rapids, MI: Eerdmans, 2005.

———. *Martin Luther as Prophet, Teacher, and Hero: Images of the Reformer, 1520–1620.* Grand Rapids, MI: Baker Books, 1999.

———. *Nicholas Von Amsdorf (1483–1565): Popular Polemics in the Preservation of Luther's Legacy.* Nieuwkoop, Netherlands: B. De Graaf, 1978.

Kolb, Robert, and Timothy J. Wengert. *The Book of Concord: The Confessions of the Evangelical Lutheran Church.* Minneapolis, MN: Fortress Press, 2000.

Köstlin, Julius. *The Life of Martin Luther.* Translated by John G. Morris. 2 vols. Philadelphia: Lutheran Publication Society, 1883. Originally published as *Martin Luther: Sein Lebel und seine Schriften. Leben und ausgewählte schriften der väter und Begründer der lutherischen Kirche* 1, 2 (Elberfeld: R.L. Friderichs, 1875).

———. *The Theology of Martin Luther.* Translated by Charles E. Hay. Philadelphia: Lutheran Publication Society, 1897. Originally published as *Luthers Theologie* (Stuttgart: Steinkopf, 1875).

Kusukawa, Sachiko. *A Wittenberg University Library Catalogue of 1536.* Binghamton, NY: Medieval & Renaissance Texts & Studies, 1995.

Kvam, Kristen. "Luther, Eve, and Theological Anthropology." PhD diss., Emory University, 1992.

Lau, Franz. "Der Bauernkrieg und das angebliche Ende der lutherischen Reformation als spontaner Volksbewegung." *Lutherjahrbuch* 26 (1959): 109–34.

Leppin, Volker. "Luther-Literatur seit 1983." *Theologische Rundschau* 65 (2000): 350–57, 431–54.

Lienhard, Marc. *Luther, Witness to Jesus Christ.* Translated by Edwin H. Robertson. Minneapolis, MN: Fortress Press, 1982. Originally published as *Luther: Témoin de Jésus Christ* (Paris: Editions du Cerf, 1973).

Lindberg, Carter. *Beyond Charity: Reformation Initiatives for the Poor.* Minneapolis, MN: Fortress, 1993.

———. *The European Reformations.* Oxford, UK: Blackwell, 1996.

———. "Luther's Critique of the Ecumenical Assumption That Doctrine Divides but Service Unites." *Journal of Ecumenical Studies* 27 (1990): 679–96.

———. *The Reformation Theologians.* Oxford, UK: Blackwell, 2002.

———. "Tainted Greatness: Luther's Attitudes toward Judaism and Their Historical Reception." In *Tainted Greatness: Antisemitism and Cultural Heroes,* edited by Nancy A. Harrowitz. Philadelphia: Temple University Press, 1994.

Loehr, Joanna, ed. *Dona Melanchthoniana: Festgabe für Heinz Scheible.* Stuttgart-Bad Cannstatt: Fromann-Holzboog, 2001.

Loewenich, Walter von. *Luther's Theology of the Cross.* Translated by Herbert J. A. Bouman. Minneapolis, MN: Augsburg, 1976. Originally published as *Luthers Theologia Crucis* (Munich: Kaiser, 1954).

Lohse, Bernhard, ed. *Der Durchbruch der reformatorischen Erkenntnis bei Luther.* Darmstadt: Wissenschaftliche Buchgesellschaft, 1958.

———, ed. *Der Durchbruch der reformatorischen Erkenntnis bei Luther: Neuere Untersuchungen.* Wiesbaden: Steiner, 1988.

———. *Martin Luther.* Translated by Robert C. Schultz. Philadelphia: Fortress Press, 1986. Originally published as *Martin Luther* (Munich: C. H. Beck, 1980).

———. *Martin Luther's Theology: Its Historical and Systematic Development*. Translated by Roy A. Harrisville. Minneapolis, MN: Fortress Press, 1999. Originally published as *Martin Luthers Theologie* (Göttingen: Vandenhoeck and Ruprecht, 1995).

Lortz, Joseph. *Die Reformation in Deutschland*. Freiburg im Breisgau: Herder, 1940.

Luther, Martin. *D. Martin Luthers Werke: Kritische Gesamtausgabe, Abteilung Werke*. Weimar: H. Böhlau, 1883–1993.

———. *Luthers Werke in Auswahl*. Edited by Albert Leitzmann and Otto Clemen. 8 vols. Berlin: de Gruyter, 1959–67.

———. *Luther's Works*. St. Louis: Concordia/Philadelphia: Fortress Press, 1958–86.

———. *Sermons of Martin Luther*. Edited by John Nicolaus Lenker. 8 vols. Grand Rapids, MI: Baker Books, 1993.

Luther's Lives: Two Contemporary Accounts of Martin Luther. Translated and annotated by Elizabeth Vandiver, Ralph Keen, and Thomas D. Frazel. Manchester, UK: Manchester University Press, 2002. Distributed in the USA by Palgrave.

Maag, Karin. *Melanchthon in Europe*. Grand Rapids, MI: Baker Books, 1999.

Maltby, William S., ed. *Reformation Europe: A Guide to Research, 2*. St. Louis, MO: Center for Reformation Research, 1992.

Mannermaa, Tuomo. *Christ Present in Faith: Luther's View of Justification*. Minneapolis, MN: Fortress, 2005. Originally published as *In ipsa fide Christus adest: Luterilaisen ja ortodoksisen kritinuskonkäsityksen leikkauspiste* (Hannover: Lutherisches Verlagshaus, 1989).

———. *Der im Glauben gegenwärtige Christus, Rechtfertigung und Vergottung: Zum ökumenischen Dialog*. Hannover: Lutherisches Verlagshaus, 1989.

Marius, Richard. *Martin Luther: The Christian Between God and Death*. Cambridge, MA: Belknap, 1999.

Mattox, Mickey. *Defender of the Most Holy Matriarchs: Martin Luther's Interpretation of the Women of Genesis in the* Enarrationes in Genesin, *1535–1545*. Leiden: Brill, 2003.

McGrath, Alister E. *The Intellectual Origins of the European Reformation*. Oxford, UK: Blackwell Press, 1987.

———. *Luther's Theology of the Cross*. Oxford, UK: Basil Blackwell, 1985.

———. *Reformation Thought: An Introduction*. 2nd edition. Cambridge, MA: Blackwell Press, 1993.

McKim, Donald K. *The Cambridge Companion to Martin Luther*. Cambridge: Cambridge University Press, 2003.

McSorley, Harry J. *Luther: Right or Wrong? An Ecumenical-Theological Study of Luther's Major Work, The Bondage of the Will*. New York: Newman/Minneapolis: Augsburg, 1969.

Melanchthon, Philipp. *Corpus Reformatorum: Philippi Melanchthonis Opera quae Supersunt Omnia*. 28 vols. Halle: Schwetschke et Filium, 1834–60.

Miller, Gregory. "Fighting like a Christian: The Ottoman Advance and the Development of Luther's Doctrine of Just War." In *Caritas et Reformatio: Essays in Honor of Carter Lindberg*, edited by David M. Whitford, 89–102. St. Louis: Concordia, 2002.

———. "Luther on the Turks and Islam." *Lutheran Quarterly*, n.s. 14, no. 1 (2000): 79–97.

Ngien, Dennis. *The Suffering of God According to Martin Luther's "Theologia Crucis."* New York: Lang, 1995.

Oberman, Heiko A., *The Dawn of the Reformation: Essays in Late Medieval and Early Reformation Thought*. Edinburgh: T & T Clark, 1986.

———. *The Harvest of Medieval Theology: Gabriel Biel and Late Medieval Nominalism*. Cambridge, MA: Harvard University Press, 1963.

——. *The Impact of the Reformation*. Grand Rapids, MI: Eerdmans, 1994.

——. *Luther: Man Between God and the Devil*. Translated by Eileen Walliser-Schwarzbart. New Haven, CT: Yale University Press, 1989. Originally published as *Luther: Mensch zwischen Gott und Teufel* (Berlin: Severin and Seidler, 1982).

——. *The Reformation: Roots & Ramifications*. Translated by Andrew Colin Gow. Grand Rapids, MI: Eerdmans, 1994.

——. Review of *Martin Luther: The Christian Between God and Death*, by Richard Marius. *The New Republic* 221, no. 7 (August 16, 1999): 40–45.

Ocker, Christopher. *Church Robbers and Reformers, 1525–1547: Confiscation and Religious Rurpose in the Holy Roman Empire*. Leiden: Brill, 2006.

Oettinger, Rebecca Wagner. *Music as Propaganda in the German Reformation*. Burlington, VT: Ashgate, 2001.

Olivier, Daniel. *Luther's Faith*. Translated by John Tonkin. St. Louis, MI: Concordia, 1982. Originally published as *Le foi de Luther* (Paris: Beauchesne, 1978).

Ozment, Steven. *The Age of Reform: 1250–1550: An Intellectual and Religious History of Late Medieval and Reformation Europe*. New Haven, CT: Yale University Press, 1980.

——. *Protestants: The Birth of a Revolution*. New York: Doubleday, 1992.

——, ed. *Reformation Europe: A Guide to Research*. St. Louis, MO: Center for Reformation Research, 1982.

Pelikan, Jaroslav. *The Christian Tradition: A History of the Development of Doctrine*. Vol. 4, *Reformation of Church and Dogma (1300–1700)*. Chicago: University of Chicago Press, 1984.

Pesch, Otto H. *Theologie der Rechtfertigung bei Martin Luther und Thomas von Aquin*. Mainz: Grünewald, 1967.

Peters, Albrecht. *Kommentar zu Luthers Katechismen*. Edited by Gottfried Seebaß. 5 vols. Göttingen: Vandenhoeck & Ruprecht, 1990–94.

Peura, Simo. *Mehr als Mensch? Die Vergöttlichung als Thema der Theologie Martin Luthers von 1513 bis 1519*. Mainz: Zabern, 1994.

Rieth, Ricardo. *"Habsucht" bei Martin Luther: Ökonomisches und Theologisches Denken*. Weimar: Böhlau, 1996.

Rublack, Hans-Christoph, ed. *Die lutherische Konfessionalisierung in Deutschland*. Gütersloh: Mohn, 1992.

Saarinen, Rusto. *Gottes Wirken auf Uns*. Wiesbaden: Steiner, 1989.

Saarnivaara, Uuras. *Luther Discovers the Gospel: New Light upon Luther's Way from Medieval Catholicism to Evangelical Faith*. St. Louis, MO: Concordia, 1951.

Safley, Thomas Max. *The Reformation of Charity: The Secular and the Religious in Early Modern Poor Relief*. Boston: Brill, 2003.

Sasse, Herman. *This Is My Body: Luther's Contention for the Real Presence*. Minneapolis, MN: Augsburg, 1959.

Scheible, Heinz, ed. *Melanchthon: Eine Biographie*. Munich: Verlag C.H. Beck, 1997.

——. *Melanchthons Briefwechsel*. Stuttgart-Bad Cannstatt: Fromann-Holzboog, 1977–95.

Schilling, Heinz. "Confessional Europe." In *Handbook of European History 1400–1600: Late Middle Ages, Renaissance and Reformation*, edited by Thomas A. Brady Jr., Heiko A. Oberman, and James D. Tracy, 2:641–70. Leiden: Brill, 1995.

Schneider, John. *Melanchthon's Idea of Biblical Authority as It Developed under the Influence of His Rhetorical Theory to 1521*. Cambridge: Cambridge University Press, 1986.

——. *Philip Melanchthon's Rhetorical Construal of Biblical Authority: Oratio Sacra*. Lewiston, ME: Mellen, 1990.

Schofield, John. *Philip Melanchthon and the English Reformation.* Aldershot: Ashgate, 2006.

Schwarz, Hans. *True Faith in the True God: An Introduction to Luther's Life and Thought.* Translated by Mark William Worthing. Minneapolis, MN: Augsburg, 1996.

Schwarz, Reinhard. *Luther.* Göttingen: Vandenhoeck & Ruprecht, 1986.

Schwarzwäller, Klaus. *Kreuz und Auferstehung.* Göttingen: Vandenhoeck & Ruprecht, 2000.

———. *Shibboleth: Die Interpretation von Luthers Schrift* De servo arbitrio *seit Theodosius Harnack.* Munich: Kaiser, 1969.

———. "Verantwortung des Glaubens, Freiheit und Liebe nach der Dekalogauslegung Martin Luthers." In *Freiheit als Liebe bei/Freedom as Love in Martin Luther,* edited by Dennis D. Bielfeldt and Klaus Schwarzwäller, 133–58. Frankfurt: Lang, 1995.

Scribner, Robert. W. *For the Sake of Simple Folk: Popular Propaganda for the German Reformation.* Cambridge: Cambridge University Press, 1981.

Sider, Ronald J. *Andreas Bodenstein von Karlstadt: The Development of His Thought.* Leiden: Brill, 1974.

Siemon-Netto, Uwe. *The Fabricated Luther: The Rise and Fall of the Shirer Myth.* Foreword by Peter L. Berger. St. Louis, MO: Concordia, 1995.

Siggins, Ian. *Martin Luther's Doctrine of Christ.* New Haven, CT: Yale University Press, 1970.

Spitz, Lewis. *The Religious Renaissance of the German Humanists.* Cambridge, MA: Harvard University Press, 1963.

Stayer, James M. *Martin Luther, German Saviour: German Evangelical Theological Factions and the Interpretation of Luther, 1917–1933.* Montreal: McGill-Queens University Press, 2000.

Steinmetz, David C. *The Bible in the Sixteenth Century.* Durham, NC: Duke University Press, 1990.

———. *Luther in Context.* Bloomington: Indiana University Press, 1998.

———. *Misericordia Dei: The Theology of Johannes von Staupitz in Its Late Medieval Setting.* Leiden: Brill, 1968.

Stolt, Birgit. *Martin Luther, människohjärtat och Bibeln.* Stockholm: Verbum, 1994.

Strauss, Gerald. *Luther's House of Learning: Indoctrination of the Young in the German Reformation.* Baltimore: Johns Hopkins University Press, 1978.

Trigg, Jonathan. *Baptism in the Theology of Martin Luther.* Leiden: Brill, 1994.

Verzeichnis der im deutschen Sprachbereich ershienenen Drucke des XVI. Jahrhunderts [VD 16]. Stuttgart: Hiersemann, 1983–.

Vogel, Heinrich. *Vogel's Cross Reference and Index to the Contents of Luther's Works: A Cross Reference between the American Edition and the St. Louis, Weimar, and Erlangen Editions of Luther's Works.* Milwaukee, WI: Northwestern Publishing House, 1983.

Wabel, Thomas. *Sprache als Grenze in Luthers theologischer Hermeneutik und Wittgensteins Sprachphilosophie.* Berlin: W. de Gruyter, 1998.

Wengert, Timothy. *Human Freedom, Christian Righteousness: Philip Melanchthon's Exegetical Dispute with Erasmus of Rotterdam.* Oxford: Oxford University Press, 1998.

———. *Law and Gospel: Philip Melanchthon's Debate with John Agricola of Eisleben over Poenitentia.* Grand Rapids, MI: Baker Books, 1997.

———. *Philip Melanchton's Annotationes in Johanem in Relation to Its Predecessors and Contemporaries.* Geneva: Droz, 1987.

———. Review of *Union with Christ,* by Carl Bratten and Robert Jenson. *Theology Today* 56/3 (1999): 433.

———, ed., *Harvesting Martin Luther's Reflections on Theology, Ethics, and the Church.* Grand Rapids, MI: Eerdmans, 2003.

————. and M. P. Graham. *Philip Melanchthon (1497–1560) and the Commentary.* Sheffield: Sheffield Academic Press, 1997.

————, and Scott Hendrix, eds., *Philip Melanchthon: Then and Now (1497–1997): Essays Celebrating the 500th Anniversary of the Birth of Philip Melanchthon, Theologian, Teacher and Reformer.* Columbia, SC: Lutheran Theological Southern Seminary, 1999.

Wenz, G. *Theologie der Bekenntnisschriften der evangelisch-lutherischen Kirche,* 2 vols. Berlin: Aldine de Gruyter, 1996, 1998.

Whitford, David. "*Cura Religionis* or Two Kingdoms: The Late Luther on Religion and the State." *Church History* 71, no. 1 (2004): 41–62.

————. Review of *One with God: Salvation as Deification and Justification,* by Veli-Matti Kärkkäinen. *Reviews in Religion and Theology* 13, no. 2 (2006): 185–87.

————. *Tyranny and Resistance: The Magdeburg Confession and the Lutheran Tradition.* St. Louis, MO: Concordia, 2001.

Wicks, Jared. *Man Yearning for Grace: Luther's Early Spiritual Teaching.* Washington, DC: Corpus, 1968.

Wingren, Gustaf. *Luther on Vocation,* Translated by Carl C. Rasmussen. Philadelphia: Muhlenberg, 1957.

Wolgast, Eike. *Die Wittenberger Theologie und die Politik der evangelischen Stände.* Gütersloh: Gütersloher Verlagshaus, 1977.

Wriedt, Markus. *Gnade und Erwählung: Eine Untersuchung zu Johann von Staupitz und Martin Luther.* Mainz: Zabern, 1991.

Yeago, David. "Ecclesia Sancta, Ecclesia Peccatrix: The Holiness of the Church in Martin Luther's Theology." *Pro Ecclesia* 9, no. 3 (2000): 331–54.

Zachman, Randall. *The Assurance of Faith: Conscience in the Theologies of Martin Luther and John Calvin.* New ed. Grand Rapids, MI: Eerdmans, 2005.

Zur Mühlen, Karl-Heinz. *Nos extra nos: Luthers Theologie und zwischen Mystik und Scholastik.* Tübingen: Mohr/Siebeck, 1972.

2

Contributors to the Reformed Tradition

Amy Nelson Burnett

Anyone wishing to know how research on the Reformed tradition has changed in the past fifty years need only compare the 1954 standard work by John T. McNeill (*The History and Character of Calvinism*) with Philip Benedict's 2002 *Christ's Churches Purely Reformed: A Social History of Calvinism*. After an introductory section devoted to Ulrich Zwingli and Zurich, McNeill's book concentrates on John Calvin and developments in Geneva, then traces the spread of Calvinism in Europe and the American colonies. McNeill briefly discusses other theologians and churchmen such as Johannes Oecolampadius, Martin Bucer, and Heinrich Bullinger; however, his treatment of the Zurich Reformation as a precursor to that in Geneva, as well as his persistent use of the term "Calvinism" to describe the religious movement of the later sixteenth and seventeenth centuries, tends to make Calvin the definitive figure within the Reformed tradition. His final section, "Calvinism and Modern Issues," traces the development of the Calvinist churches into the nineteenth and twentieth centuries and argues for the relevance of Calvinism to the present day.

In contrast, although Benedict also uses the term "Calvinism" in his subtitle, he clarifies his terminology in the book's introduction, preferring the term "Reformed" for the larger religious tradition of which Calvin was a part and restricting "Calvinism" to those ideas directly traceable to Calvin. This distinction enables Benedict both to highlight the contribution of other figures, particularly Bullinger, to the Reformed tradition and to emphasize the significant diversity within that tradition with regard to issues such as ecclesiastical polity, liturgical practices, and church-state relations. Benedict also discusses the distinctive characteristics of the Reformed tradition concerning the ministry, the exercise of discipline, and the practice of piety in the early modern period. He closes with a much more ambivalent assessment of Calvinism's contribution to liberal democracy and capitalism and highlights the centrality of the Reformed tradition to early modern history rather than its continuing contribution to the (post-) modern world.

Benedict's masterful overview demonstrates the shift in the historiography of the Reformed tradition away from theology and great men, and toward a new concern with social and political context and with the impact of religious reform on common people. Because the book synthesizes much recent research on institutional development, popular piety, and the national characteristics of the various Reformed churches, this essay will not address these topics. Instead, it will concentrate on Continental theologians who contributed to the development of the Reformed tradition in the sixteenth century, and particularly on those from what is now Germany and Switzerland.

Sources, Scholarly Aids, and Sponsoring Institutions

The previous research guides reveal the growing recognition of theological diversity within the Reformed tradition. Ozment's 1982 research guide contained an essay by David Steinmetz titled "The Theology of Calvin and Calvinism" that focused entirely on the Genevan Reformer. Brian Armstrong's contribution, "Calvin and Calvinism," in Maltby's 1992 guide broadened the scope to include recent works on Zwingli, Bullinger, Bucer, and Theodore Beza, as well as on both Genevan and French Calvinism. In the same volume, J. Wayne Baker ("The Reformation at Zurich") looked more specifically at recent research on Zwingli, Bullinger, and the Zurich Reformation.

Over the past fifteen years, research on these and other contributors to the Reformed tradition has seen a renaissance of sorts, made possible by the publication of correspondence, critical editions, and bibliographies of works by and about various Reformed theologians. Armstrong described several of these editorial projects, particularly those concerning the works of individual reformers; some of these are highlighted below. In addition, there are other projects of broader interest to those studying the history of the Reformed tradition. Chief among these is a new critical edition (by Eberhard Busch et al.) of Reformed confessions, *Reformierte Bekenntnisschriften*.[1] When complete, this edition will include Reformed confessions and church ordinances from all of Europe and extending from Zwingli's 1523 Synod Articles through the Barmen Declaration of 1934. Another project of interest to scholars is the publication of the records of the Geneva Consistory, which begin in 1542. Four volumes are now in print, and the first volume has been translated into English.[2]

The critical editions described below have been augmented by microfiche versions of sixteenth-century imprints and out-of-print older monographs commercially available through IDC Publishers.[3] In addition to their series devoted to Calvin, Zwingli, and Bullinger, IDC offers microfiche reproductions of works dealing with the Reformation in Heidelberg and with Reformed Protestantism in Switzerland/Geneva, France/Strasbourg, the Netherlands and Germany, and more specifically in East Frisia and northwestern Germany. Of particular value are microfiche reproductions of two major letter collections preserved in Zurich's Zentralbibliothek. The Simler Sammlung, assembled by the eighteenth-century pastor and school superintendent Johann Jakob Simler, contains over two hundred volumes of documents related to Swiss church history, about one-third of which were transcribed from the originals in various archives and libraries throughout Switzerland and Germany. The Thesaurus Hottingerianus, collected by the seventeenth-century Orientalist Johann Heinrich Hottinger, contains both originals and later transcriptions of the letters of many Reformed church leaders and pastors from the sixteenth and seventeenth centuries as well.

The Thesaurus Hottingerianus microfiche series, as well as several others related to Reformed Protestantism published by IDC, are owned by the H. Henry Meeter Center for Calvin Studies in Grand Rapids. The Meeter Center also owns microfilm copies of correspondence not available elsewhere from the Bibliothèque Sainte Geneviève in Paris and the Zurich

---

[1]Volume 1 covers 1523 through 1549, and was published in two parts, in 2002 and 2006. Compare the older, partial collections of Reformed confessions: Müller, *Die Bekenntnisschriften der reformierten Kirche*; and Niesel, *Bekenntnisschriften und Kirchenordnungen der nach Gottes Wort reformierten Kirche* (translated into English by Cochrane as *Reformed Confessions of the Sixteenth Century*).

[2]Lambert et al., *Registres du Consistoire de Genève*; and Kingdon et al., *Registers of the Consistory of Geneva*.

[3]IDC Publishers can be found online at www.idcpublishers.com.

Staatsarchiv. In addition, they have microfilms of over sixty manuscript volumes of correspondence and synodical records pertaining to the French church preserved in the Bibliothèque publique et universitaire of Geneva. These films include the protocols of the Genevan Consistory and Small Council meetings, some records from the Genevan Company of Pastors, and a significant part of the Archives Tronchin, which contain manuscript letters and other documents from the late sixteenth through the early eighteenth century pertaining to Genevan and French Calvinism.

Another important microfilmed correspondence collection is the Thesaurus Baumianus, which can be consulted in the library of Concordia Seminary in St. Louis, Missouri. The Thesaurus Baumianus, preserved in Strasbourg's Bibliothèque nationale et universitaire, was copied in the nineteenth century by J. W. Baum, one of the editors of Calvin's *Opera*. Although many of its letters are themselves copies of those in the Simler Sammlung, the Thesaurus Baumianus's focus on the Alsatian reformers and its transcriptions of letters preserved only in Strasbourg make it a valuable supplement to the Zurich collections. An index of the Thesaurus Baumianus, published by Johannes Ficker in 1905, illustrates the value of this collection.

Despite the problems inherent in working with later manuscript transcriptions of sixteenth-century letters, all of these microform collections have the advantage of making more easily available to North American scholars the correspondence not only of major figures, but also of individuals such as Konrad Pellikan and Leo Jud, Zwingli's and Bullinger's associates in Zurich, and Oswald Myconius, Oecolampadius's successor in Basel, all of whom contributed to the shaping of the early Reformed church. In this respect, these letter collections supplement the older editions of the correspondence of the French-speaking reformers, of Joachim Vadian, of Ambrosius and Thomas Blarer, of Bucer with Landgraf Philipp of Hesse, and of Bullinger with the reformers of Graubünden.[4]

The most recent addition to the variety of sixteenth- and seventeenth-century sources now available to North American scholars is the Digital Library of Classic Protestant Texts created by Ad Fontes and now owned by Alexander Street Press. The Digital Library will eventually contain

---

[4]Herminjard, *Correspondance des Réformateurs dans les pays de langue française*; Arbenz and Wartmann, *Vadianische Briefsammlung, 1508–1540*; Schiess, *Briefwechsel der Brüder Ambrosius und Thomas Blarer, 1509–1548*; Lenz, *Briefwechsel Landgraf Philipps des Großmüthigen von Hessen mit Bucer*; and Schiess, *Bullingers Korrespondenz mit den Graubündnern*.

approximately 1500 works, emphasizing confessional documents, commentaries, and polemical treatises. Although it includes Lutheran and Anabaptist writers, the library is weighted towards works within the Reformed tradition. A relatively new venture, this searchable, full-text database is available to libraries through the Internet either for purchase or for an annual subscription fee.

Beyond ready access to their sources, scholars also need annual bibliographies to keep informed about the most recent publications in their field. Along with the yearly literature supplement of the *Archive for Reformation History*, students of the Reformed tradition can draw on two more specialized annual bibliographies now at least partially available via the web. The Bibliography of the Swiss/Zwinglian Reformation published in *Zwingliana* has an online version with limited search capabilities that begins in 1995.[5] The Calvin and Calvinism Bibliography, published annually since 1971 in *Calvin Theological Journal*, also has an online version beginning with 1997.[6] The Calvinism Resources Database, maintained by the Meeter Center, provides a searchable way of consulting all of the entries in the Calvinism bibliography.

Finally, the leadership of the institutes and congresses listed by Armstrong has changed during the past decade, but all of them continue to promote research on the Reformed tradition, whether in its Genevan or its Zurich form. Many of these now have websites that provide information regarding programs, resources, and publications. The Meeter Center's website is particularly useful because it contains links to most of these other organizations.

Two other research libraries in Germany deserve special mention. Since its inauguration in 1997, the Jan à Lasco Bibliothek in Emden has become another center for research on the Reformed tradition through its sponsorship of, and publication of proceedings from, conferences on Reformed topics. Its specialized collection of works on the Reformed tradition builds on the library of Emden's Reformed church, which dates back to the sixteenth century and includes the personal libraries of Albert Hardenberg and his contemporary, the Emden Bürgermeister Petrus Medmann. The books in Hardenberg's library have been digitized and are

---

[5]*Archive for Reformation History*; and Bächtold, Haag, and Ruetschi, "Neue Literatur zur zwinglischen Reformation."

[6]Tylenda, "Calvin Bibliography"; de Klerk and Fields, "Calvin [and Calvinism] Bibliography"; and Fields, "Calvin Bibliography," at www.calvin.edu/meeter/bibliography.

accessible online through the library's website. The Jan à Lasco Bibliothek also owns more recent source collections, such as the microfiche copy of the Simler Sammlung. Although the Herzog August Bibliothek in Wolfen-büttel is generally associated more with German Lutheranism than with the Reformed tradition, that library also has significant holdings of works by many Reformed theologians. In addition, it has invested in microfiche reproductions such as the Thesaurus Hottingerianus. Like the Meeter Center, both the à Lasco Bibliothek and the Herzog August Bibliothek offer stipends to scholars wanting to make use of their collections. Their websites give information on their programs and are the gateways to each library's online catalog.

Origins of the Reformed Tradition: Calvin, the Zurich Reformers, and Bucer

Scholars first began to look more broadly at the founding figures of the Reformed tradition a generation ago. David Steinmetz's collection of short biographies, *Reformers in the Wings* (originally published in 1971), has recently been updated and includes chapters on Bullinger, Beza, Bucer, and Peter Martyr Vermigli. The chapters on Zwingli, Bullinger, Calvin, and Beza in Carter Lindberg's edited volume, *Reformation Theologians*, summarize each individual's thought. Jill Raitt's edited volume, *Shapers of Religious Traditions in Germany*, also contains brief biographies of Bullinger and Beza, as well as of the lesser-known figures Lambert Daneau and Zacharias Ursinus. All three books provide convenient starting points in English for anyone doing research on these individuals.

It would be easy to devote an entire essay to scholarship on Calvin, leaving no room to discuss other significant Reformed figures. Fortunately, there is no need for such competition, since Maag and Fields have published elsewhere a useful overview of Calvin resources.[7] Those wanting a sense of current directions in Calvin research should also look at the recently published proceedings of the 2002 meeting of the International Congress on Calvin Research and of the 2003 and 2005 colloquia of the Calvin Studies Society.[8] Perhaps the most important addition to the primary sources available for work on Calvin is the searchable, full-

---

[7]Maag and Fields, "Calvin in Context."

[8]Selderhuis, *Calvinus Praeceptor Ecclesiae*; Foxgrover, *Calvin and the Company of Pastors*; and Foxgrover, *Calvin, Beza, and Later Calvinism*.

text version of the *Calvini Opera* (Corpus Reformatorum) on DVD-ROM.[9] The *Cambridge Companion to John Calvin*, in which the Maag and Fields article is published, contains several other essays introducing the reader to various aspects of Calvin's life and thought. Randall Zachman's *John Calvin as Pastor, Teacher, and Theologian* is a valuable introduction to Calvin.

In the last three years, several other important contributions to the literature on Calvin have appeared, including Paul Helm's *John Calvin's Ideas*, which approaches the reformer from a philosophical perspective, and Stephen Edmondson's *Calvin's Christology*. Three other works are devoted to Calvin's exegesis of scripture: E. A. De Boer examines Calvin's sermons in *John Calvin on the Visions of Ezekiel*, Ward Holder (*John Calvin and the Grounding of Interpretation*) studies Calvin's exegetical method in his early commentaries on the Pauline epistles, and Raymond Blacketer, in *The School of God*, looks at Calvin's use of rhetoric in his sermons and commentary on Deuteronomy. Finally, Jean-François Gilmont's study of Calvin and the printed book is now available in English translation, as is Herman Selderhuis's study of Calvin's Psalms commentary.[10]

Elsewhere in this volume, Bruce Gordon has summarized recent research on the two founders of the second source of Reformed theology, the Zurich reformers Ulrich Zwingli and Heinrich Bullinger, but mention should be made here of the wealth of information available to scholars in Bullinger's correspondence. Consisting of over twelve thousand letters, it is larger than the correspondence of Luther, Calvin, and Zwingli combined. Bullinger wrote only about two thousand letters out of that total; the remainder are from his correspondents and shed light on Zurich's influence throughout the Continent. The critical edition of this correspondence, consisting of twelve volumes as of 2007, has now reached the 1540s, and publication is proceeding at the rate of a volume a year. The Institute for Swiss Reformation History at the University of Zurich sponsors an Internet databank of the entire correspondence searchable by correspondent and geographical location.[11]

---

[9]*Calvini Opera Database*, ed. Selderhuis. This project was sponsored by the Institute for Reformation Research, affiliated with the Theological University in Apeldoorn, the Netherlands.

[10]Gilmont, *John Calvin and the Printed Book*; and Selderhuis, *Calvin's Theology of the Psalms*.

[11]Bullinger, *Briefwechsel*; and Bullinger Letters Database, online at http://www.unizh.ch/irg/briefwechseldb/ index_engl.html.

The third major source of the Reformed tradition was the Strasbourg reformer Martin Bucer. Progress on a critical edition of Bucer's works has been slow. *De Regno Christi*, the first volume of *Martini Buceri Opera Latina*, was published in 1954, but a second volume did not appear until 1982, and only four more volumes have been published since then. *Deutsche Schriften* have received more financial support, with twelve out of a projected seventeen volumes in print, either fully or in part. Publication of Bucer's correspondence has proven to be more difficult because of his infamously illegible handwriting—the first volume did not appear until 1979; the sixth volume, which extends into 1531, has only recently been published.[12] Little of Bucer's work has been translated into English, but there is a collection of theological loci drawn from his commentaries, as well as an abridged translation of *De Regno Christi*.[13] The recently published descriptive bibliography prepared at the Bucer-Forschungsstelle at the University of Heidelberg has sections devoted to Bucer's works published during the reformer's lifetime, to those published after his death, to those parts of his correspondence that have been printed, and to literature about Bucer from the sixteenth century through 2002.[14]

The four hundredth anniversary of Bucer's birth in 1991 occasioned two collections of essays that summarized much Bucer research to date. The two-volume *Martin Bucer and Sixteenth Century Europe* (edited by Christian Krieger and Mark Leinhard) resulted from a conference in Strasbourg that brought together almost everyone then working on the Alsatian reformer. David Wright's *Martin Bucer* looked more specifically at aspects of Bucer's ecclesiology and sacramental theology. Martin Greschat's outstanding biography (*Martin Bucer*) was also published to coincide with the commemoration. This biography has been translated into English with a new concluding chapter that surveys works on Bucer published since 1990, providing an up-to-date overview in English of Bucer research; it therefore complements Seebaß's "Bucer-Forschung seit dem Jubilaümsjahr 1991," which includes works published during the 1990s. To these, two further works should be added: Nicholas Thompson's *Eucharistic Sacrifice and Patristic Tradition*, which examines Bucer's interpretation of the sacrifice of the mass at the time of the religious colloquies and the attempted reformation of Cologne, and *Martin Bucer zwischen Luther und Zwingli* (edited

---

[12]Bucer, *Correspondance de Martin Bucer.*
[13]Bucer, *Common Places of Martin Bucer*; and Bucer, "De Regno Christi."
[14]Seebaß, *Martin Bucer (1491–1541): Bibliographie.*

by Arnold and Hamm), a collection of papers loosely related to Bucer's emerging concord efforts in the months between the Marburg Colloquy and the Diet of Augsburg.

Several recent studies have demonstrated that through the 1540s the relations between Zurich on the one hand and Geneva and Strasbourg on the other were not as smooth as they have traditionally been portrayed.[15] These tensions made the agreement between Calvin and Bullinger embodied in the Consensus Tigurinus of 1549 even more significant, for the Consensus and the second eucharistic controversy that resulted would identify Calvin with the Zurich theologians rather than with Bucer and, through him, with the German Lutherans. Ulrich Gäbler and Paul Rorem have described the political context and the theological negotiations that led to the Consensus Tigurinus, which can in this respect be seen as the founding document of the Reformed tradition.[16]

Other Reformed Theologians

Calvin's successor Theodore Beza has never received as much attention as his mentor. The critical edition of Beza's correspondence, the first volume of which was published in 1960, has now reached the mid-1580s.[17] These letters, many of them with churches and individuals in France, highlight Beza's importance for the Huguenot church, as do *Registres de la Compagnie des Pasteurs de Genève* (edited by Bergier), whose thirteen volumes extend to 1618. Unfortunately, there is no plan to begin a critical edition of Beza's own writings, and all that is available to scholars is an edition of his previously unpublished lectures on Romans and Hebrews given during the mid-1560s.[18] Frédéric Gardy and Alain Dufour's *Bibliographie des oeuvres théologiques* is somewhat unusual in that the secondary literature concerning Beza is given not separately at the end but is interspersed through the descriptive bibliography of Beza's work. The annual "Calvin and Calvinism" bibliography described above is the best guide to more recent publications on Beza.

Paul Geisendorf's 1949 biography, *Théodore de Bèze*, is still the standard work on Beza. After a number of publications in the 1970s on Beza's

---

[15]Heron, "Calvin and Bullinger"; van Stam, "Das Verhältnis zwischen Bullinger und Calvin"; Burnett, "Basel and the Wittenberg Concord"; and Burnett, "Myth of the Swiss Lutherans."

[16]Gäbler, "Das Zustandekommen des Consensus Tigurinus"; and Rorem, *Calvin and Bullinger on the Lord's Supper.*

[17]Dufour, Nicollier-De Weck, and Bodenmann, *Correspondance de Théodore de Bèze.*

[18]Fraenkel and Perrotet, *Théodore de Bèze.*

eucharistic theology, his ecclesiology, his views on predestination, his influence on the English New Testament, and on the relationship of reason and revelation, there were no further monographs on Beza until Jill Raitt's study, *The Colloquy of Montbéliard,* which discussed Beza's role during this confrontation between Reformed and Lutheran theologians.[19] In the last few years, four more works have appeared on Beza's relations with the French church, his religious epistemology, his text-critical work on the New Testament, and on the pastoral aspects of his understanding of God's sovereignty.[20] The papers delivered at a conference commemorating the four hundredth anniversary of Beza's death in 1605 have also just been published, and we can hope that they will stimulate further study of the man who led Geneva's church through the last third of the sixteenth century.[21]

Other contributors to the Reformed tradition have also gradually begun to receive more attention, often in the form of conference volumes that combine bibliographical aids, historiographical surveys and individual studies. A 1980 colloquium devoted to Guillaume Farel, for example, resulted in the two-volume *Actes du Colloque Farel Neuchâtel,* volume 1 containing essays devoted to his life and influence, the second containing a register of his correspondence and a bibliography of his published works.[22] The 1930 biography *Guillaume Farel* is the most detailed description of Farel's life, but it is plagued by inconsistencies and contradictions that stem from the fact that it was written by a committee of scholars without a general editor. Its characterizations of Farel's theology are also open to revision. Elfriede Jacobs, for instance, has argued that Farel's view of the sacraments was not derived from Zwingli but developed instead in dialogue with Oecolampadius and Bucer and was already close to Calvin's before the latter came to Geneva.[23]

The relationship between Farel and Calvin has been examined from various perspectives by David Wiley, Heiko Oberman, and Cornelis Augustijn.[24] Similarly, Calvin's friendship with Pierre Viret has been the

---

[19]See Maruyama, *Ecclesiology of Theodore Beza*; Bray, *Theodore Beza's Doctrine of Predestination*; Backus, *Reformed Roots of the English New Testament*; Kickel, *Vernunft und Offenbarung bei Theodore Beza*; and Raitt, *Eucharistic Theology of Theodore Beza.*

[20]Manetsch, *Theodore Beza and the Quest for Peace in France*; Mallinson, *Faith, Reason, and Revelation*; Krans, *Beyond What Is Written*; and Wright, *Our Sovereign Refuge.*

[21]Backus, *Théodore de Bèze.*

[22]Volume 2 contains "Répertoire de la correspondance de Guillaume Farel" by Rémy Scheurer and Dominique Quadioni, and "L'oeuvre imprimé de Guillaume Farel" by Jean-François Gilmont.

[23]Jacobs, "Die Sakramentslehre Wilhelm Farels."

[24]Wiley, "Calvin's Friendship with Guillaume Farel"; Oberman, "Calvin and Farel"; and Augustijn, "Farel und Calvin in Bern."

subject of essays by Robert Linder and Willem Balke.[25] Jean Barnaud's 1911 biography, *Pierre Viret*, has been updated by two recent articles looking at Viret's career in France.[26] Georges Bavaud has explored Viret's theology as a whole, while Linder has looked more closely at Viret's political thought.[27] Dominique-A. Troilo's "L'oeuvre de Pierre Viret" not only lists other secondary works about Viret but also considers questions relating to Viret's published writings and correspondence.

In contrast to Calvin's associates, Zwingli's closest colleague, Oecolampadius, has drawn little scholarly attention. Ernst Staehelin's bibliography of the Basel reformer's publications, as well as his biography and his edition of Oecolampadius's correspondence, are still the standard works.[28] The only monograph to appear since Staehelin's biography is Olaf Kuhr's work on Oecolampadius's view of church discipline.[29] The rewards to be gained from a closer study of Oecolampadius are illustrated by the articles of Irena Backus, Hughes Oliphant Old, and Martin Jung on the Basel reformer's use of the church fathers, his commentaries on the Bible, and his role in the eucharistic controversy, respectively.[30]

Bucer's colleague Wolfgang Capito has also been generally neglected. Since the publication of Beate Stierle's *Capito als Humanist* and James Kittelson's *Wolfgang Capito*, there have been no new monographs on the Strasbourg reformer. The closest approximation is *Der Berner Synodus von 1532* (edited by Gottfried Locher), which commemorates the Bern Synod of 1532. The first volume includes a combination church ordinance and theology primer written by Capito, while the essays in the second volume touch on aspects of the Strasbourger's theology and so update Otto Erich Strasser's 1928 work, *Capitos Beziehungen zu Bern*, on Capito's influence in Bern. Research on Capito has been hindered by the lack of scholarly tools such as bibliographies or editions, although one can find much related to Capito in the works cited in the Bucer bibliographies discussed above. Olivier Millet's *Correspondance de Wolfgang Capiton*, which includes a

---

[25]Linder, "Brothers in Christ"; and Balke, "Jean Calvin und Pierre Viret."

[26]Roussel, "Pierre Viret en France"; and Chareyre, "Les derniers miracles de Viret."

[27]Bavaud, *Le réformateur Pierre Viret*; and Linder, *Political Ideas of Pierre Vinet*.

[28]Staehelin, "Bibliographische Beiträge zum Lebenswerk Oekolampads"; Staehelin, "Oekolampad-Bibliographie"; Staehelin, *Das theologische Lebenswerk Johannes Oekolampads*; and Staehelin, *Briefe und Akten zum Lebel Oekolampads*.

[29]Kuhr, "*Die Macht des Bannes und der Buße*." For a summary of his views in English, see Kuhr, "Significance of Oecolampadius."

[30]Backus, "What Prayers for the Dead"; Backus, "Disputations of Baden and Berne"; Old, "Homiletics of John Oecolampadius"; and Jung, "Abendmahlsstreit."

brief summary of each letter's contents, is a starting point for further research, although it is not widely available. It is being supplanted by *Correspondence of Wolfgang Capito*, a new translation by Erika Rummel, the first volume of which is now in print. The editors are also making the original Latin or German letters available online for subscribers to the Iter gateway (which includes not only many research libraries but also individual members of the Renaissance Society of America).[31] This editorial project may generate new interest in the man who was the most prominent reformer in Strasbourg until he deferred to Bucer's more vigorous personality.

Another reformer strongly influenced by Bucer during his formative years was Wolfgang Musculus, who underwent a short apprenticeship in Strasbourg before he was sent to Augsburg as a pastor. The Augsburg Interim forced Musculus to flee the Swabian city, and for the remainder of his life he taught theology at Bern's academy. Musculus was the first Reformed theologian to write a *Loci Communes*, a theology textbook that went through several editions over the last third of the sixteenth century.

Until fairly recently, only Musculus's political theology had received any scholarly attention because it was seen as one of the influences on the English state church.[32] A conference in 1996 helped give greater prominence to other aspects of Musculus's life and thought.[33] The biographical sketches by Rudolf Dellsperger and Marc van Wijnkoop Lüthi have now been joined by Reinhard Bodenmann's full-length biography.[34] Lüthi is also assembling a register of Musculus's correspondence, much of which is located in either Bern or Zofingen, with an eye to future publication.[35] The list of Musculus's printed works reveals his importance both as a translator of patristic works and as a biblical exegete.[36] Craig Farmer's *Gospel of John in the Sixteenth Century*, places Musculus's exegesis in the context of patristic, Scholastic, and contemporary interpretations of the Gospel.

The most important of the Zurich theologians after Bullinger was Peter Martyr Vermigli, the Italian Augustinian who fled the Roman Inquisition in 1542 and died in Zurich in 1562 after teaching theology in both

---

[31]Electronic Capito Project: http://www.itergateway.org/index.cfm.

[32]Kreßner, *Schweizer Ursprünge*; and Bäumlin, "Naturrecht und obrigkeitliches Kirchenregiment."

[33]Papers from the conference were published in Dellsperger et al., *Wolfgang Musculus*.

[34]Dellsperger, "Wolfgang Musculus"; Dellsperger, "Wolfgang Musculus: Leben und Werk"; Lüthi, "Wolfgang Musculus in Bern"; and Bodenmann, *Wolfgang Musculus*.

[35]Weber, "Wolfgang und Abraham Musculus."

[36]Lüthi, "Druckwerkeverzeichnis des Wolfgang Musculus."

Strasbourg and Oxford. J. Patrick Donnelly's *Bibliography of the Works of Peter Martyr Vermigli* not only contains information on all of the Italian theologian's works, but also includes a register of his correspondence and a bibliography of secondary sources on Vermigli. It therefore supersedes the checklist of correspondence included in Marvin Anderson's otherwise still useful study, *Peter Martyr: A Reformer in Exile*. Vermigli is the only Reformed theologian besides Calvin whose works are available in English translation: the Peter Martyr Library now has nine volumes published;[37] supplementing this series is Robert Kingdon's *The Political Thought of Peter Martyr Vermigli: Selected Texts and Commentary*.

A few studies devoted to Vermigli were written before 1970, most notably Joseph McLelland's work on his sacramental theology and Philip McNair's study of his formative years in Italy.[38] The current interest in Vermigli more properly dates from the 1970s, however, when most of those now responsible for the bibliography and English translations began their research. In addition to Anderson's book, that decade saw publications on Vermigli's first stay in Strasbourg, on his eucharistic theology, and on the influence of Scholasticism on his thought.[39] A conference held in 1977 brought together many of those then studying Vermigli to share their research and stimulated work on the bibliography and translations mentioned above.[40] Frank James III's study of Vermigli's doctrine of predestination is the most recent contribution to this line of scholarship.[41] Both these established scholars and a new generation of researchers gathered at another conference in 1999, and the essay collection that resulted is a useful introduction to the current state of Vermigli studies. McLelland's essay looks back to developments since 1977, while Emidio Campi combines a brief biographical sketch with a discussion of Vermigli's broader influence; both essays point to several areas for future research.[42] Last but not least, the essays edited by James consider Vermigli's relations with other reformers as well as important aspects of his exegetical and theological work.[43]

---

[37]See the bibliography for a listing of the volumes of Vermigli's works published thus far. The Peter Martyr Library has fifteen additional volumes projected to be published in the future.

[38]McLelland, *Visible Words of God*; and McNair, *Peter Martyr in Italy*.

[39]Sturm, *Die Theologie Peter Martyr Vermiglis*; Corda, *Veritas Sacramenti*; and Donnelly, *Calvinism and Scholasticism in Vermigli's Doctrine of Man and Grace*.

[40]McLelland, *Peter Martyr Vermigli and Italian Reform*.

[41]James, *Peter Martyr Vermigli and Predestination*.

[42]Campi, "Streifzug durch Vermiglis Biographie"; and McLelland, "From Montreal to Zurich." The essays from this conference are collected in Campi et al., *Peter Martyr Vermigli*.

[43]James, *Peter Martyr Vermigli and the European Reformations*.

Zurich's influence outside Switzerland is illustrated in the thought of yet another late convert to the Reformed faith, the Polish nobleman Jan à Lasco. Like Vermigli, à Lasco was already in his forties when he broke with the Roman church, but in the remaining seventeen years of his life, he became one of the most international of all reformers. After seven years as superintendent of the church of East Frisia, he went to London where he became head of the Strangers' Church. Following Mary's accession to the English throne, à Lasco returned to Emden briefly, then became pastor of the refugee church in Frankfurt, and finally returned to his homeland in Poland in 1557, where he died three years later.

A nineteenth-century edition of à Lasco's works and correspondence edited by Abraham Kuyper is still the basis for any study of the Polish-born reformer; to this should be added Cornel Zwierlein's recent edition of à Lasco's 1548 treatise on the Lord's Supper.[44] Basil Hall's *John à Lasco* provides a brief overview of à Lasco's life in English. Oskar Bartel's lengthier biography, *Jan Laski*, is a problematic German translation from the original Polish. Bartel's biography has been largely supplanted by Henning Jürgens's careful study, *Johannes à Lasco in Ostfriesland*, which, despite its title, is devoted almost equally to the period before à Lasco's open break with Rome and his first stay in East Frisia, and by Dirk Rodgers's *John à Lasco in England*. The seventeen conference papers contained in Strohm's 2000 *Johannes à Lasco* reflect the range of à Lasco's contacts and his influence.

À Lasco's friend Albert Hardenberg later claimed at least partial credit for à Lasco's conversion, but their relationship was not untroubled. Wim Janse has demonstrated that Hardenberg, who was driven from his post as cathedral preacher in Bremen because of his "Zwinglian" view of the Lord's Supper, was actually a faithful student of Bucer. Janse's work illustrates the many theological currents influencing the development of the Reformed tradition in northwestern Germany. J.-V. Pollet also discusses Bucer's relationships with à Lasco and Hardenberg in his study of religious developments in the Low Countries and the lower Rhineland.[45]

Further south in Germany, the conversion of the Electoral Palatinate to the Reformed confession in 1563 raised Heidelberg's theology faculty to prominence. Despite its importance as the outpost of the Reformed

---

[44]Kuyper, *Joannis à Lasco opera*; and Zwierlein, "Ein verschollen geglaubter Abendmahlstraktat Johannes à Lascos von 1548."

[45]Janse, *Albert Hardenberg als Theologe*; Janse, "À Lasco und Albert Hardenberg"; and Pollet, *Martin Bucer*.

Church within the Holy Roman Empire, the theological developments in the Palatinate have received relatively little scholarly attention. Derk Visser has published a full-length biography, *Zacharias Ursinus, the Reluctant Reformer*, while Erdmann Sturm's *Der junge Zacharias Ursin* includes a list of his correspondence from 1551 to 1563. Christopher Burchill has also written a biographical sketch of Ursinus, as well as another on his colleague Hieronymus Zanchi.[46] Discussions of Zanchi have focused on his view of predestination and his conflict with Johannes Marbach in Strasbourg; John Farthing, in particular, has written several articles on various aspects of Zanchi's thought.[47] Kaspar Olevianus has received less attention, but two articles on his life and career, as well as a bibliography of his works, were published in commemoration of the four hundredth anniversary of his death.[48] In addition to these works on individual theologians, research on the Reformed tradition in Heidelberg has clustered around three issues: the development of covenant theology, the theology and influence of the Heidelberg Catechism, and the conflict over church discipline that pitted Thomas Erastus, as spokesman for the Zurich position, against the Calvinist position defended by Olevianus.[49]

The absence of French and Dutch theologians from this survey may be striking, but it is not surprising in view of the political turmoil and warfare as well as the relatively late establishment of Reformed academies and universities in both countries. The most significant French theologian besides Beza during this time, Lambert Daneau, spent considerable time in Geneva and the Netherlands. Paul de Félice's brief nineteenth-century biography also includes an edition of Daneau's surviving correspondence. Olivier Fatio's study of Daneau's years in Leiden was followed by a larger study of Daneau's use of dialectic for exegesis and theology.[50] Most recently, Christoph Strohm has examined Daneau's work to demonstrate

---

[46]Burchill, "On the Consolation of a Christian Scholar"; and Burchill, "Girolamo Zanchi."

[47]Moltmann, *Predestination und Perseveranz*; Gründler, *Die Gotteslehre Girolamo Zanchis*; and Spijker, "Bucer als Zeuge Zanchis im Strassburger Prädestinationsstreit." Works by Farthing include "'De coniugio spirituali,'" "'Foedus Evangelicum,'" "Christ and the Eschaton," "Holy Harlotry," and "Patristics, Exegesis, and the Eucharist."

[48]Müller, "Caspar Olevian"; Menk, "Casper Olevian"; and Goeters, "Bibliographia Oleviana."

[49]Visser, "Covenant in Zacharias Ursinus"; Strehle, *Calvinism, Federalism, and Scholasticism*; Weir, *Origins of Federal Theology*; Bierma, *German Calvinism in the Confessional Age*; Hollweg, *Neue Untersuchungen zur Geschichte und Lehre*; Henss, *Der Heidelberger Katechismus*; Bierma, "Doctrine of the Sacraments"; Wesel-Roth, *Thomas Erastus*; and Walton, "Der Streit zwischen Thomas Erastus und Caspar Olevian."

[50]Félice, *Lambert Daneau*; Fatio, *Nihil pulchrius ordine*; and Fatio, *Méthode et théologie*.

the blending of humanism, both Aristotelian and Stoic philosophy, and legal training on the development of Reformed ethical thought.[51]

In *Frühorthodoxie und Rationalismus*, Ernst Bizer used Daneau, as well as Beza, Ursinus, and Zanchi, to illustrate the growing emphasis on reason within early Reformed orthodoxy. His argument brings us to the broader development of Reformed orthodoxy over the course of the sixteenth century, an issue that has received considerable attention in the last fifteen years, thanks to the revisionism of Richard Muller.

The Development of Reformed Orthodoxy

The older interpretation of early Reformed orthodoxy is best presented by Wilhelm Neuser's contribution to volume 2 of the *Handbuch der Dogmen- und Theologiegeschichte*. The fact that Neuser is unable to cite other literature besides his own research on many of the developments he describes attests both to the dearth of studies and to Neuser's own significant contribution to a better understanding of the development of the Reformed tradition; Goeters's survey of Reformed confessions in Germany is the only parallel treatment. Neuser's synthesis is shaped by an understanding of Reformed Scholasticism first laid out by Brian Armstrong and widely adopted by other scholars.[52] This definition characterizes Reformed Scholasticism as emphasizing deductive reasoning based on Aristotelian philosophy, attributing to reason a place of equal standing with faith in theology, viewing scripture as a unified and comprehensive account used as the norm for determining orthodoxy, and having a pronounced interest in metaphysics.

Muller has criticized this definition, arguing instead that Protestant Scholasticism was a methodology used in the schools rather than a specific philosophy, that it made eclectic use not only of Aristotle but of other philosophical traditions as well, and that early Reformed orthodoxy was as indebted to the philological and exegetical priorities of humanism as it was to Scholastic method and the use of metaphysics.[53] Muller is equally adamant in his rejection of the older view that predestination served as the central organizing doctrine of Reformed orthodoxy. In a sense, Muller's approach to the development of Reformed theology is the counterpart to

---

[51]Strohm, *Ethik im frühen Calvinismus.*

[52]Neuser, "Dogma und bekenntnis in der Reformation"; Goeters, "Genesis, Formen und Hauptthemen"; and Armstrong, *Calvinism and the Amyraut Heresy.*

[53]Muller, "Problem of Protestant Scholasticism"; and Muller, "Reformation, Orthodoxy, 'Christian Aristotelianism.'"

Benedict's reappraisal of the development of the Reformed Church more generally. Much of his vehemence is directed against an older generation of scholars who interpreted Calvin and his successors within a neo-orthodox framework and who held the Genevan Reformer up as the standard by which all subsequent theologians should be judged.[54] As a consequence, he is extremely critical of many of the works cited above.

Muller's two-part discussion of "Calvin and the 'Calvinists,'" updated in *After Calvin*, a collection of his previously published essays, is a provocative survey of the historiography of the transition from Reformation to Reformed orthodoxy that closes with an agenda for the reappraisal of the development of orthodoxy. He presents his own overview of that development in the same book and at greater length in the first volume of his four-volume *Post-Reformation Reformed Dogmatics*. Muller links the development of orthodoxy to generational change. The deaths of the first and second generation of theologians, most of them during the 1560s, coincided with a burst of doctrinal codification, as embodied in the Heidelberg Catechism and the many national confessions written during that decade. The writings of these reformers, and the confessions derived from them, in turn laid the foundation for all future developments in Reformed orthodoxy, as later generations elaborated on them and drew out their implications. The 1560s thus signaled the beginning of Protestant orthodoxy, whose first phase continued into the early seventeenth century. It was only during this phase that Reformed theology began to move outside of its south German and Swiss roots to become truly international. This early phase ended with the death of many of its leading figures and the resolution of the Arminian controversy at the Synod of Dort. The next generation constituted a second phase of early orthodoxy that was succeeded in the mid-seventeenth century by the high orthodoxy that extended well into the eighteenth century.

Muller's redefinition of Protestant Scholasticism and his interest in Reformed orthodoxy has been taken up by other scholars, as is reflected by the essays in *Protestant Scholasticism: Essays in Reassessment* edited by Carl Trueman and R. Scott Clark and *Reformation and Scholasticism: An Ecumenical Enterprise*, edited by Willem van Asselt and Eef Dekker. Donald Sinnema's studies of Scholastic method in the writings of Andreas

---

[54]Muller, *Unaccommodated Calvin*. For another presentation of the relationship between Calvin and later Calvinism, strongly influenced by Muller, see Trueman, "Calvin and Calvinism."

Hyperius and Antoine de la Roche Chandieu, and his examinations of the discussion on the use of Ramist logic and Aristotelian ethics and physics in theology are particularly worth noting.[55] Common to the reappraisal of Protestant Scholasticism in these essays is greater sensitivity to intellectual and cultural context, emphasis on the importance of the exegetical tradition, and the recognition of continuities between the later Middle Ages, the Reformation, and orthodoxy.

What does this survey suggest about further directions for research on the Reformed tradition? As Muller has pointed out, very little work has been done on even the major figures of the later sixteenth and seventeenth century, let alone their more obscure contemporaries. The increasing availability of correspondence, commentaries, and other theological writings has opened the door for further research not only on the individuals described here but also on their successors and heirs. Just as important as the contribution of individual theologians to the development of the Reformed tradition is the establishment of the academies and universities within which those theologians worked. Muller is correct in arguing that Protestant Scholasticism can only be properly understood within the academic context that produced it. Schindling's book on the Strasbourg academy, *Humanistische Hochschule und freie Reichsstadt*, is a detailed examination of a school that served as a model for many other Reformed schools, while Menk's study of the academy at Herborn, Maag's work on the Academy of Geneva and the French Huguenot academies, Clotz's book on the university of Leiden, and Burnett on the university of Basel are examples of how to approach the study of institutions responsible for training Reformed pastors.[56] A recent conference volume highlights the connections between Reformed theology, philosophy, and law at the University of Heidelberg at the end of the sixteenth century, while Howard Hotson's study of the Reformed encyclopedist Johann Heinrich Alsted illustrates the interplay between institutional factors and the intellectual currents of late humanism among Reformed intellectuals more generally. Hotson is one of several scholars who have discussed the attraction of

---

[55]Sinnema, "Aristotle and Early Reformed Orthodoxy"; Sinnema, "Discipline of Ethics"; Sinnema, "Antoine de Chandieu's Call for a Scholastic Reformed Theology": and Sinnema, "Distinction between Scholastic and Popular."

[56]Menk, *Die Hohe Schule Herborn*; Maag, *Seminary or University?*; Maag, "Huguenot Academies"; Clotz, *Hochschule für Holland*; and Burnett, *Teaching the Reformation.*

Reformed intellectuals towards Ramism and Ramism's place within Reformed academies and universities.[57]

Yet another area that offers significant potential for future research is that of Reformed liturgy and worship. *The Oxford History of Christian Worship* (by Geoffrey Wainwright and Karen B. Westerfield Tucker) has three chapters on Reformed worship in various areas of Europe; two recent essay collections are also concerned either wholly or in part with Reformed worship, while the eucharistic liturgies used in a variety of Reformed churches throughout Europe are available in a modern edition.[58] In addition to the works on worship in German-speaking Switzerland described in Bruce Gordon's essay in this volume, Bernard Roussel, Christian Grosse, and Andrew Spicer have published stimulating articles on reformed ritual and liturgical space in France and Geneva through the sixteenth and seventeenth centuries.[59]

Finally, scholars might consider the pastoral impact of Reformed orthodoxy as embodied in its sermons. Most studies of Reformed preaching focus on the major figures—Bullinger for German-speaking Switzerland, and Calvin and Beza for Geneva—but H. O. Old has provided brief overviews of the preaching of Oecolampadius and the Strasbourg reformers, as well as longer discussions of Zwingli and Calvin, within his larger work on preaching during the Reformation.[60] The only work to match the broader picture drawn by current research on Lutheran preaching in Germany is Françoise Chevalier's study of French Reformed sermons.[61] Although they do not exist in the same quantity as Lutheran sermons, there are sufficient numbers of published Reformed sermons, especially from the later sixteenth and seventeenth century, to merit closer study. For

---

[57]Strohm et al., *Späthumanismus und reformierte Konfession*; Hotson, *Johann Heinrich Alsted*; Freedman, "Diffusion of the Writings of Petrus Ramus"; Freedman, "Ramus and the Use of Ramus at Heidelberg"; Strohm, "Theologie und Zeitgeist"; Feingold et al., *Influence of Petrus Ramus*; and Hotson, *Commonplace Learning*.

[58]Pitassi, *Edifier ou instruire?*; and Maag and Witvliet, *Worship in Medieval and Early Modern Europe* (which includes translations of primary sources with each essay, making them particularly useful for teaching). Eucharistic liturgies are available in Pahl, *Coena Domini I*.

[59]Roussel, "Ensevelir honnestement les corps"; Grosse, "Anthropologie historique" ; Grosse, "'En spirit et en vérite'?"; Grosse, "Places of Sanctification"; and Spicer, "'Qui est de Dieu.'"

[60]Büsser, "Bullingers Festtagspredigten"; Büsser, "H. Bullingers 100 Predigten"; Stephens, "Bullinger's Sermons on the Apocalypse"; Parker, *Calvin's Preaching*; Delval, "La Prédication d'un Réformateur"; Delval, "Orthodoxie et Prédication"; DeVries, "Calvin's Preaching"; and Old, *Reading and Preaching of the Scriptures*.

[61]Chevalier, *Prêcher sous l'édit des Nantes*. Cf. Burnett, "'To Oblige My Brethren'"; and the essays in Taylor, *Preachers and People*.

instance, both Bullinger and his younger colleague Rudolf Gwalther produced commentaries on most of the books of the Bible in the form of Latin
homilies. Examination of these sermons would give new insights into the
implications of stylistic differences between Lutheran and Reformed sermons, as well as into Zurich's specific theological contribution to the development of Reformed orthodoxy.

These few suggestions demonstrate that the development of the
Reformed tradition in the later sixteenth and seventeenth centuries provides a wide open field for research. There is still much to learn for those
willing to move beyond Calvin to recognize the broad roots and tremen-
dous diversity that existed within the movement most properly known as
Reformed.

Bibliography

ELECTRONIC RESOURCES

Bächtold, Hans Ulrich, Hans Jakob Haag, and Kurt Jacob Rüetschi. *Neue Literatur zur
zwinglischen Reformation*: http://www.unizh.ch/irg/biblio.html.
Bullinger Letters Database: http://www.unizh.ch/irg/briefwechseldb/index_engl.html
Calvini Opera Database 1.0. Edited by Herman J. Selderhuis. CD-ROM. Apeldoorn, Neth-
erlands: Instituut voor Reformatieonderzoek, 2005.
Calvinism Resources Database: http://www.calvin.edu/library/database/card/
Concordia Seminary, St. Louis, MO: http://www.csl.edu/
Digital Library of Classic Protestant Texts: http://solomon.tcpt.alexanderstreet.com/.
Electronic Capito Project (Iter gateway): http://www.itergateway.org/index.cfm.
Fields, Paul. *Calvin Bibliography* [1997–]: http://www.calvin.edu/meeter/bibliography.
Herzog August Bibliothek, Wolfenbüttel, Germany: http://www.hab.de.
H. Henry Meeter Center for Calvin Studies, Grand Rapids, MI:
    http://www.calvin.edu/meeter.
IDC Publishers: http://www.idcpublishers.com.
Institute for Reformation Research, Theological University in Apeldoorn, the Netherlands:
    http://www.instituutreformatieonderzoek.nl/english.
Jan à Lasco Bibliothek, Emden, Germany: http://www.jalb.de/flshmenu/frameset.html.

PRIMARY SOURCES

Arbenz, Emil, and Hermann Wartmann, eds. *Vadianische Briefsammlung, 1508–1540*. Mit-
    teilungen zur Vaterländischen Geschichte 24–30a. St. Gallen, Switzerland: Fehr,
    1884–1913.
Bergier, Jean-François, et al., eds. *Registres de la Compagnie des Pasteurs de Genève*.
    Travaux d'humanisme et renaissance. Geneva: Droz, 1962–.
Bucer, Martin. *Common Places of Martin Bucer*. Translated and edited by David F. Wright.
    Courtenay Library of Reformation Classics 4. Abingdon, UK: Sutton Courtenay
    Press, 1972.

———. *Correspondance de Martin Bucer.* Edited by Jean Rott et al. Martini Buceri Opera Omnia, Series 3. Leiden: Brill, 1979–.

———. "De Regno Christi." In *Melanchthon and Bucer,* translated and edited by Wilhelm Pauck, 155–394. Library of Christian Classics 19. Philadelphia: Westminster, 1969.

———. *Deutsche Schriften.* Edited by Robert Stupperich et al. Martini Buceri Opera Omnia, Series 1. Gütersloh, Germany: Gütersloher Verlagshaus G. Mohn, 1960–.

———. *Martini Buceri Opera Latina.* Edited by François Wendel et al. Martini Buceri Opera Omnia, Series 2. Paris: Presses universitaires; 1954; Leiden: Brill, 1982–.

Bullinger, Heinrich. *Briefwechsel.* Edited by Fritz Büsser et al. Heinrich Bullinger Werke, Part 2. Zurich: Theologischer Verlag, 1973–.

Busch, Eberhard, et al., eds. *Reformierte Bekenntnisschriften.* Neukirchen-Vluyn, Germany: Neukirchener Verlag, 2002–.

Cochrane, Arthur C., ed. *Reformed Confessions of the Sixteenth Century.* Philadelphia: Westminster, 1966.

Dufour, Alain, et al., eds. *Correspondance de Théodore de Bèze: Recueillie par Hippolyte Aubert.* Travaux d'humanisme et renaissance 40–. Geneva: Droz, 1960–.

Fraenkel, Pierre, and Luc Perrotet, eds. *Théodore de Bèze: Cours sur les Epîtres aux Romains et aux Hébreux 1564–66 d'après les Notes de Marcus Widler. Thèses disputées à Genève, 1564–1567.* Travaux d'humanisme et renaissance 226. Geneva: Droz, 1988.

Herminjard, A.-L., ed. *Correspondance des Réformateurs dans les pays de langue Française.* 9 vols. 1878–97. Reprint, Nieuwkoop, Netherlands: de Graaf, 1965–66.

Kingdon, Robert M. *The Political Thought of Peter Martyr Vermigli: Selected Texts and Commentary.* Geneva: Droz, 1980.

———, et al., eds. *The Registers of the Consistory of Geneva at the Time of Calvin.* Grand Rapids, MI: Eerdmans, 2000.

Kuyper, Abraham, ed. *Joannis à Lasco opera tam edita quam inedita duobus voluminibus comprehensa.* Amsterdam: Muller, 1866.

Lambert, Thomas, Isabella M. Watt, Robert M. Kingdon, and Jeffrey R. Watt. *Registres du Consistoire de Genève au temps de Calvin.* Travaux d'humanisme et renaissance. Geneva: Droz, 1996–.

Lenz, Max, ed. *Briefwechsel Landgraf Philipps des Großmüthigen von Hessen mit Bucer.* 3 vols. Publikationen aus den königlichen preussischen Stattsarchiven 5, 28, 47. Leipzig: Hirzel, 1880–91.

Müller, E. F. Karl, ed. *Die Bekenntnisschriften der reformierten Kirche: In authentischen Texten mit geschichtlicher Einleitung und Register.* Leipzig: Deichert, 1903. Reprint, Zurich: Theologischer Buchhandlung, 1987.

Niesel, Wilhelm, ed. *Bekenntnisschriften und Kirchenordnungen der nach Gottes Wort reformierten Kirche.* Zurich: Evangelischer Verlag, 1938.

Pahl, Irmgard, ed. *Coena Domini I. Die Abendmahlsliturgie der Reformationskirchen im 16./ 17. Jahrhundert.* Spicilegium Friburgense 29. Fribourg, Switzerland: Universitätsverlag, 1983.

Rummel, Erika, ed. *The Correspondence of Wolfgang Capito.* Toronto: University of Toronto Press, 2005–.

Schiess, Traugott, ed. *Briefwechsel der Brüder Ambrosius und Thomas Blaurer, 1509–1548.* 3 vols. Freiburg im Breisgau: Fehsenfeld, 1908–12.

———, ed. *Bullingers Korrespondenz mit den Graubündnern.* 3 vols. Quellen zur Schweizergeschichte 23–25. 1904–6. Reprint, Nieuwkoop, Netherlands: de Graaf, 1968.

Staehelin, Ernst, ed. *Briefe und Akten zum Leben Oekolampads, zum vierhundertjährigen Jubiläum der Basler Reformation.* 2 vols. Quellen und Forschungen zur Reformationsgeschichte 10, 19. Leipzig: Heinsius, 1927–34.

Vermigli, Peter Martyr. *Commentary on Aristotle's Nicomachean Ethics,* edited by Emidio Campi and Joseph McLelland. Peter Martyr Library 9; Sixteenth Century Essays and Studies 73. Kirksville, MO: Truman State University Press, 2006.

———. *Commentary on the Lamentations of the Prophet,* translated and edited by Dan Shute. Peter Martyr Library 6; Sixteenth Century Essays and Studies 55. Kirksville, MO: Truman State University Press, 2002.

———. *Dialogue on the Two Natures in Christ,* translated and edited by John Patrick Donnelly. Peter Martyr Library 2; Sixteenth Century Essays and Studies 31. Kirksville, MO: Truman State University Press, 1995.

———. *Early Writings: Creed, Scripture, Church,* translated and edited by Mario Di Gangi and Joseph C. McLelland. Peter Martyr Library 1; Sixteenth Century Essays and Studies 30. Kirksville, MO: Truman State University Press, 1994.

———. *Life, Letters, and Sermons,* translated and edited by John Patrick Donnelly. Peter Martyr Library 5; Sixteenth Century Essays and Studies 42. Kirksville, MO: Truman State University Press, 1999.

———. *The Oxford Treatise and Disputation on the Eucharist,* translated and edited by Joseph C. McLelland. Peter Martyr Library 7; Sixteenth Century Essays and Studies 56. Kirksville, MO: Truman State University Press, 2000.

———. *The Peter Martyr Reader,* edited by John Patrick Donnelly, Frank James III, and Joseph C. McLelland. Kirksville, MO: Truman State University Press, 1999.

———. *Philosophical Works: On the Relation of Philosophy to Theology,* translated and edited by Joseph C. McLelland. Peter Martyr Library 4; Sixteenth Century Essays and Studies 39. Kirksville, MO: Truman State University Press, 1996.

———. *Predestination and Justification: Two Theological Loci,* translated and edited by Frank James III. Peter Martyr Library 8; Sixteenth Century Essays and Studies 68. Kirksville, MO: Truman State University Press, 2003.

———. *Sacred Prayers Drawn from the Psalms of David,* translated and edited by John Patrick Donnelly. Peter Martyr Library 3; Sixteenth Century Essays and Studies 34. Kirksville, MO: Truman State University Press, 1996.

Zwierlein, Cornel A. "Ein verschollen geglaubter Abendmahlstraktat Johannes à Lascos von 1548." *Archiv für Reformationsgeschichte* 92 (2001): 43–86.

SELECTED SECONDARY WORKS

Actes du Colloque Farel Neuchâtel, 29 Sept.–1er Oct. 1980. 2 vols. Cahiers de la Revue de Théologie et de Philosophie 9. Geneva: Revue de Théologie et de Philosophie, 1983.

Anderson, Marvin W. *Peter Martyr: A Reformer in Exile (1542–1562): A Chronology of Biblical Writings in England and Europe.* Bibliotheca humanistica et reformatorica 10. Niewkoop, Netherlands: de Graaf, 1975.

Archive for Reformation History [Archiv für Reformationsgeschichte]. Literature review supplement nos. 1– (1972–).

Armstrong, Brian G. "Calvin and Calvinism." In *Reformation Europe: A Guide to Research II,* edited by William S. Maltby, 75–103. St. Louis, MO: Center for Reformation Research, 1992.

———. *Calvinism and the Amyraut Heresy: Protestant Scholasticism and Humanism in Seventeenth-Century France.* Madison: University of Wisconsin Press, 1969.

Arnold, Matthieu, and Berndt Hamm, eds. *Martin Bucer zwischen Luther und Zwingli.* Spätmittelalter und Reformation, Neue Reihe 23. Tübingen: Mohr Siebeck, 2003.

Asselt, Willem J. von, and Eef Dekker, eds. *Reformation and Scholasticism: An Ecumenical Enterprise.* Grand Rapids, MI: Baker Academic, 2001.

Augustijn, Cornelis. "Farel und Calvin in Bern 1537–1538." In *Calvin im Kontext der Schweizer Reformation,* edited by Peter Opitz, 9–23. Zurich: Theologischer Verlag, 2003.

Bächtold, Hans Ulrich, et al. "Literatur zur schweizerischen/zwinglischen Reformation." *Zwingliana* 13– (1969–). Available online at http://www.unizh.ch/irg/biblio.html.

Backus, Irena. "The Disputations of Baden, 1526, and Berne, 1528: Neutralizing the Early Church." *Studies in Reformed Theology and History* 1/1 (1993): 1–130.

———. *The Reformed Roots of the English New Testament: The Influence of Theodore Beza on the English New Testament.* Pittsburgh, PA: Pickwick Press, 1980.

———. "What Prayers for the Dead in the Tridentine Period? [Pseudo-] John of Damascus, 'De his qui in fide dormierunt' and its 'Protestant' Translation by Johannes Oecolampadius." In *Das reformierte Erbe. Festschrift für Gottfried W. Locher zu seinem 80. Geburtstag,* edited by Heiko A. Oberman et al., 2:13–24. Zwingliana 19/2. Zurich: Theologischer Verlag, 1992.

———, ed. *Théodore de Bèze (1519–1605). Actes du Colloque de Genève (septembre 2005).* Geneva: Droz, 2007.

Baker, J. Wayne. "The Reformation at Zurich in the Thought and Theology of Huldrych Zwingli and Heinrich Bullinger." In *Reformation Europe: A Guide to Research II,* edited by William S. Maltby, 46–73. St. Louis, MO: Center for Reformation Research, 1992.

Balke, Willem. "Jean Calvin und Pierre Viret." In *Calvin im Kontext der Schweizer Reformation,* edited by Peter Opitz, 57–92. Zurich: Theologischer Verlag, 2003.

Barnaud, Jean. *Pierre Viret. Sa vie et son oeuvre (1511–1571).* St.-Amans, France: Carayol, 1911. Reprint, Nieuwkoop, Netherlands: de Graaf, 1973.

Bartel, Oskar. *Jan Łaski.* Translated by Arnold Starke. Berlin: Evangelische Verlagsanstalt, 1981.

Bäumlin, R. "Naturrecht und obrigkeitliches Kirchenregiment bei Wolfgang Musculus." In *Für Kirche und Recht. Festschrift für Johannes Heckel,* edited by Sigfried Grundmann, 120–43. Cologne/Graz: Böhlau, 1959.

Bavaud, Georges. *Le réformateur Pierre Viret (1511–1571): Sa théologie.* Histoire et société 10. Geneva: Labor et Fides, 1986.

Benedict, Philip. *Christ's Churches Purely Reformed: A Social History of Calvinism.* New Haven, CT: Yale University Press, 2002.

Bierma, Lyle D. "The Doctrine of the Sacraments in the Heidelberg Catechism: Melanchthonian, Calvinist or Zwinglian?" *Studies in Reformed Theology and History* 4 (1999): 1–48.

———. *German Calvinism in the Confessional Age: the Covenant Theology of Caspar Olevianus.* Grand Rapids, MI: Baker Books, 1996.

Bizer, Ernst. *Frühorthodoxie und Rationalismus.* Theologische Studien 71. Zurich: EVZ-Verlag, 1963.

Blacketer, Raymond A. *The School of God: Pedagogy and Rhetoric in Calvin's Interpretation of Deuteronomy.* Dordrecht: Springer, 2006.

Bodenmann, Reinhard. *Wolfgang Musculus (1497–1563): Destin d'un autodidacte lorrain au siècle des Réformes.* Travaux d'humanisme et renaissance 343. Geneva: Droz, 2000.

Bray, John S. *Theodore Beza's Doctrine of Predestination.* Bibliotheca humanistica et reformatorica 12. Nieuwkoop, Netherlands: de Graaf, 1975.

Büsser, Fritz. "Bullingers Festtagspredigten (1558). Die Zürcher Reformation zwischen Tradition und Erneuerung." In *Oratio: Das Gebet in patristischer und reformatorischer Sicht. Festschrift Alfred Schindler*, edited by Emidio Campi, Leif Grane, and Adolf Martin Ritter, 175–83. Göttingen: Vandenhoeck & Ruprecht, 1999.

———. "H. Bullingers 100 Predigten über die Apokalypse." *Zwingliana* 27 (2000): 117–31.

Burchill, C. J. "Girolamo Zanchi: Portrait of a Reformed Theologian and His Work." *Sixteenth Century Journal* 15 (1984): 185–207.

———. "On the Consolation of a Christian Scholar: Zacharius Ursinus (1534–83) and the Reformation in Heidelberg." *Journal of Ecclesiastical History* 37 (1986): 565–83.

Burnett, Amy Nelson. "Basel and the Wittenberg Concord." *Archiv für Reformationsgeschichte* 96 (2005): 33–56.

———. "The Myth of the Swiss Lutherans: Martin Bucer and the Eucharistic Controversy in Bern." *Zwingliana* 32 (2005): 45–70.

———. *Teaching the Reformation: Ministers and Their Message in Basel, 1529–1629*. Oxford Studies in Historical Theology. New York: Oxford University Press, 2006.

———. "'To Oblige My Brethren': The Reformed Funeral Sermons of Johann Brandmüller." *Sixteenth Century Journal* 36 (2005): 37–54.

Campi, Emidio. "Streifzug durch Vermiglis Biographie." In *Peter Martyr Vermigli*, edited by Campi et al., 17–36.

Campi, Emidio, et al., eds. *Peter Martyr Vermigli: Humanism, Republicanism, Reformation*, Travaux d'Humanisme et renaissance 365. Geneva: Droz, 2002.

Chevalier, Françoise. *Prêcher sous l'édit de Nantes: La prédication réformée au XVIIe siècle en France*. Histoire et société 30. Geneva: Labor et Fides, 1994.

Chareyre, Philippe. "'Les derniers miracles de Viret vivant et mourant.' Pierre Viret et la réformation du Béarn (1567–1571)." *Bulletin de la Société de l'Histoire du Protestantisme Français* 144 (1998): 841–80.

Clotz, Henrike L. *Hochschule für Holland: Die Universität Leiden in Spannungsfeld zwischen Provinz, Stadt und Kirche, 1575–1619*. Stuttgart: Franz Steiner, 1998.

Corda, Salvatore. *Veritas Sacramenti: A Study in Vermigli's Doctrine of the Lord's Supper*. Zürcher Beiträge zur Reformationsgeschichte 6. Zurich: Theologischer Verlag, 1975.

De Boer, E. A. *John Calvin on the Visions of Ezekiel: Historical and Hermeneutical Studies in John Calvin's 'Sermons Inédits,' Especially on Ezekiel 36–48*. Leiden: Brill, 2004.

De Klerk, Peter, and Paul Fields. "Calvin [and Calvinism] Bibliography." *Calvin Theological Journal* 7– (1972–).

Dellsperger, Rudolf. "Wolfgang Musculus (1497–1563), Prädikant bei Hl. Kreuz von 1531 bis 1548." In *Die Augsburger Kirchenordnung von 1537 und ihr Umfeld*. Edited by Reinhard Schwarz, 91–111. Gütersloh: Gerd Mohn, 1988.

———. "Wolfgang Musculus (1497–1563): Leben und Werk." In *Wolfgang Musculus (1497–1563) und die oberdeutsche Reformation*. Edited by Rudolf Dellsperger et al., 23–41. Colloquia Augustana 6. Berlin: Akademischer Verlag, 1997.

Dellsperger, Rudolf, et al., eds. *Wolfgang Musculus (1497–1563) und die oberdeutsche Reformation*. Colloquia Augustana 6. Berlin: Akademischer Verlag, 1997.

Delval, Michel. "Orthodoxie et Prédication: Théodore de Bèze." *Bulletin de la Société de l'Histoire du Protestantisme Français* 134 (1988): 693–97.

———. "La Prédication d'un Réformateur au XVIe Siècle: L'activité homilétique de Théodore de Bèze." *Mélanges de Science Religieuse* 41 (1984): 61–86.

DeVries, Dawn. "Calvin's Preaching." In McKim, *Cambridge Companion to John Calvin*, 106–24.

Donnelly, John Patrick. *Calvinism and Scholasticism in Vermigli's Doctrine of Man and Grace*. Studies in Medieval and Renaissance Thought 18. Leiden: Brill, 1976.

Donnelly, John Patrick, Robert M. Kingdon, and Marvin W. Anderson, eds. *A Bibliography of the Works of Peter Martyr Vermigli*. Sixteenth Century Essays and Studies 13. Kirksville, MO: Sixteenth Century Journal Publishers, 1990.

Edmondson, Stephen. *Calvin's Christology*. Cambridge: Cambridge University Press, 2004.

Farmer, Craig S. *The Gospel of John in the Sixteenth Century: The Johannine Exegesis of Wolfgang Musculus*. Oxford Studies in Historical Theology. New York: Oxford University Press, 1997.

Farthing, John L. "Christ and the Eschaton: The Reformed Eschatology of Jerome Zanchi." In *Later Calvinism: International Perspectives*, edited by W. Fred Graham, 333–54. Sixteenth Century Essays and Studies 22. Kirksville, MO: Sixteenth Century Journal Publishers, 1994.

———. "'De coniugio spirituali': Jerome Zanchi on Ephesians 5:22–33." *Sixteenth Century Journal* 24 (1993): 621–52.

———. "'Foedus Evangelicum': Jerome Zanchi on the Covenant." *Calvin Theological Journal* 29 (1994): 149–67.

———. "Holy Harlotry: Jerome Zanchi and the Exegetical History of Gomer (Hosea 1–3)." In *Biblical Interpretation in the Era of the Reformation: Essays Presented to David C. Steinmetz in Honor of His Sixtieth Birthday*, edited by Richard A. Muller and John L. Thompson, 292–312. Grand Rapids, MI: Eerdmans, 1996.

———. "Patristics, Exegesis, and the Eucharist in the Theology of Girolamo Zanchi." In *Protestant Scholasticism, Essays in Reassessment*, edited by Trueman and Clark, 79–95.

Fatio, Olivier. *Méthode et Théologie: Lambert Daneau et les débuts de la scholastique réformée*. Travaux d' humanisme et renaissance 147. Geneva: Droz, 1976.

———. *Nihil pulchrius ordine: Contribution à l'étude de l'établissement de la discipline ecclésiastique aux Pays-Bas ou Lambert Daneau aux Pays-Bas (1581–1583)*. Leiden: Brill, 1971.

Feingold, Mordechai, et al., eds. *The Influence of Peter Ramus: Studies in Sixteenth and Seventeenth Century Philosophy and the Sciences*. Schwabe-Philosophica 1. Basel: Schwabe, 2001.

Félice, Paul de. *Lambert Daneau (de Beaugency-sur-Loire), pasteur et professeur en théologie, 1530–1595: Sa vie, ses oeuvrages, ses lettres inédites*. Geneva: Slatkine Reprints, 1971.

Ficker, Johannes. *Thesaurus Baumianus: Verzeichnis der Briefe und Akten*. Strasbourg: Kaiserliche Universitäts- und Landesbibliothek Selbstverlag, 1905.

Foxgrover, David, ed. *Calvin and the Company of Pastors: Papers Presented at the 14th Colloquium of the Calvin Studies Society*. Grand Rapids, MI: CRC Product Services, 2004.

———, ed. *Calvin, Beza and Later Calvinism: Papers Presented at the 15th Colloquium of the Calvin Studies Society*. Grand Rapids, MI: CRC Product Services, 2006.

Freedman, Joseph S. "The Diffusion of the Writings of Petrus Ramus in Central Europe, c. 1570–c. 1630." *Renaissance Quarterly* 46 (1993): 98–152.

———. "Ramus and the Use of Ramus at Heidelberg within the Context of Schools and Universities in Central Europe, 1572–1622." In Strohm et al., *Späthumanismus und reformierte Konfession*, 93–126.

Gäbler, Ulrich. "Das Zustandekommen des Consensus Tigurinus vom Jahre 1549." *Theologische Literaturzeitung* 104 (1979): 321–332.

Gardy, Frédéric, and Alain Dufour, eds. *Bibliographie des oeuvres théologiques, littéraires, historiques et juridiques de Th. de Bèze*. Travaux d'humanisme et renaissance 41. Geneva: Droz, 1960.

Geisendorf, Paul-F. *Théodore de Bèze*. Geneva: Labor et Fides, 1949.

Gilmont, Jean François. *John Calvin and the Printed Book*. Translated by Karin Maag. Kirksville, MO: Truman State University Press, 2005. Originally published as *Jean Calvin et le livre imprimé* (Geneva: Droz, 1997).

——. "L'oeuvre imprimé de Guillaume Farel." In *Actes du Colloque Farel Neuchâtel, 29 Sept.–1er Oct. 1980*. Cahiers de la Revue de Theologie et de Philosophie 9/2. Geneva: Revue de Théologie et de Philosophie, 1983.

Goeters, J. F. G. "Bibliographia Oleviana." *Monatshefte für evangelische Kirchengeschichte des Rheinlandes* 37/38 (1988/89): 320–37.

——. "Genesis, Formen und Hauptthemen des reformierten Bekenntnisses in Deutschland. Eine Übersicht." In *Die reformierte Konfessionalisierung in Deutschland—das Problem der "Zweiten Reformation": Wissenschaftliches Symposion des Vereins für Reformationsgeschichte 1985*, edited by Heinz Schilling, 44–59. Schriften des Vereins für Reformationsgeschichte 195. Gütersloh, Germany: Gerd Mohn, 1986.

Greschat, Martin. *Martin Bucer: Ein Reformator und seine Zeit 1491–1551*. Munich: Beck, 1990. Translated by Stephen E. Buckwalter as *Martin Bucer: A Reformer and His Times* (Louisville, KY: Westminster John Knox Press, 2004).

Grosse, Christian. "Anthropologie historique: Les rituels réformés (XVIe–XVIIe siècles)." *Bulletin de la Société de l'histoire du Protestantisme Français* 148 (2002): 979–1009.

——. "'En esprit et en vérité'? La part du rituel dans la culture religieuse réformé (Genève, XVI siècle)." In Selderhuis, *Calvinus Praeceptor Ecclesiae*, 303–21.

——. "Places of Sanctification: The Liturgical Sacrality of Genevan Reformed Churches, 1535–1566." In *Sacred Space in Early Modern Europe*, edited by Will Coster and Andrew Spicer, 60–80. Cambridge: Cambridge University Press, 2005.

Gründler, Otto. *Die Gotteslehre Girolamo Zanchis und ihre Bedeutung für seine Lehre von der Prädestination*. Beiträge zur Geschichte und Lehre der Reformierten Kirche 20. Neukirchen-Vluyn, Germany: Neukirchener Verlag, 1965.

Guillaume Farel, 1489–1565: Biographie nouvelle, écrite d'après les documents originaux par un groupe d'historiens, professeurs et pasteurs de Suisse, de France et d'Italie. Neuchâtel/Paris, 1930. Reprint, Geneva: Slatkine, 1978.

Hall, Basil. *John à Lasco (1499–1560). A Pole in Reformation England*. Friends of Dr. Williams's Library Lectures 25. London: Dr. Williams's Trust, 1971.

Helm, Paul. *John Calvin's Ideas*. 2nd edition. Oxford: Oxford University Press, 2004.

Henss, Walter. *Der Heidelberger Katechismus im konfessionspolitischen Kräftespiel seiner Frühzeit: Historisch-bibliographische Einführung der ersten vollständigen deutschen, der sogenannten 3. Auflage von 1563 und der darzugehörigen lateinischen Fassung*. Zurich: Theologischer Verlag, 1983.

Heron, Alasdair. "Calvin and Bullinger 1536–1549." In *Profile des reformierten Protestantismus aus vier Jahrhunderten. Vorträge der ersten Emder Tagung zur Geschichte des reformierten Protestantismus*, edited by Matthias Freudenberg, 49–69. Wuppertal, Germany: Foedus, 1999.

Holder, R. Ward. *John Calvin and the Grounding of Interpretation: Calvin's First Commentaries*. Leiden: Brill, 2006.

Hollweg, Walter. *Neue Untersuchungen zur Geschichte und Lehre des Heidelberger Katechismus*. Beiträge zur Geschichte und Lehre der Reformierten Kirche 13. Neukirchen, Germany: Neukirchener Verlag, 1961.

Hotson, Howard. *Commonplace Learning: Ramism and Its German Ramifications, 1543–1630*. Oxford: Oxford University Press, 2007.

———. *Johann Heinrich Alsted 1588–1638: Between Renaissance, Reformation, and Universal Reform*. Oxford Historical Monographs. Oxford: Clarendon, 2000.

Jacobs, Elfriede. *Die Sakramentslehre Wilhelm Farels*. Zürcher Beiträge zur Reformationsgeschichte 10. Zurich: Theologisches Verlag, 1978.

James, Frank A., III. *Peter Martyr Vermigli and Predestination: The Augustinian Inheritance of an Italian Reformer*. Oxford Theological Monographs. Oxford: Clarendon, 1998.

———. ed. *Peter Martyr Vermigli and the European Reformations*. Studies in the History of Christian Traditions 115. Leiden: Brill, 2004.

Janse, Wim. "À Lasco und Albert Hardenberg: Einigkeit im Dissens." In Strohm, *Johannes à Lasco*, 261–82.

———. *Albert Hardenberg als Theologe: Profil eines Bucer-Schülers*. Studies in the History of Christian Thought 57. Leiden: Brill, 1994.

Jung, Martin H. "Abendmahlsstreit: Brenz und Oekolampad." *Blätter für württembergische Kirchengeschichte* 100 (2000): 143–61.

Jürgens, Henning P. *Johannes à Lasco in Ostfriesland: Der Werdegang eines europäischen Reformators*. Spätmittelalter und Reformation Neue Reihe 18. Tübingen, Germany: Mohr Siebeck, 2002.

Kickel, W. *Vernunft und Offenbarung bei Theodore Beza; Zum Problem des Verhältnisses von Theologie, Philosophie und Staat*. Beiträge zur Geschichte und Lehre der Reformierten Kirche 25. Neukirchen-Vluyn, Germany: Neukirchener Verlag, 1978.

Kittelson, James M. *Wolfgang Capito, From Humanist to Reformer*. Studies in Medieval and Reformation Thought. Leiden: Brill, 1975.

Krans, Jan. *Beyond What Is Written: Erasmus and Beza as Conjectural Critics of the New Testament*. Leiden: Brill, 2006.

Kreßner, Helmut. *Schweizer Ursprünge des anglikanischen Staatskirchentums*. Schriften des Vereins für Reformationsgeschichte 170. Gütersloh: Bertelsmann, 1953.

Krieger, Christian, and Marc Lienhard, eds. *Martin Bucer and Sixteenth Century Europe. Actes du colloque de Strasbourg, 28–31 août 1991*. 2 vols. Studies in Medieval and Reformation Thought 52–53. Leiden: Brill, 1993.

Kuhr, Olaf. *"Die Macht des Bannes und der Buße": Kirchenzucht und Erneuerung der Kirche bei Johannes Oekolampad (1482–1531)*. Basler und Berner Studien zur historischen und systematischen Theologie 68. Bern: Peter Lang, 1999.

———. "The Significance of Oecolampadius and the Basel Discipline Ordinance for the Institution of Ecclesiastical Discipline in Geneva." *Scottish Bulletin of Evangelical Theology* 16 (1998): 19–33.

Lindberg, Carter, ed. *The Reformation Theologians: An Introduction to Theology in the Early Modern Period*. Oxford: Blackwell, 2002.

Linder, Robert. "Brothers in Christ: Pierre Viret and John Calvin as Soul-Mates and Co-Laborers in the Work of the Reformation." In *Calvin Studies Society Papers 1995, 1997*. Edited by David Foxgrover, 134–58. Grand Rapids, MI: CRC Product Services, 1998.

———. *The Political Ideas of Pierre Viret*. Travaux d'humanisme et renaissance 64. Geneva: Droz, 1964.

Locher, Gottfried W., ed. *Der Berner Synodus von 1532: Edition und Abhandlungen zum Jubiläumsjahr 1982*. 2 vols. Neukirchen-Vluyn: Neukirchener Verlag, 1984–88.

Lüthi, Marc van Wijnkoop. "Druckwerkeverzeichnis des Wolfgang Musculus (1497–1563)." In *Wolfgang Musculus (1497–1563) und die oberdeutsche Reformation*, edited by Rudolf Dellsperger, 351–414. Colloquia Augustana 6. Berlin: Akademischer Verlag, 1997.

———. "Wolfgang Musculus in Bern (1549–1563)." In Dellsperger, *Wolfgang Musculus,* 281–98.

Maag, Karin. "The Huguenot Academies: Preparing for an Uncertain Future." In Mentzer and Spicer, *Society and Culture in the Huguenot World,* 139–56.

———. *Seminary or University? The Genevan Academy and Reformed Higher Education, 1560–1620.* St. Andrews Studies in Reformation History. Aldershot, Hants: Scolar Press, 1995.

———, and John D. Witvliet, eds. *Worship in Medieval and Early Modern Europe: Change and Continuity in Religious Practice.* Notre Dame, IN: University of Notre Dame Press, 2004.

———, and Paul Fields. "Calvin in Context: Current Resources." In *The Cambridge Companion to John Calvin,* edited by Donald K. McKim, 317–29. Cambridge: Cambridge University Press, 2004.

Mallinson, Jeffrey. *Faith, Reason, and Revelation in Theodore Beza (1519–1605).* Oxford Theological Monographs. Oxford: Oxford University Press, 2003.

Manetsch, Scott M. *Theodore Beza and the Quest for Peace in France, 1572–1598.* Studies in Medieval and Reformation Thought 79. Leiden: Brill, 2000.

Maruyama, Tadataka. *The Ecclesiology of Theodore Beza.* Travaux d'humanisme et renaissance 166. Geneva: Droz, 1978.

McKim, Donald K., ed. *The Cambridge Companion to John Calvin.* Cambridge: Cambridge University Press, 2004.

McLelland, Joseph C. "From Montreal to Zurich (1949–1999): Vermigli Studies Today." In Campi et al., *Peter Martyr Vermigli,* 9–16.

———. *The Visible Words of God: An Exposition of the Sacramental Theology of Peter Martyr Vermigli.* Grand Rapids, MI: Eerdmans, 1957.

———, ed. *Peter Martyr Vermigli and Italian Reform.* Waterloo, Ontario: Wilfrid Laurier University Press, 1980.

McNair, Philip M. J. *Peter Martyr in Italy: An Anatomy of Heresy.* Oxford: Clarendon, 1967.

McNeill, John T. *The History and Character of Calvinism.* New York: Oxford University Press, 1954.

Menk, Gerhard. "Caspar Olevian während der Berleburger und Herborner Zeit (1577–1587): Ein Beitrag zum Selbstverständnis des frühen deutschen Kalvinismus." *Monatsheft für evangelische Kirchengeschichte des Rheinlandes* 37/38 (1988/89): 139–204.

———. *Die Hohe Schule Herborn in ihrer Frühzeit (1584–1660): Ein Beitrag zum Hochschulwesen des deutschen Kalvinismus im Zeitalter der Gegenreformation.* Wiesbaden: Historische Kommission für Nassau, 1981.

Mentzer, Raymond A., and Andrew Spicer, eds. *Society and Culture in the Huguenot World, 1559–1685.* Cambridge: Cambridge University Press, 2002.

Millet, Olivier. *Correspondance de Wolfgang Capiton (1478–1541). Analyse et index (D'après le Thesaurus Baumianus et autres sources).* Publications de la Bibliothèque nationale et universitaire de Strasbourg 8. Strasbourg: [Bibliothèque nationale et universitaire de Strasbourg], 1982.

Moltmann, Jürgen. *Prädestination und Perseveranz, Geschichte und Bedeutung der reformierten Lehre "de perseverantia sanctorum."* Beiträge zur Geschichte und Lehre der Reformierten Kirche 12. Neukirchen-Vluyn, Germany: Neukirchener Verlag, 1961.

Müller, Karl. "Caspar Olevian—Reformator aus Leidenschaft. Zum 400. Todestag am 5. März 1987." *Monatsheft für evangelische Kirchengeschichte des Rheinlandes* 37/38 (1988/89): 13–138.

Muller, Richard A. *After Calvin: Studies in the Development of a Theological Tradition.* Oxford Studies in Historical Theology. New York: Oxford University Press, 2002.

————. *Post-Reformation Reformed Dogmatics: The Rise and Development of Reformed Orthodoxy, ca. 1520 to ca. 1725.* 4 vols. 2nd ed. Grand Rapids, MI: Baker, 2003.

————. "The Problem of Protestant Scholasticism: A Review and Definition." In Asselt and Dekker, *Reformation and Scholasticism*, 45–64.

————. "Reformation, Orthodoxy, 'Christian Aristotelianism,' and the Eclecticism of Early Modern Philosophy." *Dutch Review of Church History* 81 (2001): 306–25.

————. *The Unaccommodated Calvin: Studies in the Foundation of a Theological Tradition.* Oxford Studies in Historical Theology. New York: Oxford University Press, 2000.

Neuser, Wilhelm H. "Dogma und Bekenntnis in der Reformation: Von Zwingli und Calvin bis zur Synode von Westminster." In *Handbuch der Dogmen- und Theologiegeschichte*. Vol. 2, *Die Lehrentwicklung im Rahmen der Konfessionalität*, edited by Carl Andresen and Adolf Martin Ritter, 167–352. Göttingen, Germany: Vandenhoeck & Ruprecht, 1998.

Oberman, Heiko A. "Calvin and Farel: The Dynamics of Legitimation in Early Calvinism." *Journal of Early Modern History* 2 (1998): 32–60.

Old, Hughes Oliphant. "The Homiletics of John Oecolampadius and the Sermons of the Greek Fathers." In *Communio sanctorum: Mélanges offerts à Jean-Jacques von Allemen*. Edited by Yves Congar et al., 239–50. Geneva: Labor et Fides, 1982.

————. *The Reading and Preaching of the Scriptures in the Worship of the Christian Church.* Vol. 4, *The Age of the Reformation*. Grand Rapids, MI: Eerdmans, 2002.

Opitz, Peter, ed. *Calvin im Kontext der Schweizer Reformation.* Zurich: Theologischer Verlag, 2003.

Parker, Thomas H. L. *Calvin's Preaching.* Louisville, KY: Westminster/John Knox Press, 1992.

Pitassi, Maria Cristina. *Edifier ou instruire? Les avatars de la liturgie réformée du XVIe au XVIIIe siècle.* Paris: Campion, 2000.

Pollet, J. V. *Martin Bucer: Études sur les relations de Bucer avec les Pays-Bas, l'Électorat de Cologne et l'Allemagne du Nord.* 2 vols. Studies in Medieval and Reformation Thought 33–34. Leiden: Brill, 1985.

Raitt, Jill. *The Colloquy of Montbéliard: Religion and Politics in the Sixteenth Century.* New York: Oxford University Press, 1993.

————. *The Eucharistic Theology of Theodore Beza: Development of the Reformed Position.* AAR Studies in Religion 4. Chambersburg, PA: American Academy of Religion, 1972.

————, ed. *Shapers of Religious Traditions in Germany, Switzerland and Poland, 1560–1600.* New Haven, CT: Yale University Press, 1981.

Rodgers, Dirk. *John à Lasco in England.* American University Studies, Series 7; Theology and Religion 168. New York: Peter Lang, 1994.

Rorem, Paul. *Calvin and Bullinger on the Lord's Supper.* Nottingham, UK: Grove Books, 1989.

Roussel, Bernard. "'Ensevelir honnestement les corps': Funeral Corteges and Huguenot Culture. In Mentzer and Spicer, *Society and Culture in the Huguenot World*, 193–208.

————. "Pierre Viret en France (septembre 1561–aout 1565)." *Bulletin de la Société de l'Histoire du Protestantisme Français* 144 (1998): 803–39.

Scheurer, Rémy, and Dominique Quadioni. "Répertoire de la Correspondance de Guillaume Farel." In *Actes du Colloque Farel Neuchâtel, 29 Sept.–1er Oct. 1980.* Cahiers de la Revue de Théologie et de Philosophie 9/2. Geneva: Revue de Théologie et de Philosophie, 1983.

Schindling, Anton. *Humanistische Hochschule und freie Reichsstadt: Gymnasium und Akademie in Straßburg 1538–1621*, Veröffentlichungen des Instituts für europäische Geschichte Mainz 77. Wiesbaden: Franz Steiner, 1977.

Seebaß, Gottfried. "Bucer-Forschung seit dem Jubiläumsjahr 1991." *Theologische Rundshau* 62 (1997): 271–300.

———. *Martin Bucer (1491–1551). Bibliographie.* Gütersloh, Germany: Mohn, 2005.

Selderhuis, Herman J. *Calvin's Theology of the Psalms.* Grand Rapids, MI: Baker Academic, 2007.

———, ed. *Calvinus Praeceptor Ecclesiae: Papers of the International Congress of Calvin Research.* Geneva: Droz, 2004.

Sinnema, Donald. "Antoine de Chandieu's Call for a Scholastic Reformed Theology (1580)." In *Later Calvinism: International Perspectives*, edited by W. Fred Graham, 159–90. Sixteenth Century Essays and Studies 22. Kirksville, MO: Sixteenth Century Publishers, 1994.

———. "Aristotle and Early Reformed Orthodoxy: Moments of Accommodation and Antithesis." In *Christianity and the Classics: The Acceptance of a Heritage*, edited by Wendy E. Helleman, 119–48. Lanham, MD: University Press of America, 1990.

———. "The Discipline of Ethics in Early Reformed Orthodoxy." *Calvin Theological Journal* 28 (1993): 10–44.

———. "The Distinction between Scholastic and Popular: Andreas Hyperius and Reformed Scholasticism." In Trueman and Clark, *Protestant Scholasticism*, 127–43.

Spicer, Andrew. "'Qui est de Dieu, oit la parole de Dieu': The Huguenots and Their Temples." In Mentzer and Spicer, *Society and Culture in the Huguenot World*, 175–92.

Spijker, Willem van't. "Bucer als Zeuge Zanchis im Strassburger Prädestinationsstreit." In *Reformiertes Erbe, Festschrift für G.W. Locher*, edited by Heiko A. Oberman et al., 327–42. Zwinglia 19/1. Zurich: Theologischer Verlag, 1992.

Staehelin, Ernst. "Bibliographische Beiträge zum Lebenswerk Oekolampads." *Basler Zeitschrift für Geschichte und Altertumskunde* 27 (1928): 191–234.

———. "Oekolampad-Bibliographie (Verzeichnis der im 16. Jahrhundert erschienenen Oekolampaddrücke)." *Basler Zeitschrift für Geschichte und Altertumskunde* 17 (1918): 1–119.

———. *Das theologische Lebenswerk Johannes Oekolampads.* Quellen und Forschungen zur Reformationsgeschichte. Leipzig: Heinsius, 1939.

Stam, Frans Pieter van. "Das Verhältnis zwischen Bullinger und Calvin während Calvins erstem Aufenthalt in Genf." In Opitz, *Calvin im Kontext*, 25–40.

Steinmetz, David C. *Reformers in the Wings: From Geiler von Kaysersberg to Theodore Beza.* 2nd ed. Oxford: Oxford University Press, 2001.

———. "The Theology of Calvin and Calvinism." In *Reformation Europe: A Guide to Research*, edited by Steven Ozment, 211–32. St. Louis, MO: Center for Reformation Research, 1982.

Stephens, W. Peter. "Bullinger's Sermons on the Apocalypse." In *Die Zürcher Reformation: Ausstrahlungen und Rückwirkungen; Wissenschaftliche Tagung zum hundertjährigen Bestehen des Zwinglivereins (29. Oktober bis 2. November 1997 in Zürich)*, edited by Alfred Schindler and Hans Stickelberger, 261–80. Zürcher Beiträge zur Reformationsgeschichte 18. Bern: Peter Lang, 2001.

Stierle, Beate. *Capito als Humanist.* Gütersloh, Germany: Mohn, 1974.

Strasser, Otto Erich. *Capitos Beziehungen zu Bern.* Quellen und Abhandlungen zur Schweizerischen Reformationsgeschichte n.s. 4, no. 7. Leipzig: Heinsius, 1928.

Strehle, Stephen. *Calvinism, Federalism, and Scholasticism: A Study of the Reformed Doctrine of the Covenant.* Basler und Berner Studien zur historischen und systematischen Theologie 58. New York: Lang, 1988.

Strohm, Christoph. *Ethik im frühen Calvinismus: Humanistische Einflüsse, philosophische, juristische und theologische Argumentationen sowie mentalitätsgeschichtliche Aspekte am Beispiel des Calvinschülers Lambertus Danaeus.* Arbeiten zur Kirchengeschichte 65. Berlin: de Gruyter, 1996.

———. "Theologie und Zeitgeist: Beobachtungen zum Siegeszug der Methode des Petrus Ramus am Beginn der Moderne." *Zeitschrift für Kirchengeschichte* 110 (1999): 352–71.

———, ed. *Johannes à Lasco: Polnischer Baron, Humanist und europäischer Reformator.* Spätmittelalter und Reformation Neue Reihe 14. Tübingen: Mohr Siebeck, 2000.

———, et al., eds. *Späthumanismus und reformierte Konfession. Theologie, Jurisprudenz und Philosophie in Heidelberg an der Wende zum 17. Jahrhundert.* Tübingen: Mohr Siebeck, 2006.

Sturm, Erdmann Karl. *Der junge Zacharias Ursin: Sein Weg vom Philippismus zum Calvinismus (1534–1562).* Beiträge zur Geschichte und Lehre der Reformierten Kirche 33. Neukirchen-Vluyn, Germany: Neukirchener Verlag, 1972.

Sturm, Klaus. *Die Theologie Peter Martyr Vermiglis während seines ersten Aufenthalts in Strassburg 1542–1547.* Beiträge zur Geschichte und Lehre der Reformierten Kirche 31. Neukirchen, Vluyn, Germany: Neukirchener Verlag, 1971.

Taylor, Larissa, ed. *Preachers and People in the Reformations and Early Modern Period.* History of the Sermon 2. Leiden: Brill, 2001.

Thompson, Nicholas. *Eucharistic Sacrifice and Patristic Tradition in the Theology of Martin Bucer 1534–1546.* Studies in the History of Christian Traditions 119. Leiden: Brill, 2005.

Troilo, Dominique-A. "L'oeuvre de Pierre Viret: Le problème des sources." *Bulletin de la Société de l'Histoire du Protestantisme Français* 144 (1998): 759–90.

Trueman, Carl R. "Calvin and Calvinism." In McKim, *Cambridge Companion to John Calvin,* 225–44.

———, and R. Scott Clark, eds. *Protestant Scholasticism: Essays in Reassessment.* Carlisle, UK: Paternoster, 1999.

Tylenda, Joseph N. "Calvin Bibliography, 1960–1970." *Calvin Theological Journal* 6 (1971): 156–93.

Visser, Derk. "The Covenant in Zacharias Ursinus." *Sixteenth Century Journal* 18 (1987): 531–44.

———. *Zacharias Ursinus, the Reluctant Reformer: His Life and Times.* New York: United Church Press, 1983.

Wainwright, Geoffrey, and Karen B. Westerfield Tucker. *The Oxford History of Christian Worship.* Oxford: Oxford University Press, 2006.

Walton, Robert C. "Der Streit zwischen Thomas Erastus und Caspar Olevian über die Kirchenzucht in der Kurpfalz in seiner Bedeutung für die internationale reformierte Bewegung." *Monatshefte für evangelische Kirchengeschichte des Rheinlandes* 37/38 (1988/89): 205–46.

Weber, Rudolf. "Wolfgang und Abraham Musculus: Die Sammler der Zofinger Humanistenbriefe." *Zofinger Neujahrsblatt* 69 (1984): 5–19.

Weir, David. *The Origins of Federal Theology in Sixteenth Century Reformation Thought.* New York: Oxford University Press, 1990.

Wesel-Roth, Ruth. *Thomas Erastus: Ein Beitrag zur Geschichte der reformierten Kirche und zur Lehre von der Staatssouveränität.* Veröffentlichungen des Vereins für Kirchengeschichte in der evangelischen Landeskirche Badens 5. Lahr/Baden: M. Schauenburg, 1954.

Wiley, David N. "Calvin's Friendship with Guillaume Farel." In *Calvin Studies Society Papers 1995, 1997,* edited by David Foxgrover, 187–204. Grand Rapids, MI: CRC Product Services, 1998.

Wright, David F., ed. *Martin Bucer: Reforming Church and Community.* Cambridge: Cambridge University Press, 1994.

Wright, Shawn D. *Our Sovereign Refuge: The Pastoral Theology of Theodore Beza.* Carlisle, UK: Paternoster, 2004.

Zachman, Randall. *John Calvin as Pastor, Teacher and Theologian: The Shape of His Writings and Thought.* Grand Rapids, MI: Baker Academic, 2006.

3

Early Modern Catholicism

Robert Bireley

Interest in the study of Catholicism of the early modern period began to burgeon in the 1970s and has continued to grow to the present day. In *Trent and All That*, John W. O'Malley has masterfully outlined the longer historiography of the subject. This recent study has displayed the Catholicism of the period as anything but the stereotypical monolith often found in textbooks, and has revealed a rich variety of colors both bright and dark. Spanish Catholicism under Philip II differed from that of France under the last Valois, and recusant Catholicism in England in the seventeenth century differed from that in the Habsburg Monarchy as it emerged from the Thirty Years' War. How then does one denominate this period of Catholic history? The question has long stood out as a controversial one, and rightly so because terminology serves to reflect historical interpretation. Since at least the late nineteenth century "Catholic Reform" and "Counter-Reformation" have vied with each other as the two principal terms to define the period, with Catholics generally preferring the former and Protestants the latter. In Hubert Jedin's classic 1946 essay, the great historian of the Council of Trent suggested a compromise. Both terms named essential elements of early modern Catholicism, he proposed, with Catholic Reform denoting its "soul" and Counter-Reformation its "body."[1] His suggestion proved satisfactory to many, especially in an increasingly ecumenical age, yet it did not remain without its critics. Recently O'Malley himself, while admitting

[1]Jedin, *Katholische Reform*, 38.

that both Catholic Reform and Counter-Reformation do indicate important elements of the Catholicism of the period, has rejected them as inadequate to the rich reality. First of all, he argues, they define the period
excessively with reference to the Protestant Reformation and so exclude
developments like the missionary expansion across the seas in Asia and the
Americas and the emergence of new spiritualities like that of the Jesuits.
Secondly, for O'Malley the word "reform" seems to indicate that the church
found itself in a state of notable decline at the end of the fifteenth century, a
state of affairs he considers unsupported by recent research, which has
tended to upgrade the status of the late medieval church. Nor did the early
Jesuits, certainly a significant force in the Catholicism of the period, consider themselves as church reformers. O'Malley also finds a similar inade-
quacy in the term "Tridentine Catholicism" as exaggerating the role of the
council, important though it was. Instead, he has endorsed the simple, pro-
saic, yet inclusive term "early modern Catholicism" to denote this period in
the history of Catholicism. That his proposal currently is gathering acceptance is suggested by the very title of this essay.[2]

Periodization as well as terminology follows from interpretation.
When did early modern Catholicism begin? To what extent did it represent continuity with medieval Catholicism? Ronnie Hsia, who does not
use the term early modern Catholicism, titled his 1998 book *The World of
Catholic Renewal*, dating this movement from 1540. Michael A. Mullett in
his 1999 *The Catholic Reformation* points up the continuity of Trent with
an earlier tradition of "reform in head and members" that gathered steam
at the Council of Constance and continued throughout the fifteenth century into the sixteenth. Indeed, this issue of periodization overlaps with
the still broader interpretative question of the end of the Middle Ages and
the beginning of the Renaissance or early modern times. In a pathbreaking essay first published in 1929, Lucien Febvre contended that the Protestant Reformation could not be explained as a reaction to decline and
abuses within the medieval church, but must have resulted from a change
in religious sentiment or mentality at a deeper level.[3] H. Outram Evennett,
then, in a series of insightful lectures delivered in 1951 (but only published
in 1968) proposed that "if the Counter-Reformation was, at bottom, the
total process of adaptation to new world conditions which Catholicism

---

[2]O'Malley's subtitle highlights this view: *Trent and All That: Renaming Catholicism in the Early
Modern Era.*

[3]Febvre, "The Question of the French Reformation."

underwent in the first two centuries of the post-medieval age, a modernization, in the sense of the establishment of a new 'modus vivendi' of the
Church with the world, then it would seem that this effort can be said to
have reached an end somewhere in the age of Louis XIV."[4]

Both these themes—adaptation and modernization—have subsequently been taken up and developed by others. Robert Bireley, in his 1999
The Refashioning of Catholicism, 1450–1700, has interpreted early modern
Catholicism as a response to the changing world of the late fifteenth and
sixteenth centuries and as a continuation of the church's tradition of adaptation, where the church both acts upon contemporary cultures and societies and is acted upon by them. Following Theodore K. Rabb's classic *The
Struggle for Stability in Early Modern Europe*, Bireley has identified five
changes that distinguish the transition from medieval to early modern
Europe: (1) a decisive stage in the development of the modern state both in
the larger monarchies of England, France, and Spain and in the territorial
states of Italy and Germany; (2) demographic growth and economic
expansion along with social dislocation that accompanied a growing
imbalance between the rich and poor; (3) European expansion into Asia,
the Americas, and to a lesser extent, Africa; (4) the Renaissance, including
the new technology of printing; and (5) the Protestant Reformation. All
these developments except the last began before 1500 or 1517.

The theory of confessionalization as first developed chiefly by Ernst
Walter Zeeden, Wolfgang Reinhard, and Heinz Schilling has influenced the
study of early modern Catholocism. Its focus on the similar and parallel
features of the three principal confessions or churches—Lutheran, Calvinist, and Catholic—as they developed in the sixteenth century constitutes its
strength.[5] When does Catholic confessionalization begin, and does it overlap with the emergence of early modern Catholicism? Working with Germany as a model, Reinhard, in his 1989 article "Reformation, Counter-
Reformation, and the Early Modern State," proposed that the first years of
the Protestant Reformation (from 1517 to 1525) be viewed as an evangelical period that ended with the Peasants' Revolt and the intervention of the
princes. The era of confessionalization began properly with the Lutheran
Confession of Augsburg of 1530, the first of the confessions of faith that
make up the initial step in the formation of a confession or church. The
Calvinists and the Catholics then followed (the decisive years being the

[4]Evennett, *Spirit of the Counter-Reformation*, 20.
[5]Ute Lotz-Heumann's contribution to this volume deals in detail with confessionalization.

1550s and 1560s), with the Catholic equivalent of the Confession of Augsburg being the Tridentine Profession of Faith that followed the Council of
Trent in 1564. The recent multivolume French *Histoire du Christianisme*
takes over this interpretation, breaking at 1530 between the seventh volume, *De la réforme à la Réformation (1450–1530)*, and the eighth volume,
Le temps des confessions (1530–1620) rather than at 1517, as might have
been expected.

Yet a solid argument exists for beginning the process of confessionalization earlier, especially when Reinhard closely associates it with the
growth of the state, as does Paolo Prodi. In fact, Prodi finds the start of
confessionalization in the middle of the fifteenth century with the advance
of territorial states in Germany and Italy, the extension of their control
over the church, and the alliance of the papacy with states through concor-
dats aimed at checking the conciliarist movement, for example the Con-
cordat of Vienna of 1448 between the pope and Emperor Frederick III.[6]
The year 1450 also saw the permanent return of the pope to Rome after the
long absences of the fourteenth and fifteenth centuries, a new policy aimed
at the restoration of the city of Rome, and a new emphasis on the pope's
role as ruler of an Italian state that became the principal source of papal
revenue with the decline of income from the European states. For Prodi,
this signaled an increasing secularization of the church and sacralization of
the state. In sum, one can propose provisionally that both early modern
Catholicism and Catholic confessionalization started in the middle of the
fifteenth century, and lasted well past the traditional endpoint of 1648, the
year of the Peace of Westphalia, into the eighteenth century and perhaps
up to the cataclysm of the French Revolution. Any more precise date, it
seems, is open to question.

In a seminal article of 1977, Wolfgang Reinhard argued that the
Counter-Reformation in its accommodation to contemporary culture and
society—to be sure, an anachronistic concept but one that fits reality—constituted a force for modernization in the Western world. So he rejected the
long-standing Whiggish stereotype that the Protestant Reformation represented progress in the West and the Counter-Reformation the forces of
reaction.[7] Ever since, the issue of the "modern" character of the Counter-
Reformation has remained a lively one especially since the term "modern"

[6]Prodi, "Introduzione," in Kellebenz and Prodi, *Fisco, religione, Stato nell'età confessionale*, 7–20.
[7]Reinhard, "Gegenreformation als Modernisierung?"

has many and varying connotations. In 1996, *Il concilio di Trento e il Moderno,* a significant volume edited by Reinhard and Prodi, took up the issue with a narrower focus on the council itself. In his contribution, Prodi made an important controversial argument for the modern character of the council, whose decrees have now been published anew in Latin and English.[8] According to Prodi, Trent marked a transition from the medieval *respublica Christiana* to the world of the modern states. The older medieval universalism saw Europe as one society with two forces competing for leadership: the spiritual (the pope) and the temporal (the emperor or other rulers). This conception was well represented in the late medieval councils of Constance and Basel, which were both strongly conciliarist in sentiment. The councils met in nations that were still cultural groups rather than states and not only bishops, but also members of corporations like cathedral chapters and universities, took an active role. Representatives of governments played a major part. Indeed, these were assemblies of Christendom.

Trent, on the other hand, was an ecclesiastical council where only bishops, superiors general of religious orders, and abbots were allowed to vote. Representatives of governments, though present, had much less influence than in previous councils. Both the council and the church were clericalized. The Council of Trent envisioned, not one universal Christendom, but interlocking societies where the church stood as the *respublica Christiana,* in its own right a "perfect society." The new dualism was not of one society with two leaders but of two competing societies, one with the goal of man's temporal welfare, the other with the goal of his eternal well-being. Crucial for this development, according to Prodi, was the council's decision not to publish the planned decree on the reform of princes, which would have required them also to take an oath to uphold the council's doctrinal decisions, and instead merely to issue a simple call for the cooperation of rulers. So the council recognized the new sovereignty of the princes, and the church, for its part, took on features of a state, such as expanding the tasks of nuncios to include church reform. Canon law, apart from marriage, now applied for the most part only to clerics. The church no longer sought to influence society through law; that it left to the states, though it certainly continued to defend clerical privileges. Instead, it aimed to influence society through the establishment of moral standards and the use of the internal forum and the confessional (see the discussion of confession below).

---

[8]Tanner, *Decrees of the Ecumenical Councils.*

Intellectually, this position of the council was influenced by the theory of the pope's indirect power in temporal affairs that was first outlined by Dominican theologians Pedro de Soto and Francisco Vitoria in the early part of the century, and developed later by the Jesuits Francisco Suarez and Robert Bellarmine. This theory recognized explicitly the temporal sovereignty of princes but allowed for papal intervention in the event that a prince obstructed the pursuit of his subjects' eternal goal. It is against this backdrop of the Council of Trent, Prodi maintains, that one must view the subsequent jurisdictional conflicts between state and church in the seventeenth and eighteenth centuries. The extent to which his position about the modern character of Trent wins acceptance remains to be seen.[9]

French historian Alain Tallon finds in Trent's complete neglect of contemporary millenarianism one feature of its modernity.[10] But his major contribution, a marvelous volume of 821 pages, investigates the relationship of France to the Council of Trent and so fills a gap that Jedin himself recognized. Tallon looks at France's policy toward the council, the French understanding of the council, and finally the role of the French at Trent itself and only briefly its impact on the kingdom. "In the dramatic situation of religious crisis," he concludes, "despite all the faults one might find with it, the Council of Trent seemed to be the plank of salvation for Gallicanism, for it permitted the invocation of authority of a general council, so dear to the French, to defend the old faith against any compromise with the innovators without at the same time yielding completely to Roman absolutism."[11] Furthermore, adherence to the council secured a greater independence for the French church from the crown and helped create a national consciousness apart from the monarchy. According to Joseph Bergin's thorough study, "the years from Henry IV to the death of Mazarin represent a crucial stage in the emergence of an episcopate which by the later seventeenth century had in many ways become a model for much of Catholic Europe."[12]

The papacy continues to attract scholarship. According to Prodi's *Papal Prince*, the Papal States initially led the way to the formation of a

---

[9]Prodi and Reinhard, *Il concilio di Trento e il moderno*, 7–22. See also Prodi with Müller-Luckner, *Glaube und Eid*, vii–xxix; and Prodi, *Una storia della giustizia*, 195–255. For an updating of Reinhard's "Gegenreformation als Modernisierung?" with respect to the Council of Trent, see Prodi and Reinhard, *Il concilo di Trento e il moderno*.

[10]Tallon, *Concile de Trente*.

[11]Tallon, *La France et le Concile de Trente*, 815.

[12]Bergin, *Making of the French Episcopate*, 557.

modern state with its administrative structure and system of taxation, a further example of the church's adaptation to a changing world. Jean Delumeau considered the Papal States at the end of the sixteenth century to be administratively "the equal, if not the superior of any other state in Europe," and it had in the course of the century developed from the lowest taxed to "probably the most heavily taxed" state in Italy.[13] But subsequently it faltered for a number of reasons. Among them were the demands on the papal treasury by Catholic governments engaged in the religious wars and the replacement of laymen with temporal authority by clerics, and the resulting reduction in the pool of officeholders and failure to nurture a class of lay civil servants. The College of Cardinals declined in influence as it increased in numbers from twenty-four at the conclusion of the Council of Constance to an increasingly Italianized seventy under Sixtus V. By the early seventeenth century, the college provided the central figures of a model baroque court where the chief concern of the cardinals often became family power and wealth. Studies by Volker Reinhardt, Wolfgang Reinhard, and more recently Brigit Emich[14] have looked from different perspectives at Cardinal Scipione Borghese, nephew of Paul V (1605–21). Additional biographies of the early modern popes would be useful and valuable; for many, there seems to be more than enough material at hand. Gianvittorio Signorotto and Maria Antonietta Visceglia have edited a valuable volume of essays on the early modern papal court.[15]

The nunciature reports (the correspondence between the papal secretariat of state and its nuncios in the field) are a major source for the papacy; however, all the historical institutes in Rome save the German Historical Institute have suspended or greatly reduced their publication. A major innovation took place in 1984 with the publication of the *Hauptinstruktionen Clemens VIII für die Nuntien und Legaten an den europäischen Fürstenhöfen (1592–1605)* edited by Klaus Jaitner. Until then, the various series of the correspondence of the nuncios had been published in great detail for individual courts, with a volume rarely covering more than two or three years. This continues for nunciatures in Germany. Usually these series aimed to serve as sources primarily for the history of the state to which the nuncio was posted and only secondarily for papal policy. The

---

[13]Delumeau, "Rome," 298, 302.

[14]Reinhardt, *Kardinal Scipione Borghese*; Reinhard, "Papal Power and Family Strategy"; and Emich, *Bürokratie und Nepotismus*.

[15]Signorotto and Visceglia, *Court and Politics in Papal Rome*.

Hauptinstruktionen publish all the principal instructions for nuncios and legates of a pontificate; they tell much more about the general policy of a particular pope, but they do not so easily reveal the compromises and modifications made as policy was implemented. As with the earlier series, they contain a mine of references to primary and little-known secondary sources. In 1997, Jaitner published the *Hauptinstruktionen* for the papacy of Gregory XV (1621–23). In 2003, Silvano Giordano published the three-volume *Le instruzioni generali di Paolo V ai diplomatici pontifici (1605–1621)*, and he has begun work on the principal instructions of Urban VIII (1623–44). Scholars navigating the Vatican Archives will find Francis X. Blouin's *Vatican Archives: An Inventory and Guide to Historical Documents of the Holy See* extremely valuable.

Early modern Catholicism saw the birth of numerous religious orders, both male and female, with an intensified commitment to new types of pastoral ministry as well as to traditional apostolic works, and they created new forms and styles of religious life to support that commitment. Pastoral practice diversified and extended its reach as preachers, missionaries, and confessors were supplemented by writers, hospitalers, "social workers," catechists, and, above all, schoolmasters and schoolmistresses. Education became for the first time a major work of many religious congregations. Until recently, traditional histories have not adequately noticed this development, perhaps because they were little connected directly with Trent and Tridentine reform on which historians have generally concentrated.[16]

Richard Demolen's *Religious Orders of the Catholic Reformation* continues to serve as a fine introduction to the new male religious orders of the sixteenth and seventeenth centuries. The Jesuits have been well served by the literature. Of great importance for their history is the long-awaited four-volume *Diccionario histórico de la Compañía de Jésus* edited by Charles E. O'Neill and Joaquin M. Dominguez, which appeared (unfortunately, in Spanish only) in 2001. John O'Malley's prizewinning *The First Jesuits* and *The Mercurian Project: Forming Jesuit Culture, 1573–1580*, thirty essays written by a variety of scholars and edited by Thomas McCoog, carry the narrative of Jesuit history nearly up to 1600. Contributions in *The Mercurian Project* often extend beyond the narrow limits indicated in the title, and the volume is also rich in both primary source material and bibliography. Robert Bireley in *The Jesuits and the Thirty*

---

[16]See Bireley, *Refashioning of Catholicism*; and O'Malley, "Priesthood, Ministry, and Religious Life."

Years War: Kings, Courts and Confessors, has investigated Jesuit activity in politics from the perspective of the Jesuit superior general in Rome, Muzio Vitelleschi. *The Jesuits: Cultures, Sciences and the Arts, 1540–1773,* thirty-two essays edited by a team headed by John O'Malley, appeared in 1999 and a sequel (*The Jesuits II*) followed in 2005. Along with Jeffrey Chipps Smith's *Sensuous Worship: Jesuits and the Art of the Early Catholic Reformation in Germany,* these volumes represent an increasing scholarly attention to the arts as a feature of Jesuit activity.

The publication of the three-volume *I Frati Cappuccini: Documenti e Testimonianze del primo secolo,* edited by Costanzo Cargnoni, will, it is hoped, stimulate the study of the Capuchins, the new branch of the Franciscan order that first received papal approbation in 1528. The Capuchins exercised an enormous influence on early modern Catholicism, especially in the seventeenth century, their golden age, when their numbers increased to 30,000. But there is much work to be done on the other orders that emerged in the sixteenth century and especially on the older orders, both the monastic orders like the Benedictines and Cistercians and the mendicants like the Franciscans, Dominicans, and Augustinians, who still vastly outnumbered the new orders. For all religious orders and congregations, old and new, male and female, the ten-volume *Dizionario degli Istituti di Perfezione* edited by Guerrino Pelliccia and Giancarlo Rocca remains an indispensable research tool. The first volume of a welcome new multivolume series dealing with male and female religious orders in Germany in the early modern period appeared in 2005; it treats principally the Benedictines and Cistercians.[17]

Two new phenomena of the late sixteenth and early seventeenth centuries that deserve attention are the societies of common life and male, nonclerical congregations. The former were associations primarily of priests who wished to live in community according to the evangelical counsels, but without taking vows. They omitted vows principally, it seems, because of a desire to identify with and provide a model for secular priests who were recognized to be in need of reform. Generally speaking, their spirituality focused on the priesthood itself, and not surprisingly, they became deeply involved with the education of priests. Apart from the Roman Oratory of Philip Neri, which first received papal recognition in 1575, they were concentrated in France. Pierre de Bérulle founded the

---

[17]Jürgensmeier and Schwerdtfeger, *Orden und Klöster im Zeitalter von Reformation und katholischer Reform.*

French Oratory in Paris in 1611. By 1702, it comprised seventy-eight communities with 581 priests. Under pressure from Pope Paul V, the French Oratorians undertook the work of secondary education and by 1631, conducted thirty-one colleges.[18] Vincent de Paul's Congregation of the Mission (or Lazarists after the hospital complex of Saint Lazaire given them on the outskirts of Paris) first came into existence in 1625 for the purpose of conducting missions in rural areas and educating the secular clergy, and by 1660 it counted 229 members in twenty-five houses, chiefly in France.[19]

Two important nonclerical male congregations originated during this period, the Hospitalers of St. John of God, who were devoted to ministry to the sick, and the Brothers of Christian Schools, committed to the growing ministry of education. The Hospitalers continued a medieval tradition of aid to the sick. Founded by the Spaniard John of God, who has been called "the creator of the modern hospital" after his construction of a hospital in Granada just prior to his death in 1550, the society had 288 hospitals spread over most of Catholic Europe as well as Latin America and Canada by the early eighteenth century.[20] The Brothers of the Christian Schools founded by John Baptist de la Salle devoted themselves to free elementary education for poor boys, opening their first school at Rheims in 1679. They were recognized by Rome in 1725, and by 1789 they opened 116 schools, thus creating "the first program of national primary education in France."[21] They developed a spirituality of the Christian teacher, which drew on the resources of baptism and confirmation for their pastoral mission. Other groups would follow in the traditions of both the Hospitalers and the Brothers of the Christian Schools.

The influx of male religious into ministry had an effect on church structures that bears further study. In particular, the founding of the Capuchins and the Jesuits, who were particularly favored by the papacy, strengthened Rome vis-à-vis bishops and national churches. With their centralized international organizations and their continued widespread exemptions, these two groups generally supported papal authority at a time when Trent had emphasized the role of bishops and aimed to regulate exemptions from episcopal authority. Their allegiance to Rome would cost

---

[18]Clavel, "Oratorio di Gesù e di Maria Immacolata," in *Dizionario degli Istituti di Perfezione,* 6:775–80; and Lemoine, *Le droit des religieux du concile de Trente,* 108–16.

[19]Chierotti, "Congregazione della Missione," in *Dizionario degli Istituti di Perfezione,* 2:1543–51.

[20]Botifoll, "Giovanni di Dio, santo," in *Dizionario degli Istituti di Perfezione,* 4:1266–71; and Botifoll, "Ospedalieri di San Giovanni di Dio," in *Dizionario degli Istituti di Perfezione,* 6:982–88.

[21]De Viguerie, *L'institution des enfants,* 64–65.

both orders dearly as the papacy became embattled in the eighteenth century. The full story of the suppression of the Jesuits in 1773 remains to be told, but a recent translation of an account by the eighteenth-century Jesuit Giulio Cesare Cordara has made it more accessible.[22] The new involvement of religious in the church's pastoral mission also exacerbated rivalry between regulars and seculars over their respective roles. In 1601, Clement VIII assigned to the Congregation for Bishops and Religious the mediation of disputes between the two and between religious orders themselves. Massimo Carlo Giannini has edited *Religione, conflittualità e cultura*, which deals with these issues regarding the regular clergy of Europe in the early modern period.

Interest in the women religious of the early modern period has grown apace with the popularity of women's history. Olwen H. Hufton's *The Prospect before Her: A History of Women in Western Europe* describes succinctly the situation of religious women against the general background of women's history. During this period, the number of women religious surpassed that of men and Elizabeth Rapley writes of the "feminization" of religious life in France in the course of the seventeenth century.[23] Female religious life acquired a new style and an apostolic spirituality often related to that of the Jesuits with whom the women were frequently associated. The many new active congregations represented a novel phenomenon as they sprouted in Italy, France, the Netherlands, and the Rhineland. Indeed, a question that needs further investigation is the extent to which these new foundations were rooted in the medieval period, that is, in third orders and in lay congregations. Gabriella Zarri, in "From Prophecy to Discipline," has taken up this issue for Italy, and Craig Harline, in "Actives and Contemplatives," for the Netherlands. These developments took place, if not in spite of, then certainly not because of the Council of Trent or the papacy. At its close, the council issued reform measures for female monasteries, insisting in particular on the observance of enclosure. Pius V followed this up in 1566 with a rigorous bull, Circa Pastoralis, in which he required that all female monasteries accept enclosure, even where entrants had not foreseen this as a part of their way of life, and that all third orders with simple rather than solemn vows either take solemn vows and accept enclosure or remain as they were. Should they choose the latter, they could accept no new novices and so were sentenced to extinction. Eventually however, with social

---

[22]Cordara, *On the Suppression of the Socety of Jesus*, trans. Murphy.
[23]Rapley, *The* Dévotes, 20–21.

change, some episcopal support, and a clever strategy, female religious congregations with simple vows and at least modified cloister came to be tolerated by Rome, as Rapley has shown for the many female congregations that sprouted in France in the seventeenth century.[24] Of all the women's congregations, the Ursulines (founded in 1535 by Angela Merici [1474–1540], a laywoman of Brescia) were undoubtedly the most numerous and probably the most influential. Though many of their convents in France accepted enclosure willingly due to the enthusiasm for the contemplative life engendered by the Carmelite reform of Teresa of Avila coming from Spain, they became the first women's congregation vowed to the apostolate of education and in France "the feminine teaching congregation par excellence," where they reportedly numbered nearly ten thousand in 1750.[25] Henriette Peters's 1994 biography describes the life of Englishwoman Mary Ward (1585–1645). As founder of the Institute of the Blessed Virgin Mary (or "English Ladies" as they were called in South Germany), an order modeled on the Jesuits, Ward encountered many difficulties with church authorities and met only limited success.

Traditional contemplative nuns remained the great majority of women religious and they continue to be a popular subject of research, which often takes up their struggle with the new emphasis on enclosure as well as the attempt of church officials to acquire greater control over their houses in the wake of Trent. Charlotte Woodford and K. J. P. Lowe provide insights into the nuns' understanding of themselves through studies of their chronicles from Germany and Italy, respectively.[26]

The Catholic Church, however one might define it, in this period (as always) saw its principal aim as leading its members and those beyond to a deeper faith, hope, and charity, and thus preparing them for eternal life. Historians in recent years have used different terms to name this overall process; before looking at the methods or procedures employed to achieve the goal, it is crucial to clarify the terms applied to the process. As these overlap in varying degrees, but reveal vastly different historical outlooks, it is important that scholars remain aware of the differences as they go about their work. French historians have frequently employed the terms "evangelization" or "Christianization"—clearly religious terms that envision growth

[24]See also Conrad, *Zwischen Kloster und Welt*; and Conrad, "Ehe, Semireligiosentum und Orden."
[25]Rapley, *The Dévotes*, 48.
[26]Woodford, *Nuns as Historians*; and Lowe, *Nuns' Chronicles and Convent Culture*. See also the chapter in this volume by Merry Wiesner-Hanks for further treatment of women in early modern Catholicism.

in faith, hope, and charity. Such growth is difficult to determine since one cannot directly measure these virtues, though it is possible to draw some conclusions from religious observance and knowledge. The second term (or pair of terms)—confessionalism or confessionalization—has rather an ecclesiastical ring, looking more to the formation of the church as an institution; their elaboration has been closely associated with the emergence of the modern state, so they also connote the political. The third term, "social discipline," rather social and political in tone, is farthest removed from the religious. It derives from sociological modernization theory via Gerhard Oestreich's understanding of the rise of absolutism.[27] Social discipline implies an understanding of religion chiefly as a means of social control. In this essay, for convenience, evangelization and confessionalization are used interchangeably.

Scholarship has now generally retreated from a sharp distinction between elite and popular religion as well as a rigid top-down model for confessionalization, as Marc Forster has illustrated in *The Counter-Reformation in the Villages* and *Catholic Revival in the Age of the Baroque*. But there remains much to be investigated about the negotiation between authorities and communities. Craig Harline and Eddy Put's *A Bishop's Tale* tells poignantly the story of a conscientious Flemish bishop's efforts to apply church norms to a sometimes recalcitrant flock. Who was ultimately the responsible agent for confessionalization from above? Was it the pope, the bishop, or the prince who took his religious responsibility seriously and who, as Philip II is supposed to have asserted, considered "religion too important to be left to the pope"? At a local level, was it the parish priest or the Jesuit missionary preacher? Issues of jurisdiction regularly plagued efforts at confessionalization. Catholics differed sharply from Protestants in this regard, in that they also looked to the pope in Rome as well as to local or national authorities. One thinks of the conflict from 1605 to 1607 between Paul V and Venice that provoked the famous interdict over the Most Serene Republic.

Researchers have looked at the many means used to confessionalize or evangelize: preaching, education, the administration of the sacraments (especially penance), confraternities, inquisitorial prosecution, and censorship, to name a few. The last four come in for comment here.[28] Confession, or the sacrament of penance, has attracted considerable attention

---

[27]See Reinhard, "Disciplinamento sociale."
[28]For a discussion of preaching and education, see Bireley, *Refashioning of Catholicism*.

recently. W. David Myers (in *"Poor, Sinning Folk"*) has found that, in Counter-Reformation Bavaria, confession became more frequent—often monthly and even weekly among the devout—and more private with the introduction of the confessional box in 1600; he finds no evidence in the pre-Reformation era of the widespread anxiety some scholars have attributed to confession. According to John O'Malley, the early Jesuits, who considered the hearing of confessions a principal ministry, stressed its consolatory features, and others have seen the regular use of confession and the examination of conscience as a source of developing individualism and sense of the self.[29] On the other hand, Wietse de Boer has emphasized the use of the sacrament as a means of social control, especially by Archbishop Carlo Borromeo in Counter-Reformation Milan. This was done by the imposition of public penances and by the archbishop's reservation to himself or his cathedral penitentiaries of absolution from certain public sins such as participation in popular entertainments. In a famous incident of 1579, the Jesuit preacher Giulio Mazarino clashed with the archbishop over his alleged rigorism and the event escalated into a jurisdictional dispute involving eventually Pope Gregory XIII and Philip II.[30] Adriano Prosperi has contended that in the 1560s and 1570s, the church in Italy used confession in its campaign against heresy by requiring penitents to denounce suspect heretics to the Inquisition and, in the process, infringed on the secrecy of confession.[31] Prodi argues that the church, with the development of moral theology and casuistry and the emphasis at Trent on the judicial character of confession, created an alternative system of justice to both the law of the state and the canon law of the church and so fostered the distinction between sin and crime.[32] Many of these issues come to the fore in *Penitence in the Age of Reformations*, a series of essays edited by Katherine Jackson Lualdi and Anne Thayer.

The religious, social, and charitable organizations called confraternities have elicited substantial interest in recent years; in 1989 the Society for Confraternity Studies was founded, and it now publishes its own bulletin and regularly organizes sessions at historical conferences. Nicholas Terpstra, a leading scholar of confraternities, has shown that many of the early

[29]O'Malley, *The First Jesuits*, 141. See also Tentler, "Postscript," in Lualdi and Thayer, *Penitence in the Age of Reformations*, 253–55.

[30]De Boer, *Conquest of the Soul*, 248–49, 252.

[31]Prosperi, *Tribunali della coscienza*.

[32]Prodi, *Una storia della giustizia*.

modern orders and congregations started out as groupings at least similar to confraternities, and he calls for the study of analogous confraternal organizations in the Protestant and even Jewish and Muslim milieu. Terpstra writes, "As we absorb the implications of recent works and look ahead, how can we plot an agenda for future research into confraternities that takes these brotherhoods—and the scholars studying them—out of the institutional niche and captures their character as a form of spiritual community which is ubiquitous, fluid, and even provisional?"[33]

Two questions seem key for the role of confraternities in early modern Catholicism. To what extent was there a continuity between the late medieval confraternities with their normal lay leadership and early modern confraternities, especially after the Tridentine measures subordinating confraternities to the control of the hierarchy? And more important still, how did confraternities, often associated with religious orders, relate to the parish after Trent's vigorous assertion of the importance of the parish as the basic unit of church organization? Christopher Black takes up these issues with regard to Italy in his "Confraternities and the Parish in the Context of Italian Catholic Reform." According to Black, early modern confraternities grew out of their medieval forerunners, contributed significantly to the nascent religious revival in Italy in the early sixteenth century, and continued to represent a vigorous lay piety. But he qualifies this statement with a reference to the wide variety of confraternities and the complexity of the situation in Italy. John Patrick Donnelly and Michael Maher, editors of *Confraternities and Catholic Reform in Italy, France, and Spain*, in which Black's article appears, imply the same when they remind us that if all politics is local, so much the more is church reform, and that generalizations "must pay close attention to the local conditions that encouraged, discouraged, and shaped the direction of reform efforts affecting confraternities."[34]

The study of the confraternities has implications for both the role of the layperson in the church and the often tense relationship between religious and secular clergy, both issues of major significance for early modern Catholicism. Louis Châtellier's *Europe of the Devout* remains the key study of the principal confraternity conducted by the Jesuits, the Marian congregations, and Lance Lazar's recent study of Jesuit confraternities in Italy, *Working in the Vineyard of the Lord*, stands out as a major contribution.

---

[33]Terpstra, "Ignatius, Confratello: Confraternities as Modes of Spiritual Community in Early Modern Society," in Cornerford and Pabel, *Early Modern Catholicism*, 163.

[34]Donnelly and Maher, *Confraternities and Catholic Reform*, vii.

The Inquisition, or better, Inquisitions (that is, the medieval, the Spanish, the Portugese, and the Roman) have long stimulated both scholarship and curiosity. Recent work has tended to demythologize them, making them more understandable as instruments of confessionalization and social discipline and perhaps even evangelization in light of their alleged ultimate pastoral purpose; generally, toward the end of the sixteenth century, they turned more to the prosecution of moral offenses, magic, and superstition rather than strict heresy. Only Francisco Bethencourt, in *L'inquisition à l'époque moderne,* has attempted a comparative study of the Spanish, the Portuguese, and the Roman Inquisitions. Henry Kamen's *The Spanish Inquisition: A Historical Revision* synthesizes much recent research on this fearsome institution and generally revises downward its impact on Spanish society. The 1998 opening of the archives of the Holy Office in Rome has undoubtedly given new impetus to the study of the Roman Inquisition, and already the contributions to two symposia marking the event have been published, an October 1998 symposium sponsored by the Vatican and another in June 1999 sponsored by the Academia Nazionale dei Lincei.[35] Closely associated with the Inquisition was the Roman Congregation of the Index, which assumed censorship and control of books in 1571. Important to the study of this body, as well as of all the Indices of Prohibited Books issued by various authorities in the early modern period is the multivolume series *Index des livres interdits* edited by J. M. De Bujanda and colleagues at the Centre d'études de la Renaissance at Quebec's University of Sherbrooke. In *La Bibbia al rogo,* Gigliola Fragnito has demonstrated the different attitudes of church authorities in southern and northern Europe toward the publication of the vernacular Bible. For example, no vernacular Bible was published in Italy between 1567 and 1773, while translations did appear in areas inhabited by Catholics and Protestants.

The Inquisition did not function in the Habsburg lands in central Europe where, apart from pockets of crypto-Protestantism, Catholicism was restored by 1700 by a mixture of peaceful evangelization and forced confessionalization; the degree to which each was involved in the process remains controverted. Significant contributions to the discussion have come from Joseph Patrouch for Upper Austria, Regina Pörtner for Styria,

---

[35]The proceedings have been published in Borromeo, *L'Inquisizione: Atti del Simposio internazionale;* and *L'Inquisizione e gli storici.*

and Thomas Winkelbauer for the Austrian lands and Bohemia; the last-named deftly applies the concept of confessionalization to the landed estates of the nobility.[36]

Consciousness of belonging to a now worldwide church added a decidedly new element to the sense of identity of early modern Catholics, as seen in the colonnades outside Saint Peter's in Rome reaching out to embrace the world and in the American Indian headdress worn by a cherub above a choir stall in the baroque Praemonstratensian church at Steingaden in Bavaria. With its missionary expansion into Asia and the Americas, Catholicism had become a global religion. The letters of Francis Xavier (1506–52) from the East were copied, recopied, translated, and circulated widely throughout all Catholic Europe; the first (from India) was dated 15 January 1544. According to the German Jesuit Peter Canisius and the French Jesuit Edmond Auger writing in the middle of the sixteenth century, Francis Xavier's letters encouraged Catholics who underwent reverses at the hands of Protestants in Europe.[37] Often, the gains for the church across the seas were interpreted as providential compensation for the losses in Europe. An enormous literature exists on this missionary outreach of the early modern era, but is beyond the scope of this essay. It should be noted, however, that access to and exploitation of indigenous sources as well as the application of sophisticated anthropological methods has made it increasingly possible to learn about the impact of the missionary advance from the side of the local peoples themselves, as can be seen in the work, for example, of Nicholas Standaert for China and Sabine Mac-Cormack for the Inca civilization in Peru.[38] The mission field also provided opportunities for evangelization, confessionalization, and social discipline. The 1999 publication of *Relazione delle Quattro parti del mondo* provides a vision of the missions as seen from Rome. This report dating from 1649 is now clearly attributed to Francesco Ingoli, a longtime advocate of the foreign missions and secretary of the Congregation for the Propagation of the Faith from its establishment in 1622 until his death in 1649.

Theology and spirituality deserve greater recognition and integration into the study of early modern Catholicism, especially since they emphasize its distinctiveness. Despite a renewed insistence on doctrinal

---

[36]Patrouch, *A Negotiated Settlement*; Pörtner, *Counter-Reformation in Central Europe*; and Winkelbauer, *Ständefreiheit und Fürstenmacht*.

[37]Xavier, *Letters and Instructions of Francis Xavier*, ed. and trans. Costolloe, xi, xxiv.

[38]Standaert, *Handbook of Christianity in China*; and MacCormack, *Religion in the Andes*.

orthodoxy following Trent and expressed in the Tridentine Profession of Faith, the Catholicism of the period displayed a remarkable variety of spiritualities or ways of living the Christian life. In major European cities and towns and even in colonial centers, one could find churches of various religious orders each representing a particular approach to God. In the late seventeenth century, Guadalajara, Mexico, hosted communities of Dominicans, Franciscans, Augustinians, Mercedarians, Oratorians (of Philip Neri), and Jesuits, plus four convents of nuns—two Dominican, one Carmelite (of the Teresian reform), and one Augustinian—and two hospitals, one conducted by the Hospitalers of St. John of God and another by the Bethlehemites, a congregation first founded as a confraternity in Guatemala City in 1663. Early modern Catholicism was characterized by the conviction that the Christian life could be lived in the world, despite a vigorous Augustinian view to the contrary represented after the mid-seventeenth century by Jansenism. A paradigmatic figure for the age, Niccolò Machiavelli, had asserted or was understood to have asserted, in his 1513 *The Prince,* that the moral Christian could not succeed in politics and, by extrapolation, in the world. His theory was, in the words of German historian Friedrich Meinecke, "a sword which was plunged into the flank of the body politic of Western humanity, causing it to shriek and rear up."[39] The reaction was not long in coming, rooted in a world-affirming Thomism that predominated in early modern theology. An extensive anti-Machiavellian literature struck back, led by Giovanni Botero's 1589 *Reason of State,* which claimed that an intelligent, moral politics generated political success and that an immoral politics brought, in the long run, only failure.[40] Francis de Sales, the saintly Bishop of Geneva, contended in his immensely popular *Introduction to the Devout Life* (1609) that one could live the Christian life to the full in any state of life, and Ignatius Loyola's *Spiritual Exercises* pointed in the same direction.[41] A bevy of books appeared in the seventeenth century attempting to show how one could live the Christian life in varying states, like Nicholas Caussin's *Holy Court,* which first came off in the press in 1624 and went through many editions and translations into all the major European languages. The often vilified casuistry of the seventeenth century aimed to help the Christian live in the

[39]Meinecke, *Machiavellism: The Doctrine of* Raison d'État *and Its Place in Modern History,* trans. Douglas Scott (New York: Praeger, 1965), 49.

[40]Bireley, *Counter-Reformation Prince,* passim.

[41]Both of these works are available in English in many editions.

world, and it may at times have gone too far. But an underappreciated legacy of early modern Catholicism is its positive evaluation of the world, and its influence on the coming Enlightenment deserves investigation.

Bibliography

ELECTRONIC RESOURCES
Internet sites devoted to early modern Catholicism run in the hundreds, if not thousands. Sites are dedicated to individuals as well as movements. Some recommended sites are:
Vatican Library and Archives: http://www.vatican.va/
Digital Library of the Catholic Reformation: http://solomon.dlcr.alexanderstreet.com
The Jesuit Portal (directs users to other sites on Jesuit history): http://www.sjweb.info/

PRINTED SOURCES
Bergin, Joseph. *The Making of the French Episcopate, 1589–1661.* New Haven, CT: Yale University Press, 1996.
Bethencourt, Francisco. *L' Inquisition à l'époque moderne: Espagne, Italie, Portugal, XVe–XIXe Siècle.* Paris: Fayard, 1995.
Bireley, Robert. *The Counter-Reformation Prince: Anti-Machiavellianism or Catholic Statecraft in Early Modern Europe.* Chapel Hill: University of North Carolina Press, 1990.
———. *The Jesuits and the Thirty Years War: Kings, Courts and Confessors.* Cambridge, UK: Cambridge University Press, 2003.
———. *The Refashioning of Catholicism, 1450–1700: A Reassessment of the Counter-Reformation.* Washington, DC: Catholic University of America Press, 1999.
Blouin, Francis X., Jr., et al., eds. *Vatican Archives: An Inventory and Guide to Historical Documents of the Holy See.* New York: Oxford University Press, 1998.
Borromeo, Agostino, ed. *L'Inquisizione: Atti del Simposio internationale, Città del Vaticano, 29–31 Ottobre 1998.* Vatican City: Bibliotheca Apostolica Vaticana, 2003.
Cargnoni, Costanzo, ed. *I Frati Cappuccini. Documenti e testimonianze del primo secolo.* 3 vols. Perugia: Edizioni Frate Indovino, 1988–91.
Châtellier, Louis. *The Europe of the Devout: The Catholic Reformation and the Formation of a New Society.* Translated by Jean Birrell. Cambridge: Cambridge University Press, 1989.
Comerford, Kathleen M., and Hilmar M. Pabel, eds. *Early Modern Catholicism: Essays in Honor of John W. O'Malley, S.J.* Toronto: University of Toronto Press, 2002.
Conrad, Anne. "Ehe, Semireligiosentum und Orden: Frauen als Adressatinnen und Aktivistinnen der Gegenreformation," in "Aspekte der Gegenreformation," edited by Victoria von Flemming, special issue, *Zeitsprüngen: Forschungen zur frühen Neuzeit 1,* no. 3/4 (1997): 529–45.
———. *Zwischen Kloster und Welt: Ursulinen und Jesuiten in der katholischen Reformbewegung des 16/17. Jarhunderts.* Institut für europäische Geschichte Mainz, Abteilung Religionsgeschichte 142. Mainz: Zabern, 1991.
Cordara, Giulio Cesare. *On the Suppression of the Society of Jesus: A Contemporary Account.* Translated and annotated by John P. Murphy. Chicago: Loyola Press, 1999.
De Boer, Wietse. *The Conquest of the Soul: Confession, Discipline, and Public Order in Counter-Reformation Milan.* Leiden: Brill, 2001.

De Bujanda, J. M. et al. *Index des livres interdits.* 11 vols. Montreal: Médiaspaul; Geneva: Librairie Droz, 1984–2002.

Delumeau, Jean. "Rome: Political and Administrative Centralization in the Papal State in the Sixteenth Century." In *The Late Italian Renaissance, 1525–1630,* edited by Eric Cochrane, 288–302. New York: Harper and Row, 1970.

Demolen, Richard L. *Religious Orders of the Catholic Reformation: In Honor of John C. Olin on His Seventy-fifth Birthday.* New York: Fordham University Press, 1994.

De Viguerie, Jean. *L'institution des enfants: L'éducation en France, XVIe–XVIIIe siècles.* Paris: Calman-Levy, 1978.

Diccionario Historico de la Compañía de Jésus. Edited by Charles E. O'Neill and Joaquin M. Dominguez. 4 vols. Rome: Institutum Historicum Societatis Iesu; Madrid: Universidad Pontificia Comillas, 2001.

Dizionario degli Istituti di Perfezione. Edited by Guerrino Pellicia and Giancarlo Rocca. 10 vols. Rome: Edizione paoline, 1974–97.

Donnelly, John Patrick, and Michael Maher, eds. *Confraternities and Catholic Reform in Italy, France and Spain.* Sixteenth Century Essays and Studies 44. Kirksville, MO: Truman State University Press, 1998.

Emich, Birgit. *Bürokratie und Nepotismus unter Paul V (1605–1621): Studien zur frühneuzeitlichen Mikropolitik in Rom.* Päpste und Papsttum 30. Stuttgart: Anton Hiersemann, 2001.

Evennett, H. Outram. *The Spirit of the Counter-Reformation.* Edited with a postscript by John Bossy. Notre Dame, IN: University of Notre Dame Press, 1970.

Febvre, Lucien. "The Question of the French Reformation: A Badly-Put Question?" In *A New Kind of History: From the Writings of Lucien Febvre,* edited by Peter Burke and translated by K. Folca, 44–107. New York: Harper and Row, 1973.

Forster, Marc. *Catholic Revival in the Age of the Baroque: Religious Identity in Southwest Germany, 1550–1750.* Cambridge: Cambridge University Press, 2001.

———. *The Counter-Reformation in the Villages: Religion and Reform in the Bishopric of Speyer, 1560–1720.* Ithaca, NY: Cornell University Press, 1992.

Fragnito, Gigliola. *La Bibbia al rogo: La censura ecclesiastica e il volgarizzamento della Scrittura 1471–1605.* Bologna: Il Mulino, 1997.

Francis De Sales. *Introduction to the Devout Life.* Translated with an introduction and notes by John K. Ryan. 2nd edition, revised. New York: Image Books Doubleday, 1989.

Giannini, Massimo Carlo, ed. *Religione, conflittualità e cultura: Il clero regolare nell'Europa d'antico regime.* Cheiron 33–34. Rome: Bulzone, 2006.

Giordano, Silvano, ed. *Le istruzioni generali di Paolo V ai diplomatici pontifici 1605–1621.* 3 vols. Instructiones Pontificum Romanorum. Tübingen: Max Niemeyer, 2003.

Harline, Craig. "Actives and Contemplatives: The Female Religious of the Low Countries before and after Trent." *Catholic Historical Review* 81 (1995): 541–67.

———, and Eddy Put. *A Bishop's Tale: Mathias Hovius among His Flock in Seventeenth-Century Flanders.* New Haven, CT: Yale University Press, 2000.

Hsia, R. Po-Chia. *The World of Catholic Renewal 1540–1770.* Cambridge, UK: Cambridge University Press, 1998.

Hufton, Olwen H. *The Prospect before Her: A History of Women in Western Europe.* London: Harper Collins, 1995.

Ingoli, Francesco. *Relazione delle quattro parti del mundo.* Edited by Fabio Tosi with an introduction by Josef Metzler. Rome: Urbaniana University Press, 1999.

L'inquisizione e gli storici: Un cantiere aperto: Tavola rotonda nell'ambito della conferenza annuale della ricerca, Roma 24–25 giugno 1999. Rome: Accademia dei Lincei, 2000.

Jaitner, Klaus, ed. *Die Hauptinstruktionen Clemens VIII. für die Nuntien und Legaten an den europäischen Fürstenhöfen 1592–1605.* Vols. 1 and 2. Instructiones Pontificum Romanorum. Tübingen: Max Niemeyer, 1984.

———, ed. *Die Hauptinstruktionen Gregors XV. für die Nuntien und Gesandten an den Europäischen Fürstenhöfen 1621–1623.* 2 vols. Instructiones Pontificum Romanorum. Tübingen: Max Niemeyer, 1997.

Jedin, Hubert. *Geschichte des Konzils von Trient.* 4 vols. in 5. Freiburg im Breisgau: Herder, 1949–75. Vols. 1 and 2 translated by Ernest Graf as *A History of the Council of Trent* (London: Thomas Nelson and Sons, 1957–61).

———. *Katholische Reform oder Gegenreformation? Ein Versuch zur Klarung der Begriffe nebst einer Jubiläumsbetrachtung über das Trienter Konzil.* Lucerne: Josef Stocker, 1946.

Jürgensmeier, Friedhelm, and Regina Elisabeth Schwerdtfeger, eds. *Orden und Klöster im Zeitalter von Reformation und katholischer Reform 1500–1700.* I. Katholisches Leben und Kirchenreform im Zeitalter der Glaubensspaltung 65. Münster: Aschendorff, 2005.

Kamen, Henry. *The Spanish Inquisition: A Historical Revision.* New Haven, CT: Yale University Press, 1998.

Kellenbenz, Hermann, and Paolo Prodi, eds. *Fisco, religione, stato nell'età confessionale.* Bologne: Il Mulino, 1989.

Lazar, Lance. *Working in the Vineyard of the Lord: Jesuit Confraternities in Early Modern Italy.* Toronto: University of Toronto Press, 2005.

Lowe, K. J. P. *Nuns' Chronicles and Convent Culture in Renaissance and Counter-Reformation Italy.* Cambridge, UK: Cambridge University Press, 2003.

Loyola, St. Ignatius of. *Personal Writings.* Translated and edited by Joseph A. Munitz and Philip Endean. Harmondsworth, UK: Penguin Books, 1996.

Lualdi, Katharine Jackson, and Anne T. Thayer, eds. *Penitence in the Age of Reformations.* Aldershot, UK: Ashgate, 2001.

MacCormack, Sabine. *Religion in the Andes: Vision and Imagination in Early Colonial Peru.* Princeton, NJ: Princeton University Press, 1991.

Mayeur, Jean Marie, Marc Venard, and Viviane Barrie-Curien. *Histoire du Christianisme des origines à nos jours.* Vol. 7, *De la Réforme à la Réformation, 1450–1530.* Paris: Desclée, 1994.

Mayeur, Jean Marie, Charles Pietri, André Vauchez, and Marc Venard. *Histoire du Christianisme des origines à nos jours.* Vol. 8, *Le Temps des Confessions (1530–1620/30).* Paris: Desclée, 1992.

McCoog, Thomas M., ed. *The Mercurian Project: Forming Jesuit Culture 1573–1580.* Rome: Institutum Historicum Societatis Jesu; St. Louis, MO: Institute of Jesuit Sources, 2004.

Minnich, Nelson H. *The Fifth Lateran Council: Studies on Its Membership, Diplomacy, and Proposals for Reform.* Aldershot/Brookfield, VT: Variorum, 1993.

Mullett, Michael A. *The Catholic Reformation.* London: Routledge, 1999.

Myers, W. David. *"Poor, Sinning Folk": Confession and Conscience in Counter-Reformation Germany.* Ithaca, NY: Cornell University Press, 1996.

O'Malley, John W. *The First Jesuits.* Cambridge, MA: Harvard University Press, 1993.

———. "Priesthood, Ministry, and Religious Life: Some Historical and Historiographical Reflections." *Theological Studies* 49 (1988): 223–57. Reprinted in O'Malley, *Tradition and Transition: Historical Perspectives on Vatican II,* 127–71. Wilmington, DE: M. Glazier, 1989.

————. *Trent and All That: Renaming Catholicism in the Early Modern Era*. Cambridge, MA: Harvard University Press, 2000.

————, et al., eds. *The Jesuits: Cultures, Sciences, and the Arts, 1540–1773*. Toronto: University of Toronto Press, 1999.

————, et al., eds. *The Jesuits II: Cultures, Sciences, and the Arts, 1540–1773*. Toronto: University of Toronto Press, 2006.

O'Neill, Charles E., and Joaquin M. Dominguez, eds. *Diccionario historico de la Compañía de Jésus*. 4 vols. Rome: Institutum Historicum Societatis Iesu; Madrid: Universidad Pontificia Cornillas, 2001.

Patrouch, Joseph. *A Negotiated Settlement: The Counter-Reformation in Upper Austria under the Habsburgs*. Studies in Central European History. Boston: Humanities Press, 2000.

Peters, Henriette. *Mary Ward: A World in Contemplation*. Translated by Helen Butterworth. Leominster, UK: Gracewing, 1994.

Pörtner, Regina. *The Counter-Reformation in Central Europe: Styria 1580–1630*. Oxford: Clarendon Press, 2001.

Prodi, Paulo. *The Papal Prince, One Body and Two Souls: The Papal Monarchy in Early Modern Europe*. Translated by Susan Haskins. Cambridge, UK: Cambridge University Press, 1987. Originally published as *Il sovrano pontefice: Un corpo e due anime, la monarchia papale nella prima età moderna* (Bologna: Il Mulino, 1982).

————. *Una storia della giustizia: Dal pluralismo dei fori al moderno dualismo tra scienza e diritto*. Bologna: Il Mulino, 2000. Translated into German as *Eine Geschichte der Gerechtigkeit: Vom Recht Gottes zum modernen Rechtstaat* (Munich: Beck, 2003).

————, with Elisabeth Müller-Luckner, eds. *Glaube und Eid: Treueformeln, Glaubensbekenntnisse und Sozialdisziplinierung zwischen Mittelalter und Neuzeit*. Munich: Oldenbourg, 1993.

————, and Wolfgang Reinhard, eds. *Il concilio di Trento e il moderno*. Annali dell'Istituto storico italo-germanico in Trento. Quademo 45. Bologna: Il Mulino, 1996. Translated into German as *Das Konzil von Trient und die Moderne* (Berlin: Duncker und Humblot, 2001).

Prosperi, Adriano. *Tribunali della coscienza. Inquisitori, confessori, missionari*. Turin: Einaudi, 1996.

Rabb, Theodore K. *The Struggle for Stability in Early Modern Europe*. New York: Oxford University Press, 1975.

Rapley, Elizabeth. *The Dévotes: Women and Church in Seventeenth-Century France*. Montreal: McGill University Press, 1990.

————. *Social History of the Cloister: Daily Life in the Teaching Monasteries of the Old Regime*. Montreal: McGill-Queen's University Press, 2001.

Reinhard, Wolfgang . "Disciplinamento sociale, confessionalizzazione, modernizzazione: Un discorso storiografico." In *Disciplina dell'anima, disciplina del corpo, disciplina della società tra medioevo ed età moderna*, edited by Paolo Prodi with Carla Penuti, 101–24. Annali dell'Istituto storico italo-germanico 40. Bologna: Il Mulino, 1994. Translated into German as "Sozialdisziplinierung—Konfessionalisierung—Modernisierung: Ein historiographischer Diskurs." In *Die Frühe Neuzeit in der Geschichtswissenschaft. Forschungstendenzen und Forschungserträge*, edited by Nada Boskovska Leimgruber, 39–55 (Paderbom: Ferdinand Schöningh, 1997).

————. "Gegenreformation als Modernisierung? Prolegomena zu einer Theorie des konfessionellen Zeitalters." *Archiv für Reformationsgeschichte* 68 (1977): 226–52.

———. "Das Konzil von Trient und die Modernisierung der Kirche: Einführung." In Prodi and Reinhard, *Das Konzil von Trient und die Moderne*, 23–42.

———. "Papal Power and Family Strategy in the Sixteenth and Seventeenth Centuries." In *Princes, Patronage, and the Nobility: The Court at the Beginning of the Modern Age, 1450–1650*, edited by Ronald G. Asch and Adolph M Burke, 329–56. Oxford, UK: Oxford University Press. 1991.

———. "Reformation, Counter-Reformation, and the Early Modern State: A Reassessment." *Catholic Historical Review* 75 (1989): 383–404. Reprinted in David M. Luebke, ed., *The Counter-Reformation: The Essential Readings*. Oxford, UK: Blackwell, 1999.

———, and Heinz Schilling, eds. *Die katholische Konfessionalisierung*. Reformationsgeschichtliche Studien und Texte 135. Münster: Aschendorff, 1995.

Reinhardt, Volker. *Kardinal Scipione Borghese (1605–1633). Vermögen, Finanzen und sozialer Aufstieg eines Papstnepoten*. Bibliothek des Deutschen Historischen Instituts zu Rome 58. Tübingen, Germany: Max Niemeyer, 1984.

Signorotto, Gianvittorio, and Maria Antoinetta Visceglia, eds. *Court and Politics in Papal Rome, 1492–1700*. Cambridge Studies in Italian History and Culture. Cambridge: Cambridge University Press, 2002.

Smith, Jeffrey Chipps. *Sensuous Worship: Jesuits and the Art of the Early Catholic Reformation in Germany*. Princeton, NJ: Princeton University Press, 2002.

Standaert, Nicolas, ed. *Handbook of Christianity in China*. Vol. 1, *635–1800*. Handbook of Oriental Studies, Section 4, China 15/1. Leiden: Brill, 2001.

Tallon, Alain. *La France et le Concile de Trente, 1518–1563*. Paris: École française de Rome, 1997.

———. *Le Concile de Trente*. Paris: Cerf, 2000.

Tanner, Norman P., ed. *Decrees of the Ecumenical Councils*. 2 vols. Washington, DC: Georgetown University Press, 1990.

Winkelbauer, Thomas. *Ständefreiheit und Fürstenmacht: Länder und Untertanen des Hauses Habsburg im konfessionellen Zeitalter*. 2 parts. Österreichische Geschichte 8: 1522–1699. Vienna: Ueberreuter, 2003.

Woodford, Charlotte. *Nuns as Historians*. Oxford Modern Languages and Literature Monographs Series. Oxford: Clarendon Press, 2002.

Xavier, Francis. *The Letters and Instructions of Francis Xavier*. Edited and translated by M. Joseph Costolloe. St. Louis, MO: Institute of Jesuit Sources, 1992.

Zani, Gabriella. "From Prophecy to Discipline." In *Women and Faith: Catholic Religious Life in Italy from Late Antiquity to the Present*, edited by Lucetta Scaraffia and Gabriella Zarri, 83–112. Cambridge, MA: Harvard University Press, 1999.

4

Radicals

R. Emmet McLaughlin

Although the designation "Radical Reformation" first appeared in the book of the same name by George H. Williams in 1962, the historical category was created fifty years earlier when Ernst Troeltsch combined Max Weber's ideal type of the "sect" with Alfred Hegler's discovery of Spiritualism in Sebastian Franck (1499–1542).[1] Up to that point, Luther's catchall term *Schwärmer* (fanatic) had promiscuously combined all Protestant reformers to Luther's left, originally including Zwingli and other Sacramentarians, into a single movement of raving murder-prophets whose appeal to the spirit led inevitably to assaults on both true religion and legitimate authority. Heinrich Bullinger, Zwingli's successor, generously contributed the Zurich Anabaptists by attributing their rise to the Saxon archprophet and executed leader of the Peasants' Revolt, Thomas Müntzer, thereby conveniently moving the blame for Anabaptism far from Zurich and its first reformer. The Münsterite Kingdom, in any event, proved to Bullinger that Müntzer's spirit inspired the Anabaptists despite their hypocritical meekness and pacifism.

Troeltsch's threefold typology of Christian social forms—church, sect, and spiritualism—not only distinguished between sects like the Anabaptists and individualists like Franck, it also credited the sectarians and spiritualists with helping to create the modern world with its separation of church and state, religious toleration, and individual freedom of conscience.

[1] Hegler, *Geist und Schrift bei Sebastian Franck*; and Troeltsch, *Soziallehren der christlichen Kirchen und Gruppen.*

Putting the Schwärmer in the vanguard of progress and relegating Luther to the retrograde church and its medieval *corpus christianorum* predictably provoked outrage and response from Lutherans. The most important rebuttal, Karl Holl's "Luther und die Schwärmer" reasserted the traditional view, but gave it theological and historical solidity. Medieval mysticism lay at the root of all the Schwärmer, and they were important in constructing an Anglo-Saxon modernity that Holl condemned as selfishly individualistic, greedy, and immoral.

Despite Holl, the conception of a legitimate, and perhaps more legitimate, movement of reform took hold, particularly in the United States where many of the groups descended from the Schwärmer had found refuge. A variety of names (e.g. "left wing of the Reformation," or "stepchildren of the Reformation") were proposed before George H. Williams coined the term "Radical Reformation." The name had the virtue of ambiguity. Radical could mean that these reformers were simply more consistent or extreme forms of Lutheranism or Reformed Protestantism. It could also mean that they were socially or politically radical; for example, supporting revolutionary social change, or seeking to separate church and state, or arguing for complete religious freedom. This second meaning would not necessarily require the Radicals to be extreme forms of Protestantism. They could have derived directly from medieval or other sources. The question whether the Anabaptists or individual Radical Spiritualists were ever truly followers of Luther or Zwingli remains controverted because the heirs of the latter were not happy with the idea that the Radicals were more faithful to the Reformation principles or because those heirs still wish to dissociate the eccentricities and perversions of the Schwärmer from the socially responsible and religiously sensible Reformation with which they identified.

Williams' *Radical Reformation* was fortunate in its timing. The 1960s and 1970s proved very congenial to any historical figures that were socially progressive, revolutionary, countercultural, or simply outrageous. For social historians, who were themselves trying to overcome entrenched ideological opposition to their goals and methods, the Radicals offered a chance to crack open sixteenth-century society to see what was happening beneath the surface both in the sense of accessing the lower classes and in the sense of laying bare social dynamics that were invisible to those who were driven by them. Because it was innovative and critical of their elders, young scholars were drawn to social history and hence, sometimes, to the

Radicals. The field attracted some very talented young historians who would remain prominent for decades. Although, predictably, proponents criticized both the term and the underlying conceptual basis, they made the Radical Reformation an accepted part of the historical landscape. In fact, they encountered remarkably little resistance.

Time and history have caught up with them, as it always does to the young and avant-garde. The collapse of Communism beginning in 1989 discredited Marxism and put in question the progressive social agenda that lay at the root of social history. After all, social history originally was not just meant to study society, but to change it. The lurch rightward in the United States and Europe left social history stranded. Postmodernism provided weapons to social history's opponents, some of whom did not in fact share postmodernism's epistemological presuppositions, but were quite willing to use it to clear the way for conservative or even reactionary visions of reality. And time conspired with social history's opponents as well, since the sixties generation is now retiring. But since there is as yet no clear successor to social history—cultural history has not established a comparable hegemony—certainly not in Reformation studies, Radical Reformation scholarship finds itself without a clear direction. Individual scholars are doing fine work, but there is no common agenda. This may allow for variety and creativity. It will surely lessen manifest ideological deflections that warp historical judgments. But the lack of questions that "matter" and on which there are serious theoretical or political clashes, could enervate the field and leave it to slide into irrelevance. There does seem to be a drift toward the later sixteenth century, as there is in Reformation studies as a whole. Confessionalization has also cropped up. The outsider status of the Radicals makes them interesting test cases for both the program and the reality. The Radicals may prove interesting in the question of social disciplining since, in the case of the Anabaptists, there was a more heightened level of communal discipline than even in the surrounding established churches, and with the Spiritualists the step to individual self-disciplining had already taken place. The study of Radical Spiritualism is also testing the waters of seventeenth-century cultural history. And there is always the intriguing question of the relationship between it and the early Enlightenment.

This essay will deal only with the Saxon Radicals (Karlstadt, Müntzer), the Radical Spiritualists and the Anabaptists. Unitarianism,

Williams' third subset, is neglected here, as it is in most treatments of the Radical Reformation, because its geographical centers were outside of Germany and because the denial of Christ's divinity shifted its theological center of gravity outside the orbit of the other Radicals, even those who had doubts about the Trinity (e.g., Franck). The Anabaptists and Spiritualists, however, share three traits that alienated them from the major Protestant reformers and led to their segregation from Troeltsch's church-type Protestants. The Radicals were thoroughly dissatisfied with the lack of visible moral improvement in the wake of the gospel. While almost all continued to hold *sola fide* justification, they rejected a merely imputed forensic righteousness.[2] They condemned the latter as a "counterfeit faith" and insisted that true faith remade the believer into a new person capable of a manifestly Christian life. Secondly, they claimed direct access to the word unmediated by the learned Protestant clergy. Whether that entailed a clear literal Bible, or possession of the Spirit, or both, often determined where an individual stood on a continuum stretching from Radical Spiritualism, through spiritualizing Anabaptism, to biblicistic Anabaptism. Thirdly, they all rejected infant baptism, although Weigel, who had no choice in the matter, found a use for the sacraments as signs pointing inward away from themselves. The Radical Spiritualists and the Anabaptists split over the question of believers' baptism and rebaptism. The Radical Spiritualists saw no point in either and thought they gave baptism undue importance. It is unclear whether Karlstadt and Müntzer experimented with postponing baptism until children reached the age of reason. The access to the word and baptism make clear both the common front presented by the Radicals and their significant divisions.

Andreas Bodenstein von Karlstadt (1486–1541)

Karlstadt is perhaps the least understood of the Radical Reformers because he does not fit easily into the categories developed to describe later Radicals. Although by the end of his life, he was clearly a Radical Spiritualist, during his early career when he held center stage with Luther his theology was still inchoate. He had the makings of an Anabaptist, but never accepted rebaptism. He is best compared with the spiritualizing Anabaptists such as Hans Denck or Johannes Bünderlin.

Karlstadt was second only to Luther in influence during the early years of the Reformation when he published approximately ninety works

---

[2]Beachy, *Concept of Grace.*

in more than two hundred editions. Especially important were his writings regarding iconoclasm and the Lord's Supper. In general, he often anticipated both Luther and the Reformation as a whole in converting theory into reality. His writings, particularly those that drew upon late medieval mysticism, remained a staple for religious dissenters from Valentin Weigel to eighteenth-century Pietism.[3]

However, the common historical verdict on Karlstadt simply repeated Luther's condemnations. There was little or no attempt to actually investigate him or his writings until the beginning of the twentieth century. The modern study of Karlstadt began with Hermann Barge (1905).[4] Barge argued for Karlstadt's independence as a thinker and credited him with offering a lay Puritanism that constituted an important alternative to Luther, although Karlstadt continued to agree with Luther on fundamental theological issues. Karl Müller replied by repristinating the traditional Lutheran stereotype.[5] For half a century, Karlstadt research followed one of these two approaches. Some scholars viewed Karlstadt as derived from and in basic agreement with Luther; their clash would then simply reflect personal antagonism or disagreement on the pace of reform.[6] Other scholars adopted Luther's condemnation by positing a fundamental difference between the two that made Karlstadt an alien element in the Reformation proper. They usually emphasized the medieval and mystical elements in his theology.[7] But it must be noted that even those like Barge, who wrote positively about Karlstadt, assumed Luther as the standard against which to measure Karlstadt, rather than examining Karlstadt's theology on its own terms.

Close examination of Karlstadt's writings did not necessarily preclude a Lutheran frame of reference. Ernst Kähler's study of Karlstadt's commentary on Augustine's *De spiritu et litera* not surprisingly tended to overemphasize the Augustinian character of Karlstadt's entire theology.[8] However, his conclusion that Karlstadt was a Schwärmer and a mystic simply repeated Luther and rendered the entire exercise superfluous. American historians in the 1950s and 1960s finally broke out of the entrenched ideological fronts. Gordon Rupp saw in Karlstadt a forerunner of Puritanism

[3]Bubenheimer, "Karlstadtrezeption von der Reformation bis zum Pietismus."
[4]Barge, *Andreas Bodenstein von Karlstadt.*
[5]Müller, *Luther und Karlstadt.*
[6]Hertzsch, *Karlstadt und seine Bedeutung.*
[7]For example, Kriechbaum, *Grundzüge der Theologie Karlstadts.*
[8]Kähler, *Karlstadt und Augustin.*

and placed him on the left wing of the Reformation.[9] More importantly, Hans Hildebrand used Karlstadt to argue that the Protestant theology of grace could assume more than one, Lutheran, form.[10] The 1970s saw further substantial contributions by Americans to Karlstadt scholarship. James Preus's study of Karlstadt, the Wittenberg movement, and Luther's response presented Luther as a practitioner of *Realpolitik* confronted by a Karlstadt who brought the Bible to bear in practice on the institutional form of the church and society.[11] In the latter efforts, Karlstadt foreshadowed developments in the cities of Switzerland and southern Germany. While emphasizing Karlstadt's dependence on Augustine, Preus found no substantive disagreement between Luther and Karlstadt. Rather, the two men split because of personal antagonisms and differing perceptions of the political situation and the pace of reform. Ronald Sider's examination of Karlstadt's Orlamünde theology reached much the same conclusion.[12] Although he emphasized Karlstadt's independent development of mystical themes (in particular, rebirth and *Gelassenheit*), on the central theological issues, Sider viewed Karlstadt as being at one with Luther.

Calvin Augustine Pater was the first to truly depart from the traditional categories and concerns of earlier scholarship. Pater touted Karlstadt's deviance from Luther and christened him the "father of the Baptist movement."[13] Karlstadt's influence reached to both Ulrich Zwingli and the earliest Anabaptists in Zürich, in particular Felix Mantz and Conrad Grebel. Pater also used Karlstadt's brief cooperation with Melchior Hoffman as evidence of Karlstadt's influence upon northern Anabaptism and, eventually, on Dutch Anabaptist leader Menno Simmons. While Pater's research has raised awareness of Karlstadt's influence, thereby rescuing him from Luther's shadow, much of his argumentation is highly speculative and tends to discount evidence that runs counter or does not contribute to his thesis.

More solid, if less venturesome, Ulrich Bubenheimer tended to ignore the concerns of earlier scholarship to pursue a research program focused on biographical detail, new sources, and Karlstadt's place in his late medieval academic context.[14] Bubenheimer sought to appreciate the full range of

[9]Rupp, "Andrew Karlstadt and Reformation Puritanism"; and Rupp, *Patterns of Reformation*.
[10]Hildebrand, "Andreas Bodenstein of Karlstadt."
[11]Preus, *Carlstadt's "Ordinationes" and Luther's Liberty*.
[12]Sider, *Andreas Bodenstein von Karlstadt*.
[13]Pater, *Karlstadt as the Father of the Baptist Movement*.
[14]Bubenheimer, *Consonantia theologiae et iurisprudentiae*; and Bubenheimer, "Karlstadt."

Karlstadt's intellectual sources, not just Luther and mysticism. In particular, he reminded scholars that Karlstadt was a doctor of both canon and Roman laws and showed how Karlstadt's legal training affected his intellectual development as a professor and as a reformer. Further, Bubenheimer claimed Karlstadt's influence upon Müntzer's appropriation of Johannes Tauler and raised the spiritualistic profile of Karstadt as a counterpart to his biblicism. Bubenheimer also emphasized Karlstadt's significance in the Wittenberg movement as well as his experiment in *Gemeindereformation*.

More recent scholarship investigated Karlstadt as an independent reformer rather than merely as a thinker and writer in Luther's wake. For example, Stefan Oehmig's Berlin dissertation examined the provisions for care of the poor in Wittenberg in the later Middle Ages and Reformation.[15] Oehmig placed Karlstadt into the context of European efforts to manage the growing phenomenon of urban poverty. Volkmar Joestel recovered Karlstadt's career as a radical preacher of reform not only in Orlamünde, but in eastern Thüringen generally.[16] Karlstadt's communal Reformation fell victim to the territorial state's absorption of the church within its borders. Alejandro Zorzin's study of Karlstadt as a pamphlet writer made clear the importance of Karlstadt in the early years of the Reformation.[17] Only Luther published more extensively. In his research, Zorzin unearthed an anonymous 1527 publication from Worms that he identified with the Karlstadt baptism pamphlet mentioned in Anabaptist correspondence.[18] Since the Worms text did not resemble the contents of Felix Mantz's *Protestation*, Calvin Pater's case for Karlstadt's central role in early Anabaptist thought was greatly weakened. Pater responded by ascribing the newly discovered pamphlet to Gerhard Westerburg, Karlstadt's brother-in-law.[19] This claim has found little acceptance.

Research on Karlstadt's theology continued in detailed studies that may eventually lead to its general reevaluation. The mystical roots of Karlstadt's theology still attracted attention.[20] The Platonism in Karlstadt's eucharistic theology has finally received some attention.[21] Other new

---

[15]Oehmig, "Studien zum Armen- und Fürsorgewesen der Lutherstadt Wittenberg."
[16]Joestel, *Ostthüringen und Karlstadt*.
[17]Zorzin, *Karlstadt als Flugschriftenautor*.
[18]Zorzin, "Zur Wirkungsgeschichte einer Schrift aus Karlstadts Orlamünde Tätigkeit."
[19]Pater, "Westerburg." Zorzin has since responded; Zorzin, "Karlstadts 'Dialogus vom Tauff der Kinder.'"
[20]Hasse, *Karlstadt und Tauler*.
[21]Ponader, "Die Abendmahlslehre des Andreas Bodenstein von Karlstadt"; and Ponader, "'Caro nichil prodest.'"

research demonstrated that Karlstad was a trilingual humanist, having not only Greek and Latin but Hebrew as well.[22] His linguistic ability lends added importance to his establishment of the Protestant biblical canon, as well as its significance for modern biblical criticism.[23] The picture of Karlstadt that emerges has greater complexity and depth. Clearly Luther and his Reformation discovery was only one factor, though perhaps the most important, in Karlstadt's development as a theologian and practical reformer. Released from Luther's tutelage and Lutheran confessionalism, Karlstadt became a very interesting subject for investigation.[24] A measure of his newfound attractiveness (and his earlier neglect) are the plans to finally produce a critical edition of his collected works.[25] There is still much to understand about his thought and reform program. His contemporary impact and place in the dissident tradition of the next two centuries also need to be pursued. What we now know may be only the tip of the iceberg.

Thomas Müntzer (d. 1525)

Although the extent of Müntzer's impact in his own time can probably not compare with Karlstadt's, his reputation has overshadowed Karlstadt's since the sixteenth century. For this Müntzer could thank both his enemies and eventual admirers. Luther made him the tar with which to brush all the other Radicals; Marxists would heroicize him for exactly the same reason.

Thoroughly demonized by Luther and the Lutheran church, Müntzer's name became a byword for rebellion and religious violence.[26] He was portrayed as a deadly heretic, a bloodthirsty murderer, a raving fanatic, and an enemy to all that was good and decent. Only in the eighteenth century did Gottfried Arnold finally find words of praise for Müntzer and his mystically inspired theology.[27] However it was Friedrich Engels' rediscovery of Müntzer as the protagonist of the early bourgeois revolution (*frühbürgerliche Revolution*) that made the sixteenth-century theologian and preacher into a social revolutionary in the war between the classes.[28] For Engels, Müntzer was the hero that Luther would have been had he not sold out to the feudal princes. A clear-eyed visionary, Müntzer

---

[22]Rüger, "Karlstadt als Hebräist."
[23]Walter, "'Bücher: So night der heiligen Schrifft gleik gehalten.'"
[24]Bubenheimer and Oehmig, *Querdenker der Reformation.*
[25]On this see Looß, "Desiderat der Forschungen zur Reformationsgeschichte."
[26]Steinmetz, *Das Müntzerbild von Martin Luther bis Friedrich Engels.*
[27]Härtwig, "Gottfried Arnolds Müntzerbild."
[28]Engels, "Der deutsche Bauernkrieg."

was a modern thinker. In the sixteenth century, theology was simply the appropriate vehicle to legitimate an essentially secularizing revolution aimed at a this-worldly utopia. The glorification of Müntzer by Marxists served only to reinforce the dark legend of Müntzer in conservative Germany. The figures of Luther and Müntzer became symbols of two ideological visions.[29]

Protestant historians in the nineteenth century maintained and updated the Luther version of Müntzer making him a thinly disguised representative for the modern revolutions that threatened state and church, and discovering profound psychological or character flaws that explained his "madness" and, by implication, that of modern malcontents.[30] It was only in the early twentieth century that a new more sophisticated Lutheran analysis of Müntzer made an appearance. Karl Holl's Müntzer was not a caricature, even if Holl judged Müntzer harshly.[31] For Holl, Müntzer's theology was derivative of Luther's, but Müntzer intensified the elements of medieval mysticism to give Müntzer's theology great personal intensity, at the cost of loosing the restraints provided by holy scripture. Holl also argued that Müntzer's political and social action brought a tension into Müntzer's thought since Holl was convinced that mystically based theology did not accord well with social activism. In a way, Holl agreed with the Marxists that Müntzer's revolutionary activities were not theologically based. Having conceded a Lutheran base to Müntzer's theology, Holl had to isolate it from social consequences in order to distance both Luther and the Reformation from the social unrest that the Catholics had always laid to their charge.

Another Lutheran, Heinrich Böhmer, disagreed with Holl concerning the theological roots of Müntzer's violent agenda.[32] For Böhmer, the key to Müntzer's thought and behavior was to be found in an apocalypticism derived from Taborite chiliasm. The only thing that Müntzer had gotten from mysticism was his insistence upon mortification of the believer. But that was bound up in an apocalyptic vision based upon the Old Testament in which Müntzer plays the role of a *Mordprophet* proclaiming a renewed kingdom of God. An apocalyptic preacher, Müntzer was not a leading figure in the Peasants' War. Unlike Holl, Böhmer

---

[29]Goertz, *Das Bild Thomas Müntzers.*
[30]For example, von Baczko, *Thomas Müntzer*; and Leo, *Thomas Müntzer.*
[31]Holl, "Luther und die Schwärmer."
[32]Böhmer, "Thomas Müntzer und das jüngste Deutschland."

rejected completely the Marxist Müntzer as social revolutionary. Between them, the two Lutheran church historians and the Marxists provided the templates for Müntzer for the rest of the century: the mystic, the apocalyptic, and the revolutionary.

Carl Hinrichs' study of Müntzer's right of resistance published just after World War II was a milestone in Müntzer research.[33] Neither a church historian nor a Marxist, Hinrichs placed Müntzer firmly into his historical setting and emphasized his gradual development into the Radical. Müntzer turned to the people to wield the sword against the godless only after losing out to Luther for the support of the Saxon princes. Employing the same passage from Romans 13:1 that Luther used to demand submission to authority, Müntzer argued that rulers who failed to serve God were to be replaced. As this example shows, Müntzer's theological insights had revolutionary potential, a potential that was realized when he faced official opposition. For Hinrichs, Müntzer envisioned a new democratic and communist state under the guise of the kingdom of God. Unlike Luther, who expected the end of the world, Müntzer preached a new earthly age. Hinrichs' interpretation bound together the religious and social revolutionary that others had resolutely separated since he recognized that such a separation was foreign not only to Müntzer, but to Luther as well.

As with much else, the study of Müntzer began to shift its ground in the 1960s. The Marxist historian Manfred Bensing presented a Müntzer who was first and foremost a theologian, but whose failure as a revolutionary was the product of his erroneous assessment of the times. His utopian vision was too far ahead of the historical timetable.[34] The triumph of the bourgeois, not the establishment of communist communities, was necessary to move society forward to a later denouement in which capitalism would be overcome. Despite Bensing's appreciation of Müntzer the theologian and preacher, in the end Bensing offered a split picture of Müntzer in which the religious and the secular ran parallel but did not coincide. Müntzer was clearly the social revolutionary and not the apocalyptic. By contrast, Walter Elliger, whose biography of Müntzer was both massive and based on detailed research, maintained the Lutheran confessional position.[35] His Müntzer was not the social revolutionary. He was the Murder

---

[33]Hinrichs, *Luther und Müntzer.*
[34]Bensing, *Thomas Müntzer und der Thüringer Aufstand*; and Bensing, *Thomas Müntzer.*
[35]Elliger, *Thomas Müntzer.*

Prophet (*Mordprophet*) and delusional Servant of God (*Knecht Gottes*) whose goal was not social upheaval and justice for the lower classes, but a radical reform of church and Christianity ushering in the kingdom of God. The mystical Müntzer reappeared with the work of Hans-Jürgen Goertz.[36] Unlike Holl, who believed that Luther had mediated the mystical elements in Müntzer's thought, Goertz demonstrated Müntzer's thorough and direct knowledge of Tauler. Goertz also argued that Müntzer went beyond his sources to produce a mysticism that fueled Müntzer's social engagement rather than subverting it. As Goertz would later admit, he failed to give the apocalyptic element its due weight. By contrast, Gottfried Maron refurbished the apocalyptic Müntzer by drawing attention to Müntzer's focus upon the "judgment of God" (*Gericht Gottes*).[37] For Maron, apocalypticism was what bound together Müntzer theology and made sense of his biography. Reinhard Schwarz pursued the Taborite connection suggested by Böhmer and argued that chiliasm (that is, the dawning thousand-year reign of saints, not the apocalyptic reign of God) formed the center of Müntzer's theology.[38] Unfortunately, Schwarz could present no evidence that Müntzer in fact knew Taborite teachings, which in any event differed significantly from Müntzer's own positions.

In general, while Western historians tended to give greater weight to the social revolutionary side of Müntzer than they had previously, and Marxist historians increasingly conceded the theological cast of Müntzer thought and career, no consensus could be achieved in the 1970s and 1980s. The period was productive, instead, of detailed studies of isolated aspects of Müntzer. The most important results came, as in the case of Karlstadt, from Bubenheimer.[39] His careful archival work filled gaps in Müntzer's early life and education. Müntzer's family had some connection with the goldsmith's trade and may have held much the same position in society as Luther's. In other words, Müntzer was not a man of the people (the lower classes). Bubenheimer also made clear that humanism played a greater role in Müntzer's early development than is customarily believed. Bubenheimer established Müntzer's presence in Wittenberg in 1517 through 1518, though Bubenheimer argued Müntzer may have associated more with Melanchthon and Karlstadt than Luther. The young Müntzer was still innocent of revolutionary tendencies when he arrived in Zwickau in 1520.

[36]Goertz, *Innere und äußere Ordnung in der Theologie Thomas Müntzers.*
[37]Maron, "Thomas Müntzer als Theologe des Gerichts."
[38]Schwarz, *Die apokalyptische Theologie Thomas Müntzers und der Taboriten.*
[39]Bubenheimer, *Thomas Müntzer.*

The celebration in 1989 of Müntzer's putative birth five hundred years before produced a raft of biographies and other studies, though it could not be said that they moved the field forward very much. Müntzer the bloodthirsty apocalyptic, the earnest mystic, and the committed revolutionary made their appearances. The best and most balanced treatment came from the Marxist historian Günter Vogler.[40] By contrast, Abraham Friesen recreated the traditional *Mordprophet* Müntzer. But Friesen also directed attention to a new mystical source, the apocryphal life of Tauler that accompanied early editions.[41] Tom Scott's entry is valuable for his treatment of the covenants and leagues that Müntzer inspired. Defensive in nature, they were designed to protect the reform movement from threatening Catholic princes.[42] Rather than leading a worldwide revolution of the saints, Müntzer's expressed goal in 1525 was to conquer lands in a 50-mile radius from Mühlhausen. Hans-Jürgen Goertz's biography maintained the primacy of the mystical roots of Müntzer's theology, but accommodated both apocalyptic and revolutionary strands as well.[43] Finally, Gerhard Brendler's effort to incorporate Müntzer's theology into the standard Marxist interpretation, foundered on Brendler's weak theological grounding and resulted in an apocalyptic Müntzer much like Friesen's.[44]

The most important product of the Müntzer year was a volume of essays on *The Theologian Thomas Müntzer* edited by Siegfried Bräuer and Helmar Junghans.[45] This remarkable collection of substantive essays on every aspect of Müntzer's theology clearly established him as a theologian with a sophisticated body of doctrine and a figure in his own right, not merely a counterweight to Martin Luther. While the social revolutionary did not disappear in the collection, he did recede into the background. Given the reunification of Germany in the years following this volume's publication, the theological heft given to Müntzer makes probable a continuing focus on his religious profile.

The 1989 commemoration marked the highwater mark of scholarly interest in Müntzer. The collapse of the SED regime in East Germany eliminated much of the ideological motivation, although this had in fact already begun to ebb. More importantly, material support disappeared. A

---

[40]Vogler, *Thomas Müntzer.*
[41]Friesen, *Thomas Müntzer.*
[42]Scott, *Thomas Müntzer.*
[43]Goertz, *Thomas Müntzer.*
[44]Brendler, *Thomas Müntzer.*
[45]Bräuer, *Der Theologe Thomas Müntzer.*

continued interest in Müntzer would also not help an East German scholar's integration into the West German academic establishment. The general shift of interest to the later Reformation and confessionalization also took its toll. Since 1990 the production of Müntzer scholarship has collapsed. Even my piece on Müntzer's apocalypticism owed its inception to the occasion of the millennium.[46] There have been some exceptions including the 1999 dissertation of William McNiel on both Müntzer and Karlstadt.[47] And there is renewed interest in Müntzer's relationship to the Grebel circle in Zurich.[48] Müntzer research may need the coattails of Anabaptism whose modern heirs guarantee continuing interest. Müntzer research is also hobbled to some extent by a not quite critical edition by Günther Franz.[49] Because its shortcomings are widely recognized, scholars have produced critical editions of selected works in connection with their own research interests.[50] In his English translation of Müntzer's collected works, Peter Matheson also corrected some of the texts.[51] Serious researchers would be advised to consult the originals of works that lack a critical edition.

The Radical Spiritualists

Radical Spiritualism was born in the late nineteenth century, at least historiographically speaking. The term and the religious category was first applied to Sebastian Franck by Alfred Hegler in 1892.[52] In 1912, Ernest Troeltsch incorporated the Spiritualists as the third ideal type in his taxonomy.[53] The Quaker Rufus Jones in 1914 recognized a group of "spiritual reformers," while Johannes Kuhn (1923) included them as one of the five basic forms of Protestantism.[54] George Williams (1957) filled out the picture of Radical Spiritualism and proposed three subcategories: Revolutionary (Müntzer, Karlstadt, and the Zwickau prophets), Rationalist

---

[46]McLaughlin, "Müntzer and Apocalypticism."

[47]McNiel, "Andreas von Karlstadt and Thomas Müntzer"; and McNiel, "Andreas von Karlstadt as a Humanist Theologian."

[48]Stayer, "Sächsischer Radikalismus und Schweizer Täufertum"; and Goertz, "'A Common Future Conversation.'"

[49]Müntzer, *Schriften und Briefe*, ed. Franz and Kirn.

[50]See for example, Müntzer, *Theologische Schriften*, ed. Brauer and Ullmann.

[51]Müntzer, *Collected Works*, ed. and trans. Matheson.

[52]Hegler, *Geist und Schrift bei Sebastian Franck*. For a good example of traditional treatments of Franck, see Hase, *Sebastian Franck von Wörd der Schwarmgeist*.

[53]Troeltsch, *Soziallehren der christlichen Kirchen und Gruppen*.

[54]Jones, *Spiritual Reformers in the Sixteenth and Seventeenth Centuries*; and Kühn, *Toleranz und Offenbarung*.

(Sebastian Franck, Paracelsus, and Valentin Weigel), and Evangelical (Schwenckfeld).[55] Recently, I offered a refinement of the Williams typology based upon the natures, characteristics, and sources of two understandings of "Spirit": Biblical/Charismatic (Müntzer), Platonic/Noetic (Franck and Dirck Volkertszoon Coornhert), and Platonic/Sacramental (Schwenckfeld, Weigel).[56] Despite the inherently individualistic character of Radical Spiritualism, the four main Radical Spiritualists form a tightly clustered group of thinkers who often knew and used each other's works. What they shared was an extreme form of the tendency shared by all Protestant reformers to diminish or dismiss human or material mediation between God and the individual.

SEBASTIAN FRANCK

Sebastian Franck's 1531 letter to Johannes Campanus is the classic exposition of Radical Spiritualism.[57] Franck argued that the church had disappeared shortly after the apostles, but that reestablishing the apostolic church made no sense because mature Christians no longer needed the "toys" that God had conceded to the young church. Instead, the Christian should focus upon the "divine spark" (*funklein*) within, a concept Franck had taken from the *Theologia Deutsch* that lay at the heart of Franck's spiritualism. A printer, Franck compiled and printed a number of standard reference works on history, geography, and aphorisms, each of which was also a vehicle for his spiritualistic views.[58] Franck's contributions to the writing of history, geography, and German literature have made it difficult to encompass the man.[59] Both his own works and those he reprinted by writers such as Erasmus and Agrippa von Nettesheim reflected his increasing epistemological and religious skepticism. In the *Paradoxes* (1534), he would conclude that scripture itself served only to confuse, thereby driving the Christian inward to the inner word.[60] Although very much the loner in his life, his books made him the second most influential radical after Karlstadt.[61]

---

[55]Williams, *Spiritual and Anabaptist Writers.*

[56]McLaughlin, "Reformation Spiritualism."

[57]Williams, *Spiritual and Anabaptist Writers.* On the dating of the letter to Campanus, see Dejung, "Sebastian Franck."

[58]Dipple, "Sebastian Franck and the Münster Anabaptist Kingdom."

[59]Bischof, *Sebastian Franck*; Dejung, *Wahrheit und Häresie.* See also Dejung, "Geschichte lehrt Gelassenheit"; and Müller, *Sebastian Franck.*

[60]Franck, *Paradoxa.*

[61]His secular and religious history, for example, influenced Bernard Rothman, the theologian of

There has been little doubt since Alfred Hager's pioneering work on Franck that late medieval mysticism, especially the *Theologia Deutsch* and Johannes Tauler's *Sermons*, lies at the root of most Radical Spiritualism.[62] Karl Holl and Steven Ozment reaffirmed that interpretation.[63] Parallel to the religious Franck, however, there quickly developed a secularized version: Franck as forerunner of modern German idealism.[64] While a Franck shorn of his religious context and character clearly is misconstrued, the secular version of Franck made him an interesting subject for the philosophers, who produced a number of penetrating studies of his thought.[65] Less helpful was Franck's adoption by German Romantics and nationalists in a spate of publications of dubious value, particularly in the Nazi era.

Everhard Teufel's work served as a bridge between earlier scholarship and the new. His 1954 biography grounded Franck in the cities of southern Germany and the Reformation milieu. It provided a solid historical platform for further research on his intellectual and religious development.[66] Horst Weigelt's study of Franck's early development remains foundational for any later treatment of him as a religious figure.[67] Christoph De Jung's analysis of the library that Franck left at his death has proven particularly useful.[68] Most recently Patrick Hayden-Roy has produced an updated biography.[69] Franck's varied educational background and voracious reading meant that other traditions exercised influence as well, in particular Erasmian humanism and Scholastic nominalism, both of which reinforced the impact of the *Theologia Deutsch*'s negative theology on the most salient aspect of Franck's thought—thoroughgoing skepticism.[70] His skepticism played a large role in his support for religious toleration.[71]

The trajectory for Franck studies is not clear. The tension between the religious/theological interpretation of Franck and the secular/philo-

---

the Münster Anabaptists. See Dipple, "Sebastian Franck and the Münster Anabaptist Kingdom"; and Kaczerowsky, *Sebastian Franck*.

[62]Teufel, "Die 'Deutsche Theologie' und Sebastian Franck."

[63]Ozment, *Mysticism and Dissent*.

[64]Wollgast, *Der deutsche Pantheismus*; and Séguenny, *Les Spirituels*.

[65]Joachimsen, "Zur inneren Entwicklung Sebastian Francks."

[66]Teufel, *"Landräumig": Sebastian Franck*.

[67]Weigelt, *Sebastian Franck und die lutherische Reformation*.

[68]Dejung, "Sebastian Francks nachgelassene Bibliothek."

[69]Hayden-Roy, *Inner Word and the Outer World*.

[70]McLaughlin, "Sebastian Franck and Caspar Schwenckfeld."

[71]See for example, Barbers, *Toleranz bei Sebastian Franck*; and Goldhammer, "Der Toleranzgedanke bei Franck und Wiegel."

sophical can still be seen in the work of Siegfried Wollgast, the foremost proponent of the pantheistic Franck.[72] The question of Franck's influence has not been exhausted.[73] The general shift of interest to the later Reformation and the seventeenth century is moving research on Franck forward in time to his impact on theosophical literature and Pietism.[74] And there are intriguing questions concerning his relationship to—of all things—the debacle at Münster that could presage some revision of the rationalist saint.[75] The new critical edition that began to appear in 1992 will doubtless open up new avenues of research and facilitate conversation among the many disciplines interested in Franck.[76] As with Dirck Volkertszoon Coornhert, so with Franck, we are dealing with a phenomenon that reaches far into the intellectual life of the sixteenth and seventeenth century in the Netherlands and Germany. A connection between Radical Spiritualism and the Enlightenment, particularly regarding toleration, has often been claimed. Only such a broader cultural approach can establish a relationship between the Reformation religious movement and the secular turn of the Enlightenment.[77]

CASPAR SCHWENCKFELD

Unlike Franck, Caspar Schwenckfeld (1489–1561) already enjoys a full modern edition because Schwenckfeld (paradoxically for a Radical Spiritualist) left a church that still bears his name.[78] Schwenckfeld differed from the other Radical Spiritualists in a number of other ways: his social status (noble), the sources of his theological vision, and his irenic temper.[79] The first and last were doubtless closely related.

Schwenckfeld's noble status shielded him from many of the dangers confronting other Radicals in his own time, but also offered him some protection from later scholarly vitriol. Beginning in the nineteenth century, he

---

[72]Wollgast, "Sebastian Francks theologisch-philosophische Auffassungen."

[73]Becker, "Nederlandische Vertalingen van Sebastian Franks Geschriften." See most recently, van Gemert, "Zur Funktionalisierung Franckchen Gedankenguts."

[74]Williams, "Gelächter vor Gott."

[75]Stupperich, "Sebastian Franck." More recently, see Dipple, "Sebastian Franck and the Münster Anabaptist Kingdom."

[76]Franck, *Sämtliche Werke.*

[77]See for example, Wollgast, "Valentin Weigel und seine Stellung"; Fix, *Prophecy and Reason*; and Brecht, "Der Beitrag des Spiritualismus der Reformationszeit."

[78]Schwenckfeld, *Corpus Schwenckfeldianorum.*

[79]Schultz, *Caspar Schwenckfeld von Ossig,* is hagiographical, but still quite useful. See also McLaughlin, 1986; and Eberlein, *Ketzer oder Heiliger?*

was well served by local historians in Silesia who established the basic outline of his early life and career. Research in the twentieth century has concentrated on his relationship to Luther, the sources of his thought, the
influence of Krautwald, and the key components of his theology. Despite
Schwenckfeld's claims to the contrary, some scholars have denied that
Schwenckfeld was ever truly a follower of Luther.[80] Others have admitted
his reliance upon Luther's theology, but believe he misunderstood and misconstrued it in ways that presage his later spiritualism.[81] Still others have
argued that Schwenckfeld remained a loyal and well-informed Lutheran
until 1524.[82] Mysticism, in particular Tauler (*Theologia Deutsch* is
strangely absent from Schwenckfeld's writings), has often been credited,
wrongly, as an important source either before or after Schwenckfeld's break
with Luther.[83] Humanism has also been suggested.[84] In the Eucharistic
controversy, both Karlstadt and Zwingli have been seen as the sources of
Schwenckfeld's own position.[85] Unlike Karlstadt and Zwingli, however,
Schwenckfeld argued for the necessity of a real spiritual participation in
Christ. He appealed to John 6:54–57, while they cited John 6:63. There has
been some speculation about influence from the Bohemian Brethren's
teaching on the Eucharist.[86] I have argued that Schwenckfeld's Eucharistic
theology developed out of late medieval Eucharistic piety, in particular the
practice and doctrine of spiritual communion.[87]

The exact relationship between Krautwald's teaching and Schwenckfeld's theology has troubled some scholars who correctly believe that
Krautwald has not received recognition for developing much of their common theology.[88] Krautwald's Augustinian spiritualism was less thoroughgoing than Schwenckfeld's and that allowed Krautwald to retain a greater
commitment to the visible church than would his colleague. Schwenckfeld
denied the existence of a Christian church but, unlike Franck, he expected

---

[80]Kluge, "Leben und Entwicklungsgang Schwenckfelds"; and Erb, "Role of Late Medieval Spirituality."

[81]Maron, *Individualismus und Gemeinschaft bei Caspar Schwenckfeld.*

[82]Hirsch, "Zum Verständnis Schwenckfelds"; and McLaughlin, *Reluctant Radical.*

[83]Weigelt, *Spiritualistische Tradition im Protestantismus.*

[84]Sciegienny, "Réforme érasmienne ou Réforme luthérienne?"; and Sciegienny, *Homme charnel,
homme spirituel.*

[85]Köhler, *Zwingli und Luther*; and Shantz, *Crautwald and Erasmus.*

[86]Urner, "Die Taufe bei Caspar Schwenckfeld."

[87]McLaughlin, "Genesis of Schwenckfeld's Eucharistic Doctrine."

[88]Eberlein, "Zur Würdigung des Valentin Krautwald"; Weigelt, *Valentin Krautwald*; and Shantz,
Crautwald and Erasmus. McLaughlin, *Reluctant Radical*; and *Freedom of the Spirit*, agrees except for
Schwenckfeld's initial Eucharistic position and his Christology. See also Erb, "Valentin Crautwald."

the reinstitution of the apostolic church at Christ's second coming.[89] Schwenckfeld also believed scripture had a positive value for those with the spirit.[90] The "knowledge of Christ" (*Erkenntnis Christi*) played a central role in his thought. Schwenckfeld's peculiar heavenly flesh Christology denying the creaturehood of the humanity of Christ has attracted attention.[91] What has not been studied as it should are the decades after 1540. Schwenckfeld published ceaselessly during those years and clashed with opponents as different as Pilgram Marpeck and Matthias Flaccius.[92]

The Schwenckfelder movement in southern Germany and the Schwenckfelder communities in Silesia have been studied.[93] More work should be done in other regions, in particular Poland and the Baltic littoral, the middle and lower Rhine, and Switzerland. The sizable collection of his works in the library of Sir David Lindsay (ca. 1490–1555), known as the Bibliotheca Lindesiana, in Wigan, England, the birthplace of Gerrard Winstanley, suggests that this might also be a fruitful area of study. Because of the remarkable prominence of women among Schwenckfeld's followers, his theology offers an interesting object of gender analysis, something that is rare elsewhere in Radical Reformation historiography.[94] The paradoxical existence of a spiritualist "church" in southern Germany presents a unique opportunity to track the social context and significance of what would otherwise be an almost invisible phenomenon. The Schwenckfelders present an interesting example of the limits of confessionalization and the ways in which individuals eluded political and social enforcement of religious conformity.[95] That the southern German branch can be traced well into the seventeenth century (the Silesian branch continues to this day in North America) also helps to fill the gap between Reformation and early Enlightenment that is of increasing interest to scholars. Even more than Franck, Schwenckfeld was kept in play by his followers in theosophical and pietistic circles.

---

[89]Maron, *Individualismus und Gemeinschaft bei Caspar Schwenckfeld*; Pietz, *Die Gestalt der zukünftigen Kirche*; and Ecke, *Schwenckfeld, Luther*.

[90]McLaughlin, "Spiritualism and the Bible."

[91]Hirsch, "Zum Verständnis Schwenckfelds"; Maier, *Caspar Schwenckfeld on the Person and Work of Christ*; McLaughlin, *Reluctant Radical*; and McLaughlin, "Schwenckfeld-Vadian Christological Debate."

[92]Loserth, *Pilgram Marpecks Antwort auf Caspar Schwenckfelds*.

[93]Weigelt, *Spiritualistische Tradition im Protestantismus*; Clasen, "Schwenckfeld's Friends"; and McLaughlin, "Schwenckfeld-Vadian Christological Debate."

[94]Gouldbourne, "Theology and Gender."

[95]Gritschke-Grossman, *Via media*.

VALENTIN WEIGEL

The second-generation spiritualist and Nicodemite pastor of Zscho-
pau in Meissen, Valentin Weigel (1533–88), is the most striking evidence of
a lively intellectual insurgency beneath the enforced conformity of the confessionalizing Saxon state church. He is also the most important medium
through which spiritualistic impulses were transmitted to Paracelsian and
theosophical circles. At the same time, he was the crucial link in the chain
leading from Radical Spiritualism to both Pietism and reformers who
remained within the pale of orthodoxy.[96]
    Weigel lived the confessionalization of Lutheran Saxony.[97] Despite
the thoroughly heretical cast of his thought, however, Weigel faced questions only once, in the year (1572) Lutheran rulers imposed a Formula of
Concord to end the controversies that had wracked the Lutheran churches
since the Augsburg Interim. Weigel's unwilling subscription to the formula
left a bad taste in his mouth that only grew with time. His one brush with
the authorities also taught him to conceal his discontent and his secret
rejection of the reigning orthodoxy, and perhaps of Lutheranism itself.
With each passing year, the radicalness of his critique and the boldness of
his speculation increased.
    The most pressing issue in Weigel studies concerns the separation of
Weigel's own work from that of his first editors, admirers, and imitators.
Much has passed under his name that probably stemmed from his colleague Benedikt Biedermann, his cantor Christoph Weickhart, and the
publisher of Paracelsus' theological works, Johann Staricius.[98] After a false
start, a new critical edition has begun to appear.[99] In the meantime, since
some of Weigel's most influential works remain under suspicion, interpretations of his thought are in some sense provisional. But the impact of
Weigeliana, both authentic and spurious, cannot be doubted.[100] Among
others, two seminal figures of the seventeenth century, Jacob Boehme

---

[96]Brecht, "Der Beitrag des Spiritualismus der Reformationszeit."
    [97]For a good introduction to Weigel, see Weeks, *Valentin Weigel*. On his theology, see Ozment,
Mysticism and Dissent.
    [98]Lieb, *Valentin Weigels Kommentar*; Weigel, *Handschriftliche Predigtensammlung*, ed. Zeller;
Pfefferl, "Die Überlieferung der Schriften Valentin Weigels"; Pfefferl, "Christoph Weickhart as
Paracelsist"; Pfefferl, "Zum Wirkungsgeschichte des Paracelsus"; Zeller, *Die Schiften Valentin Weigels*;
and Zeller, "Der frühe Weigelianismus."
    [99]Weigel, *Sämtliche Schriften*, ed. Peuckert and Zeller; and Weigel, *Sämtliche Schriften*, ed. Pfef-
ferl. See also Weigel, *Ausgewählte Werke*, ed. Wollgast; and Pfefferl, "Die kritische Ausgabe der
'Sämtlichen Schriften' Valentin Weigels."
    [100]Opel, *Valentin Weigel*; and van Dülmen, *Schwärmer und Separatisten*.

(1575–1624) and, especially, Johannes Arndt (1555–1621), were in his debt, and through them he contributed to the theosophical current and Pietism. A measure of his influence is the fact that "Weigelian" replaced "Schwenckfelder" as the worst form of Lutheran opprobrium.

Although Weigel drew upon many and varied sources—his wide reading at University shows that he already harbored heterodox notions—a few stand out: Luther, medieval mysticism, Radical Spiritualism, Platonism, and Paracelsus. Weigel skillfully played the young Luther against his orthodox epigones in a way that foreshadows Johannes Arndt and Pietism. It remains unclear if his appeal to Luther was disingenuous. Weigel drew upon a number of other Radical Spiritualists, but he was the follower of none. His theology resembled Schwenckfeld's, but he more frequently appealed to Franck, and even had kind things to say about Müntzer. Wiegel held a heavenly flesh Christology as had Schwenckfeld, but gave it a Paracelsian twist. He was also less categorical in his rejection of the church and scripture than Franck.[101] His criticism of the collusion of church and state to oppress the poor laity sounds much like Müntzer—he even appealed to Müntzer's Daniel statue from the Sermon to the Princes—although Weigel completely rejected the use of force in religion.[102] His pacifism on the eve of the Thirty Years' War was prescient and drew the attention of contemporaries and later scholars. Among the Radical Spiritualists whose conception of spirit was Platonic in nature, he alone read deeply in the Neoplatonists, particularly Proclus, and understood the foundational metaphysical assumptions underpinning the Radical Spiritualist spirit/matter dualism. Despite that, Weigel was drawn to Paracelsus whose works Weigel was among the first to appreciate.[103] Paracelsus' fundamental insights, however, put in question any spirit/matter dualism. Recapitulating developments in ancient Neoplatonism, Weigel borrowed Paracelsus' mediating "sidereal" cosmos to bridge the gap whose maintenance, however, was essential to his entire religious approach. In fact, Weigel's cosmological speculations are hard to reconcile with the Radical Spiritualists' disinterest in the physical universe.

Given Weigel's intellectual location at the intersection of so many crosscurrents, it is not surprising that there are sharp disagreements over

---

[101]Schoep, *Von Himmlischen Fleisch Christi.*

[102]Ozment, *Mysticism and Dissent*; and Goldhammer, "Der Toleranzgedanke."

[103]Pfefferl, "Valentin Weigel und Paracelsus"; and Pfefferl, "Die Rezeption der paracelsischen Schriftums bei Valentin Weigel."

where to place him in the religion and culture of the age. Horst Pfefferl, for example, argued that despite the Saxon state church's condemnation, Weigel remained a Lutheran, though one closer to Luther himself than to the orthodoxy of Weigel's own time.[104] Martin Brecht, by contrast, makes of him a proto-Pietist.[105] Hans Maier took more seriously both Weigel's debt to medieval mysticism and his Radical Spiritualism.[106] Maier and Heinz Längin both claimed that Weigel's epistemology foreshadowed Kant's.[107] Going further, Siegfried Wollgast argued that Weigel was first and foremost a philosopher who was critical not only of the established church, but of religion generally.[108] Wollgast assigned Weigel a prominent place in the same progressive pantheist tradition as Sebastian Franck. Weigel's Paracelsianism, however, threatens to undermine both Wollgast's thesis and the various religious interpretations of it as well. The polymath Franck was difficult to categorize because of the breadth and variety of his interests. Weigel poses even greater challenges because of his contributions to competing explanatory disciplines (theology vs. "science") with contradictory primal assumptions (dualism vs. materialism). His conceptual elusiveness, the unresolved identification of his authentic writings, the general shift to the later Reformation, and the new prominence of cultural history will make Weigel a continuing subject of research and debate.

Dirck Volkertszoon Coornhert

In turning to Dirck Volkertszoon Coornhert (1522–90), we leave rarified German mystical-philosophical-cosmological speculation for bracing Dutch common sense. Though contemporaries, Coornhert and Weigel shared little but their opposition to overweening clerically dominated established churches. If Weigel looked forward to Pietism and theosophism, Coornhert foreshadowed modern religious individualism and religious freedom. And while Weigel maintained a subtle Nicodemite subterfuge in the "belly of the beast," Coornhert was the most public of Radical Spiritualists whose own views and criticism of others were to be found in the bookshops of Holland.

---

[104]Pfefferl, "Das neue Bild Valentin Weigels."

[105]Brecht, *Geschichte des Pietismus.*

[106]Maier, *Der Mystische Spiritualismus Valentin Weigels.*

[107]Längin, "Grundlinien der Erkenntnislehre Valentin Weigels."

[108]Wollgast, "Valentin Weigel und Jakob Boehme"; and Wollgast, "Valentin Weigel und seine Stellung."

Coornhert was born into a wealthy Amsterdam merchant family.[109] He received a solid basic education, though unlike the other Spiritualists, he never attended university. Even more than they, he was an autodidact, but immensely well read. At the age of twenty-two, his reading of Luther, Calvin, Menno Simons, and Franck made him a Radical Spiritualist. Only later would he find the *Theologia Deutsch,* but it would remain his favorite and he reread it often. Erasmus would also be valued. Protestantism, Radical Spiritualism, mysticism, and humanism provided the basic stock of his intellectual storehouse, although constant reading continually added to the store.

Coornhert is best known for his defense of religious freedom.[110] He recognized in the Calvinists a new threat to religious liberty and opposed their teachings on original sin, bondage of the will, *sola fide* justification, and predestination. They, for their part, sought to silence him, but were forced to meet his criticism both in print and public disputation. His *Synod on the Freedom of Conscience* (1582) was the most extensive treatment of religious freedom in the sixteenth century. Although Coornhert did not deny the existence of heresy, he argued that it could not be prosecuted without injustice and that toleration benefited both church and state. He rejected Franck's skepticism and equated the "divine spark" with reason, laying the groundwork for a transition from Radical Spiritualism to Enlightenment rationalism.[111] He also denied that the church had disappeared from the earth, as most Radicals and certainly Franck argued. The Catholic Church remained the only true church since none of the Protestant churches could prove their divine calling, but the Catholic Church was so encrusted with error and abuse as to be useless. Coornhert never formally left the Catholic Church nor did he join any other. Coornhert wrote the first book of ethics in a modern language, and did so without appealing to scripture, but only at the request of his editor. His rejection of original sin and his condemnation of predestination as blasphemous accompanied a vigorous defense of human freedom and the teaching of human perfectibility ("perfectism," "perfectibilism"). He even admitted to agreement with the arch-heretic Pelagius. Arminius may well have learned much from Coornhert, as the Contra-Remonstrants claimed.

---

[109]For his biography, see Bonger, *Life and Work of Dirck Volckertszoon Coornhert.* See also Voogt, *Constraint on Trial.*

[110]See most recently, Voogt, *Constraint on Trial.*

[111]Fix, *Prophecy and Reason.*

Reading Coornhert, it is difficult to believe that the Zwickau Prophets appeared in Wittenberg the year he was born, or that the Anabaptist Kingdom of Münster fell in his thirteenth year, or that his adult life coincided with the surge of confessionalization, or that he died twenty-eight years before the Synod of Dort. As much as the other Radical Spiritualists looked forward to modern developments, Coornhert's thought *is* modern in important ways. Recognition of his modernity has led some to see him as a purely secular thinker, much as it has for both Franck and Weigel. Because his nontheological *Ethics* was intellectually more accessible to modern scholars, many have based their judgments of him upon it alone. The *Ethics* relied entirely upon human reason, so some nineteenth-century writers claimed him as a representative of universal theism, though it is clear that he was a convinced Christian.[112] Others thought him a Stoic.[113] Still others have seen him as a pure rationalist and humanist.[114] German scholars, on the other hand, attempted to bring him into the main arena of the Reformation, by claiming his dependence on Erasmus, Zwingli, and Schwenckfeld.[115]

The twentieth century saw a continuation of many of these questions. For example, the role of the classics and Coornhert's access to them has revived questions concerning how Christian he was.[116] But it has also finally seen the rediscovery of the religious Coornhert in the work of Bruno Becker during the 1920s and 1930s.[117] Nonetheless, since World War II Coornhert scholarship has focused upon his role in the history of religious toleration.[118] Promisingly, a collection of essays published in 1989 for the four-hundredth anniversary of Coornhert's death presents a wider, richer picture of his thought.[119]

Coornhert remains little known outside of Holland since he wrote in Dutch. But that he wrote in his native tongue and may be said to have laid the foundations for modern Dutch, made him a factor to be reckoned with

---

[112]Land, *De wijsbegeerte in de Nederlanden*; and Dilthey, *Weltanschauung und Analyse*.

[113]Moorrees, *Dirk Volkertszoon Coornhert*.

[114]Lindenboom, *Stiefkinderen van het Christendom*.

[115]Troeltsch, *Soziallehren der christlichen Kirchen und Gruppen*; Dilthey, *Weltanschauung und Analyse*; and Kühn, *Toleranz und Offenbarung*.

[116]van der Meer, *Bijdrage tot het onderzoek*. Cf. Kuiper, *Orbis Artium en Renaissance*.

[117]Becker, *Bronnen tot de kennis*. His studies appeared mostly in articles that began to appear in 1923. For a list, see Bonger, *Life and Work of Coornhert*.

[118]Bonger, *De motivering van den godsdienstvrijheid*; Voogt, 2000; Lecler, *Histoire de la tolerance*; Lecler and Valkhoff, *Les premiers défenseurs*; and Güldner, *Das Toleranz-Problem*.

[119]Bonger, *Dirck Volckertszoon Coornhert*.

in his own time.[120] He rivals Schwenckfeld in the volume of his writings and he surpasses Franck in the range of his genres: engraving, poetry, drama, ethics, translations, philosophy, theology, penology, and politics. It would be too much to say that Coornhert is virgin territory, but he remains relatively unexplored. The recent efforts of Gerrit Voogt to bring him to the attention of English-speaking scholars may help remedy the neglect. Sources are not lacking, but they are rarely found in modern editions. His 1630 collected works contain most but not all of his writings. Some have been republished, but others are missing.[121] We may not have a full accounting of his *oeuvre* in any event. Most importantly, the engravings need study. Although his plays and poems are well known to Dutch literary historians, analyzing them for religious, philosophical, or political content largely remains to be done. The new interest in the later sixteenth century and the increased attention to the Netherlands in the larger narrative of Europe,[122] give Coornhert studies great promise.

Anabaptism

Twentieth-century Anabaptist historiography is a story of the rise and fall of Harold Bender's "Anabaptist Vision."[123] Published in 1944, Bender's "Anabaptist Vision" was both a manifesto and a blueprint for a new positive understanding of sixteenth-century Anabaptism. Bender identified three defining characteristics of what he called "normative Anabaptism": discipleship, sectarian separatism, and pacifism. Such a definition excluded, and was meant to exclude, "aberrant" Anabaptists like Hans Hut and Balthasar Hubmaier in the south and the Melchiorites/Münsterites in the north. The legitimate line of succession began with Conrad Grebel and his colleagues in Zurich, achieved its classic expression in the 1527 Schleitheim Confession of the martyred Michael Sattler, and found its abiding expression in the Dutch Mennonites and the Moravian Hutterites.

Another term Bender used, "Evangelical Anabaptism," reveals an agenda within an agenda. Modern Mennonitism, he believed, had fallen

---

[120]Zijlstra, "Anabaptists, Spiritualists, and the Reformed Church"; and van Veen, "Spiritualism in the Netherlands."

[121]Coornhert, *Werken* (1630) has all of the most important works. Coornhert, *Weet of Rust* (1985) is limited to prose and therefore does not include the poetry, drama, or engravings. In 1942, Bruno Becker published an edition of Coornhert's ethical treatise, the *Zedekunst*.

[122]See Israel, *Dutch Republic*; Israel, *Radical Enlightenment*; Kaplan, *Calvinists and Libertines*; Fix, *Prophecy and Reason*; and Oestreich, *Antiker Geist und moderner Staat bei Justus Lipsius*.

[123]Bender, "Anabaptist Vision."

victim to a Pietistic spirituality that threatened true Bible Christianity. A conservative American Protestant himself, Bender's "Anabaptist Vision" presented an Anabaptism that was Protestantism carried to its logical conclusion, and that was a purely religious phenomenon lacking any social roots, agenda, or implications. In a word, the Anabaptists were not sixteenth-century Bolsheviks. The "Anabaptist Vision" sold well in 1950s America. It should be noted, however, that even at this early stage, the Canadian Mennonite Walther Klaassen (in 1963) had shown a diversity of opinions among the early Anabaptists concerning the dangerous topic of the Holy Spirit. And Bender's friend and colleague Robert Friedmann, an Austrian Jewish convert to Mennonitism, offered an alternative understanding of Anabaptism as being neither Catholic nor Protestant, to borrow the title of Klaassen's later book.[124]

Although never unchallenged, Bender's "normative Anabaptism" was only undone by revisionist historians beginning in the 1970s. The revisionists rejected confessionally defined "normative Anabaptism" and took cognizance of the geographical and theological diversity characteristic of the first generation of Anabaptists. James Stayer's *Anabaptists and the Sword* showed that pacificism and apoliticalism were not characteristic of all Anabaptists, that each group responded to their immediate circumstances, and that even the Zurich Anabaptists only gradually accepted nonviolence. Gottfried Seebass and Werner Packull established the medieval mystical origins and apocalyptic character of South German Anabaptism that derived from Thomas Müntzer by way of Hans Hut.[125] Stephen Ozment had already argued for the decisive role of mysticism, in particular the *Theologia Deutsch*, in promoting religious and political dissent, including Hans Hut and Hans Denck as well as Müntzer, Franck, Weigel, and Sebastian Castellio.[126] Kenneth Davis retained Bender's "normative Anabaptism," but revived Albrecht Ritschl's thesis of a medieval ascetic origin.[127] Klaus Deppermann's study of Melchior Hoffmann established both Hoffmann's Anabaptist credentials and his contribution to the apocalyptic theocracy of Münster.[128] For the revisionists, "polygenesis" had replaced

---

[124]See Klaassen, "Spiritualization in the Reformation"; Friedman, *Theology of Anabaptism*; and Klaassen, *Anabaptism: Neither Catholic Nor Protestant*.

[125]Seebass, "Müntzers Erbe"; and Packull, *Mysticism and the Early South German-Austrian Anabaptist Movement*.

[126]Ozment, *Mysticism and Dissent*.

[127]Davis, *Anabaptism and Asceticism*. See also Snyder, *Life and Thought of Michael Sattler*.

[128]Deppermann, *Melchior Hoffman*.

"monogenesis,"[129] theological diversity had replaced the normative vision, and Protestant biblicism now competed with medieval mysticism and asceticism as genetic explanations.

The initial assault on the "Anabaptist Vision" had been conducted with the weapons of intellectual history at a time when social history was already asserting itself. Claus Peter Clasen's brash *Anabaptism: A Social History* combined quantification with a principled disinterest in the religious dimension. His conclusions were unsettling, to say the least. Initially most Anabaptists were in the cities, but as persecution eliminated its educated leadership and drove the rank and file into the countryside, it became a predominantly peasant movement. The earlier urban character made any connection to the Peasants' War unlikely, and Clasen denied it. While the Bender school may have welcomed that conclusion, they could not have been happy that Clasen reduced the extent of persecution and argued that the Anabaptist phenomenon was neither numerically nor historically significant, estimating a total of 30,000 adherents (exclusive of the Melchiorite north, which he did not study) up to the Thirty Years' War. Although Clasen's method, failure to consider the religious elements of the movement, and conclusions were challenged, his study had a sobering effect.

The Marxists, of course, had long offered the explanation that Anabaptism represented disillusioned sectarian withdrawal after the shattering defeat of the early bourgeois revolution.[130] Albert Mellinck's findings on Holland, an area not studied by Clasen, contradicted Clasen on Anabaptist connections to revolutionary violence.[131] Mellinck found that a revolutionary form of Anabaptism had enjoyed a very large following for quite some time in the 1530s, that is, the era of Münster. Mellinck's work began a process in Dutch Mennonite studies that paralleled that going on for the south. The Melchiorites were increasingly accepted as central to Dutch Anabaptism. It was also conceded that Menno came from their ranks and even that he had retained a version of Hoffman's "heavenly flesh" Christology.[132] David Waite's work on David Joris reaffirmed that Joris, not Menno, was the most prominent leader of Dutch Anabaptists in the immediate post-Münster period.[133]

---

[129]Deppermann, Packull, and Stayer, "From Monogenesis to Polygenesis."
[130]Zschäbisch, *Zur mitteldeutschen Wiedertäuferbewegung.*
[131]Mellinck, *De Wederdopers*; and Mellinck, *De radikale Reformatie.*
[132]Klaassen, "Menno Simons Research."
[133]Waite, *David Joris and Dutch Anabaptism.*

Despite their differences, Clasen, the Marxists, and Mellinck did agree that Anabaptism was primarily a lower-class phenomenon, appealing to poorer elements in society. Karl-Heinz Kirchhoff undid that comfortable assumption by showing that in Münster the Anabaptists enjoyed relative prosperity and that their leadership was drawn from the traditional elites.[134] The belief that Anabaptism was linked with the Peasants' War has fared better. Earlier research establishing the involvement of later Anabaptists in the Peasants' War was confirmed.[135] J. F. G. Goeters had already shown links between Anabaptism and peasant resistance to Zurich's policy of centralization.[136] Stayer and Martin Haas followed that up by arguing that the earliest Anabaptists had participated in the efforts by rural congregations to abolish the tithe, or perhaps apply it to local needs, in order to independently cleanse the church and institute truly evangelical worship.[137] Hans-Jürgen Goertz elevated anticlericalism from a minor side effect to a powerful force expressing important religious and social interests, and not only for the peasantry.[138] This entire line of inquiry culminated with Peter Blickle's 1985 *Communal Reformation* (*Gemeindereformation*), which argued for a peasant Reformation of the "common man" intent on fulfilling the long-held desire of rural communities to take control of churches, and religion, in the villages.[139]

Beginning in the 1990s, a subtle shift began that may, or may not, presage a course correction for the field of Anabaptist studies. The revisionist school's research had focused on the disparate origins of Anabaptism and had distinguished three loci: Switzerland, southern Germany, and the lower Rhine and Low Countries. Each had a distinctive theological profile in large measure determined by its historical *Sitz im Leben*. New books by Stayer, Packull, and Arnold Snyder, however, emphasized a longer time line and the convergence or commonalities of the three centers. Stayer's *Peasants War and the Anabaptist Community of Goods* argued that the peasants

---

[134]Kirchhoff, *Die Täufer in Münster*.

[135]Zschäbisch, *Zur mitteldeutschen Wiedertäuferbewegung*; Oyer, *Lutheran Reformers against Anabaptists*; Stayer, "Anabaptists and Future Anabaptists"; Stayer, *German Peasants' War and Anabaptist Community of Goods*; Stayer, *Reublin und Brötli*; Goertz, "Aufständischen Bauern und Täufer in der Schweiz"; and Packull, "Die Anfänge des Täufertums in Tirol."

[136]Goeters, "Die Vorgeschichte des Täufertums in Zürich."

[137]Haas, "Der Weg der Täufer"; and Stayer, "Die Anfänge des schweizerischen Täufertums."

[138]Goertz, *Pfaffenhass und gross Geschrei*.

[139]Blickle, *Gemeindereformation*.

had shared a goal of establishing a just and egalitarian society based upon the Bible. In the wake of their defeat, some of the most religiously and socially committed became Anabaptists and sought to pursue the same goal through instantiating the communism of goods of Acts 2 and 4. The Hutterites most closely approximated the ideal, while the Swiss Brethren and Mennonites converted it into stewardship of wealth and readiness to aid the needy brethren. Lacking the experience of the Peasants' War, the Melchiorites in Münster, under enormous pressure, produced a caricature. Werner Packull's *Hutterite Beginnings* carefully traced the movement from its origins in the Peasants' War in the Tyrol through innumerable internecine struggles and divisions in Moravia to the communitarian experiment of the Hutterite communities. But along the way, Packull made clear the close interconnection of Anabaptist groups all over southern Germany and Switzerland in the years after 1525. C. Arnold Snyder's *Anabaptist History and Theology* sought to synthesize the findings of the preceding twenty years to extract an essence of Anabaptism, but this time ex post facto and not a priori as Bender had done. His aligning of Anabaptism with medieval asceticism would not have pleased Bender, nor would his choice of the nonpacifistic and nonseparatist Hubmaier as representative. Hubmaier is in fact something of a bellweather (see Strübind below). Some other Mennonites severely criticized Snyder on this point. Some of the criticism reflected the rise of a conservative (or reactionary, in the original sense of the term) American Evangelicalism among Mennonites that would turn its back on social activism and history to focus on theology, Jesus Christ, the family, and sexual morality.[140] It will bear watching to see how this new factor affects the historical study of Anabaptism.

The years since 1995 have seen attempts to overturn or at least to substantially revise the revisionists. Although of the same vintage, Abraham Friesen simply dismisses the revisionists and the work of a generation of scholars. Friesen had already (1989) produced a portrait of Thomas Müntzer that revived the Lutheran "murder prophet" tradition. Overturning decades of Dutch Mennonite historiography, Friesen denied (1998) that Menno Simons owed anything to Hoffmann, the Melchiorites, and Münster.[141] His *Erasmus, the Anabaptists, and the Great Commission*

---

[140]A comparison of Steve Nolt ("Anabaptist Visions of Church and Society") and Levi Miller ("Reconstruction of Evangelical Anabaptism") in the same issue of the *Mennonite Quarterly Review* is quite revealing.

[141]Friesen, "Present at the Inception." Cf. Klaassen, "Menno Simons Research."

(1998) ascribed the rise of adult baptism and hence Anabaptism to a theological insight derived from the biblical scholarship of the great humanist, Desiderius Erasmus.[142] Theologian Andrea Strübind (2003) also emphasized the Grebel circle as a Bible study group that continued the work of earlier humanist sodalities.[143] According to her careful reading of the evidence, Anabaptism was a purely theological phenomenon produced by faithful engagement with scripture alone and unconnected with the contemporary social upheaval. Her exclusion, however, of Balthasar Hubmaier and Waldshut on Zurich's northern border from a work on the "The Early Baptist Movement in Switzerland" is dubious and detracts substantially from her claims.

Although the historical analysis that Strübind offers is traditional intellectual history, her book's lengthy theoretical prolegomenon borrows from postmodern hermeneutic theory. She challenges the revisionist approach as just as much a faith-based normative vision as that which they criticized. But the warning, "He who sups with the devil should have a long spoon," applies since the logic of her hermeneutic critique precludes meaningful discussion above the level of basic textual issues, perhaps not even that, and produces competing "faith communities" or disciplines that could do little but rail against each other. Her own prolegomenon savors of Reformation polemic as the author smites her opponents hip and thigh. While undoing the revisionist social history Strübind has no other history with which to replace it. Rather, she argues that Church History be reconceived as historical theology. What that would do with institutional history, history of missions, liturgical history, or history of piety is not clear. But neither theology nor historical theology is history. They serve different purposes—useful purposes, but different.

Brad Gregory's impressive *Salvation at Stake* also does not provide an alternative.[144] His reaffirmation of a nonreducible category of the religious is congenial, although one would be hard-pressed to find any of the revisionists denying the proposition. But what follows from that reaffirmation? Are we left with Leibnizian monads that coincide but don't interact? Is it a one-way street from the religious to the social? Or are the religious and social in constant conversation, an approach that would allow for the retrieval of much that was useful from thirty years of revisionist social his-

---

[142]Friesen, *Erasmus, the Anabaptists, and the Great Commission.*
[143]Strübind, *Eifriger als Zwingli.*
[144]Gregory, *Salvation at Stake.*

tory? But how does one recognize which partner in the conversation is speaking? Are the sources to be taken at their word? Do historical actors always know what motivates them? Or are there larger social forces, movements, or connections that are invisible to the individuals who are part of them? Psychology and the social sciences presume this. Should historians? These daunting questions must be addressed before a new paradigm, rather than simply a revival of an older one, can take place.

There is in fact no evidence yet of a new paradigm.[145] If there is a shift it is toward intellectual history.[146] Dissertations in the United States in the past fifteen years are either straight intellectual history or a form of social history much like the revisionists'. Reprints of intellectual or theological histories from the 1960s and 1970s have been popular. But then such histories had never been lacking. There is renewed interest in the spiritualizing Anabaptists—Denck, Ludwig Hätzer, Bünderlin, Entfelder, Kautz, Obbe Phillips, Joris.[147] Geoffrey Dipple's recent book does for the Anabaptist vision of history and restitution of the church what Stayer did for the doctrine of the sword in 1972, although over a longer time span and with an interest in Anabaptist confessionalism.[148] Moving with the larger field of Reformation studies, Michael Driedger has studied the response of Hamburg's Mennonites to Lutheran confessionalization, and developments in the Mennonite community that parallel it.[149] As with the Radical Spiritualists, the late sixteenth and seventeenth centuries beg to be explored.[150]

The greatest change in Anabaptist studies is the retirement of the generation that brought about the revision of the 1970s. That, more than postmodern critiques, changes the landscape dramatically and leaves a void that may not be filled. For three decades scholars such as Stayer, Packkull, Goertz, Klaassen, and Snyder have put Anabaptism on the Reformation map. Without the intellectual energy and academic respectability that social history provided, not to mention the close relationship to the Peasants' War that reconnected Anabaptism with the larger society, there is a real danger that the field will become again an historical backwater in

---

[145]Stayer, "A New Paradigm in Anabaptist/Mennonite Historiography?"; Strübind, "Stayer, 'A New Paradigm': A Response"; and Packull, "Between Paradigms." It should be noted that Packull's two paradigms are the earlier Bender and the new revisionist, not the revisionist and some postrevisionist paradigm.

[146]Chudaska, *Peter Riedemann*.

[147]Waite, *David Joris and Dutch Anabaptism*; and Dipple, "The Spiritualist Anabaptists."

[148]Dipple, "Just as in the Time of the Apostles."

[149]Driedger, *Obedient Heretics*.

[150]von Schlachta, *Hutterische Konfession und Tradition*.

which justifiable Mennonite concerns for identity and faith will over-shadow the historians' commitment to understand the past, warts and all. Social history will certainly not disappear, if only because capitalist socie-ties agree with the Marxists in ascribing great importance to economic motives.

On the hopeful side, Anabaptist studies are well provided with source collections and editions. The *Täuferakten* pursue the Anabaptists into the governmental records where they most often surface. One caveat: that research project owes a great deal to the Bender school, and the principle of selection may not provide all the documents of interest to those with different approaches. There are critical editions of many of the Anabaptist leaders and English translations of most. And new manuscript sources await discovery in the archives, especially in Eastern Europe. Martin Roth-kegel's work in Moravia has done much to revise the history of Anabaptism there and to point the way to a geographical expansion of Anabaptist stud-ies.[151] The works of Michael Driedger and Astrid von Schlachta, for exam-ple, show the promise of a "long" Radical Reformation. Despite an opening to gender studies in the 1970s and 1980s culminating in a 1996 collection of essays, the postrevisionist era seems to have turned its back on the his-tory of gender, perhaps because of the "progressive" agenda it shares with social history.[152] Nonetheless, it is a promising field for future research. In general, despite Andrea Strübind's challenge to the early Zurich narrative, Anabaptist studies seem to be moving beyond the beachhead of the revo-lutionary early German and Dutch Radical Reformations.

Bibliography

ELECTRONIC RESOURCES

Available English Translations of 16th Century Anabaptist Documents:
http://www.goshen.edu/mqr/enganbib.html
Global Anabaptist Mennonite Encyclopedia Online: http://www.gameo.org
Guide to Schwenkfelder Library Holdings and Translations:
http://www.rpc.ox.ac.uk/sfld/sfldindx.htm
Links for Radical Reformation: http://cat.xula.edu/tpr/links/radical/

PRIMARY SOURCES

Coornhert, Dirck Volckszoon. *Weet of Rust: Proza van Coornhert*, edited by H. Bonger and A. J. Gelderbloom. Amsterdam: Querido, 1985.

[151]Rothkegel, "Anabaptism in Moravia and Silesia."
[152]Haude, "Gender Roles and Perspectives."

———. *Wercken.* 3 vols. Amsterdam: Iacob Aertsz. Colom, 1630.

———. *Zedekunst. dat is wellevenkunst,* edited by Bruno Becker. Leiden: Brill, 1942.

Die älteste Chronik der hutterischen Brüder. Edited by A. J. F. Zieglschmid. Ithaca, NY: Cayuga Press, 1943.

Die Schriften der Münsterischen Täufer und ihrer Gegner, edited by Robert Stupperich. 3 vols. Münster: Aschendorff, 1970, 1980, 1983.

Documenta anabaptistica Neerlandica. Leiden: Brill, 1975–.

Franck, Sebastian. *Paradoxa,* edited by Siegfried Wollgast. Berlin: Akademie-Verlag, 1966.

———. *Sämtliche Werke: Kritische Ausgabe mit Kommentar,* edited by Peter Klaus Knauer and Hans Gert Roloff. Bern: P. Lang, 1992–.

———. *Sebastian Francks lateinische Paraphrase der Deutschen Theologie und seine holländisch erhaltene Traktate,* edited by Alfred Hegler. Tübingen: G. Schnürlen, 1901.

Müntzer, Thomas. *The Collected Works of Thomas Müntzer,* edited and translated by Peter Matheson. Edinburgh: T. & T. Clark, 1988.

———. *Schriften und Briefe: Kritische Gesamtausgabe,* edited by Günther Franz and Paul Kirn. Gütersloh: G. Mohn, 1968.

———. *Theologische Schriften aus dem Jahr 1523,* edited by Siegfried Brauer and Wolfgang Ullmann. 2nd ed. Berlin: Evangelische Verlagsanstalt, 1982.

Quellen zur Geschichte der Täufer. Gütersloh: C. Bertelsmann, 1930–.

Quellen zur Geschichte der Täufer in der Schweiz. 3 vols. Zurich: Theologischer Verlag, 1973–74.

Schwenckfeld, Caspar. *Corpus Schwenckfeldianorum.* 19 vols. Leipzig: Breitkopf and Härtel, 1907–61.

Weigel, Valentin. *Ausgewählte Werke,* edited by Siegfried Wollgast. Berlin: Union-Verlag, VOB, 1977.

———. *Handschriftliche Predigtensammlung, 1573–1574,* edited by Winfried Zeller. Stuttgart: Frommann, 1977–78.

———. *Sämtliche Schriften,* edited by Will-Erich Peuckert and Winfried Zeller. Stuttgart-Bad Cannstatt: Frommann-Holzboog, 1966–78.

———. *Sämtliche Schriften,* edited by Horst Pfefferl. Stuttgart-Bad Cannstatt: Frommann-Holzboog, 1996–.

SECONDARY SOURCES

Barbers, Meinulf. *Toleranz bei Sebastian Franck.* Bonn: L. Röhrscheid, 1964.

Barge, Hermann. *Andreas Bodenstein von Karlstadt.* 2 vols. Leipzig: Friedrich Brandstetter, 1905.

Beachy, Alvin J. *The Concept of Grace in the Radical Reformation.* Nieuwkoop: De Graaf, 1977.

Becker, Bruno. "Nederlandische Vertalingen van Sebastiaan Francks Geschriften." *Nederlandsch Archief voor Kerkgeschiedenis* 21 (1928): 149–60.

———, ed. *Bronnen tot de kennis van het leven en de werken van D. V. Coornhert.* 's-Gravenhage: M. Nijhoff, 1928.

Bender, Harold S. "The Anabaptist Vision." *Church History* 13 (1944): 3–24.

Bensing, Manfred. *Thomas Müntzer.* 3rd ed. Leipzig: Bibliographisches Institut, 1983.

———. *Thomas Müntzer und der Thüringer Aufstand 1525.* Berlin: Deutscher Verlag der Wissenschaften VEB, 1966.

Bischof, Hermann. *Sebastian Franck und deutsche Geschichtschreibung: Beitrag zur culturgeschichte vorzuglich des XVI. Jahrhunderts.* Tübingen: Ernst Riecker, 1857.

Blickle, Peter P. *Gemeindereformation: Die Menschen des 16. Jahrhunderts auf dem Weg zum Heil.* Munich: Oldenbourg, 1985. Translated by Thomas Dunlap as *Communal Reformation: The Quest for Salvation in Sixteenth-Century* (Atlantic Highlands, NJ: Humanities Press, 1992).

Böhmer, Heinrich H. "Thomas Müntzer und das jüngste Deutschland." In Böhmer, *Gesammelte Aufsätze,* 187–222. Gotha: Flamberg, 1927.

Bonger, Henk. *The Life and Work of Dirck Volkertszoon Coornhert.* Translated and edited by Gerrit Voogt. Amsterdam: Rodopi, 2004. Originally published as *Leven en werk van D. V. Coornhert* (Amsterdam: G. A. van Oorschot, 1978).

———. *De motivering van de godsdienstvrijheid bij Dirck Volckertszoon Coornhert.* Arnhem: Van Loghum Slaterus, 1954

———, ed. *Dirck Volckertszoon Coornhert: Dwars maar recht.* Zutphen: De Walburg Pers, 1989.

Bräuer, Siegfried, and Helmar Junghans, H. *Der Theologe Thomas Müntzer. Untersuchungen zu seiner Entwicklung und Lehr.* Berlin: Evangelische Verlagsanstalt, 1989.

Brecht, Martin. "Der Beitrag des Spiritualismus der Reformationszeit zur Erneuerung der lutherischen Kirche im 17. Jahrhundert." In *Wegscheiden der Reformation,* edited by Günter Vogler, 369–79. Weimar: H. Böhlaus Nachfolger, 1994.

———, ed. *Geschichte der Pietismus.* Vol 1, *Der Pietismus vom siebzehnten bis zum frühen achtzehnten Jahrhundert.* Göttigen: Vandenhoeck & Ruprecht, 1993.

Brendler, Gerhard. *Thomas Müntzer: Geist und Faust.* Berlin: Deutscher Verlag der Wissenschaften, 1989.

Bubenheimer, Ulrich. *Consonantia theologiae et iurisprudentiae: Andreas Bodenstein von Karlstadt als Theologe und Jurist zwischen Scholastik und Reformation.* Tübingen: Mohr, 1977.

———. "Karlstadt, Andreas Rudolf Bodenstein von (1486–1541)." *Theologische Realenzyklopedia* 17 (1988): 649–55.

———. "Karlstadtrezeption von der Reformation bis zum Pietismus." In *Andreas Bodenstein von Karlstadt (1486–1541),* edited by Sigrid Looß and Markus Matthias, 24–71. Wittenberg: Drei Kastanien Verlag, 1998.

———. *Thomas Müntzer: Herkunft und Bildung.* Leiden: Brill, 1989.

———, and Stefan Oehmig, eds. *Querdenker der Reformation: Andreas Bodenstein von Karlstadt und seine frühe Wirkung.* Würzburg: Religion und Kultur Verlag, 2001.

Chudaska, Andrea. *Peter Riedemann: Konfessionbildendes Täufertum im 16. Jahrhundert.* Gütersloh: Gütersloher Verlagshaus, 2003.

Clasen, Claus-Peter. *Anabaptism: Social History, 1525–1618.* Ithaca, NY: Cornell University Press, 1972.

———. "Schwenckfeld's Friends: A Social Study." *Mennonite Quarterly Review* 46 (1972): 58–69.

Davis, Kenneth R. *Anabaptism and Asceticism: A Study in Intellectual Origins.* Scottsdale, PA: Herald Press, 1974.

Dejung, Christoph. "Geschichte lehrt Gelassenheit, Über den Historiker Sebastian Franck." In *Beiträge zum 500. Geburtstag von Sebastian Franck,* edited by Siegfried Wollgast, 89–126. Berlin: Weidler Buchverlag, 1999.

———. "Sebastian Franck." *Bibliotheca Dissidentium* 7 (1986): 39–119.

———. "Sebastian Francks nachgelassene Bibliothek." *Zwingliana* 16 (1984): 315–36.

———. *Wahrheit und Häresie: Untersuchungen zur Geschichtsphilosophie bei Sebastian Franck.* Zurich: Samisdat, 1980.

Deppermann, Klaus. *Melchior Hoffman: Soziale Unruhen und apokalyptische Visionen im Zeitalter der Reformation.* Göttingen: Vandenhoeck und Ruprecht, 1979. Translated by Benjamin Drewery as *Melchior Hoffman: Social Unrest and Apocalyptic Visions in the Age of Reformation* (Edinburgh: T. & T. Clark, 1987).

Deppermann, Klaus, Werner O. Packull, and James M. Stayer. "From Monogenesis to Polygenesis: The Historical Discussion of Anabaptist Origins." *Mennonite Quarterly Review* 49 (1975): 83–121.

Dilthey, Wilhelm. *Weltanschauung und Analyse des Menschen seit Renaissance und Reformation.* Leipzig: Teubner, 1914.

Dipple, Geoffrey. *"Just as in the Time of the Apostles": Uses of History in the Radical Reformation.* Kitchener, Ont.: Pandora Press, 2005.

———. "Sebastian Franck and the Münster Anabaptist Kingdom." In *Radical Reformation Studies: Essays presented to James M. Stayer,* edited by Werner Packull and Geoffrey Dipple, 91–105. Aldershot, UK: Ashgate, 1999.

———. "The Spiritualist Anabaptists." In *A Companion to Anabaptism and Spiritualism, 1521–1700,* edited by John D. Roth and James M. Stayer, 257–97. Leiden: Brill, 2007.

Driedger, Michael D. *Obedient Heretics: Mennonite Identities in Lutheran Hamburg and Altona during the Confessional Age.* Aldershot, UK: Ashgate, 2002.

Eberlein, G. "Zur Würdigung des Valentin Krautwald." *Correspondenzblatt des Vereins für Geschichte der Evangelischen Kirche Schlesiens* 8 (1903): 268–80.

Eberlein, Paul Gerhard. *Ketzer oder Heiliger? Caspar von Schwenckfeld: Der schlesische Reformator und seine Botschaft.* Metzingen: Ernst Franz Verlag, 1998.

Ecke, Karl. *Schwenckfeld, Luther und der Gedanke einer apostolischen Reformation.* Berlin: Martin Warneck, 1911.

Elliger, Walter. *Thomas Müntzer: Leben und Werk.* Berlin-Friedenau: Wichern-Verlag, 1960.

Engels, Friedrich. "Der deutsche Bauernkrieg." In *Karl Marx, Friederich Engels: Werke,* 7:327–413. Berlin: Deitz, 1960.

Erb, Peter. "The Role of Late Medieval Spirituality in the Work of Gottfried Arnold (1666–1714)." 2 vols. PhD dissertation, University of Toronto, 1976.

———. "Valentin Crautwald." *Bibliotheca Dissidentium* 6 (1985): 1–70.

———, ed. *Schwenckfeld and Early Schwenkfeldianism: Papers Presented at the Colloquium on Schwenckfeld and the Schwenkfelders.* Pennsburg, PA: Schwenckfelder Library, 1986.

Fix, Andrew C. *Prophecy and Reason: The Dutch Collegiants in the Early Enlightenment.* Princeton, NJ: Princeton University Press, 1991.

Friedmann, Robert. *The Theology of Anabaptism.* Scottsdale, PA: Herald Press, 1973.

Friesen, Abraham. *Erasmus, the Anabaptists, and the Great Commission.* Grand Rapids, MI: Eerdmans, 1998.

———. "Present at the Inception: Menno Simons and the Beginnings of Dutch Anabaptism." *Mennonite Quarterly Review* 72 (1998): 351–88.

———. *Thomas Müntzer, a Destroyer of the Godless: The Making of a Sixteenth-Century Religious Revolutionary.* Berkeley: University of California Press, 1990.

Goertz, Hans-Jürgen. "Aufständischen Bauern und Täufer in der Schweiz." In *Zugänge zur bäuerlichen Reformation,* edited by Peter Blickle, 263–85. Zurich: Chronos, 1987.

———. "'A Common Future Conversation': A Revisionist Interpretation of the September 1524 Grebel Letters to Thomas Müntzer." In *Radical Reformation Studies: Essays presented to James M. Stayer,* edited by Werner Packull and Geoffrey Dipple, 73–90. Aldershot, UK: Ashgate, 1999.

———. *Das Bild Thomas Müntzers in Ost und West*. Hannover: Niedersächsische Landeszentrale für Politische Bildung, 1988.

———. *Innere und äußere Ordnung in der Theologie Thomas Müntzers*. Leiden: Brill, 1967.

———. *Pfaffenhass und gross Geschrei: Die Reformatorischen Bewegungen 1517–1529*. Munich: C. H. Beck, 1987.

———. *Thomas Müntzer: Mystiker, Apokalyptiker, Revolutionär*. Munich: Beck, 1989. Translated by Jocelyn Jaquiery as *Thomas Müntzer: Apocalyptic, Mystic, and Revolutionary* (Edinburgh: T & T Clark, 1993).

Goeters, J. F. G. "Die Vorgeschichte des Täufertums in Zürich." In *Studien zur Geschichte und Theologie der Reformation. Festschrift für Ernst Bizer*, edited by Luise Abramowski and J. F. G. Goeters, 239–81. Neukirchen: Neukirchener Verlag, 1969.

Goldhammer, Kurt. "Der Toleranzgedanke bei Franck und Wiegel." *Archiv für Reformationsgeschichte* 47(1956): 180–211.

Gouldbourne, R. M. B. "Theology and Gender in the Writings of Caspar Schwenckfeld." PhD diss., University of London, 2000.

Gregory, Brad S. *Salvation at Stake: Christian Martyrdom in Early Modern Europe*. Cambridge, MA: Harvard University Press, 1999.

Gritschke-Großmann, C. *Via media: Spiritualistische Lebenswelten und Konfessionalisierung. Das süddeutsche Schwenckfeldertum im 16. und 17. Jahrhundert*. Berlin: Akademie-Verlag, 2006.

Güldner, G. *Das Toleranz-Problem in den Niederlanden im Ausgang des 16. Jahrhunderts*. Lübeck: Matthiesen, 1968.

Haas, Martin. "Der Weg der Täufer in die Absonderung. Zur Interdependenz von Theologie und sozialem Verhalten." In *Umstrittenes Täufertum, 1525–1975: Neue Forschungen*, edited by Hans-Jürgen Goertz, 50–78. Göttingen: Vandenhoeck und Ruprecht, 1975.

Härtwig, Christiane. "Gottfried Arnolds Müntzerbild: Eine Alternative zu früheren Müntzerdarstellungen." In *Wegscheiden der Reformation*, edited by Günter Vogler, 463–77. Weimar: H. Böhlaus Nachfolger, 1994.

Hase, Karl Alfred von. *Sebastian Franck von Wörd der Schwarmgeist: Ein Beitrag zur Reformationsgeschichte*. Leipzig: Breitkopf und Härtel, 1869.

Hasse, Hans-Peter. *Karlstadt und Tauler: Untersuchungen zur Kreuzestheologie*. Güterloh: G. Mohn, 1993.

Haude, Sigrun. "Gender Roles and Perspectives among Anabaptist and Spiritualist Groups." In *A Companion to Anabaptism and Spiritualism, 1521–1700*, edited by John D. Roth and James M. Stayer, 425–65. Leiden: Brill, 2007.

Hayden-Roy, Patrick Marshall. *The Inner Word and the Outer World: A Biography of Sebastian Franck*. New York: P. Lang, 1994.

Hegler, Alfred. *Geist und Schrift bei Sebastian Franck. Eine Studie zur Geschichte des Spiritualismus in der Reformationszeit*. Freiburg: J. C. B. Mohr, 1892.

Hertzsch, Erich. *Karlstadt und seine Bedeutung für das Luthertum*. Gotha: L. Klotz, 1932.

Hildebrand, Hans. "Andreas Bodenstein of Karlstadt. Prodigal Reformer." *Church History* 35 (1966): 379–98.

Hinrichs, Carl. *Luther und Müntzer: Ihre Auseinandersetzung über Obrigkeit und Widerstandsrecht*. Berlin: W. De Gruyter, 1952.

Hirsch, Emanuel. "Zum Verständnis Schwenckfelds." In *Festgabe Karl Müller*, edited by Otto Scheel, 145–70. Tübingen: J. C. B. Mohr, 1922: 145–70.

Holl, Karl. "Luther und die Schwärmer." In *Gesammelte Aufsätze zur Kirchengeschichte*, 1:420–67. Tübingen: J. C. Mohr, 1923.

Israel, Jonathan I. *The Dutch Republic: Its Rise, Greatness, and Fall 1477–1806.* Oxford: Clarendon Press, 1995.

———. *Radical Enlightenment: Philosophy and the Making of Modernity, 1650–1750.* Oxford: Oxford University Press, 2001.

Joachimsen, Paul. "Zur inneren Entwicklung Sebastian Francks." *Blätter für deutsche Philosophie* 2 (1928): 1–28.

Joestel, Volkmar V. *Ostthüringen und Karlstadt: Soziale Bewegungen und Reformation im mittleren Saaletal am Vorabend des Bauernkrieges (1522–1524).* Berlin: Schelzky & Jeep, 1996.

Jones, Rufus M. *Spiritual Reformers in the Sixteenth and Seventeenth Centuries.* 2nd ed. Boston: Beacon Press, 1959.

Kaczerowsky, Klaus. *Sebastian Franck: Bibliographie.* Wiesbaden: G. Pressler, 1976.

Kähler, Ernst. *Karlstadt und Augustin: Der Kommentar des Andreas Bodenstein von Karlstadt zu Augustins Schrift de spiritu et litera.* Halle: M. Niemeyer, 1952.

Kaplan, Benjamin J. *Calvinists and Libertines: Confession and Community in Utrecht 1578–1620.* Oxford: Clarendon Press, 1995.

Kirchhoff, Karl-Heinz. *Die Täufer in Münster 1534–1535: Untersuchungen zum Umfang und zur Sozialstruktur der Bewegung.* Münster: Aschendorff, 1973.

Klaassen, Walther. *Anabaptism: Neither Catholic nor Protestant.* Waterloo, Ont.: Conrad Press, 1973.

———. "Menno Simons Research, 1937–1986." *Mennonite Quarterly Review* 60 (1986) 483–96.

———. "Spiritualization in the Reformation." *Mennonite Quarterly Review* 37 (1963): 67–77.

Kluge, A. "Leben und Entwicklungsgang Schwenckfelds." *Correspondenzblatt des Vereins für Geschichte der Evangelischen Kirche Schlesiens* 15 (1917): 220–44.

Köhler, Walther. *Zwingli und Luther: Der Streit über das Abendmahl nach seinen politischen und religiösen Beziehungen.* 2 vols. Leipzig: Verein für Reformationsgeschichte, 1924, 1953.

Kriechbaum, Friedel. *Grundzüge der Theologie Karlstadts: Eine systematische Studie zur Erhellung der Theologie Karlstadts.* Hamburg-Bergstedt: H. Reich, 1967.

Kühn, Johannes. *Toleranz und Offenbarung.* Leipzig: F. Meiner, 1923.

Kuiper, G. *Orbis Artium en Renaissance, I: Cornelius Valerius en Sebastianus Foxius Morzillus als bronnen van Coornhert.* Harderwijk: Drukkerij "Flevo," 1941.

Land, J. P. N. *De wijsbegeerte in de Nederlanden,* edited and translated by C. van Vollenhoven. s'Gravenhage: M. Nijhoff, 1899.

Längin, Heinz. "Grundlinien der Erkenntnislehre Valentin Weigels." *Archiv für Geschichte der Philosophie* 41 (1932): 435–78.

Lecler, Joseph. *Histoire de la tolérance au siècle de la Réforme.* 2 vols. Paris: Aubier, 1955.

———, and Marius Valkhoff, eds. *Les premiers défenseurs de la liberté religieuse.* 2 vols. Paris: Aubier, 1969.

Leo, Heinrich. *Thomas Müntzer.* Berlin: Gustav Schlawitz, 1856.

Lieb, Fritz. *Valentin Weigels Kommentar zur Schöpfungsgeschichte und das Schrifttum seines Schülers Benedikt Biedermann.* Zurich: EVZ-Verlag, 1962.

Lindeboom, Johannes. *Stiefkinderen van het Christendom.* The Hague: Nijhoff, 1929.

Looß, Sigrid S. "Desiderat der Forschungen zur Reformationsgeschichte—eine Werkausgabe des Andreas Bodenstein aus Karlstadt (1486–1541)." In *Editionsdesiderate zur Frühen Neuzeit,* edited by Hans-Gert Roloff, 1:553–65. Amsterdam: Rodopi, 1997.

Loserth, Johann. *Pilgram Marpecks Antwort auf Caspar Schwenckfelds Beurteilung des Buches des Beundesbezeugung von 1542*. Vienna: Carl Fromme, 1929.

Maier, Hans. *Der Mystische Spiritualismus Valentin Weigels*. Gütersloh: C. Bertelsmann, 1926.

Maier, Paul. *Caspar Schwenckfeld on the Person and Work of Christ: A Study of Schwenckfeldian Theology at Its Core*. Assen: Van Gorcum, 1959.

Maron, Gottfried. *Individualismus und Gemeinschaft bei Caspar Schwenckfeld*. Stuttgart: Evangelisches Verlagwerk, 1961.

———. "Thomas Müntzer als Theologe des Gerichts. Das 'Urteil': Ein Schlüsselbegriff seines Denkens." *Zeitschrift für Kirchengeschichte* 83 (1972): 195–225.

McLaughlin, Robert Emmet. *Caspar Schwenckfeld, Reluctant Radical: His Life to 1540*. New Haven, CT: Yale University Press, 1986.

———. *The Freedom of the Spirit, Social Privilege, and Religious Dissent: Caspar Schwenckfeld and the Schwenckfelders*. Baden-Baden: V. Koerner, 1996.

———. "The Genesis of Schwenckfeld's Eucharistic Doctrine." *Archiv für Reformationsgeschichte* 74 (1983): 94–121.

———. "Müntzer and Apocalypticism." *Archiv für Reformationsgeschichte* 95 (2004): 98–131.

———. "Reformation Spiritualism: Typology, Sources and Significance." In *Radikalität und Dissent im 16. Jahrhundert*, edited by Hans-Jürgen Goertz and James M. Stayer, 127–40. Berlin: Duncker & Humblot, 2002.

———. "Schwenckfeld and the Schwenckfelders in South Germany." In *Schwenckfeld and Early Schwenckfeldianism: Papers Presented at the Colloquium on Schwenckfeld and the Schwenckfelders*, edited by Peter Erb, 145–80. Pennsburg, PA: Schwenckfelder Library, 1987.

———. "The Schwenckfeld-Vadian Christological Debate." In *Schwenckfeld and Early Schwenckfeldianism: Papers Presented at the Colloquium on Schwenckfeld and the Schwenckfelders*, edited by Peter Erb, 237–58. Pennsburg, PA: Schwenckfelder Library, 1987.

———. "Sebastian Franck and Caspar Schwenckfeld: Two Spiritualist Viae." In *Sebastian Franck (1499–1542)*, edited by J.- D. Müller, 71–86. Wiesbaden: Harrassowitz, 1993.

———. "Spiritualism and the Bible: The Case of Caspar Schwenckfeld." *Mennonite Quarterly Review* 53 (1979): 282–98.

McNiel, William. "Andreas von Karlstadt and Thomas Müntzer: Relatives in Theology and Reformation." PhD diss., Queen's University, 1999.

———. "Andreas von Karlstadt as a Humanist Theologian." In *Radical Reformation Studies: Essays presented to James M. Stayer*, edited by Werner Packull and Geoffrey Dipple, 106–19. Aldershot, UK: Ashgate, 1999.

Mellink, Albert F. *De radikale Reformatie als Thema van social-relieuze Geschiedenis*. Nijmegen: Socialistiese Uitgeverij Nijmegen, 1979.

———. *De Wederdopers in de Noordelijke Nederlanden, 1531–1544*. Groningen: Wolters, 1954.

Miller, Levi L. "A Reconstruction of Evangelical Anabaptism." *Mennonite Quarterly Review* 69 (1995): 295–306.

Moorrees, F. D. J. *Dirk Volkertszoon Coornhert: Notaris te Haarlem, de Libertijn, bestrijder der Gereformeerde predikanten ten tijde van Prins Willem I: Leves- en karakterschets*. Schoonhoven: S. & W. N. van Nooten, 1887.

Müller, Jan-Dirk, ed. *Sebastian Franck (1499–1542)*. Wiesbaden: Harrassowitz, 1993.

Müller, Karl. *Luther und Karlstadt: Stücke aus ihrem gegenseitigen Verhältnis.* Tübingen: J. C. B. Mohr, 1907.

Nolt, Steve. "Anabaptist Visions of Church and Society." *Mennonite Quarterly Review* 69 (1995): 283–94.

Oehmig, Stefan. "Studien zum Armen- und Fürsorgewesen der Lutherstadt Wittenberg am Ausgang des Mittelalters und in der Reformationszeit." PhD diss., University of Berlin, 1990.

Oestreich, Gerhard. *Antiker Geist und moderner Staat bei Justus Lipsius (1547–1606): Der Neustoizismus als politische Bewegung.* Göttingen: Vandenhoeck & Ruprecht, 1989.

Opel, Julius Otto. *Valentin Weigel: Ein Beitrag zur Literatur- und Culturgeschichte Deutschlands im 17. Jahrhunderts.* Leipzig: T. O. Weigel, 1864.

Oyer, John S. *Lutheran Reformers against Anabaptists. Luther, Melanchthon and Menius and the Anabaptists of Central Germany.* The Hague: M. Nijhoff, 1964.

Ozment, Steven. *Mysticism and Dissent: Religious Ideology and Social Protest in the Sixteenth Century.* New Haven, CT: Yale University Press, 1973.

Packull, Werner O. "Between Paradigms: Anabaptist Studies at a Crossroads." *Conrad Grebel Review* 8 (1990): 1–22.

———. "Die Anfänge des Täufertums in Tirol." In *Wegscheiden der Reformation,* edited by Günter Vogler, 179–209. Weimar: H. Böhlaus Nachfolger, 1992.

———. *Hutterite Beginnings.* Baltimore: Johns Hopkins University Press, 1995.

———. *Mysticism and the Early South German-Austrian Anabaptist Movement, 1525–1531.* Scottsdale, PA: Herald Press, 1977.

Pater, Calvin A. *Karlstadt as the Father of the Baptist Movements: The Emergence of Lay Protestantism.* Toronto: University of Toronto Press, 1984.

———. "Westerburg: The Father of Anabaptism; Author and Content of the Dyalogus of 1527." *Archive for Reformation History* 85 (1994): 138–62.

Pfefferl, Horst. "Christoph Weickhart als Paracelsist... Zu Leben und Persönlichkeit eines Kantors Valentin Weigels." In *Analecta Paracelsica: Studien zum Nachleben Theophrast von Hohenheim im deutschen Kulturgebiet der frühen Neuzeit,* edited by Joachim Telle, 27–41. Stuttgart: F. Steiner, 1994.

———. "Das neue Bild Valentin Weigels—Ketzer oder Kirchenmann: Aspekte einer erforderlichen Neubestimmung seiner kirchen- und theologiegeschichtliche Position." *Jahrbuch für deutsche Kirchengeschichte* 18 (1993–94): 67–79.

———. "Die kritische Ausgabe der 'Sämtlichen Schriften' Valentin Weigels." *Chloe* (supplement to *Daphnis)* 24 (1997): 577–87.

———. "Die Rezeption des paracelsischen Schrifftums bei Valentin Weigel: Probleme ihre Erforschung am Beispiel der kompilatorischen Schrift 'Viererlei Auslegung von der Schöpfung.'" In *Neue Beiträge zur Paracelsus-Forschung,* edited by Peter Dilg and Hartmut Rudolph, 151–65. Hohenheimer Protokolle 47. Stuttgart: Akademie der Diözese Rottenburg-Stuttgart, 1995.

———. "Die Überlieferung der Schriften Valentin Weigels." PhD diss., University of Marburg/Lahn, 1991.

———. "Valentin Weigel und Paracelsus." *Paracelsus und sein dämonengläubiges Jahrhundert: Salzburger Beiträge zur Paracelsusforschung* 26 (1988): 77–95.

———. "Zum Wirkungsgeschichte des Paracelsus am Ende des 16. Jahrhunderts: Neue Aspekte zu einem Kantor Winfried Weigels." In *Nachlese zum Jubiläumskongress: 500 Jahre Paracelsus,* 27–41. Vienna: Österreichischer Kunst- und Kulturverlag, 1995.

Pietz, Reinhold. *Die Gestalt der zukünftigen Kirche: Schwenckfelds Gespräch mit Luther, Wittenberg 1525*. Stuttgart: Calwer Verlag, 1959.

Ponader, Ralf. "'Caro nichil prodest. Joan.vi. Das fleisch ist nicht nutz/ sonder der geist.' Karlstadts Abendmahlsverständnis in der Auseinandersetzung mit Martin Luther 1521–1524." In *Andreas Bodenstein von Karlstadt (1486–1541)*, edited by Sigrid Looß and Markus Matthias, 223–45. Wittenberg: Drei Kastanien Verlag, 1998.

———. "Die Abendmahlslehre des Andreas Bodenstein von Karlstadt in den Jahren 1521–1524: Die Kritik an der Realpräsenz durch Karlstadt, untersucht vor dem Hintergrund dor Khorismus-Problematik." PhD diss., University of Greifswald, 1994.

Preus, James. *Carlstadt's 'Ordinationes' and of Luther's Liberty: A Study of the Wittenberg Movement*. Cambridge, MA: Harvard University Press, 1974.

Rothkegel, M. "Anabaptism in Moravia and Silesia." In *A Companion to Anabaptism and Spiritualism, 1521–1700*, edited by John D. Roth and James M. Stayer, 163–215. Leiden: Brill, 2007.

Rüger, Hans-Peter. "Karlstadt als Hebräist an der Universität Wittenberg." *Archiv for Reformationsgeschichte* 75 (1984) 297–308.

Rupp, Gordon. "Andrew Karlstadt and Reformation Puritanism." *Journal of Theological Studies*, n.s. 10 (1959): 308–26.

———. *Patterns of Reformation*. London: Epworth Press, 1969.

Schoep, Hans J. *Vom Himmlischen Fleisch Christi*. Tübingen: J. C. B. Mohr, 1951.

Schultz, Selina Gerhard. *Caspar Schwenckfeld von Ossig (1489–1561)*. Introduction by Peter Erb, 4th ed. Pennsburg, PA: Board of Publication of the Schwenkfelder Church, 1977.

Schwarz, Reinhard. *Die apokalyptische Theologie Thomas Müntzers und der Taboriten*. Tübingen: Mohr, 1977.

Sciegienny, André. *Homme charnel, homme spirituel: Etude sur la christologie de Caspar Schwenckfeld (1489–1561)*. Wiesbaden: Steiner, 1975.

———. "Réforme érasmienne ou Réforme luthérienne? Caspar Schwenckfeld et Erasme." *Revue d'Histoire et de Philosophie Religieuse* 54 (1974): 309–24.

Scott, Tom. *Thomas Müntzer. Theology and Revolution in the German Reformation*. New York: St Martin's Press, 1989.

Seebass, Gottfried, "Müntzers Erbe: Werk, Leben und Theologie des Hans Hut." Habilitationsschrift, Erlangen, 1972. Originally published as *Müntzers Erbe: Werk, Leben und Theologie des Hans Hut* (Göttingen: Gütersloher Verlagshaus, 2002).

Séguenny, André. *Les Spirituels: Philosophie et religion chez les jeunes humanistes allemands au seizième siècle*. Baden-Baden: V. Koerner, 2000.

Shantz, D. H. *Crautwald and Erasmus : A Study in Humanism and Radical Reform in Sixteenth Century Silesia*. Baden-Baden: V. Koerner, 1992.

Sider, Ronald J. *Andreas Bodenstein von Karlstadt. The Development of His Thought 1517–1525*. Leiden: Brill, 1974.

Snyder, C. Arnold. *Anabaptist History and Theology*. Kitchener, Ont.: Pandora Press, 1995.

———. *The Life and Thought of Michael Sattler*. Scottsdale, PA: Herald Press, 1984.

Stayer, James M. "Anabaptists and Future Anabaptists in the Peasants' War." *Mennonite Quarterly Review* 62 (1988): 99–139.

———. *Anabaptists and the Sword*. Lawrence, KS: Coronado Press, 1972.

———. "Die Anfänge des schweizerischen Täufertums im reformierten Kongregationalismus." In *Umstrittenes Täufertum, 1525–1975: Neue Forschungen*, edited Hans-Jürgen Goertz, 19–49. Göttingen: Vandenhoeck und Ruprecht, 1975.

——. *The German Peasants' War and Anabaptist Community of Goods*. Montreal: McGill-Queen's University Press, 1991.

——. "A New Paradigm in Anabaptist/Mennonite Historiography?" *Mennonite Quarterly Review* 78 (2004): 297–307.

——. "Reublin und Brötli, the Revolutionary Beginnings of Swiss Anabaptism." In *The Origins and Characteristics of Anabaptism*, edited by Marc Lienhard, 83–102. Den Haag: Nijhoff, 1977.

——. "Sächsischer Radikalismus und Schweizer Täufertum: Die Wiederkehr des Verdrängten." In *Wegscheiden der Reformation*, edited by Günter Vogler, 151–78. Weimar: H. Böhlaus Nachfolger, 1994.

Steinmetz, Max. *Das Müntzerbild von Martin Luther bis Friedrich Engels*. Berlin: Deutscher Verlag der Wissenschaften, 1971.

Strübind, Andrea. *Eifriger als Zwingli: Die frühe Täuferbewegung in der Schweiz*. Berlin: Duncker & Humblot, 2003

——. "James M. Stayer, 'A New Paradigm in Anabaptist/Mennonite Historiography?' A Response." *Mennonite Quarterly Review* 78 (2004): 308–13.

Stupperich, Robert. "Sebastian Franck und das münsterische Täufertum." In *Dauer und Wandel der Geschichte: Festgabe für Kurt von Aumer zum 15. Dezember 1965*, edited by Rudolf Vierhaus and Mansfred Botzenhart, 144–62. Münster: Aschendorff, 1966.

Teufel, Eberhard. "Die 'Deutsche Theologie' und Sebastian Franck im Lichte der neueren Forschung." *Theologische Rundschau* 11(1939): 304–25.

——. *'Landräumig': Sebastian Franck: Ein Wanderer am Donau, Neckar, und Rhein*. Neustadt a. d. Aisch: Degener & Co., 1954.

Troeltsch, Ernst. *Soziallehren der christlichen Kirchen und Gruppen*. 2 vols. Tübingen: J. C. B. Mohr, 1912.

Urner, Hans. "Die Taufe bei Caspar Schwenckfeld." *Theologische Literaturzeichnung* 23 (1948): 329–42.

van der Meer, S. *Bijdrage tot het onderzoek naar klassieke elementen in Coornherts Wellevenskunste*. Amsterdam: Gebr. Huisman en Hanenburg, 1934.

van Dülmen, Richard. "Schwärmer und Separatisten in Nürnberg (1618–1648): Ein Beitrag zum Problem des 'Weigelianismus.'" *Archiv für Sozialgeschichte* 55 (1973): 107–37.

van Gemert, Guillaume. "Zur Funktionalisierung Franckischen Gedankenguts in den Niederlanden: Der Traktat 'Van het Rycke Christi' (1611) und sein Stellenwert." In *Beiträge zum 500. Geburtstag von Sebastian Franck*, edited by Siegfried Wollgast, 209–47. Berlin: Weidler Buchverlag, 1999.

van Veen, Mirjam G. K. "Spiritualism in the Netherlands from David Joris to Dirk Volkertz. Coornhert." *Sixteenth Century Journal* 33 (2002): 129–50.

Vogler, Günter. *Thomas Müntzer*. Berlin: Dietz, 1989.

von Baczko, Ludwig. *Thomas Müntzer, dessen Charakter und Schicksale*. Halle: Ruff, 1812.

von Schlachta, Astrid. *Hutterische Konfession und Tradition (1578–1619): Etabliertes Leben zwischen Ordnung und Ambivalenz*. Mainz: Von Zabern, 2003.

Voogt, Gerrit. *Constraint on Trial: Dirck Volckhertsz Coornhert and Religious Freedom*. Kirksville, MO: Truman State University Press, 2000.

Waite, Gary K. *David Joris and Dutch Anabaptism, 1524–1543*. Waterloo, ON: Wilfrid Laurier Press, 1990.

Walter, Nikolaus. "'Bücher: So nicht der heiligen Schrifft gleick gehalten...'? Karlstadt, Luther und die Folgen." In *Tragende Tradition: Festschrift für Martin Seils zum 65. Geburtstag*, edited by Nannegret Freund, 173–97. Frankfurt a.M.: P. Lang, 1992.

Weeks, Andrew. *Valentin Weigel (1533–1588): German Religious Dissenter, Speculative Theorist, and Advocate of Tolerance*. Albany: State University of New York Press, 2000.

Weigelt, Horst. *Sebastian Franck und die lutherische Reformation*. Gütersloh: Gütersloher Verlagshaus, 1972.

———. *Spiritualistische Tradition im Protestantismus: Die Geschichte des Schwenckfeldertums in Schlesien*. Berlin: De Gruyter, 1973. Translated by Peter C. Erb as *Schwenckfelders in Silesia* (Pennsburg, PA: Schwenkfelder Library, 1985).

———. *Valentin Krautwald: Der führende Theologe des frühen Schwenckfeldertums. Biographisches und kirchenpolitische Aspeckte*. Baden-Baden: V. Koener, 1983.

Williams, George H. *Radical Reformation*. Philadelphia: Westminster Press, 1962.

———, ed. *Spiritual and Anabaptist Writers*. Philadelphia: Westminster Press, 1957.

Williams, Gerhild Scholz. "Gelächter vor Gott: Mensch und Kosmos bei Franck und Paracelsus." *Daphnis: Zeitschrift für Mittler Deutsche Literatur* 15 (1986): 463–81.

Wollgast, Siegfried. *Der deutsche Pantheismus im 16. Jahrhundert. Sebastian Franck und seine Wirkungen auf die Entwicklung der pantheistischen Philosophie in Deutschland*. Berlin: Deutscher Verlag der Wissenschaften, 1972.

———. "Sebastian Francks theologisch-philosophische Auffassungen. Aspekte." In Wollgast, *Beiträge zum 500. Geburtstag von Sebastian Franck,* 15–87. Berlin: Weidler Buchverlag, 1999.

———. "Valentin Weigel und Jakob Boehme: Vertreter einer Entwicklungslinie progressiven Denkens in Deutschland." In *Protokolband: Jakob-Böhme-Sumposium* (Görlitz 1974), 67–86. Görlitz: Rat der Stadt Görlitz, 1977.

———. "Valentin Weigel und seine Stellung in der deutschen Philosophie- und Geistesgeschichte." In Wollgast, *Vergessene und Verkannte: Zur Philosophie und Geistesentwicklung in Deutschland zwischen Reformation und Frühaufklärung*, 229–53. Berlin: Akademie Verlag, 1993.

Zeller, Winfried. "Der frühe Weigelianismus—Zur Literaturkritik der PseudoWeigeliana." In *Theologie und Frömmigkeit. Gesammelte Aufsätze,* edited by Bernd Jaspert, 197–229. Marburg: N. B. Elwert, 1971.

———. *Die Schriften Valentin Weigels: Eine literarkritische Untersuchung*. Berlin Ebering, 1940.

Zijlstra, Samme. "Anabaptists, Spiritualists and the Reformed Church in East Frisia." *Mennonite Quarterly Review* 75 (2001): 57–73.

Zorzin, Alejandro. *Karlstadt als Flugschriftenautor*. Göttingen: Vandenhoeck & Ruprecht, 1990.

———. "Karlstadts 'Dialogus vom Tauff der Kinder' in einem anonymen Wormser Druck aus dem Jahr 1527." *Archive for Reformation History* 79 (1988): 27–57.

———. "Zur Wirkungsgeschichte einer Schrift aus Karlstadts Orlamünde Tätigkeit: Der 1527 in Worms gedruckte *Dialog vom fremden Glauben, Glauben der Kirche, Taufe der Kinder*. Fortsetzung einer Diskussion." In *Andreas Bodenstein von Karlstadt (1486-1541)*, edited by Sigrid Looß und Markus Matthias, 143–58. Wittenberg: Drei Kastanien Verlag, 1998.

Zschäbitz, G. *Zur mitteldeutschen Wiedertäuferbewegung nach dem grossen Bauernkrieg*. Berlin: Rüttem & Loening, 1958.

Schwarz, *Die apokalyptische Theologie Thomas Müntzers und der Taboriten*.

5

Jewish History and Thought

Matt Goldish

Jewish history has been an extremely active field in recent years. While a quick look at book catalogues might lead one to think most of this productivity is connected with the Holocaust, there have in fact been numerous excellent studies on the early modern period. These have expanded the range of disciplines and approaches familiar from traditional Jewish historiography, bringing Jewish history more closely into the larger context of its various environments. This survey will begin by mentioning some overall trends in the field, then move on to a group of the more active subfields, focusing primarily on materials in English and on books, unless journal articles or book chapters are particularly relevant.

One of the strongest new directions in the past few decades of Jewish historical research has been toward social history. Jacob Katz of Hebrew University and Salo Baron of Columbia University were pioneers who greatly expanded the interest and tool chest of historians working in this area.[1] While a number of scholars (especially Robert Bonfil and Kenneth Stow, both working on Italy) have headed toward a consciously *mentalité* approach, many more have begun to examine the rhythms and assumptions of everyday life for early modern Jews.[2] The Jews' lack of a homeland with permanent archives makes the kind of social history done by historians of European Christian communities extremely difficult. Some of the

---

[1] See, for example, Katz, *Exclusiveness and Tolerance*; Katz, *Tradition and Crisis*; and Baron, *Social and Religious History of the Jews*.

[2] On Bonfil and Stow, see below in the section on Italy. See also Fine, *Judaism in Practice*.

slack created by a lack of baptismal and death records or regular court proceedings can be made up through judicious use of *responsa* collections (queries on Jewish law sent to rabbis, along with their responses), sermons, inquisitional files, and personal documents.

Closely related to the rise in social history is a corresponding interest in the social contexts of religious and intellectual history. Whereas older generations of Jewish historians were often content to note the development of, say, a conflict between rabbis over a questionable divorce or ritual bath, basing their work solely on legal documents, the new generation of historians will look for the contextual human elements involved. Often this type of study includes comparison and contrast with attitudes in the surrounding majority culture, based on a good knowledge of the literature in those fields.

This nuanced analysis of interactions between Jews and non-Jews is another of the truly revolutionary changes in recent historiography. Older literature often focused on oversimplified relationship models, particularly the "lachrymose" model made famous by Baron, according to which Jewish history is a litany of suffering at gentile hands, and what might be styled the "sanguine" model cultivated by Cecil Roth, according to which happy coexistence or *convivencia* was the norm in certain settings. While these outlooks have by no means disappeared, the prevalent scholarly approach today is to examine cases individually, study the lives and backgrounds of the specific people involved, and try to determine motivations that go beyond an artless dichotomy between "anti-Semitism" and "philo-Semitism." Some of the most interesting work has been done on settings or fields in which Jews and non-Jews interacted. These include physical spaces, such as the printing house, the alchemical laboratory, sometimes the classroom, and occasionally even the bedroom. They also include areas of mutual interest in which relations were mainly literary: biblical exegesis, messianic expectations, science, and commercial enterprises.

In the same way that European history in general has become more interdisciplinary in the past generation, so has the historiography of the Jews. Some scholars, most notably Sergio della Pergola, have focused on demographic statistics and other numerical methods. Moshe Idel and others have introduced anthropological techniques such as models to historical situations involving Jews. Postmodernist analysis borrowed from literature and cultural studies has its adherents in this field. Some very interesting work has been done by historians studying Jews from an economic perspective. In a few cases, edited volumes or journals have undertaken the analysis of one episode or group by scholars of various disciplines.[3]

Some other trends in historiography of the Jews are notable as well. There is a distinct turn toward focus on primary documents at all levels of research. The increasing crossover between historic studies of the Jews and their majority neighbors has made the publishing and translating of primary document collections an especially useful development. Another trend has been toward focusing on formerly marginalized groups in Jewish society. This includes women, of course, but also poor people, communities in commonly overlooked regions, individuals straddling the boundaries between Judaism and Christianity or Islam, homosexuals, and slaves. Finally, like many other historians, scholars of early modern Jewish history have begun to think in terms of a Mediterranean world and an Atlantic world, rather than in continental or political divisions.[4] Sometimes the breakdown is even more general: the Sephardi diaspora, the lands of Ashkenaz, or Jewish maritime networks, for example.

One study stands alone in its sweeping survey of early modern Jewish history in the West. That is Jonathan Israel's *European Jewry in the Age of Mercantilism, 1550–1750*, which has gone through three editions since its original appearance in 1985.[5] Israel commands a huge range of material, composed in a number of languages and genres, which he brings together to present an overview of Jewish settlement, culture, economics, self-government, religion, and relations with the Christian majority. *European Jewry* is the most appropriate starting point for anyone first approaching the Jewish presence in western and central Europe during the early modern period. While the book focuses on the larger developments of Jewish fate and does not generally probe the lived experience of individual Jews, it is an indispensable work.

The study of Jewish mysticism and messianism has been tremendously active in recent decades. While Gershom Scholem, who essentially established this field as an academic discipline, apparently felt he had done

---

[3]Unfortunately, most of Sergio della Pergola's work on premodern Jewry is in Hebrew. See Idel, *Between Ecstasy and Magic*; Beitchman, *Alchemy of the Word*; Israel, *Diasporas Within a Diaspora*; Arbel, *Trading Nations*; and Goldish, *Spirit Possession in Judaism*.

[4]See, for example, Toaff, *Mediterranean and the Jews*; Bernardini and Fiering, *Jews and the Expansion of Europe*.

[5]Israel, *European Jewry in the Age of Mercantilism*. See also Cooperman, *Jewish Thought in the Sixteenth Century*; and Twersky and Septimus, *Jewish Thought in the Seventeenth Century*.

most of what there was to do, it turns out that his work was only the beginning.[6] His famous thesis concerning early modern Jewish kabbalah (mystical philosophy and practice) was that the expulsion of the Jews from Spain in 1492 caused a massive shift in Jewish thinking, placing the experience of exile and hopes for redemption at the center. Rationalism was largely cast aside as a wave of messianic pretenders appeared in the wake of the expulsion. When these failed, the impulse shifted to the speculative plane and reappeared in the kabbalah of Rabbi Isaac Luria and his school in Safed in the late sixteenth century, then jumped back to an active mode with the messianic movement of Shabbatai Zvi in the seventeenth century.

Scholem's students, such as Joseph Dan and Isaiah Tishby, have continued this historical approach. Others have struck out in different directions. Zvi Werblowsky published an excellent English account of the mystical life of Rabbi Joseph Karo, the greatest Jewish legal scholar of the age, whose life spanned the exile from Spain through the Safed experience.[7] Karo was one of several early modern rabbis to be visited by a *maggid*, or mentoring spirit, a topic explored by Jeffrey H. Chajes.[8] Elliot Wolfson has introduced a very strong gender component into mystical studies, in several English volumes dealing partially with the early modern period.[9] Lawrence Fine places a greater emphasis on the role of mystical practice and personality in the Safed circle.[10] Moshe Idel and Yehuda Liebes question many of Scholem's assumptions about the role of the Spanish expulsion and his emphasis on exile and redemption in early modern Jewish thought.[11] Matt Goldish has argued against the centrality of mystical theology in the Sabbatean movement.[12] Several good collections of essays and sources in English dealing with all this material are available.[13] A very strong Christian interest in kabbalah arose in the late fifteenth century and lasted for hundreds of years, which will be discussed below in the context of Christian Hebraism.

---

[6]See, for example, Scholem, *Major Trends in Jewish Mysticism*; Scholem, *Messianic Idea in Judaism*; and Scholem, *Sabbatai Sevi*.

[7]Werblowsky, *Joseph Karo*.

[8]Chajes, *Between Worlds*.

[9]See, for example, Wolfson, *Circle in the Square*.

[10]Fine, *Physician of the Soul*.

[11]Idel, *Messianic Mystics*; and Liebes, *Studies in Jewish Myth*.

[12]Goldish, *Sabbatean Prophets*.

[13]See, for example, Fine, *Essential Papers on Kabbalah*; Lenowitz, *Jewish Messiahs*; and Jacobs, *Jewish Mystical Testimonies*.

Just as European historiography in recent decades has traced the development of occult and magical mentalities into early science, historians of the Jews have been similarly exploring Jewish engagement with scientific thought in the sixteenth through eighteenth centuries in relationship to philosophy and mysticism. David Gans, a rabbi who spent time with Tycho Brahe and Johannes Kepler and wrote extensively about astronomy in the early sixteenth century, has been the subject of two major studies.[14] David Ruderman's research on Jews and early modern science has opened up the field as a major topic of discussion and laid the groundwork for future research. He has written both a synthetic study of the subject and monographs on individual Jews engaged in scientific study.[15] Raphael Patai's book on Jews and alchemy deals extensively with the early modern period.[16] A new journal on Jews and the sciences, *Aleph*, often features papers on early modern topics as well. The general conclusion of all these studies is that early modern Jews were engaged with science to the degree that they were able, but being barred from most universities (Padua and, later, Leiden were limited exceptions), they did not have opportunities to participate in much pathbreaking work. Ruderman has emphasized that there was little or no religious objection to these studies in the Jewish world.

Regional studies have been quite active, with those concerning early modern Poland, Italy, and Germany especially noticeable. Jews first arrived in Poland in significant numbers at the beginning of the early modern period; during the seventeenth and eighteenth centuries, Poland became the largest Jewish population center in the world. Poland was also the site of major Jewish religious upheavals in the eighteenth century, namely, Frankism (a radical messianic sect vaguely connected with earlier Sabbateanism), and Hasidism (a popular mystical and charismatic sect still very much alive today). Polish Jewry is the exclusive subject of the journals *Polin* and *Gal-ed* (the latter in Hebrew with English summaries). Recent studies have emphasized the experiences of ordinary Jews in Polish towns and villages, on the one hand, and of Polish rabbinic scholars, on the other. Some of the most innovative work has been done in an effort to understand the historical origins of the legendary early Hasidic leaders. This pursuit, in

---

[14]Neher, *Jewish Thought and the Scientific Revolution*; and Efron, "R. David b. Solomon Gans and Natural Philosophy."

[15]Ruderman, *Jewish Thought and Scientific Discovery*; Ruderman, *Kabbalah, Magic, and Science*; and Ruderman, *World of a Renaissance Jew*.

[16]Patai, *Jewish Alchemists*.

which Moshe Rosman excels, takes advantage of local Polish archives and other Polish sources little used by earlier historians of the Jews.[17]

Scholarship on Italian Jewry also has its own journals. *Italia*, published in Israel, usually contains articles in Hebrew, English, and Italian, many of them focusing on the early modern period. *La Rassegna Mensile de Israel* is a more popular journal containing a mixture of scholarly and popular material. A series of volumes called *Italia Judaica* contains a lot of early modern material. Kenneth Stow's work on the Jews of sixteenth-century Rome, using notarial archive material, has shown previously little-known facets of daily life in the ghetto.[18] Other important recent studies focus on the Jews in early modern Florence and Venice, among other places.[19] Robert Bonfil has written about both the Renaissance rabbinate in Italy, and the overall experience of Italian Jewry in the Renaissance period. Bonfil attempts to correct perspectives from an earlier generation of scholarship that tended to oversimplify the attitudes of Jews toward their complex situation around the time walled ghettos began to appear in 1516.[20] Many other specialized studies on early modern Italian Jewry and specific individuals within it have also been published in recent years.[21] A handy place to begin is with *Essential Papers on Jewish Culture in Renaissance and Baroque Italy*, edited by Ruderman.[22] The essays in this volume reflect the recent scholarly focus on Jewish intellectual life and popular culture in Italy.

Relations between Jews and Christians in early modern Germany and Italy, particularly those negative relationships that resulted in accusations of ritual murder and host desecration, have received extensive treatment. Ronnie Po-chia Hsia has examined the Trent ritual murder case in depth, as well as explaining the religious and political motivations of blood libels throughout the period. Miri Rubin presents a study of the formal tropes and contexts in which these accusations appeared and what they reveal about the accusers. These works share a common focus on the precise

---

[17]Among these recent works, see Dynner, *Men of Silk*; Fram, *Ideals Face Reality*; Shulman, *Authority and Community*; Hundert, *Jews in Poland-Lithuania*; Rosman, *The Lord's Jews*; Rosman, *Founder of Hasidism*; Teter, *Jews and Heretics*.

[18]Stow, *Jews in Rome*; and Stow, *Theater of Acculturation*.

[19]See Siegmund, *Medici State and the Ghetto of Florence*; Arbel, *Trading Nations*; Malkiel, *A Separate Republic*.

[20]Bonfil, *Rabbis and Jewish Communities*; and Bonfil, *Jewish Life in Renaissance Italy*.

[21]See, for example, Ruderman and Veltri, *Cultural Intermediaries*; Ruderman, *Preachers of the Italian Ghetto*; and de' Rossi, *Light of the Eyes*.

[22]Ruderman, *Essential Papers on Jewish Culture*.

background of malfeasance accusations against Jews within Christian society.[23] Several other recent works about relations between Jews and Christians in early modern Germany present both benign and sinister aspects of their interactions. Some of this writing reflects a sort of historical response to the thesis of Daniel Jonah Goldhagen, who famously claimed that Germany had a long legacy of particularly violent anti-Semitism for centuries before the Holocaust.[24] The volumes of the series *Germania Judaica* are now reaching the early modern period as well, and will be an invaluable resource.

Jewish life in Spain and the expulsion in 1492 continue to be an enormous topic of research. While the standard work on the centuries leading up to the expulsion remains Yitzhak Baer's two-volume *History of the Jews in Christian Spain* (re-released in 1992), a great deal has been added since Baer first appeared.[25] Ben-zion Netanyahu has studied the Jewish responses to expulsion and conversion, and the developments leading up to the establishment of the Inquisition and the expulsion from the Spanish perspective.[26] Mark Meyerson's *Jewish Renaissance in Fifteenth-Century Spain* claims that, contrary to the views of Baer and others, Spanish Jewry actually experienced a cultural flowering in the fifteenth century.[27] Norman Roth examines the phenomenon of *conversos* (converted Jews) in Spain from before the expulsion, their relationship with the Inquisition, and the decision to expel the Jews.[28] Renée Levine Melammed treats the role of women in *converso* society.[29] A spate of edited works, many connected to the five hundredth anniversary of the expulsion, deal with the expulsion decree, the fate of Jews in exile from Spain, and the problem of the *conversos*.[30]

The study of Sephardic (Spanish, or Iberian) Jewry after the expulsion has exploded in recent years. While much of this material deals with

[23]Hsia, *Myth of Ritual Murder*; Hsia, *Trent, 1475*; and Rubin, *Gentile Tales*.

[24]See, for example, Bell, *Sacred Communities*; Hsia and Lehmann, *In and Out of the Ghetto*; Carlebach, *Divided Souls*; Gow, *Red Jews*; and Bell and Burnett, *Jews, Judaism, and the Reformation*.

[25]Baer, *History of the Jews in Christian Spain*. The 1992 edition has an important introduction by Benjamin Gampel.

[26]Netanyahu, *Marranos of Spain*; Netanyahu, *Origins of the Inquisition*; and Netanyahu, *Toward the Inquisition*. Originally published in 1966, *Marranos of Spain* was reissued in 1993 and 1999.

[27]Meyerson, *Jewish Renaissance*.

[28]Roth, *Conversos, Inquisition, and the Expulsion of the Jews*.

[29]Melammed, *Heretics or Daughters of Israel?*

[30]See, for example, Gampel, *Crisis and Creativity*; Waddington and Williamson, *Expulsion of the Jews*; Lazar and Haliczer, *Jews of Spain*; Beinart, *Sephardi Legacy*; Kedourie, *Spain and the Jews*.

the Ottoman Empire and North Africa, studies of the western Sephardi Diaspora are relevant to the topic of early modern Europe. A very interesting biography of the fabulously wealthy Portuguese *conversa*, Doña Gracia Nasi, featuring her travels around Europe and the Mediterranean, was published recently by the journalist Andrée Aelion Brooks. Equally interesting, if somewhat more dry in style, is Mercedes García-Arenal's and Gerard Wiegers' biography of Samuel Pallache, a Moroccan Jew who carried on many intrigues and adventures in Europe.[31]

About a century after the expulsion, communities of escaped *conversos* had formed in several western European cities that banned Jews. Many of these *conversos* were secret Judaizers, and several of them were wealthy merchants. Their secret Jewish lives inevitably became known to their Christian neighbors. Some cities' leaders allowed economic motives (the utility of Sephardi merchants) to triumph over religious bias and permitted these people to remain as Jews. This was the genesis of the western Sephardi Diaspora, whose centers were in Amsterdam, London, Hamburg, Venice, Livorno, Bayonne, and Bordeaux. Satellite communities of former *conversos* also appeared in Barbados, Goa, Recife, and other locations. The real differentiation of Western Sephardic communities from those in the East, and the analysis of their differences, has largely been the work of Yosef Kaplan, whose biography of Isaac Orobio de Castro traces the complex career of this important *converso* intellectual. Kaplan's subsequent work has laid the conceptual groundwork for specialized studies in the western Sephardi Diaspora.[32] An equally absorbing biography by Yosef Hayim Yerushalmi follows the life of Isaac Cardoso, another complicated *converso* personality, who ended up in Livorno.[33] Several other important works on the western Sephardim, especially those of Amsterdam, have enriched this field considerably. Miriam Bodian's survey of the Amsterdam Portuguese Jewish community, in particular, has been very popular in modern Jewish history courses.[34] David Katz focuses on the English perspective concerning the *converso* group in London and the readmission of Jews to England.[35] Several important works on Rabbi Menasseh ben Israel of Amsterdam, the learned Jew who begged Cromwell to accept Jewish settlement in England,

---

[31]Brooks, *Woman Who Defied Kings*; and García-Arenal and Wiegers, *Man of Three Worlds*.
[32]Kaplan, *From Christianity to Judaism*; and Kaplan, *Alternative Path to Modernity*.
[33]Yerushalmi, *From Spanish Court to Italian Ghetto*.
[34]Bodian, *Hebrews of the Portuguese Nation*; and Swetschinski, *Reluctant Cosmopolitans*.
[35]Katz, *Philo-Semitism*; and Katz, *Jews in the History of England*.

have also been published in recent years. They deal with his mystical views and correspondence with Christians, as well as his mission to Cromwell.[36]

A sort of subgenre has developed in the study of Amsterdam Sephardim, focused on the most famous scion of that community, Barukh d'Espinosa, or Benedict Spinoza. Scholarship has slowly come around to the realization that Spinoza's background in the Jewish world is critical to understanding his philosophy. Harry Austryn Wolfson and Leo Strauss touched on this issue, but the new Spinoza biography by Steven Nadler brings it to the fore. Richard H. Popkin, Yirmiyahu Yovel, Stephen Smith, and others also focus on the Jewish element in Spinoza's thought.[37]

Spinoza is the key figure in Jonathan Israel's massive *Radical Enlightenment*, which is just one of a number of recent works that stress the role of Jewish ideas in early Enlightenment thought. Popkin wrote a group of essays on topics such as the use of Jewish anti-Christian arguments by Enlightenment authors, the adoption of a position on the boundary between Judaism and Christianity by members of both faiths, and attempts by early Enlighteners to "reform" Judaism. Israel's student, Adam Sutcliffe, crafted a detailed study of Enlightenment attitudes toward Jews and Judaism that suggests that Jews were an important subject for Enlightenment ideologues, but a trying one as well, because the "Jewish Question" forced them to struggle with their biases.[38] This emphasis on intellectual influences running between Judaism and Christianity in the late seventeenth and early eighteenth centuries was seldom touched on by older historiography and raises many new questions about the changing role of the Jewish presence in Europe.

The Enlightenment entanglement of Judaism in European thought was a late phase of Renaissance Christian Hebraism, a trend that began in the Catholic Church during the fifteenth century and grew widely from there. Hebraists recognized the Hebrew language as the "third classical tongue," but they were also interested in what Jewish texts could teach them about Christianity. This interest became much more pronounced in the Reformation, with a slowly growing recognition that one needed to

---

[36]Kaplan, Méchoulan, and Popkin, *Menasseh Ben Israel*; and Coppenhagen, *Menasseh ben Israel*.

[37]Nadler, *Spinoza*; Nadler, *Spinoza's Heresy*; Popkin, *Spinoza*; Smith, *Spinoza, Liberalism, and the Question of Jewish Identity*; and Yovel, *Spinoza and Other Heretics*.

[38]Israel, *Radical Enlightenment*; Popkin, "Late Seventeenth-Century Gentile Attempt to Convert the Jews"; Popkin, "Role of Jewish-Christian Arguments"; Popkin, "Jewish Anti-Christian Arguments"; Popkin, "Marranos, New Christians, and the Beginnings of Modern Anti-Trinitarianism"; Popkin, "Christian Jews and Jewish Christians"; and Sutcliffe, *Judaism and Enlightenment*.

learn about the Jewish life of Jesus and the apostles in order to return to apostolic Christian practice. Even before the Reformation, Giovanni Pico della Mirandola and his circle had discovered the Jewish Kabbalah, which they construed to be a repository of ancient wisdom along with Hermetic and Platonic texts. Christian Kabbalah studies, as well as general Hebraic studies of ancient Judaism and biblical interpretation, remained strong well into the eighteenth century. While this field was not unexplored earlier, the present generation of scholarship has excelled in uncovering the contexts and intentions of Hebraism.[39]

These, then, are among the topics in early modern historiography of the Jews that have been most active and creative in recent decades. The study of early modern Jewish history and thought will undoubtedly continue to develop in the directions that have been described. The highly fruitful comparative focus on larger cultural, political, and religious contexts of Jewish life promises to enrich not only this field, but also fields in which the Jews have previously been marginal. Studies of anti-Semitism will continue to give way to the more specific and nuanced approaches made possible by local conditions. The expansion of the study of early modern Jews to include more emphasis on the Mediterranean, Adriatic, North African, and Asian regions will bring these communities toward the center of scholarly discussion. The availability of long-closed archives in Central and Eastern Europe promises to yield more information about the Jews of those communities as well. More generally, social history will continue to gain ground, but intellectual and religious history will remain vigorous fields.

Bibliography

ELECTRONIC RESOURCES

Jewish National and University Library, Digitized Book Repository (primary sources):
   http://www.jnul.huji.ac.il/dl/books/html/bk_all.htm
Jewish National and University Library, Index of Articles on Jewish Studies (RAMBI):
   http://jnul.huji.ac.il/rambi/

---

[39]See Manuel, *Broken Staff*; Burnett, *From Christian Hebraism to Jewish Studies*; Van Rooden, *Theology, Biblical Scholarship, and Rabbinical Studies*; Friedman, *Most Ancient Testimony*; Jones, *Discovery of Hebrew*; Katchen, *Christian Hebraists and Dutch Rabbis*; Beitchman, *Alchemy of the Word*; Coudert, *Impact of the Kabbalah*; Coudert, *Leibniz and the Kabbalah*; Coudert and Shoulson, *Hebraica Veritas?*; Reuchlin, *On the Art of Kabbalah*; Swietlicki, *Spanish Christian Kabbalah*; Wirszubski, *Pico della Mirandola's Encounter*; Dan, *Christian Kabbalah*; de León Jones, *Giordano Bruno and the Kabbalah*; Petry, *Gender, Kabbalah, and the Reformation*; Bell & Burnett, *Jews, Judaism, and the Reformation*.

PRINTED SOURCES

Arbel, Benjamin. *Trading Nations: Jews and Venetians in the Early Modern Eastern Mediterranean.* Leiden: Brill, 1995.

Baer, Yitzhak. *A History of the Jews in Christian Spain.* 2 vols. Translated by Louis Schoffman, with introduction by Benjamin R. Gampel. Philadelphia: Jewish Publication Society, 1992.

Baron, Salo. *A Social and Religious History of the Jews.* 18 vols. New York: Columbia University Press, 1952–83.

Beinart, Haim, ed. *The Sephardi Legacy.* 2 vols. Jerusalem: Magnes Press, Hebrew University, 1992.

Beitchman, Philip. *Alchemy of the Word: Cabala of the Renaissance.* New York: State University of New York Press, 1998.

Bell, Dean Phillip. *Sacred Communities: Jewish and Christian Identities in Fifteenth-Century Germany.* Leiden: Brill, 2001.

———, and Stephen Burnett, eds. *Jews, Judaism, and the Reformation in Sixteenth Century Germany.* Leiden: Brill, 2006.

Bernardini, Paolo, and Norman Fiering, eds. *The Jews and the Expansion of Europe to the West, 1450 to 1800.* European Expansion and Global Interaction 2. New York: Berghahn Books, 2001.

Bodian, Miriam. *Hebrews of the Portuguese Nation: Conversos and Community in Early Modern Amsterdam.* Bloomington: University of Indiana Press, 1997.

Bonfil, Roberto. *Jewish Life in Renaissance Italy.* Berkeley: University of California Press, 1994.

———. *Rabbis and Jewish Communities in Renaissance Italy.* Oxford: Littman Library, 1990.

Brooks, Andrée Aelion. *The Woman Who Defied Kings: The Life and Times of Doña Gracia Nasi, A Jewish Leader during the Renaissance.* St. Paul, MN: Paragon House, 2002.

Burnett, Stephen. *From Christian Hebraism to Jewish Studies: Johannes Buxtorf (1564–1629) and Hebrew Learning in the Seventeenth Century.* Leiden: Brill, 1996.

Carlebach, Elisheva. *Divided Souls: Converts from Judaism in Germany, 1500–1750.* New Haven, CT: Yale University Press, 2001.

Chajes, Jeffrey Howard. *Between Worlds: Dybbuks, Exorcists, and Early Modern Judaism.* Jewish Culture and Contexts. Philadelphia: University of Pennsylvania Press, 2003.

Cooperman, Bernard Dov, ed. *Jewish Thought in the Sixteenth Century.* [Cambridge, MA]: Harvard University Center for Jewish Studies, 1983. Distributed by Harvard University Press.

Coppenhagen, J. H. *Menasseh ben Israel: Manuel Dias Soeiro, 1604–1657: A Bibliography.* Jerusalem: Misgav Yerushalayim, 1990.

Coudert, Allison. *The Impact of the Kabbalah in the Seventeenth Century: The Life and Thought of Francis Mercury van Helmont (1614–1698).* Leiden: Brill, 1999.

———. *Leibniz and the Kabbalah.* Dordrecht, Netherlands: Kluwer, 1995.

———, and Jeffrey S. Shoulson, eds. *Hebraica Veritas? Christian Hebraists and the Study of Judaism in Early Modern Europe.* Philadelphia: University of Pennsylvania Press, 2004.

Dan, Joseph, ed. *The Christian Kabbalah: Jewish Mystical Books and Their Christian Interpreters.* Cambridge, MA: Harvard College Library, 1997.

de León Jones, Karen Silva. *Giordano Bruno and the Kabbalah: Prophets, Magicians, and Rabbis.* New Haven, CT: Yale University Press, 1997.

de' Rossi, Azariah. *The Light of the Eyes.* Translated, with introduction and annotations by Joanna Weinberg. New Haven, CT: Yale University Press, 2001.

Dynner, Glenn. *Men of Silk: The Hasidic Conquest of Polish Jewish Society.* Oxford: Oxford University Press, 2006.

Efron, Noah. "R. David b. Solomon Gans and Natural Philosophy in Jewish Prague." PhD diss., Tel-Aviv University, 1995.

Fine, Lawrence. *Physician of the Soul, Healer of the Cosmos: Isaac Luria and His Kabbalistic Fellowship.* Stanford, CA: Stanford University Press, 2003.

———, ed. *Essential Papers on Kabbalah.* New York: New York University Press, 1995.

———, ed. *Judaism in Practice, From the Middle Ages through the Early Modern Period.* Princeton, NJ: Princeton University Press, 2001.

Fram, Edward. *Ideals Face Reality: Jewish Law and Life in Poland, 1550–1655.* Cincinnati, OH: Hebrew Union College Press, 1997.

Friedman, Jerome. *The Most Ancient Testimony: Sixteenth-Century Christian-Hebraica in the Age of Renaissance Nostalgia.* Athens: Ohio University Press, 1983.

Gampel, Benjamin R., ed. *Crisis and Creativity in the Sephardic World, 1391–1648.* New York: Columbia University Press, 1997.

García-Arenal, Mercedes, and Gerard Wiegers. *A Man of Three Worlds: Samuel Pallache, A Moroccan Jew in Catholic and Protestant Europe.* Translated by Martin Beagles. Baltimore: Johns Hopkins University Press, 2003.

Germania Judaica, Vol. 3, pts. 1–3, *1350–1519.* Edited by Arye Maimon, Mordechai Breuer, and Yacov Guggenheim. Tübingen: Mohr-Siebeck, 1987–2003.

Goldish, Matt. *The Sabbatean Prophets.* Cambridge, MA: Harvard University Press, 2004.

———, ed. *Spirit Possession in Judaism: Cases and Contexts from the Middle Ages to the Present.* Detroit, MI: Wayne State University Press, 2003.

Gow, Andrew. *The Red Jews: Antisemitism in an Apocalyptic Age, 1200–1600.* Leiden: Brill, 1995.

Hsia, R. Po-chia. *The Myth of Ritual Murder: Jews and Magic in Reformation Germany.* New Haven, CT: Yale University Press, 1988.

———. *Trent, 1475: Stories of a Ritual Murder Trial.* New Haven, CT: Yale University Press, 1992.

———, and Hartmut Lehmann, eds. *In and Out of the Ghetto: Jewish-Gentile Relations in Late Medieval and Early Modern Germany.* Cambridge: Cambridge University Press, 1995.

Hundert, Gershon David. *Jews in Poland-Lithuania in the Eighteenth Century: A Genealogy of Modernity.* Berkeley: University of California Press, 1994.

Idel, Moshe. *Hasidism: Between Ecstasy and Magic.* New York: State University of New York Press, 1995.

———. *Messianic Mystics.* New Haven, CT: Yale University Press, 1998.

Israel, Jonathan. *Diasporas Within A Diaspora: Jews, Crypto-Jews and the World Maritime Empires (1540–1740).* Leiden: Brill, 2002.

———. *European Jewry in the Age of Mercantilism, 1550–1750.* 3rd ed. London: Littman Library, 1998.

———. *The Radical Enlightenment: Philosophy and the Making of Modernity, 1650–1750.* Oxford: Oxford University Press, 2001.

Jacobs, Louis, ed. *Jewish Mystical Testimonies.* New York: Schocken, 1976.

Jones, G. Lloyd. *The Discovery of Hebrew in Tudor England: A Third Language.* Manchester, UK: Manchester University Press, 1983.

Kaplan, Yosef. *An Alternative Path to Modernity: The Sephardi Diaspora in Western Europe.* Leiden: Brill, 2000.

————. *From Christianity to Judaism: The Story of Isaac Orobio de Castro*. Oxford: Littman Library, 1989.

————, Richard H. Popkin, and Henry Méchoulan, eds. *Menasseh Ben Israel and His World*. Brill Studies in Intellectual History 15. Leiden: Brill, 1989.

Katchen, Aaron. *Christian Hebraists and Dutch Rabbis: Seventeenth Century Apologetics and the Study of Maimonides' Mishneh Torah*. Cambridge, MA: Harvard University Press, 1984.

Katz, David. *The Jews in the History of England, 1485–1850*. Oxford: Oxford University Press, 1994.

————. *Philo-Semitism and the Readmission of the Jews to England*. Oxford: Clarendon Press, 1982.

Katz, Jacob. *Exclusiveness and Tolerance: Studies in Jewish-Gentile Relations in Medieval and Modern Times*. New York: Schocken, 1962.

————. *Tradition and Crisis: Jewish Society at the End of the Middle Ages*. Translated and edited by Bernard Dov Cooperman. New York: New York University Press, 1993.

Kedourie, Elie, ed. *Spain and the Jews: The Sephardi Experience 1492 and After*. London: Thames & Hudson, 1992.

Lazar, Moshe, and Stephen Haliczer, eds. *The Jews of Spain and the Expulsion of 1492*. Lancaster, CA: Labyrinthos, 1997.

Lenowitz, Harris. *The Jewish Messiahs, From the Galilee to Crown Heights*. New York: Oxford University Press, 1998.

Liebes, Yehuda. *Studies in Jewish Myth and Jewish Messianism*. Albany: State University of New York Press, 1993.

Malkiel, David. *A Separate Republic: The Mechanics and Dynamics of Venetian Jewish Self-Government, 1607–1624*. Jerusalem: Magnes Press, 1991.

Manuel, Frank. *The Broken Staff: Judaism Through Christian Eyes*. Cambridge, MA: Harvard University Press, 1992.

Melammed, Renée. *Heretics or Daughters of Israel? The Crypto-Jewish Women of Castile*. New York: Oxford University Press, 1999.

Meyerson, Mark. *A Jewish Renaissance in Fifteenth-Century Spain*. Princeton, NJ: Princeton University Press, 2004.

Nadler, Seven. *Spinoza: A Life*. Cambridge: Cambridge University Press, 1999.

————. *Spinoza's Heresy: Immortality and the Jewish Mind*. Oxford: Clarendon Press, 2001.

Neher, André. *Jewish Thought and the Scientific Revolution of the Sixteenth Century: David Gans (1541–1613) and His Times*. Oxford: Littman Library, 1986.

Netanyahu, Benzion. *The Marranos of Spain from the Late XIVth to the Early XVIth Century, According to Contemporary Hebrew Sources*. New York: American Academy for Jewish Research, 1966 (2nd ed., 1972). Reprint, Millwood, NY: Kraus Reprint, 1973. 3rd ed., Ithaca, NY: Cornell University Press, 1999.

————. *The Origins of the Inquisition in Fifteenth-Century Spain*. New York: Random House, 1995.

————. *Toward the Inquisition: Essays on Jewish and Converso History in Late Medieval Spain*. Ithaca, NY: Cornell University Press, 1997.

Patai, Raphael. *The Jewish Alchemists: A History and Source Book*. Princeton, NJ: Princeton University Press, 1994.

Petry, Yvonne. *Gender, Kabbalah, and the Reformation: The Mystical Theology of Guillaume Postel (1510–1581)*. Leiden: Brill, 2004.

Popkin, Richard. "Christian Jews and Jewish Christians in Spain, 1492 and After." *Judaism* 41 (1992): 248–67.

———. "Jewish Anti-Christian Arguments as a Source of Irreligion from the 17th to the Early 19th Century." In *Atheism from the Reformation to the Enlightenment*, edited by Michael Hunter and David Wootton, 159–81. Oxford: Clarendon Press, 1992.

———. "A Late Seventeenth-Century Gentile Attempt to Convert the Jews to Reformed Judaism." In *Israel and the Nations: Essays Presented in Honor of Shmuel Ettinger*, edited by Shmuel Almog, 25–45. Jerusalem: Historical Society of Israel, 1987.

———. "Marranos, New Christians and the Beginnings of Modern Anti-Trinitarianism." In *Jews and Conversos at the Time of the Expulsion*, edited by Yom Tov Assis and Yosef Kaplan, 143–60. Jerusalem: Zalman Shazar Center for Jewish History, 1999.

———. "The Role of Jewish-Christian Arguments in the Rise of Scepticism." In *New Perspectives on Renaissance Thought: Studies in Intellectual History in Memory of Charles Schmitt*, edited by John Henry and Sarah Hutton, 1–12. London: Duckworth, 1990.

———. *Spinoza*. Oxford: Oneworld, 2004.

Reuchlin, Johann. *On the Art of the Kabbalah = De arte cabalistica*. Translated by Martin and Sarah Goodman. Lincoln: University of Nebraska Press/Bison Books, 1993.

Rosman, Murray. *Founder of Hasidism: A Quest for the Historical Ba'al Shem Tov*. Berkeley: University of California Press, 1996.

———. *The Lord's Jews: Magnate-Jewish Relations in the Polish-Lithuanian Commonwealth During the Eighteenth Century*. Cambridge, MA: Harvard University Press, 1990.

Roth, Norman. *Conversos, Inquisiton, and the Expulsion of the Jews from Spain*. Madison: University of Wisconsin Press, 1995.

Rubin, Miri. *Gentile Tales: The Narrative Assault on Late Medieval Jews*. New Haven, CT: Yale Univrsity Press, 1999.

Ruderman, David. *Essential Papers on Jewish Culture in Renaissance and Baroque Italy*. New York: New York University Press, 1993.

———. *Jewish Thought and Scientific Discovery in Early Modern Europe*. New Haven, CT: Yale University Press, 1995.

———. *Kabbalah, Magic, and Science: The Cultural Universe of a Sixteenth Century Jewish Physician*. Cambridge, MA: Harvard University Press, 1988.

———. *Preachers of the Italian Ghetto*. Berkeley: University of California Press, 1992.

———. *The World of a Renaissance Jew: The Life and Thought of Abrham ben Mordecai Farrisol*. Cincinnati, OH: Hebrew Union College Press, 1981.

———, and G. Veltri, eds., *Cultural Intermediaries: Jewish Intellectuals in Early Modern Italy*. Philadelphia: University of Pennsylvania Press, 2004.

Scholem, Gershom. *Major Trends in Jewish Mysticism*. New York: Schocken, 1941.

———. *The Messianic Idea in Judaism and Other Essays on Jewish Spirituality*. New York: Schocken, 1971.

———. *Sabbatai Sevi, The Mystical Messiah, 1626–1676*. Princeton, NJ: Princeton University Press, 1973.

Shulman, Nisson. *Authority and Community: Polish Jewry in the Sixteenth Century*. Hoboken, NJ: Ktav, 1986.

Siegmund, Stefanie B. *The Medici State and the Ghetto of Florence: The Construction of an Early Modern Jewish Community*. Stanford, CA: Stanford University Press, 2005.

Smith, Steven. *Spinoza, Liberalism, and the Question of Jewish Identity*. New Haven, CT: Yale University Press, 1997.

Stow, Kenneth. *The Jews in Rome*, 2 vols. Leiden: Brill, 1995.

———. *Theater of Acculturation: The Roman Ghetto in the Sixteenth Century*. Seattle: University of Washington Press, 2001.

Sutcliffe, Adam. *Judaism and Enlightenment.* Cambridge: Cambridge University Press, 2003.

Swetschinski, Daniel. *Reluctant Cosmopolitans: The Portuguese Jews of Seventeenth-Century Amsterdam.* London: Littman Library, 2000.

Swietlicki, Catherine. *Spanish Christian Kabbalah: The Works of Luis de León, Santa Teresa de Jesús, and San Juan de la Cruz.* Columbia: University of Missouri Press, 1986.

Teter, Magda. *Jews and Heretics in Catholic Poland: A Beleaguered Church in the Post-Reformation Era.* Cambridge: Cambridge University Press, 2006.

Toaff, Ariel. *The Mediterranean and the Jews.* 2 vols. Ramat-Gan: Bar-Ilan University Press, 1989.

Twersky, Isadore, and Bernard Septimus. *Jewish Thought in the Seventeenth Century.* Harvard Judaic Texts and Studies 6. Cambridge, MA: Harvard University Center for Jewish Studies, 1987. Distributed by Harvard University Press.

Van Rooden, Peter. *Theology, Biblical Scholarship and Rabbinical Studies in the Seventeenth Century: Constantijn L'Empereur (1591–1648), Professor of Hebrew and Theology at Leiden.* Leiden: Brill, 1989.

Waddington, Raymond B., and Arthur H. Williamson, eds. *The Expulsion of the Jews: 1492 and After.* New York: Garland, 1994.

Werblowsky, R. J. Zwi., *Joseph Karo, Lawyer and Mystic.* London: Oxford University Press, 1962.

Wirszubski, Chaim. *Pico della Mirandola's Encounter With Jewish Mysticism.* Cambridge, MA: Harvard University Press, 1989.

Wolfson, Elliot. *Circle in the Square: Studies in the Use of Gender in Kabbalistic Symbolism.* New York: State University of New York Press, 1995.

Yerushalmi, Yosef Hayim. *From Spanish Court to Italian Ghetto: Isaac Cardoso; A Study in Seventeenth-Century Marranism and Jewish Apologetics.* Seattle: University of Washington Press, 1981.

Yovel, Yirmiyahu. *Spinoza and Other Heretics.* 2 vols. Princeton, NJ: Princeton University Press, 1989.

6

Confessionalization

Ute Lotz-Heumann

In the 1982 *Reformation Europe: Guide to Research*, James M. Kittelson wrote a chapter entitled "The Confessional Age: The Late Reformation in Germany," in which he called the research situation with regard to the second half of the sixteenth century "a virtual wasteland."[1] That situation has since changed dramatically, not least as a result of the influence of the concept of confessionalization introduced by Wolfgang Reinhard and Heinz Schilling in books and articles published in the early and mid-1980s. This concept has shifted historiographical interest from its emphasis on the early Reformation toward the second half of the sixteenth and the seventeenth centuries. Between 1986 and 1995, three volumes on Reformed (Calvinist), Lutheran, and Catholic confessionalization appeared that set the scene for a lively historiographical debate.[2] From the beginning, the concept of confessionalization had been met with positive reception as well as strong criticism, which has grown over time. The critique of the concept is closely connected with the move away from societal history (*Gesellschaftsgeschichte*) and structural history toward microhistory and cultural history. This essay will first give an overview of the genesis and contents of the concept of confessionalization. The second part will explain the historiographical critique that has resulted from an intensive discussion of the concept as well as its application to different case studies.

---

[1]Kittelson, *Confessional Age*, 361.
[2]See Schilling, *Die reformierte Konfessionalisierung*; Rublack, *Die lutherische Konfessionalisierung*; and Reinhard and Schilling, *Die katholische Konfessionalisierung*.

The third and final part will explore the question of future directions for the field and argue that a more flexible concept of confessionalization can still serve as a useful research tool.

Development of the Concept of Confessionalization

In nineteenth-century German historiography, not least through the influence of Leopold von Ranke, the terms *Reformation* and *Gegenreformation* were established and came to be understood as two distinct historical periods in the sixteenth century. *Gegenreformation* was translated into other languages (as, for example, "Counter-Reformation," "contre-réforme," "Controriforma," "Contrareforma") and spread in European historiography. However, as Counter-Reformation implies a mere reaction to Protestantism and neglects the aspect of reform within Catholicism, the term was repeatedly criticized.[3] Responding to this state of affairs, the Catholic theologian Hubert Jedin in 1946 suggested the compromise terminology "Catholic reform and Counter-Reformation," which has remained influential in historical research ever since.[4]

In 1958, the Catholic historian Ernst Walter Zeeden suggested a new approach. He stressed that in the second half of the sixteenth century, the major creeds developing out of medieval Christianity—Catholicism, Lutheranism, and Calvinism—started to build modern, clearly defined confessional churches, which centered on written confessions of faith. Zeeden called this process "confession-building" or "confessional formation" (*Konfessionsbildung*), a neutral term that could be applied to all churches.[5]

In the late 1970s and early 1980s, two historians of the next generation, Wolfgang Reinhard and Heinz Schilling, from Catholic and Protestant backgrounds respectively, widened the concept of confession-building into "confessionalization." While Reinhard developed the concept of confessionalization from his criticism of the negative and antimodern implications of the term Counter-Reformation, Schilling developed the paradigm out of his research on the interactions of Calvinism and Lutheranism in northwestern Germany.[6]

---

[3]See Lotz-Heumann, "Confessionalization in Ireland."
[4]See Jedin, *Katholische Reformation*; and O'Malley, *Trent and All That*.
[5]See Zeeden, "Grundlagen und Wege der Konfessionsbildung."
[6]See Reinhard, "Gegenreformation als Modernisierung?"; idem, "Konfession und Konfessionalisierung in Europa"; idem, "Zwang zur Konfessionalisierung?"; idem, "Reformation, Counter-Reformation, and the Early Modern State"; idem, "Was ist katholische Konfessionalisierung?"; Schilling,

The Concept of Confessionalization

How do Schilling and Reinhard conceptionalize confessionalization? They see it as a paradigm of societal history (*Gesellschaftsgeschichte*). In their view, the religious and ecclesiastical developments of the early modern period, in particular the confessional divisions, deeply affected society and politics as well. The concept of confessionalization thus proceeds from the general observation that during the Middle Ages and the early modern period, the religious and the secular, church and state, were closely linked. As a consequence, Reinhard and Schilling stress the connections between confession-building and state formation, processes that could interact in different ways. According to Reinhard and Schilling, confessionalization in most cases "enabled states and societies to integrate more tightly."[7] When medieval Christianity was broken up by the Reformation, the principle *cuius regio, eius religio* (whose territory, his religion), which had been established in the Holy Roman Empire by the Peace of Augsburg in 1555, was enforced by the German princes in their territories, resulting in the creation of unified confessional states. Reinhard and Schilling see confessionalization as the first phase of early modern state formation and social disciplining (*Sozialdisziplinierung*).[8] As a result, one aspect of the original formulation of the concept, that of opposition and conflict, has taken a backseat: "confessionalization could also provoke confrontation with religious and political groups fundamentally opposed to this...integration of state and society."[9]

In contrast to the older historiography, Reinhard and Schilling stress parallel developments and "functional similarities"[10] between the confessional churches. Instead of the differences in doctrine and ritual, the concept of confessionalization focuses on the comparative aspects between the confessional churches: the aim of confessional homogenization, or maybe even the Christianization of popular religion; the connection between confession-building and state formation; the confessional churches' contribution to the process of social disciplining; the development of cultural and

---

Konfessionskonflikt und Staatsbildung; idem, "Die Konfessionalisierung im Reich"; idem, "Confessionalization in the Empire"; idem, "Confessional Europe"; idem, "Die Konfessionalisierung von Kirche"; and idem, "Confessionalization."

[7]Schilling, "Confessionalization in the Empire," 208.
[8]The term is Gerhard Oestreich's. See Schulze, "Gerhard Oestreichs Begriff."
[9]Schilling, "Confessionalization in the Empire," 209.
[10]Schilling, "Confessionalization in the Empire," 210.

political—often national—identities in which the confessional factor played a key role. Reinhard and Schilling have also introduced a new terminology. The terms traditionally used by German historians to describe the developments of the three confessional churches in the second half of the sixteenth and at the beginning of the seventeenth centuries—Catholic reform/Counter-Reformation, Lutheran orthodoxy, and Second Reformation (for the introduction of Calvinism in Lutheran territories)—have been replaced by the parallel terms Catholic, Lutheran, and Calvinist (or Reformed) confessionalization.

All in all, Reinhard and Schilling see confessionalization as "a fundamental process of society, which had far-reaching effects upon the public and private life of individual European societies."[11] They assume that the process of confessionalization affected all areas of life, from the state and its institutions to gender relations and personal lives. In addition, Reinhard and Schilling emphasize the modernizing impetus of the process of confessionalization. In order to contradict the antimodern implications of the term Counter-Reformation, Reinhard stresses the intentional and unintentional modernizing effects of Tridentine reform, for instance the rationality of the Jesuits. Schilling rejects the established notion that the Reformation was the decisive turning point toward the modern age, holding rather that the age of confessionalization brought about deep-rooted changes on the way to modernity. For example, in his view, the social control exercised by church and state led to a modern, disciplined society. Moreover, because the process of confessionalization resulted in war and destruction, reducing confessional formation to absurdity, confessionalization eventually resulted in secularization.

Reinhard and Schilling have put different emphases in their definitions of confessionalization. Schilling has developed a periodization for the process of confessionalization in the Holy Roman Empire between the Peace of Augsburg in 1555 and the Thirty Years' War.[12] He defines four phases. The first is the "preparatory phase," from the late 1540s until the early 1570s. Although confessions of faith had already been formulated in the Reformation period, during this time, the Augsburg peace system was still functioning; however, Tridentine reform and Calvinism entered the empire and made the confessional situation more precarious. The second

[11]Schilling, "Confessionalization in the Empire," 209.
[12]See Schilling, "Die Konfessionalisierung im Reich"; and Schilling, "Confessionalization in the Empire."

phase, the 1570s, brought the "transition to confessional confrontation." After the conflicts within Lutheranism following Martin Luther's death in 1546, the Lutheran concord movement once again defined Lutheranism unambiguously through the Formula of Concord of 1577 and the Book of Concord of 1580–81. As a result, Lutheran orthodoxy was defined in clear contrast to Calvinism, and Protestant princes were increasingly forced to choose between Lutheranism and Calvinism. In this phase, Catholicism also became more dynamic as princes and prince bishops embraced the Tridentine decrees and introduced the Jesuit order to their lands. This period marked the onset of a "pressure for confessionalization" (*Zwang zur Konfessionalisierung*), a phrase coined by Reinhard.[13] The third phase, the "apogee of confessionalization," occurred between the 1580s and the 1620s. Several German princes became Calvinist during this period, the concord movement was vibrant in Lutheran Germany, and Tridentine Catholicism had become a major force in Catholic territories. These developments took place against a political background increasingly characterized by confrontation and conflict on all levels of imperial politics. The new generation of politicians was clearly lacking a will for compromise. Pope Gregory XIII introduced his calendar reform in 1582, but Protestants in the empire did not accept the new calendar until 1699/1700. Even time had become confessionalized. Schilling describes the fourth phase as "the end of confessionalization under the conditions of war and in the basis of the Peace of Westphalia." This last period began in the 1620s when people realized that confessional conflict led to destruction and devastation. As a result, irenicism and new religious movements such as Pietism were on the rise.

Wolfgang Reinhard has identified seven methods or mechanisms of confessionalization used by church and state to establish confessional homogeneity and to implement the *cuius regio, eius religio* principle.[14] First, the establishment of pure doctrine and its formulation in a confession of faith: this meant distinguishing one confessional church from other churches and eliminating possible sources of confusion. Second, the distribution and enforcement of these new norms, for example through confessional oaths and subscription. In this way, the religious orthodoxy of personnel in key positions—for instance theologians, clergy, teachers,

---

[13]Reinhard, "Zwang zur Konfessionalisierung?" For the translation, see Schilling, "Confessionalization in the Empire," 224.

[14]For the following see Reinhard, "Konfession und Konfessionalisierung in Europa"; Reinhard, "Zwang zur Konfessionalisierung?"; and Reinhard, "Reformation, Counter-Reformation, and the Early Modern State."

midwives, and secular officials—was to be ensured and "dissidents" were to be removed. Third, propaganda and censorship, meaning, on the one hand, using the printing press for propaganda purposes and preventing rival churches and religious movements from making use of the printing press on the other hand. Although scholars used controversial theology as a propaganda weapon, catechesis, preaching, and processions (in the Catholic Church) were used to influence the people. All confessional churches practiced censorship, the most famous being the Roman index, the *index librorum prohibitorum*. Fourth, internalization of the new norms through education: by founding new educational institutions, especially universities, the confessional churches wanted to keep their flock from attending rivaling institutions and to indoctrinate future generations. Fifth, disciplining the people: visitations and church discipline were used in order to create a confessionally homogenous population. The expulsion of confessional minorities also served as a means to this end. Sixth, rites and control of participation in rites: in view of the importance of rites for the coherence of the confessional group, participation in rites like baptism and marriage was ensured through the keeping of registers. Rites that served as markers of confessional differences were cultivated in particular. Seventh, the confessional regulation of even language: this is a field in which little research has been done so far. As an example, Reinhard mentions Christian names: while saints' names were particularly appealing to Catholics, they were forbidden in Geneva, with Calvinists preferring names from the Old Testament.

Historiography of the Concept of Confessionalization
The discussions about and critique of the concept of confessionalization fall broadly within six categories:[15] (1) the discussion about the periodization of the confessionalization process; (2) macrohistorical criticism of confessionalization as a fundamental process of society; (3) the critique of confessionalization as a modernization process; (4) the controversy about the neglect of the characteristics of the confessional churches; (5) the microhistorical critique of the "top-to-bottom approach" or "etatistic narrowing" of the concept of confessionalization; and (6) criticism or suggestions for modifications of the concept resulting from research on early modern countries and regions outside of Germany.

---

[15]See Lotz-Heumann, "Concept of 'Confessionalization.'"

Periodization of the Confessionalization Process

With regard to periodization, even Wolfgang Reinhard and Heinz Schilling are not in agreement. As seen above, Schilling has proposed a periodization of confessionalization in Germany that spans the period between the Peace of Augsburg in 1555 and the Thirty Years' War. In contrast, Reinhard has extended the confessionalization process much further, although he has not suggested a detailed periodization. He sees the beginning of the age of confessionalization in the 1520s with the development of written confessions of faith and the *Confessio Augustana* of 1530 as a first climax of this process. And he argues that the Thirty Years' War was not the end point of confessionalization, but that this came only with the expulsion of the Salzburg Protestants in 1731–32, which was, according to Reinhard, the last confessionally motivated act of expulsion in the Holy Roman Empire.[16] In Reinhard's view, therefore, the age of confessionalization is understood as a *longue durée* process; however, he also defines Catholic, Lutheran, and Reformed confessionalization as developments that were largely chronologically parallel.[17]

With Reinhard and Schilling not agreeing on periodization, it is not surprising that later historians have presented very different opinions. Harm Klueting, for instance, argues in favor of 1525 as the end of the Reformation as a popular movement and thus the beginning of confessionalization as a state-sponsored process.[18] Similarly, Erika Rummel has argued that the confessionalization of humanism had already begun in the 1520s.[19] Other historians have rejected the idea of a parallel development of the confessional churches. The Catholic historian Walter Ziegler, for instance, argues that the Catholic Church was in a special position because of its unbroken continuity with the medieval period.[20] The Protestant church historian Thomas Kaufmann stresses the importance of the Protestant Reformation as an upheaval and turning point in early modern society that will be underestimated if the development of the three confessional churches is regarded as parallel.[21] Studies on early modern Catholicism, in particular, have shown that the process of confessionalization did not end

---

[16]See Reinhard, "Konfession und Konfessionalisierung in Europa"; and Reinhard, "Was ist katholische Konfessionalisierung?"
[17]See Reinhard, "Zwang zur Konfessionalisierung?"
[18]See Klueting, *Das Konfessionelle Zeitalter.*
[19]See Rummel, *Confessionalization of Humanism.*
[20]See Ziegler, "Kritisches zur Konfessionalisierungsthese."
[21]See Kaufmann, "Die Konfessionalisierung von Kirche und Gesellschaft."

with the Thirty Years' War. In their works on Catholic areas in Germany, Marc Forster, Werner Freitag, and Andreas Holzem have made very clear that Catholic confessionalization was a vibrant process after 1650 and far into the eighteenth century.[22] As a result, collections of essays have now also begun to extend the framework of confessionalization at least until the beginning of the eighteenth century.[23]

Criticism of Confessionalization as a Fundamental Process of Society

From the very beginning, historians have doubted Schilling's and Reinhard's thesis that the role of religion in the sixteenth and seventeenth centuries was so important that confessionalization was a fundamental process of society. Scholars have identified numerous elements and developments in the age of confessionalization that were unconfessional or could not be confessionalized, such as Roman law and many aspects of matrimonial law, the mystic-spiritual tradition, alchemy, and astrology. As Anton Schindling has pointed out, the boundaries of the concept of confessionalization in today's research are thus defined by those areas of early modern life that were not affected by confessionalization.[24] In addition, as Hartmut Lehmann and others have stressed, popular religion and the influence of other processes like the "little ice age" on popular religion have not yet been sufficiently analyzed to gauge the relationship between confessionalization and other processes in sixteenth- and seventeenth-century society.[25]

Winfried Schulze, one of the earliest critics of the concept of confessionalization, has also argued that many historical subjects and processes of the sixteenth and seventeenth centuries existed independent of, and can therefore be described without reference to, confessionalization. He holds that Reinhard and Schilling have overestimated the "pressure for confessionalization." Schulze stresses ideas and phenomena of tolerance and religious freedom, but also those of skepticism and unbelief as well as secularized ideas of peace in the sixteenth and seventeenth centuries. In his

[22]See Forster, *Counter-Reformation in the Villages*; Forster, *Catholic Revival*; Freitag, *Pfarrer, Kirche und ländliche Gesellschaft*; and Holzem, *Religion und Lebensformen*.

[23]See Headley, Hillerbrand, and Papalas, *Confessionalization in Europe*; and Dietz and Ehrenpreis, *Drei Konfessionen in einer Region*.

[24]See Schindling, "Konfessionalisierung und Grenzen von Konfessionalisierbarkeit." On literature and confessionalization see Lotz-Heumann and Pohlig, "Confessionalization and Literature in the Empire."

[25]See Lehmann, "Grenzen der Erklärungskraft der Konfessionalisierungsthese."

opinion, this period was marked by pluralization and paved the way for secularization, rather than being characterized by confessionalization.[26] This critique has been reinforced from the point of view of the history of law. Martin Heckel and Michael Stolleis have stressed aspects like the secularization of imperial law and the "detheologizing of politics" by political theorists and lawyers.[27] Rudolf Schlögl has argued that confessionalization as such was not a fundamental process. Rather, proceeding from system theory, he sees confessionalization only as a symptom of a more far-reaching fundamental process in society, in which the form of differentiation of society gradually changed from the preeminence of social hierarchy with the nobility at the top into independent spheres of social action such as the state and the church.[28]

Confessionalization as a Modernization Process

Reinhard's and Schilling's view of confessionalization as a modernization process has also come under criticism. While authors like Schulze and Schlögl do not doubt that a modernization process took place in the early modern period, even if they do not see confessionalization as being at the forefront of modernization, other historians doubt the concept of modernization altogether. They regard this thesis as an expression of the historiography of the 1970s, when German historians proceeded on the assumption that there was a teleological process of social change, moving toward improved social and political structures. Luise Schorn-Schütte has stressed that, because the notion of Western modernity has now been replaced by the idea of multiple modernities in which western civilization no longer plays a leading role, the modernization aspect of the concept of confessionalization can no longer be maintained.[29] A younger generation of scholars, therefore, is more skeptical about the long-term implications of processes in early modern church, state, and society and is more inclined to concentrate on the period and its characteristics as such.

Characteristics of Confessional Churches

Both Protestant and Catholic scholars (for example, Thomas Kaufmann and Walter Ziegler) have criticized the concept of confessionalization for

---

[26]See Schulze, "Konfessionalisierung als Paradigma."
[27]See Stolleis, "'Konfessionalisierung' oder 'Säkularisierung'"; and Heckel, *Deutschland im konfessionellen Zeitalter*.
[28]See Schlögl, "Differenzierung und Integration."
[29]See Schorn-Schütte, "Konfessionalisierung als wissenschaftliches Paradigma?"

ignoring the specific characteristics—the so-called *propria*—of the confessional churches in theology, piety, and spirituality.[30] Kaufmann regards the treatment of religion in the context of the paradigm of confessionalization as "functional-reductionist":[31] functional because the concept looks only at the function of religion within state and society and reductionist because the *propria* of the confessional churches are thus leveled. Already during the first symposium on Calvinist confessionalization in the Holy Roman Empire (held in 1985), participants argued that the concept of confessionalization did not sufficiently consider the characteristics of the Calvinist (Reformed) Church in Germany.[32] Kaufmann, whose research focuses on the development of Lutheranism in the seventeenth century, has proposed the concept of *Konfessionskulturen* (confessional cultures) as an alternative to confessionalization. He concentrates on the "internal perspective" of the confessions and looks at how a confessional church variously shaped social and cultural life. His emphasis on diversity in Lutheran confessional culture, rather than uniformity, has led him to introduce a new term, *binnenkonfessionelle Pluralität* (inner-confessional plurality).[33]

Confessionalization and State Formation

Younger historians have also expressed doubts about the close connection between confessionalization and state formation postulated by Reinhard and Schilling. This point of criticism impinges on the general debate about the relationship between macro- and microhistory, between societal history and cultural history in Germany. As noted above, Reinhard and Schilling proceed from the assumption that confessionalization was decisively influenced by the early modern state and was therefore a top-to-bottom process; state and church worked together to confessionalize and discipline the people. However, historians have increasingly drawn attention to conflict and resistance to confessionalization by the estates, the nobility, local officials, clergymen, burghers, and the populace. For example, Werner Freitag has drawn attention to the Anhalt principalities, and Bodo Nischan has shown how conflict-ridden confessionalization really was in seventeenth-century Brandenburg.[34]

[30]See Kaufmann, "Die Konfessionalisierung von Kirche und Gesellschaft"; and Ziegler, "Kritisches zur Konfessionalisierungsthese."

[31]Kaufmann, "Die Konfessionalisierung von Kirche und Gesellschaft," 1121.

[32]See Schilling, *Die reformierte Konfessionalisierung.*

[33]See Kaufmann, *Dreißigjähriger Krieg und Westfälischer Friede*; and Kaufmann,"Einleitung."

[34]See Freitag, "Konfliktfelder und Konfliktparteien"; Nischan, *Prince, People, and Confession*; and Nischan, *Lutherans and Calvinists.*

Luise Schorn-Schütte has stressed that confessionalization from above did not automatically take effect below; confessional disciplining measures by state and church failed more often than not. Thus, according to Schorn-Schütte, the concept of confessionalization has been shown to be a self-fulfilling prophecy: it interprets intentions of disciplining and confessionalizing the population in early modern society as having been successful and as actually having influenced behavior, while in reality this did not happen.[35] Andreas Holzem, a Catholic church historian who has published a major study on the prince-bishopric of Münster, has also drawn attention to the interaction between confessionalization from above and the reactions and the processes of appropriation and rejection in the local communities. However, in contrast to Schorn-Schütte, he concludes that by the eighteenth century confessionalization measures eventually had a disciplining effect on the population, if only partially.[36]

Territories of mixed confessional makeup or with a weak state have proven to be suitable test cases for critiquing the concept of confessionalization. For example, Marc Forster has drawn attention to the bishopric of Speyer and other smaller Catholic territories in southwestern Germany, where the communities developed a Catholic identity from below without much influence either by Tridentine reform or by confessionalization measures instituted by the state.[37] Confessional cultures and identities could, therefore, develop without confessionalization from above. In a collection of essays on the duchy of Berg, a multiconfessional region in northwestern Germany, the concept of confessionalization as a successful top-to-bottom process is also called into question. Because Catholics, Lutherans, and Calvinists coexisted in the region, the etatistic version of confessionalization can clearly not be applied to this case. However, the editors of the volume, Stefan Ehrenpreis and Burkhard Dietz, have interpreted confessional formation on the local level, which resulted in many conflicts among communities, as competing processes of confessionalization from below.[38]

The European Perspective: Modifications of the Concept of Confessionalization

Suggestions to modify the concept of confessionalization have also been put forward by historians working on European countries other than Germany.

---

[35]See Schorn-Schütte, "Konfessionalisierung als wissenschaftliches Paradigma?"
[36]See Holzem, "Die Konfessionsgesellschaft"; and Holzem, *Religion und Lebensformen*.
[37]See Forster, *Counter-Reformation in the Villages*.
[38]See Dietz and Ehrenpreis, *Drei Konfessionen in einer Region*.

From a microhistorical viewpoint as well as from the perspective of research into the workings of church discipline in the early modern period, Heinrich Richard Schmidt has criticized the etatistic focus and overestimation of the role of the state in the concept of confessionalization. Drawing on his research on church courts (*Chorgerichte*) in the rural communities of the Reformed territory of Berne, Schmidt concluded that successful social disciplining—if it existed at all—was not due to pressure from state and church, but rather was based on mechanisms of self-regulation and self-disciplining in the village communities. Although Schmidt does not deny that there were pressures toward confessionalization from above, he argues that the process of confessionalization could be successful only if it fit in with the need for regulation within society.[39] Randolph Head has also used a Swiss territory, Graubünden, as a case study to test the concept of confessionalization. He comes to the conclusion that, although the state "was absent," confessional identities emerged in Graubünden which were strong enough to disrupt the "power communal solidarity created by the Bündner political system." Head formulates three conclusions: first, "agents besides institutional states or churches could have instigated the confessionalization process"; second, "confessional conflict became an arena for carrying out underlying struggles that derived from both internal and exogenous forces"; and third, "confessionalization…may have been only one version of a broader process of social and ideological transformation."[40]

The aspects of agency beyond state and church and of confessionalization from below have proven to be an important modification or supplement when the concept of confessionalization is applied to other European case studies. For example, Olaf Mörke has made clear that the concept cannot be applied to the Dutch Republic as a whole because it was a multiconfessional state and because—by early modern European standards—it was very tolerant. However, Mörke drew attention to the fact that in the Netherlands, it was the individual religious communities that experienced processes of confessionalization. Although the Netherlands do not fit the etatistic model, this does not mean that processes of confessionalization did not take place there.[41] Similar results have been presented by historians working on east central Europe, notably Winfried Eberhard, who has shown that the German model of confessionalization from above cannot be

---

[39]See Schmidt, *Dorf und Religion*; and Schmidt, "Sozialdisziplinierung?"
[40]Head, "Catholics and Protestants in Graubünden," 341–42.
[41]See Mörke, "Die politische Bedeutung"; and Kaplan, *Calvinists and Libertines*.

applied to these territories. Rather, confessionalization processes in east central Europe took place in a multiconfessional framework and were thus regionalized and localized. In addition, they were not initiated centrally by the state, but by the estates or, as Michael G. Müller has shown regarding Gdańsk, Elblag, and Toruń, by urban elites.[42]

Historians have also increasingly discussed the application of the concept of confessionalization to France. Philip Benedict, James Farr, Gregory Hanlon, and Mack Holt[43] have concluded that the "strong theory of confessionalization", which postulates that state-building and confessionalization were mutually reinforcing processes, cannot be applied to France. However, a "weak theory of confessionalization" is regarded as a useful research tool for the French case: in Benedict's words, the weak theory "defines confessionalization as a process of rivalry and emulation by which the religions that emerged from the upheavals of the Reformation defined and enforced their particular versions of orthodoxy and orthopraxy, demonized their rivals, and built group cohesion and identity." In terms of the role of the state, different views have been put forward. On the one hand, Benedict argues that "France's wars of religion…illustrate how the division of Christendom into rival confessions could bring even the era's strongest states to the very brink of dissolution."[44] On the other hand, Farr has observed that, if the time frame is broadened to 1530 through 1685 and if confessionalization is understood as an intention of state policy and not necessarily as a success, "then we can see that there *was* a relatively consistent state policy of catholicization"[45] in France.[46]

For the cases of England and Scotland, Andrew Pettegree has also rejected the strong theory of confessionalization, arguing that "the process of confessionalism (*Konfessionsbildung*), the internal consolidation of the different confessions in parallel, competing churches, went forward strongly."[47] My own research on Ireland has led to the conclusion that the

---

[42]See Eberhard, "Voraussetzungen und strukturelle Grundlagen der Konfessionalisierung"; Müller, *Zweite Reformation und ständische Autonomie*; Müller, "Unionsstaat und Region"; and Plaggenborg, "Konfessionalisierung in Osteuropa."

[43]See Benedict, "Confessionalization in France?"; Farr, "Confessionalization and Social Discipline in France"; Hanlon, *Confession and Community*; and Holt, "Confessionalization Beyond the Germanies."

[44]Benedict, "Confessionalization in France?" 48, 50.

[45]Farr, "Confessionalization and Social Discipline in France," 291.

[46]For Italy and Iberia, see Comerford, "Did Tuscan Dioceses Confessionalize?"; Reinhardt, "Rom im Zeitalter der Konfessionalisierung"; and Poska, "Confessionalization and Social Discipline in the Iberian World."

[47]Pettegree, "Confessionalization in North Western Europe," 119.

development in Ireland is best described as a process of double or dual confessionalization. Ireland became biconfessional after the introduction of the Protestant Reformation because the majority of the population remained Catholic, which led to two competing confessionalization processes in the late sixteenth and early seventeenth centuries. While the Protestant process of confessionalization was state-sponsored, the Catholic process of confessionalization came from below, initiated by the traditional elites who used Parliament or rebellion to voice their demands.[48]

All in all, it becomes clear that applying the concept of confessionalization to case studies of German territories and other European areas has resulted in some refinement—or redefinition—of the concept. Above all, it is striking that historians with very different specialties agree that there was hardly ever a successful connection between confession-building and state formation. Rather, different constellations have to be taken into account: confessionalizing intentions by the state with no or little success; different forms of resistance and opposition to state-sponsored processes of confessionalization; different agents such as estates, urban elites, and the populace; and above all, various forms of confession-building; and the formation of confessional identities independent of state influence. These last two points have inspired recent research,[49] so that on the one hand, religious communities like the Mennonites or the Jews, which (according to the original definition of the concept) were not considered to have gone through a process of confessionalization, have been described as confessionalized communities.[50] On the other hand, some authors have rejected the concept of confessional identity altogether.[51]

The question is: where do we go from here?

Future Directions

In the light of recent research, it is no longer possible to see confessionalization as a fundamental process of society, as a modernizing force, or as a process successfully integrating state-building and confessional formation. The result is a concept more limited in scope. And there is, of course, always the question whether and how far a theoretical concept can be redefined, supplemented, or handled more flexibly before there is nothing left

---

[48]See Lotz-Heumann, *Die doppelte Konfessionalisierung in Irland*; and Lotz-Heumann, "Confessionalization in Ireland."

[49]See Pohlig, *Zwischen Gelehrsamkeit*; and Rau, *Geschichte und Konfession*.

[50]See Driedger, *Obedient Heretics*; and Lauer, "Die Konfessionalisierung des Judentums."

[51]See Grochowina, *Indifferenz und Dissens*; and Volkland, *Konfession und Selbstverständnis*.

of the original concept. However, the concept of confessionalization can still serve as a useful heuristic research tool.

It is of course true that questions about popular religiosity, about early modern religion as a phenomenon between individual experience and social communication, about religion as everyday practice, and so forth, can best be answered by employing methods of microhistory. These include thick description and the close analysis of ego-documents and sources that provide glimpses of the everyday life of early modern common people. However, in this way, history and history-writing run the danger of becoming fragmented. Therefore, if we still wish to attempt comparative approaches beyond individual case studies, look at structures, ask macrohistorical questions, and examine long-term developments, the concept of confessionalization can help us do so. By integrating the discussion of political, social, and cultural developments in the sixteenth and seventeenth centuries, this concept enables us to see, for example, possible connections among these different spheres.

Confessionalization also has the advantage of being defined as a process. Thus, "confessionalization" is not the same as "confessionalism" (as it is sometimes translated into English). The term "confessionalization" draws attention to the developments that led to confession-building and the construction of confessional cultures and identities by different agents. Moreover, the development of confessional *propria*, of different confessional cultures, was an essential ingredient of confessionalization as a process of confessional differentiation. Applying the concept of confessionalization should therefore entail analyzing parallels between, as well as specifics of, the early modern confessional churches and cultures; for example, parallel strategies could be effected by different means. In this context, the methods of confessionalization identified by Wolfgang Reinhard remain useful as a guideline. At the same time, new research—and in particular new case studies—can identify other methods of confessionalization and gauge their effectiveness, as well as discuss and categorize the reactions and possible strategies of avoidance they provoked.

Scholars now know that opposition to centralized state-building and confessionalization from above was widespread, possibly even universal, in early modern Europe. We have also come to realize that confessional conflicts and confessional cultures could be the result of local and regional developments, rather than of state influence from above. As a consequence, the relationship between state formation and confession-building as part of the concept of confessionalization must be construed much more flexibly. First, opposition and resistance to measures by state and church must move to the forefront of research. Second, we must ask whether even measures from above that were not effective did in fact have unintended effects: even if such measures remained only declarations of intent, they were perceived as potentials or threats to which people may have reacted in some way. Third, we will have to look away from the question of "success and failure" of confessionalization altogether and look instead at different agents and their interests in the process of confessionalization. Social formations like confessional churches, cultures, or identities could, after all, only come into being and continue to exist if they were reinforced again and again through interaction and communication. As research into the state is also changing, so that the early modern state is seen not as an entity but as fragmented into different agents, it becomes possible to look at various agents and their interests in state and society and thus at the role of individuals and different social groups. Consequently, a microhistory of the state can be combined with a microhistory of social and cultural phenomena to describe the process of confessionalization as one of conflict, negotiation, and accommodation. Fourth, such a modified approach raises, among others, the question of horizontal confessionalization within social groups[52] and of self-confessionalization, about which little is known so far. It is clear that elites on all levels of society played an important role in the process, but it is so far largely unknown how confessional identities and confessional cultures—on the eventual existence of which current research largely agrees—came into being.

Finally, research into the creation of confessional cultures and identities can profit from using confessionalization as a framework and research tool because the concept offers a wide approach. It integrates political, social, and cultural developments, analyzing their interaction, and as a developmental concept, it focuses on processes of cultural construction and (attempted) diffusion in society. Recent research has shown that the process of confessionalization extended far into the eighteenth century. Scholars can therefore ask questions like "What is the relationship between confessionalization and secularization?" again, but from a different angle—not as a macrohistorical thesis, but as a research problem that looks in detail at the processes and agents that constructed religious and secular meanings in the early modern period.

---

[52]Schnabel-Schüle, "Vierzig Jahre Konfessionalisierungsforschung," 37.

Bibliography

ELECTRONIC RESOURCES

Forum "Confessionalization". *H-German* (April 2005):
http://www.h-net.org/~german/discuss/Confessionalization/Confess_index.htm

PRINTED SOURCES

Bahlcke, Joachim, and Arno Strohmeyer, eds. *Konfessionalisierung in Ostmitteleuropa: Wirkungen des religiösen Wandels im 16. und 17. Jahrhundert in Staat, Gesellschaft und Kultur.* Stuttgart: Steiner, 1999.

Benedict, Philip. "Confessionalization in France? Critical Reflections and New Evidence." In *Society and Culture in the Huguenot World 1559–1685,* edited by Raymond A. Mentzer and Andrew Spicer, 44–61. Cambridge: Cambridge University Press, 2002.

Brady, Thomas A., Jr. "Confessionalization: The Career of a Concept." In *Confessionalization in Europe, 1555–1700: Essays in Memory of Bodo Nischan,* edited by John M. Headley, Hans J. Hillerbrand, and Anthony Papalas, 1–20. Aldershot: Ashgate, 2004.

Chaix, Gérald. "La confessionnalisation. Note critique." *Bulletin de la Société de l'Histoire du Protestantisme Français* 148 (2002): 851–65.

Comerford, Kathleen M. "Did Tuscan Dioceses Confessionalize in the Sixteenth and Seventeenth Centuries?" *Journal of Early Modern History* 7 (2003): 312–31.

Dietz, Burkhard, and Stefan Ehrenpreis, eds. *Drei Konfessionen in einer Region: Beiträge zur Geschichte der Konfessionalisierung im Herzogtum Berg vom 16. bis zum 18. Jahrhundert.* Cologne: Rheinland-Verlag, 1999.

Driedger, Michael D. *Obedient Heretics: Mennonite Identities in Lutheran Hamburg and Altona during the Confessional Age.* Aldershot: Ashgate, 2002.

Eberhard, Winfried. "Voraussetzungen und strukturelle Grundlagen der Konfessionalisierung in Ostmitteleuropa." In *Konfessionalisierung in Ostmitteleuropa: Wirkungen des religiösen Wandels im 16. und 17. Jahrhundert in Staat, Gesellschaft und Kultur,* edited by Joachim Bahlcke and Arno Strohmeyer, 89–103. Stuttgart: Steiner, 1999.

Ehrenpreis, Stefan. "Konfessionalisierung von unten: Konzeption und Thematik eines bergischen Modells?" In *Drei Konfessionen in einer Region: Beiträge zur Geschichte der Konfessionalisierung im Herzogtum Berg vom 16. bis zum 18. Jahrhundert,* edited by Burkhard Dietz and Stefan Ehrenpreis, 3–13. Cologne: Rheinland-Verlag, 1999.

———, and Ute Lotz-Heumann. *Reformation und konfessionelles Zeitalter.* Kontroversen um die Geschichte. Darmstadt: Wissenschaftliche Buchgesellschaft, 2002.

Farr, James R. "Confessionalization and Social Discipline in France, 1530–1685." *Archiv für Reformationsgeschichte* 94 (2003): 276–93.

Forster, Marc R. *Catholic Revival in the Age of the Baroque: Religious Identity in Southwest Germany, 1550–1750.* Cambridge: Cambridge University Press, 2001.

———. *The Counter-Reformation in the Villages: Religion and Reform in the Bishopric of Speyer, 1560–1720.* Ithaca, London: Cornell University Press, 1992.

Freitag, Werner. "Konfliktfelder und Konfliktparteien im Prozeß der lutherischen und reformierten Konfessionalisierung—das Fürstentum Anhalt und die Hochstifte Halberstadt und Magdeburg im 16. Jahrhundert." *Archiv für Reformationsgeschichte* 92 (2001): 165–94.

———. *Pfarrer, Kirche und ländliche Gesellschaft: Das Dekanat Vechta 1400–1803.* Bielefeld: Verlag für Regionalgeschichte, 1998.

Frieß, Peer, and Rolf Kießling, eds. *Konfessionalisierung und Region*. Konstanz: Universitätsverlag Konstanz, 1999.

Greyerz, Kaspar von, Manfred Jakubowski-Tiessen, Thomas Kaufmann, and Hartmut Lehmann, eds. *Interkonfessionalität—Transkonfessionalität—binnenkonfessionelle Pluralität: Neue Forschungen zur Konfessionalisierungsthese*. Gütersloh: Gütersloher Verlagshaus, 2003.

Grochowina, Nicole. *Indifferenz und Dissens in der Grafschaft Ostfriesland im 16. und 17. Jahrhundert*. Frankfurt am Main: Lang, 2003.

Hanlon, Gregory. *Confession and Community in Seventeenth-Century France: Catholic and Protestant Coexistence in Aquitaine*. Philadelphia: University of Pennsylvania Press, 1993.

Harrington, Joel F., and Helmut Walser Smith. "Confessionalization, Community, and State Building in Germany, 1555–1870." *Journal of Modern History* 69 (1997): 77–101.

Head, Randolph C. "Catholics and Protestants in Graubünden: Confessional Discipline and Confessional Identities without an Early Modern State?" *German History* 17 (1999): 321–45.

Headley, John M., Hans J. Hillerbrand, and Anthony Papalas, eds. *Confessionalization in Europe, 1555–1700: Essays in Memory of Bodo Nischan*. Aldershot: Ashgate, 2004.

Heckel, Martin. *Deutschland im konfessionellen Zeitalter*. Deutsche Geschichte 5. Göttingen: Vandenhoeck & Ruprecht, 1983.

Holt, Mack P. "Confessionalization beyond the Germanies: The Case of France." In *Confessionalization in Europe, 1555–1700: Essays in Memory of Bodo Nischan*, edited by John M. Headley, Hans J. Hillerbrand, and Anthony Papalas, 257–73. Aldershot: Ashgate, 2004.

Holzem, Andreas. "Die Konfessionsgesellschaft: Christenleben zwischen staatlichem Bekenntniszwang und religiöser Heilshoffnung." *Zeitschrift für Kirchengeschichte* 110 (1999): 53–85.

———. *Religion und Lebensformen: Katholische Konfessionalisierung im Sendgericht des Fürstbistums Münster 1570–1800*. Paderborn: Schöningh, 2000.

Jedin, Hubert. *Katholische Reformation oder Gegenreformation? Ein Versuch zur Klärung der Begriffe nebst einer Jubiläumsbetrachtung über das Trienter Konzil*. Luzern: Stocker, 1946.

Kaplan, Benjamin J. *Calvinists and Libertines: Confession and Community in Utrecht, 1578–1620*. Oxford: Clarendon Press, 1995.

Kaufmann, Thomas. "Die Konfessionalisierung von Kirche und Gesellschaft: Sammelbericht über eine Forschungsdebatte." *Theologische Literaturzeitung* 121 (1996): 1008–25, 1112–21.

———. *Dreißigjähriger Krieg und Westfälischer Friede: Kirchengeschichtliche Studien zur lutherischen Konfessionskultur*. Tübingen: Mohr Siebeck, 1998.

———. "Einleitung: Transkonfessionalität, Interkonfessionalität, binnenkonfessionelle Pluralität—Neue Forschungen zur Konfessionalisierungsthese." In *Interkonfessionalität—Transkonfessionalität—binnenkonfessionelle Pluralität: Neue Forschungen zur Konfessionalisierungsthese*, edited by Kaspar von Greyerz, Manfred Jakubowski-Tiessen, Thomas Kaufmann, and Hartmut Lehmann, 9–15. Gütersloh: Gütersloher Verlagshaus, 2003.

Kittelson, James M. "The Confessional Age: The Late Reformation in Germany." In *Reformation Europe: A Guide to Research*, edited by Steven Ozment, 361–81. St. Louis: Center for Reformation Research, 1982.

Klueting, Harm. *Das Konfessionelle Zeitalter 1525–1648*. Stuttgart: Ulmer, 1989.

———. "'Zweite Reformation'—Konfessionsbildung—Konfessionalisierung: Zwanzig Jahre Kontroversen und Ergebnisse nach zwanzig Jahren." *Historische Zeitschrift* 277 (2003): 309–41.

La confessionnalisation dans le Saint Empire XVIe–XVIIe siècles: Journées d'étude de novembre 2001 (Sorbonne/CIÉRA). Edited by Patrice Veit and Jean-Marie Valentin. *Études Germaniques* 57 (2002): 395–576.

Lauer, Gerhard. "Die Konfessionalisierung des Judentums: Zum Prozeß der religiösen Ausdifferenzierung im Judentum am Übergang zur Neuzeit." In *Interkonfessionalität— Transkonfessionalität—binnenkonfessionelle Pluralität: Neue Forschungen zur Konfessionalisierungsthese*, edited by Kaspar von Greyerz, Manfred Jakubowski-Tiessen, Thomas Kaufmann, and Hartmut Lehmann, 250–83. Gütersloh: Gütersloher Verlagshaus, 2003.

Lehmann, Hartmut. "Grenzen der Erklärungskraft der Konfessionalisierungsthese." In *Interkonfessionalität—Transkonfessionalität—binnenkonfessionelle Pluralität: Neue Forschungen zur Konfessionalisierungsthese*, edited by Kaspar von Greyerz, Manfred Jakubowski-Tiessen, Thomas Kaufmann, and Hartmut Lehmann, 242–49. Gütersloh: Gütersloher Verlagshaus, 2003.

Lotz-Heumann, Ute. "The Concept of "Confessionalization": A Historiographical Paradigm in Dispute." *Memoria y Civilización* 4 (2001): 93–114.

———. "Confessionalization." In *The Encyclopedia of Protestantism*, edited by Hans J. Hillerbrand, 1:497–501. New York: Routledge, 2004.

———. "Confessionalization in Ireland. Periodization and Character." In *The Origins of Sectarianism in Early Modern Ireland, 1500–1700*, edited by Alan Ford and John McCafferty, 24–53. Cambridge: Cambridge University Press, 2005.

———. *Die doppelte Konfessionalisierung in Irland: Konflikt und Koexistenz im 16. und in der ersten Hälfte des 17. Jahrhunderts*. Tübingen: Mohr Siebeck, 2000.

———, and Matthias Pohlig. "Confessionalization and Literature in the Empire, 1555–1700." *Central European History* 40 (2007): 35–61.

Mörke, Olaf. "Die politische Bedeutung des Konfessionellen im Deutschen Reich und in der Republik der Vereinigten Niederlande. Oder: War die Konfessionalisierung ein 'Fundamentalvorgang'?" In *Der Absolutismus—ein Mythos? Strukturwandel monarchischer Herrschaft in West- und Mitteleuropa (ca. 1550–1700)*, edited by Ronald G. Asch and Heinz Duchhardt, 125–64. Cologne: Böhlau, 1996.

Müller, Michael G. *Zweite Reformation und ständische Autonomie im Königlichen Preußen: Danzig, Elbing und Thorn in der Epoche der Konfessionalisierung (1557–1660)*. Berlin: Akademie-Verlag, 1997.

Müller, Michael G. "Unionsstaat und Region in der Konfessionalisierung: Polen-Litauen und die großen Städte des Königlichen Preußen." In *Konfessionalisierung in Ostmitteleuropa: Wirkungen des religiösen Wandels im 16. und 17. Jahrhundert in Staat, Gesellschaft und Kultur*, edited by Joachim Bahlcke and Arno Strohmeyer, 123–37. Stuttgart: Steiner, 1999.

Nischan, Bodo. *Lutherans and Calvinists in the Age of Confessionalism*. Aldershot: Ashgate, 1999.

———. *Prince, People and Confession: The Second Reformation in Brandenburg*. Philadelphia: University of Pennsylvania Press, 1994.

Ohlidal, Anna. "'Konfessionalisierung': Ein historisches Paradigma auf dem Weg von der Sozialgeschichte zur Kulturwissenschaft?" *Acta Comeniana* 15–16 (2002): 327–42.

O'Malley, John W. *Trent and All That: Renaming Catholicism in the Early Modern Period*. Cambridge, MA: Harvard University Press, 2000.

Pettegree, Andrew. "Confessionalization in North Western Europe." In *Konfessionalisierung in Ostmitteleuropa: Wirkungen des religiösen Wandels im 16. und 17. Jahrhundert in Staat, Gesellschaft und Kultur*, edited by Joachim Bahlcke and Arno Strohmeyer, 105–20. Stuttgart: Steiner, 1999.

Plaggenborg, Stefan. "Konfessionalisierung in Osteuropa im 17. Jahrhundert: Zur Reichweite eines Forschungskonzeptes." *Bohemia* 44 (2003): 3–28.

Pohlig, Matthias. *Zwischen Gelehrsamkeit und konfessioneller Identitätsstiftung: Lutherische Kirchen- und Universalgeschichtsschreibung 1546–1617*, Tübingen: Mohr Siebeck, 2007.

Poska, Allyson M. "Confessionalization and Social Discipline in the Iberian World." *Archiv für Reformationsgeschichte* 94 (2003): 308–19.

Rau, Susanne. *Geschichte und Konfession: Städtische Geschichtsschreibung und Erinnerungskultur im Zeitalter der Reformation und Konfessionalisierung in Bremen, Breslau, Hamburg und Köln*. Hamburg: Dölling und Galitz, 2002.

Reinhard, Wolfgang. "Gegenreformation als Modernisierung? Prolegomena zu einer Theorie des konfessionellen Zeitalters." *Archiv für Reformationsgeschichte* 68 (1977): 226–52.

———. "Konfession und Konfessionalisierung in Europa." In *Bekenntnis und Geschichte: Die Confessio Augustana im historischen Zusammenhang*, edited by Wolfgang Reinhard, 165–89. Munich: Vögel, 1981.

———. "Reformation, Counter-Reformation, and the Early Modern State: A Reassessment." *The Catholic Historical Review* 75 (1989): 383–404.

———. "Was ist katholische Konfessionalisierung?" In *Die katholische Konfessionalisierung: Wissenschaftliches Symposion der Gesellschaft zur Herausgabe des Corpus Catholicorum und des Vereins für Reformationsgeschichte*, edited by Wolfgang Reinhard and Heinz Schilling, 419–52. Gütersloh: Gütersloher Verlagshaus, 1995.

———. "Zwang zur Konfessionalisierung? Prolegomena zu einer Theorie des konfessionellen Zeitalters." *Zeitschrift für historische Forschung* 10 (1983): 257–77.

Reinhard, Wolfgang, and Heinz Schilling, eds. *Die katholische Konfessionalisierung: Wissenschaftliches Symposion der Gesellschaft zur Herausgabe des Corpus Catholicorum und des Vereins für Reformationsgeschichte*. Gütersloh: Gütersloher Verlagshaus, 1995.

Reinhardt, Volker. "Rom im Zeitalter der Konfessionalisierung: Kritische Überlegungen zu einem Epochendeutungskonzept." *Zeitsprünge: Forschungen zur Frühen Neuzeit* 7 (2003): 1–18.

Rublack, Hans-Christoph, ed. *Die lutherische Konfessionalisierung in Deutschland: Wissenschaftliches Symposion des Vereins für Reformationsgeschichte 1988*. Gütersloh: Gütersloher Verlagshaus, 1992.

Rummel, Erika. *The Confessionalization of Humanism in Reformation Germany*. Oxford: Oxford University Press, 2000.

Schilling, Heinz. "Confessional Europe." In *Handbook of European History 1400–1600: Late Middle Ages, Renaissance and Reformation*. Vol. 2, *Visions, Programs and Outcomes*, edited by Thomas A. Brady, Jr., Heiko A. Oberman, and James D. Tracy, 641–75. Leiden: Brill, 1995.

———. "Confessionalization: Historical and Scholarly Perspectives of a Comparative and Interdisciplinary Paradigm." In *Confessionalization in Europe, 1555–1700: Essays in*

Memory of Bodo Nischan, edited by John M. Headley, Hans J. Hillerbrand, and Anthony Papalas, 21–35. Aldershot: Ashgate, 2004.

———. "Confessionalization in the Empire: Religious and Societal Change in Germany between 1555 and 1620." In Schilling, *Religion, Political Culture and the Emergence of Early Modern Society: Essays in German and Dutch History*, 205–45. Leiden: Brill, 1992.

———. "Die Konfessionalisierung im Reich: Religiöser und gesellschaftlicher Wandel in Deutschland zwischen 1555 und 1620." *Historische Zeitschrift* 246 (1988): 1–45.

———. "Die Konfessionalisierung von Kirche, Staat und Gesellschaft: Profil, Leistung, Defizite und Perspektiven eines geschichtswissenschaftlichen Paradigmas." In *Die katholische Konfessionalisierung: Wissenschaftliches Symposion der Gesellschaft zur Herausgabe des Corpus Catholicorum und des Vereins für Reformationsgeschichte*, edited by Wolfgang Reinhard and Heinz Schilling, 1–49. Gütersloh: Gütersloher Verlagshaus, 1995.

———. *Konfessionskonflikt und Staatsbildung: Eine Fallstudie über das Verhältnis von religiösem und sozialem Wandel in der Frühneuzeit am Beispiel der Grafschaft Lippe.* Gütersloh: Gütersloher Verlagshaus, 1981.

———, ed. *Die reformierte Konfessionalisierung in Deutschland—Das Problem der "Zweiten Reformation": Wissenschaftliches Symposion des Vereins für Reformationsgeschichte 1985.* Gütersloh: Gütersloher Verlagshaus, 1986.

Schindling, Anton. "Konfessionalisierung und Grenzen von Konfessionalisierbarkeit." In *Die Territorien des Reichs im Zeitalter der Reformation und Konfessionalisierung: Land und Konfession 1500–1650.* Vol. 7, *Bilanz—Forschungsperspektiven—Register*, edited by Anton Schindling and Walter Ziegler, 9–44. Münster: Aschendorff, 1997.

Schlögl, Rudolf. "Differenzierung und Integration: Konfessionalisierung im frühneuzeitlichen Gesellschaftssystem: Das Beispiel der habsburgischen Vorlande." *Archiv für Reformationsgeschichte* 91 (2000): 238–84.

Schmidt, Heinrich Richard. *Dorf und Religion: Reformierte Sittenzucht in Berner Landgemeinden der Frühen Neuzeit.* Stuttgart: Gustav Fischer, 1995.

———. *Konfessionalisierung im 16. Jahrhundert.* Munich: Oldenbourg, 1992.

———. "Sozialdisziplinierung? Ein Plädoyer für das Ende des Etatismus in der Konfessionalisierungsforschung." *Historische Zeitschrift* 265 (1997): 639–82.

Schnabel-Schüle, Helga. "Vierzig Jahre Konfessionalisierungsforschung: Eine Standortbestimmung." In *Konfessionalisierung und Region*, edited by Peer Frieß and Rolf Kießling, 23–40. Konstanz: Universitätsverlag Konstanz, 1999.

Schorn-Schütte, Luise. "Konfessionalisierung als wissenschaftliches Paradigma?" In *Konfessionalisierung in Ostmitteleuropa: Wirkungen des religiösen Wandels im 16. und 17. Jahrhundert in Staat, Gesellschaft und Kultur*, edited by Joachim Bahlcke and Arno Strohmeyer, 63–77. Stuttgart: Steiner, 1999.

Schulze, Winfried. "Gerhard Oestreichs Begriff 'Sozialdisziplinierung in der Frühen Neuzeit.'" *Zeitschrift für historische Forschung* 14 (1987): 265–302.

———. "Konfessionalisierung als Paradigma zur Erforschung des konfessionellen Zeitalters." In *Drei Konfessionen in einer Region: Beiträge zur Geschichte der Konfessionalisierung im Herzogtum Berg vom 16. bis zum 18. Jahrhundert*, edited by Burkhard Dietz and Stefan Ehrenpreis, 15–30. Cologne: Rheinland-Verlag, 1999.

Stolleis, Michael. "'Konfessionalisierung' oder 'Säkularisierung' bei der Entstehung des frühmodernen Staates." *Ius Commune: Zeitschrift für Europäische Rechtsgeschichte* 20 (1993): 1–23.

Volkland, Frauke. *Konfession und Selbstverständnis: Reformierte Rituale in der gemischtkonfessionellen Kleinstadt Bischofszell im 17. Jahrhundert.* Göttingen: Vandenhoeck & Ruprecht, 2005.

Zeeden, Ernst Walter. "Grundlagen und Wege der Konfessionsbildung im Zeitalter der Glaubenskämpfe." *Historische Zeitschrift* 185 (1958): 249–99.

Ziegler, Walter. "Kritisches zur Konfessionalisierungsthese." In *Konfessionalisierung und Region,* edited by Peer Frieß and Rolf Kießling, 41–53. Konstanz: Universitätsverlag Konstanz, 1999.

Reformation and Early Modern Europe

a guide to research

PART 2
Regional Trends

7

Central Europe, 1550–1700

Howard Hotson

An Expanding Field

GEOGRAPHICAL SCOPE

No area of Reformation studies has witnessed such profound transformation during the past fifteen years as the region of central Europe. One might even say that when the previous research guide was conceived, "central Europe" did not even exist. In the late 1980s as for decades previously, Europe was sharply divided down the middle by a political, ideological, military, and physical barrier into "eastern Europe" and "western Europe." Then, in the last few months of the decade, these barriers vanished with astonishing speed. By the time the previous research guide was published in 1992, the Berlin Wall had crumbled, East and West Germany had precipitously reunited, the Warsaw Pact had been dissolved, and the Soviet Union had collapsed. As this volume was in the making, the European Union was radically enlarged in 2004 by the accession of a swath of countries reaching from the Baltic to the Adriatic, most of which did not even exist as independent states fifteen years earlier. With the once razor-sharp distinction between "eastern" and "western" Europe thereby rendered permanently anachronistic, a fresh conception of "central Europe" has emerged in its place, with the subcategory of east central Europe conveniently reserved—for the time being at least—for the new accession countries.

The repercussions of these dramatic developments for the study of the equally momentous events of the Reformation period, though by no means instantaneous, promise over the longer term to be profound. For almost half a century during which western historical scholarship was transformed, eastern and western Europe were separated by the most significant political and ideological barrier in the world. While ideology distorted historiography, particularly on the eastern side of that barrier, the barrier itself distorted historiography on the western side. For evidence of the latter distortion, one need look no further than the previous two research guides, where no room was found for a chapter on the Reformation in Germany's eastern neighbors: Poland, Bohemia, or Hungary.[1]

A distortion that was half a century in the making will take decades to correct, but this process is now well under way.[2] As a new generation of historians from this region revisits neglected aspects of their own history and absorbs recent developments in western historiography, "eastern" and "western" scholars have more and more to communicate with one another. As the linguistic orientation of east central Europe shifts from Russian to German and English, scholarly communication across the Slavic language barrier is being enhanced. As the European Union embraces east central Europe, west European scholars are bound to take a greater interest in east central European history. Already, chapters on this region have become obligatory in collaboratively authored surveys of the Reformation era.[3] More recently, histories of the reformations in Poland,[4] the Czech lands,[5] and Hungary[6] have begun to appear in English and German, superseding

[1]In attempting to make good this deficit here, this chapter is much beholden to Karin Friedrich (Aberdeen), Graeme Murdock (Birmingham), and Vladimír Urbánek (Prague) for guidance on Polish, Hungarian, and Czech material, respectively.

[2]For a recent historiographic stocktaking, see Murdock, "Central and Eastern Europe."

[3]On Bohemia, see, for instance, Eberhard, "Bohemia, Moravia and Austria"; Kavka, "Bohemia"; and Palmitessa, "Reformation in Bohemia and Poland." On Hungary, see Daniel, "Hungary"; Peter, "Hungary"; and Tóth, "Old and New Faith in Hungary, Turkish Hungary, and Transylvania." On Poland, see Tazbir, "Poland"; and Palmitessa, "Reformation in Bohemia and Poland." And on east central Europe in general, see Eberhard, "Reformation and Counterreformation in East Central Europe"; and Murdock 2000, "Eastern Europe." Historians have also, per force, made more progress in this difficult task; cf. Evans, "Calvinism in East Central Europe"; Benedict, *Christ's Churches Purely Reformed*, 255–80; and Murdock, *Beyond Calvin*.

[4]Janusz Tazbir's *A State Without Stakes* and Ambrose Jobert's *De Luther à Mohila* can now be supplemented with Jerzy Kłoczowski's *History of Polish Christianity* and Magda Teter's *Jews and Heretics in Catholic Poland*. Christoph Schmidt's *Auf Felsen gesät* should be used with caution. Also useful is Jill Raitt's *Shapers of Religious Traditions in Germany, Switzerland, and Poland*.

[5]For Bohemia, original works in English (e.g., Evans and Thomas, *Crown, Church and Estates*; Fudge, *Magnificent Ride*; and David, *Finding the Middle Way*) are complemented by major Czech works in translation (e.g., Říčan, *History of the Unity of Brethren*; and Šmahel, *Die Hussitische Revolution*).

[6]In addition to older works on Hungary by Mihály Bucsay (*Der Protestantismus in Ungarn*) and Alexander Sándor Unghváry (*Hungarian Protestant Reformation*), see Murdock, *Calvinism on the Frontier*, on Hungary-Transylvania.

or supplementing the isolated works that afforded access to these subjects for decades previously.[7] General surveys of most of these regions in the early modern period have also begun to appear,[8] which, together with similar works on Austria,[9] now provide unprecedented access by non-Slavicists to basic information on east central Europe in the early modern period. A series of massive volumes has also undertaken to survey the cultural history of many of these regions,[10] while the ten-volume series Deutsche Geschichte im Osten Europas, published between 1993 and 1999, has been something of a publishing sensation in Germany.[11] Yet while the potential harvest is plenteous, for the time being the laborers remain rather few. The richest crop of literature accessible to nonspecialists discusses those parts of east central Europe of most immediate concern to their German-speaking neighbors: the Bohemian kingdom within the Holy Roman Empire, the Hungarian dominions of the Austrian Habsburgs, and the extensive Pomeranian and Prussian territories on the southern shore of the Baltic. As a consequence, this essay will also focus on materials pertaining to Germany in the first instance, and to literature on its central European neighbors accessible to nonspecialists in the second.

CHRONOLOGICAL SCOPE

The opening of the eastern frontiers of German Reformation scholarship, however, is only the most dramatic respect in which historical research on

---

[7]For east central Europe in general, see Maag, Reformation in Eastern and Central Europe; and Bahlcke, Lambrecht, and Maner, Konfessionelle Pluralität.

[8]On Poland-Lithuania, see Butterwick, Polish-Lithuanian Monarchy; Niendorf, Das Grossfürstentum Litauen; and Müller, Handbuch für Geschichte Polens. For Bohemia, the older work edited by Karl Bosl (Handbuch der Geschichte der böhmischen Länder) can be updated with reference to Joachim Bahlcke's 1994 Regionalismus und Staatsintegration im Widerstreit. For Hungary, cf. Fata, Ungarn, das Reich der Stephanskrone; and Kosa, Cultural History of Hungary. Competing three-volume histories of Transylvania—one Hungarian, the other Romanian—are currently appearing in English translation: Köpeczi, History of Transylvania; and Pop and Nägler, History of Transylvania.

[9]R. J. W. Evans' Making of the Habsburg Monarchy (easily the richest synthesis on this subject for a quarter century) has been joined by Thomas Winkelbauer's Ständfreiheit und Fürstenmacht (a massive survey of all the lands and subjects of the House of Austria in the confessional era, with extensive and up-to-date bibliographies).

[10]Garber, Komorowski, and Walter, Kulturgeschichte Ostpreußens in der Frühen Neuzeit; Garber and Klöker, Kulturgeschichte der baltischen Länder; Beckmann and Garber, Kulturgeschichte Preußens königlich polnischen Anteils; and Garber, Kulturgeschichte Schlesiens. Cf. Kosa, Cultural History of Hungary.

[11]Volumes in this series include Boockmann, Ostpreußen und Westpreußen; Prinz, Böhmen und Mähren; Pistohlkors, Baltische Länder; Conrads, Schlesien; Schödl, Land an der Donau; Rogall, Land der großen Ströme: Von Polen nach Litauen; Stricker, Rußland; Suppan, Zwischen Adria und Karawanken; Röskau-Rydel, Galizien, Bukowina, Moldau; and Buchholz, Pommern.

this region has been transformed in the past fifteen years. The chronological as well as geographical scope of this field has also radically expanded. In the single chapter on this region in Ozment's and Maltby's previous guides to Reformation Europe, James M. Kittelson described the historiography of the latter sixteenth century in Germany as "a virtual wasteland."[12] In the past fifteen years, however, the concentration of attention has palpably shifted. For the first time since modern study of the Reformation era began, the chronological focus of research on Germany has moved from the dramatic events of the early sixteenth century to the traditionally neglected processes of the subsequent period. In a general sense, this shift is in line with a broader European trend stemming from the Annales school, which has devoted increasing attention to the popular reception of the Reformation over the longer term (the very topic examined by Kittelson), and which has tended to regard Protestant and Catholic reforms as parallel rather than antithetical.[13] Within Germany, this shift of emphasis and chronological focus has been stimulated in particular by the confessionalization thesis—a thesis of such widespread influence on the study of religion, society, and politics in post-Reformation Germany in recent years that it has rightly been afforded separate treatment in this volume. Noteworthy here is the fact that both the confessionalization thesis itself and the broader investigation of religious and confessional identities have spread to east central Europe as well.[14]

TOPICAL RANGE

This widening chronological scope has also helped create space for a commensurate expansion of thematic breadth. As even the title of this current guide to research suggests, this expansion is in keeping with broader European trends; but here again these have been reinforced by peculiarly German developments. The first half of the sixteenth century in Germany was undeniably dominated by the drama of the Reformation, the ramifications of which continued to unfold in the subsequent period. Yet when the early Reformation is placed in the context of early modern German history as a whole, a host of other issues and developments traditionally neglected by Reformation scholars immediately clamor for attention. Despite the fact

---

[12]Kittelson, "Confessional Age," 361.

[13]Milestones in this tradition include Delumeau, *Catholicisme entre Luther et Voltaire*; and Bossy, *Christianity in the West*. For a recent synthesis, see Wallace, *The Long European Reformation*.

[14]Notably in Bahlcke, *Konfessionalisierung in Ostmitteleurop*; Andor and Tóth, *Frontiers of Faith*; and Craciun, Ghitta, and Murdock, *Confessional Identity in East-Central Europe*.

that the shift in chronological focus was propelled by the restrictive agenda of the confessionalization thesis and focused on issues directly related to the Reformation, its longer-term effect has been progressively to enrich the range of themes being pursued in the field of early modern central European studies.

A first stage of this thematic expansion is clearly evident in an innovative historical project that has become a central fixture of historical education in Germany over the past fifteen years: the *Enzyklopädie deutscher Geschichte* (hereafter *EDG*).[15] The *EDG* is not an encyclopedia of the traditional kind, but a series of about one hundred similarly structured volumes which collectively attempt to analyze the whole of German history in systematic fashion. The series as a whole divides German history into three traditional periods: medieval, early modern, and modern. Each period is then split into six major topics: society, economy, culture, religion, politics, and international relations. These topics are further subdivided into particular themes, and each theme is explored in a brief volume of about 150 pages consisting of three parts: an encyclopedic overview of the topic in question, a central historiographical discussion of basic problems and current research trends, and a systematically organized bibliography. The strengths of this approach are considerable. The basic format offers the researcher an extremely efficient introduction to a new field, further accelerated by the fact that the topics of each paragraph are identified by marginal headings. The individual volumes are quite up-to-date: of the thirty-three early modern volumes planned, twenty-eight have now been published (most during the early 1990s), while some are now in their second or even third impression. The division of all three periods into similar topics also facilitates the study of longer historical developments. The three volumes on the Jews, for instance, survey the troubled history of that community in medieval, early modern, and modern Germany. For researchers exploring specializations tangential to their own, whether at the undergraduate, graduate, or postdoctoral level, these volumes are an invaluable resource.

The extreme systematization of this approach, however, also has its drawbacks. The imposition of a uniform set of topics onto radically different periods inevitably distorts developments peculiar to individual epochs. There is little room in such a system, for instance, for the enormous

---

[15]For detailed descriptions of individual volumes, see http://www.oldenbourg.de/verlag/lehr-buch-prospekt.

proliferation of literature surrounding the Thirty Years' War[16] or witch-hunting in early modern Germany,[17] to mention only two of the best-established topics in post-Reformation German history. Moreover, since the system of organization underlying the series was conceived in the 1980s, the distribution of emphasis within the series as a whole is more dated than the individual volumes that comprise it. In keeping with the social-scientific tendency of much previous postwar German historiography (including the confessionalization thesis itself), a dozen volumes—over a third of the entire early modern series—are devoted to society, including princely courts, the nobility, cities, the peasantry (two volumes), poverty and marginal groups, women and gender, the Jews, riot and revolt, military developments, demography, and the environment. Ten further volumes are devoted to economic history (including the agrarian economy, manufacturing, and commerce) and the political and constitutional topics previously dominant (the constitution of the Reich and its constituent parts, and its place within the evolving international state system).[18] Surprisingly, this leaves only four volumes for religion and church: one on the Reformation itself, another on confessionalization, a third on church, state, and society in the seventeenth and eighteenth centuries, and a fourth on religious movements. Only half a dozen volumes are reserved for "Kultur, Alltag, Mentalitäten," and half of these are on well-established topics ("Bildung und Wissenschaft" and the Enlightenment), leaving only three volumes for the more innovative subjects of media, and the everyday lives and cultures of urban elites and of the lower social orders respectively.

Needless to say, traditional narrative history (long spurned by serious German historians) has virtually no place within this encyclopedia at all. More importantly still, a huge range of topics and approaches fit uncomfortably within this rigid conceptual matrix and have been marginalized within the *EDG* or excluded altogether. Moreover, if one is to judge from the more compact introduction to early modern history published by the same press and coauthored by a large number of mostly younger German

---

[16]Literature on the Thirty Years' War ranges from fresh new synopses (Asch, *Thirty Years' War*; and Parker, *Thirty Years' War*) to the three huge and beautifully illustrated volumes marking the three hundred fiftieth anniversary of the Peace of Westphalia (Bußman and Schilling, *1648: War and Peace in Europe*). The parallel military events in northeastern Europe have also been the subject of a pioneering synthesis in Frost, *The Northern Wars*.

[17]See the essay by Erik Midelfort in this volume.

[18]A major addition to the English literature on these subjects is Scribner and Ogilvie, *Germany: A New Social and Economic History*.

historians, German historiography is rapidly moving beyond the structuralist assumptions underlying the *EDG*.[19] After the exhausting labors of attempting, with the help of tools and methods from the social sciences, to reach generalizations about parallel developments within the innumerable political entities of the Holy Roman Empire, a younger generation of historians appears to have embraced microhistory as a fresh approach to old problems that liberates them from the necessity of reaching generalized conclusions.

The proliferation of fresh topics and approaches in early modern central European studies, it therefore appears, is an ongoing process that is still gaining ground. Unlike the confessionalization thesis and the broader structuralist historiography of which it is a part, this thematic expansion is not being driven by any one interpretive paradigm and is therefore far too variegated to be adequately surveyed here. Using as a touchstone the extension and expansion of a few topics related to previous Reformation historiography will nevertheless provide some impression of its scope and potential importance. Protestant Scholasticism, for instance, once universally decried as a degeneration from the evangelical insights of the great reformers, is now being rehabilitated as a flexible and creative intellectual tradition, especially among historians of Reformed theology.[20] Renaissance humanism, once pronounced dead with the death of Erasmus, is now seen by many scholars as undergoing a final flourishing in the decades around 1600, though a consensus regarding its vitality has as yet proved elusive.[21] The irenical, conciliatory strands of contemporary thought and practice—formerly associated with humanism and seemingly running counter to the confessional imperatives of the age—have also attracted a surge of recent work,[22] due not least to the expansion of the

---

[19]Völker-Rasor, *Frühe Neuzeit*.

[20]See especially the massive statement in Muller, *Post-Reformation Reformed Dogmatics*, and his complementary *Dictionary of Latin and Greek Theological Terms*. See also Trueman and Clark, *Protestant Scholasticism*; and Asselt and Dekker, *Reformation and Scholasticism*.

[21]For a fresh restatement of the older approach, see Rummel, *Confessionalization of Humanism in Reformation Germany*. Explorations of alternative perspectives include Fleischer, "Komm in den totgesagten Park und Schau"; Fleischer, *Harvest of Humanism in Central Europe*; Hammerstein and Walther, *Spähumanismus*; Seidel, *Spähumanismus in Schlesien*; Walter, *Spähumanismus und Konfessionspolitik*; Caspary, *Spähumanismus und Reichspatriotismus*; and Strohm, Selderhuis, and Freedman, *Spähumanismus und reformierte Konfession*.

[22]Greyerz, Jakubowski-Tiessen, Kaufmann, and Lehmann, *Interkonfessionalität—Transkonfessionalität—binnenkonfessionelle Pluralität*; Klueting, *Irenik und Antikonfessionalismus*; Louthan and Zachman, *Conciliation and Confession*; and Racaut and Ryrie, *Moderate Voices in the European Reformation*.

field to include the outstanding examples of ethnic and confessional pluralism provided by east central Europe in this period.[23] Far from being
marginal to the period, moreover, much of the most influential irenicism
has been traced to the courts of successive Habsburg emperors Maximilian
II and Rudolf II.[24] In Rudolfine Prague in particular, universalist and irenical strivings were part and parcel of an extraordinarily rich mannerist culture that can be profusely documented in many of the other leading
princely courts of the empire as well.[25] Alongside courts, the innumerable
cities of the empire have become the focus of a scholarly industry.[26] The
intense competition of these archipelagoes of free cities, princely courts,
and religious houses produced an extraordinary proliferation of artistic
and architectural traditions in this region, relatively free from the dominance of a single court style experienced in more centralized monarchies
to the west.[27] In the intellectual sphere, this same competition was
reflected in the foundation of numerous universities and immediately sub-
university *gymnasia illustria* in early modern Germany, which—while still
deplored by many as mere indices of confessional disunity, territorial fragmentation, and incipient princely absolutism—are also increasingly
regarded as the seedbeds of pedagogical and philosophical developments
of great intrinsic richness and international importance.[28] This dense network of competing and collaborating courts and universities also gave rise
to all manner of philosophical currents, including those such as alchemy,

---

[23]Bietenholz, *Daniel Zwicker*; David, *Finding the Middle Way*; Müller, *Irenik als Kommunikations-reform*; and Korthaase, Hauff, and Fritsch, *Comenius und der Weltfriede.*

[24]The paradigm established in Evans' classic portrait *Rudolf II and His World* has been applied to his predecessor, Maximilian II, in Louthan, *Quest for Compromise*; and Fichtner, *Emperor Maximilian II.*

[25]This topic is particularly well illustrated by a series of exhibition catalogs on Prague (Schultze and Fillitz, *Prag um 1600*; and Fučíková, *Rudolf II and Prague*), Braunschweig-Wolfenbüttel (Gatenbröker, *Hofkunst der Spätrenaissance*), Kassel (Borggrefe, Lüpkes, and Ottomeyer, *Moritz der Gelehrte*), Heidelberg (Wolf, *Der Winterkönig*), and Dresden (Syndram and Scherner, *Princely Splendor*; and Watanabe-O'Kelly, *Court Culture in Dresden*). On German courts generally, see also Müller, *Der Fürstenhof in der Frühen Neuzeit.*

[26]For a crisp overview, see Schilling, *Die Stadt in der Frühen Neuzeit.* For an enormous bibliogra-phy, see Stoob, *Bibliographie zur deutschen historischen Städteforschung.*

[27]For a splendid synopsis, see Kaufmann, *Court, Cloister and City.* For bibliographical guidance, see Kaufmann, *Art and Architecture in Central Europe.*

[28]Valuable introductions include Hammerstein, *15. bis 17. Jahrhundert*; Hammerstein, *Bildung und Wissenschaft*; and Schindling, *Bildung und Wissenschaft in der frühen Neuzeit.* For international comparisons, see Ridder-Symoens, *Universities in Early Modern Europe.* A leading monograph series in the history of German universities is Contubernium, published by Franz Steiner Verlag in Stuttgart. On pedagogical developments, see, for instance, Freedman, *Philosophy and the Arts in Central Europe*; and Hotson, *Commonplace Learning.* A sequel to the latter work will follow these developments into the intellectual crisis of the mid-seventeenth century.

astrology, spiritualism, Paracelsianism, and Rosicrucianism which challenge and complicate the characterization of this period as a static and sterile era of orthodoxy.[29] Many of these themes are related in important respects to a fresh set of topics that emerged from the mid-seventeenth century onwards: the international community of pansophists and universal reformers inspired above all by the great Moravian pedagogue and pansophist Jan Amos Comenius, the movement of religious revival known in Germany as Pietism, and the extraordinary synthesis of the greatest German philosophical mind of the era, Gottfried Wilhelm Leibniz.[30]

Clearly, the field described here is not only far larger geographically and chronologically than the older unit of Reformation Germany; it also embraces a far more diverse set of themes and traditions. Equally clearly, much of this rapidly developing field lacks clear synthetic statements and a great deal of exploration is still waiting to be done. But already it is possible to grasp the lineaments of a fresh and synoptic account of the religious, intellectual, and cultural history of central Europe, emancipated from nationalist and confessional historiographies, and relishing the enormous cultural variety created by the very territorial fragmentation that previous historians have so often deplored.

POLITICAL CONTEXT

This enhanced awareness of the rich variety of cultural trends simultaneously present in the innumerable polities of central Europe is, in turn, part of a fourth major development: the growing appreciation of the sprawling political entity that united so many of them, the Holy Roman Empire. Here too, the historiographical tide is responding to profound tectonic shifts in late twentieth-century German history. The empire began its early modern history as the most prestigious political institution in Christendom, at least as far as the formalities of international diplomacy were concerned. Yet as the confessional fragmentations issuing from the Reformation consolidated existing political divisions within the empire, and as these divisions entered into imperial law provisionally in 1555 and perma-

---

[29]Two voluminous and comprehensive surveys are Wollgast, *Philosophie in Deutschland*; and Holzhey and Schmidt-Biggemann, *Das Heilige Römische Reich Deutscher Nation*. See also, Moran, "Patronage and Institutions."

[30]All of these are now relatively well-organized areas of study, notably in the edition of Comenius' *Opera* being produced by the Czech Academy of Sciences, in the *Deutsche Comenius-Gesellschaft*, in the *Historische Kommission zur Erforschung des Pietismus*, and in the Gottfried Wilhelm Leibniz Bibliothek.

nently in 1648, this formal status rang increasingly hollow. For almost three centuries after 1648, a tradition of historical and political thinkers emanating especially from Prussia portrayed the empire's political, confessional, and cultural fragmentation as an unmitigated national disaster; and this view, codified in the mid-nineteenth century, remained dominant until the Second World War. Militarily, the nationalist historians complained, this fragmentation left Germany unable to resist the depredations of centralized and unified states like Sweden under Gustavus Adolphus and especially France under Louis XIV and Napoleon. Politically, this fragmentation diverted Germany from the high road to modernization taken by centralized nation states to the west. And since the nation state was regarded as the bearer of cultural as well as political and economic progress, political fragmentation was equated not only with political backwardness, but with cultural and intellectual backwardness as well.

Here too, relatively recent historical experiences have altered perceptions of the German past in ways that are still working themselves out. The disastrous consequences of German nationalism and militarism in the first half of the twentieth century destroyed the axiomatic association of national unification with political, cultural, and intellectual progress. The devolution of authority to individual *Länder* in the constitution of the Federal Republic of Germany represented, in a sense, a return to regional patterns of government deeply grounded in German history. Finally, the process of European unification in recent decades has provided a fresh perspective on the Holy Roman Empire as an enduring, supranational, multiethnic political institution that kept the peace in central Europe better than any other until the advent of the European Union. Against this backdrop, a wide range of specialists have begun to perceive politically sound and culturally fertile aspects of the Holy Roman Empire overlooked by previous generations of historians.

Even within Germany, this reassessment is still very much ongoing, and as yet relatively little of this new perspective has worked its way into English. For the basic institutional structure of the Holy Roman Empire and its evolution over the early modern period, Peter Wilson has provided an ideal brief introduction.[31] More detail can conveniently be found in Gerhard Oestreich's contribution to the previous edition of *Gebhardt*, the

---

[31]Wilson, *Holy Roman Empire*. Very brief introductions in English include Press, "Holy Roman Empire in German History"; and Press, "Habsburg Lands." Works in German include Schmidt, *Geschichte des Alten Reiches*; Gotthard, *Das Alte Reich*; Hartmann, *Das heilige Römische Reich Deutscher Nation*; and Stollberg-Rilinger, *Das heilige Römische Reich Deutscher Nation*.

relevant volume of the EDG, and a number of recent, brief German introductions.[32] Further introductory resources (although now somewhat
dated) are the dictionary and thematically organized annotated bibliography compiled by Jonathan Zophy.[33] The proceedings of a conference held
in Oxford in 2006 to mark the two-hundredth anniversary of the demise of
the Old Reich should shortly provide a convenient conspectus of this
emerging perspective in English.[34] In the longer term, the volume on the
Holy Roman Empire between 1495 and 1806 being prepared for the
Oxford History of Modern Europe series by Joachim Whaley promises to
provide expert guidance.

Improved Tools

Propelled by fundamental historical as well as historiographical processes,
the geographical, chronological, and thematic expansion and reassessment
of this field over the past fifteen years has opened up a vast field for exploration and analysis. If, as Kittelson rightly claimed in 1982, "Germany in
the second half of the sixteenth century [was] a land of golden opportunity
for students of the Reformation,"[35] then central Europe in the latter sixteenth and seventeenth centuries represents an even more remarkable
opportunity for students of early modern studies a quarter-century later.
The prospects for efficiently exploring this still poorly mapped territory
have been radically improved, moreover, by a fifth and—from a scholarly
point of view—even more fundamental transformation of this field: the
radical improvement during the past two decades of the basic instruments
of interdisciplinary research on early modern central Europe in general
and on Germany in particular. As a result of Germany's long history of
national fragmentation (reaching back to the Reformation era itself) and
the repeated political dislocations of the past century, historians of early
modern Germany have, until recently, had to work with a set of basic tools
inferior in many respects to those of their neighbors to the east as well as to
the west. Thanks to the technological as well as political revolutions of the
past fifteen years, this situation is also rapidly changing for the better. Since
these tools are, in effect, the preconditions for a proper exploration of this
still poorly understood cultural world, the most immediate task of this

---

[32]Oestreich, *Verfassungsgeschichte vom Ende des Mittelalters*; Neuhaus, *Das Reich in the Frühen Neuzeit*; and Duchhardt, *Deutsche Verfassungsgeschichte*.

[33]Zophy, *Holy Roman Empire*; and Zophy, *Annotated Bibliography of the Holy Roman Empire*.

[34]The proceedings are being edited for publication by R. J. W. Evans et al.

[35]Kittelson, "The Confessional Age," 361.

essay is to bring a new generation of graduate students and nonspecialists up to date with the latest basic tools of the trade in this area of early modern studies.

NATIONAL LIBRARIES

No tools of interdisciplinary scholarship are more fundamental than national libraries; and a comparative sketch of the national libraries in central Europe is indicative of the broader histories of scholarly infrastructure in Germany and her eastern neighbors. The Czech national library—the Národní knihovna ČR in Prague—was founded in 1777 on the basis of collections dating back to the foundation of the Charles University in 1348. The roots of the Austrian national library—the Österreichische National-bibliothek in Vienna—can be traced back to the collections that Duke Albrecht III began to assemble in 1349. The origins of the Polish national library, like Polish history generally, are more complicated. The Biblioteka Narodowa in Warsaw derives from the library donated by the noble family of Załuski in 1747; but it shares some of its functions as a national library with the Biblioteka Jagiellońska in Kraków, which has evolved continuously since the foundation of the university there in 1364. Without an ancient university or continuously resident native dynasty of its own, Hungary owes its national library—the Országos Széchényi Könyvtár in Budapest—to the bequest in 1802 of the Hungarian aristocrat whose name it bears, Count Ferenc Széchényi.[36]

The history of the German national library contrasts markedly with those of its neighbors to the east and this for several obvious reasons. As the birthplace of western printing, Germany witnessed a greater flood of early print than anywhere else in Europe. Territorial fragmentation simultaneously multiplied the number of early printing centers, while depriving Germany of national institutions to collect the books produced by them. Not until 1913, in fact, was a single institution—the Deutsche Bibliothek in Leipzig—assigned the task of collecting and cataloguing every book henceforth published in Germany. After the division and reunification of Germany, this function is now divided, in the best federal fashion, between institutions in Leipzig, Frankfurt am Main, and Berlin, which have collectively been rechristened the Deutsche Nationalbibliothek as recently as 2006.

---

[36]Further information on these libraries is available on their respective websites (listed in the bibliography).

In order to coordinate the collection of specialized, *international* academic literature on an ongoing basis, Germany has created a still more devolved national library system known as WEBIS (an acronym formed by combining "web" with BibliotheksInformationsSystem). WEBIS divides the whole of learning into 121 subject areas and geographical regions and then assigns to some forty libraries distributed all over Germany the task of assembling the most comprehensive collections possible of German and foreign literature in those areas. Thus, for instance, theology and religious studies are the responsibility of Tübingen, while the history of science and medicine is collected in Leipzig. Collecting literature on Britain and North America is Göttingen's task, while material on general and German history goes to Munich. As well as describing this system in detail, the central WEBIS website provides opportunities for browsing through it by subject, region, and library. The individual library websites collected there also contain lists of recent acquisitions in their subject areas, and collaborate with one another to create broader information gateways to those subject areas.[37]

More challenging still was the task of retrospectively assembling and cataloguing German books published before 1913, a difficulty which the disasters that engulfed Germany after 1914 did nothing to alleviate. Given the impossibility of bringing a full retrospective collection together in one place, the alternative solution was proposed in 1983 of sharing this responsibility among five different collections. In 1989, these entities came together to form a "virtual national library" known as the Arbeitsgemeinschaft Sammlung Deutscher Drucke (AGSDD). This division of labor bestows a special status on three especially rich German collections of early modern printed books: the Bayerische Staatsbibliothek (BSB) in Munich, which is now, in effect, the German national library for books printed in the fifteenth and sixteenth centuries; the Herzog August Bibliothek (HAB) in Wolfenbüttel, which holds the same status for the seventeenth century; and the Niedersächsische Staats- und Universitätsbibliothek (SUB) in Göttingen for the eighteenth. Together with three other libraries charged with collecting German imprints from 1800 to the present, their joint objective is to assemble, record, preserve, and make publicly available the most comprehensive collection possible of all printed works published in German-speaking countries. Partly for this reason, a good deal of the scholarly

---

[37]See the discussion below under Gateways.

infrastructure of early modern studies in Germany now centers around these three institutions.

RETROSPECTIVE NATIONAL BIBLIOGRAPHIES

The task of assembling and cataloging a comprehensive national library goes hand in hand with that of producing one of the most fundamental tools of historical research: a retrospective national bibliography. Within central Europe, those countries with access to representative collections of national imprints naturally led the way in creating basic research tools of this sort. In Poland, for instance, the director of the Jagiellonian Library, Karol Estreicher, began in 1868 the compilation of a *Bibliografia Polska*: a retrospective bibliography of Polish imprints that remains the standard work today.[38] Contemporaneously, Čeněk Zíbrt, a professor at the Charles University working under the auspices of the Royal Academy in Prague, compiled the *Bibliografie české historie*, a retrospective bibliography of sources and literature for Czech history up to 1679. In 1923, shortly after the founding of Czechoslovakia, the decision was taken to compile a more detailed catalog of all imprints in the Czech language before 1800. An enhanced version is now available on the Internet, where it will eventually be joined by a catalog of early modern Latin imprints from the Bohemian lands, extending the earlier work of Josef Hejnic and Jan Martínek.[39] By 1900, likewise, leading members of the Hungarian Academy of Sciences had compiled a comprehensive retrospective national bibliography (*Régi Magyar Könyvtar*), comprising not only 1800 titles published in Hungarian (part 1) and 2500 titles in other languages published in Hungary from 1473 to 1711 (part 2), but also over 4800 works by native Hungarians published in other languages outside Hungary (part 3). Further additions and corrections were added in 1906 and 1912.[40] All of this work is now being superseded by a chronologically

[38]As in the Hungarian case, Estreicher included not only all works in Polish irrespective of place of publication and all works published in Poland irrespective of language, but also works by Poles or concerning Poland published abroad. Of particular interest to early modernists are parts 2 (vols. 8–11, containing a chronological listing, 1455–1899) and 3 (vols. 12–34, containing an alphabetical listing, 1455–1600). An additional volume (*Bibliografja Polsia XV.–XVI. stólecia*) includes a chronological listing of 7200 fifteenth- and sixteenth-century items, and an alphabetical listing of materials in Polish libraries.

[39]The Czech-language bibliography is Tobolka and Horák, *Knihopis československých tisků od doby nejstarší až do konce 18. století*. The best guidance for Latin imprints in Czech lands is Hejnic and Martínek, *Rukověť' humanistického básnictví v Čechách a na Moravě*.

[40]Sztripszky, *Adalékok Szabó Károly Régi magyar könyvtár* includes the material previously collected by Lajos Dézsi and published in the journal *Magyar Könyvszemle* (1906): 131–53.

organized bibliography, including photographs of title pages and detailed bibliographical descriptions (*Regi Magyarországi Nyomtatványok*). Both versions are now available on CD-ROM and on the Internet (*Elektronikus Régi Magyar Könyvtár*), together with a further list of Hungarica published outside Hungary in languages other than Hungarian.[41]

In Germany, however, the compilation of a retrospective national bibliography, like the creation of a virtual national library, was a task postponed until the later twentieth century. Since 1969 the Deutsche Forschungsgemeinschaft has funded a full-scale assault on this problem aimed at creating a complete retrospective bibliography of all German-language books and of all the works in whatever language printed or published in the historically German-speaking regions of Europe. The first product of this work appeared in twenty-two large volumes between 1983 and 1995 (*Verzeichnis der im deutschen Sprachbereich erschienenen Druckschriften des XVI. Jahrhunderts*, or *VD16*), comprising a bibliography of some 75,000 sixteenth-century German imprints, assembled in Munich with collaboration from Wolfenbüttel and (since 1990) from the Landes- und Forschungsbibliothek in Gotha. To this basic alphabetical listing were added an index of editors, commentators, translators, and contributors in 1997, and an index of places of publication, printers, publishers, and years of publication in 2000. Based as it is on only a small group of leading early modern collections, *VD16* inevitably remains far from comprehensive, but further work on the project continues. More that 25,000 new titles from additional libraries in and outside Germany have been added to the database in Munich, which was made available on a CD-ROM accessible over the Internet in December 2005, and was converted into a web-mounted database in 2006. In 1996, moreover, work commenced simultaneously on a similar catalog for the seventeenth century (*Verzeichnis der im deutschen Sprachraum erschienenen Drucke des 17. Jahrhunderts*, or *VD17*). In this case, however, the database has been published online from the outset and is growing incrementally. Digital technology has also made possible refinements unthinkable in the previous catalog: the over 200,000 imprints currently cataloged in *VD17* are accompanied by over 630,000 "key pages"— that is, title pages, dedications, major section titles, colophons, and printers' marks—designed to facilitate the individuation of editions and imprints.

---

[41]The latter is Apponyi, *Hungarica*. For further guidance on east central European national bibliographies, see http://www.library.uiuc.edu/spx/class/nationalbib/natbib.htm.

CATALOGS AND GUIDES TO HISTORICAL BOOK COLLECTIONS

While these bibliographies and collections are gradually being perfected over coming decades, the student will need to supplement them from catalogs and collections elsewhere. Further bibliographical information can now be obtained with previously unimaginable ease thanks to yet another technological wonder: the online Karlsruher Virtueller Katalog, which allows the simultaneous searching of hundreds of independent libraries inside and outside Germany.

If, in the creation of a national retrospective bibliography, Germany has trailed behind many of its neighbors, in mapping out the historical dispersion and current preservation of book production in Germany since the invention of printing, it has leapt into the lead with the creation of an immense and unique work of reference, the tripartite *Handbuch der Historischen Buchbestände* edited by Bernard Fabian. The first two multivolume series offer regionally organized surveys of all the printed matter (including books, periodicals, newspapers, music, maps, and ephemera) published between 1450 and 1900 and preserved in some 1500 German (series 1) and 300 Austrian (series 2) libraries of every kind (national, regional, municipal, academic, ecclesiastical, monastic, or specialized). The third series surveys only material printed in the German language or in German-speaking countries preserved in selected libraries in seventeen countries in western, central, and eastern Europe. The entry for each library contains a brief history and detailed analysis of its holdings (organized chronologically, linguistically, and topically, with particular attention to special collections), as well as listings of published and unpublished catalogs, archival records, and other published descriptions of the collections. The first two series, and the individual volumes of the third, conclude with indexes of persons and subjects. Originally published in forty-seven large volumes between 1992 and 2001, all three series were republished in 2002 on a single CD-ROM. The resulting work offers a comprehensive survey of German book production, a massive documentation of its international dissemination, and a detailed guide to research collections both in and outside Germany itself.[42]

A major ongoing Hungarian resource in this field, *Bibliotheca Eruditionis: The History of Reading Databank (1500–1708)*, aims to document in unprecedented detail the reading culture of the Carpathian basin in the

---

[42]Further descriptions are available from the publisher (http://www.olms.de/) and the Universität Münster, which coordinated the work (http://www.anglistik.uni-muenster.de/Handbuch/).

early modern period. At the heart of the project is a set of interconnected databases collecting information on (1) 1,750 book inventories and other archival sources, (2) the roughly 200,000 copies of some 60,000 Hungarian and foreign works listed in them, (3) extant copies of these books in contemporary Hungarian collections, and (4) specialized literature on the inventories, previous possessors, contemporary collections, and some individual works. While the databases themselves have not yet been published, four series of publications generated by the project have been appearing steadily for twenty-five years. The first series provides detailed descriptions of the inventories and related documents upon which the entire project rests; the second publishes the inventories themselves, with lengthy historical introductions and detailed indexes; the third attempts the full reconstruction of important library collections; while the fourth, a supplemental series, publishes more synthetic studies that derive from the project.[43] Many of these volumes are written or summarized at length in major languages of international scholarship.

DIGITIZED SOURCE COLLECTIONS WITH UNRESTRICTED ACCESS

Given the state of the German historical bibliography, it will be some time before a collection for Germany can be assembled that is equivalent to Early English Books Online, which makes virtually every English book published in the early modern period available at the click of a mouse. Yet something of this kind is already in prospect. A discreet notice on the website of the Bayerische Staatsbibliothek (BSB) in Munich announces the commencement of a project to digitize and publish on the Internet all the library's holdings listed in *VD16*.[44] As a pilot project, the BSB proposes to begin by digitizing all its sixteenth-century holdings in the pre-Reformation period. Inevitably, however, the digitization even of the portion of sixteenth-century imprints currently listed in *VD16* would require the cooperation of many different libraries. The general strategy of the

[43]These four series are Monok, *Könyvtártörténeti Füzetek* [Bibliographies of 16th to 18th century Library History]; Keserû, *Adattár XVI–XVIII.svázadi szellemi mozgalmaink történetéhez* [Contributions to the history of the intellectual and cultural movements in the Carpathian basin in the 16th to 18th centuries]; Monok, *A Kárpátmedence Koraújkori Könyvtárai* [Libraries in the Carpathian Basin in the Early Modern Age]; and Monok, *Olvasmánytörténeti Dolgozatok* [Studies in the History of Reading], respectively. Full lists of these publications can be found at http://www.eruditio.hu/kiad_eng.html.

[44]See the link from the Münchener Digitalisierungszentrum (http://mdz1.bib-bvb.de/~mdz/sammlungen.html) to the project Digitalisierung, Erschließung und Bereitstellung im WWW von im deutschen Sprachgebiet erschienenen Drucken des 16. Jahrhunderts der Bayerischen Staatsbibliothek (VD16 digital).

Deutsche Forschungsgemeinschaft (DFG), therefore, is to divide this huge task into priority areas and assign these to individual institutions best equipped to pursue them, thereby collectively comprising a "Verteilte Digitale Forschungsbibliothek." With this strategy in mind, the DFG program for the "Retrospektive Digitalisierung von Bibliotheksbeständen" has already supported a large number of projects across the whole range of humanistic research, including many of those mentioned in this article.[45] While the default option in the Anglo-American sphere was to leave such developments to the private sector (who then sell them back to those institutions wealthy enough to afford them), in Germany the objective is apparently to fund this work publicly, and eventually to put the German-speaking world's entire literary heritage in the public domain, free of charge to the end user.

Pioneering examples of these DFG-funded efforts are the joint projects CAMENA and TERMINI, pursued since 1999 at the universities of Mannheim and Heidelberg. CAMENA stands for Corpus Automatum Multiplex Electorum Neolatinitatis Auctorum, and its aim is to build a digital library of the central European neo-Latin *respublica litterarum* during the period 1500 to 1770. The first collection, *Poemata*, has digitized some 60,000 pages of printed Latin poetry composed by German authors during this period, which is reproduced both as images and as machine-readable texts. A second collection, *Thesaurus eruditionis*, is assembling the kinds of reference works that scholarly central Europeans would have had at their elbows during the early modern era. It currently contains over sixty-five works on an encyclopedic range of subjects totaling more than 58,000 pages, accompanied by machine-readable transcriptions of either entire works or their summaries and indexes alone.[46] The TERMINI Project effectively provides a cumulative index of this *Thesaurus eruditionis* that allows the user to search the entire collection simultaneously. Since 2004 a third collection of Latin historical and political works published in early modern Germany has been added to CAMENA; this collection currently contains ninety-eight works and over 48,000 pages, accompanied by electronically searchable summaries and indexes. The most recent project, entitled CERA or Corpus Epistolicum Recentioris Aevi, aims to digitize

---

[45]Lists of these projects can be found at http://gdz.sub.uni-goettingen.de/de/vdf-d.

[46]In cooperation with Mannheim, Wolfenbüttel has begun developing its own *Thesaurus eruditionis*, concentrating initially on early modern Latin dictionaries and proposing in the future to add works in the *historia literaria*: http://www.hab.de/bibliothek/wdb/thesaurus/index.htm.

ninety printed collections of Latin learned correspondence from central Europe in the period 1530 to 1770.[47]

Pursuing the digitization of Germany's literary heritage on such a devolved basis raises the obvious necessity of coordinating efforts and collecting results so that users can readily find and use what they need most. In response to this situation, the AGSDD, together with several partner organizations and the support of the DFG, published on the Internet in 2005 a central listing of digitized publications in Germany, the *Zentrale Verzeichnis Digitalisierter Drucke*. The first phase of this project to be realized involved assembling links (with brief descriptions) to digital collections and digital libraries. Currently encompassing some 150 collections organized alphabetically by the institutions that host them, this listing ranges far beyond the field of early modern central Europe; but it also lists many collections invaluable to this field (some of them mentioned in this essay) and will only get richer with the passage of time. In due course, this basic list of collections will be complemented by a detailed listing of individual printed works digitized in their entirety to a high standard and available without cost over the Internet.

Private initiatives have also played an important role here, not least due to the specialized and international nature of many aspects of this field. Dana F. Sutton of the University of California–Irvine, for instance, has assembled the invaluable *Analytical Bibliography of On-Line Neo-Latin Titles*, which is freely available on the Internet without subscription charges or access restrictions. First posted in 1999, this listing currently approaches 22,000 records relevant to many aspects of early modern studies in and beyond central Europe.

COMMERCIAL COLLECTIONS: MICROFILM, DIGITAL, AND PRINT

In introducing the first Reformation research guide in 1982, Steven Ozment observed that "the marvels of modern technology have provided scholars with ever expanding textual resources." Within that same volume, he accordingly dedicated his own essay to the "Pamphlet Literature on the German Reformation," which was then being made readily accessible on microfilm for the first time. In this respect as well, technology has continued its astonishing advance and has consequently changed both the tools and the content of research in this field.

---

[47]A related resource is Estermann, *Verzeichnis der gedruckten Briefe deutscher Autoren des 17. Jahrhunderts*, a four-volume register of printed letters by seventeenth-century German authors.

Pride of place must go to the German *Flugschriften des 16. Jahrhunderts*, whose advent on microfilm in 1979 prompted Ozment's remarks. The first series (1979–87), containing some 5,000 German and Latin pamphlets printed in the empire between 1501 and 1530, is now complete. Thematically, it is naturally focused on the early Reformation itself, the associated disruption of the Peasants' War, and further conflicts both within western Europe and against the Turks. The second series (1990–), which will eventually include a similar number of pamphlets from the remainder of the sixteenth century, deals with a broader range of topics, including (as the catalog states) "the Turkish wars, the revolt of the Netherlands, the persecution of French Protestants, the status of Calvinists and Zwinglians in the Holy Roman Empire, the Council of Trent, the Anabaptist Kingdom of Münster, the Schmalkaldic War and the Interim, propaganda against the papacy and the Jesuits, intra-Protestant theological quarrels, the building of confessional networks, witch-hunting, anti-Jewish polemics and more." Hans Joachim Kohler's invaluable bibliography of this extraordinary resource (*Bibliographie der Flugschriften des 16. Jahrhundert*) unfortunately remains stalled midway through the first series.

Meanwhile, old-media publication in this field has continued to demonstrate its value. The influential series of nine volumes on *The German Single-Leaf Woodcut*, published in the later 1970s, is now being complemented by two equally ambitious, related projects.[48] John Roger Paas is producing *The German Political Broadsheet, 1600–1700*, a ten-volume catalog of seventeenth-century German political broadsheets in chronological order.[49] And Wolfgang Harms is creating *Deutsche illustrierte Flugblätter des 16. und 17. Jahrhunderts*, a systematic and extensively annotated catalog of major library collections of German sixteenth- and seventeenth-century illustrated pamphlets, which relate thematically not merely to religion and politics but to all areas of contemporary discourse and debate, notably ethics, physics, and history. The BSB in Munich is also preparing digital editions of similar material, while the pioneering Czech work in this field focuses on the turbulent decades of the Thirty Years' War.[50]

The provision of unprecedentedly large collections of printed sources on microfiche and the Internet has not, of course, been restricted to popu-

---

[48]Geisberg, *German Single-Leaf Woodcut, 1500–1550*, 4 vols.; Strauss, *German Single-Leaf Woodcut, 1550–1600*, 3 vols.; and Alexander and Strauss, *German Single-Leaf Woodcut, 1600–1700*, 2 vols.

[49]For more on this series, see http://www.harrassowitz-verlag.de.

[50]Bohatcová, *Irrgarten der Schicksale.*

lar ephemera. Scholarly disciplines have also been receiving their share of attention. As befits the confessional age, theology has been particularly well served in this regard, thanks largely to pioneering microfiche publications from *IDC*. A microfiche series, *The Catholic Reformation* (edited by Paul Blum), contains a large amount of central European material and includes separate sections on philosophy, theology, controversies, biographies, and foreign missions. William S. Maltby's collection of 362 sources on the Lutheran Reformation has been supplemented by Timothy J. Wengert's *Philipp Melanchthon*, a collection of thirty-one early editions designed to complement the more recent collections of Melanchthon's works. The parallel collection of 269 titles on Reformed Protestantism in the Netherlands and Germany has been complemented by two collections on Heidelberg—the first treating the first and second reformations there between 1536 and 1576, the second resuming the story between the reconversion of the Palatinate from Lutheranism in 1583 and the sack of Heidelberg in 1622.[51] A further series on the Hungarian Reformation will appear shortly under the editorial supervision of Graeme Murdock.

A still more recent development is the provision since 2001 of two related international collections of theological texts from the Reformation era in digitized form. By far the larger of the two is the *Digital Library of Classic Protestant Texts,* which currently contains over 1200 texts by over 300 authors from the sixteenth and seventeenth centuries, with a marked preference for English divinity (over 500 titles) and the Reformed tradition (ca. 475 titles). The parallel *Digital Library of the Catholic Reformation* is intended to grow to a similar size, though it is currently much smaller (272 titles by 112 authors, most from the sixteenth or early seventeenth centuries). According to the promotional material, the planned collection will include "papal and synodal decrees, catechisms and inquisitorial manuals, biblical commentaries, theological treatises and systems, liturgical writings, saints' lives, and devotional works." In addition to digital facsimiles of the original editions used, this database provides electronic texts in modernized spelling to facilitate searching, and a very user-friendly electronic index analyzing each complete corpus into some 150 standard topics.

Two other large collections have expanded the disciplinary range of this material beyond theology. From 1990 onward, a huge selection of German-language texts of a generally literary nature has been made available

---

[51]Balke and van't Spijker, *Reformed Protestantism 3: Netherlands and Germany*; Gunnoe and Muller, *Reformation in Heidelberg*; and Selderhuis, *Irenical Theology: Heidelberg 1583–1622.*

on microfiche in the *Bibliothek der Deutschen Literatur* published by K. G. Saur. This massive series—containing over 10 million pages of text from 17,225 works by 2500 authors—is overwhelmingly dominated, as one might expect, by the later periods; but the modest sections on *Humanismus/Reformation* (ca. 1450–1600, eighteen authors), and the somewhat richer one on the *Barock* (ca. 1600–1720: ca. 175 authors) can be purchased separately. The best guide is the hard-copy bibliography and index by Axel Frey, which does not, however, include the works included in the second supplement.[52] In 2002 a pan-European collection on *Philosophy and the Liberal Arts in the Early Modern Period,* edited by J. S. Freedman et al., began to appear from IDC. Eventually, it will include thousands of texts on philosophical disciplines (metaphysics, physics, ethics, politics), liberal arts (logic, rhetoric, grammar, poetics, history), mathematical disciplines, and printed curricula for individual schools and universities.[53]

MANUSCRIPTS

At the opposite end of the spectrum of user-friendliness from machine-readable digital sources are the *Urquellen* themselves: unedited manuscripts. Needless to say, the system of archives in Germany is complex, but reliable guidance can be found in the fifteenth edition of *Archive in der Bundesrepublik Deutschland, Österreich und der Schweiz,* updated in 1995 to take account of German reunification. A catalog of the extensive collection of inventories and finding aids for archives in the three countries assembled at the German Historical Institute in Washington, DC, was placed on the Internet in 1995, and further web-based guidance is available in a more recent guide to German archives compiled by Andreas Hanacek.[54] For regularly updated information, the Archiveschule Marburg (the leading German institution of its kind) hosts a neatly organized listing of German, European, and worldwide archives, as well as information on other gateways to relevant information. At a far greater level of detail, the *Kalliope* database provides an updated, digitized version of the union catalog of autographs and collections of literary papers in German collections. Though already consisting of some 1.2 million records, it is currently restricted, for the most part, to papers held in German libraries. Plans for a

---

[52]Frey, *Bibliothek der Deutschen Literatur.*

[53]For further information on this series, see http://www.idcpublishers.info/philosophy/.

[54]Skorsetz, Micunek, and Nahr, *Guide to Inventories and Finding Aids at the German Historical Institute Washington, DC;* and Hanacek, *Archive in der Bundesrepublik Deutschland/Archives in Germany.*

second phase will extend it to include collections in archives and museums as well. A similarly conceived *Repertorium der handschriftlichen Nachlässe in den Bibliotheken und Archiven der Schweiz* exists for Switzerland, though it is far from complete. In the absence of such tools, the special collections pages of the national libraries discussed above are typically a good starting point in searching for manuscript material. The website of the Hungarian National Archives (Magyar Országos Levéltár) lists their collections and holdings in reasonable detail.

QUELLENKUNDE: BIBLIOGRAPHIES OF SOURCES AND LITERATURE
Aside from bibliographical information on and practical access to original source material, the historian's second need is for similar access to secondary literature. Here, two kinds of bibliography are indispensable: retrospective bibliographies, which list the most important previously published sources and literature, and cumulative bibliographies, which regularly list recently published material in the field.

Retrospective Bibliographies
The standard, thematically organized, retrospective bibliography of major sources and literature for the whole of German history—Dalmann and Waitz's *Quellenkunde der deutschen Geschichte*—has now appeared in a tenth revised edition, in ten large volumes, continuing a tradition dating back to 1830. The end of volume 6 and the whole of volume 7 deal with the sixteenth and seventeenth centuries. Also useful for early modernists are the first section (dealing with general issues and research tools) and the second section (arranged geographically) in the first volume, and the index that concludes the entire series. Handier and slightly more recent are the volumes on *Quellenkunde zur deutschen Geschichte der Neuzeit* edited by Winfried Baumgart, which list only primary sources. Winfried Becker's volume on the period 1618 to 1715 is primarily useful for major collections of source material on German political and constitutional history, and international relations.[55] Historians of the lands now comprising Austria are more fortunate to have a thoroughly up-to-date survey of the archival and published sources that devotes over one thousand pages to the sixteenth to eighteenth centuries.[56] Recent and

---

[55]Dotzauer, *Das Zeitalter der Glaubensspaltung, 1500–1618*; and Becker, *Dreißigjähriger Krieg und Zeitalter Ludwigs XIV, 1618–1715.*

[56]Pauser, Scheutz, and Winkelbauer, *Quellenkunde der Habsburgemonarchie 16.–18. Jahrhunderte.*

voluminous retrospective bibliographies are also readily available for Czech and Slovak history and for German-Polish relations.[57]

Cumulative Bibliographies

The basic ongoing cumulative bibliography on German history remains the *Jahresberichte für deutsche Geschichte (JDG)*. Continuing a tradition dating back to 1880, and compiled annually since 1952 by the Deutsche (now Berlin-Brandenburgische) Akademie der Wissenschaften, these hefty volumes list recently published primary and secondary literature in any language pertaining (for the early modern period) to all the territories included in the Holy Roman Empire (in some cases, until the period of their permanent secession). Three years ago, listings since 1985 were made available in searchable form on the Internet. Updated daily, the online version currently contains some 326,000 entries, which also include links to the German Zeitschriftendatenbank and the Karlsruher Virtueller Katalog, as well as to book reviews and full-text publications available online.[58] The *Österreichische historische Bibliographie* (*ÖHB*) lists all historical literature (for whatever country) produced in Austria since 1945. Since 2004 it has been expanded to include a selective bibliography of work on Austrian history published outside the country between 1990 and 1995.[59] For regions further east, an equally invaluable aid is the series *Bibliographien zur Geschichte und Landeskunde Ostmitteleuropas*, published regularly by the Herder Institute in Marburg, many of them in bilingual and trilingual editions compiled in collaboration with east central European partner institutions. Included in this metaseries are bibliographies on the histories of the Bohemian lands and Slovakia, Silesia, Pomerania, East and West Prussia, Great Poland, and the Baltic countries, as well as separate volumes on the history of German-Polish relations. This too is now available online: the entire database—including 400,000 titles (mostly from about 1990 onward) collected from 780 west European and North American periodicals and a similar number of east central European publication series—is also furnished with a splendid set of search facilities.[60]

[57]Bosl, *Handbuch der Geschichte der böhmischen Länder*; Kovtun, *Czech and Slovak History*; and Lawaty and Mincer, *Deutsch-Polnische Beziehungen in Geschichte und Gegenwart*.

[58]For further information on coverage, see http://www.bbaw.de/bbaw/Forschung/Forschungsprojekte/jdg/de/Startseite.

[59]The annual cumulative bibliography began with the volume for 1965 (published in 1967). The retrospective bibliography for 1945 through 1964 appeared in 1985.

[60]The website of the Herder-Institute lists the recent publications in this series (under *Veröffentlichungen*) and provides access to the cumulative bibliography (*Literaturdokumentation zur Geschichte Ostmitteleuropas*), which is also searchable via Clio-online.

These geographically organized resources can be usefully supplemented by interdisciplinary cumulative bibliographies, published in periodical form. The well-known "Literaturbericht," published annually as a supplement to the *Archiv für Reformationsgeschichte*, provides brief reviews of a wide selection of pertinent literature, especially on the sixteenth century. The thematically organized "Bibliographie zur Barockliteratur" published in the *Wolfenbütteler Barock-Nachrichten* is extensive and richly interdisciplinary for the seventeenth century. The literature surveys on the early modern period periodically published in *Geschichte in Wissenschaft und Unterricht* naturally place their emphasis squarely on history. Another invaluable resource for keeping up to date is the Internet version of German books in print, the *Verzeichnis Lieferbarer Bücher*.

BIOGRAPHICAL BASICS

The prosopographer, like the bibliographer, has hitherto labored under particular difficulties in Germany. Shortly after unification in 1871, Germany led the way in Europe in the compilation of a massive national biography (the *Allgemeine deutsche Biographie*, or *ADB*) containing 26,500 entries in fifty-six volumes. Since 1953 a replacement has been in preparation (the *Neue deutsche Biographie*), which is intended to include 25,500 entries in twenty-eight volumes when completed around 2017.[61] As these statistics indicate, a large number of persons and families treated in the earlier work have been cut from the later one in order to make room for significant figures from the later nineteenth and twentieth centuries; so the newer work by no means entirely supersedes the older one. In a similar fasion, the work begun in the gargantuan eighteenth-century German encyclopedia of J. H. Zedler and the contemporary biographical dictionary of C. G. Jöcher (continued by Adelung, Rotermund, and Günther) contain brief entries on many individuals not listed in the *ADB*.[62] These all build, in turn, on a plethora of earlier biographical dictionaries for individual German territories, which often contain far more information that any other single source (an outstanding example is Strieder, *Grundlage an einer hessischen Gelehrten- und Schriftsteller-Geschichte*). Ready access to a comprehensive selection of such literature is rare within Germany, and nonexistent

---

[61]For further information, see http://www.ndb.badw-muenchen.de/.
[62]Zedler, *Grosses vollständiges Universal-Lexicon*; Jöcher, *Allgemeines Gelehrten-Lexicon*; and Adelung, *Allgemeines Gelehrten-Lexicon*.

outside it, making research into the communities of less well-known German historical figures very cumbersome.[63]

In this case too, technology has recently transformed the situation, at least for those able to access the expensive results. In the 1970s, the publishing firm of K. G. Saur Verlag grasped this particular nettle and set out to conflate a huge collection of biographical reference works into a single, immense scrapbook. Their project aimed, in effect, to cut out the articles on individual figures from a whole library of biographical reference works, to paste them into a single alphabetical series, and then to publish the results on microfiche. The first and, for present purposes, most useful result was the original *Deutsches biographisches Archiv* (*DBA I*), which includes 480,000 articles on 213,000 individuals, collected from 265 sources published between 1707 and 1913 (published in installments between 1982 and 1986 with a hardbound index: the *Deutscher biographischer Index* or *DBI*).[64] Subsequent years have seen the publication of similar archives for all the regions of Europe and many countries outside it— most notably, for present purposes, the Baltic countries, Poland, the Czech and Slovak Republics, and Hungary. Within the past few years, digitized versions of all the western and central European biographical archives have been made available (by subscription) on the Internet, and the plan is to add all the other archives to the online version by 2009 to create a World Biographical Information System Online (WBIS Online). The resulting work still falls short of the ideal in several significant respects. The lack of page numbers makes it impossible to cite the original works precisely without recourse to hard copies. While local biographical dictionaries are included aplenty, topical ones—such as Melchior Adam's lives of leading sixteenth- and early seventeenth-century German philosophers, theologians, lawyers, and medical doctors—are strangely lacking.[65] Also inevitably missing are a host of more recent works that are still in copyright. Such regrets notwithstanding, some forms of exploratory prosopographical and

---

[63]A stunning exception is the Heyne-Lesesaal (previously Forschungsbibliothek für Wissenschaftsgeschichte) in the SUB Göttingen, which provides open-shelf access to some 160,000 eighteenth- and nineteenth-century reference works in all branches of academic research, arranged in their original order within Göttingen's famous university library: see http://www.sub.uni-goettingen.de/ebene_1/1_forschungsls.html.de.

[64]A second series (*DBA II*) is devoted primarily to recent figures, but includes a small increment of supplementary information on early modern individuals.

[65]Thankfully, this 2,815-page collection of 546 biographies of leading German writers is available elsewhere on the Internet, partly in machine-readable form; Adam, *Vitae*, online at http://www.uni-mannheim.de.mateo/camemaref/adam.html.

biographical research will be transformed by the ability to search some 10 million entries on 5 million people collected from 8,600 reference works in forty languages, not only by name, but by gender, occupation, year of birth or death, and country as well. Even this does not exhaust the biographical material readily available on the Internet, however. Still more extensive sources of contemporary biographical information can be located, for instance, via the catalog of German-language funeral sermons compiled since 1974 by the Forschungsstelle für Personalschriften in Marburg.[66]

Technological advances such as these notwithstanding, traditional national biographies remain indispensable and are being refurbished for some countries in central Europe. The Swiss, for instance, after generations of coping with an inadequate national biography (*Historisch-Biographische Lexikon der Schweiz*), are now assembling a new historical lexicon (*Historisches Lexikon der Schweiz*), which by 2014 will include some 40,000 articles on people, families, places, and other historical topics in fourteen volumes. Despite the simultaneous appearance of this dictionary in German, French, and Italian, the publishing timetable is ticking away like a Swiss watch, with the fifth annual volume appearing in 2006. Better still, over half the full dictionary is now available in the (trilingual) Internet version, where articles are being published as soon as they are finished. The Czech situation is similar. Here too, eighteenth-century Latin and German biographical dictionaries retain some utility; but historians still turn for further biographical information to the voluminous Czech encyclopedia published at the turn of the century and to an excellent and more recent handbook limited to neo-Latin authors.[67] All this is now changing with the appearance in 2004 of the first volume of a state-of-the-art biographical dictionary of Czech and Slovak lands being produced by the Historical Institute of the Czech Academy of Science (*Biografický slovník českých zemí*). For the German reader, a four-volume biographical dictionary of the Czech lands is now nearly complete; while a similar work for southeastern Europe is also available.[68] Along with the Polish national biography (currently forty volumes and still creeping its way to completion), a compact German-language biography is available

---

[66]*Gesamtkatalog deutschsprachiger Leichenpredigten* (currently approaching 175,000 entries).

[67]Pelzel, *Abbildungen böhmischer und mährischer Gelehrten und Künstler*; Balbín, *Bohemia Docta*; Studnicka and Celakovsky, *Ottův slovník naučný: Illustrovana encyklopaedie obecnych vedomosti*; and Hejnic and Martínek, *Rukověť humanistického básnictví v Čechách a na Moravě*.

[68]Sturm, *Biographisches Lexikon zur Geschichte der böhmischen Länder*; and Bernath and Schroeder, *Biographisches Lexikon zur Geschichte Südosteuropas*.

for Prussian territories.[69] The Hungarian national biography (now available online) can be supplemented in the field of Reformation studies by the clerical biographies included in a dictionary of Hungarian Protestant ecclesiastical history.[70]

Aside from these geographically organized bibliographical dictionaries, other valuable works provide detailed information on various categories of figures active in early modern central Europe. For the humanist background, Bietenholz and Deutscher's three-volume dictionary of *Contemporaries of Erasmus* is convenient and authoritative. Four volumes of biographical entries prefaced to the ongoing edition of Melanchthon's *Briefwechsel* will serve a similar function. For major figures and issues of the Reformation period itself, the *Oxford Encyclopedia of the Reformation* (edited by Hillerbrand) is a convenient point of reference. Minor figures can also be found in Bautz and Bautz's *Biographisch-bibliographisches Kirchenlexikon*, republished at almost double its previous size since 1990 and now also available on the Internet. A further dictionary edited by Erwin Iserloh surveys fifty-two leading Catholic theologians of the Reformation period (in and outside Germany) in six up-to-date volumes, with substantial discussions of life and works, and bibliographies of primary and secondary sources.[71] For the entire theological context, the steadily published volumes of the *Theologische Realenzyclopädie* provide compelling grounds for any researcher in this field to acquire at least a rudimentary reading knowledge of German. Basic biographical and extremely rich bibliographical information on German writers of the baroque period (that is, on those who published their chief literary works in the seventeenth century) is conveniently available thanks to Gerhard Dünnhaupt's *Personalbibliographien zu den Drucken des Barock*.

TOPOGRAPHICAL NECESSITIES
The territorial fragmentation of Germany underlying these biographical and bibliographical problems previously created almost insuperable difficulties for the empirically grounded study of early modern German history more generally. As decades of research on the Reformation in the cities clearly demonstrated, any meaningful generalization regarding the reception of the Reformation in Germany must be based on the comparative

---

[69]*Polski sownik biograficzny*; and Krollmann, *Altpreußische Biographie*.
    [70]Kenyeres, *Magyar életrajzi lexicon*; and Zoványi and Ladányi, *Magyarországi protestáns egyháztörténeti lexikon*.
    [71]Iserloh, *Katholische Theologen der Reformationszeit*.

study of myriad semi-independent political and ecclesiastical entities.[72] More recently, the confessionalization thesis posed precisely the same problem for Germany's principalities: the hypothesis that fundamental similarities underlie the evolution of even confessionally antagonistic territories could only be validated by the comparative analysis of the histories of reformations in numerous individual territories. The desire to facilitate this research produced yet another of the key new reference works that have appeared during the past fifteen years: a seven-volume overview of the territories of the Holy Roman Empire in the era of Reformation and confessionalization (that is, roughly between 1500 and 1650).[73] Each of the sixty-two independently authored chapters of this invaluable handbook summarizes the basic information on one or more key imperial territories. At the outset of each chapter, a basic map is provided together with an outline of the territory's ruling house, its divisions and reunifications, and its position within the constitutional hierarchy and geographical matrix of the empire. The bulk of each chapter is then devoted to narrating the political and ecclesiastical situation around 1500, the key dynastic and confessional developments of the next half-century, the consolidation or continued disruption of confessional churches in the latter sixteenth century, and the impact of the Thirty Years' War, before concluding with selective bibliographies of sources and secondary literature. Above and beyond the issue of confessionalization itself, these volumes provide an invaluable orientation to anyone seeking the basic mastery of this extraordinarily complex and fluid landscape which is a prerequisite for filling the vital middle ground between detailed studies of individual territories and vague generalizations about the history of the empire as a whole.

Inevitably, not all of the Holy Roman Empire's hundreds of territories could be treated in adequate detail even in this substantial collaborative work. Digitized collections of historical maps are proliferating on the Internet,[74] but since most of these maps are relatively recent and the collections lack the systematic character of an integrated atlas, searching for information in these collections can be frustrating. Even more voluminous is the national database of old maps (*IKAR*) assembled since 1985 in Berlin and

---

[72]Moeller, *Reichsstadt und Reformation*; Chrisman, "Cities in the Reformation"; and Stoob, *Bibliographie zur deutschen historischen Städteforschung*.

[73]Schindling and Ziegler, *Die Territorien des Reichs im Zeitalter der Reformation und Konfessionalisierung*.

[74]*Zentrales Verzeichnis Digitalisierter Drucke* (*ZVDD*) currently lists major cartographical digitization projects in Bremen, Dresden, Freiburg, Halle, and Munich.

available online since 1991. Of over 230,000 old maps cataloged in this database, fewer than 1500 are currently provided with links to digital images. One category of smaller territories—those ruled by some thirty religious orders and monastic communities active in sixteenth- and seventeenth-century Germany—is currently being mapped in a complementary three-volume atlas, which will also complement the biographical dictionary of Catholic theologians mentioned above.[75] The history of cities in Germany has become a major industry, serviced by a massive three-volume bibliography of sources and literature.[76] For other small imperial territories—as well as for more information on significant places within larger ones—one can turn to a number of useful reference works. Gerhard Köbler's historical lexicon of German lands, updated for the third time in 1999, provides brief overviews and bibliographies for some 5000 geographical entities. Köbler's bibliographical information can be supplemented by Reinhard Oberschelp's concise and up-to-date bibliography of basic research tools in German regional historiography.[77] More detailed topographical information can be found in the regionally organized volumes of the constantly evolving *Handbuch der historischen Stätten Deutschlands,* which provide detailed information on cities, towns, markets, monasteries, castles, princely and noble residences, and other historically significant sites.[78] For the more obscure place names, one can consult *Müllers Grosses Deutsches Ortsbuch,* now in its twenty-ninth edition. For Latin place names, Graesse's wonderful *Orbis Latinus* is now available on the Internet. The Latin names of places too insignificant for inclusion in Graesse can often be identified in the indexes to the contemporary matriculation register of a nearby university.[79] A handy guide for locating cities in Germany and east central Europe on basic maps, and for unscrambling the variety of early modern and contemporary designations for them, is the *Thesaurus Locorum,* maintained in Marburg. Less a necessity for the student, perhaps, than a delight for the connoisseur is the reprint of Matthäus Merian's wonderful seventeenth-

---

[75]Jürgensmeier and Schwerdtfeger, *Orden und klösterliche gemeinschaften im Zeitalter von Reformation und katholischer Reform.*

[76]See Stoob, *Bibliographie zur deutschen historischen Städteforschung,* which continues the older work of Keyser, *Bibliographie zur Städtegeschichte Deutschlands.*

[77]Oberschelp, *Die Bibliographien zur deutschen Landesgeschichte und Landeskunde;* and Köbler, *Historisches Lexicon der deutschen Länder.*

[78]The most recent volume is Groten et al., *Nordrhein-Westfalen.* Bahlcke, *Böhmen und Mähren,* extends the series to a neighboring region.

[79]There is an excellent index of places, for instance, in Toepke, *Die Matrikel der Universität Heidelberg,* now available on the web.

century *Topographia Germaniae*—with its irresistible engravings of innumerable German cities, towns, and *Schlösser* comprising an image of the Empire in the mid-seventeenth century.

For more easterly regions, excellent historical maps can be found in the standard ten-volume history of Hungary. The polyglot lists of place-names appended to it can be supplemented by the valuable list of Hungarian names of places outside modern Hungary's borders compiled by László Sabok.[80] Another outstanding resource is the historical atlas of Czech towns, which combines surveys of archaeological, historical, geographical, political, economic, and cultural information with reproductions of old maps and town plans, specially commissioned historical maps, and comprehensive bibliographies.[81]

LINGUISTIC AIDS

Linguistic help is also now readily available on the web. The immense historical dictionary of the German language—begun by the Brothers Grimm in 1838 and finished thirty-three volumes later in 1971 (*Das Deutsche Wörterbuch*)—was republished on CD-ROM in 2004 and is now available online. No sooner was the first edition finished, than work began on a second and more homogenous revision.[82] An even more welcome innovation for the student of neo-Latin literature is Johann Ramminger's modestly titled *Neulateinische Wortliste*, which charts the development of Latin between roughly 1300 and 1700 under the influence of humanism, the invention of printing, and the needs of early modern culture. Far from a mere word list, it concentrates on and illustrates the usage of new, rare, and noteworthy terms that can be browsed in thematic groupings as well as in alphabetical and reverse-alphabetical order. Those bold enough to venture into Hungarian materials may need to know that the standard English-Hungarian dictionaries are those edited by László Országh and Tamás Magay. Also noteworthy is the five-volume German-Czech dictionary compiled on historical principles by Josef Jungmann in the nineteenth century and recently reprinted.

[80]Pach, *Magyarország tortenete*; and Sebok, *Magyar neve?*

[81]Semotanová, Šimůnek, and Žemlička, *Historický atlas měst České republiky*.

[82]First steps to an electronic edition of *DWB II* are evident on the project site of the Göttinger Akademie der Wissenschaften: http://grimm.adw-goettingen.gwdg.de/index.html. For a useful collection of other dictionaries on the Internet, see http://www.yourdictionary.com/languages/germanic.html#german.

GATEWAYS

Last but by no means least are a set of research tools that have not merely been improved but invented *de novo* in the past fifteen years: the multipurpose gateways. The oldest of these—the WWW Virtual Library—was established in 1991, one year before the previous research guide to Reformation Europe was published. Such has been the enthusiasm for assembling collections of Internet links that, for most of the intervening period, historians have been confronted with an increasingly bewildering proliferation of alternative portals for entry into this field. Yet as web-mounted digital resources have multiplied exponentially, so too has the labor required to catalog them in a professional manner. In the field of early modern German history, at least, this fertile but increasingly anarchic start-up phase has now been superseded by a more rationalized system of subject gateways, funded, yet again, by the DFG and superimposed on the national system of subject libraries described above (WEBIS).[83]

The all-embracing Internet gateway for historical study in the German-speaking world is Clio-online, sponsored by the DFG and hosted at the Humboldt University in Berlin. Like the discipline it serves, this gateway is inevitably huge, complex, and multifaceted, and the user is advised to begin exploring it via the site map off the home page. Moreover, since early modern central Europe is only a tiny fraction of the historical discipline as a whole, the researcher will often find it more profitable to visit more specialized gateways, particularly while browsing as opposed to searching. One pair linked to Clio-online is InformationsWeiser Geschichte/History Guide. History Guide has been developed by Göttingen since 1995 as part of its responsibility for organizing information on Anglo-American history. Since 2001, it has been combined with InformationsWeiser Geschichte, developed in Munich as part of its responsibility for German and general history. This project was then enlarged within Clio-online in 2003 into an official Network Subject Gateway for history. The purpose of this gateway is to assemble, organize, and thereby ease access to digital publications on the Internet in a manner analogous to JDG for print media. The DFG-funded gateway to Internet resources for Europe east of Germany and Austria is the Virtuelle Fachbibliothek Osteuropa.

---

[83]Several of the older gateways have remained on the Internet for the benefit of established users even though they are no longer being updated. New users are therefore advised to check the date of last modification before relying on more peripheral gateways.

Most of these geographically defined gateways allow searches to be restricted to early modern materials. Nevertheless, they can be usefully complemented by gateways devoted to early modern material that can be delimited geographically. Within the WWW Virtual Library, for instance, early modern German history is still ably served by the Virtual Library Frühe Neuzeit, based in the Historisches Centrum Hagen. An especially valuable register of resources recovering the entire interdisciplinary field of early modern studies, with a particular focus on German-language resources, is Frühe Neuzeit Digital (FND), maintained by the Herzog August Bibliothek in Wolfenbüttel. In addition to the predictable categories (digital sources, editions, catalogs, and databases), FND also collects links to institutions in Germany and elsewhere which foster early modern studies, and links to other gateways in the field. A gateway of a rather different sort is H-German, "a daily Internet discussion forum focused on scholarly topics in German history," and dedicated to "serving professional historians of Germany around the world." Although dominated by modernists, it also broadcasts medieval and early modern book and exhibition reviews, historiographical debates, and conference reports via email, which are archived on its website along with course syllabi, an extensive links page, and other resources.

Given the rate at which digital resources are proliferating in this field, fresh material will certainly appear on these lists while this volume is in press. Hence the need to conclude with reference to the tools best adapted to keeping abreast of future developments. Yet three general conclusions substantiated by this essay may not so rapidly be rendered obsolete. The first is that obtaining a synthetic, interdisciplinary appreciation of the history, thought, and culture of central Europe in the post-Reformation era will require a generation and more of energetic, international, and interdisciplinary effort. A second is that political conditions have never been more favorable and scholarly tools never more adequate to this demanding task. And from these two a third and most general conclusion naturally follows: the task of mapping out central Europe in the post-Reformation period offers one of the greatest challenges anywhere in the field of early modern studies to the next generation of intellectually adventurous researchers.

Bibliography

Gateways

Clio-online: http://www.clio-online.de.
Frühe Neuzeit Digital: http://www.hab.de/bibliothek/fachinfo/fnd/index.htm.
H-German: http://www.h-net.org/~german.
History Guide: http://www.historyguide.de/index.php.
InformationsWeiser Geschichte: http://mdz2.bib-bvb.de/hist/index.php.
Karlsruher Virtueller Katalog: http://www.ubka.uni-karlsruhe.de/kvk.html.
Virtual Library Frühe Neuzeit: http://www.historisches-centrum.de/index.php?id=66.
Virtuelle Fachbibliothek Osteuropa (ViFaOst): http://www.vifaost.de.
WWW Virtual Library: http://vlib.org.

Institutional Websites

Arbeitsgemeinschaft Sammlung Deutscher Drucke: http://www.ag-sdd.de.
Archivschule Marburg: http://www.archivschule.de/content.
Bayerische Staatsbibliothek, Munich: http://www.bsb-muenchen.de.
Biblioteka Jagiellońska, Kraków: http://www.bj.uj.edu.pl.
Biblioteka Narodowa / National Library, Warsaw: http://www.bn.org.pl.
Deutsche Comenius-Gesellschaft: http://www.deutsche-comenius-gesellschaft.de.
Deutsche Forschungsgemeinschaft: http://www.dfg.de/en/.
Deutsche Nationalbibliothek: http://www.d-nb.de.
German Historical Institute, Washington, DC: http://www.ghi-dc.org/index.html.
Gottfried Wilhelm Leibniz Bibliothek (formerly Niedersächsische Landesbibliothek), Hannover: http://www.gwlb.de/Leibniz.
Herder Institute, Marburg: http://www.herder-institut.de.
Herzog August Bibliothek, Wolfenbüttel: http://www.hab.de.
Historische Kommission zur Erforschung des Pietismus: http://www.pietismuskommission.de.
Magyar Országos Levéltár / Hungarian National Archives, Budapest: http://www.mol.gov.hu.
Národní knihovna eské republiky / National Library of the Czech Republic, Prague: http://www.nkp.cz.
Országos Széchényi Könyvtár / National Széchényi Library, Budapest: http://www.oszk.hu.
Österreichische Nationalbibliothek, Vienna: http://www.onb.ac.at/about/index.htm.
Staats- und Universitätsbibliothek, Göttingen: http://www.sub.uni-goettingen.de.
WEBIS —WEB BibliotheksInformationsSystem: http://webis.sub.uni-hamburg.de.

Biographical Dictionaries and Related Aids

Adam, Melchior. *Vitae.* Heidelberg, 1615, 1620. 5 parts: *Vitae Germanorum philosophorum, qui seculo superiori, et quod excurrit, philosophicis ac humanioribus literis clari floruerunt* (1615); *Vitae Germanorum medicorum...* (1620); *Vitae Germanorum iureconsultorum et politicorum* (1620); *Vitae Germanorum Theologorum* (1620); *Decades Duæ Continentes Vitas Theologorum Exteriorum Principum* (1653). Available online at http://www.uni-mannheim.de/mateo/camenaref/adam.html.
Adelung, Johann Christoph. *Allgemeines Gelehrten-Lexicon: Fortsetzung und Ergänzungen zu Christian Gottlieb Jöchers allgemeinem Gelehrten-Lexico,* continued by Heinrich Wil-

helm Rotermund (vols. 3–6) and Otto Günther (vol. 7). 7 vols. Leipzig: Gleditsch, 1784–1897.

Allgemeine deutsche Biographie. 56 vols. Leipzig: Duncker & Humblot, 1875–1912. Facsimile reprint, Berlin: Duncker and Humblot, 1967–71. Also available online at http://mdz1.bib-bvb.de/~ndb.

Balbín, Bohuslav. *Bohemia Docta.* 3 vols. Prague: Hagen, 1776–80.

Bautz, F. W., and T. Bautz, eds. *Biographisch-bibliographisches Kirchenlexikon.* 2nd enlarged ed. 25 vols. Hamm, Westphalia [later Nordhausen]: Bautz, 1990–2005. Also available online at http://www.bautz.de/bbkl.

Bernath, Mathias, and Felix von Schroeder, eds. *Biographisches Lexikon zur Geschichte Südosteuropas.* 4 vols. Munich: R. Oldenbourg, 1974–81.

Biografický slovník českých zemí. Edited by P. Vošahlíková et al. Currently 4 vols. covering A–Bez. Prague: Historický ústav AV ČR-Libri, 2004–.

Bietenholz, Peter G., and Thomas B. Deutscher, eds. *Contemporaries of Erasmus: A Biographical Register of the Renaissance and Reformation.* 3 vols. Toronto: University of Toronto Press, 1985–87.

Deutscher biographischer Index. Edited by Willi Gorzny. 4 vols. Munich: Saur, 1986.

Deutsches biographisches Archiv: Eine Kumulation aus 254 der wichtigsten biographischen Nachschlagewerke für den deutschen Bereich bis zum Ausgang des neunzehnten Jahrhunderts. Edited by Bernhard Fabian. 1421 microfiches. Munich: Saur, 1982–86.

Gesamtkatalog deutschsprachiger Leichenpredigten. Online at http://web.uni-marburg.de/fpmr//html/db/gesainfo.html.

Historisch-Biographisches Lexikon der Schweiz. Edited by Heinrich Türler et al. 7 vols. plus supplement. Neuenburg: Administration des Historisch-Biographischen Lexicons der Schweiz, 1921–34.

Historisches Lexikon der Schweiz. Edited by the Stiftung Historisches Lexikon der Schweiz. 13 vols. planned; currently 6 vols. Basle: Schwabe, 2002–. Also available online at http://www.hls-dhs-dss.ch/index.php.

Iserloh, Erwin, ed. *Katholische Theologen der Reformationszeit.* 6 vols. Münster: Aschendorff, 1984–2004.

Jöcher, Christian Gottlieb. *Allgemeines Gelehrten-Lexicon.* 4 vols. Leipzig, 1750–51.

Kenyeres, Ágnes, ed. *Magyar életrajzi lexikon* [Hungarian Biographical Dictionary]. 2 vols. Budapest: Akadémiai Kiadó, 1967–69. Supplement issues, 1981, 1994. Available online at http://mek.iif.hu/porta/szint/egyeb/lexikon/eletrajz/html/index.html.

Krollmann, Christian, ed. *Altpreußische Biographie.* 2 vols. Königsberg: Grafe und Unzer, 1941–67.

Neue deutsche Biographie. Berlin: Duncker und Humblot, 1953–. Index available online at http://mdz1.bib-bvb.de/~ndb.

Pelzel, Franz Martin. *Abbildungen böhmischer und mährischer Gelehrten und Künstler.* 4 vols. Prague: Gerle, 1773–82.

Polski sownik biograficzny. Edited by Władysław Konopczynski et al. Currently 40 vols. Kraców: Skład główny w ksieg. Gebethnera i Wolffa, 1935–.

Strieder, F. W. *Grundlage an einer hessischen Gelehrten- und Schriftsteller-Geschichte.* 21 vols. Göttingen and Marburg, 1781–1868.

Studnicka, Frantisek Josef, and Jaromir Celakovsky, eds. *Ottův slovník naučný: Illustrovana encyklopaedie obecnych vedomosti.* 28 vols. Prague: J. Otto, 1888–1909.

Sturm, Heribert, et al., eds. *Biographisches Lexikon zur Geschichte der böhmischen Länder.* 4 vols. Munich: R. Oldenbourg, 1974–.

World Biographical Information System Online: Online at http://www.saur.de/wbis-online/index.htm.

Zedler, J. H., ed. *Grosses vollständiges Universal-Lexicon.* 64 vols. Halle and Leipzig, 1732–54. Also available online at http://www.zedler-lexikon.de.

Zoványi, Jenő, and Sándor Ladányi. *Magyarországi protestáns egyháztörténeti lexikon* [Lexicon of Hungarian Church History]. 3rd rev. ed. Budapest: Magyarországi Református Egyház Zsinati Irodájának Sajtóosztálya, 1977.

BIBLIOGRAPHIES AND GUIDES TO PRIMARY SOURCES

Apponyi, Alexander. *Hungarica: Ungarn betreffende im Auslande gedruckte Bücher und Flugschriften.* 4 vols. Munich: Jacques Rosenthal, 1903, 1925–27. Reprint, Nendelm/Liechtenstein: Kraus-Reprint, 1969; Budapest: Országos Széchényi Könyvtár, 2005.

Archive in der Bundesrepublik Deutschland, Österreich und der Schweiz. Edited by the Verein deutscher Archivare. 15th ed. Münster: Ardey-Verflag, 1995–.

Baumgart, Winfried, ed. *Quellenkunde zur deutschen Geschichte der Neuzeit von 1500 bis zur Gegenwart.* Vol. 1, *Das Zeitalter der Glaubensspaltung 1500-1618,* edited by Winfried Dotzauer (1987); Vol. 2, *Dreißigjähriger Krieg und Zeitalter Ludwigs XIV. 1618-1715,* edited by Winfried Becker (1995). Darmstadt: Wissenschaftliche Buchgesellschaft, 1987, 1995.

Bibliotheca Eruditionis: The History of Reading Databank (1500-1708). Available online at http://www.eruditio.hu.

Dahlmann, F. C., and Georg Waitz. *Quellenkunde der deutschen Geschichte: Bibliographie der Quellen und der Literatur zur deutschen Geschichte.* 10th ed. by Hermann Heimpel and Herbert Geuss. 12 vols. Stuttgart: A. Hiersemann, 1965–99.

Dünnhaupt, Gerhard. *Personalbibliographien zu den Drucken des Barock.* 2nd rev. ed. 6 vols. Stuttgart: Anton Hiersemann, 1990–93.

Elektronikus régi magyar könyvtár (eRMK). Edited by Országos Széchényi Könyvtár. 1 CD-ROM. Budapest: Arcanum Adatbázis, 2001. Available online at http://www.arcanum.hu/oszk.

Estermann, Monika, ed. *Verzeichnis der gedruckten Briefe deutscher Autoren des 17. Jahrhunderts.* Part 1, *Drucke zwischen 1600 und 1750.* 4 vols. Wiesbaden: Harrassowitz, 1992–93.

Estreicher, Karol, ed. *Bibliografia Polska.* 34 vols. Kraków: Nakladem Spólkiksi, egarzy polskich, 1870–1939. Reprint, New York: Johnson Reprint Corp., 1964–65.

———, ed. *Bibliografja Polska XV.–XVI stólecia.* Kraków, 1875. Reprint, Warsaw: WAiF Reprint, 1978.

Fabian, Bernhard, ed. *Handbuch der Historischen Buchbestände.* Series 1, *Deutschland,* 27 vols. in 28 (1992–2000); Series 2, *Österreich,* edited by the Österreichische Nationalbibliothek under the direction of Helmut W. Lang, 4 vols. (1994–97); Series 3, *Europa,* 12 vols. in 15 (1997–2001). Series 1–3, CD-ROM version (2002). Hildesheim: Olms, 1992–2002.

Frey, Axel. *Bibliothek der Deutschen Literatur: Bibliographie und Register.* 2nd ed., rev. and enlarged. Munich: K. G. Saur, 1999.

Hanacek, Andreas. *Archive in der Bundesrepublik Deutschland (1995-2000).* Online at http://home.bawue.de/~hanacek/info/darchive.htm.

Hejnic, Josef, and Jan Martínek, eds. *Rukověť' humanistického básnictví v Čechách a na Moravě / Enchiridion renatae poesis Latinae in Bohemia et Moravia cultae.* 5 vols. Prague: Academia, 1966–82.

IKAR—Altkartendatenbank. Online at http://ikar.sbb.spk-berlin.de.

Kalliope: Zentraler Nachweis von Nachlässen und Autographen in Deutschland. Online at http://kalliope.staatsbibliothek-berlin.de.

Karlsruher Virtueller Katalog. Online at http://www.ubka.uni-karlsruhe.de/kvk.html.

Kohler, Hans Joachim. *Bibliographie der Flugschriften des 16. Jahrhunderts.* Part 1, *Das frühe 16. Jahrhundert (1501–1530)*, Vols. 1-3, Druckbeschreibungen A–S. Tübingen: Biblioteca Academica, 1991–.

Libraries on the Web: Germany and Central Europe. Online at http://lists.webjunction.org/libweb/central.html.

Monok, István, ed. A *Kárpátmedence Koraújkori Könyvtárai/Libraries in the Carpathian Basin in the Early Modern Age.* Szeged: Scriptum, 1996–. Currently 3 titles in series, listed at http://www.eruditio.hu/kkk_eng.html.

———, ed. *Könyvtártörténeti Füzetek/Bibliographies of 16th- to 18th-Century Library History.* Szeged: Scriptum, 1981–. Currently 11 titles in series, listed at http://www.eruditio.hu/ktf_eng.html.

Pauser, Josef, Martin Scheutz, and Thomas Winkelbauer, eds. *Quellenkunde der Habsburgermonarchie. 16.–18. Jahrhunderte: Ein exemplarisches Handbuch.* Vienna: Oldenbourg, 2004.

Régi Magyar Könyvtar (RMK) [*Old Hungarian Library*]. 3 parts. Parts 1–2 by Károly Szabó; Part 3 by Árpád Hellebrant. Budapest: Magyar Tudomanyos Akademia, 1879–98. Enhanced version in *eRMK* at http://www.arcanum.hu/oszk.

Régi Magyarországi Nyomtatványok, 1473–1600: Res Litteraria Hungariae Vetus Operum Impressorum. Budapest: Akadémiai Kiadó, 1971–. Available online in *eRMK* at http://www.arcanum.hu/oszk.

Repertorium der handschriftlichen Nachlässe in den Bibliotheken und Archiven der Schweiz. Online at http://www.nb.admin.ch/slb/dienstleistungen/online_katalog/00454/01524/index.html?lang=de.

Sutton, Dana F. *An Analytic Bibliography of On-Line Neo-Latin Titles* (1999–). Online at http://www.philological.bham.ac.uk/bibliography.

Sztripszky, Haidor, ed. *Adalékok Szabó Károly Régi magyar könyvtár: c. munkájának I–II. Kötetéhez: Pótlások és igazítások, 1472–1711 / Appendix ad I–II tomos operis Caroli Szabó Régi magyar könytár: Bibliographia hungarica vetus: Additiones et emendationes, 1472–1711.* Budapest: Országos Széchényi Könyvtár, 1912. Reprint, Budapest: Országos Széchényi Könyvtár, 1967.

Tobolka, Z. V. , and František Horák, eds. *Knihopis československých tisků od doby nejstarší až do konce 18. století.* Part 1, *Incunables*, edited by Z. V. Tobolka. Prague: Knihkupectví Fr. Topiče, 1925. Part 2, *1501–1800*, edited by Z. V. Tobolka and F. Horák, 9 vols. Prague: Komise pro knihopisný soupis českých a slovenských tisků, 1936–67. Also available online at http://www.knihopis.org/index.eng.asp.

Ulrike Skorsetz, Janine Micunek, and Luzie Nahr. *Guide to Inventories and Finding Aids at the German Historical Institute, Washington, D.C.* (1995). Online at http://www.ghi-dc.org/guide5/index.html.

Verzeichnis der im deutschen Sprachbereich ershienenen Druckschriften des XVI. Jahrhunderts (*VD 16*). 25 vols. Stuttgart: Hiersemann, 1983–2000. Enhanced version available at http://gateway-bayern.bib-bvb.de/aleph-cgi/bvb_suche?sid=VD16. See also http://www.vd16.de.

Verzeichnis der im deutschen Sprachraum erschienenen Drucke des 17. Jahrhunderts (*VD 17*). Online at http://www.vd17.de.

Zentrales Verzeichnis Digitalisierter Drucke/Central Index of Digitized Imprints. Online at http://www.zvdd.de.

Zíbrt, Č. *Bibliografie české historie* [Bibliography of Czech History]. 5 vols. Prague: Nákladem České akademie cisaře Franktiška Josefa pro vědy, slovesnost a umñí, 1900–1912.

BIBLIOGRAPHIES AND GUIDES TO SECONDARY SOURCES

"Bibliographie zur Barockliteratur." In *Wolfenbütteler Barock-Nachrichten*. Hamburg: E. Hauswedell & Co.; Wiesbaden: Harrassowitz, 1974–. Originally semi-annual, quarterly since 1988.

Bibliographien zur Geschichte und Landeskunde Ostmitteleuropas. Marburg: Verlag Herder Institut. Full list available online at http://www.herder-institut.de/index.php?lang=de&id=3118&band=16. Database, *Literaturdokumentation zur Geschichte Ostmitteleuropas,* available online at http://www.herder-institut.de/index.php?lang=de&id=3193.

Chrisman, Miriam U. "Cities in the Reformation." In William S. Maltby, ed., *Reformation Europe: A Guide to Research II,* 105–27. St Louis, MO: Center for Reformation Research, 1992.

Geschichte in Wissenschaft und Unterricht. Stuttgart: E. Klett, 1950–.

Jahresberichte für deutsche Geschichte (JDG). Neue Folge, Herausgegeben von der Berlin-Brandenburgischen Akademie der Wissenschaften. Berlin: Akademie Verlag, 1952–. Available online at http://jdgdb.bbaw.de/cgi-bin/jdg.

Kaufmann, Thomas DaCosta, with Heiner Borggrefe and Thomas Fusenig. *Art and Architecture in Central Europe, 1550–1620: An Annotated Bibliography.* Marburg: Jonas, 2003.

Keyser, Erich. *Bibliographie zur Städtegeschichte Deutschlands.* Cologne: Böhlau, 1969.

Kittelson, James M. "The Confessional Age: The Late Reformation in Germany." In Steven Ozment, ed., *Reformation Europe: A Guide to Research,* 361–81. St. Louis, CO: Center for Reformation Research, 1982.

Kovtun, George J., ed. *Czech and Slovak History: An American Bibliography.* Washington, DC: Library of Congress, 1996.

Lawaty, Andreas, and Wiesaw Mincer, eds. *Deutsch-polnische Beziehungen in Geschichte und Gegenwart: Bibliographie, 1900–1998.* 4 vols. Wiesbaden: Harrassowitz, 2000.

Literaturbericht. Annual supplement, *Archiv für Reformationsgeschichte.* Gütersloh: Gütersloher Verlagshaus, 1972–.

Oberschelp, Reinhard. *Die Bibliographien zur deutschen Landesgeschichte und Landeskunde.* 3rd rev. ed., Frankfurt am Main: Klostermann, 1997.

Österreichische historische Bibliographie: Austrian Historical Bibliography. Graz: Neugebauer; Santa Barbara, CA: Clio Press, 1967–. Available online at http://www.uni-klu.ac.at/oehb.

Stoob, Heinz, ed. *Bibliographie zur deutschen historischen Städteforschung.* 3 vols. Cologne: Böhlau, 1986–96.

Verzeichnis Lieferbarer Bücher. Online at http://www.buchhandel.de.

Zophy, Jonathan. *An Annotated Bibliography of the Holy Roman Empire.* New York: Greenwood Press, 1986.

OTHER REFERENCE WORKS

Bosl, Karl, ed. *Handbuch der Geschichte der böhmischen Länder.* 4 vols. Stuttgart: A. Hiersemann, 1967–74.

Conze, Werner, and Volker Hentschel, eds. *Ploetz, deutsche Geschichte: Epochen und Daten.* Freiburg: Ploetz, 1996; Darmstadt: Wissenschaftliche Buchgesellschaft, 1998.

Deutsches Wörterbuch von Jacob Grimm und Wilhelm Grimm. Neubearbeitung. Edited by W. Braun et al. Produced by the Deutsche Akademie der Wissenschaften in Berlin in collaboration with the Akademie der Wissenschaften in Gottingen. Leipzig [now Stuttgart]: S. Hirzel Verlag, 1965–.

Enzyklopädie deutscher Geschichte. ca. 100 vols. Munich: Oldenburg, 1988–. For details, see http://www.oldenbourg.de/verlag/lehrbuch-prospekt.

Graesse, Johann Georg Theodor. *Orbis Latinus: Lexikon lateinischer geographischer Namen des Mittelalters und der Neuzeit,* edited by Helmut Plechl and Sophie-Charlotte Plechl. 3 vols. Braunschweig: Klinkhardt & Biermann, 1972. Also available online at http://www.columbia.edu/acis/ets/Graesse/contents.html.

Grimm, Jacob, and Wilhelm Grimm (founders). *Das Deutsche Wörterbuch.* 33 vols. Leipzig: Hirzel, 1854–1971. Facsimile reprint, Gütersloh: Bertelsmann-Club, 1991. Digitized version edited by Kompetenzzentrum für Elektronische Erschließungs und Publikationsverfahren in den Geisteswissenschaften, University of Trier. 2 CD-ROMs. Frankfurt am Main: Zweitausendeins, 2004. Also available online at http://germazope.uni-trier.de/Projects/DWB.

Handbuch der historischen Stätten Deutschlands. Stuttgart: Alfred Kröner Verlag, 1958–. Complete series listed at http://www.kroener-verlag.de.

Hillerbrand, Hans J., ed. *The Oxford Encyclopedia of the Reformation.* 4 vols. New York: Oxford University Press, 1996.

Jungmann, Josef. *Slovník česko-německý,* edited by Jan Petr. 5 vols. Prague: Fetterlowá, 1835–39. Reprint, Prague: Academia, 1989–90.

Jürgensmeier, Friedhelm, and Regina E. Schwerdtfeger, eds. *Orden und klösterliche Gemeinschaften im Zeitalter von Reformation und katholischer Reform 1500–1700.* 3 vols. Münster: Aschendorff, 2005–.

Köbler, Gerhard. *Historisches Lexikon der deutschen Länder.* 6th ed. Munich: C. H. Beck, 1999.

Müller, Michael G., ed., *Handbuch für Geschichte Polens.* Stuttgart: Hiersemann-Verlag, 2007.

Muller, Richard A. *Dictionary of Latin and Greek Theological Terms, Drawn Principally from Protestant Scholastic Theology.* Grand Rapids, MI: Baker Academic, 1996.

Müllers Grosses Deutsches Ortsbuch. 29th rev. ed. Munich: Saur, 2005.

Országh, László, and Tamás Magay, eds. *Angol Magyar nagyszótár/English-Hungarian Dictionary.* Budapest: Akadémiai Kiadó, Klasszikus Nagyszótárak, 1998.

———, eds. *A Concise English-Hungarian dictionary.* 10th rev. ed. Oxford: Oxford University sity Press, 1990.

Pach, Pál Zsigmond, ed. *Magyarország története* [History of Hungary]. 10 vols., esp. Vol. 3, *1526–1686,* edited by Agnes Várkonyi (1987). Budapest: Akadémiai Kiadó, 1976–.

Ramminger, Johann. *Neulateinische Wortliste: Ein Wörterbuch des Lateinischen von Petrarca bis 1700.* Online at http://www.neulatein.de.

Schindling, Anton, and Walter Ziegler, eds. *Die Territorien des Reichs im Zeitalter der Reformation und Konfessionalisierung: Land und Konfession 1500–1650.* 7 vols. Münster: Aschendorff, 1989–97.

Sebok, László, ed. *Magyar neve? Határokon túli helységnév-szótár* [Hungarian Name? Dictionary of Place-Names beyond Hungary's Borders]. N.p.: Arany Lapok, 1990.

Semotanová, Eva, Robert Šimůnek, and Josef Žemlička, eds. *Historický atlas měst České republiky* [Historical Atlas of Towns in the Czech Republic]. Currently 14 vols.

Prague: Historický ústav Akademie ved CR, 1995–. Description available online at http://www.hiu.cas.cz/atlas.

Thesaurus Locorum: Datenbank frühneuzeitlicher Ortsnamen. Online at http://www. uni-marburg.de/fpmr/html/db/thelo_info.html.

Theologische Realenzyklopädie. Edited by G. Krause and G. Müller. Berlin: Walter de Gruyter, 1976–.

Zophy, Jonathan. *The Holy Roman Empire: A Dictionary Handbook.* Westport, CT: Greenwood Press, 1980.

PRIMARY SOURCES

Alexander, Dorothy, and Walter L. Strauss. *The German Single-Leaf Woodcut, 1600–1700.* 2 vols. New York: Abaris, 1977.

Balke, Willem, and W. van 't Spijker, eds. *Reformed Protestantism 3: The Netherlands and Germany.* 269 titles on 2550 microfiches. Leiden: IDC, n.d.

Bibliothek der deutschen Literatur: Mikrofiche-Gesamtausgabe nach den Angaben des Taschengoedeke; Eine Edition der Kulturstiftung der Länder. Edited by Axel Frey and Leopold Hirshberg. Hauptwerk and 2 supplements. Ca. 17,225 works by ca. 2500 authors on 22,810 microfiches. Munich: Saur, 1990–2005.

Blum, Paul Richard, ed. *The Catholic Reformation.* 2950 microfiches. Leiden: IDC, 1987.

Bohatcová, M. *Irrgarten der Schicksale: Einblattdrucke vom Anfang des dressigjährigen Krieges.* Translated by Peter Aschner. 2 vols. in 1. Prague: Artia, 1966.

Corpus Automatum Multiplex Electorum Neolatinitatis Auctorum. Online at http:// www.uni-mannheim.de/mateo/camenahtdocs/camena.html.

Comenius, Jan Amos. *Opera omnia.* Prague: Academia, 1969.

Digital Library of Classic Protestant Texts. Alexandria, VA: Alexander Street Press. See http://alexanderstreet.com/products/tcpt.htm.

Digital Library of the Catholic Reformation. Alexandria, VA: Alexander Street Press. See http://alexanderstreet.com/products/dlcr.htm.

Flugschriften des frühen 16. Jahrhunderts. 1956 microfiches. Zug, Switzerland: Inter Documentation Co., 1979–87.

Flugschriften des späteren 16. Jahrhunderts, 1531–1600. Leiden: IDC, 1990–.

Freedman, J. S., et al., eds. *Philosophy and the Liberal Arts in the Early Modern Period.* Currently 5 installments including 547 titles on 2100 microfiches. Leiden: IDC, 2002–.

Geisberg, Max. *The German Single-Leaf Woodcut, 1500–1550.* Revised and edited by Walter L. Strauss. 4 vols. New York: Hacker, 1974.

Gunnoe, Charles, ed., and Richard A. Muller, advisor. *Reformation in Heidelberg.* 2 parts. Pt. 1, 99 titles on 252 microfiches; Pt. 2, 78 primary and 23 secondary titles on 524 microfiches. Leiden: IDC, 1999–.

Harms, Wolfgang, ed. *Deutsche illustrierte Flugblätter des 16. und 17. Jahrhunderts.* Currently 6 vols. Vols. 1–3, *Die Sammlung der Herzog August-Bibliothek in Wolfenbüttel;* Vol. 1, *Ethica, Physica* (1985); Vol. 2, *Historica* (1980, enlarged ed. 1997); Vol. 3, *Theologica, Quodlibetica* (1989); Vol. 4, *Die Sammlungen der Hessischen Landes- und Hochschulbibliothek in Darmstadt* (1987); Vol. 5, *Die Sammlung Hermann in der Bibliothèque Nationale et Universitaire in Strassburg* (forthcoming); Vols. 6–7, *Die Sammlung der Zentralbibliothek Zürich* (1997–2005). Munich: Kraus, 1980; continued Tübingen: Niemeyer, 1985–2005.

Keserû, Bálint, ed. Adattár XVI–XVIII. századi szellemi mozgalmaink történetéhez/Contributions to the history of the intellectual and cultural movements in the Carpathian basin in the 16–18 centuries. Szeged: Scriptum, 1983–. Currently 38 vols. in series, listed online at http://www.eruditio.hu/adatt_eng.html.

Maltby, William, ed. *Lutheran Reformation: Sources, 1500–1650.* 362 works on 1,667 microfiches. Leiden: IDC, n.d.

Melanchthon, Philipp. *Melanchthons Briefwechsel: Kritische und kommentierte Gesamtausgabe,* edited by Heinz Scheible. First Series (17 vols. planned; 14 vols. completed): Vols. 1–8, Register of Letters; Vol. 9, Addenda and Concordance; Vol. 10, Index of Places and Itinerary; Vols. 11–14, Biographical Register; Vols. 15–17, Catalogue of Manuscripts. Stuttgart: Frommann-Holzboog, 1977–. Second Series: Texts (30 vols. planned; 5 vols. completed). Stuttgart: Frommann-Holzboog, 1991–.

Merian, Matthäus. *Topographia Germaniae.* 17 vols. 1642–55. Facsimile reprint in 8 vols., Braunschweig: Archiv Verlag, 2005.

Paas, John Roger. *The German Political Broadsheet 1600–1700.* 10 vols. planned. Wiesbaden: Harrassowitz, 1985–.

Selderhuis, H. J., ed. *Irenical Theology: Heidelberg 1583–1622.* 142 titles on 596 microfiches. Leiden: IDC, 2007.

Strauss, Walter L. *The German Single-Leaf Woodcut, 1550–1600.* 3 vols. New York, Abaris, 1975.

Toepke, Gustav. *Die Matrikel der Universität Heidelberg, 1386–1662.* 3 vols. Heidelberg, 1884–89. Available online at http://www.ub.uni-heidelberg.de/helios/digi/unihdmatrikel.html.

Wengert, Timothy, ed. *Philipp Melanchthon, Theologian and Humanist.* 31 works on approx. 200 microfiches. Leiden: IDC, 2001.

SECONDARY SOURCES

Andor, Eszter, and István György Tóth, eds. *Frontiers of Faith: Religious Exchange and the Constitution of Religious Identities, 1400–1750.* Budapest: Central European University/European Science Foundation, 2001.

Asch, Ronald G. *The Thirty Years War: The Holy Roman Empire and Europe, 1618–1648.* Basingstoke: Macmillan, 1997.

Bahlcke, Joachim. *Regionalismus und Staatsintegration im Widerstreit: Die Länder der Böhmischen Krone im ersten Jahrhundert der Habsburgerherrschaft (1526–1619).* Munich: Oldenbourg, 1994.

———, ed. *Konfessionalisierung in Ostmitteleuropa: Wirkungen des religiösen Wandels im 16. und 17. Jahrhundert in Staat, Gesellschaft und Kultur.* Wiesbaden: Steiner, 1999.

———, Karen Lambrecht, and Hans-Christian Maner, eds. *Konfessionelle Pluralität als Herausforderung: Koexistenz und Konflikt in Spätmittelalter und Früher Neuzeit.* Leipzig: Leipziger Universitäts-Verlag, 2006.

Beckmann, Sabine, and Klaus Garber, eds. *Kulturgeschichte Preußens königlich polnischen Anteils in der Frühen Neuzeit.* Tübingen: Niemeyer, 2005.

Benedict, Philip. *Christ's Churches Purely Reformed: A Social History of Calvinism.* New Haven, CT: Yale University Press, 2002.

Bietenholz, Peter G. *Daniel Zwicker, 1612–1678: Peace, Tolerance and God the One and Only.* Florence: Olschki, 1997.

Borggrefe, Heiner, Vera Lüpkes, and Hans Ottomeyer, eds. *Moritz der Gelehrte: Ein Renaissancefürst in Europa.* Eurasberg: Minerva, 1997.

Bossy, John. *Christianity in the West, 1400–1700.* Oxford: Oxford University Press, 1985.

Brady, Thomas A., Jr., Heiko A. Oberman, and James D. Tracy, eds. *Handbook of European History, 1400–1600: Late Middle Ages, Renaissance and Reformation*. 2 vols. Leiden: Brill, 1994–95; Grand Rapids, MI: Eerdmans, 1996.

Bucsay, Mihály. *Der Protestantismus in Ungarn, 1521–1978*. 2 vols. Vol. 1, *Im Zeitalter der Reformation, Gegenreformation und katholischer Reform* (1977). Cologne: Böhlau, 1977–79.

Bußman, Klaus, and Heinz Schilling, eds. *1648: War and Peace in Europe*. 3 vols. Munich: Bruckmann, 1998.

Butterwick, Richard, ed. *The Polish-Lithuanian Monarchy, 1500–1795*. London: Palgrave, 2001.

Caspary, Gundula. *Späthumanismus und Reichspatriotismus: Melchior Goldast und seine Editionen zur Reichsverfassungsgeschichte*. Göttingen: Vandenhoeck & Ruprecht, 2006.

Craciun, Maria, Ovidiu Ghitta, and Graeme Murdock, eds. *Confessional Identity in East-Central Europe*. Aldershot: Ashgate, 2002.

Daniel, David. "Hungary." In Pettegree, *Early Reformation in Europe*, 49–69.

David, Zdenek V. *Finding the Middle Way: The Utraquists' Liberal Challenge to Rome and Luther*. Washington, DC: Woodrow Wilson Center Press, 2003.

Delumeau, Jean. *Le Catholicisme entre Luther et Voltaire*. Paris: Nouvelle Clio, 1971. Translated as *Catholicism between Luther and Voltaire: A New View of the Counter-Reformation*. London: Burnes & Oates, 1978.

Deutsche Geschichte im Osten Europas. 10 vols. *Ostpreußen und Westpreußen*, edited by Hartmut Boockmann (1993); *Böhmen und Mähren*, edited by Friedrich Prinz (1993); *Baltische Länder*, edited by Gert von Pistohlkors (1994); *Schlesien*, edited by Norbert Conrads (1994); *Land an der Donau*, edited by Günter Schödl (1995); *Land der großen Ströme: Von Polen nach Litauen*, edited by Joachim Rogall (1996); *Ruß-land* edited by Gerd Stricker (1997); *Zwischen Adria und Karawanken*, edited by Arnold Suppan (1998); *Galizien, Bukowina, Moldau* edited by Isabel Röskau-Rydel (1999); *Pommern*, edited by Werner Buchholz (1999). Berlin: Siedler, 1993–99.

Duchhardt, Heinz. *Deutsche Verfassungsgeschichte, 1495–1806*. Stuttgart: Kohlhammer, 1991.

Eberhard, Winfried. "Bohemia, Moravia and Austria." In Pettegree, *Early Reformation in Europe*, 23–48.

———. "Reformation and Counterreformation in East Central Europe." In Brady, Oberman, and Tracy, *Handbook of European History*, 551–84.

Evans, R. J. W. "Calvinism in East Central Europe: Hungary and Her Neighbours, 1540–1700." In Menna Prestwich, ed. *International Calvinism*, 167–96. Oxford: Oxford University Press, 1985.

———. *The Making of the Habsburg Monarchy, 1550–1700*. Oxford: Oxford University Press, 1979.

———. *Rudolf II and His World: A Study in Intellectual History, 1576–1612*. Oxford: Clarendon Press, 1973. Reprint, London: Thames & Hudson, 1983, 1997.

———, and T. V. Thomas, eds. *Crown, Church and Estates: Central European Politics in the Sixteenth and Seventeenth Centuries*. Basingstoke: Macmillan, 1991.

Fata, Márta. *Ungarn, das Reich der Stephanskrone im Zeitalter der Reformation und Konfessionalisierung: Multiethnizität, Land und Konfession, 1500 bis 1700*. Edited by F. Brendle and A. Schindling. Münster: Aschendorff, 2000.

Fichtner, Paula Sutter. *Emperor Maximilian II*. New Haven, CT: Yale University Press, 2001.

Fleischer, Manfred P. "Komm in den totgesagten Park und Schau. Der deutsche Humanismus nach 1550." *Zeitschrift für Religions- und Geistesgeschichte* 42 (1990): 136–54.

———, ed. *The Harvest of Humanism in Central Europe: Essays in Honor of Lewis Spitz*. St. Louis, MO: Concordia, 1992.

Freedman, Joseph S. *Philosophy and the Arts in Central Europe, 1500–1700: Teaching and Texts at Schools and Universities*. Aldershot: Ashgate, 2000.

Frost, Robert I. *The Northern Wars: War, State and Society in Northeastern Europe, 1558–1721*. Harlow: Longman, 2000.

Fučíková, Eliška, ed., *Rudolf II and Prague: The Court and the City*. Prague: Prague Castle Administration; London: Thames and Hudson, 1997.

Fudge, Thomas A. *The Magnificent Ride: The First Reformation in Hussite Bohemia*. Aldershot: Ashgate, 1998.

Garber, Klaus, ed. *Kulturgeschichte Schlesiens in der Frühen Neuzeit*. 2 parts. Tübingen: Niemeyer, 2005.

———, and Martin Klöker, eds. *Kulturgeschichte der baltischen Länder in der Frühen Neuzeit*. Tübingen: Niemeyer, 2003.

———, Manfred Komorowski, and Axel E. Walter, eds. *Kulturgeschichte Ostpreußens in der Frühen Neuzeit*. Tübingen: Niemeyer, 2001.

Gatenbröker, Silke, ed. *Hofkunst der Spätrenaissance: Braunschweig-Wolfenbüttel und das kaiserliche Prag um 1600*. Braunschweig: Herzog Anton Ulrich-Museum, 1998.

Gotthard, Axel. *Das Alte Reich, 1495–1806*. Darmstadt: Wissenschaftliche Buchgesellschaft, 2003.

Greyerz, Kaspar von, Manfred Jakubowski-Tiessen, Thomas Kaufmann, and Harmut Lehmann, eds. *Interkonfessionalität—Transkonfessionalität—binnenkonfessionelle Pluralität: Neue Forschungen zur konfessionalisierungsthese*. Gütersloh: Gütersloher Verlaghaus, 2003.

Hammerstein, Notker. *Bildung und Wissenschaft vom 15. bis zum 17. Jahrhundert*. Enzyclopädie deutscher Geschichte 64. Munich: Oldenbourg, 2003.

———, ed. *15. bis 17. Jahrhundert: Von der Renaissance und der Reformation bis zum Ende der Glaubenskämpfe*. Vol. 1 of *Handbuch der deutschen Bildungsgeschichte*, edited by Christa Berg et al. Munich: C. H. Beck, 1996.

———, and Gerrit Walther, eds. *Späthumanismus: Studien über das Ende einer kulturhistorischen Epoche*. Göttingen: Wallstein, 2000.

Hartmann, Peter Claus. *Das Heilige Römische Reich deutscher Nation in der Neuzeit 1486–1806*. Stuttgart: Reclam, 2005.

Holzhey, Helmut, and Wilhelm Schmidt-Biggemann, eds. *Das Heilige Römische Reich Deutscher Nation. Nord- und Ostmitteleuropa*, 2 parts. Vol. 4 of *Die Philosophie des 17. Jahrhunderts*. Grundriss der Geschichte der Philosophie, founded by Friedrich Ueberweg. Basle: Schwabe, 2001.

Hotson, Howard. *Commonplace Learning: Ramism and Its German Ramifications, 1543–1630*. Oxford: Oxford University Press, 2007.

Hsia, Ronnie Po-chia, ed. *A Companion to the Reformation World*. Oxford: Blackwell, 2004.

Jobert, Ambroise. *De Luther à Mohila: La Pologne dans la crise de la chrétienté, 1517–1648*. Paris: Institut d'Etudes Slaves, 1974.

Kaufmann, Thomas DaCosta. *Court, Cloister and City: The Art and Culture of Central Europe 1450–1800*. London: Weidenfeld and Nicolson, 1995.

Kavka, František. "Bohemia." In Scribner, Porter, and Teich, *Reformation in National Context*, 131–54.

Koczowski, Jerzy. *A History of Polish Christianity*. Cambridge: Cambridge University Press, 2000.

Klueting, Harm, ed. *Irenik und Antikonfessionalismus im 17. und 18. Jahrhundert*. Hildesheim: Olms, 2003.

Köpeczi, Béla, ed. *History of Transylvania*. Edited by B. Kovrig. 3 vols. Boulder, CO: Social Science Monographs, 2001–.

Korthaase, Werner, Sigurd Hauff, and Andreas Fritsch, eds. *Comenius und der Weltfriede: Comenius and World Peace*. Berlin: Deutsche Comenius-Gesellschaft, 2005.

Kosa, László, ed. *A Cultural History of Hungary*. 2 vols. Budapest: Osiris-Corvina, 2000.

Kulturstiftung Ruhr Essen. *Prag um 1600: Kunst und Kultur am Hofe Rudolfs II*. 2 vols. Freren: Luca, 1988.

Louthan, Howard P. *The Quest for Compromise: Peacemakers in Counter-Reformation Vienna*. Cambridge: Cambridge University Press, 1997.

———, and Randall C. Zachman, eds. *Conciliation and Confession: The Struggle for Unity in the Age of Reform, 1415–1648*. Notre Dame, IN: University of Notre Dame Press, 2004.

Maag, Karin, ed. *The Reformation in Eastern and Central Europe*. Aldershot: Ashgate, 1997.

Moeller, Bernd. *Reichsstadt und Reformation*. Gütersloh: Mohn, 1962. Rev. ed., Berlin: Evangelische Verlagsanstalt, 1987. Partial English translation in *Imperial Cities and the Reformation*. Edited and translated by H. C. Eric Midelfort and Mark U. Edwards Jr. Philadelphia: Fortress Press, 1972; Durham, NC: Labyrinth Press, 1982.

Monok, István, ed. *Olvasmánytörténeti Dolgozatok* [Studies in the History of Reading]. Szeged: Scriptum, 1991–. Titles in series available at http://www.eruditio.hu/odolg_eng.html.

Moran, Bruce T. "Patronage and Institutions: Courts, Universities, and Academies in Germany: An Overview, 1550–1750." In Moran, ed., *Patronage and Institutions: Science, Technology, and Medicine at the European Court, 1500–1750*, 169–83. Rochester, NY: Boydell, 1991.

Müller, Hans-Joachim. *Irenik als Kommunikationsreform: Das Colloquium Charitativum in Thorn 1645*. Göttingen: Vandenboeck and Ruprecht, 2004.

Müller, Rainer A. *Der Fürstenhof in der Frühen Neuzeit*. Enzyclopädie deutscher Geschichte 33. Munich: Oldenbourg, 1995.

Muller, Richard A. *Post-Reformation Reformed Dogmatics: The Rise and Development of Reformed Orthodoxy, ca. 1520 to ca. 1725*. 2nd ed. 4 vols. Grand Rapids, MI: Baker Academic, 2003.

Murdock, Graeme. *Beyond Calvin: The Intellectual, Political and Cultural World of Europe's Reformed Churches*. Basingstoke: Palgrave, 2004.

———. *Calvinism on the Frontier, 1600–1660: International Calvinism and the Reformed Church in Hungary and Transylvania*. Oxford: Oxford University Press, 2000.

———. "Central and Eastern Europe." In *Palgrave Advances in the European Reformations*, edited by Alec Ryrie, 36–56. Basingstoke: Palgrave Macmillan, 2006.

———. "Eastern Europe." In *The Reformation World*, edited by Andrew Pettegree, 190–210. London: Routledge, 2000.

Neuhaus, Helmut. *Das Reich in der Frühen Neuzeit*. Enzyclopädie deutscher Geschichte 42. Munich: Oldenbourg, 1997.

Niendorf, Mathias. *Das Grossfürstentum Litauen: Studien zur Nationsbildung in der Frühen Neuzeit (1569–1795)*. Wiesbaden: Harrassowitz, 2006.

Oestreich, Gerhard. *Verfassungsgeschichte vom Ende des Mittelalters bis zum Ende des alten Reiches*. Munich: Deutscher Taschenbuch-Verlag, 1974.

Palmitessa, James R. "The Reformation in Bohemia and Poland." In Hsia, *Companion to the Reformation World*, 185–204.

Parker, Geoffrey, ed. *The Thirty Years' War*. 2nd rev. ed. London: Routledge, 1997.

Peter, Katalin. "Hungary." In Scribner, Porter, and Teich, *Reformation in National Context*, 155–67.

Pettegree, Andrew, ed. *The Early Reformation in Europe*. Cambridge: Cambridge University Press, 1992.

Pop, Ioan-Aurel. and Thomas Nägler, eds. *The History of Transylvania*. 3 vols. Translated and revised by Bogdan Aldea and Richard Proctor. Cluj-Napoca: Romanian Cultural Institute, 2005–.

Press, Volker. "The Habsburg Lands: The Holy Roman Empire." In Brady, Oberman, and Tracy, *Handbook of European History*, 437–66.

———. "The Holy Roman Empire in German History." In *Politics and Society in Reformation Europe*, edited by E. I. Kouri and T. Scott, 51–77. Houndmills: Macmillan; New York: St. Martin's Press, 1987.

Racaut, Luc, and Alex Ryrie, eds. *Moderate Voices in the European Reformation*. Aldershot: Ashgate, 2005.

Raitt, Jill, ed. *Shapers of Religious Traditions in Germany, Switzerland and Poland, 1560–1600*. New Haven, CT: Yale University Press, 1981.

Říčan, Rudolf. *The History of the Unity of Brethren: A Protestant Hussite Church in Bohemia and Moravia*. Translated by C. Daniel Crews. Bethlehem, PA: Moravian Church in America, 1992.

Ridder-Symoens, Hilde de, ed. *Universities in Early Modern Europe (1500–1800)*. History of the University in Europe 2. Cambridge: Cambridge University Press, 1996.

Rummel, Erika. *The Confessionalization of Humanism in Reformation Germany*. Oxford: Oxford University Press, 2000.

Schilling, Heinz. *Die Stadt in der Frühen Neuzeit*. Enzyclopädie deutscher Geschichte 24. Munich: Oldenbourg, 1993.

Schindling, Anton. *Bildung und Wissenschaft in der frühen Neuzeit 1650–1800*. Munich: Oldenbourg, 1994.

Schmidt, Christoph. *Auf Felsen gesät: Die Reformation in Polen und Livland*. Göttingen: Vandenhoeck and Ruprecht, 2000.

Schmidt, Georg. *Geschichte des Alten Reiches: Staat und Nation in der Frühen Neuzeit 1495–1806*. Munich: Beck, 1999.

Scribner, Robert W., and Sheilagh C. Ogilvie, eds. *Germany: A New Social and Economic History*. 2 vols. Vol. 1, *1450–1630*; Vol. 2, *1630–1800*. London: Arnold, 1996.

———, Roy Porter, and Mikuláš Teich, eds. *The Reformation in National Context*. Cambridge: Cambridge University Press, 1994

Seidel, Robert. *Späthumanismus in Schlesian: Caspar Dornau (1577–1631), Leben und Werk*. Tübingen: Niemeyer, 1994.

Šmahel, František. *Die Hussitische Revolution*. 3 vols. Hannover: Hahn, 2002.

Stollberg-Rilinger, Barbara. *Das Heilige Römische Reich Deutscher Nation: Vom Ende des Mittelalters bis 1806*. Munich: Beck, 2006.

Strohm, Christoph, Herman J. Selderhuis, and Joseph S. Freedman, eds. *Späthumanismus und reformierte Konfession: Theologie, Jurisprudenz und Philosophie in Heidelberg an der Wende zum 17. Jahrhundert*. Tübingen: Mohr Siebeck, 2006.

Syndram, Dirk, and Antje Scherner, eds. *Princely Splendor: The Dresden Court 1580–1620*. Dresden: Staatliche Kunstsammlungen Dresden, 2004.

Tazbir, Janusz. "Poland." In Scribner, Porter, and Teich, *Reformation in National Context*, 168–80.

———. *A State Without Stakes: Polish Religious Tolerance in the Sixteenth and Seventeenth Centuries.* [New York]: Kosciuszko Foundation, 1973.

Teter, Magda. *Jews and Heretics in Catholic Poland: A Beleaguered Church in the Post-Reformation Era.* Cambridge: Cambridge University Press, 2006.

Tóth, István György. "Old and New Faith in Hungary, Turkish Hungary, and Transylvania." In Hsia, *Companion to the Reformation World*, 205–21.

Trueman, Carl R., and R. S. Clark, eds. *Protestant Scholasticism: Essays in Reinterpretation.* Carlisle, UK: Paternoster Press, 1999.

Unghváry, Alexander Sándor. *The Hungarian Protestant Reformation in the Sixteenth Century under the Ottoman Impact.* Lewiston: Edwin Mellen Press, 1989.

van Asselt, Willem J., and Eef Dekker, eds. *Reformation and Scholasticism: An Ecumenical Enterprise.* Grand Rapids, MI: Baker Academic, 2001.

Völker-Rasor, Anette, ed. *Frühe Neuzeit.* Munich: Oldenbourg, 2000.

Wallace, Peter G. *The Long European Reformmation.* Houndsmills, Basingstoke: Palgrave Macmillan, 2004.

Walter, Axel E. *Späthumanismus und Konfessionspolitik: Die europäische Gelehrtenrepublik um 1600 im Spiegel der Korrespondenzen Georg Michael Lingelsheims.* Tübingen: Niemeyer, 2004.

Watanabe-O'Kelly, Helen. *Court Culture in Dresden: From Renaissance to Baroque.* Basingstoke: Palgrave, 2002.

Wilson, Peter H. *The Holy Roman Empire, 1495–1806.* New York: St. Martin's Press, 1999.

Winkelbauer, Thomas. *Ständefreiheit und Fürstenmacht: Länder und Untertanen des Hauses Habsburg im konfessionellen Zeitalter.* 2 vols. Vienna: Ueberreuter, 2003.

Wolf, Peter, ed. *Der Winterkönig—Friedrich V., der letzte Kurfürst aus der oberen Pfalz: Amberg, Heidelberg, Prag, Den Haag.* Katalog zur Bayerischen Landesausstellung 2003, Stadtmuseum Amberg, 9. Mai bis 2. November 2003. Augsburg: Haus der Bayerischen Geschichte, 2003.

Wollgast, Siegfried. *Philosophie in Deutschland, 1500–1650.* 2nd rev. ed. Berlin: Akademie Verlag, 1993.

8

France

Barbara B. Diefendorf

As in many other areas of early modern religious history, historians of France are still working to fill out the picture that began to emerge more than thirty years ago, when attention shifted from the reformers' message to the reception of this message on the part of the laity. French historians continue fruitfully to explore the religious choices men and women made, the pious practices in which they engaged, and the social, political, and cultural implications of these choices and practices. This is not to say that important work has ceased on the ideas of the major reformers, but this scholarship too has been imbued with a different spirit, with historians asking not just *what* the reformers' message was but *how* it was delivered and *why* it was (or was not) attractive to its audience.

This increased attention to religious practice and belief has produced fundamental shifts in historians' understanding of late medieval piety and, as a consequence, of the nature of religious dissent and origins of the Protestant Reformation in France. A new attention to the spread of ideas through both the pulpit and the printing press has produced fresh insights into the dissemination of Protestant ideas and their adoption or rejection, with attention to both the formal creation of Calvinist institutions and the success of these institutions in forging a distinct Calvinist culture. At the same time, attention to religious propaganda and to the social and cultural aspects of belief has brought the religious dimension of the Wars of Religion into focus. Narratives stressing political tensions within the nobility have given way to studies of popular religious enthusiasm and religious violence. The latter current, moreover, has already produced a reaction on the part of scholars who seek to turn our attention from the brutal episodes in which people killed one another over their religious differences to those longer periods when Protestants and Catholics lived side by side in relatively peaceful, if sometimes tense, coexistence. It seems then that, far from having exhausted themselves, the avenues of inquiry into religious practice and belief continue to produce useful questions and agendas for further research.

The Roots of the Reformation in France

More than seventy-five years ago, Lucien Febvre challenged traditional narratives that rooted the Protestant Reformation in the fertile soil of disaffection from a corrupt church poorly served by an ignorant clergy. Pointing to the many new churches and chapels built in the Flamboyant Gothic style during the late fifteenth and early sixteenth centuries, he called on these "witnesses made of stone" to testify "not only that fidelity to the old beliefs remained intact, but also that the traditional piety was manifest with a very special fervor" during the late fifteenth and early sixteenth centuries in France.[1] Taking up Febvre's suggestion that late medieval religious culture remained both vibrant and popular, A. N. Galpern, Nicole Lemaître, Larissa Taylor, Virginia Reinburg, and Moshe Sluhovsky, among others, have given a far more positive assessment of the ways that Catholic ritual, teachings, and forms of association served the broader community than the previous literature allowed.[2] A notable dissenter from this view, Jean Delumeau, has argued that, owing to the ignorance of the clergy, mechanical repetition of ritual, and lack of instruction in doctrine, the mass of the European population was only superficially Christianized on the eve of the Protestant and Catholic Reformations.[3] Although Delumeau's thesis that the mass of the people remained virtually pagan, practicing a mixture of superstition and magic, has been taken up by some historians of witchcraft and popular culture, historians of religion have generally preferred Jean-Claude Schmitt's more nuanced view of local religion as capable of absorbing folkloric elements and customs without

---

[1]Febvre, *Au cœur religieux* , 27.

[2]Galpern, *Religions of the People*; Lemaître, *Le Rouergue flamboyant*; Taylor, *Soldiers of Christ*; Reinburg, "Liturgy and the Laity"; Reinburg, "Hearing Lay People's Prayer"; and Sluhovsky, *Patroness of Paris*.

[3]Delumeau, *Catholicism between Luther and Voltaire*.

thereby becoming pagan or losing its foundational core of Christian beliefs.[4]

In keeping with this interest in popular belief, historians of the early Reformation have paid relatively less attention to evangelical reformers such as Jacques Lefèvre and more to the character of popular heresy. David Nicholls suggests that the religious fervor of the later Middle Ages was not incompatible with the skepticism and questioning of fundamental Catholic beliefs that characterized popular heresy in the pre-Calvinist era. He finds this period characterized by "innumerable quests for religious truth" and believes that this chaotic situation hindered the Calvinists' attempt to impose their vision of a reformed church and society.[5] Recent studies of publishing and religious propaganda also point to the diversity—and doctrinal confusion—apparent in the early stage of French religious dissent.[6] If this diversity hindered early Calvinists in their quest for theological unity, it also hindered efforts on the part of Catholic authorities to stamp out dissent in its entirety because, as Timothy Watson argues for Lyon, "there was no clear target to aim at."[7]

Interest in the character of popular religious dissent is also evident in Gabriel Audisio and Euan Cameron's productive rethinking of the relationship between Calvinism and France's long-established dissenters, the Waldensians.[8] If the Calvinists succeeded in gaining the adherence of this group, they suggest, this is not because the Waldensians already shared key elements of Calvinist theology but rather because, after a new round of persecution in the 1540s, they preferred to ally with another outcast group than to rejoin the church that had persecuted them for centuries. Meanwhile, William Monter has profoundly reshaped historians' understanding of prosecution of heresy by the high courts of Parlement.[9] Demolishing the long-accepted belief that the repression of heresy by French courts intensified with the organization and growth of Calvinist churches in France, he shows that, from the 1520s, French courts were eager to act against heresy. Their ability do so was impeded by both internal and external (i.e., political) factors. Convictions for heresy peaked during the reign of François I and not, as has usually been assumed, after Henri II's introduction of the

---

[4]Schmitt, *The Holy Greyhound.*
[5]Nicholls, "Nature of Popular Heresy," 274.
[6]For example, Higman, *Lire et découvrir.*
[7]Watson, "Preaching, Printing, Psalm-Singing," 18.
[8]Audisio, *Waldensian Dissent*; and Cameron, *Reformation of the Heretics* and *Waldenses.*
[9]Monter, *Judging the French Reformation.*

infamous *Chambre ardente.*[10] Despite their inclusion in Reformed mar-
tyrologies, most of France's convicted heretics thus belong to the theologically diverse period before Calvinism was effectively introduced into
France.

The Creation of Calvinist Churches and Culture

Catholic authorities and Protestant martyrologists made very different use
of the spectacularly staged public executions of convicted heretics to reinforce their conceptions of community and faith.[11] Conviction for heresy
was, however, only one measure of religious persecution. Even if Catherine
de Médici's policies of limited toleration made it very difficult successfully
to prosecute heresy cases, suspects continued to be arrested and frequently
could be prosecuted on the alternative charge of sedition. Suspected Protestants were vulnerable to attack in religious riots and individual or collective acts of popular violence.[12] Recent work on the creation of Calvinist
churches stresses the impact of this troubled political climate. The essays
published by Raymond Mentzer and Andrew Spicer, for example, illustrate
well the vital role that the threat and reality of persecution played in shaping the Huguenots' social and cultural values, as well as determining their
political priorities.[13]

It was not, however, just the danger of persecution that caused many
of those who were initially drawn to Protestant teachings to return to the
Catholic Church. Natalie Davis demonstrated forty years ago that the institutionalization of the Calvinist reform in Lyon drove journeymen printers,
who had been leaders of the early movement, back into the arms of the
mother church. Finding themselves not only excluded from participation
in the consistory but also the objects of its moralizing scrutiny, the journeymen, angered by both the church's reinforcement of traditional social
hierarchies and its disciplining function, returned "somewhat lukewarmly"
to the Catholic fold.[14] Recent studies have confirmed the tendency for the

---

[10]Heresy accusations, however, follow a different curve. Mentzer, "Heresy Proceedings in
Languedoc, 1500–1560," reveals a cyclical but rising pattern of heresy accusations in Languedoc that
peaks in the 1550s, just when Calvinist churches were beginning to be organized.

[11]Nicholls, "Theatre of Martyrdom."

[12]Davis's "Rites of Violence," originally published in 1973 (reprinted in her *Society and Culture in
Early Modern France*), is the pioneering essay. See also Greengrass, "Anatomy of a Religious Riot";
Crouzet, *Les guerriers de Dieu*; and Diefendorf, *Beneath the Cross*.

[13]Mentzer and Spicer, *Society and Culture*; also Diefendorf, "Huguenot Psalter."

[14]Davis's "Strikes and Salvation in Lyon" was originally published in 1965, and reprinted in her
Society and Culture in Early Modern France.

roles of elder and even deacon to be reserved for men with a higher social profile; they have also stressed the tensions resulting from attempts on the part of Calvinist consistories to impose moral discipline. Mentzer's articles on the regulation of morals by Reformed consistories are especially useful here.[15] Kevin Robbins's study of La Rochelle and Philip Conner's book on Montauban also give precious insights into the relationship between the consistory and the urban elite and the role these institutions played in creating a "godly society."[16] Conner finds that even when consuls and consistory collaborated, as they did in Montauban, "the initial burst of reforming zeal was not sustained," and pastors had to temper their enthusiasm for regulating public behavior—especially when it came to pastimes such as dancing, favored by elite as well as popular culture.[17] Philippe Chareyre's study of Nîmes arrives at similar conclusions. The "tireless activity" of the Reformed consistory in Nîmes peaked between 1578 and 1614, a period Chareyre qualifies as the "golden age of censure among southern French Protestants."[18] Even during this period, however, the consistory was significantly more successful in reinforcing the family unit and resolving disputes than in repressing traditional festivities and forms of urban sociability.

More work remains to be done to broaden historians' understanding of the impact of Calvinist moral discipline both chronologically and geographically. With the completion of the catalogue of consistory records Mentzer is compiling, the scattered sources for this necessary research will be markedly easier to find. Exploiting and interpreting these records will nevertheless remain a major challenge. There is a need for comparative studies that look at a single question or type of social issue across a number of consistories, but also for more community-based studies in which consistory records are augmented with careful research in city and notarial archives so as to firmly ground the analysis of Calvinist culture within the existing dynamics of family and class. A related theme deserving of more research is the practice of piety among the Calvinist laity. Here again, Mentzer has made a valuable contribution by exploring ways in which ritual and ceremony reinforced Calvinist identity in France.[19] More can be

---

[15]Mentzer, *Blood and Belief*; "Persistence of 'Superstition and Idolatry'"; "Morals and Moral Regulation"; and "Notions of Sin and Penitence."

[16]Robbins, *City on the Ocean Sea*; and Conner, *Huguenot Heartland*.

[17]Conner, *Huguenot Heartland*, 65.

[18]Chareyre, "The Great Difficulties," 64–65.

[19]Mentzer, "Laity and Liturgy."

done, however, to fill out this picture, identify local variations, and trace changes over time.

Historians' understanding of the institutional context of French Protestantism has benefited from Glenn Sunshine's emphasis on the importance of equality—a refusal to put one church over another—in the evolution of French synodical structures.[20] This collegiality was a necessary development, in Sunshine's view, given the need to unite churches that were originally highly local and insisted on retaining a large measure of autonomy. It nevertheless resulted in the creation of a church that offended the monarchy by its "republican" character, as well as by its theology. The crown's reaction to Calvinism has also received thoughtful treatment by Christopher Elwood, who identifies the doctrine of the Eucharist as the subversive heart of Calvinist theology.[21] When Calvinists rejected Catholic notions of divine immanence as idolatrous, they challenged fundamental notions about the way power worked and undermined the sacred status of the king. Despite their protestations of loyalty and acceptance of monarchical authority, their self-presentation as a holy community around shared participation in the Eucharist identified them as a people apart, awakening suspicion on the part of the king but also violent anger on the part of Catholic preachers and people. The acts of iconoclasm through which some Protestants demonstrated their belief that Catholic worship was idolatrous further exacerbated the already tense situation. Although Protestant leaders distanced themselves from these acts, recent research suggests that at least some ministers secretly encouraged them—just as Catholic crowds suspected.[22]

The Wars of Religion

Surveys by Mack Holt and Robert Knecht offer very good introductions to France's religious wars.[23] Both offer balanced interpretations, with the former emphasizing the religious character of the conflicts and the latter placing more stress on the way aristocratic quarrels played into the religious tensions.[24] Knecht's book has a particularly extensive and useful

---

[20]Sunshine, *Reforming French Protestantism*.

[21]Elwood, *Body Broken*.

[22]On Protestant iconoclasm, see Davis, *Society and Culture*; Sauzet, "L'iconoclasme dans le diocèse"; Crouzet, *Les guerriers de Dieu*, chaps. 7–10; and Christin, *Une révolution symbolique*.

[23]Holt, *French Wars of Religion*; and Knecht, *French Civil Wars*.

[24]Holt also discusses the role that religion played in the wars in a useful review article, "Putting Religion Back into the Wars of Religion."

annotated bibliography. David Potter has produced a useful collection of documents.[25] J. H. M. Salmon's *Society in Crisis* remains useful on the social and political tensions behind the wars.[26] Philip Benedict's essay on "The Dynamics of Protestant Militancy, 1555–1563" offers an excellent analysis of the period between the formation of the first Calvinist congregations and the outbreak of civil war. In contrast to previous historians who saw French Protestants as merely desiring "recognition," or freedom of worship, Benedict argues that they wanted to complete the civic reformation they believed necessary to the regeneration of church and society alike and that "once the initial step of assembling in defiance of the law had been taken, other steps came to be seen as justifiable to counter the way in which the government or Catholic opinion reacted to the initial assemblies."[27] Fearing they would be attacked by Catholic crowds or else shut down by government officials, the rapidly growing congregations began to create paramilitary structures, while still stridently insisting on their loyalty to the crown. These structures provided the basis for the Huguenots' mobilization in 1562, when events surrounding the massacre of Vassy pushed both sides into war. Jérémie Foa, Penny Roberts, and Kevin Gould have also offered useful insights into the fundamental issues prompting the wars by demonstrating the profound impact that conflicts over urban space and places of worship had on both Protestant and Catholic militance.[28]

James Wood's history of the royal army helps explain why the wars were so inconclusive and why they dragged on so long.[29] It was extremely expensive to keep an army in the field and budget problems repeatedly forced the crown to negotiate with the Huguenots, whose tactic of seizing walled towns allowed them to maintain a stronger defensive position than their overall numbers would predict. The Huguenots' ability to make the crown pay for the mercenaries they hired to help fight their wars also increased the cost of the wars to the king, as well as to the Catholic subjects whose taxes time and again went to pay off armies that had made war against them. Because the actual fighting was widely scattered, having a far greater impact on some regions than others, the history of the French civil

[25]Potter, *French Wars of Religion*.

[26]Salmon, *Society in Crisis*.

[27]Benedict et al., *Reformation, Revolt and Civil War*, 38 and 42. For the contrasting view, see Sutherland, *Huguenot Struggle*.

[28]Foa, "An Unequal Apportionment"; Roberts, "Most Crucial Battle"; and Gould, *Catholic Activism*.

[29]Wood, *King's Army*.

wars is often approached on a regional basis. Michel Cassan has studied the Limousin, and Mark Konnert the towns of Champagne.[30] Other urban studies have been done by Joan Davies for Toulouse, Philip Benedict for Rouen, Barbara Diefendorf for Paris, Wolfgang Kaiser for Marseille, David Nicholls for Tours, and Penny Roberts for Troyes.[31] Stuart Carroll's study of the Guise affinity takes a different organizing principle and enriches scholars' understanding of how the Guise family organized support in the areas of their greatest strength.[32] His recent book on early modern violence shows the impact of the Wars of Religion on the moral code of the French nobility.[33]

Luc Racaut makes a strong case for the role Catholic polemics played in stirring religious hatreds to a fever pitch.[34] The classic works on popular polemics nevertheless remain Denis Crouzet's *Guerriers de Dieu* and Denis Pallier's study of the Parisian printing trades during the Holy League. In addition, Philip Benedict has examined the use of images as propaganda during the religious wars; Keith Cameron, Kathleen Crawford, and Alexander Wilkinson have examined the propaganda campaign waged against Henri III; and Michael Wolfe has shown how Henri IV's image evolved in the contemporary media.[35] Of course, the pulpit played as crucial a role as the printing press in stirring popular emotions during the wars.[36]

Two phases of the Wars of Religion continue to attract special attention. The first is the Saint Bartholomew's Day Massacre; the second the wars of the League. On the former, Philip Benedict's 1978 article on the provincial massacres remains the standard. Barbara Diefendorf focuses on the popular killings in Paris and the religious hatreds that prompted them; Denis Crouzet rethinks the role of Catherine de Medici and Charles IX; and Robert Kingdon traces the propaganda value of the massacre at home and abroad.[37] Jean-Louis Bourgeon's works on the massacre should be used with caution; his thesis that the massacre represented a Guise-led

---

[30]Cassan, *Le temps des guerres*; and Konnert, *Local Politics*.

[31]Davies, "Persecution and Protestantism"; Benedict, *Rouen during the Wars*; Diefendorf, *Beneath the Cross*; Kaiser, *Marseille au temps de troubles*; Nicholls, "Protestants, Catholics, and Magistrates"; Roberts, *City in Conflict*; and Konnert, *Civic Agendas*.

[32]Carroll, *Noble Power*.

[33]Carroll, *Blood and Violence*.

[34]Racaut, *Hatred in Print*.

[35]Benedict, "Of Marmites and Martyrs" and *Graphic History*; Benedict, Bryant, and Neuschel, "Graphic History"; Cameron, "Satire, Dramatic Stereotyping"; Crawford, "Love, Sodomy, and Scandal"; Wilkinson, "'Homicides Royaux'"; and Wolfe, "Henry IV and the Press."

[36]Baumgartner, *Radical Reactionaries*; and Armstrong, *Politics of Piety*.

[37]Diefendorf, *Beneath the Cross*; Crouzet, *La nuit de la Saint-Barthélemy*; and Kingdon, *Myths*.

revolt of the Parisian bourgeoisie against the crown is based on a very partial and selective use of sources.[38]

The climactic stage of the Wars of Religion—when ultra-Catholics formed a Holy League and rebelled against a crown that seemed unwilling or unable to put a stop to the Protestant heresy—continues to occasion lively debate about the character of the rebellion and underlying motives of the rebels. Elie Barnavi's characterization of the Paris Holy League as a sociopolitical revolution on the part of middling classes excluded from urban power structures has been contested by Robert Descimon, who views the revolt as an attempt to reclaim traditional communal values on the part of the same social group, and Denis Crouzet, who interprets it rather as an apocalyptic and millenarian movement.[39] Rather than resolving the debate about Paris, studies of provincial cities reinforce a sense of the league as a diverse movement rooted in local conditions and concerns.[40] Many cities adopted a moderate course, allying with the league or rejecting it only after much debate and without the sort of violent upheaval experienced in Paris. The intense religious passions and zeal for moral reform demonstrated by Parisian leaguers were absent in many provincial cities as well. It seems important, then, not to generalize too broadly from the Parisian case. Jean-Marie Constant's *La Ligue* avoids this problem, while incorporating many insights produced by specialized studies, and shows how thin support for the league was outside of a handful of major cities.[41] Henri IV was in a stronger position when he came to the crown than is usually assumed. This does not alter the fact that Henri's conversion to Catholicism was a necessary step in pacifying the kingdom, as were the steps he subsequently took to buy off his enemies and gain legitimacy.[42] Moreover, only in retrospect does his 1594 entry into Paris appear to have been a decisive turning point in the league's fall from power. At the time, many hard-core leaguers looked upon it as a temporary setback and not a permanent defeat.[43]

---

[38]Cf. Diefendorf, "La Saint-Barthélemy."

[39]Barnavi, *Le parti de Dieu*; Descimon, *Qui étaient les Seize?*; and Crouzet, *Les guerriers de Dieu.* Diefendorf, "The Catholic League," sums up the debates.

[40]Benedict, *Rouen during the Wars*; Harding, "Revolution and Reform"; Greengrass, "Anatomy of Religious Riot"; Kaiser, *Marseille au temps*; Cassan, *Le temps des guerres*; Konnert, *Civic Agendas*; and Gal, *Grenoble au temps.*

[41]Constant, *La Ligue.*

[42]Wolfe, *Conversion of Henry IV*; Wolfe, "Protestant Reactions to the Conversion of Henry IV"; Love, *Blood and Religion*; and Finley-Croswhite, *Henry IV and the Towns.*

[43]Descimon and Ruiz Ibáñez, *Les ligueurs de l'exil.*

The difficult search for an end to the religious wars has been approached from a variety of perspectives. A number of scholars have looked at the theoretical constructs of civil harmony used to justify an end to the quarrels.[44] By contrast, Jérémie Foa and Penny Roberts have attempted to reassess the actual work of the royal commissions sent out to negotiate enforcement of the pacification edicts in the provinces.[45] Both argue convincingly that peacemaking was taken more seriously under the Valois kings than is usually assumed and that Henri IV's ability to stabilize his kingdom built in important ways on the success of his predecessors in maintaining the rule of law. Foa's article "Making Peace" offers a particularly impressive demonstration of the efforts of royal commissioners pragmatically to negotiate compromise by adjudicating a wide variety of disputes but also issuing guidelines that local authorities could follow. His soon-to-be-completed thesis promises to revise our understanding of the role of the crown during the early stages of the religious wars in important ways.

The study of individuals who sought out a middle path in the wars has also yielded productive results. Thierry Wanegffelen's massive *Ni Rome ni Genève* examines a number of prominent individuals who tried to find a middle way and offers a most interesting perspective on attempts to broker a compromise during the reign of Henri IV.[46] For Theodore Beza, by contrast, there could be no middle ground. Like Calvin before him, Beza strongly condemned any compromise that touched on Protestant doctrine. Beza's position with regard to the religious wars nevertheless evolved significantly over time. As Scott Manetsch has shown, "Beza himself played a more significant role in subversive activities than is generally recognized," at least during the 1570s. Ten years later, however, "Beza was advising friends in France to desist from armed confrontation, convinced that it was better to suffer 'under the cross' than to be held responsible for the plague of anarchy in the kingdom and the dissipation in the churches." He continued to be a voice for "patience and political accommodation" after Henri IV's conversion.[47]

The impact of the Edict of Nantes on the lives of both Protestants and Catholics during the period following its promulgation remains

---

[44]Turchetti, *Concordia o tolleranza*; Turchetti, "Religious Concord"; Christin, *La paix de religion*; Christin, "La réception de l'Édit"; Grandjean and Roussel, *Coexister dans l'intolérance*; Crouzet, *La sagesse et le malheur*; Wanegffelen, *Ni Rome ni Genève*; and Wanegffelen, *De Michel de L'Hospital*.

[45]Foa, "Making Peace"; and Roberts, "Royal Authority and Justice."

[46]Wanegffelen, *Ni Rome ni Genève*.

[47]Manetsch, *Theodore Beza*, 339.

understudied, despite useful case studies of Protestant-Catholic coexistence and conversion by Gregory Hanlon, Keith Luria, Raymond
Mentzer, and Philip Benedict.[48] Benedict has also done important work
on Huguenot social demography.[49] Diane Margolf has studied the adjudi-
cation of legal disputes under the terms of the Edict of Nantes.[50]

The Catholic Revival

Early modern Catholicism is the subject of another essay in this volume.
The paragraphs that follow will attempt only to round out this essay's
theme of a historiographical shift from top-down histories of the Reformations to works focusing more on popular piety and religious practice. Even
more than for the Protestant movement, the Catholic Reformation has traditionally been seen as initiated and controlled by the clergy. For France,
moreover, it has generally been seen as a belated movement whose arrival
was delayed by the disruption caused by the religious wars. Only when
peace returned could the church begin setting its house in order, imple-
menting the decrees passed half a century earlier at Trent, and beginning
the reform of both secular clergy and religious. For René Taveneaux, for
example, the Catholic Reformation only begins in 1610, at least in its "positive phase."[51] There is of course some validity to the traditional perspective. The Catholic Church was undeniably centralized and hierarchical in
organization, and the spread of new, reformed religious orders largely took
place only after the Wars of Religion had ended. The wars, moreover,
heightened the customary independence of the Gallican church. The
decrees issued from the Council of Trent never were officially accepted by
the French government, and they were only belatedly adopted by its Catholic Church in 1615.[52]

These traditional views are, however, too limited and limiting. The
Catholic Church never achieved the centralization to which it aspired.
Moreover, as Denis Richet showed in a pioneering essay first published in
1977, already during the Wars of Religion, the Protestant challenge promoted a reinvigoration of popular piety and a new concern with living out

---

[48]Hanlon, *Confession and Community*; Luria, "Rituals of Conversion"; Luria, "Separated by
Death"; Luria, *Sacred Boundaries*; Mentzer, *Blood and Belief*; and Benedict, *Faith and Fortunes*.
[49]Benedict, *Faith and Fortunes*.
[50]Margolf, *Religion and Royal Justice*.
[51]Taveneaux, *Le catholicisme*, 8.
[52]On France's role at the Council of Trent, see Tallon, *La France et le Concile*.

one's faith on the part of Catholic elites.[53] Robert Schneider's essay on penitential processions illustrates this point well. As Schneider demonstrates, participants in these processions did not see themselves as reviving the flagellant confraternities of the later Middle Ages and wanted rather to counter Protestantism by displaying "a Church militant, unified, numerous and purified" but also to mark themselves out as a "spiritual elite."[54] Mark Venard has also stressed the "successful marriage" between popular piety and the Counter-Reformation during the era of the religious wars. "It was only later, during the course of the seventeenth century, that a divorce would grow and deepen."[55]

Diefendorf also locates the roots of the Catholic revival of the seventeenth century in the penitential and ascetic spirituality that characterized the religious wars, especially during the Wars of the League.[56] Not only did Capuchins, Feuillants, and other Counter-Reformation orders play an important role as preachers during the wars, but admiration for their penitential piety helped spark the desire to reform lax religious orders and found austere new ones in the wake of the wars. In Paris alone, fifty new religious congregations for women were founded during the first half of the seventeenth century. As the penitential impulse that prompted the first of these foundations waned, it gave way to the more extroverted desire for Christian service evident in the foundation of uncloistered teaching and nursing congregations and charitable confraternities. Whether cloistered contemplative convents, active teaching congregations, or lay charities, these institutions were almost invariably created on women's initiative and with money supplied by female benefactors.[57] Elizabeth Rapley's works on the active orders similarly stress the importance of women's initiative. She argues, moreover, that these new orders should not be seen as "an integral part of the Tridentine reform. The burst of feminine agency was neither foreseen nor welcomed."[58] Diefendorf finds more evidence of productive collaboration between male clergy and lay and religious women. More research is needed, however, to clarify women's role in the Catholic Church

---

[53]"Aspects socio-culturels des conflits religieux à Paris dans la seconde moitié du xviᵉ siècle," reprinted in Richet, *De la réforme.*

[54]Schneider, "Mortification on Parade," 125, 140.

[55]Venard, *Le catholicisme à l'épreuve,* 217. See also Venard, *Réforme protestante, réforme catholique.*

[56]Diefendorf, "An Age of Gold"; and Diefendorf, *From Penitence to Charity.*

[57]Diefendorf, *From Penitence to Charity.*

[58]Rapley, *The Dévotes,* 21; see also Rapley, *Social History of the Cloister.*

of the Reformation. Susan Dinan's new book on the Daughters of Charity is particularly welcome on this account.[59]

The extent to which the Catholic Reformation penetrated the French countryside is another subject that remains in dispute. Philip Hoffman attributes the movement's successes to an alliance between devout urban elites and the urban clergy and its failures to the resistance rural groups posed to the social discipline these initiatives implied.[60] Robin Briggs also emphasizes the controlling impulses of the Counter-Reformation church.[61] By contrast, Keith Luria finds both peasants and city dwellers creatively adapting religious rituals and practices to suit their needs.[62] These questions of peasant and elite mentalities go beyond the limits of this essay. It is nevertheless clear that, for Protestants and Catholics alike, religion remained a vital component of the early modern world; it framed the way people saw their roles, relationships, and responsibilities, but always within a broader context framed also by social, economic, and political variables.

Future Directions

Where is the field headed? There are two main trends in current research. The first is a continuation of the efforts sketched out in this essay to examine the religious choices early modern French people made and the social, political, and cultural implications of these choices. More specifically, researchers are continuing efforts to question and revise long-held generalizations about the impact of the Reformation, the place that religion held in people's lives, the origins and character of the Wars of Religion, and the role of monarchy in these troubles. At the same time, scholars are going beyond the study of religious divisions and the conflicts they provoked to ask about coexistence and compromise across religious lines. This essay has cited some results from these efforts, but more research is under way and still more needs to be undertaken

This work demands both intensive archival research and imaginative use of old and new sources. Fortunately, finding aids for French archives are increasingly being put online. The Archives nationales (available at http://www.archivesnationales.culture.gouv.fr) and many departmental archives have posted general inventories of their holdings to the Internet. More detailed repertories of documents are still regrettably rare, but they too are

---

[59]Dinan, *Women and Poor Relief.*
[60]Hoffman, *Church and Community.*
[61]Briggs, *Communities of Belief.*
[62]Luria, *Territories of Grace.*

gradually becoming available. Many library catalogs can also be consulted from a distance. The Bibliothèque nationale's useful site (http://www.bnf.fr) allows convenient searches of not only that library's collections (through the BN-OPALE PLUS link) but also those of many municipal and specialized libraries (through the CCFr link). The Catalogue Collectif de France is incomplete—the holdings of many libraries and special collections can still be known only by visiting them in person—but increasingly worth consulting. Much more preliminary work can be done before heading off to French archives and libraries than was possible just a few years ago.

Much more sophisticated research can also now be done without ever leaving home, thanks to the proliferation of electronic texts available online. It is now possible to download from the Bibliothèque nationale's electronic text collection, not just literary texts and dictionaries but also important historical sources, including, for example, the *Histoire ecclésiastique* attributed to Theodore Beza, Pierre de L'Estoile's *Mémoires-journaux*, and François Hotman's juridical and polemical works. These are searchable through the GALLICA link on the BNF home page but also now appear in the regular catalog. Two special GALLICA projects will also be of interest to early modern historians. The first is the online publication of periodicals published by regional *sociétés savantes*, many of which contain *livres de raison* and other precious archival sources.[63] The second, entitled Voyages en France, contains a number of classic works for the early modern period, including, among many other things, accounts of royal entries into provincial cities. Only a few manuscript documents are currently available, but these include Pierre de L'Estoile's fascinating *Les belles figures et drolleries de la Ligue* (through GALLICA or OPALE-PLUS) and a small but growing collection of pacification edicts and related documents on the Wars of Religion (available at http://www.culture.gouv.fr/documentation/archim/desguerresdereligion.htm). These expanding resources will serve as valuable aids to professional historians as well as greatly expand the possibilities for serious research by graduate and even undergraduate students previously hampered by limited library resources.

Bibliography

Armstrong, Brian G. "Semper Reformanda: The Case of the French Reformed Church, 1559–1620." In *Later Calvinism: International Perspectives*, edited by W. Fred Graham, 119–40. Kirksville, MO: Sixteenth Century Journal Publishers, 1992.

[63]As this goes to press, only periodicals from Aquitaine and Lorraine are available, but more will be available with time.

Armstrong, Megan C. *The Politics of Piety: Franciscan Preachers during the Wars of Religion, 1560–1600.* Rochester, NY: University of Rochester Press, 2004.

Audisio, Gabriel. *The Waldensian Dissent: Persecution and Survival, c. 1170–c.1570.* Translated by Claire Davison. Cambridge, UK: Cambridge University Press, 1999.

Barnavi, Elie. *Le parti de Dieu: Etude sociale et politique des chefs de la Ligue parisienne, 1585–1594.* Brussels: Nauwelaerts, 1980.

Baumgartner, Frederic J. *Change and Continuity in the French Episcopate: The Bishops and the Wars of Religion, 1547–1610.* Durham: University of North Carolina Press, 1986.

———. *Radical Reactionaries: The Political Thought of the French Catholic League.* Geneva: Droz, 1976.

Benedict, Philip. *Christ's Churches Purely Reformed: A Social History of Calvinism.* New Haven, CT: Yale University Press, 2002.

———. *The Faith and Fortunes of France's Huguenots, 1600–85.* Aldershot: Ashgate, 2001.

———. *Graphic History: The "Wars, Massacres and Troubles" of Tortorel and Perrissin.* Geneva: Librairie Droz, 2007.

———. "Of Marmites and Martyrs: Images and Polemics in the Wars of Religion." In *The French Renaissance in Prints from the Bibliothèque Nationale de France,* 109–38. Los Angeles: Grunwald Center for the Graphic Arts, 1994.

———. *Rouen during the Wars of Religion.* Cambridge, UK: Cambridge University Press, 1980.

———. "The Saint Bartholomew's Massacres in the Provinces." *Historical Journal* 21 (1978): 205–25.

———, Lawrence M. Bryant, and Kristen B. Neuschel. "Graphic History: What Readers Knew and Were Taught in the *Quarante Tableaux* of Perrissin and Tortorel." *French Historical Studies* 28, no. 2 (Spring 2005): 175–229.

———, Guido Marnef, Henk van Nierop, and Marc Venard, eds. *Reformation, Revolt and Civil War in France and the Netherlands, 1555–1585.* Amsterdam: Royal Netherlands Academy of Arts and Sciences, 1999.

Blaisdell, Charmarie. "Religion, Gender, and Class: Nuns and Authority in Early Modern France." In Wolfe, *Changing Identities in Early Modern France,* 147–68.

Bourgeon, Jean-Louis. *Charles IX devant la Saint-Barthélemy.* Geneva: Droz, 1995.

Briggs, Robin. *Communities of Belief: Cultural and Social Tensions in Early Modern France.* Oxford: Oxford University Press, 1989.

Cameron, Euan. *The Reformation of the Heretics: The Waldenses of the Alps, 1480–1580.* Oxford: Oxford University Press, 1984.

———. *Waldenses: Rejections of Holy Church in Medieval Europe.* Oxford: Blackwell Publishers, 2000.

Cameron, Keith. "Satire, Dramatic Stereotyping and the Demonizing of Henry III." In Pettegree, Nelles, and Connor, *Sixteenth-Century Religious Book,* 157–76.

Carroll, Stuart. *Blood and Violence in Early Modern France.* Oxford: Oxford University Press, 2006.

———. *Noble Power during the French Wars of Religion: The Guise Affinity and the Catholic Cause in Normandy.* Cambridge: Cambridge University Press, 1998.

Cassan, Michel. *Le temps des guerres de Religion: Le cas du Limousin (vers 1530–vers 1630).* Paris: Editions Publisud, 1996.

Chareyre, Philippe. "The Great Difficulties One Must Bear to Follow Jesus Christ: Morality at Sixteenth-Century Nîmes." In Mentzer, *Sin and the Calvinists,* 63–96.

Christin, Olivier. *La paix de religion: L'autonomisation de la raison politique au XVIᵉ siècle.* Paris: Seuil, 1997.

————. "La réception de l'Édit de Nantes: Illusions et désillusions de la 'tolérance.'" In Pettegree, Nelles, and Connor, *Sixteenth-Century Religious Book*, 197–209.

————. *Une révolution symbolique: L'Iconoclasme huguenot et la reconstruction catholique.* Paris: Les Éditions de Minuit, 1991.

Conner, Philip. *Huguenot Heartland: Montauban and Southern French Calvinism during the Wars of Religion.* Aldershot: Ashgate, 2002.

Constant, Jean-Marie. *La Ligue.* Paris: Fayard, 1996.

Crawford, Katherine B. "Love, Sodomy, and Scandal: Controlling the Sexual Reputation of Henry III." *Journal of the History of Sexuality* 12 (2003): 513–42.

Crouzet, Denis. *La genèse de la Réforme française, 1520–1562.* Paris: SEDES, 1996.

————. *Les guerriers de Dieu: La violence au temps des troubles de religion, vers 1525–vers 1610.* 2 vols. Seyssel: Champ Vallon, 1990.

————. *La nuit de la Saint-Barthélemy: Un rêve perdu de la Renaissance.* Paris: Fayard, 1994.

————. *La sagesse et le malheur: Michel de L'Hospital, chancelier de France.* Seyssel: Champ Vallon, 1998.

Davies, Joan M. "Persecution and Protestantism: Toulouse, 1562–1575." *Historical Journal* 22 (1979): 31–51.

Davis, Natalie Zemon. "The Sacred and the Body Social in Sixteenth-Century Lyon." *Past and Present* 90 (1981): 40–70.

————. *Society and Culture in Early Modern France.* Stanford, CA: Stanford University Press, 1975.

Delumeau, Jean. *Catholicism between Luther and Voltaire: A New View of the Counter-Reformation.* Translated by Jeremy Moiser. London: Burns & Oates, 1977.

Descimon, Robert. *Qui étaient les Seize? Mythes et réalités de la Ligue parisienne, 1585–1594.* Paris: Klincksieck, 1983.

————, and José Javier Ruiz Ibáñez. *Les ligueurs de l'exil: Le refuge catholique français après 1594.* Seyssel: Champ Vallon, 2005.

Diefendorf, Barbara B. "An Age of Gold? Parisian Women, the Holy League, and the Roots of Catholic Renewal." In Wolfe, *Changing Identities in Early Modern France*, 169–90.

————. *Beneath the Cross: Catholics and Huguenots in Sixteenth-Century Paris.* New York: Oxford University Press, 1991.

————. "The Catholic League: Social Crisis or Apocalypse Now?" *French Historical Studies* 15 (1987): 332–44.

————. *From Penitence to Charity: Pious Women and the Catholic Reformation in Paris.* New York: Oxford University Press, 2004.

————. "Houses Divided: Religious Schism in Sixteenth-Century Parisian Families." In Zimmerman and Weissman, *Urban Life in the Renaissance*, 80–99. Newark: University of Delaware Press, 1989.

————. "The Huguenot Psalter and the Faith of French Protestants in the Sixteenth Century." In Diefendorf and Hesse, *Culture and Identity in Early Modern Europe*, 41–64.

————. "La Saint-Barthélemy et la bourgeoisie parisienne." *Histoire, économie, et société* 17 (1998): 341–53.

————, and Carla Hesse, eds. *Culture and Identity in Early Modern Europe (1500–1800): Essays in Honor of Natalie Zemon Davis.* Ann Arbor: University of Michigan Press, 1993.

Dinan, Susan. "Confraternities as a Venue for Female Activism during the Catholic Reformation." In John Patrick Donnelly and Michael W. Maher, eds., *Confraternities and Catholic Reform in Italy, France, and Spain*, 191–214. Kirksville, MO: Thomas Jefferson University Press, 1999.

———. "Overcoming Gender Limitations: The Daughters of Charity and Early Modern Catholicism." In Kathleen Comerford and Hilmar Pabel, eds., *Early Modern Catholicism: Essays in Honour of John O'Malley, S.J.*, 97–113. Toronto: University of Toronto Press, 2001.

———. *Women and Poor Relief in Seventeenth-Century France: The Early History of the Daughters of Charity*. Aldershot: Ashgate, 2006.

Dolan, Claire. *Entre tours et clochers: Les gens d'église à Aix en Provence au XVIe siècle*. Sherbrooke: Les Éditions de l'Université de Sherbrooke, 1981.

Elwood, Christopher. *The Body Broken: The Calvinist Doctrine of the Eucharist and the Symbolization of Power in Sixteenth-Century France*. New York: Oxford University Press, 1999.

Febvre, Lucien. *Au cœur religieux du XVIe siècle*. 2nd ed. Paris: SEVPEN, 1968.

———. *The Problem of Unbelief in the Sixteenth Century: The Religion of Rabelais*. Translated by Beatrice Gottlieb. Cambridge, MA: Harvard University Press, 1982.

Finley-Croswhite, Annette. *Henry IV and the Towns: The Pursuit of Legitimacy in French Urban Society, 1589–1610*. Cambridge: Cambridge University Press, 1999.

Foa, Jérémie. "Making Peace: The Commissions for Enforcing the Pacification Edicts in the Reign of Charles IX (1560–1574)." *French History* 18 (2004): 256–74.

———. "An Unequal Apportionment: The Conflict over Space between Protestants and Catholics at the Beginning of the Wars of Religion." *French History* 20 (2006): 369–86.

Gal, Stéphane. *Grenoble au temps de la Ligue: Étude politique, sociale et religieuse d'une cité en crise (vers 1562–vers 1598)*. Grenoble: Presses universitaires de Grenoble, 2000.

Galpern, A. N. *The Religions of the People in Sixteenth-Century Campagne*. Cambridge, MA: Harvard University Press, 1976.

Garrisson-Estèbe, Janine. *Protestants du Midi, 1555–98*. New ed. Toulouse: Privat, 1991.

Gould, Kevin. *Catholic Activism in South-West France, 1540–1570*. Aldershot: Ashgate, 2006.

Grandjean, Michel, and Bernard Roussel, eds. *Coexister dans l'intolérance: L'édit de Nantes (1598)*. Geneva: Labor et Fides, 1998.

Greengrass, Mark. "The Anatomy of a Religious Riot in Toulouse in May 1562." *Journal of Ecclesiastical History* 34 (1983): 367–91.

———. "The Calvinist Experiment in Béarn." In Andrew Pettegree, Alastair Duke, and Gillian Lewis, eds., *Calvinism in Europe, 1540–1620*, 119–42. Cambridge: Cambridge University Press, 1994.

———. "The Sainte Union in the Provinces: The Case of Toulouse." *Sixteenth Century Journal* 14 (1983): 469–96.

Hanlon, Gregory. *Confession and Community in Seventeenth-Century France: Catholic and Protestant Coexistence in Aquitaine*. Philadelphia: University of Pennsylvania Press, 1993.

Harding, Robert. "Revolution and Reform in the Holy League: Angers, Rennes, Nantes." *Journal of Modern History* 53 (1981): 379–416.

Heller, Henry. *The Conquest of Poverty: The Calvinist Revolt in Sixteenth-Century France*. Leiden: Brill, 1986.

———. *Iron and Blood: Civil Wars in Sixteenth-Century France*. Montreal: McGill-Queen's University Press, 1991.

Higman, Francis. *Lire et découvrir: La circulation des idées au temps de la Réforme*. Geneva: Droz, 1998.

———. *Piety and the People: Religious Printing in French, 1511–1551*. Aldershot: Ashgate, 1996.

Hoffman, Philip. *Church and Community in the Diocese of Lyon, 1500–1789*. New Haven, CT: Yale University Press, 1984.

Holt, Mack P. "Burgundians into Frenchmen: Catholic Identity in Sixteenth-Century Burgundy." In Wolfe, *Changing Identities in Early Modern France*, 345–70.

———. *The Duke of Anjou and the Politique Struggle during the Wars of Religion*. Cambridge: Cambridge University Press, 1986.

———. *The French Wars of Religion, 1562–1629*. Cambridge: Cambridge University Press, 1995.

———. "Putting Religion Back into the Wars of Religion." *French Historical Studies* 18 (1993): 524–51.

———. "Wine, Community and Reformation in Sixteenth-Century Burgundy." *Past and Present* 138 (1993): 58–93.

Kaiser, Wolfgang. *Marseille au temps de troubles: Morphologie sociale et luttes de factions, 1559–1595*. Translated by Florence Chaix. Paris: EEHESS, 1992.

Kelley, Donald. *The Beginning of Ideology: Consciousness and Society in the French Reformation*. Cambridge: Cambridge University Press, 1981.

Kingdon, Robert M. *Consolidation of the French Protestant Movement, 1564–1572*. Geneva: Droz, 1967.

———. *Geneva and the Coming of the Wars of Religion in France, 1555–1563*. Geneva: Droz, 1956.

———. *Myths about the St. Bartholomew's Day Massacres, 1572–1576*. Cambridge, MA: Harvard University Press, 1988.

Knecht, Robert J. *The French Civil Wars, 1562–1598*. Harlow: Longman, 2000.

Konnert, Mark W. *Civic Agendas and Religious Passion: Châlons-sur-Marne during the French Wars of Religion*. Kirksville, MO: Sixteenth Century Journal Publishers, 1997.

———. *Local Politics in the French Wars of Religion: The Towns of Champagne, the Duc de Guise, and the Catholic League (1560–95)*. Aldershot: Ashgate, 2006.

Lemaître, Nicole. *Le Rouergue flamboyant: Le clergé et les fidèles du diocèse de Rodez (1418–1563)*. Paris: Cerf, 1988.

Love, Ronald S. *Blood and Religion: The Conscience of Henri IV, 1553–1593*. Montreal: McGill-Queen's University Press, 2001.

Luria, Keith P. "Rituals of Conversion: Catholics and Protestants in Seventeenth-Century Poitou." In Diefendorf and Hesse, *Culture and Identity in Early Modern Europe*, 65–82.

———. *Sacred Boundaries: Religious Coexistence and Conflict in Early-Modern France*. Washington, DC: Catholic University of America Press, 2005.

———. "Separated by Death? Burials, Cemeteries, and Confessional Boundaries in Seventeenth-Century France." *French Historical Studies* 24 (2001): 185–222.

———. *Territories of Grace: Cultural Change in the Seventeenth-Century Diocese of Grenoble*. Berkeley: University of California Press, 1991.

Manetsch, Scott M. *Theodore Beza and the Quest for Peace in France*. Leiden: Brill, 2000.

Margolf, Diane C. *Religion and Royal Justice in Early Modern France: The Paris Chambre de l'Édit, 1598–1665*. Kirksville, MO: Truman State University Press, 2003.

Mentzer, Raymond A. *Blood and Belief: Family Survival and Confessional Identity among the Provincial Huguenot Nobility*. West Lafayette, IN: Purdue University Press, 1994.

———. "Heresy Proceedings in Languedoc, 1500–1560." Special issue, *Transactions of the American Philosophical Society* 74/5 (1984).

———. "Laity and Liturgy in the French Reformed Tradition." In Lee Palmer Wandel, ed., *History Has Many Voices*, 71–92. Kirksville, MO: Truman State University Press, 2003.

———. "Morals and Moral Regulation in Protestant France." *Journal of Interdisciplinary History* 31 (2000): 1–20.

———. "Notions of Sin and Penitence within the French Reformed Community." In Katharine Jackson Lualdi and Anne T. Thayer, eds., *Penitence in the Age of Reformations*, 84–100. Aldershot: Ashgate, 2000.

———. "The Persistence of 'Superstition and Idolatry' among Rural French Calvinists." *Church History* 65 (1996): 220–33.

———, ed. *Sin and the Calvinists: Morals Control and the Consistory in the Reformed Tradition*. Kirksville, MO: Sixteenth Century Journal Publishers, 1994.

———, and Andrew Spicer, eds. *Society and Culture in the Huguenot World, 1559–1685*. Cambridge: Cambridge University Press, 2002.

Monter, William. *Judging the French Reformation: Heresy Trials by Sixteenth-Century Parlements*. Cambridge, MA: Harvard University Press, 1999.

Nicholls, David. "France." In Andrew Pettegree, ed., *The Early Reformation in Europe*, 120–41. Cambridge: Cambridge University Press, 1992.

———. "The Nature of Popular Heresy in France, 1520–1542." *Historical Journal* 26 (1983): 261–75.

———. "Protestants, Catholics, and Magistrates in Tours, 1562–1572: The Making of a Catholic City during the Religious Wars." *French History* 8 (1994): 14–33.

———. "The Theatre of Martyrdom in the French Reformation." *Past and Present*, 121 (1988): 49–73.

Pallier, Denis. *Recherches sur l'imprimerie à Paris pendant la Ligue (1585–1594)*. Geneva: Droz, 1976.

Pettegree, Andrew, Paul Nelles, and Philip Connor, eds. *The Sixteenth Century Religious Book*. Aldershot: Ashgate, 2001.

Potter, David, ed. and trans. *The French Wars of Religion: Selected Documents*. New York: St. Martin's Press, 1998.

Racaut, Luc. *Hatred in Print: Catholic Propaganda and Protestant Identity during the French Wars of Religion*. Aldershot: Ashgate, 2002.

Rapley, Elizabeth. *The Dévotes: Women and Church in Seventeenth-Century France*. Montreal: McGill-Queen's University Press, 1990.

———. *A Social History of the Cloister: Daily Life in the Teaching Monasteries of the Old Regime*. Montreal: McGill-Queen's University Press, 2001.

Reinburg, Virginia. Hearing Lay People's Prayer. In Diefendorf and Hesse, *Culture and Identity in Early Modern Europe*, 19–40.

———. "Liturgy and the Laity in Late Medieval and Reformation France." *Sixteenth Century Journal* 23 (1992): 526–47.

Richet, Denis. *De la réforme à la Révolution: Etudes sur la France moderne*. Paris: Aubier, 1991.

Robbins, Kevin. *City on the Ocean Sea: La Rochelle 1530–1650: Urban Society, Religion, and Politics on the French Atlantic Frontier*. Leiden: Brill, 1997.

Roberts, Penny. *A City in Conflict: Troyes during the French Wars of Religion*. Manchester: Manchester University Press, 1996.

———. "The Most Crucial Battle of the Wars of Religion? The Conflict over Sites for Reformed Worship in Sixteenth-Century France." *Archive for Reformation History* 89 (1998): 247–67.

———. "Royal Authority and Justice during the French Religious Wars." *Past and Present* 184 (2004): 3–32.

Roelker, Nancy Lyman. "The Appeal of Calvinism to French Noblewomen in the Sixteenth Century." *Journal of Interdisciplinary History* 2 (1971–72): 391–413.

———. *One King, One Faith: The Parlement of Paris and the Religious Reformations of the Sixteenth Century.* Berkeley: University of California Press, 1996.

———. "The Role of Noblewomen in the French Reformation." *Archive for Reformation Research* 63 (1972): 168–95.

Salmon, John H. M. *Society in Crisis: France in the Sixteenth Century.* London: St. Martin's, 1975.

Sauzet, Robert. "L'iconoclasme dans le diocèse de Nîmes au XVIᵉ siècle." *Revue de l'histoire de l'église de France* 66 (1980): 5–16.

Schmitt, Jean-Claude. *The Holy Greyhound: Guinefort, Healer of Children since the Thirteenth Century.* Translated by Martin Thom. Cambridge: Cambridge University Press, 1983.

Schneider, Robert A. "Mortification on Parade: Penitential Processions in Sixteenth- and Seventeenth-Century France." *Renaissance and Reformation* 10 (1986): 123–46.

Sluhovsky, Moshe. *Patroness of Paris: Rituals of Devotion in Early Modern Paris.* Leiden: Brill, 1998.

Sunshine, Glenn S. *Reforming French Protestantism: The Development of Huguenot Ecclesiastical Institutions, 1557–1572.* Kirksville, MO: Truman State University Press, 2003.

Sutherland, N. M. *The Huguenot Struggle for Recognition.* New Haven, CT: Yale University Press, 1980.

Tallon, Alain, *La France et le Concile de Trente, 1518–1563.* Rome: École française de Rome, 1997.

Taveneaux, René. *Le catholicisme dans la France classique, 1610–1715.* 2 vols. Paris: SEDES, 1980.

Taylor, Larissa. *Soldiers of Christ: Preaching in Late Medieval and Reformation France.* New York: Oxford University Press, 1992.

Turchetti, Mario. *Concordia o tolleranza: François Baduin (1520–1573) e i 'moyenneurs.'* Milan: F. Angeli, 1984.

———. "Religious Concord and Political Tolerance in Sixteenth- and Seventeenth-Century France." *Sixteenth Century Journal* 22 (1991): 15–25.

Venard, Marc. *Le catholicisme à l'épreuve dans la France du XVIᵉ siècle.* Paris: Éditions du Cerf, 2000.

———. *Réforme protestante, réforme catholique dans la province d'Avignon au XVIe siècle.* Paris: Éditions du Cerf, 1993.

Wanegffelen, Thierry. *Ni Rome ni Genève: Des fidèles entre deux chaires en France au XVIe siècle.* Paris: Honoré Champion, 1997.

———, ed. *De Michel de L'Hospital à l'édit de Nantes: Politique et religion face aux Églises.* Clermont-Ferrand: Presses Universitaires Blaise-Pascal, 2002.

Watson, Timothy. "Preaching, Printing, Psalm-Singing: The Making and Unmaking of the Reformed Church in Lyon, 1550–1572." In Mentzer and Spicer, *Society and Culture in the Huguenot World,* 10–28.

Wilkinson, Alexander. "Homicides Royaux: The Assassination of the Duc and Cardinal de Guise and the Radicalization of French Public Opinion." *French History* 18 (2004): 129–53.

Wolfe, Michael. *The Conversion of Henry IV: Politics, Power, and Religious Belief in Early Modern France.* Cambridge, MA: Harvard University Press, 1993.

———. "Henry IV and the Press." In Pettegree, Nelles, and Conner, *The Sixteenth Century Religious Book*, 177–96.

———. "Protestant Reactions to the Conversion of Henry IV." In Wolfe, *Changing Identities in Early Modern France*, 371–90.

———, ed. *Changing Identities in Early Modern France*. Durham: Duke University Press, 1997.

Wood, James B. *The King's Army: Warfare, Soldiers and Society during the Wars of Religion in France, 1562–1576*. Cambridge: Cambridge University Press, 1996.

9
Italy

Nicholas Terpstra

Bonifacio dalle Balle, youngest and most shiftless of the three sons of a merchant family, walked the night streets of Bologna's red light district and had a religious experience. Falling in step behind a prostitute who was walking with a companion, he overheard her sigh, "Who will deliver me from this life?" Jolted by her distress, and conscious of his own misspent youth, dalle Balle embarked on a path that would see him devote his fortune, his properties, and his life to developing a shelter for prostitutes' daughters. Was it this prostitute's distress that moved him? He wrote elsewhere of coming across a twelve-year-old girl, in the same seedy quarter, who was holding off a mob of taunting boys with a stick. Thinking perhaps of the dangers facing his own illegitimate daughter, Anna (conceived with a servant), he found the girl's mother and persuaded her to let him place her with a woman who would raise her at dalle Balle's expense. Dalle Balle would later write a third account of finding another girl abandoned on the city street and of also placing her with another female guardian. Dalle Balle's rescue work developed, by the early 1580s, into the Casa di Santa Croce—a home for abandoned and vulnerable girls. But it was also his own life that dalle Balle was rescuing, and he wrote the three differing accounts of his moment of conversion in order to get the narrative right. He adopted a personal lay vocation, never marrying or joining a religious order, signing his share of the family business over to his brothers, studying theology intently, and devoting his energies to his charitable shelter for young illegitimate girls like his own daughter (who was, however, sent off

228

to a convent). He preached to the girls in Santa Croce, wrote sermons and tracts that paid scant regard for the intermediary role of saints and clerics, and wrote the multiple—and sometimes contradictory—autobiographical fragments that cast his life and work as a morality tale. Intensely Christo-centric—in all three narratives his conversion occurs at age thirty-three—his orphanage was the only one in Bologna not dedicated to the Virgin Mary or a saint, but to Christ's cross. Dalle Balle determined to "work in the world for the greater glory of God and to establish a current of love between the creation and the Creator."

Was dalle Balle a Protestant? a Catholic Reformer? Counter-Reformer? a *spirituale* or "aspiring saint"? These questions are likely unan-swerable and certainly moot. It is not even clear whether he wrote or merely transcribed the sermons and spiritual writings that fill his personal papers and that he shared with the girls in his care. Yet he is a type who recurs across late sixteenth-century Italy, practicing a biblically simple faith, adapting the model of Christ to lay life, and directing charity to the spiritually and morally vulnerable. He is also a type encountered more fre-quently in current research on the Reformation in Italy, which has been deeply influenced by the methods of microhistory, and even more by its orientation to the individual, the marginal and dispossessed, and above all, the local.

In their chapters in the 1992 Reformation research guide, Elisabeth G. Gleason and Frederick J. McGinness explored the archaeology and dif-fusion of new religious ideas through communities such as the Oratories of Divine Love, individuals such as Juan de Valdes and Reginald Pole, and books such as the *Beneficio di Cristo*, along with the institutional Catholic response to them in the Index, the Inquisition, and the Council of Trent. These areas of research tested one of the fundamental questions bandied back and forth by those tracking the shifting religious climate of sixteenth-century Italy: when did the chill set in? Following Delio Cantimori, the early leader among Italian historians of religious dissent, many historians pointed to the 1540s—and specifically, 1542—as the turning point when orthodox hard-liners began getting the upper hand over Erasmian-*spiritu-ali* moderates. According to Cantimori, the ideas of these latter had been ascendant since circa 1513, but experienced a crisis-inducing reaction from the 1540s to the 1560s, before inspiring a second generation from the 1560s to the 1580s, and finally mutating into some very personal com-pounds by thinkers like Giordano Bruno and Tommasso Campanella from the 1580s to 1620s. This periodization, and the question and dating of a turning point, focused attention on intellectual and institutional history and, to a lesser extent, on the fates of high-profile male and clerical reformers. It assumed a move from openness to repression.

The debate continues, though with relaxed temporal boundaries and without the urgency brought to it by those shaped by the sharp, ideological struggles of the mid-twentieth century—ranging from the fascist/communist debates of the 1930s to the upheavals following Vatican II. Anne J. Schutte's article on "The Post-Cantimori Paradigm Shift" helped reorient the field by suggesting that historians should consider a different set of markers, which she has elsewhere described as "the shape of sanctity, the contours of holiness."[1] These markers point to the lived religious experience of laypeople, women, children, and marginal groups. They highlight the drawn-out processes of Christianization and confessionalization by which political and ecclesiastical authorities attempted, with mixed results and against significant resistance, to direct that sometimes free-flowing experience into orthodox channels. For some historians, these processes implied the allied concepts of social discipline and centralization, worked out through the Council of Trent and a reinvigorated papacy and episcopacy.[2] Others have questioned whether such concepts lead inevitably to simplified dichotomies of center vs. periphery, clergy vs. laity, and high vs. low culture, and so obscure the shifting identities of the parties, the inefficiencies of the process, and the reciprocations of influence. They would ask, apropos of the question noted above, whether it is valid to say that a chill set in at all.[3]

An allied fundamental question posed by historians of sixteenth-century Italian religious history has been: what shall we call it—Catholic Reform? Counter-Reform? Tridentine Catholicism? Reminiscent of an earlier generation's preoccupations and relevant across Europe, the question takes on broader social, political, and cultural relevance in Italy, because from the later sixteenth century we are dealing with a more deliberately *Roman* Catholic Church. John O'Malley's concise and authoritative discussion in *Trent and All That*, argues for the phrase "early modern Catholicism" in part on the basis that it more easily accommodates the

---

[1]Schutte, "Periodization of Sixteenth-Century Italian Religious History"; and idem, *Aspiring Saints*.

[2]Prodi, *Disciplina dell'anima, disciplina del corpo, e disciplina della società*; Prosperi, *Tribunali della conscienza*; and idem, *Salvezza delle anima, disciplina dei corpi*.

[3]Ditchfield, "In Search of Local Knowledge."

new focus on the social history of religion and the understanding that the Catholic Church was not simply a monolithic agency handing down norms at absolutism's dawn.[4] It was itself caught up, taken by surprise, altered, and internally divided by the social, economic, and political changes that characterized the early modern period.

The narrative of sixteenth-century Italian religious history is different now. In place of epic Manichean struggles between darkness and light, we now have the twisting Foucauldian dynamics of power and negotiation. In place of a Reformation focused on dramatic flights by high-profile Reformers eluding the Inquisition, we now have the slow twisting of the screws of social discipline in areas like convent enclosure, marriage law, and charity that "supports and redeems"—and the determined resistance of those fighting for "the preservation of the particular."[5] In place of binary oppositions between high and low culture, or center and periphery, we have intensely negotiated reciprocations. And we have the likes of Bonifacio dalle Balle, launching his personal rescue mission and discovering firsthand how tricky the dynamics of power and negotiation could be.

In the balance of this article, the aim will be more to supplement than revisit the authoritative treatments by Gleason and McGinness. Recent surveys of early modern Catholicism[6] and of early modern Italy[7] update and contextualize their studies. O'Malley's *Trent and All That* offers an indispensable orientation to the historiographical big picture, while Salvatore Caponnetto's *The Protestant Reformation in Sixteenth Century Italy* and Christopher Black's *Church, Religion, and Society in Early Modern Italy* offer excellent starting points for a detailed investigation of the social and cultural history of early modern Italian Protestantism and Catholicism.[8] The focus here will be on three interlinked areas that received less attention in the earlier research guides, but have expanded rapidly in the past fifteen years: local and lay religion, current institutional history (with an emphasis, in particular, on women's religious communities), and Jewish-Catholic relations.

---

[4]O'Malley, *Trent and All That*.

[5]Pullan, *Poverty and Charity*; and Ditchfield, *Liturgy, Sanctity and History*.

[6]Po-Chia Hsia, *World of Catholic Renewal*; Bireley, *Refashioning of Catholicism*; Peterson, "Out of the Margins"; Wright, *Early Modern Papacy*; Comerford and Pabel, *Early Modern Catholicism*.

[7]Black, *Early Modern Italy*; Hanlon, *Early Modern Italy*; Marino, *Early Modern Italy*; and Najemy, *Italy in the Age of the Renaissance*.

[8]Caponnetto, *Protestant Reformation in Sixteenth Century Italy*; and Black, *Church, Religion, and Society*.

Local and Lay Religion

A critical issue in current research involves measuring local religion in the early modern period, and determining what its continuing vitality may say about the Council of Trent's supposed centralizing effects on local traditions, institutions, and relations. In its medieval roots, local religion assumes that while the dogmas, catechisms, and hierarchy of Catholicism provide the grammar of religion, the lived faith of believers is always expressed in a vernacular of confraternities, shrines, processions, hospitals, and cults. These are the elements out of which towns and cities write the pious narrative of God's tough love (expressed through prosperity or punishment as local devotion and deviance require), of the Virgin Mary's enduring favor, and of their own efforts to negotiate between the two. Each of these elements emerges out of thanks or propitiation, and becomes a marker in a local sacred history that forms in conversation with local political, economic, and social changes. These civic religions are deeply rooted in the mendicant piety and factional politics of the communal period, are often strongly lay, and can generate affective, emotive, and superstitious elements that the more educated find troubling. A good deal of sixteenth-century Catholic Reform is aimed not simply at rooting out nascent (philo-)Protestant heresies, but at correcting or even extirpating these overly enthusiastic, but unorthodox, Catholic practices. The tools studied in recent works for Italy, as indeed for elsewhere in Europe, are confessionalization and social discipline.[9] They have become such dominant motifs in recent studies of late sixteenth-century Catholicism and Protestantism that it takes an effort of will—and determined research—to recover the local dimension of religious life.[10]

The models for studying urban religion as a communal expression that engaged laity and clergy, and that was shaped by local sociopolitical realities, were set in the pioneering studies of Florence by Richard Trexler and Ronald Weissman,[11] and of Venice by Brian Pullan and Edward Muir.[12] Their ambitious morphologies of Renaissance urban religious life centered significantly on confraternities, the lay brotherhoods that organized much of local devotional worship, and charitable service. Nicholas Eckstein followed with the best study yet of Florentine confraternities in their neigh-

---

[9]Prodi, *Disciplina dell'anima, disciplina del corpo, e disciplina della società.*

[10]Ditchfield, "In Search of Local Knowledge."

[11]Trexler, *Public Life in Renaissance Florence*; and Weissman, *Ritual Brotherhood in Renaissance Florence.*

[12]Pullan, *Rich and Poor in Renaissance Venice*; and Muir, *Civic Ritual in Renaissance Venice.*

borhood context, showing how artisans used them to organize areas of local social life ranging beyond religion as traditionally conceived, and how Medici political priorities narrowed this scope through the later fifteenth century.[13] A similar process was at work in contemporary Bolognese confraternities, whose success in framing a lay civic-religious ideology, in distinction from papal overlords, led to their gradual infiltration by highborn elements, who marginalized the original artisanal male and female membership while expanding cultic and charitable activities.[14] Recent essay collections confirm that political and social priorities shaped confraternally directed local religious life through the ancien régime.[15] Highborn members fundamentally altered confraternal community activities without changing institutional forms, but they also brought the ambitions and resources that kept the brotherhoods at the center of the artistic, architectural, and musical patronage of the baroque.[16]

The active participation of laity in framing a spiritual life, which worked with and beyond conventional elements provided by the hierarchy, is explored for rural areas by David Gentilcore's study of the "system of the sacred" in the southern region of Otranto, and Angelo Torre's work on "devotional consumption" in Piedmont.[17] Both reject an easy division between subordinate and hegemonic groups in favor of investigating how lay believers manipulated for subsistence, health, and fertility in liturgical and sacramental dialogue with clergy, who either were willing participants or, if not, aimed more often to persuade or co-opt than to challenge or discipline.[18] Similarly, studies of Milan and Lombardy demonstrate that urban reformers necessarily adapted their goals and strategies to a countryside that moved to different rhythms and expectations, and that frequently frustrated the efforts of those who aimed for confessionalizing reform.[19]

These studies cast their largely sociological and anthropological analysis over a *longue*—or at least medium—*durée*. The purely civic studies have tended to focus on a particular century, and on the intersection of

[13]Eckstein, *District of the Green Dragon.*

[14]Terpstra, *Lay Confraternities and Civil Religion.*

[15]Zardin, *Corpi, "fraternità," mestieri nella storia della società europea*; Donnelly and Maher, *Confraternities and Catholic Reform*; Terpstra, *Politics of Ritual Kinship*; and Black and Gravestock, *Early Modern Confraternities.*

[16]O'Regan, *Institutional Patronage*; Wisch & Ahl, *Confraternities and the Visual Arts*; and Glixon, *Honoring God and City.*

[17]Gentilcore, *From Bishop to Witch*; and Torre, *Il consumo di devozioni.*

[18]Gentilcore, *Healers and Healing.*

[19]Zardin, *Confraternite e Vita di Pietà*; idem, *Riforma cattolica e resistenze nobiliari*; and de Boer, *Conquest of the Soul.*

Renaissance or early modern religious and cultural values with particular
political processes and evolving charitable networks.[20] The rural studies
have demonstrated that the implications of "Christianization" as a reciprocal rather than top-down process can only be understood when plotted
through the length of the ancien régime. Both have shown that the boundary between orthodoxy and unorthodoxy was porous at best.

Was unorthodox belief necessarily heretical? Carlo Ginzburg's
famous studies of the *benandanti* and the miller Menocchio attempted to
demonstrate the reciprocation of intellectual influences between high and
low, and how an extended process of Inquisitorial prosecution could shift
locals' understandings of where the boundary lay between orthodoxy and
heresy, and where they, as believers, stood in relation to them. In both
cases, his results have been challenged on the basis of closer examination
of the now-published trial records.[21] "Heresy" in Venice mutated in
response to local repression. A broad civic consensus for social and ecclesiastical reform built around evangelism engaged men and women of different classes and particularly artisans. But this consensus progressively
narrowed with an Inquisitorial winnowing that began with *spirituali*, mil-
lenarians, antitrinitarians, and Anabaptists, before moving to those who
aspired in ways deemed unorthodox by the Tridentine hierarchy, to reach
the higher levels of Catholic sanctity.[22] In Florence, Savonarola's shadow
stretched to the mid-sixteenth century and animated the visionaries of a
holy and charitable republic as their delicate dance with the Medici moved
from opposition to accommodation to (by the end of the ancien régime)
orthodoxy.[23] More tellingly, it was the dovetailing of Savonarolan religious
politics with Medici absolutist politics and local charitable and confraternal traditions that shaped Florence's nascent system of social charity very
differently from the neighboring city of Bologna, whose own antipapal
politics and traditions dictated a more broad-based, lay-directed, and
civic-oriented system.[24] The comparative approach allows closer examination of how local "systems of the sacred," both urban and rural, played

---

[20]Carboni, *Le doti della "povertà"*; Muzzarelli, *Il denaro e la salveza*; Garbellotti, *Le risorse dei poveri*; Gazzini, *Confraternite e società cittadina*; and D'Andrea, *Civic Christianity in Renaissance Italy.*
    [21]Ginzburg, *Cheese and the Worms*; idem, *Night Battles*; Del Col, *Domenico Scandella*; and Nar-don, *Benandanti e inquisitori.*
    [22]Martin, *Venice's Hidden Enemies*; idem, *Myths of Renaissance Individualism*; Schutte, *Aspiring Saints*; and Russell, *Giulia Gonzaga and Religious Controversies.*
    [23]Polizzotto, *Elected Nation*; idem, *Children of the Promise*; and Eisenbichler, *Boys of the Archan-gel Raphael.*
    [24]Terpstra, *Abandoned Children of Italian Renaissance.*

on the boundary between orthodoxy and unorthodoxy, and dictated the implementation and fate of peninsular or Europe-wide movements for devotional, educational, or charitable change.

Two agents found in many analyses of sixteenth-century Italian religious history are a centralizing papacy and a reformed episcopacy—sometimes working together, sometimes apart, but always key players in the process of social discipline. Simon Ditchfield suggests that they are caricatures generated by the desire to locate the Catholic Church in the process of bureaucratic and state modernization that led to the modern state.[25] He argues for more reciprocation between center and periphery, and for recognizing that the three-way dynamics between local clergy, reforming bishop, and papal curia were constantly shifting. Rome was more a divided court than an absolutist monarchy; the papacy was neither as effective nor as single-minded as the tropes would have it, and the Roman Congregation of Rites was "closer to a referee than a policeman" in its efforts to secure adherence to the new liturgical forms.[26]

Ditchfield offers a valuable corrective to the centralizing, disciplinary, and top-down tropes, and recovers the dialogue between interested parties in the Roman center and the local periphery regarding cults, missals, and liturgy. He demonstrates that the curia's willingness to tolerate local liturgical particularities of demonstrated antiquity stimulated scholarship by clergy aiming to preserve a form of the mass distinct from the new Roman model. He thus aims to recover engagement and dialogue among the parties who were constructing early modern Catholicism. Recent work on saints' lives and sermons shows how this drive had started transforming the traditional forms of communication in the fifteenth century.[27] Likewise, Henry Stone asserts the existence of a "public square" in the disputes of scholars, local clergy, and Roman clergy surrounding St. Augustine's bones, and the efforts of all to sway public opinion with their writing.[28] Yet real access to that square was limited, and if many Catholics of artisanal and merchant rank experienced a tightening of screws, it was because they fell outside the politically engaged classes. As lay and clerical elites found their community of interests around a more educated and disciplined Catholicism, they co-opted those institutional forms (such as

[25]Ditchfield, *Liturgy, Sanctity and History*; and idem, "In Search of Local Knowledge."

[26]Ditchfield, "In Search of Local Knowledge," 279; and Signorotto and Visceglia, *Court and Politics in Papal Rome*.

[27]Frazier, *Possible Lives*; and Muzzarelli, *Pescatori di uomini*.

[28]Stone, *St. Augustine's Bones*.

confraternities and hospitals) that had traditionally expressed the local religion of middling and subordinate classes. The institutions retained a voice in the public square, but the speakers were of a decidedly superior *qualità*, and frequently had a more distinctly confessionalizing agenda. Further, disciplinary institutions like the Holy Office might have had more bark than bite, but despite their inefficiencies, internal divisions, and occasional mercies, they did not lack for teeth.[29]

The Institutional Church

The Catholic Church was not a monolithic institution before the Council of Trent, and recent studies have emphasized that it was not one afterwards either. Although not quite "localized," the study of the Catholic Church as an Italian institution has devolved into a study of its various constituent parts. New biographies have moderated the reputation of the fearsome Julius II and boosted that of the underrated Clement VII—though it remains surprising how few papal biographies there are for this entire period.[30] Thanks to superb recent biographies, we now have a fuller picture of key moderates like Gasparo Contarini and Reginald Pole, and of deeply engaged power brokers like Francesco Soderini.[31] Few scholars have explored hard-liners like Gian Pietro Carafa, much less the negligent bishops or incompetent clerics who, to judge by their reforming peers' complaints, clogged the hierarchy. On the other hand, more studies explore how higher clergy became critical to framing local cultural life through their own publishing and patronage in expanding educational institutions like seminaries and universities (where theology faculties expanded as canon law studies declined), and by the discipline of external or self-censorship.[32] Financial and political realities forced the church to become ever more engaged in local Italian politics, and much recent institutional history explores these links. Paolo Prodi set the tone with an examination of the Papal State that cast it as the prototype of early modern absolutism, thoroughly engaged with the political priorities of local elites to the frequent frustration of local bishops who were pushing spiritual

---

[29]Prosperi, *Tribunali della coscienza*; Fragnito, *La Bibbia al rogo*; idem, *Church, Censorship, and Culture*; de Boer, *Conquest of the Soul*; Prosperi, *Il Concilio di Trento*; and Schutte, *Aspiring Saints*.

[30]Shaw, *Julius II*; Murphy, *The Pope's Daughter*; and Gouwens and Reiss, *Pontificate of Clement VII*.

[31]Gleason, *Gasparo Contarini*; Lowe, *Church and Politics in Renaissance Italy*; and Mayer, *Reginald Pole*.

[32]Logan, *Venetian Upper Clergy*; Comerford, *Ordaining the Catholic Reformation*; Fragnito, *Church, Censorship, and Culture*; and Grendler, *Universities of the Italian Renaissance*.

reform.[33] The papal administration expanded rapidly in scale and scope, and in the efficiency of its financial apparatus, even as methods of curial appointment and office holding remained traditionally patronal and venal and closely tied to Roman politics.[34]

The area of church institutional history most changed over the past two decades by the emphasis on the local and the microhistorical is the study of religious orders and communities, particularly convents. Studies of sixteenth-century Catholicism traditionally emphasized new religious orders such as the Theatines, Barnabites, and Somaschans, but dealt largely with male groups and emphasized institutional history.[35] The current wave of research on convents focuses on individual houses or the houses of a particular city, and contextualizes them deliberately into domestic and civic politics. Moreover, while the studies of new male orders emphasized their expanding missionary outreach, studies of convents explore the diminishing scope afforded by the gradually lowering boom of enforced enclosure, and the nuns' efforts to resist, avoid, or resign themselves to it.

A common theme is that nuns entered convents less out of their own devotion than out of their families' marriage strategies. Dowry inflation secured this result in most cities in the fifteenth century, and it was this inflation rather than any increase in piety that spurred the growth in houses and professions through the sixteenth and into the seventeenth centuries. Becoming a bride of Christ also required a dowry, albeit lower than that required on the marriage market, but the spiritual marriage was still shaped by kin politics. Families frequently favored particular houses and aimed to make their daughter's profession a means of gaining and advertising familial honor. Before Trent, nuns maintained more active contact with their families: making visits, receiving kin, and even participating discreetly in local politics.[36] Houses exercised greater or lesser enclosure, and women adopted different types of vocation when professing by informal (as *pinzochere*), formal, or third order vows.[37]

While the Council of Trent ordered more strict enclosure of convents, compliance was no more immediate or complete than with any other Tri-

---

[33]Prodi, *Papal Prince*.

[34]Partner, *The Pope's Men*; Nussdorfer, *Civic Politics in the Rome of Urban VIII*; and Signorotto and Visceglia, *Court and Politics in Papal Rome*.

[35]De Molen, *Religious Orders of the Catholic Reformation*.

[36]Sperling, *Convents and the Body Politic*; Baernstein, *A Convent Tale*; Laven, *Virgins of Venice*; Lowe, *Nuns' Chronicles and Convent Culture*; Strocchia, "Taken into Custody."

[37]Gill, "Open Monasteries for Women."

dentine decree. Yet Craig Monson documents the progression of steps by which the walls enclosing a convent like Santa Cristina della Fondazza in Bologna, famous for musical skill and innovation, became less porous in the late sixteenth century; music teachers could not come in to teach, nuns could not go out to perform, and audiences could listen only from behind a screen. The nuns protested in local ecclesiastical courts, arguing that these restrictions constituted an arbitrary and illegitimate alteration of the terms under which they had first professed. This slowed but did not reverse the process, which moved ahead as the older nuns died off. Having been a focal point of a lively local music scene, the convent became ever more conservative musically as the nuns' access was gradually cut off.[38] Caroline Reardon paints a radically different picture in Siena, where a local bishop determined to maintain more open access in and out, and where the nuns remained active participants in the local musical culture.[39]

The creativity shown in these studies finds roots, in part, in their authors' determination to broaden the range of sources employed in order to convey more thoroughly the culture that women created together. Current convent studies deal extensively with the theater performed by nuns, with their artistic production, and with their literature as a means of recovering nuns' own voices.[40] This last area embraces the chronicles through which they recorded their history, the letters nuns sent to relatives, and the devotional literature that plots the active engagement of some in the new models of sanctity developing after Trent—models shared by both nuns and women living outside the convent walls. Cultural patronage and performance became a significant bridge connecting women within and outside the convents in common pursuit of spiritual and patronal goals.[41] Some authors have explored this internal production in conjunction with external sources produced by tribunals (such as the Inquisition), which tested the professed or aspiring sanctity of nuns and laywomen against the tighter behavioral standards that obtained after Trent—hence Judith Brown's microhistorical study of one nun's efforts to negotiate and perhaps exploit the intersections of spirituality and sexuality

---

[38]Monson, *Disembodied Voices*.

[39]Reardon, *Holy Concord within Sacred Walls*.

[40]Monson, *Crannied Wall*; Kendrik, *Celestial Sirens*; Lowe, *Nuns' Chronicles and Convent Culture*; Reardon, *Holy Concord within Sacred Walls*; Weaver, *Convent Theatre in Early Modern Italy*; and Thomas, *Art and Piety in Female Religious Communities*.

[41]Zarri, *Le sante vive*; Valone, "Women on the Quirinal Hill"; and Schutte et al., *Time, Space, and Women's Lives*.

that figured large in medieval convents, and Anne Jacobson Schutte's nuanced studies of laywomen's (and men's) aspirations to sanctity in the changed temper of baroque Italy.[42]

In the past fifteen years, there has been surprisingly little new scholarship on the new male orders. The exception is Jesuit historiography, which has demonstrated exceptional quantity and breadth. John O'Malley inaugurated the recent wave with, appropriately, *The First Jesuits*, a study that effectively conveys the fluidity of Loyola's early followers and of his own intentions. Beginning initially as an informal confraternity, they metamorphosed into an order and took on their educational and charitable missions more by happenstance and seized opportunity than by any deliberate plan. Yet once seized, the opportunities multiplied and the Jesuits expressed the emerging baroque ethos as effectively as the Franciscans and Dominicans had expressed the medieval communal ethos of the thirteenth and fourteenth centuries. More than any of their contemporaries, they used art and architecture to persuasively express a form of belief that engaged emotion in order to capture the will. A great deal of recent work explores this broadly cultural approach to missions.[43] Jesuit missions also aimed to "support and redeem" through schools and wide-ranging charities, and achieved a rapid diffusion of institutions by turning the confraternal form to their needs for administration and fund-raising, and to the broader cultural project of Christianization.[44]

Jews

The themes of locality and enclosure intersected with the development in Italy of Jewish ghettos in Venice (1516), Rome (1555), Bologna (1556), Florence (1571), and elsewhere. The ghettos added physical form to long-standing legal restrictions, and underlined the extent to which Jewish communities were seen as potentially contagious elements in the Christian body politic. Some, such as the Venetian ghetto, aimed largely to contain, while others, as in Rome, intended to convert. An earlier tradition of Jewish historiography focused on Jewish exclusion from Christian society, fueled in part by the fact that many of the sources used were generated by

---

[42]Brown, *Immodest Acts*; Ferrazzi, *Autobiography of an Aspiring Saint*; and Schutte, *Aspiring Saints*.

[43]O'Malley et al., *The Jesuits*; Bailey, *Art on the Jesuit Missions*; idem, *Between Renaissance and Baroque*; and Levy, *Propaganda and the Jesuit Baroque*.

[44]Grendler, *Schooling in Renaissance Italy*; Selwyn, *Paradise Inhabited by Devils*; and Lazar, *Working in the Vineyard of the Lord*.

Catholic inquisitorial and secular prosecutions. Recent work has probed the expanding legal, social, and cultural institutions of Jewish communities in the ghettos, and explored how some Christian social and cultural forms were adapted selectively by Jews[45]—although research has also continued into more antagonistic relations, particularly with regard to forced conversion.[46]

Robert Bonfil's early survey developed the theme of cultural reciprocation across the peninsula, and more recent work explores local implications.[47] Kenneth Stow's extensive and detailed investigations into the Roman community—working particularly with notarial documents—explores its emerging forms of internal arbitration and its interactions and negotiations with a Christian culture that was alternately fascinated and repelled by it.[48] Elliott Horowitz's numerous studies into aspects of communal life across northern Italy have shown, for instance, how Catholic funeral rituals influenced burial rituals in Jewish communities, and how Jewish confraternities acted much like their Catholic counterparts to socialize and educate youths and to organize charity and devotions when communities lacked a synagogue.[49] This interest in agency, negotiation, and culture echoes investigations more generally into the broader meaning and effects of the early modern stage of the *grand renfermement*. Moreover, new work aims to expand the contexts for Christian-Jewish relations by examining the long history of engagement between Christian and Muslim individuals, groups, and states.[50] Cross-cultural traffic and opportune conversion were widespread, particularly by merchants. Contemporaries sometimes called merchant-converts a "boat with two rudders," but it seems they were more like a ship with many sails.

Postscript

Catholics of 1650 found themselves shepherded by a more disciplined and cohesive church than their counterparts of 1500. If not uniform, it was more deliberate and consistent in its liturgies, its educational efforts, and

---

[45]Ioly-Zorattini, *Processo di S. Uffizio di Venezia contro ebrei e guidaizzanti*; Stow, *Jews in Rome*; and Siegmund, *Medici State and the Ghetto of Florence*.

[46]Caffiero, *Battesimi forzati*.

[47]Bonfil, *Jewish Life in Renaissance Italy*.

[48]Stow, *Theater of Acculturation*.

[49]Horowitz, "Speaking of the Dead"; and idem, "Processions, Piety, and Jewish Confraternities."

[50]Davis, *Christian Slaves, Muslim Masters;* Davis, *Trickster Travels*, Dursteler, *Venetians in Constantinople;* and Epstein, *Transgressing Boundaries in the Eastern Mediterranean*.

its moral codes. Its churches were more grand, its confraternities more numerous and more effectively connected to local parishes, and its charitable institutions larger. There was greater discipline among clergy and laity alike, and fewer divergent voices and practices. What explains these changes?

Financial necessity forced Bonifacio dalle Balle to bring Franciscan tertiaries into his charitable rescue mission in Bologna by 1592. Together they built and staffed larger quarters, and fought off Franciscan conventuals who were eying the property. Dalle Balle's confreres recruited highborn patrons (who could place girls in the home) and found piecework contracts in the silk industry to keep the girls busy and the bottom line healthy. When dalle Balle protested the erosion of Santa Croce's spiritual purpose, the tertiaries wrote statutes that pushed him to the side and instituted an administrative model that had been framed locally decades earlier and widely adopted in Bologna's charities. This model improved accountability, efficiency, and political oversight and was endorsed by the local archbishop and senate. It was this community of interests between highborn laity and clergy—expressed almost too perfectly by the tertiaries— that squeezed dalle Balle, as indeed it was squeezing confraternities, convents, Jews, and the traditional institutions of artisanal civil society in early modern Italy. Clergy may have disliked dalle Balle's spiritual freelancing, but lay elites were more concerned with preserving the social institution it had brought into being. They believed, not without reason, that the home needed the discipline of patrons, statutes, and income if it was to survive at all. One person's enthusiasms or qualms could not stand in the way of building a holy and a safe society.

Terms like "discipline," "confessionalization," and "Christianization" can quickly feed into negative evaluations that perpetuate, at a diplomatically indirect remove, the parochial fights of earlier generations of church historians. Yet they also express the continuities between the efforts of many Italians of the fifteenth, sixteenth, and seventeenth centuries to perfect humanity by promoting an educated spirituality (informed by classical and patristic learning), civil values (framed around self-control), and governance by those whose *qualità* and *carità* made them most fit to rule. For many, discipline began in the heart and at home, where they prayed, fasted, and flagellated devoutly. Equally, devotion demanded expression in the local public square, where sometimes unlikely coalitions formed in pursuit of a more Christian social order. And if there is a tendency to emphasize clerical elites' disciplining laity, work on contemporary Spain, France, and Bavaria has emphasized that these roles could frequently be reversed as animated laity held their priests to higher standards. Local, microhistorical, and biographical studies can allow us better to understand how a community of interests formed around the needs, convictions, aspirations, and self-interest of professionals, prosperous merchants and artisans, patricians, and clergy, and on terms distinct from those that had animated late medieval and Renaissance civic religion. Such studies analytically unravel the peninsular and local economic and political realities that gave this community of interests a different face, focus, and priorities in cities, towns, and regions. They also reveal how stubborn individuals and groups and still-vibrant traditions and institutions shaped the reciprocations and negotiations that characterized the religio-political culture of the ancien régime. There was a broad consensus among early moderns that all of life is religion. Even if this begs the question of just what religion is, it reminds us to integrate spiritual and ecclesiological questions into our analysis of early modern social, political, and cultural history.

Research Aids

The electronic resources available when the previous research guide was published were modest, but their rapid expansion has made it significantly easier to plan and conduct library and archival research. Most of the major Italian archives have websites, bibliographical finding aids for secondary sources have multiplied, specialized listservs have made it easier to pursue questions, and a steadily expanding number of books and manuscripts are being digitized and made accessible through the worldwide web.

Since 1997 an Italian government ministry has mounted the Archivi portal, which, among other services, provides links to the websites of all the state archives and to many other local archives (http://archivi.beniculturali.it/). It hosts a similar site for Italian libraries (http://www.sbn.it). These are of varying utility. Some convey little more than information on access and services, while others include whole or partial inventories, searchable catalogues of holdings, digitized documents, and the libraries' website links to searchable catalogues of Latin manuscripts and Italian sixteenth-century editions held in Italian libraries. In some instances, scholars can register online and order materials in advance. Among the most helpful of these is the website for the Florentine State Archive (http://www.archiviodistato.firenze.it), which provides links to a broader range of archives across Italy, than those found in the Archivi portal. This website also offers links to further international portals that in turn link to an expanded range of civic, ecclesiastical, and institutional archives. At the time of writing, there is no single portal that provides links to all the websites for archdioceses, religious orders, ecclesiastical institutions, and church historical study centers; indeed, not all of these have websites.

Research help can be gained through a number of specialized proprietary, online bibliographies, which are accessed by subscription, by membership in scholarly societies, or through some university libraries. Among the most helpful are ITER (http://www.itergateway.org) and a comprehensive bibliography of English and French works on early modern Italy (http://www.EarlyModernItaly.com). Both list a large number of journal articles and essay collections, and while they do not yet post texts, in many instances these are available electronically through J-STOR (http://www.jstor.org). Research help in Q & A format can be gained by posting queries on listservs hosted by societies dedicated to research in Italian or early modern religious history. Among the most helpful are H-Italy (http://www.h-net.org/~italy), the Society for Early Modern Catholic Studies (http://www.georgetown.edu/users/ael3/semcs), and FICINO at the Center for Reformation and Renaissance Studies at the University of Toronto (http://www.crrs.ca/publications/electronic/ficino/htm).

The digitization of manuscripts and texts is the area of greatest promise, providing ease of access far beyond existing microfilm and microfiche series. As previously noted, a number of Italian archives are expanding their offerings in this area. The Florentine State Archive is steadily digitizing and posting manuscript materials, while Bologna's civic library of the Archiginnasio has posted an entire collection of printed broadsheets from the seventeenth and eighteenth centuries (http://www.archiginnasio.it). Two more ambitious projects are the Medici Archive Project, which is creating the searchable online database Documentary Sources for the Arts and the Humanities in the Medici Granducal Archive: 1537–1743 (http://www.medici.org), and the Ad Fontes Digital Libraries of the Catholic and Protestant Reformations (http://www.ad-fontes.com), which is making available fully searchable collections of key texts published in sixteenth- and seventeenth- century Europe.

Bibliography

ELECTRONIC SOURCES

Ad Fontes Digital Libraries of the Catholic and Protestant Reformations: http://www.ad-fontes.com
Archivi portal, with links to state and local archives: http://archivi.beniculturali.it/
Biblioteca comunale dell'Archiginnasio: http://www.archiginnasio.it
Documentary Sources for the Arts and the Humanities in the Medici Granducal Archive (1537–1743): http://www.medici.org
Early Modern Italy, bibliography of English and French works: http://www.EarlyModernItaly.com
FICINO, Center for Reformation and Renaissance Studies at the University of Toronto: http://www.crrs.ca/publications/electronic/ficino/htm
Florentine State Archive: http://www.archiviodistato.firenze.it
H-Italy: http://www.h-net.org/~italy
ITER: http://www.itergateway.org
J-STOR: http://www.jstor.org
Servizio Bibliotecario Nazionale, links to Italian libraries: http://www.sbn.it
Society for Early Modern Catholic Studies: http://www.georgetown.edu/users/ael3/semcs

PRINTED SOURCES

Baernstein, P. Renée. *A Convent Tale: A Century of Sisterhood in Spanish Milan.* New York: Routledge, 2002.
Bailey, Gauvin Alexander. *Art on the Jesuit Missions in Asia and Latin America, 1542–1773.* Toronto: University of Toronto Press, 2001.
———. *Between Renaissance and Baroque: Jesuit Art in Rome, 1565–1610.* Toronto: University of Toronto Press, 2003.
Bireley, Robert. *The Refashioning of Catholicism, 1400–1750: A Re-Assessment of the Counter-Reformation.* Washington, DC: Catholic University Press, 1999.
Black, Christopher F. *Church, Religion and Society in Early Modern Italy.* Basingstoke: Palgrave Macmillan, 2004.
———. *Early Modern Italy: A Social History.* London: Routledge, 2001.
———. *Italian Confraternities in the Sixteenth Century.* Cambridge: Cambridge University Press, 1989.
———, and Pamela Gravestock. *Early Modern Confraternities in Europe and the Americas.* Aldershot: Ashgate, 2005.
Bonfil, Robert. *Jewish Life in Renaissance Italy.* Berkeley: University of California Press, 1994.
Brown, Judith C. *Immodest Acts: the Life of a Lesbian Nun in Renaissance Italy.* New York: Oxford University Press, 1986.
Caffiero, Marina. *Battesimi forzati: Storie di ebrei, cristiani e convertiti nella Roma dei papi.* Rome: Viella, 2004.
Caponnetto, Salvatore. *The Protestant Reformation in Sixteenth Century Italy.* Kirksville, MO: Truman State University Press, 1999.
Carboni, Mauro. *Le doti della "povertà": Famiglia, risparmio, previdenza: il Monte del Matrimonio di Bologna, 1583–1796.* Bologna: il Mulino, 1999.

Cavallo, Sandra. *Charity and Power in Early Modern Italy: Benefactors and Their Motives in Turin, 1541–1789*. Cambridge: Cambridge University Press, 1994.

Comerford, Kathleen M. *Ordaining the Catholic Reformation: Priest and Seminary Pedagogy in Fiesole (1575–1675)*. Florence: L. S. Olschki, 2001.

———, and Hilmar Pabel. *Early Modern Catholicism*. Toronto: University of Toronto Press, 2001.

D'Andrea, David M. *Civic Christianity in Renaissance Italy. The Hospital of Treviso, 1400–1530*. Rochester: University of Rochester Press, 2007.

Davis, Natalie Zemon. *Trickster Travels: A Sixteenth-Century Muslim Between Worlds*. New York: Hill & Wang, 2006.

Davis, Robert C. *Christian Slaves, Muslim Masters: White Slavery in the Mediterranean, the Barbary Coast, and Italy, 1500–1800*. New York: Palgrave Macmillan, 2003.

De Boer, Wietse. *The Conquest of the Soul: Confession, Discipline, and Public Order in Counter-Reformation Milan*. Leiden: Brill, 2001.

Del Col, Andrea. *Domenico Scandella Known as Menocchio: His Trials before the Inquisition*. Binghamton: MRTS, 1996.

De Molen, Richard. *Religious Orders of the Catholic Reformation*. New York: Fordham University Press, 1994.

Ditchfield, Simon. "In Search of Local Knowledge: Rewriting Early Modern Italian Religious History." *Cristianesimo nella Storia* 19 (1998): 255–96.

———. *Liturgy, Sanctity and History in Tridentine Italy: Pietro Maria Campi and the Preservation of the Particular*. Cambridge: Cambridge University Press, 1995.

Donnelly, John P., and Michael W. Maher. *Confraternities and Catholic Reform in Italy, France, and Spain*. Kirksville, MO: Truman State University Press, 1998.

Dursteler, Eric R. *Venetians in Constantinople: Nation, Identity, and Co-existence in the Early Modern Mediterranean*. Baltimore: Johns Hopkins University Press, 2006.

Eckstein, Nicholas. *The District of the Green Dragon: Neighbourhood Life and Social Change in Renaissance Florence*. Florence: L. S. Olschki, 1995.

Eisenbichler, Konrad. *The Boys of the Archangel Raphael: A Youth Confraternity in Florence, 1411–1785*. Toronto: University of Toronto Press, 1998.

Epstein, Steven A. *Transgressing Boundaries in the Eastern Mediterranean, 1000–1400*. Baltimore: Johns Hopkins University Press, 2006.

Ferrazzi, Cecilia. *Autobiography of an Aspiring Saint*. Edited and translated by Anne J. Schutte. Chicago: University of Chicago Press, 1996.

Fragnito, Gigliola. *La Bibbia al rogo: La censura ecclesiastica e i volgarizzamenti della Scrittura (1471–1605)*. Bologna: il Mulino, 1997.

———, ed. *Church, Censorship and Culture in Early Modern Italy*. Cambridge: Cambridge University Press, 2001.

Frazier, Alison Knowles. *Possible Lives: Authors and Saints in Renaissance Italy*. New York: Columbia University Press, 2005.

Garbellotti, Marina. *Le risorse dei poveri: Carità e tutela della salute nel principato vescovile di Trento in età moderna*. Bologna: il Mulino, 2006.

Gazzini, Marina. *Confraternite e società cittadina nel medioevo italiano*. Bologna: CLUEB, 2006.

Gentilcore, David. *From Bishop to Witch: The System of the Sacred in Early Modern Terra d'Otranto*. Manchester: Manchester University Press, 1992.

———. *Healers and Healing in Early Modern Italy*. Manchester: Manchester University Press, 1998.

———. "Methods and Approaches in the Social History of the Counter-Reformation in Italy: A Review Essay." *Social History* 17 (1992): 73–98.

Gill, Katherine. Open Monasteries for Women in Late Medieval and Early Modern Italy. In *The Crannied Wall: Women, Religion, and the Arts in Early Modern Europe*, edited by Craig Monson, 15–47. Ann Arbor: University of Michigan Press, 1992.

Ginzburg, Carlo. *The Cheese and the Worms: The Cosmos of a Sixteenth Century Miller.* Baltimore: Johns Hopkins University Press, 1980.

———. *The Night Battles: Witchcraft and Agrarian Cults in the Sixteenth and Seventeenth Centuries.* Baltimore: Johns Hopkins University Press, 1983.

Gleason, Elisabeth, *Gasparo Contarini: Venice, Rome, and Reform*. Berkeley: University of California Press, 1993.

Glixon, Jonathan. *Honoring God and the City: Music at the Venetian Confraternities, 1260–1806.* Oxford: Oxford University Press, 2003.

Gouwens, Kenneth, and Sheryl E. Reiss. *The Pontificate of Clement VII: History, Politics, Culture.* Aldershot: Ashgate, 2005.

Grendler, Paul. *Schooling in Renaissance Italy: Literacy and Learning, 1300–1600.* Baltimore: Johns Hopkins University Press, 1989.

———. *The Universities of the Italian Renaissance.* Baltimore: Johns Hopkins University Press, 2002.

Hanlon, Gregory. *Early Modern Italy, 1550–1800.* London: Palgrave Macmillan, 2000.

Horowitz, Elliott. "Processions, Piety, and Jewish Confraternities." In *The Jews of Early Modern Venice*, edited by R. C. Davis and B. Ravid, 231–47, 295–301. Baltimore: Johns Hopkins University Press, 2001.

———. "Speaking of the Dead: The Emergence of the Eulogy among Sixteenth Century Italian Jewry." In *Preachers of the Italian Ghetto*, edited by D. Ruderman, 129–62. Berkeley: University of California Press, 1992.

Ioly Zorattini, Pier Cesare. *Processo di S. Uffizio di Venezia contro ebrei e giudaizzanti.* 14 vols. Florence: L. S. Olschki, 1980–99.

Kendrik, Robert. *Celestial Sirens: Nuns and Their Music in Early Modern Milan.* Oxford: Clarendon Press, 1996.

Laven, Mary. *Virgins of Venice: Enclosed Lives and Broken Vows in the Renaissance Convent.* London: Viking, 2003.

Lazar, Lance. *Working in the Vineyard of the Lord: Jesuit Confraternities in Early Modern Italy.* Toronto: University of Toronto Press, 2005.

Levy, Evonne. *Propaganda and the Jesuit Baroque.* Berkeley: University of California Press, 2004.

Logan, Oliver. *The Venetian Upper Clergy in the Sixteenth and Seventeenth Centuries: A Study in Religious Culture.* Lewiston, NY: Edwin Mellen, 1995.

Lowe, Katherine. *Church and Politics in Renaissance Italy: The Life and Career of Cardinal Francesco Soderini, 1453–1524.* Cambridge: Cambridge University Press, 1993.

———. *Nuns' Chronicles and Convent Culture in Renaissance and Counter-Reformation Italy.* Cambridge: Cambridge University Press, 2002.

Marino, John A., ed. *Early Modern Italy: 1550–1796.* Oxford: Oxford University Press, 2002.

Martin, John Jeffries. *Myths of Renaissance Individualism.* Basingstoke: Palgrave Macmillan, 2004.

———. "Religion, Renewal, and Reform in the Sixteenth Century." In *Early Modern Italy: 1550–1796*, edited by John A. Marino, 30–50. Oxford: Oxford University Press, 2002.

————. *Venice's Hidden Enemies: Italian Heretics in a Renaissance City.* Berkeley: University of California Press, 1993.

Mayer, Thomas. F. *Reginald Pole: Prince and Prophet.* Cambridge: Cambridge University Press, 2000.

Monson, Craig. *Disembodied Voices. Music and Culture in Early Modern Convents.* Berkeley: University of California Press, 1995.

————, ed. *The Crannied Wall: Women, Religion, and the Arts in Early Modern Europe.* Ann Arbor: University of Michigan Press, 1992.

Muir, Edward. *Civic Ritual in Renaissance Venice.* Princeton, NJ: Princeton University Press, 1981.

Murphy, Caroline P. *The Pope's Daughter: The Extraordinary Life of Felice della Rovere.* London: Faber & Faber, 2005.

Muzzarelli, Maria Giuseppina. *Il denaro e la salvezza: L'invenzione del Monte di Pietà.* Bologna: il Mulino, 2001.

————. *Pescatori di uomini: Predicatori e piazze alla fine del Medioevo.* Bologna: il Mulino, 2005.

Najemy, John, ed. *Italy in the Age of the Renaissance: 1300–1550.* Oxford: Oxford University Press, 2004.

Nardon, Franco. *Benandanti e inquisitori nel Friuli del Seicento.* Trieste: Edizioni Università di Trieste, 1999.

Nussdorfer, L. *Civic Politics in the Rome of Urban VIII.* Princeton, NJ: Princeton University Press, 1992.

O'Malley, John W. *The First Jesuits.* Cambridge, MA: Harvard University Press, 1993.

————. *Trent and All That: Renaming Catholicism in the Early Modern Era.* Cambridge, MA: Harvard University Press, 2000.

————, Gauvin Alexander Bailey, Steven J. Harris, and T. Frank Kennedy, eds. *The Jesuits: Cultures, Sciences, and the Arts, 1540–1773.* Toronto: University of Toronto Press, 2000.

O'Regan, Noel. *Institutional Patronage in Post-Tridentine Rome: Music at Santissima Trinità dei Pellegrini 1550–1650.* London: Royal Music Association, 1995.

Partner, Peter. *The Pope's Men: The Roman Court and the Papal Civil Service.* Oxford: Oxford University Press, 1990.

Peterson, David. "Out of the Margins: Religion and the Church in Renaissance Italy." *Renaissance Quarterly* 53 (2000): 835–79.

Po-Chia Hsia, R. *The World of Catholic Renewal, 1540–1770.* Cambridge: Cambridge University Press, 1998.

Polizzotto, Lorenzo. *Children of the Promise: The Confraternity of the Purification and the Socialization of Youths in Florence, 1427–1785.* Oxford: Oxford University Press, 2004.

————. *The Elect Nation: The Savonarolan Movement in Florence, 1494–1545.* Oxford: Oxford University Press, 1994.

Prodi, Paolo. *The Papal Prince: One Body and Two Souls.* Cambridge: Cambridge University Press, 1988.

————, ed. *Disciplina dell'anima, disciplina del corpo, e disciplina della società tra medioevo ed età moderna.* Bologna: il Mulino, 1994.

Prosperi, Adriano. *Il Concilio di Trento: Una introduzione storica.* Turin: Einaudi, 2001.

————. *Tribunali della coscienza: Inquisitori, Confessor, Missionari.* Turin: Einaudi, 1996.

————, ed. *Salvezza delle anime, disciplina dei corpi: Un seminario sulla storia del battesimo.* Pisa: Edizioni della Normale, 2006.

Pullan, Brian., *Poverty and Charity: Europe, Italy, Venice, 1400–1700.* Aldershot: Variorum, 1994.

———. *Rich and Poor in Renaissance Venice: The Social Institutions of a Renaissance State to 1620.* Oxford: Oxford University Press, 1971.

Reardon, Colleen. *Holy Concord within Sacred Walls: Nuns and Music in Siena, 1575–1700.* Oxford: Oxford University Press, 2002.

Russell, Camilla. *Giulia Gonzaga and the Religious Controversies of Sixteenth Century Italy.* Turnhout: Brepols, 2006.

Schutte, Anne J. *Aspiring Saints: Pretense of Holiness, Inquisition, and Gender in the Republic of Venice, 1618–1750.* Baltimore: Johns Hopkins University Press, 2001.

———. "Periodization of Sixteenth-Century Italian Religious History: The Post-Cantimori Paradigm Shift." *Journal of Modern History* 61 (1989): 269–84.

———. "Religion, Spirituality, and the Post-Tridentine Church." In *Early Modern Italy: 1550–1796,* edited by John A. Marino, 125–42. Oxford: Oxford University Press, 2002.

———, Thomas Kuehn, and Silvana Seidel Menchi, eds. *Time, Space, and Women's Lives in Early Modern Europe.* Kirksville, MO: Truman State University Press, 2001.

Selwyn, Jennifer D. *A Paradise Inhabited by Devils: The Jesuit Civilizing Mission in Early Modern Naples.* Aldershot: Ashgate, 2004.

Shaw, Christine. *Julius II: The Warrior Pope.* Oxford: Basil Blackwell, 1993.

Siegmund, Stefanie B. *The Medici State and the Ghetto of Florence: The Construction of an Early Modern Jewish Community.* Stanford, CA: Stanford University Press, 2006.

Signorotto, Gianvittorio, and Maria Antonietta Visceglia. *Court and Politics in Papal Rome, 1492–1700.* Cambridge: Cambridge University Press, 2002.

Sperling, Jutte. *Convents and the Body Politic in Late Renaissance Venice.* Chicago: University of Chicago Press, 1999.

Stone, Harold. *St. Augustine's Bones: A Microhistory.* Amherst: University of Massachusetts Press, 2002.

Stow, Kenneth. *The Jews in Rome.* 2 vols. Leiden: Brill, 1995, 1997.

———. *Theater of Acculturation: The Roman Ghetto in the Sixteenth Century.* Seattle: University of Washington Press, 2001.

Strocchia, Sharon. *Nuns and Nunneries in Renaissance Florence.* Baltimore, MD: Johns Hopkins University Press, forthcoming.

———. "Taken into Custody: Girls and Convent Guardianship in Renaissance Florence." *Renaissance Studies* 17 (2003): 177–200.

Tedeschi, John, and James M. Lattis. *The Italian Reformation of the Sixteenth Century and the Diffusion of Renaissance Culture: A Bibliography of the Secondary Literature (ca. 1750–1997).* Modena: Franco Cosimo Panini Editore, 2000.

Terpstra, Nicholas. *Abandoned Children of the Italian Renaissance: Orphan Care in Florence and Bologna.* Baltimore: Johns Hopkins University Press, 2005.

———. *Lay Confraternities and Civic Religion in Renaissance Bologna.* Cambridge: Cambridge University Press, 1995.

———. *The Politics of Ritual Kinship: Confraternities and Social Order in Early Modern Italy.* Cambridge: Cambridge University Press, 2000.

Thomas, Anabel. *Art and Piety in the Female Religious Communities of Renaissance Italy: Iconography, Space, and the Religious Woman's Perspective.* Cambridge: Cambridge University Press, 2003.

Torre, Angelo. *Il consumo di devozioni: Religione e communità nelle campagne dell'Ancien Regime.* Venice: Marsilio, 1995.

Trexler, Richard. *Public Life in Renaissance Florence*. New York: Academic Press, 1979.

Valone, Carolyn. "Women on the Quirinal Hill: Patronage in Rome, 1560–1630." *Art Bulletin* 76 (1994): 129–46.

Weaver, Elissa B. *Convent Theatre in Early Modern Italy: Spiritual Fun and Learning for Women*. Cambridge: Cambridge University Press, 2002.

Weissman, Ronald F. E. *Ritual Brotherhood in Renaissance Florence*. New York: Academic Press, 1982.

Wisch, Barbara, and Diane Cole Ahl, eds. *Confraternities and the Visual Arts in Renaissance Italy: Ritual, Spectacle, Image*. Cambridge: Cambridge University Press, 2000.

Wright, A. D. *The Early Modern Papacy: From The Council of Trent to the French Revolution, 1564–1789*. London: Longman, 2000.

Zardin, Danilo. *Confraternite e Vita di Pietà nelle campagne lombarde tra '500 e '600*. Milan: NED, 1981.

———. *Riforma cattolica e resistenze nobiliari nella diocesi di Carlo Borromeo*. Milan: Jaca Book, 1984.

———, ed. *Corpi, 'fraternità,' mestieri nella storia della società europea*. Rome: Bulzoni, 1998.

Zarri, Gabriella. *Le sante vive: Cultura e religiosità femminili nella prima eta moderna*. Turin: Rosenberg & Sellier, 1990.

10

England

Peter Marshall

Historians' understanding of the weave of political, cultural, and religious developments that can still usefully be called the English Reformation has changed in important ways in the quarter-century since Paul Seaver skillfully surveyed the field for the 1982 Reformation research guide. New sources have been opened up, new interpretations have been applied to old sources, and a new chronology for the topic is starting to emerge. In 1982, Seaver warned that "if we see the English Reformation as still an ongoing process until the godly lost their hope for the reform of Church and State...we will find ourselves incorporating into a single process what [A. G.] Dickens with some reason has dubbed 'the second Reformation' of the mid-seventeenth century."[1] In large measure, this has now come to pass: the English Reformation, once an exclusively mid-Tudor business, has become a "long Reformation" and a process, not an event.[2]

    Important interpretative shifts were already starting to become visible by the late 1970s. For over a decade, A. G. Dickens's 1964 survey, *The English Reformation*, had seemed to most observers to be a near definitive account. Dickens departed from the dominant "Reformation as act of state" interpretation of the earlier twentieth century, stressing instead its credentials as a genuine religious movement and its substantial achievements by the middle of the sixteenth century. He effectively finished his

---

[1]Seaver, "English Reformation."

[2]Tyacke, *England's Long Reformation*; Jones, *English Reformation*; and Marshall, *Reformation England*.

account with the Elizabethan settlement of 1559. While steering clear of the open anti-Catholic bias that had marked some earlier studies, Dickens's account was in many ways heir to a Protestant narrative that had emerged in the Reformation period itself. He evinced limited sympathy for the pre-Reformation church and stressed the prevalence of anticlericalism and humanist criticism in preparing the ground for the actions of Henry VIII.[3]

A full-scale revisionist assault on the hegemony of Dickens began with Christopher Haigh's study of *Reformation and Resistance in Tudor Lancashire*, a book with rather more to say about resistance than it does about reformation. In Haigh's view, the church before the 1530s commanded very widespread popular allegiance, Protestantism only ever made a small number of converts, and Catholic practices long continued in defiance of the law. In subsequent articles, Haigh sought to show that the model was broadly similar for other parts of the country outside London. Almost everywhere there seemed to be complaints from Protestant clergy that the people were unteachable and church court records throughout the country revealed the longevity of Catholic customs well into the reign of Elizabeth. Protestantism, it seemed, was simply unsuited to making much genuine progress in a largely illiterate, agricultural society. Protestant teaching, based around long sermons and catechism classes, was too demanding (and too dull) for a population accustomed to the colorful rituals of Catholicism, and the Calvinist doctrine of predestination (the official theology of the Elizabethan church) was an unattractive one.[4] In a general survey of 1993, Haigh made the memorable suggestion that the Reformation may eventually have succeeded in "creating a Protestant nation, but not a nation of Protestants."[5]

Haigh's was not for long a lone voice. Powerful support came in 1982 when the prestigious Ford lectures in Oxford were given by J. J. Scarisbrick, hitherto best known as the biographer of Henry VIII. Scarisbrick's thesis was that "English men and women did not want the Reformation and most of them were slow to accept it when it came."[6] He painted a vibrant picture of religious life in pre-Reformation England, devoting a chapter, for example, to a theme entirely neglected by Dickens: the guilds, or voluntary religious brotherhoods, that thrived in most English parishes until they were

---

[3]There were remarkably few modifications to the essential picture in a second edition that was published in 1989.

[4]See Haigh, *English Reformation Revised.*

[5]Haigh, *English Reformations.*

[6]Scarisbrick, *Reformation and the English People.*

put down in the late 1540s.[7] Scarisbrick's book was controversial, though the picture received broad endorsement from a series of local and regional studies. Even in London, as Susan Brigden demonstrated, Catholic sentiment remained strong and the Reformation was no walkover.[8] It was not until the mid-1990s, however, that the revisionist cause seemed to be sweeping all before it. In 1992 Eamon Duffy applied both immense theological learning and profound historical imagination to what is probably the most important book yet to be written on pre-Reformation religion, *The Stripping of the Altars*. The book is a diptych: the first half describes religious life in English parishes in the fifteenth and early sixteenth centuries, and the second half, the impact of the Reformation on parish religion up to 1580. An extraordinary range and volume of primary evidence—in particular, the vernacular religious output of the early printing press—is deployed to demonstrate widespread devotion to the mass and sacraments of the Catholic Church, huge financial investment in church building and church furnishings, the great popularity of saints' cults and pilgrimage, and an almost universal concern with praying for the souls of the dead. The Reformation itself appears as an immensely destructive force, sweeping away all kinds of practices and ideas that had exhibited no signs of preemptive decay. It is moving and tragic.[9]

The effect of what some commentators have not hesitated to call "Catholic revisionism"[10] has been to deal a fatal blow to Whiggish and progressivist narratives of the early Reformation in England. Although the emphasis in Haigh's, Scarisbrick's, and Duffy's work is on lay and parish religion with little attention to such topics as the religious orders, a recent trend has been toward the rehabilitation of the institutions as well as the devotional ethos of the pre-Reformation church.[11] Even Cardinal Wolsey, for long the exemplar of late medieval ecclesiastical corruption, has

---

[7]See Barron, "Parish Fraternities of Medieval London"; and Farnhill, *Guilds and the Parish Community*.

[8]Bowker, *Henrician Reformation*; Whiting, *Blind Devotion of the People*; and Brigden, *London and the Reformation*.

[9]Duffy, *Stripping of the Altars*. For elaborations of the thesis, see Duffy, *Voices of Morebath*; and idem, *Marking the Hours*.

[10]For example, Daniell, *William Tyndale*. Haigh has been at pains to point out that he is not a Roman Catholic: *English Reformations*, vii–viii. It is worth observing too that revisionists hardly present a unified interpretative front. Duffy's overall view of the Reformation is of a drastic cultural watershed, whereas Haigh's emphasis on the failure of Protestant evangelism leads him to conclude that in important ways not much changed.

[11]Clark, *Religious Orders in Pre-Reformation England*; and Rushton, "Monastic Charitable Provision."

received sympathetic reinterpretation as a serious-minded and humanist-influenced reformer, as well as for his allegedly sensible and pragmatic response to the emerging Lutheran threat in the 1520s.[12]

Yet all is not quite quiet on the early Reformation front. The significance of Lollardy and the nature of the contribution it was able to make to the first stirrings of the Reformation remains an interpretative flashpoint and a focus of lively research. Here an interpretation that regards late medieval Lollardy as an essentially fragmentary, incoherent, and numerically weak phenomenon, hardly deserving the epithet "movement," remains pitted against a more optimistic view that stresses organizational networks, the preservation of a Wycliffite doctrinal inheritance, and the growing ability of late fifteenth- and early sixteenth-century Lollardy to make converts across the social scale.[13] There is a growing awareness that the lines between heresy and orthodoxy were blurred in the immediately pre-Reformation decades: suspected Lollards used orthodox vernacular texts, attended church, and served as churchwardens; educated and pious Catholics sometimes possessed copies of the unsanctioned Wycliffite Bible and were capable of searing anticlerical critiques. But Lollardy is not merely a historians' construct: R. G. Davies has identified the crucial importance of personal and family connections rather than formal doctrine in sustaining Lollardy ("if Wycliffism was *what* you knew, Lollardy was *who* you knew"), and Shannon McSheffrey rightly stresses the issue of authority—Lollards were those, irrespective of the precise content of their beliefs, who consciously rejected the religious superintendence of the hierarchy and priesthood.[14]

The debates over Lollardy will continue, though they will remain in some ways peripheral to a more pressing question thrown up by the increasingly normative revisionist paradigm. If traditional Catholicism was so well integrated into community life, commanding high levels of both financial and emotional investment, how does one account for the relative ease with which successive mid-Tudor governments were able to dismantle the system? Christopher Marsh has termed this the "compliance

---

[12]Gwynn, *King's Cardinal*; Gunn and Lindley, *Cardinal Wolsey*; and D'Alton, "Suppression of Lutheran Heretics."

[13]For the former view, see Swanson, *Church and Society*; and Rex, *Lollards*. For the latter, see Hudson, *Premature Reformation*; and Aston and Richmond, *Lollardy and the Gentry*.

[14]Davies, "Lollardy and Locality"; and McSheffrey, "Heresy, Orthodoxy and English Vernacular Religion."

conundrum."[15] The question is sharpened by a growing recognition of just how radical the Henrician, Edwardian, and Elizabethan reformations were in their impact on popular religious practice and the fabric of churches. Margaret Aston's meticulous scholarship on the theory and practice of iconoclasm has illuminated a religious environment in sixteenth-century England that was much more hostile to sacred imagery than that in Lutheran Germany or even Zwinglian Zürich.[16] The intensity of the assault on another central pillar of late medieval Catholicism—prayer for the dead in purgatory—has also recently come under the spotlight.[17]

Revisionist scholars are apt to point to the coercive power of the Tudor state, though others have not found this to be a fully satisfactory explanation. Could there have been, despite the undoubted popular commitment to pre-Reformation belief and practice, a paradoxical sense of relief among people as the officially driven Reformation removed the potentially burdensome obligations of fasting, mandatory confession, and intercessory prayer? Marsh and Alec Ryrie have suggested so.[18] Colin Richmond, George Bernard, and Peter Marshall have, in different ways, pointed to the possibility of growing fissures between elite and popular religious mind-sets at the close of the Middle Ages, which may have encouraged the educated and landed classes (from Henry VIII downward) to collude in the destruction of aspects of traditional religion, such as saints' cults, shrines, and pilgrimage, even if they did not always impel them to adopt reforming ideas.[19] That such collaboration may have been the accompaniment to religious change at all social levels is the main theme of a 2003 book by Ethan Shagan (though he is inclined to emphasize material inducements rather than idealistic conviction): the opportunity to acquire monastic assets and chantry lands, or to be able to smear a quarrelsome neighbor as a papist. The English Reformation, Shagan suggests, was "not done *to* people, it was done *with* them."[20] Yet too insistent a focus on compliance risks obscuring the extent to which the Reformation *was* resisted on the ground and in the parishes. A major lacuna of the scholarship of a generation ago—a proper

---

[15]Marsh, *Popular Religion in Sixteenth-Century England.*

[16]Aston, *England's Iconoclasts.*

[17]Marshall, *Beliefs and the Dead.*

[18]Marsh, *Popular Religion in Sixteenth-Century England*; and Ryrie, "Counting Sheep, Counting Shepherds."

[19]Richmond, "Religion and the Fifteenth-Century English Gentleman"; Bernard, "Vitality and Vulnerability"; and Marshall, "Forgery and Miracles."

[20]Shagan, *Popular Politics and the English Reformation.*

study of the Northern Rebellions of 1536–37—has now been plugged by the labors of Michael Bush and Richard Hoyle.[21] The smaller-scale but still highly significant Catholic rebellions of 1549 and 1569 await similarly close investigation.[22]

In the wake of revisionist rehabilitation of traditional Catholicism and anguished considerations of popular response to official reform, the study of early Protestantism itself was threatening to become a moribund field. But there are hopeful signs here. Diarmaid MacCulloch's magisterial biography of Thomas Cranmer has brought a key figure into sharp focus, and a recent collection of essays has emphasized the variety and creativity of heterodox religious expression in the first half of the sixteenth century.[23] The tenor of much current work here is to point to the fluidity of religious positions in what was effectively a pre-confessional age. For the first half of the sixteenth century at least, "Protestant" is an anachronistic term, and "evangelical" better conveys a sense both of the linkages to pre-Reformation culture and of the nondenominational character of a fissiparous movement for religious renewal.[24]

A recognition that there was no preordained denominational outcome to the early Reformation years offers the prospect for fruitful reassessment of the religious politics of the period. The nature and directions of Henrician reform, and the parameters of Henry's personal religion, have been the subject of lively debate. Where some scholars see the ebb and flow of factional conflicts around the opinionated idiosyncrasies of an unpredictable monarch, others detect the working out of a coherent middle way in religious policy, one that looks anomalous only from later confessionalized perspectives.[25] Yet even at his imperious best, Henry was not the sole author of religious policy: a key restraining influence was the conservative bishop of Winchester, Stephen Gardiner.[26] On the evangelical side, Henry's second queen, Anne Boleyn, has emerged as a major patroness of reform in her own right, rather than merely the femme fatale of the

---

[21] Bush, *Pilgrimage of Grace*; and Hoyle, *Pilgrimage of Grace*.

[22] See Fletcher and MacCulloch, *Tudor Rebellions*.

[23] MacCulloch, *Thomas Cranmer*; and Marshall and Ryrie, *Beginnings of English Protestantism*. See also Ryrie, *Gospel and Henry VIII*.

[24] Marshall, *Religious Identities in Henry VIII's England*.

[25] Compare Rex, *Henry VIII and the English Reformation*; MacCulloch, "Henry VIII and the Reform of the Church"; McEntegart, *Henry VIII*; McEntegart, *Rethinking Catholicism*; Bernard, "Making of Religious Policy"; and idem, *King's Reformation*.

[26] Redworth, *In Defence of the Church Catholic*.

English Reformation.[27] With the possible exception of Cranmer, however, there is little doubt that the most important ally of the evangelicals in the upper reaches of the Henrician state was Thomas Cromwell. The former doyen of Tudor political history, G. R. Elton, regarded Cromwell as an essentially secular and modernizing figure, architect of a Tudor "revolution in government," or at best, as someone who regarded religious reform as a means to an end.[28] But more recent work has made a compelling case for Cromwell's real ideological commitment.[29] Remarkably, there is still no substantial scholarly life of the man who must on any reckoning count as one of the half dozen most influential politicians of the century. By contrast, biographies of Cromwell's heroic adversary Thomas More, both admiring and iconoclastic, have continued to roll off the presses in the last two decades: John Guy's recent study achieves a kind of synthesis.[30]

Neither Cromwell nor More lived to see the fulfillment of hopes, or the realization of nightmares, in the heady years of Edward VI's reign. In 1982, Seaver noted that work by Michael Bush, Barrett Beer, and Dale Hoak was revising the reputations of the dukes of Somerset (negatively) and Northumberland (positively), but also observed that these historians "have given scant attention to the Edwardian religious Reformation."[31] This has started to change. Viewed negatively in the work of revisionist historians like Duffy and Haigh (the former sees it as ideologically driven and ruthlessly destructive; the latter, as patchy and pragmatic), Edwardian religious policy is now being assessed more sympathetically on its own terms. Catharine Davies has analyzed Edwardian Protestant thought to find an internally coherent, if occasionally rather paranoid, "Reformation of the Word."[32] Diarmaid MacCulloch's superb account gives due prominence to the zealous iconoclasm implied by Edward's ascribed role as a Josiah-figure, but integrates this with consideration of another biblical prototype, Solomon, builder of the temple. In other words, the Edwardian regime was embarked on a coherent program of cleansing the realm in order to establish a reformed commonwealth, and MacCulloch partially

---

[27]Dowling, "Anne Boleyn and Reform"; Ives, "Anne Boleyn and the Early Reformation"; and idem, *Life and Death of Anne Boleyn*. For a skeptical view, see Bernard, "Anne Boleyn's Religion."
[28]Elton, *Reform and Reformation*.
[29]Brigden, "Thomas Cromwell and the 'Brethren'"; and Underwood, "'Thomas Cromwell and William Marshall's Protestant Books."
[30]Marius, *Thomas More*; Martz, *Thomas More*; Ackroyd, *Life of Thomas More*; and Guy, *Thomas More*.
[31]Seaver, "The English Reformation."
[32]Davies, *Religion of the Word*.

rehabilitates Somerset as the "good duke" who was genuinely concerned with social and economic reform. The tensions between moderately cautious reformers such as Cranmer and Nicholas Ridley, and proto-Puritans such as John Hooper, were disagreements over the pace rather than the substance of reform, over means rather than ends.[33] A further important aspect of MacCulloch's approach is his insistence on the internationalism of mid-Tudor Protestantism. Far from being an insular process (geared ultimately toward the evolution of something called Anglicanism), the Edwardian reformation positioned itself at the heart of a beleaguered European Protestant movement. Cranmer maintained close relations with the great networker of the Reformed Protestant world, Heinrich Bullinger of Zürich. In this area, MacCulloch's work complements that of Andrew Pettegree, who has highlighted the importance of the London stranger churches, as well as the myriad international connections of English Protestants under Mary.[34]

Just how historians should assess the short reign of Mary Tudor (1553–58) has become perhaps the most gaping fault line in the current historiography. The traditional interpretation (first fully articulated in the sixteenth century by the martyrologist John Foxe) is firmly established in the English historical psyche: the efforts by Queen Mary—"Bloody Mary"—to reverse the progress of the Reformation were a doomed attempt to reverse the inexorable tide of history, and her cruel persecution of Protestants merely united the nation in a hatred of Spain and of Catholicism. In a slightly (though not greatly) nuanced version, this was Dickens's characterization of the reign as "the Marian reaction." But the revisionists' thoroughgoing reassessment of the state of the Catholic Church in the 1520s has inevitably undermined the old assumption that there could be but little popular support for a Catholic restoration in the succeeding generation. Haigh, Duffy, and Jennifer Loach have found much evidence of popular enthusiasm for the restoration of the mass and other sacraments in 1553, and are inclined to regard the defeat of Northumberland's attempt to place Lady Jane Grey on the throne as the outcome of an overtly Catholic (and for once successful) rebellion.[35] Other historians, however, hold to a more

---

[33]MacCulloch, *Tudor Church Militant*; and Shagan, "Protector Somerset and the 1549 Rebellions." On the attention to religious ideology in a political study, see Alford, *Kingship and Politics*.

[34]Pettegree, *Foreign Protestant Communities*; and idem, *Marian Protestantism*. See also Euler, *Couriers of the Gospel*.

[35]Duffy, *Stripping of the Altars*; Haigh, *English Reformations*; and Loach, *Parliament and the Crown*.

traditional view that Mary fatally misinterpreted dynastic loyalism as ideological support.[36] Whereas Dickens identified Mary's tragedy as her having "failed to discover the Counter-Reformation," revisionists point to an apparent shift in the devotional priorities of Marian Catholicism away from the luxuriant growth of the late Middle Ages toward a more parochially and sacramentally centered style of worship, as well as to official initiatives (such as the planned establishment of diocesan seminaries) that in crucial respects actually anticipated the reforms of the Council of Trent.[37] The much-derided Spanish influence on Marian Catholicism appears in some accounts as modernizing and theologically creative.[38] Even the notorious failure of Cardinal Pole to accept Ignatius Loyola's offer of Jesuits to work in England is now seen as good sense, rather than shortsightedness.[39]

It is hard to spend much time surveying the Marian scene without contemplating a blunt counterfactual question: if Mary had lived longer, or been able to secure a Catholic heir, could the Reformation have been permanently reversed in England? For all the undoubted difficulties the regime encountered—the financial problems of the church, the scale of hostility to the Spanish marriage, the political disaster of the accession of the virulently anti-Habsburg Pope Paul IV in 1555—it is now impossible to answer this with an emphatic negative. Nonetheless, it remains true that revisionist accounts of the reign have tended to gloss over the least attractive aspect of official religious policy, the burnings of around three hundred Protestant men and women beginning in February 1555. Yet, thanks largely to the impact of John Foxe's *Actes and Monumentes*, it was principally for this that the reign would be remembered. In laying the foundations for a long tradition of popular and official anti-Catholicism, the Marian persecution was of immense cultural and political significance. Since 1993 a collaborative research project has been preparing accurate and annotated editions of the four editions of the *Actes and Monuments* published in Foxe's lifetime (displacing the unreliable Victorian editions of Foxe on which scholars have previously generally relied). This will undoubtedly continue to serve as a

---

[36]Dickens, *English Reformation*; Loades, *Reign of Mary Tudor*; Pogson, "Legacy of the Schism"; and MacCulloch, *Later Reformation in England*.

[37]Dickens, *English Reformation*; Duffy, *Stripping of the Altars*; Mayer, *Reginald Pole*; Duffy and Loades, *Marian Church*; and Wizeman, *Theology and Spirituality*.

[38]Edwards and Truman, *Reforming Catholicism*.

[39]McCoog, "Ignatius Loyola and Reginald Pole"; and Mayer, "Pole, Loyola and the Jesuits in England."

stimulus to research, not just on Foxe, but also on the religion and politics of his age.[40]

The accession of Elizabeth in 1558 and her church settlement of the following year, were once regarded as the happy final destination of the English Reformation. It now seems barely a midway point on the journey. Historians have moved far from the perspective that enabled Dickens to view the religious tensions of Elizabeth's reign merely as "residual problems."[41] A new agenda for research here was heralded, not by Catholic revisionists, but by the leading historian of later sixteenth-century Protestantism, Patrick Collinson. In 1988 Collinson wrote that he was now prepared to assert "crudely and flatly, that the Reformation was something which happened in the reigns of Elizabeth and James I."[42] The insight reflected a seminal category shift among Reformation historians, away from the legislative framework and toward the complex social processes by which England acquired a Protestant culture.

Yet readings of the legislative process itself have been thrown wide open in the past two decades. It had long been axiomatic that the purpose and result of the 1559 Acts of Uniformity and Supremacy was to create a consensual, Anglican *via media* (middle way) between the excesses of Rome and Geneva, though J. E. Neale had (as it seemed) convincingly argued in the 1950s that Elizabeth was forced into a more Protestant settlement than she desired by returning Puritan exiles in parliament.[43] In the early 1980s studies by Winthrop Hudson and Norman Jones turned this interpretation on its head, casting doubt on the existence of a supposed Puritan choir in the House of Commons and arguing that Elizabeth was all along aiming for a thoroughly Protestant settlement, though one nearly derailed by Catholic opposition in the Lords.[44] More recently, the pendulum has swung partway back, with assertions that Elizabeth was maneuvered into a Protestant position by her own chief minister William Cecil, rather than by Puritan parliamentarians.[45] This certainly helps to account

[40]Since 2004, an electronic edition of the parts of Foxe's work dealing with the Marian persecutions has been available in a free online format. The project has also generated four volumes of essays: Loades, *John Foxe and the English Reformation*; idem, *John Foxe: An Historical Perspective*; Highley and King, *John Foxe and His World*; and Loades, *John Foxe at Home and Abroad*. On the inadequacies of the Victorian editions, see Freeman, "Texts, Lies and Microfilm."

[41]Dickens, *English Reformation*.

[42]Collinson, *Birthpangs of Protestant England*.

[43]Neale, "Elizabethan Acts."

[44]Jones, *Faith by Statute*; and Hudson, *Cambridge Connection*.

[45]Collinson, "Monarchical Republic"; Guy, "Tudor Monarchy"; and Alford, *Early Elizabethan Polity*.

for the "thus far and no further" attitude the queen subsequently adopted in religious matters. Though attempts to penetrate to the heart of Elizabeth's sphinxlike personal religion are inevitably speculative, there is no question that, unlike the majority of her bishops and advisers, she saw the settlement of 1559 as a terminus, rather than a way station to further reform.[46]

Those pressing hardest for further reformation of the liturgy and structures of the church have conventionally been called Puritans, in contradistinction to Anglican defenders of the Elizabethan establishment.[47] This now looks unconvincing. "Anglicanism" (the word and the thing) is an anachronism in a late-sixteenth-century context, when the vast majority of English churchmen saw themselves simply as Protestants and, moreover, as part of the Reformed family of European churches. In terms of theology, scholars like Collinson and Nicholas Tyacke have argued that a Calvinist consensus prevailed in the Elizabethan and Jacobean (or, as it is sometimes termed, Jacobethan) church. Collinson in particular has made a compelling case for seeing Puritans not as members of an oppositional movement but merely as the "hotter sort" of Protestants, whose attitudes and aspirations were in many ways close to the mainstream.[48] Yet the nature and potential of Puritanism remain controversial.[49] While accepting the broad outlines of the Collinsonian model, Peter Lake in particular has laid emphasis on the theological fractiousness of Puritans driven by a distinctively introspective adherence to the doctrine of predestination.[50] Collinson too, in later work, has amply recognized the socially divisive character of Puritanism, emphasizing, as social historians tend to do, its attacks against popular festive culture in a reformation of manners.[51]

Puritans termed themselves "the godly," but historians have become increasingly sensitized to the fact that their local opponents were not necessarily the ungodly. The religion of the conformist majority of the population has come under the microscope, despite the inherent difficulties of studying people whose behavior by definition leaves little mark in the dis-

---

[46]Collinson, "Windows into a Woman's Soul"; and Doran, "Elizabeth I's Religion." For the queen's blocking of episcopal reform proposals in 1563, see Crankshaw, "Preparations for the Canterbury Provincial Convocation."

[47]An approach still visible, for example, in Greaves, *Society and Religion.*

[48]See in particular Collinson, *Religion of Protestants*; and Tyacke, *Anti-Calvinists.* For the argument that Sabbatarianism was by no means a specifically Puritan concern, see Parker, *English Sabbath.*

[49]The most helpful current guide is Durston and Eales, *Culture of English Puritanism.*

[50]Lake, "Calvinism and the English Church"; and idem, *Boxmaker's Revenge.*

[51]Collinson, *Birthpangs of Protestant England*; idem, "Cohabitation of the Faithful"; idem, "Ben Jonson's *Bartholomew Fair*"; Wrightson and Levine, *Poverty and Piety*; and Hunt, *Puritan Moment.*

ciplinary record.[52] Judith Maltby has identified a seam of "Prayer Book Protestants" in England's parishes—people committed to the institution of episcopacy and the rhythms of Cranmer's liturgies, and opposed equally to Puritan nonconformity (over issues such as the wearing of surplices) and to Laudian innovation in the 1630s.[53] Christopher Haigh prefers the label "parish anglicans" and doubts that such people had internalized the Protestant message in any meaningful way. He further suggests that pressure from instinctive conservatives in the localities served to blunt the Protestant message of the preachers.[54] Ian Green's herculean surveys of English print culture in the late sixteenth and seventeenth centuries find the best-selling items among both catechisms and other religious works to reflect the emergence of a broad consensual Protestantism (akin to the "unspectacular orthodoxy" that Martin Ingram sees being upheld by lay cooperation with the church courts). Others have questioned whether the methodology of focusing only on works in multiple editions is likely to create a false impression of harmony and consensus in the world of print.[55]

Increasingly it is to printed text, rather than to manuscript, that historians are turning in attempts to gauge the religious temperature of Protestant England—a trend likely to be encouraged by the current wide availability of the digitalized texts of EEBO (Early English Books Online). Seaver's complaint in 1982 that the "popular literature which historians have readily to hand has been largely neglected" is no longer valid.[56] A pioneering work here was Tessa Watt's survey of religious themes in ballads and chapbooks up to 1640. She found there a patchwork of beliefs that "may be described as distinctively 'post-Reformation,' but not thoroughly 'Protestant.'"[57] Characteristic of such post-revisionist studies is an emphasis on the paradoxical success of the Reformation through its linkages to the unreformed past. David Cressy and Ronald Hutton have traced the laying of a Protestant and nationalistic calendar of seasonal celebrations on top of the old cycle of saints' days.[58] Alexandra Walsham has identified a pervasive interest in divine providences as a point of connection between

---

[52]On the methodological difficulties, see Spufford, "Can We Count the 'Godly'"; and idem, *World of Rural Dissenters*.

[53]Maltby, *Prayer Book and People*.

[54]Haigh, "Church of England"; and idem, "Taming of Reformation."

[55]Green, *Christian's ABC, Print and Protestantism*; Ingram, *Church Courts*; idem, "From Reformation to Toleration"; and Lake with Questier, *Antichrist's Lewd Hat*.

[56]Seaver, "English Reformation," 286.

[57]Watt, *Cheap Print and Popular Piety*, 327.

[58]Cressy, *Bonfires and Bells*; and Hutton, *Rise and Fall of Merry England*.

Protestant elites and the long-held assumptions of the people, and Peter Marshall has found continuities, as well as sharp caesuras, in attitudes toward commemoration of the dead and the afterlife.[59] None of these approaches confirms the impression, once familiar from the work of Keith Thomas, Christopher Hill, and Peter Clark, of widespread ignorance, irreverence, or skepticism toward orthodox religion on the part of the common people.[60] Indeed, in his insightful analyses of murder pamphlets Peter Lake has found distinctly godly themes in the most sensational productions of the yellow press.[61]

An overdue attention to religious conformists is fortunately not diverting attention from the most conspicuous nonconformists on the Elizabethan and early Stuart religious scene: the Catholics. In the past, Catholic history was usually the preserve of (often amateur) practitioners from within the tradition itself, confined to the margins by mainstream accounts of the Reformation process (one of Dickens's "residual problems"). But Catholicism is at last beginning to be integrated into the master narrative of religious and political change. In the late 1970s and 1980s John Bossy and Christopher Haigh argued over whether Elizabethan Catholicism was characterized by continuity or discontinuity with the medieval and Marian past, but both agreed that by the end of the reign it had settled down to become a small and inward-looking seigneurial sect under the protection of the Catholic gentry, posing little threat to the stability of the Protestant regime.[62] Newer approaches make this view problematic. Michael Questier's work on conversion shows considerable numbers of individuals passing in and out of allegiance to Rome, and numerous families divided by religion. Both he and Peter Lake have studied the internal politics of English Catholicism—especially tensions over how far Catholics could compromise with the demands of the state—and have found the Protestant regime and its agents more than ready to fish in these troubled waters.[63]

Perhaps the most important development in recent studies of Catholicism is a recognition that Catholicism and recusancy are not two words for the same thing. The small minority of recusants who refused to go to

---

[59]Walsham, *Providence in Early Modern England*; and Marshall, *Beliefs and the Dead*.

[60]Thomas, *Religion and the Decline of Magic*; Hill, "Irreligion in the 'Puritan' Revolution"; and Clark, "Alehouse and the Alternative Society."

[61]Lake, "Deeds against Nature"; and idem, "Popular Form, Puritan Content?"

[62]Bossy, *English Catholic Community*; and Haigh, *English Reformation Revised*.

[63]Questier, *Conversion, Politics and Religion*, *Catholicism and Community*; Lake with Questier, *Antichrist's Lewd Hat*; and Lake and Questier, "Margaret Clitherow."

Church of England services were complemented by an amorphous body of church papists who attended in accordance with the law. The suggestion of Bossy and others that church papistry was a transitional phase that had effectively run its course by the end of Elizabeth's reign has been effectively questioned by Alexandra Walsham, Bill Sheils, and others, who note the ability of Catholics to move in and out of formal conformity as political and personal circumstances dictated—something they observe happening well into the seventeenth century.[64]

The prevalence and persistence of church papistry helps to account for a crucial phenomenon of early modern religious culture, one to which historians are devoting close attention: its pervasive anti-Catholicism.[65] In some ways antipopery was a culturally and politically unifying force. Protestants closed ranks in the face of an international threat headed by the papacy, which virtually all respectable theologians identified with the Antichrist foretold in scripture.[66] But there was a potentially crucial fault line between those who adopted a legalistic definition of popery as obedience to Rome, and the godly reformers apt to regard any lapse from strict Calvinist orthodoxy as tantamount to the same thing. Puritans saw popery as a pervasive, metaphysical force, liable at any time to infect the structure and ceremonies of the Church of England itself.[67]

By the 1630s, significant numbers of English people had come to believe that this had happened to an unprecedented extent—that Charles I and his ceremonializing archbishop of Canterbury, William Laud, were the witting or unwitting instruments of a popish plot to return England to subjection to Rome.[68] Few historians would now seriously contend that religious concerns were not a major factor, or even *the* major factor, in the outbreak of civil conflict in the 1640s—a struggle John Morrill has famously christened "the last of the Wars of Religion."[69] But the process by which the Calvinist consensus of the Elizabethan and Jacobean era came to unravel so badly remains a historiographical hot potato.

Nicholas Tyacke's influential view, first formulated in 1973, that Charles's counterrevolutionary promotion of a novel Arminian theology of

---

[64]Walsham, *Church Papists*; Sheils, "Household, Age, and Gender"; and Questier, "Politics of Religious Conformity."

[65]Lake, "Anti-Popery"; Walsham, "Fatal Vesper"; and Marotti, *Catholicism and Anti-Catholicism*.

[66]Lake, "Significance of the Elizabethan Identification"; and Hill, *Antichrist in Seventeenth-Century England*.

[67]Helpful discussion of this in Russell, *Causes of the English Civil War*.

[68]Hibbard, *Charles I and the Popish Plot*.

[69]Morrill, "Religious Context of the English Civil War."

grace provoked a conservative backlash has been subject to various critiques. Peter White, for example, denies that Calvinists ever held a monop-
oly of views about grace and salvation in the church, arguing instead for a
broad spectrum of views.[70] The role of Arminianism is similarly down-
played by George Bernard, Julian Davies, and Kevin Sharpe, who see in
Charles's policies of the 1630s merely a conventional concern with order,
and who are inclined to regard the meltdown of the early 1640s as a short-
term crisis stemming from Charles's 1637 decision to attempt to impose
the English Prayer Book in Scotland.[71] Tyacke, in turn, has accused his
critics of attempting to resurrect the anachronistic notion of an Anglican
via media under attack from Puritanism.[72]

A more fruitful way forward here may be to recognize the extent to
which the religious issues at stake in the 1640s had their roots in unresolved issues of the Elizabethan Reformation itself. Quarrels over whether
the communion tables in churches should be placed "altarwise" or "table-
wise" were fueled by the fact that the Elizabethan Prayer Book and Injunctions seemed to contradict each other over the issue, as they did over the
use of wafers or ordinary bread for the communion. The oddity whereby
the Elizabethan Church retained elements of Catholic structure (bishops,
cathedrals, church courts) alongside its reformed theology allowed space
for a ceremonialist, firmly anti-Puritan strain to survive within the dominant Calvinist ethos; Julia Merritt and Diarmaid MacCulloch have drawn
attention to the importance of Westminster Abbey in the process.[73]
Another potential time bomb was the theology of Richard Hooker (1554–
1600), conventionally regarded as the quintessential Anglican theologian,
but who, as Peter Lake has shown, possesses a plausible claim to have
invented Anglicanism.[74] Though doctrinally Hooker was a Calvinist, his
high doctrine of the church and its sacraments, and his assertions of the
church's continuity with its medieval predecessor, ran deeply counter to
basic assumptions of the godly. He also raised the possibility that the contemporary Roman Church might, despite its corruptions, be a true church.

[70]White, *Predestination, Policy and Polemic*. See also the debate between White and Tyacke, *Past
and Present*.
[71]Bernard, "Church of England"; Davies, *Caroline Captivity of the Church*; and Sharpe, *Personal
Rule of Charles I*.
[72]Tyacke, "Anglican Attitudes." For a survey of the debate, see the introduction to Fincham and
Lake, *Religious Politics in Post-Reformation England*.
[73]Merritt, "The Cradle of Laudianism?"; and MacCulloch, *Tudor Church Militant*.
[74]Lake, *Anglicans and Puritans?*

Anthony Milton's monumental study of early seventeenth-century attitudes toward Rome and other Protestant churches demonstrates the deeply divisive consequences of the abandonment in some quarters of conventional antipapist discourse.[75]

For all these reasons it makes conceptual sense to roll forward the English Reformation to encompass the outbreak of the civil wars of the mid-seventeenth century. For one side in the conflict, the cause involved the defense of a Protestantism of conformity and order, shaped under the uniquely English institution of the royal supremacy. For the other, it represented a chance at last to implement the agenda for godly Reformation over which Elizabeth and her successors had invariably dragged their feet. Arguably, the story should be carried through to the restoration of an Anglicanism that now dared to speak its name in 1660, or to the final defeat of the political hopes of Catholicism in 1688–89. However (devotees of *la longue durée* excepted), historians understandably feel that if periodizations are stretched too wide, their utility as organizing concepts threatens to snap.

It is as difficult to predict the future directions of Reformation research as it must have been for the parishioners of Tudor England to predict the future directions of government policy. The impression of smoothly succeeding waves of orthodoxy/revisionism/postrevisionism in fact obscures a messier reality. Historians apply different perspectives to different issues, and much important scholarship resists easy classifications. The most significant books are sometimes the least expected. It is likely, however, that traditional disciplinary demarcations will continue to be eroded; literary scholars such as Tom Betteridge and Brian Cummings are bringing the intellectual tools of their trade to the study of the poetics and rhetorics of the Reformation, while historicist critics like Stephen Greenblatt are applying historical understanding to their reading of religious themes in canonical texts.[76] There are likely to be further insights from women's history and gender studies, which, curiously, have to date made relatively little mark on the historiography of the English Reformation.[77] Attempting to view English religious history in its British dimension is a worthy objective: historians of the Tudor Reformations are starting to

[75]Milton, *Catholic and Reformed*. For the Jacobean Church as an unstable and contested polity, see Fincham, *Early Stuart Church*; and Prior, *Defining the Jacobean Church*.

[76]Betteridge, *Literature and Politics*; Cummings, *Literary Culture of the Reformation*; and Greenblatt, *Hamlet in Purgatory*.

[77]A broad agenda is sketched in Crawford, *Women and Religion*. See also Peters, *Patterns of Piety*.

follow the lead set by seventeenth-century scholars in this direction.[78] Insofar as the linguistic abilities of scholars allow it, the wider international ramifications and connections of religious reform in England (Protestant and Catholic) should similarly continue to be pursued. It is hoped that a marked feature of the best current work in the field will continue to manifest itself. Despite the abandonment of overtly confessional frameworks of interpretation and the decline (in Britain at least) of religious faith and practice in wider society, most Reformation scholars manage to engage seriously with the worldview of their subjects and to avoid crudely reductionist and functionalist models of religious belief. This empathetic encounter with difference is the mark of the good historian.

Bibliography

Ackroyd, Peter. *The Life of Thomas More*. London: Chatto and Windus, 1998.

Alford, Stephen. *The Early Elizabethan Polity: William Cecil and the British Succession Crisis, 1558–1569*. Cambridge: Cambridge University Press, 1998.

——. *Kingship and Politics in the Reign of Edward VI*. Cambridge: Cambridge University Press, 2002.

Aston, Margaret. *England's Iconoclasts: Laws Against Images*. Oxford: Oxford University Press, 1988.

——, and Colin Richmond, eds. *Lollardy and the Gentry in the Later Middle Ages*. Stroud: Alan Sutton, 1997.

Barron, Caroline. "The Parish Fraternities of Medieval London." In *The Church in Pre-Reformation Society*, edited by Caroline Barron and Christopher Harper-Bill, 13–37. Woodbridge: Boydell, 1985.

Bernard, George. "Anne Boleyn's Religion." *Historical Journal* 36 (1993): 1–20.

——. "The Church of England, c. 1529–c. 1642." *History* 75 (1990): 183–206.

——. *The King's Reformation: Henry VIII and the Remaking of the English Church*. New Haven, CT: Yale University Press, 2005.

——. "The Making of Religious Policy, 1533–1546: Henry VIII and the Search for the Middle Way." *Historical Journal* 41 (1998): 321–49.

——. "Vitality and Vulnerability in the Late Medieval Church: Pilgrimage on the Eve of the Break with Rome." In *The End of the Middle Ages? England in the Fifteenth and Sixteenth Centuries*, edited by John Watts, 199–233. Stroud: Alan Sutton, 1998.

Betteridge, Tom. *Literature and Politics in the English Reformation*. Manchester, UK: Manchester University Press, 2004.

Bossy, John. *The English Catholic Community 1570–1850*. London: Darton, Longman and Todd, 1975.

Bowker, Margaret. *The Henrician Reformation: The Diocese of Lincoln under John Longland 1521–1547*. Cambridge: Cambridge University Press, 1981.

Brigden, Susan. *London and the Reformation*. Oxford: Oxford University Press, 1989.

——. *New Worlds, Lost Worlds: The Rule of the Tudors 1485–1603*. London: Penguin, 2000.

---

[78]Brigden, *New Worlds, Lost Worlds*; and Heal, *Reformation in Britain and Ireland*.

———. "Thomas Cromwell and the 'Brethren.'" In *Law and Government under the Tudors*, edited by Claire Cross, David Loades, and J. J. Scarisbrick, 51–66. Cambridge: Cambridge University Press, 1988.

Bush, Michael. *The Pilgrimage of Grace: A Study of the Rebel Armies of October 1536*. Manchester, UK: Manchester University Press, 1996.

Clark, James, ed. *The Religious Orders in Pre-Reformation England*. Woodbridge: Boydell Press, 2002.

Clark, Peter. "The Alehouse and the Alternative Society." In *Puritans and Revolutionaries*, edited by Donald Pennington and Keith Thomas, 47–72. Oxford: Oxford University Press, 1978.

Collinson, Patrick. "Ben Jonson's *Bartholomew Fair*: The Theatre Constructs Puritanism." In *The Theatrical City: Culture, Theatre and Politics in London, 1576–1649*, edited by David Smith, Richard Strier, and David Bevington, 157–69. Cambridge: Cambridge University Press, 1995.

———. *The Birthpangs of Protestant England: Religious and Cultural Change in the Sixteenth and Seventeenth Centuries*. London: Macmillan, 1988.

———. "The Cohabitation of the Faithful with the Unfaithful." In *From Persecution to Toleration: The Glorious Revolution and Religion in England*, edited by Ole Grell, Jonathan Israel, and Nicholas Tyacke, 51–66. Oxford: Oxford University Press, 1991.

———. "The Monarchical Republic of Queen Elizabeth I." In *The Tudor Monarchy*, edited by John Guy, 110–34. London: Edward Arnold, 1997.

———. *The Religion of Protestants: The Church in English Society 1559–1625*. Oxford: Oxford University Press, 1982.

———. "Windows into a Woman's Soul: Questions about the Religion of Queen Elizabeth I." In Patrick Collinson, *Elizabethan Essays*, 87–119. London: Hambledon Press, 1994.

Crankshaw, David. "Preparations for the Canterbury Provincial Convocation of 1562–63: A Question of Attribution." In *Belief and Practice in Reformation England*, edited by Susan Wabuda and Caroline Litzenberger, 60–93. Aldershot: Ashgate Press, 1998.

Crawford, Patricia. *Women and Religion in England 1500–1720*. London: Routledge, 1993.

Cressy, David. *Bonfires and Bells: National Memory and the Protestant Calendar in Elizabethan and Stuart England*. London: Weidenfeld and Nicolson, 1989.

Cummings, Brian. *The Literary Culture of the Reformation: Grammar and Grace*. Oxford: Oxford University Press, 2002.

D'Alton, Craig. "The Suppression of Lutheran Heretics in England, 1526–1529." *Journal of Ecclesiastical History* 54 (2003): 228–53.

Daniell, David. *William Tyndale: A Biography*. New Haven, CT: Yale University Press, 1994.

Davies, Catharine. *A Religion of the Word: The Defence of the Reformation in the Reign of Edward VI*. Manchester, UK: Manchester University Press, 2002.

Davies, Cliff, Christopher Haigh, and Simon Adams. "The Eltonian Legacy." *Transactions of the Royal Historical Society*, 6th ser., 7 (1997): 177–96.

Davies, Julian. *The Caroline Captivity of the Church: Charles I and the Remoulding of Anglicanism 1625–1641*. Oxford: Oxford University Press, 1992.

Davies, R. G. "Lollardy and Locality." *Transactions of the Royal Historical Society*, 6th ser., 1 (1991): 191–212.

Dickens, A. G. *The English Reformation*. London: Batsford, 1964.

Doran, Susan. "Elizabeth I's Religion: Clues from Her Letters." *Journal of Ecclesiastical History* 52 (2001): 699–720.

Dowling, Maria. "Anne Boleyn and Reform." *Journal of Ecclesiastical History* 35 (1984): 30–46.

Duffy, Eamon. *Marking the Hours: English People and Their Prayers 1240–1570.* New Haven, CT: Yale University Press, 2006.

———. *The Stripping of the Altars: Traditional Religion in England 1400–1580.* New Haven, CT: Yale University Press, 1992.

———. *The Voices of Morebath: Reformation and Rebellion in an English Village.* New Haven, CT: Yale University Press, 2001.

———, and David Loades, eds. *The Marian Church.* Aldershot: Ashgate Press, 2005.

Durston, Christopher, and Jacqueline Eales, eds. *The Culture of English Puritanism 1560–1700.* Basingstoke: Macmillan, 1996.

Edwards, John, and R. W. Truman, eds. *Reforming Catholicism in the England of Mary Tudor: The Achievement of Friar Bartolome Carranza.* Aldershot: Ashgate Press, 2005.

Elton, G. R. *Reform and Reformation: England 1509–1558.* London: Edward Arnold, 1977.

Euler, Carrie. *Couriers of the Gospel: England and Zurich, 1531–1558.* Zurich: TVZ Theologischer Verlag, 2006.

Farnhill, Ken. *Guilds and the Parish Community in Late Medieval East Anglia c. 1470.* York: York Medieval Press, 2001.

Fincham, Kenneth, ed. *The Early Stuart Church 1603–1642.* Basingstoke: Macmillan, 1993.

———, and Peter Lake, eds. *Religious Politics in Post-Reformation England: Essays in Honour of Nicholas Tyacke.* Woodbridge: Boydell Press, 2006.

Fletcher, Anthony, and Diarmaid MacCulloch. *Tudor Rebellions.* Harlow: Pearson Education, 2004.

Freeman, Thomas. "Texts, Lies and Microfilm: Reading and Misreading Foxe's 'Book of Martyrs.'" *Sixteenth Century Journal* 30 (1999): 23–46.

Greaves, Richard. *Society and Religion in Elizabethan England.* Minneapolis: University of Minnesota Press, 1981.

Green, Ian. *The Christian's ABC: Catechisms and Catechizing in England, c. 1530–1740.* Oxford: Oxford University Press, 1996.

———. *Print and Protestantism in Early Modern England.* Oxford: Oxford University Press, 2000.

Greenblatt, Stephen. *Hamlet in Purgatory.* Princeton, NJ: Princeton University Press, 2001.

Gunn, S. J., and P. G. Lindley, eds. *Cardinal Wolsey: Church, State and Art.* Cambridge: Cambridge University Press, 1991.

Guy, John. *Thomas More.* London: Edward Arnold, 2000.

———. "Tudor Monarchy and Its Critiques." In *The Tudor Monarchy,* edited by John Guy, 78–109. London: Edward Arnold, 1997.

Gwynn, Peter. *The King's Cardinal: The Rise and Fall of Thomas Wolsey.* London: Barrie and Jenkins, 1990.

Haigh, Christopher. "The Church of England, the Catholics, and the People." In *The Impact of the English Reformation 1500–1640,* edited by Peter Marshall, 235–56. London: Edward Arnold, 1997.

———. *English Reformations: Religion, Politics, and Society under the Tudors.* Oxford: Oxford University Press, 1993.

———. *Reformation and Resistance in Tudor Lancashire.* Cambridge: Cambridge University Press, 1975.

———. "The Taming of Reformation: Preachers, Pastors and Parishioners in Elizabethan and Early Stuart England." *History* 85 (2000): 572–88.

———, ed. *The English Reformation Revised.* Cambridge: Cambridge University Press, 1987.

Heal, Felicity. *Reformation in Britain and Ireland.* Oxford: Oxford University Press, 2003.

Hibbard, Caroline. *Charles I and the Popish Plot.* Chapel Hill: University of North Carolina Press, 1983.

Highley, Christopher, and John King, eds. *John Foxe and His World.* Aldershot: Ashgate Press, 2002.

Hill, Christopher. *Antichrist in Seventeenth-Century England.* Oxford: Oxford University Press, 1971.

———. "Irreligion in the 'Puritan' Revolution." In *Radical Religion in the English Revolution,* edited by J. F. McGregor and B. Reay, 199–211. Oxford: Oxford University Press, 1984.

Hoyle, R. W. *The Pilgrimage of Grace and the Politics of the 1530s.* Oxford: Oxford University Press, 2001.

Hudson, Anne. *The Premature Reformation.* Oxford: Oxford University Press, 1988.

Hudson, W. S. *The Cambridge Connection and the Elizabethan Settlement of 1559.* Durham, NC: Duke University Press, 1980.

Hunt, William. *The Puritan Moment: The Coming of Revolution in an English County.* Cambridge, MA: Harvard University Press, 1983.

Hutton, Ronald. *The Rise and Fall of Merry England: The Ritual Year 1400–1700.* Oxford: Oxford University Press, 1994.

Ingram, Martin. *Church Courts, Sex and Marriage in England, 1570–1640.* Cambridge: Cambridge University Press, 1987.

———. "From Reformation to Toleration: Popular Religious Cultures in England, 1540–1690." In *Popular Culture in England, c. 1580–1850,* edited by Tim Harris, 95–123. Basingstoke: Macmillan, 1995.

Ives, Eric. "Anne Boleyn and the Early Reformation in England." *Historical Journal* 37 (1994): 389–400.

———. *The Life and Death of Anne Boleyn.* Oxford: Blackwell Publishing, 2004.

Jones, Norman. *The English Reformation: Religion and Cultural Adaptation.* Oxford: Blackwell Publishers, 2002.

———. *Faith by Statute: Parliament and the Settlement of Religion, 1559.* London: Royal Historical Society, 1982.

Lake, Peter. *Anglicans and Puritans? Presbyterianism and English Conformist Thought from Whitgift to Hooker.* London: Harper Collins, 1988.

———. "Anti-Popery: The Structure of a Prejudice." In *The English Civil War,* edited by Richard Cust and Ann Hughes, 181–211. London: Edward Arnold, 1997.

———. *The Boxmaker's Revenge.* Manchester, UK: Manchester University Press, 2001.

———. "Calvinism and the English Church 1570–1635." *Past and Present* 114 (1987): 32–76.

———. "Deeds against Nature: Cheap Print, Protestantism and Murder in Early Seventeenth-Century England." In *Culture and Politics in Early Stuart England,* edited by Kevin Sharpe and Peter Lake, 257–83. Basingstoke, UK: Macmillan, 1994.

———. "Popular Form, Puritan Content? Two Puritan Appropriations of the Murder Pamphlet from Mid-Seventeenth-Century London." In *Religion, Culture and Society in Early Modern Britain,* edited by Anthony Fletcher and Peter Roberts, 313–34. Cambridge: Cambridge University Press, 1994.

———. "The Significance of the Elizabethan Identification of the Pope as Antichrist." *Journal of Ecclesiastical History* 31 (1980): 161–78.

———, with Michael Questier. *The Antichrist's Lewd Hat: Protestants, Papists and Players in Post-Reformation England.* New Haven, CT: Yale University Press, 2002.

———, and Michael Questier. "Margaret Clitherow, Catholic Nonconformity, Martyrology and the Politics of Religious Change in Elizabethan England." *Past and Present* 185 (2004): 43–90.

Loach, Jennifer. *Parliament and the Crown in the Reign of Mary Tudor.* Oxford: Oxford University Press, 1986.

Loades, David. *The Reign of Mary Tudor.* London: Longman, 1991.

———, ed. *John Foxe and the English Reformation.* Aldershot: Scolar Press, 1997.

———, ed. *John Foxe: An Historical Perspective.* Aldershot: Ashgate Press, 1999.

———, ed. *John Foxe at Home and Abroad.* Aldershot: Ashgate Press, 2004.

MacCulloch, Diarmaid. "Henry VIII and the Reform of the Church." In *The Reign of Henry VIII,* edited by Diarmaid MacCulloch, 159–80. Basingstoke: Macmillan, 1995.

———. *The Later Reformation in England, 1547–1603.* Basingstoke: Palgrave, 2001.

———. *Thomas Cranmer: A Life.* New Haven, CT: Yale University Press, 1996.

———. *Tudor Church Militant: Edward VI and the Protestant Reformation.* London: Penguin, 1999. Published in the United States as *The Boy King* (New York: Palgrave, 1999).

Maltby, Judith. *Prayer Book and People in Elizabethan and Early Stuart England.* Cambridge: Cambridge University Press, 1998.

Marius, Richard. *Thomas More.* London: Dent, 1985.

Marotti, Arthur, ed. *Catholicism and Anti-Catholicism in Early Modern English Texts.* Basingstoke: Palgrave Macmillan, 1999.

Marsh, Christopher. *Popular Religion in Sixteenth-Century England.* Basingstoke: Macmillan, 1998.

Marshall, Peter. *Beliefs and the Dead in Reformation England.* Oxford: Oxford University Press, 2002.

———. "Forgery and Miracles in the Reign of Henry VIII." *Past and Present* 178 (2003): 39–73.

———. *Reformation England 1480–1642.* London: Edward Arnold, 2003.

———. *Religious Identities in Henry VIII's England.* Aldershot: Ashgate Press, 2006.

———, and Alec Ryrie, eds. *The Beginnings of English Protestantism.* Cambridge: Cambridge University Press, 2002.

Martz, Louis. *Thomas More: The Search for the Inner Man.* New Haven, CT: Yale University Press, 1990.

Mayer, Thomas. "Pole, Loyola and the Jesuits in England." In *The Reckoned Expense: Edmund Campion and the Early English Jesuits,* edited by Thomas McCoog, 21–37. Woodbridge: Boydell Press, 1996.

———. *Reginald Pole: Prince and Prophet.* Cambridge: Cambridge University Press, 2000.

McCoog, Thomas. "Ignatius Loyola and Reginald Pole: A Reconsideration." *Journal of Ecclesiastical History* 47 (1996): 257–73.

McEntegart, Rory. *Henry VIII, the League of Schmalkalden and the English Reformation.* London: Boydell Press, 2002.

McSheffrey, Shannon. "Heresy, Orthodoxy and English Vernacular Religion 1480–1525." *Past and Present* 186 (2005): 47–80.

Merritt, Julia. "The Cradle of Laudianism? Westminster Abbey, 1558–1630." *Journal of Ecclesiastical History* 52 (2001): 623–46.

Milton, Anthony. *Catholic and Reformed: The Roman and Protestant Churches in English Protestant Thought 1600–1640.* Cambridge: Cambridge University Press, 1995.

Morrill, John. "The Religious Context of the English Civil War." *Transactions of the Royal Historical Society,* 5th ser., 34 (1984): 155–78.

Neale, J. E. "The Elizabethan Acts of Supremacy and Uniformity." *English Historical Review* 65 (1950): 304–32.

Parker, Kenneth. *The English Sabbath: A Study of Doctrine and Discipline from the Reformation to the Civil War.* Cambridge: Cambridge University Press, 1988.

Peters, Christine. *Patterns of Piety: Women, Gender and Religion in Late Medieval and Reformation England.* Cambridge: Cambridge University Press, 2003.

Pettegree, Andrew. *Foreign Protestant Communities in Sixteenth-Century London.* Oxford: Oxford University Press, 1986.

———. *Marian Protestantism: Six Studies.* Aldershot: Scolar Press, 1996.

Pogson, Rex. "The Legacy of the Schism." In *The Mid-Tudor Polity, c. 1540–c.1560,* edited by Jennifer Loach and Robert Tittler, 116–36. London: Macmillan, 1980.

Prior, Charles. *Defining the Jacobean Church: The Politics of Religious Controversy, 1603–1625.* Cambridge: Cambridge University Press, 2005.

Questier, Michael. *Catholicism and Community in Early Modern England: Politics, Aristocratic Patronage and Religion, c. 1550–1640.* Cambridge: Cambridge University Press, 2006.

———. *Conversion, Politics and Religion in England, 1580–1625.* Cambridge: Cambridge University Press, 1996.

———. "The Politics of Religious Conformity and the Accession of James I." *Historical Research* 71 (1988): 14–30.

Redworth, Glyn. *In Defence of the Church Catholic: The Life of Stephen Gardiner.* Oxford: Basil Blackwell, 1990.

Rex, Richard. *Henry VIII and the English Reformation.* Basingstoke: Macmillan, 1993, 2006.

———. *The Lollards.* Basingstoke: Palgrave, 2002.

Richmond, Colin. "Religion and the Fifteenth-Century English Gentleman." In *The Church, Politics and Patronage in the Fifteenth Century,* edited by R. B. Dobson, 193–208. Gloucester: Alan Sutton, 1984.

Rushton, Neil. "Monastic Charitable Provision in Tudor England." *Continuity and Change* 16 (2001): 9–44.

Russell, Conrad. *The Causes of the English Civil War.* Oxford: Oxford University Press, 1990.

Ryrie, Alec. "Counting Sheep, Counting Shepherds: The Problem of Allegiance in the English Reformation." In *The Beginnings of English Protestantism,* edited by Peter Marshall and Alec Ryrie, 84–110. Cambridge: Cambridge University Press, 2002.

———. *The Gospel and Henry VIII.* Cambridge: Cambridge University Press, 2003.

Scarisbrick, J. J. *The Reformation and the English People.* Oxford: Oxford University Press, 1984.

Seaver, Paul. "The English Reformation." In *Reformation Europe: A Guide to Research,* edited by Steven Ozment, 271–87. St. Louis, MO: Center for Reformation Research, 1982.

Shagan, Ethan. *Popular Politics and the English Reformation.* Cambridge: Cambridge University Press, 2003.

———. "Protector Somerset and the 1549 Rebellions: New Sources and New Perspectives." In *English Historical Review* 114 (1999): 34–63.

Sharpe, Kevin. *The Personal Rule of Charles I.* New Haven, CT: Yale University Press, 1992.

Sheils, W. J. "Household, Age, and Gender among Jacobean Yorkshire Recusants." In *English Catholics of Parish and Town 1558–1778,* edited by Marie Rowlands, 131–52. London: Catholic Record Society, 1999.

Spufford, Margaret. "Can We Count the 'Godly' and the 'Conformable' in the Seventeenth Century?" *Journal of Ecclesiastical History* 36 (1985): 428–38.

———, ed. *The World of Rural Dissenters*. Cambridge: Cambridge University Press, 1995.

Swanson, R. N. *Church and Society in Late Medieval England*. Oxford: Basil Blackwell, 1989.

Thomas, Keith. *Religion and the Decline of Magic*. London: Weidenfeld and Nicolson, 1971.

Tyacke, Nicholas. "Anglican Attitudes." In Tyacke, *Aspects of English Protestantism, c. 1530–1700*, 176–202. Manchester, UK: Manchester University Press, 2001.

———. *Anti-Calvinists: The Rise of English Arminianism c. 1590–1640*. Oxford: Oxford University Press, 1987.

———, ed. *England's Long Reformation 1500–1800*. London: UCL Press, 1998.

Underwood, William. "Thomas Cromwell and William Marshall's Protestant Books." *Historical Journal* 47 (2004): 517–59.

Walsham, Alexandra. *Church Papists: Catholicism, Conformity and Confessional Polemic in Early Modern England*. Woodbridge: Boydell Press, 1993.

———. "'The Fatall Vesper': Providentialism and Anti-Popery in Late Jacobean London." *Past and Present* 144 (1994): 36–87.

———. *Providence in Early Modern England*. Oxford: Oxford University Press, 1999.

Watt, Tessa. *Cheap Print and Popular Piety, 1550–1640*. Cambridge: Cambridge University Press, 1991.

White, Peter. *Predestination, Policy and Polemic: Conflict and Consensus in the English Church from the Reformation to the Civil War*. Cambridge: Cambridge University Press, 1992.

———, and Nicholas Tyacke. "The Rise of Arminianism Reconsidered." *Past and Present* 115 (1987): 201–29.

Whiting, Robert. *The Blind Devotion of the People: Popular Religion and the English Reformation*. Cambridge: Cambridge University Press, 1989.

Wizeman, William. *The Theology and Spirituality of Mary Tudor's Church*. Aldershot: Ashgate, 2006.

Wooding, Lucy. *Rethinking Catholicism in Reformation England*. Oxford: Oxford University Press, 2000.

Wrightson, Keith, and David Levine. *Poverty and Piety in an English Village: Terling 1525–1700*. Oxford: Oxford University Press, 1995.

11

The Netherlands

Christine Kooi

It is indicative of the trajectory of early modern European historiography since the 1970s that the Netherlands had to wait until the third Reformation research guide to receive its own essay.[1] Historical study of the "long sixteenth century," especially the Reformation, has long been dominated, naturally enough, by the larger European language areas—Germany, France, England, Spain, and Italy. More peripheral regions, such as the Low Countries, Scandinavia, or the lands of eastern Europe, while hardly ignored, tended to suffer from a lack of general scholarly attention as a consequence. Happily, in the last twenty or so years, the situation has rectified itself and these regions—and their own independent historical experiences—have been assimilated more fully into the historiographical mainstream.[2]

The sixteenth century in the Netherlands, as in the rest of Europe, was dominated by two phenomena: war and religion. War meant the long revolt against Spain, that is, the region's partial detachment from the Habsburg *imperium*, and religion took the form of the introduction and spread of the Protestant Reformation, particularly its Reformed variant. The upheavals attending these events led, uniquely in Europe, to the creation of an entirely new state, the United Provinces or Dutch Republic. The Low Countries thus

---

[1]Tracy, "Calvinist Church," 253–80.
[2]See MacCulloch, *The Reformation: A History*, which brings a consciously pan-European perspective to its subject.

provide fertile soil for students of sixteenth-century dichotomies; its history abounds in such questions as the relationship between church and state, center and periphery, local and national interests, princes and parliaments, cities and countryside, nobles and burghers, and clergy and laity, to say nothing of that most familiar antipathy, Catholic and Protestant.

James D. Tracy's essay on the Dutch Reformation in the 1992 *Reformation Europe II: A Guide to Research* focused on the Reformed Church, which was certainly one of the most conspicuous products of the Netherlands' revolt and reformation. Indeed, a good portion of the scholarly literature published since then has continued to concentrate on the fortunes of Reformed Protestantism in the region, especially the independent northern provinces. Whereas an earlier generation of historians described the Reformation as a national (usually Dutch) event, more recent historiography has underscored the vital importance of local conditions in the building up of Reformed congregations. In the decentralized political culture of the Low Countries, local authority wielded the most direct influence on ecclesiastical affairs. This was true whether the location was Antwerp or Utrecht, Leiden or Lille. Consequently, historians of the Netherlands have borrowed heavily in recent years from the methodology of urban studies of the Reformation in the neighboring Holy Roman Empire; the "reformation in the cities" turned out to be a useful paradigm in the Netherlandish case as well.[3] What these civic studies, mining the rich municipal archives of the Netherlands and Belgium, have revealed is that religious change could have a broad variety of outcomes, and those outcomes depended largely on the relationships between the two principal actors in the process of reformation: municipal and ecclesiastical authorities.

In the Dutch Republic, where the Reformed Church won official recognition and the Catholic Church was disestablished by the 1570s, urban studies have shown that variations on the church-state relationship were numerous. The magistracy of Delft, for example, enjoyed a cooperative relationship with that city's Reformed consistory in the late sixteenth century, which allowed the process of reforming church life there to proceed relatively smoothly. Meanwhile not far away in Leiden, the mistrust between that city's magistracy and consistory led to repeated clashes between the two bodies on issues of church governance and autonomy.[4] In

---

[3]Spaans, *Haarlem na de Reformatie*; Roodenburg, *Onder censur*; Pol, *De reformatie te Kampen*; Wouters and Abels, *Nieuw en ongezien*; Kaplan, *Calvinists and Libertines*; and Kooi, *Liberty and Religion*.
[4]Wouters and Abels, *Nieuw en ongezien*, 1:388–414; and Kooi, *Liberty and Religion*, 55–89.

an age that considered communal harmony a paramount virtue, the magistrates of Utrecht sacrificed ecclesiastical unity for the sake of civic peace by allowing their city's Reformed Church to split, for a few years anyway, into two rival congregations.[5] Even in the most harmonious cases, however, the relationship between civic authorities and Reformed consistories tended to be complicated, arising largely from the consistories' desire to maintain a high degree of institutional autonomy, while also demanding magisterial favor and protection. For their part magistrates in all cities and towns insisted upon their right to superintend the church, reformed or not.[6] In areas where civil and ecclesiastical interests overlapped, such as poor relief, considerable negotiation and accommodation was required of both parties.[7] The alliance between political and religious rebels that had prevailed so successfully against Spain proved much more problematic in the creation of a new state. At stake was the larger question shared by all lands where the Reformation was successfully established: what precisely would the new church's place and role be within the wider polity and society?

Complicating this question was the fact that the wider society of the Dutch Republic was not uniformly receptive to the Reformed Church. Insofar as they have been able to reconstruct figures, historians of the Reformation in the Dutch cities have determined that the proportion of confessing, committed Reformed Church members in most municipalities was relatively small. Research on the Dutch urban Reformation suggests that by 1620, in most cities committed, professing church members made up an estimated 20 to 30 percent of municipal populations.[8] Thus the public church, the only officially sanctioned church of the Republic, did not even comprise a majority of the population fifty years after the start of the Revolt. The question that arises concerning the remaining four-fifths to two-thirds, of course, is this: what was their religious coloration? It is known that many fell under the category of *liefhebbers*, those who sympathized with the Reformed Church and attended its preaching, but stopped short, for whatever reason, of a full profession of faith. Who precisely these *liefhebbers* were is one of the great lacunae of Dutch Reformation historiography. Sources mention them anecdotally, but their reluctance to commit

[5]Kaplan, *Calvinists and Libertines,* 156–95.
[6]Woltjer and Mout, "Settlements," 2:403–8.
[7]Parker, *Reformation of Community.*
[8]Spaans, *Haarlem,* 104; Pol, *De reformatie te Kampen,* 346; Wouters and Abels, *Nieuw en ongezien,* 234; and Kooi, *Liberty and Religion,* 212.

fully to church membership meant that they fell outside any official record-keeping purview. Were they loath to accept consistorial discipline? Were they members in the making, or simply casual churchgoers? These sympathizers still await their historian.

The rest of the non-Reformed population included those committed to other confessions, as well as the religiously indifferent. One of the most interesting and promising developments in recent historiography has been the greater attention paid to these non-Reformed confessional groups within the formally Protestant Netherlands. Virtually every manner of early modern European Christianity seemed to find a home in the Dutch Republic (especially the metropolis of Amsterdam)—a fact that was a continuing source of pain to the Reformed worthies who led the public church. The new state guaranteed freedom of conscience to all its citizens and left the regulation of religious affairs to provincial authorities. The combination of a public church that set high standards of membership and a government unwilling to coerce religious allegiance meant that a large portion of the population was free to worship God in other ways. Thus, many communities in the Dutch Republic included significant populations of Catholics, Mennonites, and, to a lesser extent, Lutherans. Religious pluralism thus prevailed in an ostensibly Calvinist state.

The fact of this religious pluriformity is receiving more attention from historians, some of whom eschew the hoarier term *toleration*, in favor of the more neutral descriptor *coexistence*. Willem Frijhoff finds the latter term "less loaded with positive values."[9] Recent research has indeed found that the fabled tolerance of the Dutch Republic in fact comprised a complicated and shifting mix of relationships among the public church, the other confessions, and the government. The essays in the conference volume *Calvinism and Religious Toleration in the Dutch Golden Age* provide a useful window into this complexity; their breadth and variety make it clear that the degree of hostility or amity between the privileged church and the other confessions, and between the other confessions and the government, depended on a number of variables, including the attitudes of local magistrates and the course of the war against Spain. The degree of toleration also varied from province to province and town to town. And confessional coexistence took place at a range of levels—from casual everyday interaction to printed polemic to occasional judicial harassment.

[9]Frijhoff, *Embodied Belief*, 48.

The highly variegated nature of this coexistence makes it difficult to generalize about it for the Republic as a whole.[10]

Consequently, there is some debate among scholars about the nature of religious freedom in the Dutch Golden Age. In his survey *The Dutch Republic*, Jonathan Israel takes a largely skeptical view, arguing that toleration was not really acceptable to most authorities until the later seventeenth century.[11] It was certainly true that the intellectual discussion about toleration far outpaced the reality of it; Gerrit Voogt's study of Dirck Coornhert makes clear that this freethinker was championing confessional concord already by the 1570s.[12] If historians were to rely only on laws, placards, and Reformed polemics, the Republic would indeed seem to have been an inhospitable place for non-Calvinists. Frijhoff, however, argues for reframing the questions away from old paradigms of toleration toward the simpler issue of coexistence. He emphasizes what he calls the "interconfessional conviviality" of quotidian social life; that is, the peaceful interactions between adherents of different confessions that can be found in the ordinary traffic of human affairs.[13] This approach requires examining sources beyond the purely ecclesiastical, such as notarial records, popular culture, and perhaps folklore. Like all other early modern states, the Dutch Republic was publicly intolerant of religious diversity, but in the private sphere a fair degree of confessional latitude prevailed. Indeed, the publicly Reformed religious identity that the Republic maintained was a polite fiction: it masked a complicated, confessionally mixed reality.

Wiebe Bergsma's major study of the progress of the Reformed Church in the northern rural province of Friesland between 1580 and 1650 underscores this point.[14] Moving up one level from the civic study, Bergsma examines the fortunes of the public church in an entire province that possessed a reputation for Calvinist orthodoxy. Challenging this image, Bergsma instead places the Reformed Church within a multiconfessional context; Friesland was also home to considerable numbers of Mennonites and Catholics during the period. The Reformed Church, he concludes, adopted over the long term a "minority mentality" that, despite its privileges, felt threatened by the other confessions and acceded to the

---

[10]Hsia and van Nierop, *Calvinism and Religious Toleration.*
[11]Israel, *Dutch Republic*, 637.
[12]Voogt, *Constraint on Trial.* See also Berkvens-Stevelinck et al., *Emergence of Tolerance.*
[13]Frijhoff, *Embodied Belief*, 61.
[14]Bergsma, *Tussen Gideonsbende.*

toleration of them only grudgingly.[15] This study makes clear that historians who wish to research the early modern Dutch Reformed Church cannot separate it from other confessions, for religious pluralism was one of the very factors that shaped the public church, contributing to both its successes and its failures.

Bergsma's work also includes a chapter that examines, on the basis of biographical documents, the religious mentalities of four individual Reformed believers: a farmer, a nobleman, a preacher, and a scholar. This approach mirrors a recent trend in the historiography of early modern Netherlandish religious culture that focuses on particular individuals.[16] As a genre, these works fall somewhere between biography and microhistory; individual experience functions as a window onto a wider historical landscape. When done well, this kind of history is extraordinarily vivid and effective. One of the most compelling of these studies is Judith Pollmann's portrait of the Utrecht humanist lawyer Arnoldus Buchelius, whose road to God started with childhood Catholicism and traveled through religious indifference to finally reach a deeply felt Calvinism. Pollmann casts his journey in terms of the possibilities of religious choice in the Dutch Republic, where war and Reformation had created a confessionally splintered society. Buchelius, though committed to his church, nevertheless had Catholic friends, which was a common social phenomenon in the crowded cities of the Republic. This resistance to the claims of confessionalism, Pollmann argues, made it possible for the Republic's multiconfessional society to operate relatively smoothly.[17] In a similar manner, Willem Frijhoff's account of the orphan Evert Willemsz, who ultimately rose to become a Reformed preacher in the colony of New Netherland, illuminates the possibilities for religious self-fashioning that Dutch society offered. Paul Abels traces the tangled career of the doctor, priest, preacher, and sometime charlatan Pibo Ovittius Abbema, who struggled through a variety of professional metamorphoses to find a middle path through the religious polarizations of the era. And Mirjam de Baar examines the life of the Flemish mystic and prophetess Antoinette Bourignon, who found a spiritual refuge for a time in the cosmopolitanism of the seventeenth-century Dutch Golden Age. Such individual cases attest to the religious heterogeneity of

---

[15]Bergsma, *Tussen Gideonsbende.*
[16]Abels, *Ovittius' Metamorphosen*; Frijhoff, *Wegen van Willem Evertsz*; De Baar, *"Ik moet spreken"*; and Pollmann, *Religious Choice.*
[17]Pollmann, *Religious Choice,* 203.

the early modern Dutch Republic and to the confessional possibilities within that heterogeneity. Since much research on the Reformation relies heavily on formal ecclesiastical sources, which can be notably terse and formulaic, these studies of specific personalities offer a richness and human dimension that more conventional church histories often lack. Whether such colorful figures are at all typical or representative is, of course, another question; that enough documentation on each of them survived to support a monograph indicates that such figures were, at the very least, unusual. The broader point they make, however, is credible: the religious pluralism that obtained in Dutch society allowed for a considerable degree of confessional mobility. Indeed, the recent research on religious pluralism in the northern Netherlands leads one to wonder whether the Reformed Church, had it not enjoyed governmental sanction, would have succeeded there at all.

As a result of this increased emphasis on religious pluralism, non-Reformed confessions in the Dutch Republic have received greater attention than ever before. The study of Dutch Catholicism in particular seems to be undergoing something of a renaissance, with the journal *Trajecta* as its standard-bearer. A notable example of this trend is Marit Monteiro's study of spiritual virgins or *klopjes*: devout Catholic laywomen who lived together in communities but took no vows.[18] These women aided and supported the priests of the Holland Mission in their ambulant ministries to Catholics in the Republic. Monteiro examines their spirituality and their sometimes ambivalent relationship with clerical authorities, and places them in the larger context of early modern female devotion. Her two individual examples, however, lived in the Habsburg-controlled Netherlands. A study of how *klopjes* worked and worshiped within the borders of the Republic is still wanting. Gian Ackermans's prosopographical study of the secular clergy in the Holland Mission during the later seventeenth century offers a detailed portrait of these priests and their pastoral mission.[19] Ackermans concentrates on the priests' relationships with their supervisory bishops; given the complicated confessional climate in which they worked, close contact and supervision were necessary to the success of the Mission. Catholic devotion is the subject of Marc Wingens's study of pilgrimage practices among early modern Dutch Catholics, who regularly made spiritual journeys over the border to shrines in the Spanish Netherlands and

---

[18]Monteiro, *Geestelijke maagden.*
[19]Ackermans, *Herders en huurlingen.*

the Holy Roman Empire.[20] Studies such as these fall well in line with the larger historiographical interest in early modern Catholicism, which has tended to focus rather heavily on the Catholic powers of Italy, France, and Spain. The vitality of Catholicism in the Dutch Republic and the Spanish Netherlands in the seventeenth century would suggest that the phenomenon of early modern Catholicism should be viewed with the widest lens possible.[21]

Anabaptism, the other major non-Reformed confession in the Netherlands, has also received increased attention. In 2000 there appeared the first major survey of early modern Dutch Anabaptism in fifty years.[22] S. Zijlstra recounts the Anabaptists' history: their beginnings with Melchior Hoffman in the 1530s, their radicalization and subsequent persecution, the emergence of a new movement inspired by Menno Simons, the Mennonites' schisms in the late sixteenth century, and, finally, their evolution into a tolerated minority religion in the Dutch Republic in the Golden Age. A major theme of this work is that of identity; like the Reformed, the various Anabaptist groups had to define themselves in relation to other confessions. The public church in particular saw the Mennonites as serious competitors, though Zijlstra argues that their number reached, at best, perhaps 60,000 by 1650.[23] The Mennonites also suffered from the added complication of their own disputatiousness; they had to take into account not only other confessions, but their own sects and schismatics. Groups that authorities had feared as a grave threat to the social and moral order in the sixteenth century evolved during the seventeenth century into a harmless collection of small religious communities.

In the southern Netherlands, of course, the story line of revolt and reformation followed a divergent path: the Spanish *reconquista* of the 1580s ensured that Catholicism would ultimately triumph and Protestantism would be squelched. Nevertheless, some of the same historiographic trends and preoccupations are evident. Craig Harline in particular has examined the lives of specific individuals, notably Archbishop Mathias Hovius and the nun Margaret Smulders, to paint a social and cultural portrait of Catholicism in the seventeenth-century Spanish Netherlands.[24]

---

[20]Wingens, *Over de grens*.
[21]See, for example, the collection in Thomas and Duerloo, *Albert and Isabella*.
[22]Zijlstra, *Over de ware gemeente*.
[23]Zijlstra, *Over de ware gemeente*, 431.
[24]Harline, *Burdens of Sister Margaret*; and Harline and Put, *Bishop's Tale*.

Sister Margaret claimed to be possessed by demons and was driven from her convent by her co-religious, only to fight her way back in again. Together with Eddy Put in *A Bishop's Tale*, Harline uses the figure of the archbishop of Mechelen to describe the concerns of a fairly typical seventeenth-century bishop. Both studies aim to delineate the world of early modern Netherlandish Catholicism. More so than the other works cited above, their primary intention is narrative, using storytelling as a way of resurrecting the flavor of a particular era.

Like their northern counterparts, the cities in the southern Netherlands have been a focus of research as well. Because of the ultimate Habsburg triumph in this region, the southern cities naturally experienced a different outcome of revolt and reformation. For example, the southern city of Lille suffered very little from the upheavals of the sixteenth-century Netherlands.[25] Its magistracy successfully preserved the city's political stability in the midst of war, iconoclasm, and rebellion. Antwerp, the Netherlands' largest and richest city in the sixteenth century, has received especial attention. Guido Marnef has provided a detailed look at the underground Protestantism of this mercantile metropolis.[26] In the venerable Belgian tradition of social and economic history, Marnef seeks to place the various Protestant movements—Lutheran, Anabaptist, and Calvinist—in the specific urban milieu of this center of world trade. From scarce sources, he has patched together a prosopographical portrait of Antwerp's religious dissidents. He ascribes the volatility of Antwerp's reformation to the presence of a large "middle group" of citizens sympathetic to religious reform, but unwilling to commit to an illegal church. When Protestant churches were driven underground by persecution, these waverers prudently returned their allegiance to the Catholic church.[27] Marie Juliette Marinus continues the story with the next chapter in Antwerp's religious history, which is its seventeenth-century reincarnation as a bulwark of the Counter-Reformation.[28] The city's Catholic authorities worked zealously to institute the reforms and mandates of the Council of Trent in their parishes, especially in the first half of the seventeenth century. In this enterprise they had the full support of the city's elite families, who favored in particular the educational projects of various religious orders.[29] In this regard, Antwerp, which

---

[25]DuPlessis, *Lille and the Dutch Revolt*.
[26]Marnef, *Antwerp in the Age of Reformation*.
[27]Marnef, *Antwerp in the Age of Reformation*, 207.
[28]Marinus, *De contrareformatie te Antwerpen*.
[29]Marinus, *De contrareformatie te Antwerpen*, 294.

had once been the hub of Netherlandish Protestantism, joined the forefront of early modern Catholic urban reform pioneered by the Milan of
Charles Borromeo.

If religion is one of the dominant themes of the historiography of the
early modern Netherlands, then another is war—specifically, the long-run-
ning conflict with Habsburg Spain and its attendant ramifications. The
eighty-year-long revolt of the Netherlands was variously a political rebellion, a civil war, a religious revolution, and a struggle among great powers.
Different aspects of that conflict, from its sixteenth-century origins to its
seventeenth-century outcomes, remain topics of abiding interest among
scholars.[30] The recent tendency among historians is not to see the conflict
as a clear, unitary process with the creation of two separate states as its
inevitable result, but instead to see it as contemporaries did: as a complicated, shifting, and unpredictable congeries of events, groups, and outcomes. Not without good reason has a reissue of the distinguished Dutch
historian J. J. Woltjer's most important essays on the subject been titled
"Between War of Independence and Civil War."[31] A good example of this
approach is Henk van Nierop's *Het verraad van het Noorderkwartier*, which
scrutinizes episodes from the revolt in North Holland in the early 1570s.[32]
From the local inhabitants' point of view, Van Nierop argues, the conflict
brought not liberation, but terror and insecurity; Spanish and rebel troops
alike were seen as threats to good order, livelihood, and law. At best, the
revolt was something to be survived whatever its outcome, which was far
from clear in the 1570s. The inchoate and turbulent nature of the war is
accentuated in K. W. Swart's study of William the Silent's performance as
leader of the revolt. Despite his subsequent status as the heroic father of his
country, William of Orange was not uniformly successful as the com-
mander of the rebellion: he made bad decisions, had few battlefield victo-
ries, cultivated (at best) unreliable allies abroad, and was growing
increasingly unpopular by the time of his assassination in 1584. He also
failed to keep the rebel coalition intact, arguably contributing to the permanent splitting of the original seventeen provinces of the Netherlands.[33]

Jonathan Israel, however, contends in his survey of the Dutch Republic that the seeds of separation existed long before the revolt. Rejecting the

---

[30]See, for example, Darby, *Origins and Development.*
[31]Woltjer, *Tussen vrijheidsstrijd.*
[32]Nierop, *Het verraad van het Noorderkwartier.*
[33]Swart, *William of Orange.*

scholarly consensus that has prevailed since the Second World War, Israel argues that the seven northern provinces, especially Holland, were in fact culturally, economically, and politically distinct from the ten southern provinces long before the war with Spain actually broke out; the war simply made actual an already latent disconnection. These provinces had always been marginalized under the southern-oriented Burgundian-Habsburg regime, and the revolt acted as a midwife to an independent northern state.[34] Not all historians subscribe to this interpretation, however. Hugo de Schepper has posited the emergence of a modest but unambiguous national feeling in the Netherlands by the 1500s.[35] H. G. Koenigsberger's study of the parliamentary history of the late medieval and early modern Low Countries assumes at the very least a fundamental constitutional unity of all the provinces before the revolt.[36] And C. Rooze-Stouthamer's seminal research on the Reformation in Zeeland makes it abundantly clear that the culture and economy of this "northern" province was at least as heavily influenced by Flanders and Brabant as it was by Holland.[37] Perhaps it is the distinctiveness of the sixteenth-century province of Holland—its economic dynamism in particular—that tends to lead to its conflation with the entire north. "Hollandocentrism" has been a common enough phenomenon in the historiography of the Netherlands. More research on the other six northern provinces is necessary before claims can be made about the region's innate separateness.

The last major synthetic treatment of the entire revolt of the Netherlands was Geoffrey Parker's *The Dutch Revolt*, which first appeared in 1977. Since this landmark study, historians have concentrated on specific aspects of the revolt itself, especially its origins and roots. Generally, they ascribe primarily political causes to the conflict, specifically the efforts by the Habsburg government to impose greater central authority on lands long accustomed to local autonomies and privileges. It was impossible, however, to disentangle the political from the religious in the sixteenth century, and the Reformation made the conflict sharper, bloodier, and more protracted. One of the rebels' main objections to the central government was its continuing efforts to suppress Protestant heresy. Aline Goosens's two-volume study of the Inquisition in the southern Netherlands

---

[34]Israel, *Dutch Republic*, 196.
[35]De Schepper, "Burgundian-Habsburg Netherlands," 1:499–530.
[36]Koenigsberger, *Monarchies, States Generals and Parliaments*.
[37]Rooze-Stouthamer, *Hervorming in Zeeland*.

provides the latest interpretation of the subject.[38] She credits Charles V as the primary founder of this judicial apparatus, which reached the height of its activities between 1540 and 1570. The office functioned chiefly as an arm of civil rather than ecclesiastical power, Goosens argues; the government viewed it as a means both to squelch dissent and to bolster central authority and the cohesion of the state. She also makes tentative calculations about the number of victims of the Inquisition in the southern provinces during Charles V's reign: nearly 1,500 people were executed out of 4,000 to 8,000 investigated.[39] A parallel study of the Inquisition's impact on the northern provinces would provide a complete picture of the suppression of religious dissent in the entire Low Countries.

In her study, Goosens also draws comparisons with Inquisitions in other lands, joining a welcome trend in the historiography of the early modern Netherlands: the growing effort to place the Low Countries in a wider European context.[40] This comparative approach is gaining ground; Martin van Gelderen, for example, has examined the ideology of the revolt within the framework of the general European tradition of political thought.[41] An increasing number of scholars have studied the revolt in the Netherlands with an eye to contemporary events in the rest of the continent, especially the region's immediate neighbors, France and the Holy Roman Empire. The parallels between the revolt against Spain and the French civil wars are evident enough: a political contest between central and local powers, exacerbated by militant sectarianism that deeply affected the international politics of the day. A conference volume on the revolt of the Netherlands and the French civil wars, bringing together essays on the subject by a number of leading historians, makes tentative comparisons between the two conflicts.[42] Among other things, the nature of sectarian violence contrasted in both cases: in France a deeper anti-Huguenot popular backlash took place, while in the Netherlands most Catholic reaction tended to remain state-controlled. Also, an important distinction between the two crowns was that while the French monarchy was weaker than the Spanish, it ruled over a more unitary state, while the Spanish king, though more powerful, presided over a composite empire far greater than just the

---

[38]Goosens, *Les inquisitions modernes*.
[39]Goosens, *Les inquisitions modernes*, 2: 187–88.
[40]For the Dutch Republic in particular, see Davids and Lucassen, *Miracle Mirrored*.
[41]Gelderen, *Political Thought*.
[42]Benedict et al., *Reformation, Revolt and Civil War*.

Low Countries.[43] Thus, Dutch Protestants could win independence, while French Huguenots could gain, at best, toleration.

The Netherlands had a complicated relationship with its neighbor to the east, the Holy Roman Empire. With the establishment of the Burgundian Circle of 1548, the Low Countries detached themselves from direct imperial jurisdiction, but the influence of the German territories remained strong. Both Habsburg and rebel alike looked to the east for support and aid. Emden in East Friesland became a haven for Netherlandish Calvinism in exile; its printing presses served the Reformed cause and it was here that the first blueprints of the Dutch Reformed Church were drawn up.[44] Monique Weis's examination of the diplomatic correspondence between the Habsburg government in Brussels and the empire underscores Philip II's desire to be on good terms with his imperial neighbors—not least because the Spanish Road ran through their lands to bring much-needed troops to the Netherlands.[45] Johannes Arndt's important study of the empire during the Revolt of the Netherlands confirms how dependent the rebels were on the German hinterland, especially William of Orange, who desperately sought aid from the Protestant princes there.[46] Likewise the Calvinists could rely on an elaborate network of Protestant institutions within the empire (universities, printing presses) to help them in their efforts. German presses were especially adept at promoting the "black legend" of Spanish cruelty and tyranny to the European public. One of the more remarkable outcomes of the revolt, Arndt notes, was the emergence of a new state, the Dutch Republic, that in constitutional terms closely resembled the Holy Roman Empire: a decentralized confederation of officially sovereign territories.[47] Much more research needs to be done on Netherlandish-imperial relations in the early modern period; for example, the bishopric of Münster alone deserves examination for its role in Netherlandish political and religious history in the sixteenth and seventeenth centuries.

In many respects, of course, the state with which the Low Countries found themselves most entangled in this period was Spain, whose king also happened to be their sovereign. Geoffrey Parker has done much to remind us that the revolt was also a Spanish event, one of a number of crises Philip

---

[43]Benedict, *Reformation, Revolt and Civil War*, 19–20.
[44]Pettegree, *Emden and the Dutch Revolt*.
[45]Weis, *Les Pays-Bas espagnols*.
[46]Arndt, *Das Heilige Römische Reich*.
[47]Arndt, *Das Heilige Römische Reich*, 297.

II faced during his long reign. In his study of Philip's grand strategy, Parker places the revolt squarely in the context of the Spanish king's many other preoccupations with the Turks, with England, and with his global empire.[48] Religious intransigence and missteps in policy, Parker argues, cost Philip the northern part of the Low Countries. From a less monarchical perspective, Yolanda Rodríguez Pérez examines how Spanish literary culture viewed the early modern Netherlands. The image of the Netherlanders that developed in Spain during the revolt was one of heretics and traitors, stubborn, arrogant, and greedy.[49] Image and self-image intertwined; Spanish soldiery, by contrast, fought nobly for king and church. The Netherlands became a foil by which the Spanish could congratulate themselves on their superiority, and the Spanish would serve the same function for the rebels.

The placing of the early modern Netherlands within the greater European historiographical context is a welcome development that adds perspective and nuance to the interpretation of a complicated era. Many of the trends in the historiography of the sixteenth- and seventeenth-century Netherlands reflect those of scholars of other European lands: the Reformation in the cities, the problem of religious coexistence, local studies, narrative and microhistory, the revaluation of early modern Catholicism, the construction of confessional and national identities, and the growing exploration in comparative history. To be sure, there are still gaps in the literature. The iconoclastic fury of 1566, for example, still awaits a definitive treatment. There is still no detailed, scholarly, comprehensive biography of William of Orange, or, for that matter, of his successor Maurice of Nassau. Further research into the Netherlands' relationships (political, economic, and cultural) with the lands of the Holy Roman Empire will also bear significant fruit. More local studies of revolt and reformation are needed, especially outside the core provinces of Holland, Flanders, and Brabant. The Arminian controversy that rocked the Dutch Reformed Church in the 1610s—sparking the most serious religious violence in the Republic's history—would benefit from a comprehensive examination. And the whole question of nascent national identity in this period, whether northern or southern, deserves further scrutiny. The history of the early modern Netherlands remains a rich vein to be tapped; thanks to the efforts of many scholars, it has permanently joined the historiographic mainstream.

---

[48]Parker, *Reformation of Community*.
[49]Rodríguez Pérez, *De Tachtigjarige Oorlog*.

Bibliography

ELECTRONIC RESOURCES

Centre for Dutch Religious History at the Free University of Amsterdam: www.relic-vu.nl
Historisch Huis: www.historischhuis.nl
University of Leiden Library: www.dutchrevolt.leidenuniv.nl

PRINTED SOURCES

Abels, P. H. A. M. *Ovittius' Metamorphosen: De onnavolgbare gedaantewisselingen van een (zielen)dokter in de Reformatietijd.* Delft: Eburon, 2003.

Ackermans, Gian. *Herders en huurlingen: Bisschoppen en priesters in de Republiek (1663–1705).* Amsterdam: Prometheus/Bert Bakker, 2003.

Arndt, Johannes. *Das Heilige Römische Reich und die Niederlande 1566 bis 1648: Politisch-konfessionelle Verflechtung und Publizistik im Achtzigjährigen Krieg.* Köln: Böhlau, 1998.

Baar, Mirjam de. *"Ik moet spreken": Het spiritueel leiderschap van Antoinette Bourignon (1616–1680).* Zutphen: Walburg Pers, 2004.

Benedict, Philip, Henk van Nierop, Guido Marnef, and Marc Venard, eds. *Reformation, Revolt and Civil War in France and the Netherlands, 1555–1585.* Amsterdam: KNAW, 1999.

Bergsma, Wiebe. *Tussen Gideonsbende en publieke kerk: Een studie over het gereformeerde Protestantisme in Friesland, 1580–1650.* Hilversum: Verloren, 1999.

Berkvens-Stevelinck, Christiane, et al., eds. *The Emergence of Tolerance in the Dutch Republic.* Leiden: Brill, 1997.

Darby, Graham, ed. *The Origins and Development of the Dutch Revolt.* London: Routledge, 2001.

Davids, Karel, and Jan Lucassen, eds. *A Miracle Mirrored: The Dutch Republic in European Perspective.* Cambridge: University Press, 1995.

DuPlessis, Robert S. *Lille and the Dutch Revolt: Urban Stability in an Era of Revolution, 1500–1582.* Cambridge: University Press, 1991.

Frijhoff, Willem. *Embodied Belief: Ten Essays on Religious Culture in Dutch History.* Hilversum: Verloren, 2002.

———. *Wegen van Willem Evertsz: Een Hollands weeskind op zoek naar zichzelf, 1607–1648.* Nijmegen: SUN, 1995.

Gelderen, Martin van. *The Political Thought of the Dutch Revolt 1555–1590.* Cambridge: University Press, 1992.

Goosens, Aline. *Les inquisitions modernes dans les Pays-Bas méridionaux, 1520–1633.* 2 vols. Brussel: Editions de l'université de Bruxelles, 1997–98.

Harline, Craig. *The Burdens of Sister Margaret. Private Lives in a Seventeenth-Century Convent.* New York: Doubleday, 1994.

———, and Eddy Put. *A Bishop's Tale: Mathias Hovius among His Flock in Seventeenth-Century Flanders.* New Haven, CT: Yale University Press, 2000.

Hsia, Ronnie Po-chia, and H. F. K. van Nierop, eds. *Calvinism and Religious Toleration in the Dutch Golden Age.* Cambridge: Cambridge University Press, 2002.

Israel, Jonathan I. *The Dutch Republic: Its Rise, Greatness and Fall, 1477–1806.* Oxford: Clarendon, 1995.

Kaplan, Benjamin J. *Calvinists and Libertines: Confession and Community in Utrecht, 1578–1620.* Oxford: Clarendon, 1995.

Koenigsberger, Helmut Georg. *Monarchies, States Generals and Parliaments: The Netherlands in the Fifteenth and Sixteenth Centuries.* Cambridge: Cambridge University Press, 2001.

Kooi, Christine. *Liberty and Religion: Church and State in Leiden's Reformation, 1572–1620.* Leiden: Brill, 2000.

MacCulloch, Diarmaid. *The Reformation: A History.* New York: Viking, 2003.

Marinus, Marie Juliette. *De contrareformatie te Antwerpen (1585–1676): Kerkelijk leven in een grootstad.* Brussels: Paleis der Academiën, 1995.

Marnef, Guido. *Antwerp in the Age of Reformation: Underground Protestantism in a Commercial Metropolis, 1550–1577.* Baltimore, MD: Johns Hopkins University Press, 1996.

Monteiro, Marit. *Geestelijke maagden: Leven tussen klooster en wereld in Noord-Nederland gedurende de zeventiende eeuw.* Hilversum:Verloren, 1996.

Nierop, Henk van. *Het verraad van het Noorderkwartier: Oorlog, terreur en recht in de Nederlandse Opstand.* Amsterdam: Bert Bakker, 1999.

Parker, Charles H. *The Reformation of Community: Social Welfare and Calvinist Charity in Holland, 1572–1620.* Cambridge: Cambridge University Press, 1998.

Parker, Geoffrey. *The Grand Strategy of Philip II.* New Haven, CT: Yale University Press, 1998.

Pettegree, Andrew. *Emden and the Dutch Revolt: Exile and the Development of Reformed Protestantism.* Oxford: Clarendon, 1992.

Pol, Frank van der. *De reformatie te Kampen in de zestiende eeuw.* Kampen: Kok, 1990.

Pollmann, Judith. *Religious Choice in the Dutch Republic: The Reformation of Arnoldus Buchelius (1565–1641).* Manchester, UK: Manchester University Press, 1999.

Rodríguez Pérez, Yolanda. *De Tachtigjarige Oorlog in Spaanse ogen: De Nederlanden in Spaanse historische en literaire teksten (circa 1548–1673).* Nijmegen: Uitgeverij Vantilt, 2003.

Roodenburg, Herman. *Onder censuur: De kerkelijke tucht in de gereformeerde gemeente van Amsterdam, 1578–1700.* Hilversum: Verloren, 1990.

Rooze-Stouthamer, Clasina Martina. *Hervorming in Zeeland, ca. 1520–1572.* Goes: De Koperen Tuin, 1996.

Schepper, Hugo de. "The Burgundian-Habsburg Netherlands." In *Handbook of European History 1400–1600: Late Middle Ages, Renaissance and Reformation*, edited by Thomas A. Brady Jr., Heiko A. Oberman, and James D. Tracy, 1:499–530. Leiden: Brill, 1995.

Spaans, Joke. *Haarlem na de Reformatie: Stedelijke cultuur en kerkelijk leven.* Den Haag: Hollandse Historische Reeks, 1989.

Swart, Koenraad Wolter. *William of Orange and the Revolt of the Netherlands, 1572–1584.* Translated by J. C. Grayson. Aldershot: Ashgate, 2003.

Thomas, Werner, and Luc Duerloo, eds. *Albert and Isabella 1598–1621. Essays.* Turnhout: Brepols, 1998.

Tracy, James D. "The Calvinist Church of the Dutch Republic, 1572–1618/9." In *Early Modern Europe: A Guide to Research II*, edited by William S. Maltby, 253–80. St. Louis, MO: Center for Reformation Research, 1998.

Voogt, Gerrit. *Constraint on Trial: Dirck Volckertsz Coornhert and Religious Freedom.* Kirksville, MO: Truman State University Press, 2000.

Weis, Monique. *Les Pays-Bas espagnols et les États du Saint-Empire: Priorités et enjeux de la diplomatie en temps de troubles.* Brussels: Éditions de l'université de Bruxelles, 2003.

Wingens, Marc. *Over de grens: De bedevaart van katholieke Nederlanders in de zeventiende en achttiende eeuw.* Nijmegen: SUN, 1994.

Woltjer, Jan Juliaan. *Tussen vrijheidsstrijd en burgeroorlog: Over de Nederlandse Opstand.* Amsterdam: Balans, 1994.

———, and M. E. H. N. Mout. "Settlements: The Netherlands." In *Handbook of European History 1400–1600: Late Middle Ages, Renaissance and Reformation,* edited by Thomas A. Brady Jr., Heiko A. Oberman, and James D. Tracy, 2:385–416. Leiden: Brill, 1995.

Wouters, A. Ph. F., and P. H. A. M. Abels. *Nieuw en ongezien: Kerk en samenleving in de classis Delft en Delfland, 1572–1620.* 2 vols. Delft: Eburon, 1994.

Zijlstra, S. *Over de ware gemeente en de oude gronden: Geschiedenis van de dopersen in de Nederlanden 1531–1675.* Hilversum: Verloren, 2000.

12

Spain

Allyson Poska

William Maltby ended his review essay on Spain in *Catholicism in Early Modern History: A Guide to Research* on a depressing note. The study of Iberian history was in decline; few new scholars were being trained, and the impetus to new and exciting scholarship had been lost.[1] Yet although the state of Iberian scholarship may have looked dismal at the time, since the mid-1980s early modern Spanish history has flourished, driven by a wide array of academic and social factors, among them the opening of new Spanish archives and the professionalization of many others in the years since Franco's death.[2] With easier access to a wider range of materials, the field has expanded beyond the economic and demographic history that dominated earlier scholarship to address a wide range of historiographic issues. As a result, historians have moved away from the isolating notion of Spanish exceptionalism, better integrating Spain into the early modern European context and calling into question some long-held notions about the Spanish past.

Over the past two decades, interest in Spanish history has boomed, particularly in the United States. While some of this interest may be attributed to the growth of the Spanish-speaking population in the United States, Spain has also proven to be a useful historical touchstone for a wide range of scholars. Both the peninsula and the Spanish empire offer important

---

[1] I thank Tim Coates, James Tracy, Liz Lehfeldt, and Carla Rahn Phillips for their advice on this essay.

[2] Kagan, "Prescott's Paradigm."

historical precedents for understanding the dynamics of power, the creation of empire, the tensions of multicultural societies, and the complications of cross-cultural interaction. In the process, the new scholarship has dramatically transformed our understanding of early modern Spanish politics, economics, and society.

To begin with political history, scholars have significantly reevaluated many aspects of Spain's ascent to political prominence. Historians have finally begun to analyze Isabel I (1451–1504) not only as a ruler who marked a critical transition from medieval to early modern notions of monarchy, but also as a woman whose reign was constrained by contemporary notions of gender and power.[3] Moreover, for all the rhetoric about the unification of Spain under the Catholic kings, scholars now understand much more clearly how separate Isabel's Castilian realms remained from Ferdinand's Aragonese kingdoms. While the couple shared many common goals, their distinctive policies are a reminder that these were very different monarchs ruling under different social and political constraints.[4] Indeed, the complications of their reigns climaxed in a series of dynastic machinations that led to the succession of their grandson Charles rather than their daughter Juana.[5]

During the late 1980s and 1990s, interest in Charles I (Charles V, Holy Roman Emperor, 1500–58) seemed to wane.[6] However, the five hundredth anniversary of his birth in 2000 reinvigorated the scholarship and prompted a number of conferences and collections of essays on the emperor. While most of the scholarship focused on Charles's imperial activities, a few scholars used the opportunity to compose modern biographies, some of which highlight Charles's time in Spain.[7]

Traditionally, Philip II (1527–98) epitomized absolute monarchy, single-handedly and obsessively ruling his worldwide empire. However, recent research reveals a much more complicated relationship between the

---

[3]Liss, *Isabel the Queen*; Weissberger, *Isabel Rules*; Boruchoff, *Isabel La Católica*; and Lehfeldt, "Ruling Sexuality."

[4]Meyerson, *Muslims of Valencia*.

[5]Aram, *Juana the Mad*.

[6]One of the few works on Charles from this period, Rodríguez Salgado's *Changing Face of Empire*, examines Charles's foreign policy during the last years of his reign.

[7]Chaunu and Escamilla, *Charles Quint*; Lynch, *Carlos V y su tiempo*; and Pérez, *Carlos V*. Among the impressive collections of essays, see Martínez Millán and Esquerra Revilla, *Carlos V y la quiebra*; Castellano and Sánchez Montes, *Carlos V*; and Navascues Palacio, *Carolus V Imperator*. On the *comuneros* revolt, see Pérez, *Los Comuneros* (an updated version of his 1989 study); and Sánchez León, *Absolutismo y comunidad*.

sovereign and his subjects. Helen Nader's work has refuted the supposed centralization of power under both Charles and Philip. Through the sale of towns and town charters, the Habsburg monarchs attempted to both garner necessary funds for their international campaigns and maintain good relationships with their subjects. Thus, monarchical power remained the product of ongoing negotiation between the crown and local authorities.[8] Philip's power was also affected by the Castilian aristocracy, whose individual ambitions and collective power served as important checks on royal authority.[9] In terms of Philip's personality, although a number of new biographies appeared around the four hundredth anniversary of his death in 1998, he remains an enigma. Among the varied perspectives, Henry Kamen offers a sympathetic portrayal of the king, while Geoffrey Parker takes a harsher view of the relationship between Philip's management style and his foreign and domestic policy failures.[10]

Some of the most dramatic scholarly reassessments have focused on Philip III (1578–1621), whom historians had described as a lazy, incompetent, or—at best—uninterested monarch who delegated most of the governance of the kingdom to his favorite or *valido*. Expanding on John Elliott's studies of the Count-Duke of Olivares and the court of Philip IV, Antonio Feros has argued that rather than a break with the practice of government under Philip II, Philip III's reliance on the Duke of Lerma had much in common with his father's reign. Indeed, Philip III's use of a *valido* was a pragmatic response to the enormous pressures brought to bear on the king by both the size of the Spanish Empire and the weight of the Spanish bureaucracy. Moreover, Philip was actively involved in foreign policy decisions, working closely with his councils and advisors to formulate a coherent response to Spain's complicated international entanglements.[11] Lerma's power was further constrained by Philip's powerful female relatives. Although they were ensconced in the convent of the Discalced Carmelites, they pursued political agendas on behalf of their Austrian relatives that frequently clashed with those of the king's favorite.[12] Without a doubt, Philip III and his court have been rehabilitated.

---

[8]Nader, *Liberty in Absolutist Spain*. Ruth Mackay, *Limits of Royal Authority*, applies a similar argument to the seventeenth century.

[9]Boyden, *Courtier and the King*.

[10]Parker, *Grand Strategy*; and Kamen, *Philip of Spain*.

[11]Feros, *Kingship and Favoritism*; and Allen, *Philip III*. For an examination of naval reform under Philip III, see Phillips, *Six Galleons for the King of Spain*.

[12]Sánchez, *Empress, the Queen, and the Nun*.

The work of J. H. Elliott continues to dominate the scholarship on Philip IV, although in recent years scholars have begun to move beyond the study of the Count-Duke of Olivares. Historians have taken a particular interest in the years after Olivares, examining Philip as a ruler in his own right.[13] Charles II (1661–1700), the last of the Habsburg kings, has not fared as well. Although segments of his monarchy have begun to attract the attention of scholars, he and his reign still await extensive historical study.[14]

One result of this reassessment of the seventeenth-century Habsburg kings has been a reconsideration of the economic "decline" of Spain. Based on the furor created by *arbitristas*, seventeenth-century men who enthusiastically offered myriad solutions to Spain's economic ills, earlier generations of historians focused on the extent and causes of widespread depression, or at least recession. Like their seventeenth-century sources, they attributed Spain's decline to a variety of factors, including climatic and demographic events, religious dogmatism, weak monarchy, and poor fiscal policy. Certainly, the first half of the seventeenth century was marked by severe economic problems; however, based on a series of local and regional studies, economic historians now paint a much more complicated picture of the economic health of the peninsula over the century. Most importantly, these scholars have demonstrated that Castile was not Spain and that its problems were not replicated across the peninsula. Different areas experienced economic problems at different times and some regions recovered faster than others.[15] In this new context, scholars have shifted their investigations to the study of specific sectors of the Spanish economy and the economic structures of the broader Spanish empire.[16]

Long neglected, eighteenth-century Spain has become an area of interest to scholars. In particular, historians marked the three hundredth anniversary of the succession of Philip V (1683–1746) with a spate of

---

[13]Elliott and Sanz, *La España del Conde Duque*; Schaub, *Le Portugal au temps*; Sanz Camañes, *Política, hacienda y milicia*; and Stradling, *Philip IV and the Government.*

[14]For a study of taxation during this period, see Cárceles de Gea, *Reforma y fraude fiscal.*

[15]Marcos Martín, *España en los siglos*; Thompson and Yun Casalilla, *Castilian Crisis*; Yun Casalilla, "Estado y estructuras sociales"; and Phillips, "Time and Duration." For a discussion that links the early modern economy with changes in the following centuries, see Ringrose, *Spain, Europe, and the "Spanish Miracle."*

[16]For example, Ruiz Martín and García Sanz, *Mesta, transhumancia y lana*; Phillips and Phillips, *Spain's Golden Fleece*; and Thompson, *Distinctive Industrialization.* On the empire, see Yun Casalilla, *Marte contra Minerva*; Stein and Stein, *Apogee of Empire*; and Kamen, *Empire.*

biographies and works on the reign of the first Bourbon monarch.[17] However, in terms of broader social and economic issues, although Latin American historians have explored the impact of the Bourbon reforms extensively, few scholars have examined the reforms on the peninsula.[18]

Without a doubt, scholars produced some of the most important work in Spanish history leading up to and in the wake of the Columbian quincentenary. Snatched from the morass of myth and error, Christopher Columbus has finally become the subject of serious scholarly study. Rather than a hero or a conqueror, he was clearly a man, merchant, and mariner of his time.[19] Once he established contact between the two worlds, sixteenth-century thinkers quickly formulated intellectual rationales for Spanish conquest and settlement, creating new, and refashioning older, notions of empire and subjugation.[20]

Quincentenary celebrations led to the publication of a series of regionally specific quantitative studies of Spanish emigration to the Americas, but surprisingly few scholars have examined the qualitative impact of overseas migration on those who remained on the peninsula.[21] Ida Altman's works on Extremadura and Brihuega stand out as the most detailed discussions of the effects of early migration to the Americas, while Juan Javier Pescador demonstrated the impact of transoceanic ties on families and family strategies in a Basque village.[22] These studies are important because historians have largely taken for granted the connections between peoples and ideas in Spain and the development of social, political, and economic life in Spanish America. Only recently have scholars begun to focus on the ongoing intellectual and cultural dynamic.[23]

Certainly, the traditional conceptualization of Spanish "discovery" of the Americas has been consigned to the dustbin, replaced by the much more precise notion of cultural encounter.[24] From the initial contacts in the Caribbean to the last decades of the colonial period, most scholars now

[17]Calvo Poyato, *Felipe V*; Serrano, *Felipe V y su tiempo*; Kamen, *Philip V of Spain*; and García Carcel, *Felipe V y los españoles*.

[18]Herr, *Rural Change and Royal Finance*; and MacLachlan, *Spain's Empire*.

[19]Phillips and Phillips, *Worlds of Christopher Columbus*.

[20]Pagden, *Lords of All the World*; and Pagden, *Spanish Imperialism*.

[21]For example, Eiras Roel and Guimerá Ravina, *La emigración española* and *Historia de la emigración*.

[22]Pescador, *New World Inside a Basque Village*; Altman, *Transatlantic Ties*; and Altman, *Emigrants and Society*.

[23]Herzog, *Defining Nations*; and Cañizares-Esguerra, *How to Write the History of the New World*.

[24]Altman and Butler, "Contact of Cultures."

understand Spanish involvement in the Americas as a constant negotiation between Spaniards and indigenous, mixed-race, and African peoples. Non-Spaniards constantly challenged Spanish political, religious, and cultural dominance, and Spaniards provided no uniform response to those challenges as conflicts between secular and regular clergy, colonists and their governments, creoles and *peninsulares* left authority in the Indies weak and decentralized. While space does not allow a full discussion of this enormous and transformative literature, it is important to recognize the degree to which it has forced historians to reconceptualize both the Spanish and Portuguese colonial enterprises.[25]

Scholars have subjected the Spanish Catholic Church to the same rigorous inquiry as they have Spanish politics, economics, and the creation of empire; as a result, it no longer appears to have been the epitome of religious, cultural, and social power that historians once believed it to be. Much of the early historiography was mired in the propaganda of the Catholic Church that asserted both its unity and its ultimate success. However, scholars have found little evidence to support the idea of a dominant, monolithic Catholic Church. Instead, the Catholic Reformation Church in Spain was a multifaceted, often disorganized institution with varying and often conflicting priorities. Rather than a unified force in Spanish society, the church was an institution made up of individuals who continually interacted with and responded to the Spanish populace: rich and poor, literate and illiterate, pious and not so pious. In this rich drama, the prejudices, power schemes, and religious cosmologies of all those involved were central to the formation of church priorities and the progress of religious reform.

Without a doubt, the Spanish Catholic Church was not a moribund institution, paralyzed by dogmatism. The supposed dichotomy between progressive Erasmianism and regressive Scholasticism described by an earlier generation of scholars was overly simplistic. Indeed, the intellectual atmosphere of sixteenth-century Spain was diverse and highly contested.[26] Moreover, although Spanish Catholicism may have seemed homogenous, each of Spain's regional cultures experienced the Catholic Church through the lens of its local religious culture and priorities. During the late 1980s, the work of anthropologist William A. Christian Jr., the quantitative diocesan

---

[25]Some important works on Portuguese imperial expansion include Coates, *Convicts and Orphans*; Oliveira Marques, *História dos Portugueses*; and Bethencourt and Chauduri, *História da Expansão Portuguesa*.

[26]Homza, *Religious Authority*; Nieto, *El Renacimiento*; and Bouza Alvarez, *Religiosidad y cultura simbólica*.

studies undertaken by historians of religion in France, and the burgeoning history of mentalities influenced a number of scholars to examine the mechanisms employed by the Catholic Reformation Church to exert control over its parishioners. Sara Nalle's groundbreaking study of the diocese of Cuenca used both qualitative and quantitative measures to demonstrate the impressive strides that the Catholic Church made in alleviating ignorance and religious laxity among both the clergy and the laity.[27] The influence of French scholarship was also evident in a series of studies that examined religious mentalities and the pervasiveness of Catholic Reformation attitudes through the quantification of the rituals surrounding death.[28] However, as both Henry Kamen's study of Catalonia and my own study of the diocese of Ourense in Galicia reveal, the successful reform of the diocese of Cuenca was not replicated across the kingdoms. On the periphery of the peninsula, where ecclesiastical institutions were weaker, local religious beliefs and practices and illiterate clergy continued to be pervasive influences well into the seventeenth century.[29] Moreover, ecclesiastical reform did not occur outside of the context of civic life. Only by understanding the cultural milieu of Spain's urban elites can scholars fully comprehend the scope of Teresa's Carmelite reform in Avila.[30]

The research on women in early modern Spain has also contributed to the reassessment of the Catholic Reformation. Mary Elizabeth Perry's 1990 study of Seville demonstrated how the desire for religious and political order translated into a struggle for gender order.[31] Yet, women of all social strata challenged attempts by both the church and state to restrict their activity. Prostitutes continued to solicit on street corners and peasant women had sex outside of marriage. Even reformers like Teresa of Avila and members of Spain's female religious communities resisted attempts to control their religious fervor and separate them from society.[32]

Certainly the Spanish Inquisition bears little resemblance to the institution vilified for so many centuries.[33] Over the past two decades, scholars

---

[27]Nalle, *God in La Mancha.*

[28]For instance, Eire, *From Madrid to Purgatory;* and López López, *Los comportamientos religiosos.*

[29]Kamen, *Phoenix and the Flame;* and Poska, *Regulating the People.*

[30]Bilinkoff, *The Avila of St. Teresa.*

[31]Perry, *Gender and Disorder.*

[32]On prostitutes, see Perry, *Gender and Disorder.* On peasant women, see Poska, *Regulating the People.* On Teresa of Avila, see Ahlgren, *Teresa of Avila;* and Weber, *Teresa of Avila.* On opposition to enclosure, see Lehfeldt, "Discipline, Vocation, and Patronage"; and idem, *Religious Women.* On *beatas,* see the essays in Giles, *Women in the Inquisition.*

[33]For the best overview of the Inquisition, see Kamen, *Spanish Inquisition.* See also Pérez, *Spanish Inquisition;* Bethencourt, *L'Inquisition a l'époque moderne;* and Pérez Villanueva and Escandell

have come to a better understanding of the theological basis of the institution, its functioning, and its interactions with the Spanish populace. Much of the recent research on the Inquisition has been fueled by the initial results of Jaime Contreras and Gustav Henningsen's database of 44,000 Inquisition trials. The possibilities were exciting. Using statistical analysis, scholars could see the Inquisition in action at both the macro and the micro levels, and compare the activities of the various tribunals. From this perspective, the Inquisition was seen to be as diverse as the personalities of its officials, and was deeply influenced by those it sought to protect from the spread of heresy.

Some of the earliest quantitative analyses classified Inquisitional activity into a number of phases over the course of the early modern period.[34] Initially, Isabel sought the establishment of an Inquisition in her kingdoms to deal with the growing population of converted Jews (*conversos*). The old Christian population distrusted and feared *conversos*, suspecting that they secretly maintained Jewish beliefs while taking advantage of the benefits of their conversion to Christianity. The collaboration between the old Christian population and the Inquisition led to a bloody campaign to stamp out judaizing, during which more heretics were executed than faced the stake during the rest of the institution's history.[35]

During the middle of the sixteenth century, denunciations focused on other types of heresies, particularly Lutherans, *moriscos*, converted Muslims, and *alumbrados* (members of a sect who believed that by surrendering to the love of God, they could be illuminated by the Holy Spirit).[36] Then, from approximately 1560 to 1700, more Inquisition trials inquired into the beliefs of old Christians accused of minor heresies, such as blasphemy, fornication, and bigamy—a phase punctuated by a spate of anti-*converso* activity at midcentury. During the eighteenth century, the Inquisition went into decline and little is known about its last century of existence.

Within that framework, the research on individual tribunals has demonstrated the differing priorities of each tribunal, as well as their successes and failures.[37] For instance, the Aragonese and Valencian tribunals

Bonet, *Historia de la Inquisición*.

[34]For differing views of the phases of the Inquisition, see Dedieu, "Los cuatro tiempos"; and Contreras and Henningsen, "Forty-four Thousand Cases."

[35]Netanyahu, *Origins of the Inquisition*.

[36]Hamilton, *Heresy and Mysticism*.

[37]See Monter, *Frontiers of Heresy*; Haliczer, *Inquisition and Society*; and Dedieu, *L'administration de la foi*.

were far more interested in the religious activities of outsiders (French-men, *conversos,* and *morsicos*), than the heresies of old Christians, while the Murcian Inquisition became the tool of factions competing for author-ity within the city.[38]

In addition to reevaluating the institution itself, scholars have found that Inquisition trials provide a rare window into the lives of individuals. In one of the most interesting cases, the dialogue between the inquisitor, Pedro Cortes, and the accused, Bartolomé Sánchez, reveals the priorities of one inquisitor, the crazy ideas of a peasant, and evolving notions of mad-ness.[39] The trials also show new converts and their families struggling to maintain connections to their religious heritages. *Moriscos* challenged Christian law by continuing to circumcise their boys well into the six-teenth century and *conversos* transmitted Jewish knowledge from one gen-eration to the next.[40] Women's role in clandestinely preserving traditional beliefs, practices, and language has been a particularly important theme in many of these studies.[41]

The trials also provide some important evidence about sexuality and gender expectations. Clerical solicitation remained a serious problem throughout the period.[42] Contreras and Henningsen's statistical informa-tion did not include gender as a category—thus we have no comprehensive data on the numbers of women who came before the Inquisition. However, it is clear that while men made up an overwhelming majority of the accused, some heresies were clearly associated with women. Pious women, including mystics and *beatas,* who stepped out of their prescribed femi-nine roles, attracting crowds and even hinting at political discourse, often faced the condemnation of inquisitors.[43] More typically, women were denounced for less serious heretical infractions, such as having partici-pated in love magic.[44] However, the Inquisition ultimately failed to end women's activity in these spheres.[45]

[38]Contreras, *Sotos contra Riquelmes.*
[39]Nalle, *Mad for God.*
[40]Vincent, "*Moriscos* and Circumcision"; and Lazar, "Scorched Parchment and Tortured Mem-ories."
[41]On Moriscas see Perry, *Handless Maiden;* and idem, "Behind the Veil." On *conversas,* see Melammed, *Heretics or Daughters of Israel?*
[42]Haliczer, *Sexuality in the Confessional;* and Sarrión Mora, *Sexualidad y Confesión.*
[43]See Giles, *Women in the Inquisition.* On women, prophecy, and politics see Kagan, *Lucretia's Dreams.*
[44]Sánchez Ortega, *La mujer y la sexualidad.*
[45]On mystics and holy women, see Bilinkoff, *The Avila of Saint Teresa;* Surtz, *Guitar of God;* and Muñoz Fernández, *Beatas y santas neocastellanas.*

Indeed, scholars now understand that despite the reputation of the Inquisition, most Spaniards never had any interaction with its tribunals and most of those who did generally received light punishments aimed at reconciling the heretics with the Catholic Church rather than leading them towards the stake. Certainly in the context of other early modern judicial systems, it is clear that the Inquisition's ultimate goal of stopping heresy and saving souls created a complex dynamic of social discipline, religious education, and popular/elite interaction, and not a reign of religious absolutism and terror.

Because of the weaknesses of the Inquisition and Spain's other ecclesiastical institutions, the kingdoms were never as culturally homogenous as many scholars had assumed. Indeed, new understandings of the ways to access the history of subaltern peoples and their interactions with dominant political, social, and religious cultures have revealed the complex identities of Spain's minority communities. *Moriscos* were not simply rebellious subjects or opportunistic collaborators. Instead, the relationship between *moriscos* and the Christian community and its power structures was intricately connected to an ever-changing array of personal aspirations and community expectations.[46]

The study of Spain's *converso* population has generally been the realm of Jewish historians, rather than scholars of Spanish religion and society—a scholarly divide based on different understandings of religious and cultural identity. Jewish scholars have tended to see *conversos* first and foremost as former Jews who happened to be living in Spain, while historians of Spanish society generally understand them as Spaniards marginalized to different degrees by their religious heritage. However, both groups of scholars have produced a number of more nuanced explorations of Sephardic identity, connecting *conversos* to both Jewish and *converso* communities abroad as well as to the Christian communities in which they lived, thus emphasizing the fluidity of both religious belief and cultural identification.[47]

---

[46]See Meyerson, *Muslims of Valencia*; and Coleman, *Creating Christian Granada*. Although it falls outside the chronological scope of this essay, David Nirenberg's work on the relations between Muslims, Christians, and Jews during the Middle Ages has been particularly important. See Nirenberg, *Communities of Violence*.

[47]See Graizbord, *Souls in Dispute*; Martz, *Network of Converso Families*; Starr-Lebeau, *In the Shadow of the Virgin*; Meyerson and English, *Christians, Muslims, and Jews*; Bodian, *Hebrews of the Portuguese Nations*; Bodian, "Men of the Nation"; Domínguez Ortíz, *Los judeoconversos*; and Israel, *Empires and Entrepots*.

Although flawed, Inquisition trials give us remarkable insight into the history of sexualities. Historians have explored both the varieties of homosexual relationships and the sites of homosexual liaisons. They have also begun to tease out how class, race, and nationality influenced both popular expectations and Inquisitorial outcomes in sodomy cases.[48] The cases of transvestism and hermaphroditism that came before the Inquisition reveal much about early modern Spanish society's understanding of sex and gender as well as reactions to those who transgressed gender norms.[49] Heterosexual sex has proven no less intriguing. Scholars have deftly employed both Inquisition records as well as the documentation from Spain's multiple judicial systems to explore the most intimate moments of people's lives. Despite religious injunctions to the contrary and expectations of female chastity articulated by the prescriptive literature, Spaniards regularly engaged in extramarital sex, sometimes as a guarantor of a marriage promise, but also for reasons of love and lust.[50]

The history of the family in Spain remains largely the territory of historical demographers. Their careful reconstructions of marriage, residence, and inheritance patterns, household types, and family networks over the life course have demonstrated the multiple meanings of family and the adaptability of family structures to changing social and economic circumstances. Here, as noted for other areas of Spanish history, regional differences in family structures have become a prominent feature of the scholarship.[51]

Finally, the Spanish city has become a vibrant subject of intellectual inquiry. Using both traditional social history and interdisciplinary approaches, scholars have produced a remarkable array of studies of urban life.[52] Established as the capital during the sixteenth century, Madrid is an excellent example of early modern urbanization in action. Scholars have explored both the creation of the city itself and the formulation of its civic

---

[48]Garza Carvajal, *Butterflies will Burn*; Higgs, *Queer Sites*; Blackmore and Hutcheson, *Queer Iberia*; and Fernández, "Repression of Sexual Behavior."

[49]Erauso, *Lieutenant Nun*; and Velasco, *Lieutenant Nun*. See also the story of Elena de Céspedes in Kagan and Dyer, *Inquisitional Inquiries*; and Escamilla, "A propos d'un dossier inquisitorial."

[50]On heterosexuality see Barahona, *Sex Crimes, Honour, and the Law*; Fernández, "Repression of Sexual Behavior; Dubert, "Los comportamientos sexuales premaritales"; and Redondo, *Amours légitimes, amours illégitimes*.

[51]Ferrer i Alòs, "Use of the Family"; Reher, *Town and Country*; idem, *Perspectives on the Family*; Eiras Roel, *La población de Galicia*; Hernández Franco and Chacón Jiménez, *Familia y poder*; Chacón Jiménez, *Historia social*; and Pérez Moreda and Reher, *Demografía histórica en España*.

[52]Fortea Pérez, *Imágenes de la diversidad*.

identity.[53] The images of cities in both Spain and Spanish America depicted more than just a place; they were vivid descriptions of the inhabitants' sense of who they were and how they fit into the cosmos.[54]

Spain's cities were home to dynamic cross-sections of humanity, from aristocrats and bureaucrats to porters, laundresses, tradesmen, and merchants. James Amelang has described the emergence of Barcelona's elites from a combination of the city's ruling oligarchy and the traditional aristocracy. This new, relatively open ruling class then created its own distinctive culture through language, education, and control of civic festivities.[55] Barcelona's artisans were savvy political actors, who had clear ideas about their place in Spain's political hierarchy and pursued their political interests through both coalition building and violence.[56] Spanish cities were also centers of economic life that drew a steady stream of migrants from the hinterland.[57] As for the rest of urban society, scholars are only beginning to understand the lives of the poor and the institutions that served them.[58]

In the past two decades, the study of early modern Spain has come into its own. A review of the literature reveals that the peninsula was a much more complex political, economic, and social entity than most scholars realized. Spain's absolutism no longer seems as absolute; its decline seems less precipitous. The Spanish church was more vulnerable, and the Spanish people were more diverse. Yet, as exciting as the past twenty years have been, the future of the field is even brighter. From an historical perspective, early modern Spain is edging towards another new world.

Bibliography

ELECTRONIC RESOURCES
Biblioteca Virtual de Andalucía:
    http://www.catalogo.bne.es/uhtbin/webcat.
Biblioteca Virtual Miguel de Cervantes:
    http://www.cervantesvirtual.com.

[53]Escobar, *Plaza Mayor*; Río Barredo and Burke, *Madrid, Urbs Regia*; and Hernández, *A Sombra de la Corona*.

[54]Kagan, *Urban Images*.

[55]Amelang, *Honored Citizens of Barcelona*.

[56]Corteguera, *For the Common Good*.

[57]Vassberg, *Village and the Outside World*; and Reher, *Town and Country*.

[58]Barreiro Mallón and Rey Castelao, *Pobres, peregrinos y enfermos*; and Sherwood, *Poverty in Eighteenth-Century Spain*.

Catálogo Colectivo del Patrimonio Bibliográfico Español: http://www.mcu.es/bibliotecas/MC/CCPB/index.html.

Catálogo de la Biblioteca Nacional: http://www.bne.es/cgi-bin/wsirtex?FOR=WBNCONS4.

Fondos Digitalizados de la Universidad de Sevilla: http://fondosdigitales.us.es/.

National Library of Portugal, with many EM Iberian works from both Spain and Portugal: http://purl.pt/index/geral/PT/index.html.

Portal de Archivos Españoles: http://pares.mcu.es/.

Real Academia Española: http://www.rae.es.

Universidad Complutense Madrid: http://cisne.sim.ucm.es.

PRINTED SOURCES

Ahlgren, Gillian. *Teresa of Avila and the Politics of Sanctity.* Ithaca, NY: Cornell University Press, 1998.

Allen, Paul C. *Philip III and the Pax Hispanica, 1598–1621.* New Haven, CT: Yale University Press, 2000.

Altman, Ida. *Emigrants and Society: Extremadura and Spanish America in the Sixteenth Century.* Berkeley: University of California Press, 1989.

———. *Transatlantic Ties in the Spanish Empire: Brihuega, Spain and Puebla, Mexico, 1560–1620.* Stanford, CA: Stanford University Press, 2000.

———, and Reginald D. Butler, "The Contact of Cultures: Perspectives on the Quincentenary." *American Historical Review* 99, no. 2 (April 1994): 478–503.

Amelang, James S. *Honored Citizens of Barcelona: Patrician Culture and Class Relations, 1490–1714.* Princeton, NJ: Princeton University Press, 1986.

Aram, Bethany. *Juana the Mad: Sovereignty and Dynasty in Renaissance Europe.* Baltimore, MD: Johns Hopkins University Press, 2005.

———. "Juana the Mad's Signature: The Problem of Invoking Royal Authority, 1505–1507." *Sixteenth Century Journal* 29 (1998): 331–58.

Barahona, Renato. *Sex Crimes, Honour, and the Law in Early Modern Spain: Vizcaya, 1528–1735.* Toronto: University of Toronto Press, 2003.

Barreiro Mallón, Baudilio, and Ofelia Rey Castelao. *Pobres, peregrinos y enfermos: La red asistencial gallega en el antiguo régimen.* Santiago de Compostela: Edita Consorcio de Santiago, 1999.

Bethencourt, Francisco. *L'Inquisition à l'époque moderne: Espagne, Italie, Portugal, XVe–XIXe siècle.* Paris: Fayard, 1995. Translated by Federico Palomo as *La Inquisición en la época moderna: España, Portugal e Italia, siglos XV–XIX* (Madrid: Akal, 1997).

———, and Kirti Chaudhuri, eds. *História da Expansão Portuguesa—Os Portugueses no Mundo.* 3 vols. Lisbon: Círculo de Leitores, 1998.

Bilinkoff, Jodi. *The Avila of Saint Teresa: Religious Reform in a Sixteenth-Century City.* Ithaca, NY: Cornell University Press, 1989.

———. "A Spanish Prophetess and Her Patrons: The Case of María de Santo Domingo." *Sixteenth Century Journal* 23 (1992): 21–34.

Blackmore, Josiah, and Gregory S. Hutcheson. *Queer Iberia: Sexualities, Cultures, and Crossings from the Middle Ages to the Renaissance.* Durham, NC: Duke University Press, 1999.

Bodian, Miriam. *Hebrews of the Portuguese Nations: Conversos and Community in Early Modern Amsterdam.* Bloomington: Indiana University Press, 1997.

———. "Men of the Nation: The Shaping of *Converso* Identity in Early Modern Europe." *Past and Present* 143 (May 1994): 48–76.

Boruchoff, David. *Isabel La Católica, Queen of Castile: Critical Essays.* New York: Palgrave Macmillan, 2003.

Bouza Alvarez, José Luis. *Religiosidad y cultura simbólica del barroco.* Madrid: CSIC, 1990.

Boyden, James M. *The Courtier and the King: Ruy Gómez de Silva, Philip II, and the Court of Spain.* Berkeley: University of California Press, 1995.

Calvo Poyato, José. *Felipe V.* Málaga: Sarriá, 2004.

Cañizares-Esguerra, Jorge. *How to Write the History of the New World: Histories, Epistemologies, and Identities in the Eighteenth-Century Atlantic World.* Stanford, CA: Stanford University Press, 2001.

Cárceles de Gea, Beatriz. *Reforma y fraude fiscal en el reinado de Carlos II: La Sala de millones (1658–1700).* Madrid: Banco de España, 1995.

Castellano, José Luis, and F. Sánchez Montes, eds. *Carlos V: Europeismo y universalidad.* 5 vols. Madrid: Sociedad Estatal para la Conmemoración de los Centenarios de Felipe II y Carlos V, 2001.

Chacón Jiménez, Francisco, ed. *Historia social de la familia en España: Aproximación a los problemas de familia, tierra y sociedad en Castilla (ss. XV–XIX).* Alicante: Instituto de Cultura Juan Gil-Albert, Diputación de Alicante, 1990.

Chaunu, Pierre, and Michele Escamilla. *Charles Quint.* Paris: Fayard, 2000.

Coates, Timothy J. *Convicts and Orphans: Forced and State-Sponsored Colonizers in the Portuguese Empire, 1550–1755.* Stanford, CA: Stanford University Press, 2001.

Coleman, David. *Creating Christian Granada: Society and Religious Culture in an Old-World Frontier City, 1492–1600.* Ithaca, NY: Cornell University Press, 2003.

Contreras, Jaime. *Sotos contra Riquelmes: Regidores, inquisidores, y cripto-judíos.* Madrid: Anaya & Muchnik, 1992.

———, and Gustav Henningsen. "Forty-four Thousand Cases of the Spanish Inquisition (1540–1700): Analysis of a Historical Data Bank." In *The Inquisition in Early Modern Europe: Studies on Sources and Methods,* edited by Gustav Henningsen, John A. Tedeschi, and Charles Amiel, 100–129. Dekalb: Northern Illinois University Press, 1986.

Corteguera, Luis R. *For the Common Good: Popular Politics in Barcelona, 1580–1640.* Ithaca, NY: Cornell University Press, 2002.

Cruz, Anne J., and Mary Elizabeth Perry. *Culture and Control in Counter-Reformation Spain.* Minneapolis: University of Minnesota Press, 1992.

Dedieu, Jean-Pierre. *L'administration de la foi: L'Inquisition de Tolède, XVIe–XVIIIe siècles.* Madrid: Casa de Velázquez, 1989.

———. "Los cuatro tiempos de la Inquisición." In *Inquisición española: Poder político y control social,* edited by Bartolomé Benassar et al., 15–29. Barcelona: Crítica, 1984.

Domínguez Ortíz, Antonio. *Los judeoconversos en la España moderna.* Madrid: Editorial Mapfre, 1992.

Dubert, Isidro. "Los comportamientos sexuales premaritales en la sociedad gallega del antiguo régimen." *Studia Histórica: Historia moderna* 9 (1991): 117–42.

Dubert García, Isidro. *Historia de la familia en Galicia durante la época moderna, 1550–1830 (Estructura, modelos hereditarios y conflictividad).* A Coruña: Edicios do Castro, 1992.

Eiras Roel, Antonio, and Agustín Guimerá Ravina, eds. *La emigración española a Ultramar,1492–1914.* Madrid: Tabapress, Grupo Tabacalera, 1991.

———. *La población de Galicia, 1700–1860: Crecimiento, distribución espacial y estructura de la población de Galicia en los siglos XVIII y XIX.* Santiago de Compostela: Fundación CaixaGalicia, 1996.

Eire, Carlos. *From Madrid to Purgatory: The Art and Craft of Dying in Sixteenth-Century Spain.* Cambridge: Cambridge University Press, 1995.

Elliott, J. H., and Angel García Sanz. *La España del Conde Duque de Olivares: Encuentro internacional sobre la España del Conde Duque de Olivares celebrado en Toro los días 15–18 de septiembre de 1987.* Valladolid: Universidad de Valladolid, 1990.

Erauso, Catalina de. *Lieutenant Nun: Memoir of a Basque Transvestite in the New World.* Translated by Michele and Gabriel Stepto. Boston: Beacon Press, 1996.

Escamilla, Michèle. "A propos d'un dossier inquisitorial des environs de 1590: Les étranges amours d'un hermaphrodite." In *Amours légitimes, amours illégitimes en Espagne, XVIe–XVIIe siècles*, edited by Augustin Redondo, 167–82. Paris: Publications de la Sorbonne, 1985.

Escobar, Jesús. *The Plaza Mayor and the Shaping of Baroque Madrid.* Cambridge: Cambridge University Press, 2004.

Fernández, André. "The Repression of Sexual Behavior by the Aragonese Inquisition between 1560 and 1700." *Journal of the History of Sexuality* 7, no. 4 (1997): 469–501.

Feros, Antonio. *Kingship and Favoritism in the Spain of Philip III, 1598–1621.* Cambridge: Cambridge University Press, 2000.

Ferrer i Alòs, Llorenç. "The Use of the Family: Property Devolution and Well-to-do Social Groups in Catalonia (Eighteenth and Nineteenth Centuries)." *The History of the Family: An International Quarterly* 3, no. 2 (1998): 247–65.

Fortea, Pérez, José Ignacio, ed. *Imágenes de la diversidad. El mundo urbano en la Corona de Castilla (S. XVI–XVIII).* Santander: Universidad de Cantabria, 1997.

García Carcel, Ricardo. *Felipe V y los españoles.* Barcelona: Random House Mondadori, 2003.

Garza Carvajal, Federico. *Butterflies will Burn: Prosecuting Sodomites in Early Modern Spain and Mexico.* Austin: University of Texas Press, 2003.

Giles, Mary E., ed. *Women in the Inquisition: Spain and the New World.* Baltimore, MD: Johns Hopkins University Press, 1999.

Graizbord, David. *Souls in Dispute: Converso Identities in Iberia and the Jewish Diaspora, 1580–1700.* Philadelphia: University of Pennsylvania Press, 2004.

Haliczer, Stephen. *Inquisition and Society in the Kingdom of Valencia, 1478–1834.* Berkeley: University of California Press, 1990.

———. *Sexuality in the Confessional: A Sacrament Profaned.* Oxford: Oxford University Press, 1996.

Hamilton, Alastair. *Heresy and Mysticism in Sixteenth-Century Spain: The Alumbrados.* Toronto: University of Toronto Press, 1992.

Hernández, Mauro. *A Sombra de la Corona: Poder local y oligarquía urbana, Madrid, 1606–1808.* Madrid: Siglo XXI, 1995.

Hernández Franco, Juan, and Francisco Chacón Jiménez, eds. *Familia y poder: Sistemas de reproducción social en España, siglos XVI–XVIII.* Murcia: Universidad de Murcia, 1995.

Herr, Richard. *Rural Change and Royal Finance in Spain at the End of the Old Regime.* Berkeley: University of California Press, 1989.

Herzog, Tamar. *Defining Nations: Immigrants and Citizens in Early Modern Spain and Spanish America.* New Haven, CT: Yale University Press, 2003.

Higgs, David, ed. *Queer Sites: Gay Urban Histories since 1600.* London: Routledge, 1999.

Historia general de la emigración española a Iberoamérica. 2 vols. Madrid: Historia 16, 1992.

Homza, Lu Ann. *Religious Authority in the Spanish Renaissance*. Baltimore, MD: Johns Hopkins University Press, 2000.

Israel, Jonathan. *Empires and Entrepots: The Dutch, the Spanish Monarchy, and the Jews, 1585–1713*. London: Hambledon Press, 1990.

Kagan, Richard L. *Lucrecia's Dreams: Politics and Prophecy in Sixteenth-Century Spain*. Berkeley: University of California Press, 1990.

———. "Prescott's Paradigm: American Historical Scholarship and the Decline of Spain." *American Historical Review* 101, no. 2 (April 1996): 423–46.

———. *Urban Images of the Hispanic World, 1493–1793*. New Haven, CT: Yale University Press, 2000.

———, and Abigail Dyer. *Inquisitional Inquiries: Brief Lives of Secret Jews and Other Heretics*. Baltimore, MD: Johns Hopkins University Press, 2004.

Kamen, Henry. *Empire: How Spain Became a World Power, 1492–1763*. New York: Harper Collins, 2003.

———. *Philip V of Spain: The King Who Reigned Twice*. New Haven, CT: Yale University Press, 2001.

———. *Philip of Spain*. New Haven, CT: Yale University Press, 1997.

———. *The Phoenix and the Flame: Catalonia and the Counter-Reformation*. New Haven, CT: Yale University Press, 1993.

———. *The Spanish Inquisition: A Historical Revision*. New Haven, CT: Yale University Press, 1997.

Lazar, Moshe. "Scorched Parchment and Tortured Memories: The 'Jewishness' of the Anussim (Crypto-Jews)." In *Cultural Encounters: The Impact of the Inquisition in Spain and the New World*, edited by Mary Elizabeth Perry and Anne J. Cruz, 176–206. Berkeley: University of California Press, 1991.

Lehfeldt, Elizabeth A. "Discipline, Vocation, and Patronage: Spanish Religious Women in a Tridentine Microclimate." *Sixteenth Century Journal* 30, no. 4 (Winter 1999): 1009–30.

———. *Religious Women in Golden Age Spain: The Permeable Cloister*. Aldershot, UK: Ashgate Press, 2005.

———. "Ruling Sexuality: The Political Legitimacy of Isabel of Castile." *Renaissance Quarterly* 53 (2000): 31–56.

Liss, Peggy K. *Isabel the Queen: Life and Times*. Philadelphia: University of Pennsylvania Press, 2004.

López López, Roberto. *Comportamientos religiosos en Asturias durante el antiguo régimen*. Gijon: S. Cañada. 1989.

Lynch, John. *Carlos V y su tiempo*. Barcelona: Crítica, 2000.

Mackay, Ruth. *The Limits of Royal Authority: Resistance and Obedience in Seventeenth-Century Castile*. Cambridge: Cambridge University Press, 1999.

MacLachlan, Colin M. *Spain's Empire in the New World: The Role of Ideas in Institutional and Social Change*. Berkeley: University of California Press, 1988.

Maltby, William S. "Spain." In *Catholicism in Early Modern History: A Guide to Research*, edited by John W. O'Malley, 31–48. St. Louis, MO: Center for Reformation Research, 1988.

Marcos Martín, Alberto. *España en los siglos XVI, XVII y XVIII: Economía y sociedad*. Barcelona: Crítica, 2000.

Martínez Millán, José, and Ignacio J. Esquerra Revilla, eds. *Carlos V y la quiebra del humanismo político en Europa (1530–1558)*. 4 vols. Madrid: Sociedad Estatal para la Conmemoración de los Centenarios de Felipe II y Carlos V, 2001.

Martz, Linda. *A Network of Converso Families in Early Modern Toledo: Assimilating a Minority*. Ann Arbor: University of Michigan Press, 2003.

Melammed, Renée Levine. *Heretics or Daughters of Israel? The Crypto-Jewish Women of Castile*. Oxford: Oxford University Press, 1999.

Meyerson, Mark D. *The Muslims of Valencia in the Age of Fernando and Isabel: Between Coexistence and Crusade*. Berkeley: University of California Press, 1991.

———, and Edward D. English, eds. *Christians, Muslims, and Jews in Medieval and Early Modern Spain: Interaction and Cultural Change*. South Bend, IN: University of Notre Dame Press, 2000.

Monter, William E. *Frontiers of Heresy: The Spanish Inquisition from the Basque Lands to Sicily*. New York: Cambridge University Press, 1990.

Muñoz Fernández, Angela. *Beatas y santas neocastellanas: Ambivalencias de la religión y políticas correctoras del poder (ss. XIV–XVI)*. Madrid: Comunidad de Madrid, 1994.

Nader, Helen. *Liberty in Absolutist Spain: The Habsburg Sale of Towns, 1516–1700*. Baltimore, MD: Johns Hopkins University Press, 1990.

Nalle, Sara T. *God in La Mancha: Religious Reform and the People of Cuenca, 1500–1650*. Baltimore, MD: Johns Hopkins University Press, 1992.

———. *Mad for God: Bartolomé Sánchez, The Secret Messiah of Cardenete*. Charlottesville: University Press of Virginia, 2001.

Navascues Palacio, Pedro, ed. *Carolus V Imperator*. Barcelona: Editorial Lunwerg, 1999.

Netanyahu, Benzion. *The Origins of the Inquisition in Fifteenth-Century Spain*. New York: New York Review Books, 2001.

Nieto, José C. *El Renacimiento y la otra España: Visión cultural socioespiritual*. Geneva: Droz, 1997.

Nirenberg, David. *Communities of Violence: Persecution of Minorities in the Middle Ages*. Princeton, NJ: Princeton University Press, 1996.

Oliveira Marques, A. H. de, ed. *História dos Portugueses no Extremo Oriente*. 5 vols. Lisbon: Fundação Oriente, 1998–2000.

Pagden, Anthony. *Lords of All the World: Ideology of Empire in Spain, Britain, and France, c. 1500–c. 1800*. New Haven, CT: Yale University Press, 1995.

———. *Spanish Imperialism and the Political Imagination: Studies in European and Spanish-American Social and Political Theory, 1513–1830*. New Haven, CT: Yale University Press, 1990.

Parker, Geoffrey. *The Grand Strategy of Philip II*. New Haven, CT: Yale University Press, 1998.

Pérez, Joseph. *Carlos V*. Madrid: Ediciones Temas de Hoy, 1999.

———. *Los Comuneros*. Madrid: La Esfera, 2001.

———. *The Spanish Inquisition: A History*. New Haven, CT: Yale University Press, 2004.

Pérez Moreda, Vicente, and David Sven Reher, eds. *Demografía histórica en España*. Madrid: Ediciones el arquero, 1988.

Pérez Villanueva, Joaquín, and Bartolomé Escandell Bonet, eds. *Historia de la Inquisición en España y América*. 2 vols. Madrid: Biblioteca de Autores Cristianos, 1984–93.

Perry, Mary Elizabeth. "Behind the Veil: Moriscas and the Politics of Resistance and Survival." In *Spanish Women in the Golden Age: Images and Realities*, edited by Magdalena S. Sánchez and Alain Saint-Saëns, 37–54. Westport, CT: Greenwood Press, 1996.

——. *Gender and Disorder in Early Modern Seville.* Princeton, NJ: Princeton University Press, 1990.

——. *The Handless Maiden: Moriscos and the Politics of Religion in Early Modern Spain.* Princeton, NJ: Princeton University Press, 2005.

——, and Anne J. Cruz, eds. *Cultural Encounters: The Impact of the Inquisition in Spain and the New World.* Berkeley: University of California Press, 1991.

Pescador, Juan Javier. *The New World inside a Basque Village: The Oiartzun Valley and Its Atlantic Emigrants, 1550–1800.* Reno: University of Nevada Press, 2003.

Phillips, Carla Rahn. *Six Galleons for the King of Spain: Imperial Defense in the Early Seventeenth Century.* Baltimore, MD: Johns Hopkins University Press, 1986.

——. "Time and Duration: A Model for the Economy of Early Modern Spain." *American Historical Review* 92 (June 1987): 531–62.

——, and William D. Phillips Jr. *Spain's Golden Fleece: Wool Production and the Wool Trade from the Middle Ages to the Nineteenth Century.* Baltimore, MD: Johns Hopkins University Press, 1997.

Phillips, William D., Jr., and Carla Rahn Phillips. *The Worlds of Christopher Columbus.* Cambridge: Cambridge University Press, 1992.

Poska, Allyson M. *Regulating the People: The Catholic Reformation in Sixteenth-Century Spain.* Leiden: Brill, 1998.

Redondo, Augustín, ed. *Amours légitimes, amours illégitimes en Espagne (XVIe–XVIIe siècles).* Paris: Publication de la Sorbonne, 1985.

Reher, David Sven. *Perspectives on the Family in Spain, Past and Present.* Oxford: Oxford University Press, 1997.

——. *Town and Country in Pre-Industrial Spain: Cuenca, 1550–1870.* New York: Cambridge University Press, 1990.

Ringrose, David. *Spain, Europe and the "Spanish Miracle," 1700–1900.* New York: Cambridge University Press, 1996.

Río Barredo, María José del, and Peter Burke, eds. *Madrid, Urbs Regia: La capital ceremonial de la monarquía católica.* Madrid: Marcial Pons, 2000.

Rodríguez Salgado, M. J. *The Changing Face of Empire: Charles V, Philip II, and Habsburg Authority, 1551–1559.* Cambridge: Cambridge University Press, 1988.

Ruiz Martín, Felipe, and Ángel García Sanz, eds. *Mesta, transhumancia y lana en la España moderna.* Barcelona: Crítica, 1998.

Sánchez, Magdalena S. *The Empress, the Queen, and the Nun: Women and Power at the Court of Philip III of Spain.* Baltimore, MD: Johns Hopkins University Press, 1998.

Sánchez León, Pablo. *Absolutismo y comunidad: Los orígenes sociales de la guerra de los Comuneros de Castilla.* Madrid: Siglo XXI, 1998.

Sánchez Ortega, María. *La mujer y la sexualidad en el antiguo régimen: La perspectiva inquisitorial.* Madrid: Akal, 1992.

Sanz Camañes, Porfirio. *Política, hacienda y milicia en el Aragón de los últimos Austrias entre 1640 y 1680.* Zaragoza: Institución Fernando el Católico, 1997.

Sarrión Mora, Adelina. *Sexualidad y Confesión: La solicitación ante el Tribunal del Santo Oficio (siglos XVI–XIX).* Madrid: Alianza, 1994.

Schaub, Jean-Frédéric. *Le Portugal au temps du Comte-Duc d'Olivares, 1621–1640: Le conflit de juridictions comme exercice de la politique.* Madrid: Casa de Velázquez, 2001.

Serrano, Eliseo, ed. *Felipe V y su tiempo: Congreso internacional.* 2 vols. Zaragoza: Institución Fernando el Católico, 2004.

Sherwood, Joan M. *Poverty in Eighteenth-Century Spain: The Women and Children of the Inclusa.* Toronto: University of Toronto Press, 1988.

Starr-Lebeau, Gretchen D. *In the Shadow of the Virgin: Inquisitors, Friars, and Conversos in Guadalupe, Spain.* Princeton, NJ: Princeton University Press, 2003.

Stein, Stanley J., and Barbara H. Stein. *Apogee of Empire: Spain and New Spain in the Age of Charles III, 1759–1789.* Baltimore, MD: Johns Hopkins University Press, 2003.

Stradling, R. A. *Philip IV and the Government of Spain, 1621–1665.* New York: Cambridge University Press, 1988.

Surtz, Ronald. *The Guitar of God: Gender, Power, and Authority in the Visionary World of Mother Juana de la Cruz (1481–1534).* Philadelphia: University of Pennsylvania Press, 1990.

Thompson, I. A. A., and Bartolomé Yun Casalilla, eds. *The Castilian Crisis of the Seventeenth Century: New Perspectives on the Economic and Social History of Seventeenth-Century Spain.* Cambridge: Cambridge University Press, 1994.

Thompson, James. *A Distinctive Industrialization: Cotton in Barcelona, 1728–1832.* Cambridge: Cambridge University Press, 1992.

Torrents, Angels. "Actitudes públicas, actitudes privadas, 1610–1935." *Boletín de la Asociación de Demografía Histórica* 10, no. 1 (1992): 7–29.

Vassberg, David. *The Village and the Outside World in Golden Age Castile: Mobility and Migration in Everyday Rural Life.* New York: Cambridge University Press, 1996.

Velasco, Sherry. *The Lieutenant Nun: Transgenderism, Lesbian Desire, and Catalina de Erauso.* Austin: University of Texas Press, 2001.

Vincent, Bernard. "The *Moriscos* and Circumcision." In *Culture and Control in Counter-Reformation Spain,* edited by Anne J. Cruz and Mary Elizabeth Perry, 78–92. Minneapolis: University of Minnesota Press, 1992.

Weber, Alison. *Teresa of Avila and the Rhetoric of Femininity.* Princeton, NJ: Princeton University Press, 1996.

Weissberger, Barbara F. *Isabel Rules: Constructing Queenship, Wielding Power.* Minneapolis: University of Minnesota Press, 2003.

Yun Casalilla, Bartolomé. "Estado y estructuras sociales en Castilla: Reflexiones para el studio de la 'crisis del siglo XVII' en el Valle del Duero (1550–1630)." *Revista de Historia Económica* 8 (Fall 1990): 549–74.

———. *Marte contra Minerva: El precio del imperio español, c. 1450–1600.* Barcelona: Crítica, 2004.

13

The Swiss

Bruce Gordon

With plenty of well-organized archives and libraries, and an enviable survival rate of its sources—largely through the absence of war—Switzerland offers Reformation scholars extraordinary opportunities for research into institutional, social, and theological history. The possibilities are only enhanced by the relatively small amount of scholarly attention that has been paid to this crucial area of the European Reformation. It is hard to imagine a situation in England, Germany, the Low Countries, or France similar to that which exists for the Swiss, where the principal characters await fresh (or, often, any) biographies, and the largest urban centers (Zurich and Berne) lack modern studies of their reform movements. Where such accounts do exist, the narratives are often based on primary sources published over a century ago and reflect old agendas. The landscape, however, is by no means uniformly bleak. Befitting the character of the country, scholarship on the Swiss Reformation has been extremely patchy: while certain areas have witnessed considerable activity in recent years, others have lain fallow. This article will attempt to draw attention both to advances and lacunae. The current prospect reveals Heinrich Bullinger, church discipline, local studies of religious cultures, and Anabaptism to be the most active research areas. At the same time, an increasing number of sources are being made available electronically, through microfiche collections, and by traditional printed means. Much of this work is being carried out in energetic research institutes in Switzerland that have developed effective clusters of historians and theologians working within wider networks of international scholarship. The principal problem is not with the sources, but rather the shortage of scholars willing to take up the cudgel and deal with the Latin, Alemannic, and French materials that exist in such abundance.

Resources

Those wishing to engage in research on the Swiss Reformation are well served by research institutes committed to new scholarship and the fostering of international contacts. In Zurich, there is the Institute for Swiss Reformation History, which, for the most part, concentrates on the Zwinglian tradition. Currently, the Institute is very much focused on the life and work of Heinrich Bullinger. The editing of his massive correspondence remains an ongoing project, while recently there has also been a welcome return, after a long hiatus, to the production of critical editions of Bullinger's writings. The first fruit will be the publication in 2008 of the first critical edition of the Latin text of his *Decades* by Peter Opitz.[1] Many of Bullinger's key writings have been made available in modern German through a six-volume series edited by Emidio Campi, Detlef Roth, and Peter Stotz for the Theologischer Verlag Zurich. Other projects include the production of an electronic database of Zwingli's writings and a critical edition of the Baden Disputation of 1526. In Geneva, the Institut d'histoire de la Réformation Université de Genève likewise offers a combination of expertise and resources for scholars. Naturally, here the focus has been more on Calvin and the French Reformed tradition. The activities of both institutes are detailed on their websites.[2] In Basel and Berne there are no institutes of Reformation studies per se, but both have strong traditions in early modern Swiss history and are home to a number of important projects. The websites of both historical departments list the current range of research.

The major archives of the Swiss cantons are, as expected, extremely well organized and user friendly. Over the past few years, they have invested heavily in putting their resources on microfilm for purposes of preservation. While this can occasionally be irritating for those wishing to see the documents themselves, it does have the benefit of making it easier to obtain copies of material for consultation at home. In my experience, all

---

[1] Bullinger, *Dekaden (1552)*, ed. Opitz.
[2] University of Geneva, Institut d'histoire de la Réformation: http://www.unige.ch/ihr; and University of Zurich, Institut für schweizerische Reformationsgeschichte: http://www.unizh.ch/irg.

the principal libraries and archives are well equipped to assist foreign scholars and make information available. Once again, it is advisable to check their websites and make contact before arriving.

Each year the journal *Zwingliana* produces a bibliography of recently published work on the Swiss Reformation. The editors do not limit themselves to sources and literature directly on the Swiss Reformation, but also list related material pertaining to other parts of Europe that will be relevant. For those not able to access the journal itself, the bibliography is available online through the home page of the Institute in Zurich.[3] *Zwingliana* itself, which dates to the early years of the twentieth century, was traditionally a journal of Protestant church history of the Swiss Reformation. It has become a modern scholarly publication and is indispensable for those working in the field.

One of the initial obstacles facing a scholar is the paucity of critical editions of the major reformers. At the end of the nineteenth century, it was decided to undertake an edition of Zwingli's works and, almost a century later, this has been largely completed. Published in thirteen volumes, *Huldreich Zwinglis Sämtliche Werke* is part of the Corpus Reformatorum and remains one of the major intellectual achievements of Swiss Reformation scholarship. *Huldrych Zwingli Schriften* is a modern German translation of Zwingli's works edited by Thomas Brunnschweiler and Samuel Lutz. The consequences of this focus on Zwingli for the other reformers, however, have been dire. Only Johannes Oecolampadius' work received similar attention in the hands of Ernst Staehelin (*Briefe und Akten zum Leben Oekolampads*).[4] As mentioned above, there are now ambitious plans to relaunch the editions of Bullinger's works, while Peter Martyr Vermigli's writings are being translated with commentaries by a team of scholars.[5] Otherwise, one can easily list a long line of prominent Swiss reformers whose works remain unedited. The work is there for willing hands.

Apart from the writings of the reformers, there has been some important work done on other key theological sources. Of considerable importance is the recent publication of the Reformed Confessions in *Reformierte Bekenntnisschriften*, edited by Heiner Faulenbach and Eberhard Busch. The first three volumes covering the period 1523 to 1558 have

---

[3]The current Internet address for the list is http://www.unizh.ch/irg/biblio.html.

[4]Volume 1, published in 1927, covers 1499 through 1526, and volume 2, published in 1934, covers 1527 through 1593.

[5]The Peter Martyr Library is published by Truman State University Press; https://tsup.truman.edu.

appeared. These scholarly editions provide not only the texts, but a wealth of historical and theological information.

The situation for the collections of correspondence is somewhat better. In Zurich, as mentioned above, a team of scholars continues to edit and publish the massive correspondence of Heinrich Bullinger, whose collection is amongst the largest of the sixteenth-century reformers.[6] There have been editions of the correspondence of other leading figures of the Swiss Reformation, most notably the Blaur brothers, Vadianus, and the Amerbach family.[7]

IDC's publication of texts has made works of the Swiss reformers much more readily available. The most relevant collections are Reformed Protestantism, Geneva/Switzerland; Early Printed Bibles; The Anabaptist, Mennonite, and Spiritualist Reformation; Works by and about Huldrych Zwingli; and Thesaurus Hottingerianus: Zentrabibliothek Zurich. The last contains a vast body of manuscript material. Although these collections were first made available on microfiche, it is now possible to obtain them in digital format. For sixteenth-century translations of the Swiss reformers into English, it is now possible to access all the works listed in the Short-Title Catalogue through Early English Books Online (EEBO). Ad Fontes is also making electronically available works of the reformers, and among the Swiss figures included are Bullinger, Oecolampadius, Vermigli, Vadianus, and Zwingli. This system is particularly good for searching texts electronically, but it is expensive, which means that it will be largely limited to institutional subscriptions.[8]

General Works

Because the Swiss Reformation has not, on the whole, been treated as a discrete subject by German- and French-speaking scholars, there have been few attempts to provide overviews of the whole of the confederation in the sixteenth century. Two older, although key, works remain useful: Rudolf Pfister's *Kirchengeschichte der Schweiz* (vol. 2), and Gottfried W. Locher's *Die zwinglische Reformation in Rahmen der europäischen Kirchengeschichte.* The only book-length historical study is Bruce Gordon's 2002 *The Swiss*

---

[6]For an overview in English of the project, see Insitute of Swiss Reformation History, Bullinger Correspondence: http://www.unizh.ch/irg/briefwechseldb/index_engl.html.

[7]Blaur, *Briefwechsel der Brüder*; Arbenz and Wartmann, *Die Vadianische Briefsammlung*; and Hartmann and Rudolf Jenny, *Die Amerbachkorrespondenz*. To date ten volumes of the Amerbach correspondence has been published.

[8]The current Web address is http://www.ad-fontes.com/aboutus.asp.

Reformation. Gordon provides an extensive examination of the various reform movements, the theologies of the Swiss reformers, and the counter positions of the Anabaptists and radicals, as well as a list of printed primary and secondary sources. Gordon's article "Switzerland and Reformed Protestantism" provides valuable information on the historiography of the Swiss Reformation. A shorter and very useful summary of the Swiss Reformation is "Switzerland" by Mark Taplin. Philip Benedict has provided a helpful outline of the Zurich church in the first chapter of his *Christ's Churches Purely Reformed: A Social History of Calvinism*.

The Reformers

Any basic textbook on the Reformation will invoke the name of Huldrych Zwingli as one of the key reformers of the 1520s. Founder of some sort of humanist theology and opponent of Luther, he is generally regarded as the opening act for Calvin and the more mature subsequent Reformed theologians. Zwingli, however, has all but vanished from the radar screen of Reformation scholarship over the past twenty years.[9] New books recycle old nostrums, and we continue to exist with a comforting sense of a man who fits a certain pattern and place in the Reformation story. The admirable biography of Zwingli by G. R. Potter (1976) is over three decades old and the field desperately requires a replacement. Learned and beautifully written, Potter's book inhabits an older world in which history and theology kept a polite distance. More recent works on Zwingli, urban history, the Anabaptists, and the wider European Reformation, have not so much undermined Potter's conclusions as demonstrated the need for a fresh approach.[10]

That said, at least Zwingli has a relatively modern biography. Johannes Oecolampadius, Simon Grynaeus, Oswald Myconius in Basle, Berchtold Haller, Johannes Haller, Vadianus in St. Gall; and Theodor Bibliander, Konrad Pellikan, Leo Jud, Rudolf Gwalther, and Peter Martyr Vermigli in Zurich—to name a few—await scholarly assessments of their lives.[11] In the nineteenth century, a series of biographies was prepared,

---

[9]In German, highly recommended are Haas, *Ulrich Zwingli und seine Zeit*; Farner, *Ulrich Zwingli*; and Gäbler, *Ulrich Zwingli*.

[10]See, for example, Wandel, *Voracious Idols*; Bolliger, *Infiniti Contemplatio*; and Strübind, *Eifriger als Zwingli*.

[11]Still fundamental on Oecolampadius are Staehelin, *Briefe und Akten zum Leben Oekolampads*; and Staehelin,*Theologische Lebenswerk Johannes Oekolampads*. Näf, *Vadian und seine Stadt*, is very fine, but somewhat outdated. On Leo Jud, the newest work remains Wyss, *Leo Jud: Seine Entwicklung*

including Carl Pestalozzi's study of Heinrich Bullinger, but the twentieth century yielded little. Most recently, the flood of research on Heinrich Bullinger has been enriched by the publication of a two-volume biography of Bullinger by Fritz Büsser, who has devoted much of his career to the life and work of the Zurich reformer. Theodor Bibliander, an extremely important figure of the Zurich reformation, has finally received some attention with the publication of Christine Christ-von Wedel's *Theodor Bibliander: Ein Thurgauer im gelehrten Zürich der Reformationszeit*. On Vadianus, Ulrich Gaier's important new study surveys his central place in the field of Swiss humanism.[12]

Such work on individuals does, however, mask the reality that Swiss theology and reform movements were largely about networks of scholars. The Swiss Reformation was never a mass or popular movement; its progress was due to the cooperation of clerics and magistrates. It was an uneasy, and largely urban, relationship and dependent on the dynamics of personal relations. There were circles within circles: the reformers themselves worked together in humanist-style sodalities in which they shared studies, church duties, and education. A recent study of Anabaptism by Andrea Strübind has recognized the importance of these circles among the Anabaptists, but among the reformers, they await investigation. The Swiss reformers, most of whom were not Swiss, did not work in isolation, but as part of fraternities that need to be examined collectively. These networks are essential to understanding the character of the movement. They also crossed the clerical-lay boundary, which points to the urgent need for a better understanding of the roles played by the leading families in the reform movements. The Roists in Zurich, the Amerbachs in Basle, and the Tillmanns in Berne crucially supported the reform movements at moments in the 1520s when they might have failed, yet very little is known about these families. It is clear that their agendas did not always square with the aspirations of the preachers, but to what extent there were differences remains a fascinating set of tales to be told. The multiple and divided loyalties of these families reveal the complexities of the reform movements, detailing the variegated relations between religion, commerce, and familial and civic sympathies. In this respect, the publication of the Amerbach correspondence in Basle, for example, offers a gold mine of information.

---

zum Reformator 1519–1523, which treats only the early career. Konrad Pelikan is well treated by Zürcher, *Konrad Pellikans Wirken in Zürich, 1526–1556*, but the focus is largely on exegetical scholarship.

[12]Gaier, "Vadian und die Literatur des 16. Jahrhunderts."

Theology

Although research continues to appear on individual reformers, scholars await a comprehensive examination of the theology of the Swiss Reformation. Over the past twenty years, works such as Peter Stephens's *Theology of Huldrych Zwingli*, Frank James's *Peter Martyr Vermigli and Predestination*, and, most recently, Peter Opitz's *Heinrich Bullinger als Theologie*, a study of Bullinger's *Decades*, have deepened our understanding of certain figures and themes, but for the student seeking an integrated examination of what might be loosely termed *Zwinglian theology*, there is nothing. This would be an ambitious undertaking, fraught with complications, and would entail the tracing of influences and the charting of reception. Any examination of the theological culture of the Swiss reformers would need to be particularly attentive to recent trends that have identified the significant influences of Melanchthon and Oecolampadius on the early Swiss reformers. Swiss theology did not have a single source and Zwingli was not the only authority. Scholars are only beginning to understand the complexities and crosscurrents of religious thought in the 1520s. The current attention to Heinrich Bullinger reveals the extent to which he was independent of Zwingli. Likewise, centers such as Basle and the southern German cities were crucial to the formation of directions of thought that were similar to without being identical to Zwingli's theology. This is clearly demonstrated in the dissertation of James Ford, "Wolfgang Musculus and the Struggle for Confessional Hegemony in Reformation Augsburg, 1531–1548." The conference volume on Musculus edited by Rudolf Dellsperger, Rudolf Freudenberger, and Wolfgang Weber is also useful on this point.

On Zwingli the key works remain those of the Swiss scholar Gottfried W. Locher, especially his 1979 *Die zwinglische Reformation* and his 1981 *Huldrych Zwingli: New Perspectives*. In addition, *Reformiertes Erbe*, the two-volume festschrift produced for his eightieth birthday, contains a wide range of useful essays. In English, Peter Stephens's *The Theology of Huldrych Zwingli* remains the most comprehensive overview, although not very historical. Much undervalued, yet worthy of attention, are the studies of Berndt Hamm, particularly his *Zwinglis Reformation der Freiheit* and "Laientheologie zwischen Luther und Zwingli."

The start of the twenty-first century has seen the publication of outstanding work on Swiss reformers by Martin Sallmann, Daniel Bolliger, Peter Opitz, and Olaf Kuhr. The fact that all are from the German-speaking world is telling of the paucity of research, except for the above-mentioned on Vermigli, in English. What distinguishes these works are their rigorous attention to the texts and sensitivity to the place of Swiss theology within the wider matrix of Protestant thought of the sixteenth century. Sallmann's *Zwischen Gott und Mensch: Huldrych Zwinglis theologischer Denkweg im De vera et falsa religione commentarius (1525)* is a welcome and full reassessment of Zwingli's crucial early writing at the moment of the formation of the Reformed Church. Bolliger (*Infiniti Contemplatio: Grundzüge der Scotus- und Scotismusrezeption im Werk Huldrych Zwinglis*) examines Zwingli's understanding of Scholasticism, in particular Duns Scotus, and reveals the Zurich reformer to be a much more complex thinker profoundly grounded in late medieval thought. Zwingli was by no means any mere humanist rationalist. This book is far and away the most important study of Zwingli in the last thirty years. Opitz (*Heinrich Bullinger als Theologe: Eine Studie zu den Dekaden*) has studied Bullinger's *Decades* and places this most well-known of Bullinger's works within the broader scope of his enormous body of writing. Opitz provides a forensic study of how Bullinger worked with the loci method, and Opitz's conclusions reflect a growing trend to move away from Bullinger as the covenant theologian. Kuhr (*"Die Macht des Bannes und der Busse": Kirchenzucht und Erneuerung der Kirche bei Johannes Oekolampad (1482–1531)*) has produced the first major work on Oecolampadius since Staehelin in the 1930s. Although his book concentrates on the issue of church discipline, it opens a topic that needs further investigation: the pivotal influence of the Basle reformer in the early years of the Reformation. Kuhr has an English summary of his arguments in "Calvin and Basel: The Significance of Oecolampadius and the Basel Discipline Ordinance for the Institution of Ecclesiastical Discipline in Geneva."

Other especially noteworthy studies to appear recently include Irena Backus's *Reformation Readings of the Apocalypse: Geneva, Zurich, and Wittenberg*; Achim Detmers's examination of the relationships between the reformers and Judaism in his *Reformation und Judentum: Israel-Lehren und Einstellungen zum Judentum von Luther bis zum frühen Calvin*; and Peter Opitz's *Calvin im Kontext der Schweizer Reformation*. In her study of interpretations of the book of Revelation, Backus gives a great deal of attention to the work of Bibliander and Bullinger, detailing their approach to biblical texts and their readings of the material. Detmers's work makes striking use of unfamiliar sources to bring an entirely fresh approach to the discussion of Christian-Jewish relations in the sixteenth century. The Opitz volume

volume contains a large collection of essays, both historical and theological, that help place Calvin within the context of the Swiss Reformation.

In addition, recent conferences marking anniversaries of reformers have produced collections of essays that map out new directions of research. Most notable are Alfred Schindler, Hans Stickelberger, and Martin Sallmann's *Die Zürcher Reformation: Ausstrahlungen und Rückwirkungen*; Emidio Campi's *Peter Martyr Vermigli: Humanism, Republicanism, Reformation*; and Bruce Gordon and Emidio Campi's *Heinrich Bullinger: Architect of Reformation.* The papers of the 2004 conference marking the five hundredth anniversary of Bullinger's birth have been published in Campi and Opitz, *Heinrich Bullinger: Life-Thought-Influence.*

Until recently, scholarship on Swiss Reformation theology (which has meant, for the most part, Bullinger) has focused on the issues of the covenant, predestination, and the Eucharist. The role of the covenant in Swiss Reformed theology remains contested. The key work is J. Wayne Baker's *Heinrich Bullinger and the Covenant: The Other Reformed Tradition.* On the Eucharist, the best work remains Paul Rorem's *Calvin and Bullinger on the Lord's Supper.* Recently, Cornelius Venema has examined predestination in his *Heinrich Bullinger and the Doctrine of Predestination.* A welcome new departure in the examination of other crucial theologians connected with the Swiss Reformation is the two-volume edition with commentary of Girolamo Zanchi's *De religione Christiana fides—Confession of Christian Religion* prepared by Luca Baschera and Christian Moser.

Such works have been invaluable to our growing understanding of the character of theological discourse in the Swiss Confederation, but the picture remains extremely partial as long as other important areas remain untouched. Worship, liturgy, and spirituality are just three areas that urgently require attention. There have been some isolated investigations, such as Kenneth H. Marcus's "Hymnody and Hymnals in Basel, 1526–1606" and Bruce Gordon's "Transcendence and Community in Zwinglian Worship: The Liturgy of 1525 in Zurich." An important advance will be made with the publication of Roland Diethelm's Zurich dissertation on Bullinger and worship. Some of his early findings are published in Gordon and Campi's *Heinrich Bullinger: Architect of Reformation.* Another research subject to be mined is biblical scholarship in the Swiss Confederation. A major work to appear in the last decade is an extensive study of the 1531 Zurich Bible by Traudel Himmighöfer, *Die Zürcher Bibel bis zum Tode Zwinglis (1531): Darstellung und Bibliographie.*

The Cities

Next to the holes in work on the major reformers, it is perhaps most surprising that the major urban centers have not been studied, given the richness of archival material. There is an older literature that is still widely
used, including *Geschichte des Kantons Zürich*; Karl Dändliker's *Geschichte
der Stadt und des Kantons Zürich*; Richard Feller's *Geschichte Berns*; and R.
Wackernagel's *Geschichte der Stadt Basel*. Hans Guggisberg has provided a
more recent study with his *Basel in the Sixteenth Century*, but in comparison to the work that has been done on Strasbourg or Augsburg, for example, the situation for the Swiss cities is curious.

Lee Palmer Wandel has opened the door with some important work
on the nature of religious reform in Zurich and Basle in *Always Among Us:
Images of the Poor in Zwingli's Zurich* and *Voracious Idols and Violent
Hands*. For Berne, Glenn Ehrstine's excellent study of drama in the context
of urban culture, *Theater, Culture, and Community in Reformation Bern,
1523–1555*, is essential reading and offers a new perspective through its
examination of the place of drama in the civic life of Berne in the pre- and
post-Reformation periods. Alongside Ehrstine's study should be placed the
collections of essays brought together for the exhibition on iconoclasm
held in Berne and Strasbourg in 2000. *Bildersturm: Wahnsinn oder Gottes
Wille?* is a lavishly illustrated volume that contains important essays by
leading scholars on iconoclasm in Swiss and German lands in the early
Reformation.

The pioneering work of Richard Heinrich Schmidt (*Reichsstädte,
Reich und Reformation: Korporative Religionspolitik 1521–1529/30*) and
Thomas Brady Jr. (*Turning Swiss: Cities and Empire, 1450–1550*) demonstrated the close relationship between the Swiss cities and their southern
German cousins in the late medieval period. The spread of the reform
movement put all of the cities under extreme pressure as the magistrates
attempted to balance the demands of their guilds and populace with those
of the patricians and the emperor. The relations between the Swiss and the
empire are further explored by Brady in his magisterial *Protestant Politics:
Jacob Sturm (1489–1553) and the German Reformation*, which is essential
reading on the evolution of confessional relations in the 1530s and 1540s.
Yet, despite the recognized kinship between the urban cultures of the Swiss
confederation and southwestern German lands, this discussion has largely
remained in general terms; detailed case studies of the reformations in
Basle, Berne, Zurich, St. Gall, and Schaffhausen are lacking. Such work

would be entirely possible in light of the archive material, but it remains a *desideratum*.

For Zurich, the situation after Zwingli is considerably brighter with the outstanding study of Bullinger's relationship with the magistrates by Hans Ulrich Bächtold (*Bullinger vor dem Rat*). This was followed by Pamela Biel's *Doorkeepers at the House of Righteousness*; and more recently by Andreas Mühling's *Heinrich Bullingers europäische Kirchenpolitik*, which explores the political culture in Zurich in relation to the wider European developments. Two recent studies that have continued to explore the relationship between the Zurich church and England are Carrie Euler's *Couriers of the Gospel: England and Zurich, 1531–1558* and Torrance Kirby's *The Zurich Connection and Tudor Political Theology*.

Churches and Communities

Without doubt, one of the most important developments in the study of the reformation in the Swiss lands was the work of Peter Blickle and his students, *Communal Reformation: The Quest for Salvation in Sixteenth-Century Germany*, which has been perhaps the most controversial book on the Swiss Reformation of the last half century. Blickle examined the trend toward communalization in the late medieval period and put forward the thesis that Zwingli's preaching found a much more receptive audience in these lands than in Luther's, on account of his support of local autonomy. This idea of a communal reformation, Blickle argued, held sway until the brutal events of the Peasants' War of 1525, which then led to the princely reformation. Since the publication of the book, Blickle has revised some aspects of this position and his students have developed it in new directions, but it remains central to debates about Anabaptism and the early Reformation in the Swiss lands.

A project of major importance to emerge from the Blickle circle in Berne is André Holenstein's examination of rural and urban history in the late medieval and early modern periods with an emphasis on the Bernese context. Holenstein's expansive *Berns mächtige Zeit: Das 16. und 17. Jahrhundert neu entdeckt* is part of a new direction in research that is examining rural religious cultures in the Swiss Confederation in innovative ways. Francisca Loetz, in *Mit Gott handeln: Von den Zürcher Gotteslästerern der Frühen Neuzeit zu einer Kulturgeschichte des Religiösen*, explores the power and role of language through an examination of swearing and blasphemy. Her study offers a fresh perspective on popular religious mentalities in

Zurich long after the establishment of the new church order. The layers of interaction between official and popular religion are explored in Frans Mauelshagen's *Johann Wicks Wunderbücher: Reformierter Wunderglaube im Wandel der Geschichtsschreibung.* Wick collected accounts of natural disasters, wonders, and strange stories from across Europe, and Mauelshagen's book offers the first scholarly examination of this fascinating source.

Recently, important archive-based studies have greatly enhanced our understanding of the diverse ways in which the church and its clergy engaged with local communities. Randolph C. Head, in his work on the Graubünden and Thurgau, has been exploring relations between different confessions that had to live in close proximity.[13] This work also includes a useful discussion of the communalization debate. Two other areas that have drawn attention are clergy-lay relations and church discipline. Amy Nelson Burnett's *Teaching the Reformation Ministers and Their Message in Basel, 1529–1629* is the first major study of the Basle church, supplementing her earlier articles, "Preparing the Pastors" and "Controlling the Clergy." More recently, in "A Tale of Three Churches," Burnett compares clerical functions and relations in pastors and parishes in Basle, Strasbourg, and Geneva. Randolph Head examines this topic for the Graubünden in "Rhaetian Ministers, from Shepherds to Citizens." For Zurich, Bruce Gordon's *Clerical Discipline and the Rural Reformation* examines the relationship between Heinrich Bullinger and the clergy of the hundred parishes of the Zurich rural territories. On discipline, the most significant recent work is Heinrich Richard Schmidt's *Dorf und Religion: Reformierte Sittenzucht in Berner Landgemeinden der Frühen Neuzeit,* an extensive examination of the disciplinary processes in Bernese lands.[14] Roland E. Hofer, in his *Uppiges, unzüchtiges Lebwesen,* has examined the records of the disciplinary body in Schaffhausen, which in many ways was similar to Zurich's. Scholars working on church institutions will be well served by a new project supported by the Swiss Nationalfond to publish the church ordinances of Zurich and Basle from the Reformation to 1675. It is hoped that the project will ultimately extend to the other Swiss Protestant churches, opening the way for important comparative work.[15]

---

[13]Head, *Early Modern Democracy in the Grisons.* See also Head, "Nit alss zwo Gemeinden, oder Partheyen, sonder ein Gemeind"; and idem, "Shared Lordship, Authority, and Administration." Other useful studies exploring the rural religious cultures of the Swiss Reformation include Maarbjerg, "Iconoclasm in the Thurgau"; and Snyder, "Communication and the People."

[14]For a summary of his work in English, see Schmidt, "Morals Courts in Rural Berne."

[15]For further information, see the project's website: http://www.unizh.ch/irg/kio.html.

French-Speaking Areas

For the Reformation in the French-speaking parts of the Swiss Confederation, Henri Vuilleumier's *Histoire de l'Eglise Réformée du Pays de Vaud sous le Régime Bernois* remains essential reading. On the conquest of the Pays de Vaud by Berne, there is a more recent study: Charles Gilliard's *La conquête du Pays de Vaud par les Bernois*. On the imposition of the Reformation in the Vaud by the Bernese, see Michel Campiche's *La Réforme en Pays de Vaud* and Eric Junod's *La Dispute de Lausanne (1536): La théologie réformée après Zwingli et avant Calvin*. These volumes highlight the fractured world of the Vaudois Reformation as the Protestant reformers, led by Guillaume Farel, pursued an agenda too radical for both their Bernese political masters and the local population. The interactions of politics, theology, and traditional religion are usefully discussed. The architecture of the Reformed churches in the Pays de Vaud is admirably examined in Marcel Grandjean's *Les temples vaudois*. The most important recent work, however, is Michael Bruening's *Calvinism's First Battleground*. Bruening's study, based on detailed archive research, demonstrates the crucial role played by Berne and the Vaud in the development of Calvin's Reformation in Geneva.

Anabaptism and Radicals

Since the mid-1970s, research into Swiss Anabaptism has undergone a sea change through the involvement of secular historians in what was previously a highly confessional area of research. In the following decades there has been a flourishing of scholarship aided by the appearance of critical editions and source materials. As the recent study by Andrea Strübind has demonstrated, there is no consensus on key issues of the movement. Strübind's *Eifriger als Zwingli* is perhaps the most striking contribution to the field in the last decade. The very nature of Swiss Anabaptism—its relationship to Zwingli, the genesis of the movement in Zurich, the place of the Schleitheim Articles, the influence of Zurich Anabaptism on other areas, and the connections with the Peasants' War—remains active and contested in the field of scholarship. There remains a fundamental debate over how the sources should be read and interpreted.

The field is well served by works that provide both comprehensive studies of the subject and guides to historiographical issues. Of the more recent studies, most useful are C. Arnold Snyder's *Anabaptist History and Theology*; W. Packull's "The Origins of Swiss Anabaptism in the Context of the Reformation of the Common Man"; and James M. Stayer's *The German*

Peasants' War and Anabaptist Community of Goods. A particularly helpful work to appear recently is C. Arnold Snyder's *Biblical Concordance of the Swiss Brethren, 1540.*

Some extremely important studies of religious dissent in the Swiss Confederation during the Reformation have appeared recently. The most notable are Hans Guggisberg's biography, *Sebastian Castellio: Defender of Religious Freedom*; Carlos Gilly's study of Basle printing (*Spanien und der Basler Buchdruck bis 1600*); and Mark Taplin's *The Italian Reformers and the Zurich Church c. 1540–1620.* Taplin's book is a study of the covert nature of opposition to mainstream religious thought and his book provides an exhaustive bibliography of primary and secondary sources.

Communication and the Arts

The past two decades have seen the appearance of important work on cultural elements of the Swiss Reformation. Particularly notable are Peter Pfrunder's *Pfaffen Ketzer Totenfresser*: Fastnachtkultur der Reformationszeit, and Glenn Ehrstine's *Theater, Culture, and Community in Reformation Bern, 1523–1555.*[16] Other recent significant studies to appear include Manfred Vischer's *Zürcher Einblattdrucke des 16. Jahrhunderts*, Peter Blickle's *Macht und Ohnmacht der Bilder*, and Werner Meyer and Kaspar von Greyerz, *Platteriana.* The combination of Swiss and foreign writers, humanists, and artists who lived in the Swiss Confederation made it a center of cultural achievement during much of the sixteenth century. Many of these figures, such as Vadianus in St. Gall and Konrad Gesner in Zurich, offer an abundance of material for those interested in the wider dimensions of Renaissance culture.

Bibliography

ELECTRONIC RESOURCES

Ad Fontes: http://www.ad-fontes.com/aboutus.asp.
Basle University Library: http://www.ub.unibas.ch/.
Burgerbibliothek Bern: http://www.cx.unibe.ch/burgerbib/.
Canton Archive Basle: http://www.baselland.ch/docs/archive/main.htm.
Canton Archive Berne: http://www.sta.be.ch/site/staatsarchiv.
Heinrich Bullinger correspondence overview:
    http://www.unizh.ch/irg/briefwechseldb/index_engl.html.
IDS Basel Bern (linked catalogue of two of the major libraries of the two cities):
    http://www.zb.unizh.ch/.http://www.ub.unibas.ch/ibb/.

---

[16]See also Ehrstine, "Of Peasants, Women, and Bears."

Institute for Swiss Reformation Study, New Literature on Zwinglian Reformation: http://www.unizh.ch/irg/biblio.html.

Schaffhausen City Archive: www.stadtarchiv-schaffhausen.ch.

Staatsarchiv Zurich: http://www.staatsarchiv.zh.ch/index.php.

Stadtarchiv Zurich: http://www3.stzh.ch/internet/stadtarchiv/home.html.

University of Geneva, Institut d'Histoire de la Réformation: http://www.unige.ch/ihr.

Universität Zürich, Institut für schweizerische Reformationsgeschichte: http://www.unizh.ch/irg.

Zurich Central Library (serves as university library): http://www.zb.unizch.ch.

PUBLISHED SOURCES

Arbenz, Emil, Hermann Wartmann, and Joachim Vadianus, eds. *Die Vadianische Brief-sammlung der Stadtbibliothek St. Gallen.* 7 vols. St. Gallen: Huber, 1890–1913.

Bächtold, Hans Ulrich. *Bullinger vor dem Rat: Zur Gestaltung und Verwaltung des Zurcher Staatswesens in den Jahren 1531 bis 1575.* Bern: Peter Lang, 1982.

Backus, Irena. *Reformation Readings of the Apocalypse: Geneva, Zurich, and Wittenberg.* Oxford: Oxford University Press, 2000.

Baker, J. Wayne. *Heinrich Bullinger and the Covenant: The Other Reformed Tradition.* Athens: Ohio University Press, 1980.

Baschera, Luca, and Christian Moser. *Girolamo Zanchi: De religione Christiana fides—Confession of Christian Religion.* Leiden: Brill, 2007.

Benedict, Philip. *Christ's Churches Purely Reformed. A Social History of Calvinism.* New Haven, CT: Yale University Press, 2002.

Biel, Pamela. *Doorkeepers at the House of Righteousness: Henrich Bullinger and the Zürich Clergy.* Bern: Peter Lang, 1991.

Blaur, Ambrosius, and Thomas Blaur. *Briefwechsel der Brüder Ambrosius und Thomas Blaur.* 3 vols. Freiburg: F. E. Fehnsfeld, 1908–12.

Blickle, Peter. *Communal Reformation: The Quest for Salvation in Sixteenth-Century Germany.* Translated by Thomas Dunlap. Leiden: Brill, 1992.

———, ed. *Macht und Ohnmacht der Bilder: Reformatorischer Bildersturm im Kontext der europäischen Geschichte.* Munich: Oldenbourg, 2002.

Bolliger, Daniel. *Infiniti Contemplatio: Grundzüge der Scotus- und Scotismusrezeption im Werk Huldrych Zwinglis.* Leiden: Brill, 2003.

Brady, Thomas, Jr. *Protestant Politics: Jacob Sturm (1489–1553) and the German Reformation.* Atlantic Highlands, NJ: Humanities Press, 1995.

———. *Turning Swiss: Cities and Empire, 1450–1550.* Cambridge: Cambridge University Press, 1985.

Bruening, Michael. *Calvinism's First Battleground: Conflict and Reform in the Pays De Vaud.* Dordrecht: Springer, 2005.

Bullinger, Heinrich. *Dekaden (1552).* Edited by Peter Opitz. 2 vols. Zurich: Theologischer Verlag, 2008.

———. *Schriften.* Edited by Emidio Campi, Detlef Roth, and Peter Stotz. 6 vols. Zurich: Theologischer Verlag, 2004–.

Burnett, Amy Nelson. "Controlling the Clergy: The Oversight of Basel's Rural Pastors in the Sixteenth Century." *Zwingliana* 25 (1998): 129–42.

———. "Preparing the Pastors: Theological Education and Pastoral Training in Basel." In *History Has Many Voices*, edited by Lee Palmer Wandel, 131–51. Kirksville, MO: Truman State University Press, 2003.

————. "A Tale of Three Churches: Parishes and Pastors in Basel, Strasbourg, and Geneva." In *Calvin and the Company of Pastors*, edited by David L. Foxgrover, 95–124. Grand Rapids, MI: Published for the Calvin Studies Society by CRC Product Services, 2004.

————. *Teaching the Reformation: Ministers and Their Message in Basel, 1529–1629*. Oxford: Oxford University Press, 2006.

Büsser, Fritz. *Heinrich Bullinger, Leben, Werk und Wirkung*, vol. 1. Zürich: TVZ, Theologischer Verlag, 2004.

Campi, Emidio, ed. *Peter Martyr Vermigli: Humanism, Republicanism, Reformation*. Geneva: Droz, 2002.

Campi, Emidio, and Peter Opitz, eds. *Heinrich Bullinger: Life-Thought-Influence; International Congress on Heinrich Bullinger (1504–1575), Zurich, August 25–29, 2004*. Zurich: Theologischer Verlag, 2007.

Campiche, Michel. *La Réforme en Pays de Vaud*. Lausanne: L'Aire, 1985.

Christ-von Wedel, Christine, ed. *Theodor Bibliander: Ein Thurgauer im gelehrten Zürich der Reformationszeit*. Zurich: Verlag Neue Zürcher Zeitung, 2005.

Dändliker, Karl. *Geschichte der Stadt und des Kantons Zürich*. 2 vols. Zurich: Schulthess, 1908–11.

Dellsperger, Rudolf, Rudolf Freudenberger, and Wolfgang Weber, eds. *Wolfgang Musculus (1497–1563) und die oberdeutsche Reformation*. Berlin: Akademie Verlag, 1997.

Detmers, Achim. *Reformation und Judentum: Israel-Lehren und Einstellungen zum Judentum von Luther bis zum frühen Calvin*. Stuttgart: Kohlhammer, 2001.

Ehrstine, Glenn. "Of Peasants, Women, and Bears: Political Agency and the Demise of Carnival Tradition in Bernese Reformation Drama." *Sixteenth Century Journal* 30 (2000): 675–97.

————. *Theater, Culture, and Community in Reformation Bern, 1523–1555*. Leiden: Brill, 2002.

Euler, Carrie. *Couriers of the Gospel: England and Zurich, 1531–1558*. Zurich: TVZ Theologischer Verlag Zürich, 2006.

Farner, Oskar. *Ulrich Zwingli*. 3 vols. Zurich: Zwingli-Verlag, 1943–1960.

Faulenbach, Heiner, et al., eds. *Reformierte Bekenntnisschriften*, 3 vols. Neukirchener-Vluyn: Neukirchener, 2002, 2006, 2007.

Feller, Richard. *Geschichte Berns*. 3 vols. Berne: H. Lang, 1944–60.

Ford, James. "Wolfgang Musculus and the Struggle for Confessional Hegemony in Reformation Augsburg, 1531–1548." PhD diss., University of Wisconsin–Madison, 2000.

Fritzsche, Bruno W., Thomas Weibel, and Ulrich Ruoff. *Geschichte des Kantons Zürich*. 3 vols. Zurich: Werd Verlag, 1994–.

Gäbler, Ulrich. *Ulrich Zwingli: His Life and Work*. Translated by Ruth C. L. Gritsch. Philadelpia: Fortress Press, 1986.

Gaier, Ulrich. *Vadian und die Literatur des 16: Jahrhunderts*. In *St. Gallen: Geschichte einer literarischen Kultur*, edited by Werner Wunderlich, 1:265–97. St. Gallen: UVK, Fachverlag für Wissenschaft und Studium, 1999.

Gilliard, Charles. *La conquête du Pays de Vaud par les Bernois*. Lausanne: Éditions de la Concorde, 1985.

Gilly, Carlos. *Spanien und der Basler Buchdruck bis 1600*. Basel: Heilbing & Lichtenhahn, 1985.

Goertz, Hans Jürgen. *The Anabaptists*. London: Routledge, 1996.

Gordon, Bruce. *Clerical Discipline and the Rural Reformation: The Synod in Zurich 1532–1580*. Bern: Peter Lang, 1992.

————. *The Swiss Reformation*. Manchester, UK: Manchester University Press, 2002.

———. "The Swiss Reformation." In *Palgrave Advances in the European Reformations*, edited by Alec Ryrie, 57–79. Basingstoke: Palgrave Macmillan, 2005.

———. "Transcendence and Community in Zwinglian Worship: the Liturgy of 1525 in Zurich." In *Continuity and Change in Christian Worship: Papers Read at the 1997 Summer Meeting and the 1998 Winter Meeting of the Ecclesiastical History Society*, edited by R. N. Swanson, 96–128. Woodbridge, Suffolk, UK: Published for the Ecclesiastical History Society by Boydell Press, 1999.

Gordon, Bruce, and Emidio Campi, eds. *Heinrich Bullinger: Architect of Reformation*. Grand Rapids, MI: Baker Academic, 2004.

Grandjean, Marcel. *Les temples vaudois: L'architecture réformée dans le Pays de Vaud (1536–1798)*. Lausanne: Bibliothèque historique vaudoise, 1988.

Greyerz, Kaspar von, ed. *Platteriana: Beiträge zum 500: Geburtstag des Thomas Platter (1499?–1582)*. Basel: Schwabe, 2002.

Guggisberg, Hans. *Basel in the Sixteenth Century: Aspects of the City Republic before, during, and after the Reformation*. St. Louis, MO: Center for Reformation Research, 1982.

———. *Sebastian Castellio: Defender of Religious Freedom*. Aldershot: Ashgate, 2002.

Haas, Martin. *Ulrich Zwingli und seine Zeit: Leben und Werk des Zürcher Reformators*. Zurich: Zwingli-Verlag, 1969.

Hamm, Berndt. "Laientheologie zwischen Luther und Zwingli." In *Kontinuität und Umbruch. Theologie und Frömmigkeit in Flugschriften und Kleinliteratur an der Wende vom 15. zum 16. Jahrhundert*, edited by Josef Nolte, Hella Tompert, and Christof Windhorst, 222–95. Stuttgart: Klett-Cotta, 1978.

———. *Zwinglis Reformation der Freiheit*. Neukirchen-Vluyn: Neukirchener Verlag, 1988.

Hartmann, Alfred, and Beat Rudolf Jenny, eds. *Die Amerbachkorrespondenz: Im Auftrag der Kommission für die Öffentliche Bibliothek der Universität Basel*. Basel: Verlag der Universitätsbibliothek, 1942–.

Head, Randolph C. *Early Modern Democracy in the Grisons: Social Order and Political Language in a Swiss Mountain Canton, 1470–1620*. Cambridge: Cambridge University Press, 1995.

———. "Nit alss zwo Gemeinden, oder Partheyn, sonder ein Gemeind": Kommunalismus zwischen den Konfessionen in Graubünden, 1530–1620." In *Landgemeinde und Konfessionen im Zeitalter der Konfessionen*, edited by Beat Kümin and Peter Blickle, 21–57. Zurich: Chronos, 2004.

———. "Rhaetian Ministers, from Shepherds to Citizens: Calvinism and Democracy in the Republic of the Three Leagues, 1550–1620." In *Later Calvinism: International Perspectives*, edited by W. Fred Graham, 55–69. Sixteenth Century Essays and Studies 22. Kirksville, MO: Sixteenth Century Journal Publishers, 1994.

———. "Shared Lordship, Authority, and Administration: The Exercise of Dominion in the Gemeine Herrschaften of the Swiss Confederation, 1417–1600." *Central European History* 30 (1997): 489–512.

Himmighöfer, Traudel. *Die Zürcher Bibel bis zum Tode Zwinglis (1531): Darstellung und Bibliographie*. Mainz: P. von Zabern, 1995.

Hofer, Roland E. *Ueppiges, unzüchtiges Lebwesen: Schaffhauser Ehegerichtsbarkeit von der Reformation bis zum Ende des Ancien Régime (1529–1798)*. Bern: Peter Lang, 1993.

Holenstein, André, Claudie Engler, and Charlotte Gutscher-Schmid. *Berns mächtige Zeit: Das 16. und 17. Jahrhundert neu entdeckt*. Bern: Schulverlag, 2006.

James, Frank. *Peter Martyr Vermigli and Predestination: The Augustinian Influence of an Italian Reformer*. Oxford: Clarendon Press, 1998.

Junod, Eric, ed. *La Dispute de Lausanne (1536): La théologie réformée après Zwingli et avant Calvin.* Lausanne: Bibliothèque historique vaudoise, 1988.

Kirby, Torrance. *The Zurich Connection and Tudor Political Theology.* Leiden: Brill, 2007.

Kuhr, Olaf. "Calvin and Basel: The Significance of Oecolampadius and the Basel Discipline Ordinance for the Institution of Ecclesiastical Discipline in Geneva." *Scottish Bulletin of Evangelical Theology* 16 (1998): 19–33.

———. *"Die Macht des Bannes und der Busse": Kirchenzucht und Erneuerung der Kirche bei Johannes Oekolampad (1482–1531).* Bern: Peter Lang, 1999.

Locher, Gottfried W. *Die zwinglische Reformation in Rahmen der europäischen Kirchengeschichte.* Göttingen: Vandenhoeck & Ruprecht, 1979.

———. *Huldrych Zwingli: New Perspectives.* Leiden: Brill, 1981.

Loetz, Francisca. *Mit Gott handeln: Von den Zürcher Gotteslästerern der Frühen Neuzeit zu einer Kulturgeschichte des Religiösen.* Göttingen: Vandenhoeck & Ruprecht, 2002.

Maarbjerg, John P. "Iconoclasm in the Thurgau: Two Related Incidents in the Summer of 1524." *Sixteenth Century Journal* 24 (1993): 577–93.

Marcus, Kenneth H. "Hymnody and Hymnals in Basel, 1526–1606." *Sixteenth-Century Journal* 32 (2001): 723–41.

Mauelshagen, Franz. *Johann Jakob Wicks Wunderbücher: Reformierter Wunderglaube im Wandel der Geschichtsschreibung.* Zurich: Chronos-Verlag, 2006.

Meyer, Werner, and Kaspar von Greyerz. *Platteriana: Beiträge 500. Geburtstag des Thomas Platter (1499?–1582).* Basel: Schwabe, 2002.

Mühling, Andreas. *Heinrich Bullingers europäische Kirchenpolitik.* Bern: Peter Lang, 2001.

Näf, Werner. *Vadian und Seine Stadt St. Gallen.* 2 vols. St. Gall: Fehr'sche Buchhandlung, 1944–57.

Oberman, Heinz. *Reformiertes Erbe: Festschrift für Gottfried W. Locher zur seinem 80. Geburtstag.* Zurich: Theologischer Verlag, 1992–99.

Oecolampadius, Johannes. *Briefe und Akten zum Leben Oekolampads.* Edited by Ernst Staehelin. 2 vols. Leipzig: M. Heinsius Nachfolger, Eger & Sievers, 1927, 1934.

Opitz, Peter. *Heinrich Bullinger als Theologe. Eine Studie zu den "Dekaden."* Zurich: Theologischer Verlag Zürich, 2004.

———, ed. *Calvin im Kontext der Schweizer Reformation.* Zurich: Theologischer Verlag Zürich, 2003.

Packull, Werner. "The Origins of Swiss Anabaptism in the Context of the Reformation of the Common Man." *Journal of Mennonite Studies* 3 (1985): 35–59.

Pestalozzi, Carl. *Heinrich Bullinger: Leben und ausgewählte schriften. Nach handschriftlichen und gleichzeitigen quellen.* Elberfeld: R. L. Friderichs, 1858.

Pfister, Rudolf. *Kirchengeschichte der Schweiz.* 2 vols. Zurich: Theologischer Verlag, 1974.

Pfrunder, Peter. *Pfaffen Ketzer Totenfresser: Fastnachtkultur der Reformationszeit—Die Berner Spiele von Niklaus Manuel.* Zurich: Chronos-Verlag, 1989.

Potter, G. R. *Zwingli.* Cambridge: Cambridge University Press, 1976.

Rorem, Paul. *Calvin and Bullinger on the Lord's Supper.* Bramcote, Nottingham: Grove Books 1989.

Sallmann, Martin. *Zwischen Gott und Mensch: Huldrych Zwinglis theologischer Denkweg im De vera et falsa religione commentarius (1525).* Tübingen: Mohr Siebeck, 1999.

Schindler, Alfred, Hans Stickelberger, and Martin Sallmann, eds. *Die Zürcher Reformation: Ausstrahlungen und Rückwirkungen: Wissenschaftliche Tagung zum hundertjährigen Bestehen des Zwinglivereins.* Bern: Peter Lang, 2001.

Schmidt, Heinrich Richard. *Dorf und Religion: Reformierte Sittenzucht in Berner Landgemeinden der Frühen Neuzeit.* Stuttgart: G. Fischer, 1995.

———. "Morals Courts in Rural Berne during the Modern Period." In *The Reformation in Eastern and Central Europe*, edited by Karin Maag, 55–81. Aldershot, UK: Scolar Press, 1997.

———. *Reichsstädte, Reich und Reformation: Korporative Religionspolitik 1521–1529/30.* Stuttgart: F. Steiner Verlag Wiesbaden, 1986.

Snyder, C. Arnold. *Anabaptist History and Theology: An Introduction.* Kitchener, ON: Pandora Press, 1995.

———. "Communication and the People: The Case of the Reformation in St. Gall." *Mennonite Quarterly Review* 67 (1993): 152–72.

———, ed. *Biblical Concordance of the Swiss Brethren, 1540.* Kitchener, ON: Pandora Press, 2001.

Staehelin, Ernst. *Briefe und Akten zum Leben Oekolampads: Zum vierhundertjährigen Jubiläum der Basler Reformation.* 2 vols. Quellen und Forschungen zur Reformationsgeschichte 10, 19. Leipzig: M. Heinsius Nachfolger, Eger & Sievers, 1927, 1934.

———. *Das Theologische Lebenswerk Johannes Oekolampads.* Leipzig: M. Heinsius nachfolger, 1939.

———. *Oekolampad-Bibliographie: Verzeichnis der im 16. Jahrhundert erschienenen Oekolampaddrucke.* Basel, 1918. Reprint, Nieuwkoop: B. De Graaf, 1963.

Stayer, James M. *The German Peasants' War and Anabaptist Community of Goods.* Montreal: McGill-Queen's University Press, 1991.

Stephens, Peter. *The Theology of Huldrych Zwingli.* Cambridge: Cambridge University Press, 1986.

Strübind, Andrea. *Eifriger als Zwingli: Die frühe Täuferbewegung in der Schweiz.* Berlin: Duncker & Humblot, 2003.

Taplin, Mark. *The Italian Reformers and the Zurich Church c. 1540–1620.* Aldershot: Ashgate, 2003.

———. "Switzerland." In *The Reformation World*, edited by Andrew Pettegree, 169–89. New York: Routledge, 2000.

Venema, Cornelius. *Heinrich Bullinger and the Doctrine of Predestination.* Grand Rapids, MI: Baker Academic, 2002.

Vischer, Manfred. *Zürcher Einblattdrucke des 16. Jahrhunderts.* Baden-Baden: V. Koerner, 2001.

Vuilleumier, Henri. *Histoire de l'Eglise Réformée du Pays de Vaud sous le Régime Bernois.* 4 vols. Lausanne: Éditions de la Concorde, 1927–33.

Wackernagel, Rudolf. *Geschichte der Stadt Basel.* 2 vols. Basel: Heilbing and Lichtenhahn 1916.

Wandel, Lee Palmer. *Always Among Us: Images of the Poor in Zwingli's Zurich.* Cambridge: Cambridge University Press, 1990.

———. *Voracious Idols and Violent Hands.* New Haven, CT: Yale University Press, 1995.

Wyss, Karl-Heinz. *Leo Jud: Seine Entwicklung zum Reformator, 1519–1523.* Bern: Herbert Lang, 1976.

Zürcher, Christoph. *Konrad Pelikans Wirken in Zürich, 1526–1556.* Zurich: Theologischer Verlag, 1975.

Zwingli, Huldrych. *Schriften.* Edited by Thomas Braunschweiler and Samuel Lutz. 4 vols. Zurich: Theologischer Verlag, 1995.

Reformation and Early Modern Europe

a guide to research

PART 3
Social and Cultural Trends

14

Popular Religion

Kathryn A. Edwards

In the last twenty years, studies in popular religion have exploded, a situation that is somewhat ironic given debates about the term that defines the field.[1] Scholars have challenged the term *popular* as suggesting ignorant or inferior beliefs and practices, reinforcing belief in a false dichotomy between it and the equally ill-defined term *elite* and implying a common European piety at a time characterized by confessionalism.[2] While less contentious, the term *religion* has also drawn fire. Is the *religious* a belief, a practice, or a meld of the two? Does religion require an institution, or can it be expressed privately and independently?

In order to avoid such debates and clarify the parameters of their research, some authors have proposed terms like *common* or *traditional* to replace the much-maligned *popular*, substitutions that have their value but fail to address the fundamental ambiguity of the field.[3] Increasingly, scholars analyzing popular religion note the term's varied definitions and the disciplinary debates, provide a working definition that falls within the field's commonly accepted boundaries, and move on to analyzing and, to some degree, reveling in the very flexibility of the subject itself. That method will be followed in this chapter. Here, *popular religion* will have several defining characteristics: the spiritual beliefs and pious practices

---

[1]Because of the complexity in defining popular religion, many books discuss several of the themes mentioned in this article. To minimize the volume of citations, I have chosen the most appropriate location for each work and cited it only once.
[2]Burke, *Popular Culture in Early Modern Europe*.
[3]Duffy, *Stripping of the Altars*.

that a large section of a region's population support; a cosmology shared between individuals of diverse classes, genders, professions, and educational levels; and dissenting religious movements that draw on these commonalities but reformulate them in a way to appeal to the social, economic, or cultural groups comprising their movement. As this rather complex definition suggests, in some cases, popular religion may be best characterized by what it is not: religious practice and doctrine as institutional theologians primarily define them.

Although studies on popular religion include many diverse religious experiences, scholars working in this field make implicit assumptions that help to unify the discipline. Fundamental is early modern Europeans' acceptance of immanence.[4] While some theologians in later medieval Europe stressed the unknowability of God, common practices, such as blessing a farmer's field, were based on the conviction that God was directly active in this world and accessible to those using the right tools and having the right mental and spiritual state. If he could not be known, he could at least be manipulated. The holistic view of the universe implicit in these activities underlies much of later medieval popular piety and spirituality and would continue until well into the seventeenth century. Challenges to, and revisions of, this relationship were implicit in both Catholic and Protestant reform movements and are the subject of much modern scholarship on popular religion.

The place of popular religion in analyses of confessional distinctions and disputes between reformers and the general population have influenced the way in which scholars tend to present studies of popular religion. The subject of popular religion grew out of studies in the late 1970s and early 1980s on popular culture and ritual more generally; as such, it was the subject of only a chapter or two in a monograph.[5] These treatments made it clear that detailed regional studies were necessary, and much work to this day continues in this vein, concentrating on particular manifestations of popular piety (processions, pilgrimages, plays), the religious experience of distinct groups (women, villagers, dissenters), or the early modern reinterpretation of certain fundamental aspects of later medieval religion (purgatory, images, sermons) in regions throughout early modern Europe. As such, while there are many books devoted to topics in popular religion, much excellent research remains as journal articles

[4]Harline, *Miracles at the Jesus Oak.*
[5]Scribner, "Elements of Popular Belief"; and Scribner and Johnson, *Popular Religion in Germany.*

or book chapters.[6] These studies continue to emphasize the local nature of much popular religious expression and the need for thorough contextualization in its analyses—a situation that has made scholars wary of proposing big syntheses.[7]

The lack of a synthesis is not the only challenge faced by those who work in this field. Popular religion is by definition an interdisciplinary topic combining skills and involving scholars from anthropology, folklore, history, literary studies, religious studies, psychology, and sociology.[8] The diverse approaches of these disciplines enrich the field while simultaneously contributing to its fragmentation. Problems in terminology also plague research in this area. While most scholars of this subject have made their peace with the concept of popular religion, finding an appropriate vocabulary to express its intellectual and social exchanges continues to vex them. By stressing their hermeneutics, the binaries that once guided an understanding of popular religious experience (such as popular/elite and center/periphery) have been undermined, but the negotiated and polyvalent relationships that have replaced them—although more accurate—are even more difficult to synthesize. Disciplinary paradigms, such as confessionalization and social discipline, have driven much research in early modern popular religion (whether they should is another topic), and in many cases they have determined the questions asked about it.[9]

Despite these difficulties in classification, the rest of this chapter is organized according to five key approaches to early modern social and cultural history that have guided the treatment of popular religious history during the last twenty years: ritual practice; religion and community; death, the dead, and demons; reforming popular religion; and violence and toleration. As these categories make clear, many topics in popular religion incorporate related themes and rely on similar sources.

Ritual Practice

Some of the first work done in the later 1970s and 1980s on early modern popular religion focused on ritual practices, complementing a series of

---

[6]For example, Benedict and Reinburg, *Renaissance and Reformation France*; and Comerford and Pabel, *Early Modern Catholicism*. Aside from the standard journals on early modern history, the following are geared more specifically to popular religion: *Ethnohistory, Folklore, The Journal of Popular Culture, The Journal of Religion and Popular Culture*, and *Magic, Ritual, and Witchcraft*.

[7]Monter, *Ritual, Myth and Magic*.

[8]See Plongeron and Lerou, *La Piété populaire*.

[9]Hsia, *Social Discipline*; and von Greyerz, *Interkonfessionalität*.

books and articles about popular ritual and culture more generally.[10] Innovative research along these lines continues.[11] Underscoring the importance of understanding the social context of popular religious ritual, these scholars emphasize social and environmental distinctions, such as the effects of an urban or a rural setting, the influence of local or regional politics, and the interactions between artisans and burghers, in their treatment of discrete events. Discussions of appropriation and social classification frequently dominate such work. The wide possibilities for the interpretation of festivals and drama have made them particular favorites for this type of analysis. Religious processions, such as Corpus Christi celebrations or annual devotions in honor of a town's patron saint, have multiple interpretive levels that in some cases enhance orthodoxy and in others subvert it.[12] Work on religious festivals has also complemented the "history of daily life" (*Alltagsgeschichte*) through its stress on the distinctive social dynamics of individual celebrations, even if they are annual or "common" occurrences. Disputations over and changes to later medieval religious festivals point to the effects of religious reform during the sixteenth and seventeenth century on community identities and ideologies. For scholars, the ways in which communities ignore or revise religious festivals and processions illustrate the various personal and local interests affecting larger reform programs.

Fundamental to understanding changes in popular religious ritual has been research on revisions to the ritual year in Protestant Europe. Such work has stressed an obvious, but all too frequently ignored, point: time in pre-Reformation Europe was organized according to agricultural and ecclesiastical calendars. With religious reform should have come calendrical reform and thus a basic revising of the appropriate structure of time and of the relationship between those who exist in time (everything in this world, especially humans) and that which exists beyond time (God). Like the scholarship on religious festivals and processions to which it is so closely linked, research on calendrical change has stressed its gradual nature in the centuries after the Reformation.[13] Even areas that readily adopted the Gregorian calendar made few alterations to a day's significance; certain saints

---

[10]Baroja, *Las formas complejas*; and Klaniczay, *Uses of Supernatural Power.*

[11]Karant-Nunn, *Reformation of Ritual*; Lutton, *Pieties in Transition*; Parish and Naphy, *Religion and Superstition*; Plongeron, *La Piété*; Reay, *Popular Cultures in England*; van Deursen, *Plain Lives in a Golden Age*; and von Greyerz, *Religion and Culture in Early Modern Europe.*

[12]Marsh, *Popular Religion in Sixteenth-Century England*; and Rubin, *Corpus Christi.*

[13]Cressy, *Bonfires and Bells*; and Swanson, *Use and Abuse of Time.*

were still venerated on certain days, and processions and sermons continued to mark key points in the year. An examination of England, in particular, has emphasized that the annual religious calendar was the product of centuries of negotiation and was being revised right up to the beginning of the Protestant Reformation. Like the Reformation itself, calendrical change ebbed and flowed during the sixteenth century, and the calendar would never lose aspects of its pre-Reformation form, despite challenges by ecclesiastical hierarchies.[14]

The ecclesiastical calendar also affected the ritual aspects of the mass itself. Rather than focus on the Reformation's theological debates, scholars of popular religion have examined to what degree populations accepted changes in religious services and what effect these changes had on popular religiosity.[15] Moving beyond general statements about how the Reformation fragmented a "unitary" Christendom, these studies concentrate on the local appreciation of a ritual with an ostensibly universal message. For example, when an altar is changed to a simple table and the elaborate cloths, chalices, and other objects of a medieval mass are removed, many questions are left for the community so affected: Who decided that the change would occur? Who approved of the change? What happens to the objects that were once used as part of the mass? Is this new mass spiritually valid?[16] The answers to these questions and many others that could be posed stress the role of negotiation and perception in the reformation of religious ritual. Some research has carried these ideas further and examined religious ritual as a sensory experience. Arguing that later medieval religious ritual relied on the full application of all five senses, this work examines the sensory and, by implication, psychological effects of renovating churches and other sites of religious ritual during the sixteenth and seventeenth centuries.[17]

The most basic yet most complex changes to religious ritual occurred in the sacraments and sacramentals. By moving from seven to two sacraments, Protestant churches fundamentally altered the salvific system of later medieval Europe and threw into doubt the means by which individuals could be saved.[18] As might be expected, the response to such alterations

---

[14]Hutton, *Rise and Fall*; and Hutton, *Stations of the Sun*.
[15]Ditchfield, *Liturgy, Sanctity, and History*; and Duffy, *Stripping the Altars*.
[16]Duffy, *Voices of Morebath*.
[17]Scribner, *Religion and Culture in Germany*; and Wandel, *Eucharist in the Reformation*.
[18]Cressy, *Birth, Marriage, and Death*; Cressy, *Agnes Bowker's Cat*; Karant-Nunn, *Reformation of Ritual*; and Rubin, *Corpus Christi*.

was mixed. Scholars have repeatedly shown where communities resisted new impositions, with or without the help of the local clergy, and sometimes in the process created their own variants of common religious rituals. Such challenges were not confined to newly Protestant territories. Catholic reform movements condemned some aspects of popular sacramental piety while elevating others, such as the necessary place of the clergy as intercessors.[19] Particularly questioned was the role of sacramentals. Central to both later medieval and early modern popular religion, sacramentals were paraliturgical rites—means by which the laity as well as the clergy could access the sacred and the powerful. Sacramentals involved rituals such as blessing the crops and exorcism and were often used for power and security at rites of passage, such as birth and marriage.[20] Challenges to traditional sacramentals were challenges to valuable tools. As much recent scholarship has shown, communities frequently ignored ecclesiastical or secular directives about them and revised the old rite to accommodate a new sensibility, as happened when Bibles replaced the Eucharist as part of the annual blessing of the fields.

Religion and Community

John Bossy's *Christianity in the West* proposed another, but related, paradigm that has been fundamental to the analysis of popular religion.[21] Arguing that the Protestant Reformation redefined the medieval concepts of community, Bossy's work has led scholars to examine more closely the ways that popular religion depends on its communal setting and the interaction between religious rites and concepts of community. As such, these scholars are indebted to the concepts of appropriation and polyvalence described in the preceding section but use them to consider more sociological questions.

Beginning with studies of particular communal settings—villages, towns, larger cities—researchers since Bossy have explored the relationship between concepts of community and forms of popular religion. Continuity and change are the two poles by which both piety and community are often measured, and they tend to vary between urban and rural areas.[22] Perhaps not surprisingly, scholars of Catholic towns in southern Europe

---

[19]Delumeau, *Sin and Fear.*
[20]Cressy, *Birth, Marriage, and Death.*
[21]Bossy, *Christianity in the West*; and Ditchfield, *Christianity and Community.*
[22]Lake, *Boxmaker's Revenge.*

have tended to stress continuity, while those of Protestant towns in northern Europe have leaned towards change, but even this broad, denominational pattern has been challenged.[23] Work on confraternities has proven an especially useful way of combining studies of common religious beliefs and practices with analyses of community construction and perception.[24] With diverse social and spiritual functions, confraternities were an influential expression of fifteenth- and sixteenth-century popular, urban piety, and the Protestant rejection of the traditional cult of the saints undermined one of their reasons for existence. Redirection of traditional confraternal activities, such as charitable giving, in Protestant towns suggests reconstruction of community bonds and ideologies, while changing attitudes and activities among confraternities in Catholic territories calls into question the extent to which religious ideology drove aspects of early modern society and popular religious expression.[25]

Scholars working on rural communities have tended to stress continuity in popular religious beliefs and practices, while resisting a traditional dichotomy that links peasants with conservativism. Noting that it took generations for some regions to see enduring effects from Protestant reform, they also highlight "revolutionary" outbursts such as the German Peasants' Revolt, which clearly linked Reformed doctrines to concepts such as the "common man" and a sense of communal responsibility.[26] Aside from such dramatic events, most scholarship on rural communities has concentrated on durable aspects of traditional religion, although they are sometimes given an ostensibly Protestant twist. In Catholic regions, this research has assessed the extent and success of reforming missions in rural communities and the enduring manifestations of popular piety, such as local cults.[27]

In the history of later medieval Europe, pilgrimage has been seen as one means to bridge communities and create a broader sense of a Christian community. Relying as it did on the belief in an intercessory system and the efficacy of good works, two ideas anathema to Protestant reform,

---

[23]Marshall, *Religious Identities*.

[24]Black, *Italian Confraternities*; Black and Gravestock, *Early Modern Confraternities*; Donnelly and Maher, *Confraternities and Catholic Reform*; Lazar, *Working in the Vineyard*; and Terpstra, *Lay Confraternities*.

[25]D'Andrea, *Civic Charity*; and Schen, *Charity and Lay Piety*.

[26]Parish, *Monks, Miracles, and Magic*.

[27]Châtellier, *Religion of the Poor*; Dixon, *Reformation and Rural Society*; Forster, *Catholic Revival*; Fragnito, *Church, Censorship, and Culture*; and Nalle, *God in La Mancha*.

the study of its endurance, revision, or elimination during the sixteenth and seventeenth century has been used as a means of gauging the success of various reforming ideals.[28] While odysseys to Canterbury, Compostela, or Rome became the most dramatic later medieval pilgrimages, local shrines were the most frequent pilgrimage sites—an observation that has challenged the extent to which pilgrimage ever built a broad sense of Christian community. Sixteenth-century pilgrims shared the medieval emphasis on local saints, and some Protestant communities were quite reluctant to relinquish their shrines. One area that cannot be disputed, however, is that pilgrimage visibly linked key components in popular religious belief: the veneration of saints and the quest for supernatural, magical power.[29]

Veneration of saints was a fundamental part of the later medieval economy of salvation and would continue as such in Catholic regions during the sixteenth and seventeenth centuries.[30] Recent research has stressed how sanctity and the intercessory system of which saints were a part simultaneously challenged and reinforced social hierarchies and gender perceptions. Saints had such a powerful hold on the popular religious imagination that Reformers were forced to accept, and sometimes themselves embraced, constructions of Protestant martyrdom that placed Protestant martyrs in roles quite similar to those of later medieval saints.[31] Aspects of sanctity and, in some cases, Protestant martyrdom that continued to have an enormous appeal were the miracles associated with saints and martyrs. Scholarship has repeatedly shown that although Catholics and Protestants disagreed even among themselves on the sources and significance of these miracles, none could doubt their popularity. As heroes surrounded by the miraculous, or even as miracle workers, saints and martyrs both affirmed the validity of their faith and motivated others to stiffen their spiritual resolve.

In the later Middle Ages, the Virgin Mary was the ultimate saint, and in the fifteenth century veneration of the Holy Family reached new heights in popular religious expression.[32] With the reform movements of

[28]van Herwaarden, *Between Saint James and Erasmus*.

[29]Bynum, *Wonderful Blood*; and van Herwaarden, *Between St. James and Erasmus*.

[30]Christian, *Local Religion*; Sluhovsky, *Patroness of Paris*; and Vauchez, *Sainthood in the Later Middle Ages*.

[31]Covington, *Trail of Martyrdom*; Freeman and Mayer, *Martyrs and Martyrdom*; and Gregory, *Salvation at Stake*.

[32]Nixon, *Mary's Mother*.

the sixteenth and seventeenth centuries, the ontological status of the Virgin and the Holy Family changed, but each remained important examples of the religious roles and status of mothers and families.[33] The Virgin continued to have a central position in reformed Catholicism, with certain devotions (such as that of the rosary) apparently increasing, and veneration of the Virgin endured in Protestant territories longer than many Reformers would have preferred.[34] Eliminating, or even redefining, the Virgin in towns and villages whose primary church was named after Our Lady and may have been shared by Protestants and Catholics alike required a fundamental revision of the senses of hierarchy, spirituality, and gender.

Studies of the Virgin closely complement extremely productive research done on women, the feminine, and popular religion.[35] Scholars have analyzed manifestations of piety to which women were especially devoted, as well as ways in which women supported reform programs morally and financially in the sixteenth and seventeenth centuries.[36] Work on both Protestant and Catholic territories has been inspired by earlier research, which suggested that Protestantism led to a regression in women's spiritual and social status by minimizing the opportunities available to devout women. This interpretation has been strongly challenged, and a new generation of scholars has focused on ways that Catholic and Protestant reform provided opportunities for female religious expression. Among Catholics, for example, communities of religious women, such as the Daughters of Charity and the Ursulines, both accepted and challenged Counter-Reformation perceptions of female spirituality and roles.[37]

Striking among the studies of sixteenth- and seventeenth-century Catholicism have been the links between female mysticism, official Catholicism, and popular ideas of appropriate religion. The fourteenth and fifteenth centuries saw a flowering of female mysticism, and a "feminization of religious language," to use Carolyn Walker Bynum's famous phrase, was a defining characteristic of later medieval spirituality. Recent scholars have

---

[33]Ellington, *From Sacred Body to Angelic Soul*.

[34]Heal, *Cult of the Virgin Mary*; and Kreitzer, *Reforming Mary*.

[35]Bornstein and Rusconi, *Women and Religion in Italy*; and Crawford, *Women and Religion in England*.

[36]Charlton, *Women, Religion, and Education*; Harris, *Popular Culture in England*; and Luz-Sterrit, *Redefining Female Religious Life*.

[37]Conelli, "Typical Patron of Extraordinary Means"; Diefendorf, *From Penitence to Charity*; Dinan, *Women and Poor Relief*; Harline, *Burdens of Sister Margaret*; and Rapley, *The Dévotes*.

stressed the continued power of female mystics in Catholic territories during the sixteenth and seventeenth centuries but have simultaneously
emphasized the very careful path these mystics had to follow.[38] While mysticism and the feminine could lead to union with the divine, both Protestants and Catholics alike feared that mystical experiences could actually be
demonic manifestations.[39] Although both men and women could be and
were mystics, the mystics' femaleness heightened the tension between the
demonic and the divine for both herself and her community.

Death, The Dead, and Demons

The community of the later Middle Ages that Bossy described and other
scholars have found so persuasive transcended worldly bonds. His depic-
tion of a community of the living and the dead transformed by the Reformation has inspired a generation of scholarship to focus on the social and
spiritual construction of death. Influenced by the work of Philippe Ariès
and Jacques Le Goff, scholars have integrated cosmological revisions and
the practices of death and mourning. The result is research that assesses
the common experience of death and the dead, while stressing the wide
variety of ideologies that supported these practices.[40]

The later medieval intercessory system depended on a postmortem
triad: heaven, hell, and purgatory. While some theologians argued that
these were states of the soul, popular belief—and many theological
works—portrayed them as real, substantial places. In this physical, corpo-
real hell and purgatory, humans would be subject to unimaginable, albeit
frequently and graphically described, suffering.[41] Although sixteenth-century Protestant Reformers rejected purgatory, recent scholarship has
stressed that it took generations for this rejection to be reflected in popular
beliefs and practices.[42] With death ubiquitous, the rituals of death and the
practice of the good death (*ars moriendi*) retained their significance for
both Protestant and Catholic alike.[43] Although Protestant Reformers challenged the significance of tomb placement (a later medieval preoccupation), scholars have shown that location continued to matter.[44] Irregular

---

[38]Haliczer, *Between Exaltation and Infamy*; and Werner and Tanz, *Spätmittelalterliche Laienmentalitäten.*

[39]Mack, *Visionary Women.*

[40]Ariès, *Hour of our Death*; and Le Goff, *Birth of Purgatory.*

[41]Camporesi, *Fear of Hell*; Strocchia, *Death and Ritual*; and Vovelle, *Les âmes du purgatoire.*

[42]Lualdi and Thayer, *Penitence in the Age of Reformations*; and Marshall, *Beliefs and the Dead.*

[43]Eire, *From Madrid to Purgatory*; and Walsham, *Providence in Early Modern England.*

[44]Lauwers, *Naissance du cimetière*; and Reinis, *Reforming the Art of Dying.*

death, such as suicide, remained suspect, although the theological reasons for this suspicion varied between confessions.[45]

Only recently has scholarship begun analyzing one of the more widespread and contentious ideas about the dead in late medieval and early modern Europe—namely, that they could and did return.[46] Whether these dead manifested as zombies, apparitions, poltergeists, or supernatural animals, belief in these entities transcended confessional boundaries. In later medieval Christianity, such beings had a clear role confirming the existence of purgatory, the need for intercession, and the bonds between the living and the dead. They also complemented ideas about portents and prophecy, as the dead assisted prophets or manifested prophetic characteristics.[47] They found buried treasure and revealed murderers. In the sixteenth and seventeenth centuries, belief in the returning dead was remarkably durable, even when the doctrinal justification for such beliefs no longer existed.[48]

Research into the returning dead is closely tied to the extensive work that has been done about the role of demons and the devil in late medieval and early modern Europe, because one of the most common beliefs about apparitions is that they were demonic manifestations. While much of this scholarship belongs to the debates about demonology and witchcraft—and, accordingly, will be treated in that chapter—belief in demonic activity was not purely a concomitant to witchcraft trials. Heiko Oberman has convincingly stressed the place of the devil in Luther's theology and daily life, and in this Luther was very much a person of his time.[49] Late medieval and early modern Europeans commonly supported a dualistic worldview where the devil assumed the characteristics of a second divinity and the demons were his corrupted angels.[50] Although such an interpretation was at least theologically dubious and at most heretical, its existence has been repeatedly demonstrated. For this reason, possession was a real fear as well

---

[45]Watt, *Choosing Death.*

[46]Christian, *Apparitions*; Edwards, *Werewolves, Witches, and Wandering Spirits*; Gordon and Marshall, *Place of the Dead*; and Lecouteux, *Witches, Werewolves, and Fairies.*

[47]Genuth, *Comets, Popular Culture, and the Birth of Modern Cosmology*; Kagan, *Lucrecia's Dreams*; and Nalle, *Mad for God.*

[48]Barber, *Vampires, Burial, and Death.*

[49]Oberman, *Luther*; and Matheson, *Imaginative World of the Reformation.*

[50]Johnstone, *Devil and Demonism*; Maggi, *In the Company of Demons*; Matheson, *Imaginative World of the Reformation*; Muchembled, *History of the Devil*; and Thomas, *Religion and the Decline of Magic.*

as a tool in confessional battles, and exorcism was a valuable rite contended over between laity and clergy.[51]

Reforming Popular Religion

As the previous sections have suggested, key topics in early studies of popular religion were the tools by which official ideology was indoctrinated
and the extent to which indoctrination succeeded. While the work of Gerald Strauss has been particularly influential and contentious in this area,
such research also stems from the debates over social discipline.[52] Over the
last thirty years, scholars have assessed the degree to which official doctrine was designed to reconstruct and discipline society according to a
confessional ideology. While such social discipline presumes a distinction
between official and unofficial, popular and elite, that most modern scholars of popular religion insist must be nuanced, the questions of communication and interpretation that led scholars to propose the theory of social
discipline still drive modern research in this field.

Visitation records were among the first documents examined by
scholars interested in studying the reception of the Catholic and Protestant
Reformations. When comparing these records to official statements of religious belief (confessions) and catechisms, some scholars felt compelled to
echo the despair of early Lutheran and Calvinist Reformers themselves
about the "failure" of Protestant reform in village populations. More recent
work has challenged this assessment by disputing its premise that
Reformed religion was innately what its theologians determined it to be.[53]
Key to this analysis is the example of later medieval and early modern
Catholicism, where popular beliefs and practices could revise, nuance, or
even negate official doctrine. As in the Catholic Church, two of the great
challenges facing later sixteenth- and seventeenth-century Protestantism
were the enforcement of doctrine and the degree to which popular belief
and piety would mediate official doctrine and practice.

Fascinating work has been done in the last several decades on the
communication of religious messages in early modern Europe, particularly
within Protestant confessions but also in Catholic communities. Robert W.
Scribner's *For the Sake of Simple Folk* pioneered this work among historians,

---

[51]Caciola, *Discerning Spirits*; and Levi, *Inheriting Power*.
[52]Strauss, *Luther's House of Learning*. For a recent challenge to Strauss's thesis, see Rittgers, *Reformation of the Keys*.
[53]Scribner, *Popular Culture and Popular Movements*.

describing how text(s), image, symbols, and setting worked together to communicate a wide variety of orthodox Lutheran ideas to a diverse audience.[54] Given the literacy levels of early modern Europeans, such research has developed sophisticated analyses of communication systems and borrowed heavily from literary and communication theory. By using cheap literature, broadsheets, and music as the basis for their analyses, researchers in this field argue that their work is innately about popular, widespread culture and, in many cases, its potential to subvert and redefine the official.[55] The iconographic and oral elements embedded in this print culture have been traced, and recent research on manuscripts and music attempts to examine their pedagogical elements, although such influence can be much more tenuous.[56] This work has also benefited enormously from modern technologies. Services such as Early English Books Online make examples of these materials available in pdf format. Many libraries and archives are developing extensive online depositories that include early pamphlets and larger polemics. Institutions such as the Herzog August Bibliothek in Wolfenbüttel have microfilmed many of their early German broadsheets, and the St. Andrews Reformation Studies Center's Short Title Catalog for early French printed books (completed in late 2007) will make identifying and finding French sources far easier.

Sermon collections have also benefited from these technologies and methodologies and were a key means for communicating doctrine among and between literate and illiterate members of Protestant and Catholic communities. Recent research on sermons has ranged from descriptions of sermon practice and the training of preachers to linguistic analyses of sermon content.[57] Sermons may seem at first to be odd examples of popular religion, but as scholars have shown, a preacher's need to influence his audience increasingly determined the forms and presentations of early modern sermons. Effective preaching demanded accommodation to popular attitudes. Sermons themselves are consummately polyvalent documents; their audience could be quite diverse, and they could be experienced as given

---

[54]Scribner, *For the Sake of Simple Folk*.

[55]Friedman, *Battle of the Frogs and Fairford's Flies*; Soergel, *Wondrous in His Saints*; and Watt, *Cheap Print and Popular Piety*.

[56]Lake, *Anti-Christ's Lewd Hat*; Oettinger, *Music as Propaganda*; and Smith, *Acoustic World of Early Modern England*.

[57]Moeller and Stackmann, *Städtische Predigt*; Taylor, *Soldiers of Christ*; Taylor, *Preachers and People*; and Wabuda, *Preaching during the English Reformation*.

orally, as read silently or aloud, or as repeated at second- or thirdhand. Each time, they were also subject to reinterpretation and appropriation.

One of the most common means by which such religious messages were reinterpreted and made popular was through family discussion, and current scholarship continues to emphasize the role families played in the dissemination and incorporation of religious belief. In both Protestant and Catholic communities, families were a site of religious education, although official approval for this role tended to separate along confessional lines and between the clergy and laity.[58] The significance of familial religious instruction remains far more contentious. For example, while some scholars have stressed how the father's role in Lutheran religious instruction reinforced patriarchal ideals, others have questioned the extent of paternal religious instruction in the broader Lutheran community.[59]

Violence and Toleration

While the confessionalization paradigm has led to the analyses of social discipline and education as described above, it has also driven current discussions of religious violence. Such research tends to focus on the experience of persecution rather than the integration of violence and piety, which was also an aspect of early modern religious experience. Using anthropological and psychoanalytical theories, during the last several decades, scholars have proposed intriguing perspectives about the links between violence and popular religion that rely on a dialog between the prosecutor and the prosecuted.[60]

Not surprisingly for a Europe often defined by confessional difference, the prosecution of religious dissent has received considerable attention from historians. Historians of Catholicism, however, have particularly stressed the links between institutions and rituals of enforcement and popular dissent. Although excommunication was one tool for removing threats to the religious body, the subjects that have received the most thorough recent treatments and revisions are the Venetian and Spanish Inquisitions. With the opening of both the Roman and Spanish Inquisitorial archives, a new generation of scholarship on both the institutions and popular religion has emerged.[61] Rather than presenting the Inquisition as an

---

[58]Duffy, *Marking the Hours*; and Ozment, *When Fathers Ruled*.

[59]Forster and Kaplan, *Piety and Family*.

[60]Crouzet, *Les guerriers de Dieu*; and Delumeau, *L'acception de l'autre*.

[61]Fragnito, *Church, Censorship, and Culture*; Haliczer, *Inquisition and Society*; Kamen, *Spanish Inquisition*; and Rawlings, *Spanish Inquisition*.

authoritarian monolith, these works emphasize the diversity of early modern inquisitions and their need to respond to local circumstances and, at times, bow before local piety. In addition, some works stress the agency of the accused and their defenders: the ways the accused manipulated the inquisitorial environment and the unusual spirituality and piety individuals could construct from their daily exchange with official theology, lived experience, and personal interpretation.[62]

Such work on doctrinal enforcement and unofficial reconstructions complements recent studies done on religious minorities in late medieval and early modern Europe. The older concept of Radical Reform ties such groups innately to Protestant Reformed movements, but as recent scholarship has shown, such connections are misleading.[63] While some dissenting groups in the sixteenth and seventeenth centuries have clear ties to Reforming movements, others derived the bulk of their ideas and practices from later medieval communities. Europe's non-Christian minorities have also received increased treatment but in scholarship that frequently sees them through Christian eyes—asking, for example, what Christians thought of Jews—or that treats them as separate entities.[64] Recent scholarship on late medieval and early modern Spain has, in particular, been forced to grapple with the problems of popular religion about and within minority Muslim and Jewish communities and has offered intriguing insights about the effects of diversity on popular religious expression and ideologies.[65]

Research on popular religion and religious minorities, Christian or non-Christian, must often grapple with the motivations for and consequences of religious violence. Violence against heretics—that is, religious opponents—burst forth frequently in early modern Europe and could assume terrifying proportions. Not only were political and social revolts tied to popular religious beliefs, such as in the Pilgrimage of Grace and the German Peasants' War,[66] but more confined examples of religious violence and pillage could achieve recognition throughout Europe—as occurred with the St. Bartholomew's Day Massacre and the Sack of Rome.[67] Scholars of popular religion have approached these topics in diverse ways. Some

[62]Schutte, *Autobiography of an Aspiring Saint*; and Schutte, *Aspiring Saints*.

[63]Cameron, *Reformation of the Heretics*.

[64]Bell, *Jewish Identity*; Hsia, *Myth of Ritual Murder*; and Hsia and Lehmann, *In and Out of the Ghetto*.

[65]Meyerson and English, *Christians, Muslims, and Jews*; and Perry, *Handless Maiden*.

[66]Wunderli, *Peasant Fires*.

[67]Diefendorf, *Beneath the Cross*.

have concentrated on the degree to which ideas found elsewhere reappeared in widely circulated religious manifestos and the ways in which exchange between opposing camps refined and eventually revised official doctrines and practices. Others have examined the social composition of rioters to ascertain any common cultural experiences. Still others have analyzed the symbolic meaning of ritual violence. The most influential example of the latter remains Natalie Zemon Davis's distinction between popular Protestant and Catholic religious violence.[68]

As the work of Davis and those responding to her suggests, iconoclasm was a powerful manifestation of popular religious violence in early modern Europe.[69] Later medieval Catholicism viewed objects as appropriate means to guide pious reflection; early modern Protestants regarded them as misdirecting the reverence due to God alone. Recent work has stressed both the symbolic elements in iconoclasm and the practical problems communities faced when removing images. Given that families donated objects and that family sites, such as burial chapels, were covered with images in spaces that bridge any distinction modern scholars might make between the public and the private, complicated questions of ownership and patronage arose when images disappeared or were destroyed. By stressing the ritual nature of image "desecration," scholars have also pointed out the enduring nature of the symbolic systems that supported the use of images in devotions.

A more recent counterpoint to the research on religious violence has been work done on religious toleration and accommodation.[70] Responding to the vast scholarship on confessionalization, this work suggests that the oppositions within confessionalization theories are overstated.[71] Entirely practical reasons could govern moves towards religious toleration: a village might only have one church, professional or familial ties might be more significant than religious ones, or lords might be willing to deal with dissenters who could be made to pay disproportionate taxes. More spiritual emphases could also lead to accommodation, such as a sense that a peaceful example might be a more effective proselytizing tool than extermination.[72] This work rarely suggests that popular spirituality disdained

---

[68]Davis, "Rites of Violence."
[69]Kamerick, *Popular Piety and Art.*
[70]Grell and Scribner, *Tolerance and Intolerance.*
[71]Luria, *Sacred Boundaries.*
[72]Hsia and van Nierop, *Calvinism and Religious Toleration*; and Racaut and Ryrie, *Moderate Voices.*

organized religion or fell into a more *politique* or "enlightened" idea of religion; rather, it argues that diverse communities had diverse priorities. The work on toleration and accommodation in the sixteenth and seventeenth centuries even complements recent studies by scholars of the eighteenth century that challenge the extent of Enlightenment secularization.

Current research in popular religion is remarkably rich and diverse, and, as such, the answer to the question of where do we go from here might seem like an exercise in academic cheerleading: keep doing what you're doing! Certainly many of the topics discussed above have not been fully explored. There are, however, both thematic and methodological issues in the study of popular religion that especially need to be resolved. Thematically, academic studies in popular religion are only now coming to terms with subjects traditionally classified as folkloric: legends, magical practices, and supernatural beings such as werewolves, vampires, and dwarves. Individual experience of religion through senses and symbols, as advocated by the late R. W. Scribner, and the further examination of popular practices and beliefs among non-Christian and marginalized groups would also add to a greater appreciation of the diversity of early modern religious experience. Methodologically, microhistorical and local studies are still extremely valuable, but leading scholars in the field need to grapple with syntheses, if only to point out gaps in our current research. Much analysis also remains tied to, and constrained by, modern organizational boundaries—what does a particular archive tell us?—and national historiographies, which little reflect the realities of early modern experience. And, in what is perhaps the most contentious statement in this entire essay, scholars must move beyond the debates over the reality and contextualization of early modern religious experience. Of course, early modern people believed in the reality of their experience, and of course scholars need to contextualize their beliefs and experiences. The techniques applied in contextualization can, however, vary and still be legitimate. An acceptance of methodological diversity is perhaps one of the greatest contributions recent historiographical debates have given the study of popular religion in early modern Europe. The continuation of this diversity will only enhance our understanding of and appreciation for this topic.

Bibliography

Electronic Resources

While there are many websites devoted to leading authors and national histories, few concentrate specifically on popular culture. The sites listed below are quite broad, but they also contain rich sources for the study of popular religion in Reformation Europe.

Bodleian Library Broadside Ballads: http://www.bodley.ox.ac.uk/ballads/.

Elektronische Zeitschriftenbibliothek, Universitäts- und Staatbibliothek: http://www.ub.uni-koeln.de/digital/elzss/index_ger.html.

Historische Flugschriften (most are seventeenth century): http://digbib.bibliothek.uni-augsburg.de/dda/flugschriften_0001.html.

Libros antiguos hasta 1830, Biblioteca Nacional Madrid: http://www.bne.es/esp/digi/FORESBIMA.HTML.

Records of an English Village (1375–1854), Earls Colne: http://linux02.lib.cam.ac.uk/earlscolne/contents.htm.

Reformationsgeschichtliche Handschriften: http://luther.hki.uni-koeln.de/luther/pages/sucheHandschriften.html.

Réseau des Bibliothèques des Universités de Toulouse: http://www.biu-toulouse.fr/num150/accueil.htm.

Sagen (collection of European folkstories, especially Austrian): http://www.sagen.at/.

Virtuelles Archiv mitteleuropäischers Klöster und Bistumer: http://www.monasterium.net/at/.

Wolfenbütteler Digitale Bibliothek: http://www.hab.de/bibliothek/wdb/index.htm.

Printed Sources (primarily works in English or translated into English)

Ariès, Philippe. *The Hour of Our Death.* Translated by Helen Weaver. New York: Knopf, 1981.

Barber, Paul. *Vampires, Burial, and Death: Folklore and Reality.* New Haven, CT: Yale University Press, 1988.

Baroja, Julio Caro. *Las formas complejas de la vida religiosa: Religión, sociedad y carácter en la España de los siglos XVI y XVII.* Madrid: Akal, 1978.

Bell, Dean. *Jewish Identity in Early Modern Germany: Memory, Power, and Community.* Burlington, VT: Ashgate, 2007.

Benedict, Philip, and Virginia Reinberg. "Religion and the Sacred." In *Renaissance and Reformation France, 1500–1648,* edited by Mack P. Holt. New York: Oxford University Press, 2002.

Black, Christopher. *Italian Confraternities in the Sixteenth Century.* New York: Cambridge University Press, 1988.

———, and Pamela Gravestock, eds. *Early Modern Confraternities in Europe and the Americas: International and Interdisciplinary Perspectives.* Burlington, VT: Ashgate, 2005.

Bornstein, Daniel, and Roberto Rusconi. *Women and Religion in Medieval and Renaissance Italy.* Chicago: University of Chicago Press, 1996.

Bossy, John. *Christianity in the West.* New York: Oxford University Press, 1985.

Burke, Peter. *Popular Culture in Early Modern Europe.* Princeton, NJ: Princeton University Press, 1987.

Bynum, Caroline. *Wonderful Blood: Theology and Practice in Late Medieval Northern Germany and Beyond.* Philadelphia: University of Pennsylvania Press, 2007.

Caciola, Nancy. *Discerning Spirits: Divine and Demonic Possession in the Middle Ages.* Ithaca, NY: Cornell University Press, 2003.

Cameron, Euan. *The Reformation of the Heretics: The Waldenses of the Alps, 1480–1580.* New York: Oxford University Press, 1984.

Camporesi, Piero. *The Fear of Hell: Images of Damnation and Salvation in Early Modern Europe.* Translated by Lucinda Byatt. University Park: Pennsylvania State University Press, 1991.

Charlton, Kenneth. *Women, Religion, and Education in Early Modern England.* New York: Routledge, 1999.

Châtellier, Louis. *The Religion of the Poor: Rural Missions in Europe and the Formation of Modern Catholicism, c. 1500–c.1800.* Translated by Brian Pearce. New York: Cambridge University Press, 1997.

Christian, William A. *Apparitions in Late Medieval and Renaissance Spain.* Princeton, NJ: Princeton University Press, 1981.

———. *Local Religion in Sixteenth-Century Spain.* Princeton, NJ: Princeton University Press, 1981.

Comerford, Kathleen M., and Hilmar M Pabel, eds. *Early Modern Catholicism: Essays in Honour of John W. O'Malley, S.J.* Toronto: University of Toronto Press, 2001.

Conelli, Maria Ann. "A Typical Patron of Extraordinary Means: Isabella Feltria della Rovere and the Society of Jesus." *Renaissance Studies* 18, no. 3 (2004): 412–36.

Covington, Sarah. *The Trail of Martyrdom: Persecution and Resistance in England.* Notre Dame, IN: University of Notre Dame Press, 2003.

Crawford, Patricia. *Women and Religion in England, 1500–1720.* New York: Routledge, 1993.

Cressy, David. *Agnes Bowker's Cat: Travesties and Transgressions in Tudor and Stuart England.* New York: Oxford University Press, 2001.

———. *Birth, Marriage, and Death: Ritual, Religion, and the Life-Cycle in Tudor and Stuart England.* New York: Oxford University Press, 1999.

———. *Bonfires and Bells: National Memory and the Protestant Calendar in Elizabethan and Stuart England.* Berkeley: University of California Press, 1989.

Crouzet, Denis. *Les guerriers de Dieu: La violence au temps des troubles de religion, vers 1525–vers 1610.* 2 vols. Seyssel: Champ Vallon, 1990.

D'Andrea, David M. *Civic Charity in Renaissance Italy: The Hospital of Treviso, 1400–1530.* Rochester, NY: University of Rochester Press, 2007.

Davis, Natalie. "Rites of Violence: Religious Riot in Sixteenth-Century France." *Past and Present* 59, no. 1 (1973): 51–91.

Delumeau, Jean. *L'acceptation de l'autre: De l'édit de Nantes à nos jours.* Paris: Fayard, 2000.

———. *Sin and Fear: The Emergence of a Western Guilt Culture, 13th–18th centuries.* Translated by Eric Nicholson. New York: St. Martin's Press, 1990.

Diefendorf, Barbara. *Beneath the Cross: Catholics and Huguenots in Sixteenth-Century Paris.* New York: Oxford University Press, 1991.

———. *From Penitence to Charity: Pious Women and the Catholic Reformation in Paris.* New York: Oxford University Press, 2004.

Dinan, Susan E. *Women and Poor Relief in Seventeenth-Century France: The Early History of the Daughters of Charity.* Burlington, VT: Ashgate, 2006.

Ditchfield, Simon, ed. *Christianity and Community in the West: Essays for John Bossy.* Burlington, VT: Ashgate, 2001.

———. *Liturgy, Sanctity, and History in Tridentine Italy: Pietro Maria Campi and the Preservation of the Particular.* New York: Cambridge University Press, 2002.

Dixon, C. Scott. *The Reformation and Rural Society: The Parishes of Brandenburg-Ansbach-Kulmbach, 1528–1603*. New York: Cambridge University Press, 1996.

Donnelly, John Patrick, and Michael W. Maher, eds. *Confraternities and Catholic Reform in Italy, France, and Spain*. Kirksville, MO: Thomas Jefferson University Press, 1999.

Duffy, Eamon. *Marking the Hours: English People and Their Prayers, 1240–1570*. New Haven: CT: Yale University Press, 2007.

———. *The Stripping of the Altars: Traditional Religion in England, c. 1400–c.1580*. New Haven, CT: Yale University Press, 1992.

———. *The Voices of Morebath: Reformation and Rebellion in an English Village*. New Haven, CT: Yale University Press, 2001.

Edwards, Kathryn A., ed., *Werewolves, Witches, and Wandering Spirits: Traditional Belief and Folklore in Early Modern Europe*. Kirksville, MO: Truman State University Press, 2002.

Eire, Carlos M. N. *From Madrid to Purgatory: The Art and Craft of Dying in Sixteenth-Century Spain*. New York: Cambridge University Press, 1995.

Ellington, Donna Spivey. *From Sacred Body to Angelic Soul: Understanding Mary in Late Medieval and Early Modern Europe*. Washington, DC: Catholic University of America Press, 2001.

Fernandes, Maria de Lurdes Correia. *Espelhos, cartas e guias: casamento e espiritualidade na Peninsula Ibérica, 1450–1700*. Porto: Instituto de Cultura Portuguesa, 1995.

Forster, Marc R. *Catholic Revival in the Age of the Baroque: Religious Identity in Southwest Germany, 1550–1750*. New York: Cambridge University Press, 2001.

———, and Benjamin J. Kaplan, eds. *Piety and Family in Early Modern Europe: Essays in Honour of Steven Ozment*. Burlington, VT: Ashgate, 2005.

Fragnito, Gigliola, ed. *Church, Censorship, and Culture in Early Modern Italy*. Translated by Adrian Belton. New York: Cambridge University Press, 2001.

Freeman, Thomas, and Thomas Mayer. *Martyrs and Martyrdom in England, c. 1400–1700*. London: Boydell Press, 2007.

Friedman, Jerome. *Battle of the Frogs and Fairford's Flies: Miracles and the Pulp Press during the English Revolution*. New York: St. Martin's Press, 1993.

Genuth, Sara Schechner. *Comets, Popular Culture, and the Birth of Modern Cosmology*. Princeton, NJ: Princeton University Press, 1997.

Goodich, Michael. *Violence and Miracle in the Fourteenth Century: Private Grief and Public Salvation*. Chicago: University of Chicago Press, 1995.

Gordon, Bruce, and Peter Marshall. *The Place of the Dead: Death and Remembrance in Late Medieval and Early Modern Europe*. New York: Cambridge University Press, 2000.

Gregory, Brad S. *Salvation at Stake: Christian Martyrdom in Early Modern Europe*. Cambridge, MA: Harvard University Press, 1999.

Grell, Ole Peter, and Robert W. Scribner. *Tolerance and Intolerance in the European Reformation*. New York: Cambridge University Press, 1996.

Haliczer, Stephen. *Between Exaltation and Infamy: Female Mystics in the Golden Age of Spain*. New York: Oxford University Press, 2002.

———, ed. and trans. *Inquisition and Society in Early Modern Spain*. Totowa, NJ: Barnes & Noble, 1987.

Harline, Craig. *The Burdens of Sister Margaret: Inside a Seventeenth-Century Convent*. New Haven, CT: Yale University Press, 2000.

———. *Miracles at the Jesus Oak: Histories of the Supernatural in Reformation Europe*. New York: Doubleday, 2003.

Harris, Tim, ed. *Popular Culture in England, c. 1500–1850*. New York: St. Martin's Press, 1995.

Heal, Bridget. *The Cult of the Virgin Mary in Early Modern Germany: Protestant and Catholic Piety, 1500–1648.* New York: Cambridge University Press, 2007.

Hsia , R. Po-chia. *The Myth of Ritual Murder: Jews and Magic in Reformation Germany.* New Haven, CT: Yale University Press, 1988.

———. *Social Discipline in the Reformation.* New York: Routledge, 1989.

———, and Hartmut Lehmann, eds., *In and Out of the Ghetto: Jewish-Gentile Relations in Late Medieval and Early Modern Germany.* New York: Cambridge University Press, 1995.

———, and Henk van Nierop, eds. *Calvinism and Religious Toleration in the Dutch Golden Age.* New York: Cambridge University Press, 2002.

Hutton, Ronald. *The Rise and Fall of Merry England, the Ritual Year, 1400–1700.* New York: Oxford University Press, 1994.

———. *The Stations of the Sun: A History of the Ritual Year in Britain.* New York: Oxford University Press, 1996.

Johnstone, Nathan. *The Devil and Demonism in Early Modern England.* New York: Cambridge University Press, 2006.

Kagan, Richard L. *Lucrecia's Dreams: Politics and Prophecy in Sixteenth-Century Spain.* Berkeley: University of California Press, 1990.

Kamen, Henry. *The Spanish Inquisition: A Historical Revision.* New Haven, CT: Yale University Press, 1998.

Kamerick, Kathleen. *Popular Piety and Art in the Late Middle Ages: Image Worship and Idolatry in England, 1350–1500.* New York: Palgrave, 2002.

Karent-Nunn, Susan. *The Reformation of Ritual: An Interpretation of Early Modern Germany.* New York: Routledge, 1997.

———, ed. *Varieties of Devotion in the Middle Ages and Renaissance.* Turnhout: Brepols, 2003.

Klaniczay, Gábor. *The Uses of Supernatural Power: The Transformation of Popular Religion in Medieval and Early Modern Europe.* Edited by Karen Margolis. Translated by Susan Singerman. Princeton, NJ: Princeton University Press, 1990.

Kreitzer, Beth. *Reforming Mary: Changing Images of the Virgin Mary in Lutheran Sermons of the Sixteenth Century.* New York: Oxford University Press, 2004.

Lake, Peter. *The Anti-Christ's Lewd Hat: Protestants, Papists and Players in Post-Reformation England.* New Haven, CT: Yale University Press, 2002.

———. *The Boxmaker's Revenge: "Orthodoxy," "Heterodoxy," and the Politics of the Parish in Early Stuart England.* Manchester: Manchester University Press, 2001.

Lauwers, Michel. *Naissance du cimetière: Lieux sacrés et terre des morts dans l'occident médiéval.* Paris: Aubier, 2005.

Lazar, Lance. *Working in the Vineyard of the Lord: Jesuit Confraternities in Early Modern Italy.* Toronto: University of Toronto Press, 2005.

Lecouteux, Claude. *Witches, Werewolves, and Fairies: Shapeshifters and Astral Doubles in the Middle Ages.* Translated by C. Frock. Manchester, UK: Inner Traditions, 2003.

Le Goff, Jacques. *The Birth of Purgatory.* Translated by Arthur Goldhammer. Chicago: University of Chicago Press, 1984.

Levi, Giovanni. *Inheriting Power: The Story of an Exorcist.* Translated by Lydia G. Cochrane. Chicago: University of Chicago Press, 1988.

Lualdi, Katharine Jackson, and Anne T. Thayer, eds. *Penitence in the Age of Reformations.* Burlington, VT: Ashgate, 2000.

Luria, Keith P. *Sacred Boundaries: Religious Coexistence and Conflict in Early Modern France.* Washington, DC: Catholic University of America Press, 2005.

Lutton, Robert, and Elisabeth Salter, eds. *Pieties in Transition: Religious Practices and Experiences, c. 1400–1600.* Burlington, VT: Ashgate, 2007.

Luz-Sterrit, Laurence. *Redefining Female Religious Life: French Ursulines and English Ladies in Seventeenth-Century Catholicism.* Burlington, VT: Ashgate, 2006.

Mack, Phyllis. *Visionary Women: Ecstatic Prophecy in Seventeenth-Century England.* Berkeley: University of California Press, 1992.

Maggi, Armando. *In the Company of Demons: Unnatural Beings, Love, and Identity in the Italian Renaissance.* Chicago: University of Chicago Press, 2006.

Marsh, Christopher. *Popular Religion in Sixteenth-Century England: Holding Their Peace.* New York: St. Martin's Press, 1998.

Marshall, Peter. *Beliefs and the Dead in Reformation England.* New York: Oxford University Press, 2002.

———. *Religious Identities in Henry VIII's England.* Burlington, VT: Ashgate, 2005.

Matheson, Peter. *The Imaginative World of the Reformation.* Minneapolis, MN: Fortress Press, 2001.

Meyerson, Mark, and Edward English, eds. *Christians, Muslims, and Jews in Medieval and Early Modern Spain.* Notre Dame, IN: University of Notre Dame Press, 2000.

Moeller, Bernd, and Karl Stackmann. *Städtische Predigt in der Frühzeit der Reformation.* Göttingen: Vandenhoeck & Ruprecht, 1996.

Monter, William. *Ritual, Myth and Magic in Early Modern Europe.* Brighton, UK: Harvester Press, 1983.

Muchembled, Robert. *A History of the Devil, from the Middle Ages to the Present.* Translated by Jean Birrell. Malden, MA: Blackwell, 2003.

Nalle, Sara T. *God in La Mancha: Religious Reform and the People of Cuenca, 1500–1650.* Baltimore, MD: Johns Hopkins University Press, 1992.

———. *Mad for God: Bartolomé Sánchez, The Secret Messiah of Cardenete.* Charlottesville: University Press of Virginia, 2001.

Nixon, Virginia. *Mary's Mother: Saint Anne in Late Medieval Europe.* University Park: Pennsylvania State University Press, 2004.

Oberman, Heiko. *Luther: Man Between God and the Devil.* New Haven, CT: Yale University Press, 1982, 1990.

Oettinger, Rebecca Wagner. *Music as Propaganda in the German Reformation.* Burlington, VT: Ashgate, 2001.

Ozment, Steven. *When Fathers Ruled: Family Life in Reformation Europe.* Cambridge, MA: Harvard University Press, 1983.

Parish, Helen L. *Monks, Miracles, and Magic: Reformation Representations of the Medieval Church.* New York: Routledge, 2005.

———, and William G. Naphy, eds. *Religion and Superstition in Reformation.* Manchester, UK: Manchester University Press, 2003.

Perry, Mary Elizabeth. *The Handless Maiden: Moriscos and the Politics of Religion in Early Modern Spain.* Princeton, NJ: Princeton University Press, 2005.

Plongeron, Bernard, and Paule Lerou, eds. *La Piété populaire en France: Répertoire Bibliographique.* 7 vols. Paris: Cerf, 1984–.

Racaut, Luc, and Alec Ryrie, eds. *Moderate Voices in the European Reformation.* Burlington, VT: Ashgate, 2005.

Rapley, Elisabeth. *The Dévotes: Women and the Church in Seventeenth-Century France.* Montreal: McGill-Queen's University Press, 1990.

Rawlings, Helen. *The Spanish Inquisition.* Malden, MA: Blackwell, 2005.

Reay, Barry. *Popular Cultures in England, 1550–1750.* New York: Longman, 1998.

Reinis, Austra. *Reforming the Art of Dying: The* ars moriendi *in the German Reformation.* Burlington, VT: Ashgate, 2007.

Rieder, Paula. *On the Purification of Women: Churching in Northern France, 1100–1500.* New York: Palgrave, 2006.

Rittgers, Ronald. *The Reformation of the Keys: Confession, Conscience, and Authority in Sixteenth-Century Germany.* Cambridge, MA: Harvard University Press, 2004.

Rubin, Miri. *Corpus Christi: The Eucharist in Late Medieval Culture.* New York: Cambridge University Press, 1991.

Schen, Claire S. *Charity and Lay Piety in Reformation London, 1500–1620.* Burlington, VT: Ashgate, 2002.

Schutte, Anne Jacobson. *Aspiring Saints: Pretense of Holiness, Inquisition, and Gender in the Republic of Venice, 1619–1750.* Baltimore, MD: Johns Hopkins University Press, 2001.

———. *Autobiography of an Aspiring Saint: Cecilia Ferrazzi.* Chicago: University of Chicago Press, 1996.

Scribner, Robert W. "Elements of Popular Belief." In *The Handbook of European History, c. 1400–c.1600,* edited by Thomas A. Brady Jr., Heiko Oberman, and James A. Tracy, 231–62. Grand Rapids, MI: W. B. Eerdmans, 1994–96.

———. *For the Sake of Simple Folk: Popular Propaganda for the German Reformation.* New York: Cambridge University Press, 1981, 1994.

———. *Popular Culture and Popular Movements in Reformation Germany.* Ronceverte, WV: Hambledon Press, 1987.

———. *Religion and Culture in Germany (1400–1800).* Edited by Lyndal Roper. Preface by Thomas A. Brady Jr. Leiden: Brill, 2001.

———, and Trevor Johnson, eds. *Popular Religion in Germany and Central Europe, 1400–1800.* New York: St. Martin's Press, 1996.

Sluhovsky, Moshe. *Patroness of Paris: Rituals of Devotion in Early Modern France.* Boston: Brill, 1998.

Smith, Bruce R. *The Acoustic World of Early Modern England: Attending to the O-Factor.* Chicago: University of Chicago Press, 1999.

Soergel, Philip M. *Wondrous in His Saints: Counter-Reformation Propaganda in Bavaria.* Berkeley: University of California Press, 1993.

Strauss, Gerald. *Luther's House of Learning: Indoctrination of the Young in the German Reformation.* Baltimore, MD: Johns Hopkins University Press, 1978.

Strocchia, Sharon. *Death and Ritual in Renaissance Florence.* Baltimore, MD: Johns Hopkins University Press, 1992.

Swanson, R. N., ed. *The Use and Abuse of Time of Christian History.* Rochester, NY: Boydell, 2002.

Tausiet, Maria. "Excluded Souls: The Wayward and Excommunicated in Counter-Reformation Spain." *History* 88 (2003): 437–50.

Taylor, Larissa. *Soldiers of Christ: Preaching in Late Medieval and Reformation France.* New York: Oxford University Press, 1992.

———, ed. *Preachers and People in the Reformations and Early Modern Period.* Boston: Brill, 2003.

Terpstra, Nicholas. *Lay Confraternities and Civic Religion in Renaissance Bologna.* New York: Cambridge University Press, 1995.

Thomas, Keith. *Religion and the Decline of Magic.* New York: Scribner, 1971, 1997.

van Deursen, Arie. *Plain Lives in a Golden Age: Popular Culture, Religion and Society in Seventeenth-Century Holland.* Translated by Maarten Ultee. New York: Cambridge University Press, 1991.

van Herwaarden, Jan. *Between Saint James and Erasmus: Studies in Late-Medieval Religious Life : Devotions and Pilgrimages in the Netherlands.* Translated by Wendie Shaffer and Donald Gardner. Boston: Brill, 2003.

Vauchez, André. *Sainthood in the Later Middle Ages.* Translated by Jean Birrell. New York: Cambridge University Press, 1997.

von Greyerz, Kaspar. *Religion and Culture in Early Modern Europe, 1500–1800.* New York: Oxford University Press, 2000, 2007.

—— et al., eds. *Interkonfessionalität-Transkonfessionalität-binnenkonfessionelle Pluralität: Neue Forschungen zur Konfessionalisierungsthese.* Gütersloh: Gütersloher Verlagshaus, 2003.

Vovelle, Michel. *Les âmes du purgatoire, ou le travail du deuil.* Paris: Gallimard, 1996.

Wabuda, Susan. *Preaching during the English Reformation.* New York: Cambridge University Press, 2002.

Walsham, Alexandra. *Providence in Early Modern England.* New York: Oxford University Press, 1999.

Wandel, Lee. *The Eucharist in the Reformation: Incarnation and Liturgy.* New York: Cambridge University Press, 2005.

Watt, Jeffrey R. *Choosing Death: Suicide and Calvinism in Early Modern Geneva.* Kirksville, MO: Truman State University Press, 2001.

Watt, Tessa. *Cheap Print and Popular Piety, 1550–1640.* New York: Cambridge University Press, 1991.

Werner, Ernst, and Sabine Tanz. *Spätmittelalterliche Laienmentalitäten im Spiegel von Visionen, Offenbarungen und Prophezeiungen.* Bern: Lang, 1993.

Wunderli, Richard M. *Peasant Fires: The Drummer of Niklashausen.* Bloomington: Indiana University Press, 1992.

15

Witchcraft

H. C. Erik Midelfort

One of the standard scholarly exercises is the literature review, the effort to describe recent contributions to a specific field of research. Over the past generation, several useful reviews of research into the history of witchcraft, varying dramatically in ambition and scope, have appeared, ranging from the discussion of a few titles to the consideration of hundreds.[1] The literature review has become so well established in witchcraft research that the well-meaning scholar attempting this genre runs the risk of writing not secondary literature (discussions of primary sources) nor even tertiary literature (discussions of secondary sources), but what one would have to call quaternary literature (discussions of discussions of secondary sources)— an unsavory prospect. With the recent publication of Richard Golden's *Encyclopedia of Witchcraft: The Western Tradition*, moreover, students and scholars now have a remarkable and up-to-date four-volume survey of what the best researchers have discovered and concluded about the whole

[1] Midelfort, "Recent Witch Hunting Research"; idem, "Renaissance of Witchcraft Research"; idem, "Witchcraft, Magic and the Occult"; Nugent, "Witchcraft Studies"; Monter, "Historiography of European Witchcraft"; idem, "Re-contextualizing British Witchcraft"; Hess, "Hunting Witches"; Butler, "Witchcraft, Healing, and Historians' Crazes"; Estes, "Incarnation of Evil"; Behringer, "Erträge und Perspektiven der Hexenforschung"; idem, "Witchcraft Studies in Austria"; idem, "Geschichte der Hexenforschung"; Pizzini, "Aspekte der neuen Hexen-Literatur"; Becker-Cantarino, "'Feminist Consciousness' and 'Wicked Witches'"; Schwerhoff, "Vom Alltagsverdacht zur Massenverfolgung"; Hunter, "Witchcraft and the Decline of Belief"; and Barry and Davies, *Palgrave Advances in Witchcraft Studies*. Electronic resources include *Geschichtswissenschaften im Internet* (http://www.historicum.net/themen/hexenforschung/thementexte/forschungsberichte); and Schwerhoff, *Dresdner Auswahlbibliographie zur Hexenforschung* (http://rcswww.urz.tu-dresden.de/~frnz/dabhex/haupt.html).

history of witchcraft in the West.[2] There seems little point in trying to compete with so thorough a survey.

What is less clear in all this flood of information and opinion is in what direction this large field of endeavor is going and what is left to be done. This essay, therefore, will attempt to describe the future of witchcraft research—a project for which historical studies usually provide only approximate and unsteady guidance. History, however, does illuminate our present and make certain futures more likely than others. Taking one's bearings from the course or direction of research over the past circa forty years provides a better position to understand and even to predict what is coming next.

The Situation around 1960

When I began working on witchcraft in 1962 there were a few facts that seemed perfectly clear—today these facts no longer seem as solid as they did then. For example, back in those dim days, everyone "knew" that the great turn toward massive witch-hunting in the West had occurred in the first half of the fourteenth century. The great scholar Joseph Hansen wrote in 1900 that the Inquisition in southern France had detected a huge conspiracy of novel heretics in the 1330s—men and women who stood accused of sorcery (harmful magic) and of worshiping the devil.[3] It seemed that Toulouse and Carcassonne had seen perhaps as many as one thousand trials leading to over six hundred executions. This sudden eruption cried out for explanation and students of the Inquisition rushed in, for it seemed that these massive chain-reaction trials were the obvious key to understanding the whole subsequent history of witchcraft. And as a result, scholars (especially liberal scholars) concluded that inquisitorial proceedings (or, more luridly, the Inquisition) were responsible for the construction and deployment of a dangerous delusion, an amalgam of *maleficium* (harmful magic) and diabolism that came to be called the "conglomerate crime" of witchcraft. Heresy seemed to be at the very heart of this newly discovered or newly invented crime. Standard histories of witchcraft depended on Hansen's source collection and his account down into the 1970s.[4] In 1975/76, however, the major source upon which this version of the past rested was debunked as a forgery by the independent researches of

---

[2]Golden, *Encyclopedia of Witchcraft*; and Bailey, *Historical Dictionary*.
[3]Hansen, *Quellen und Untersuchungen*, 449–53, 456, 500; and idem, *Zauberwahn*.
[4]Russell, *Witchcraft in the Middle Ages*; and Kors and Peters, *Witchcraft in Europe*.

Norman Cohn and Richard Kieckhefer.[5] The result of this subtraction from what we knew about witchcraft was sensational because it now became possible to consider that heresy was only one of the historical roots of witchcraft, that the church was not the only source of witchcraft panic, and that the Inquisition was not the sole incubator of this novel crime. Indeed, historians are now finally beginning to recognize that *maleficium* remained always one of the major foci of concern, straight through the early modern period.[6]

Forty years ago, it also seemed plausible to many that the historical witch hunts had actually targeted existing groups of heretics or even surviving practitioners of pagan religions in Europe. The more flamboyant aspects of Margaret A. Murray's theories along these lines had, to be sure, been discounted for decades, but Carlo Ginzburg appeared in 1966 to give her interpretation a new and solid underpinning as he described a group of peasants in Friuli who thought that men born "with the caul" were fated to battle witches who endangered their crops. Over a period of decades, roughly 1560 to 1640, Ginzburg appeared to show that these *benandanti* were persuaded by the Venetian Inquisition to regard themselves as actual witches.[7] It seemed a perfect case of a surviving pagan agrarian cult that had been turned into witches by the overzealous inquiries of churchmen.

At that time, in the 1960s, little was known about the religious world of ordinary people. They belonged to a "world we have lost," in the famous phrase of Peter Laslett, and few historians then suspected that social historians would turn to this question with vigor and imagination, turning up heaps of hitherto neglected source material and proving, to almost everyone's satisfaction, that the common people of late medieval and early modern Europe were not pagan in any serious sense. Instead, they were Christians in the sense that they thought of themselves as Christian, attended church when they could, and partook of the rites of the church when they were available.[8] This does not at all mean that most common Christians were theologically orthodox, for many did not entertain theological convictions of any developed sort. It does mean that most of the

---

[5]Cohn, *Europe's Inner Demons*; Kieckhefer, *European Witch Trials*; and Switzer, *Étienne-Léon de Lamothe-Langon*.

[6]Behringer, "Detecting the Ultimate Conspiracy."

[7]Ginzburg, *I Benandanti*; Midelfort, "Night Battles"; Ginzburg, *Ecstasies*; and Graf, "Carlo Ginzburg's Hexensabbat."

[8]Van Engen, "Christian Middle Ages"; Cameron, *European Reformation*; Burke, "Bishop's Questions"; Febvre, *Problem of Unbelief*; Harline, "Official Religion"; Dinzelbacher, *Handbuch der Religionsgeschichte*; and Brooke and Brooke, *Popular Religion in the Middle Ages*.

time ordinary parishioners were unaware that their rituals, beliefs, and practice might (if they had been examined closely) have placed them in conflict with representatives of the official church. The mere fact that such questions have arisen in this way in the history of witchcraft suggests the importance or even the centrality of witchcraft studies to the analysis of popular religion.

Forty years ago, the prodigious works of Henry Charles Lea, Joseph Hansen, and Wilhelm Gottlieb Soldan were the standard works on the history of witchcraft—works dating from the nineteenth century or its turn to the twentieth.[9] Although these great historians worked scrupulously with original sources, their works breathe an air of liberal, anticlerical, and anti-Catholic prejudice. Lea, for example, knew better from his own research into various inquisitions, but his generation of historians often wrote as if the Inquisition had first invented the crime of witchcraft and only later discovered it all over Europe. It was not yet clear where the hot spots of witch-hunting were, and scholars were far from possessing an accurate epidemiology of proven witchcraft trials. Beginning with the assumption that the largest trials had begun in southern France in the fourteenth century, it seemed fairly simple to follow the wave of persecution northward and eastward. It was far too easy to assume that almost every European village and every region experienced high rates of suspicion, accusations, trials, and executions. It was too easy to assume that any apparent differences from region to region could be explained by the variable survival of trial records. And so, lacking better information, most historians around 1960 merely assumed that France and Germany would present roughly the same numbers of witchcraft executions, because both nations possessed the same deadly ingredients: a broadly accepted demonology, an energetic ecclesiastical organization with powers of inquisition, a tough-minded legal practice based upon a newly received Roman law (with its use of torture), and a tense religious atmosphere characterized by claims that one's enemies were working with the devil. With such general assumptions, it did not even seem worth looking at the actual trial records even if they could be located. When H. R. Trevor-Roper published his attractive summary in 1967, it seemed plausible to argue, as he did, that witchcraft trials were always to be found wherever confessional conflicts were at their fiercest. How then could there have been major differences between the French- and German-

---

[9]Soldan, *Geschichte der Hexenprozesse*; Hansen, *Zauberwahn*; Lea, *Materials toward a History of Witchcraft*, ed. Howland; and Lea, *History of the Inquisition*.

speaking parts of Europe?[10] For him, it also seemed natural that only the most courageous and enlightened persons, allies of the skeptical party of humanists such as Erasmus of Rotterdam, were able to oppose the escalating wave of witchcraft prosecutions. By the 1960s, a few of these individuals were already well known: Reginald Scot in England, Michel de Montaigne in France, and Johann Weyer and Friedrich Spee in Germany. These were men whose courage seemed as laudable as their acumen and skepticism. But courage was imagined as their most important quality, because it was commonly thought that they ran the risk of falling victim to the same panic, the same fanaticism as the witches themselves. A generation ago, it was common knowledge that four hundred years earlier, everyone believed in witchcraft and magic. Only isolated skeptics exercised an unfettered reason and saw through the "nonsense" of magic and the supposed pact with the devil. Over the intervening years, this picture has changed almost beyond recognition. Perhaps most importantly, one no longer finds leading scholars in this field claiming that witchcraft and magic were irrational. Instead, it might more easily be maintained that learned demonology suffered rather from a surfeit of (untested) reason.[11] As Stuart Clark has shown in massive detail, scholars are now better advised to conclude that demons were useful tools with which to think, not a means of evading thought.[12]

A generation ago, scholars generally knew little about witchcraft trials outside western Europe. The best national surveys were perhaps those of Notestein, Kittredge, and Ewen for England,[13] but local and regional historians had already performed excellent research for various territories of the Holy Roman Empire, such as Bavaria (by Sigmund Riezler), the Tyrol (by Ludwig Rapp and Fritz Byloff), and the Lorraine (by Etienne Delcambre), to name only three noteworthy examples.[14] Aside from a couple of Swiss dissertations, there was little known about Swiss witchcraft trials and extremely little about the crucial early trials from the fifteenth

---

[10]Trevor-Roper, *Religion, the Reformation, and Social Change*. Scholars will recall, however, that Trevor-Roper also tried to maintain that witchcraft trials persisted especially in mountainous regions—a dubious application of the global and cultural theories of Fernand Braudel.

[11]Tambiah, *Magic, Science, Religion, and the Scope of Rationality*; Duerr, *Wissenschaftler und das Irrationale*; Bertram, "Skepticism and Social Struggle"; Clack, *Wittgenstein, Frazer, and Religion*; and Waardt et al., *Dämonische Besessenheit*.

[12]Clark, *Thinking with Demons*.

[13]Notestein, *History of Witchcraft in England*; Kittredge, *Witchcraft in Old and New England*; and Ewen, *Witch Hunting and Witch Trial*.

[14]Riezler, *Geschichte der Hexenprozesse in Bayern*; Rapp, *Hexenprozesse und ihre Gegner aus Tirol*; Byloff, *Hexenglaube und Hexenverfolgung*; and Delcambre, *Le Concept de la Sorcellerie*.

century. For Scandinavia and broad tracts of eastern Europe, one would have had to write "terra incognita" on the map. The best scholars already knew that Spain and Portugal had experienced very few witchcraft trials, comparatively speaking, and that many regions of Italy, too, were virtually free of witch-hunting, but these contentions were also widely doubted. These regions were after all the core lands of a victorious Catholicism in the sixteenth and seventeenth centuries, where it was assumed that the nexus of religious zeal and awe-inspiring witchcraft trials should have been more obvious than anywhere else. Again, a few scholars knew that in Ireland among the native Irish, there had been few or actually no trials at all for witchcraft, but this fact fitted so poorly with British anticlericalism and anti-Catholicism that it was usually forgotten when larger theories were floated.[15] Until the 1970s, the black legend often overwhelmed scholars even when the evidence they were looking at pointed in other directions.[16]

A generation ago, historians were also well aware of the distinct gender bias to be found in accusations and executions for the crime of witchcraft. This subject did not have to wait for feminist or gender historians before firm (and premature) conclusions were reached, but it must be said that the reasons for the vast overrepresentation of women among those suspected of witchcraft were rarely given any searching attention. Sometimes the supposed feminine nature of witchcraft was deployed as part of a larger (and often undocumented) account of feminine power in ages past.[17] It was, however, common to read the famous *Malleus Maleficarum* as an extreme exercise in misogyny, and a few scholars attempted to examine this problem through the lens of psychoanalysis.[18] Without much careful thought, it seemed only sensible to connect the misogyny of Heinrich Kramer (and his supposed coauthor Jakob Sprenger) with their benighted Scholastic views of women and with the assumed pressures of Dominican (celibate) life. In this way, one could hit two birds with one stone: one could use the *Malleus Maleficarum* to explain the rise of mass witchcraft trials in the sixteenth century and simultaneously explain the overproportion of

---

[15]The tiny number of actual witchcraft trials conducted in Ireland were always offenses among the Anglo-Irish or English settlers, and not among the Irish. See Seymour, *Irish Witchcraft and Demonology*; and Callan, "'No such art in this land.'"

[16]Kamen, *Spanish Inquisition*: Maltby, *Black Legend in England*; and Henningsen and Tedeschi, *Inquisition in Early Modern Europe*.

[17]Michelet, *La Sorcière*; Gage, *Woman, Church and State*; Crohns, *Die Summa Theologica des Anton von Florenz*; and Hansen, *Quellen und Untersuchungen*, 416–44.

[18]Zilboorg, *The Medical Man and the Witch*; Masters, *Eros and Evil*; and Hutton, *Triumph of the Moon*, 132–50.

women among those convicted of this newly concocted crime. Working in this way, it became conventional to divide the history of witch-hunting at the *Malleus*. Before 1486, one concentrated upon the Scholastic construction of a new crime. After 1486, one watched, perhaps in horror, as the logic of persecution relentlessly unrolled in the sixteenth and seventeenth centuries.[19] An added advantage for liberal or Protestant historians lay in the fact that the authors of the accursed *Malleus* were prominent, pious members of the Dominican Order.

Scholarly Progress, 1960 to 2005

Since the 1960s, this picture has changed not only in many of its details, but also in its basic form. When I began my dissertation research in 1967, I thought I had chosen a region for study (southwest Germany) that had experienced a surprising paucity of witchcraft trials. I imagined I would be explaining why there were so few executions in this large area, but the construction of a comprehensive list of trials and victims from the surviving evidence made it plain that southwest Germany had been far from lacking in witchcraft trials. Indeed, it emerged as a region with dramatically varied rates of prosecution: here perhaps only a few convictions over the course of a century, but over there huge chain-reaction trials, such as those in Ellwangen, Marchtal, Offenburg, or Mergentheim, with hundreds of executions.[20] Since 1967, the map of witch-hunting based on the surviving trial records has slowly been filled in, so that there are today relatively few territories and cities that are still blank spots.[21]

Moreover, scholars today possess a relatively useful explanation for the varying density of the worst witchcraft trials. This model connects the intensity of witch trials to the varying development of the early modern state, especially in the form of its legal apparatus.[22] In those areas where an early modern state—such as the duchies of Bavaria or Württemberg, or

---

[19]Joseph Hansen already suggested this dichotomy by attending mainly to the early history of witchcraft, and by implying that the later sixteenth century was merely the logical extension of what had been cobbled together by the late fifteenth century. See also Russell, *Witchcraft in the Middle Ages*.

[20] Midelfort, *Witch Hunting in Southwestern Germany*.

[21]Golden, *Encyclopedia of Witchcraft*; Behringer, *Witches and Witch-Hunts*; Degn, Lehmann, and Unverhau, *Hexenprozesse*; Ankarloo and Henningsen, *Early Modern Witchcraft*; Larner, *Enemies of God*; Henningsen, *Witches' Advocate*; Klaniczay, *Uses of Supernatural Power*; Pocs, *Between the Living and the Dead*; and Lorenz and Schmidt, *Wider alle Hexerei und Teufelswerk*.

[22]This explanation was first fully expounded by Brian Levack in *The Witch-Hunt in early Modern Europe*. For village accusations, see especially Rummel, *Bauern, Herren und Hexen*. For the contempt shown by elite jurists, see especially Soman, *Sorcellerie et Justice Criminelle*. For a survey pulling these perspectives together, see Briggs, *Witches and Neighbors*.

kingdoms such as France or England—enjoyed control over a well-central-
ized judicial apparatus with an established appeals process, jurists in the
central courts might look with contempt upon the ugly rumors and superstitious accusations bubbling up from villages.[23] The closer jurists were to
the local conflicts that generated angry accusations, the more likely they
were to believe and follow up on claims of *maleficium* (harmful magic).
Thus, territories with better developed judicial systems were often better
able to resist village demands for witchcraft trials. Such states did not necessarily resist or abolish such trials, but the greater social distance between
village headmen and élite jurists often did nurture a certain haughty dis-
dain for, or indifference and skepticism toward what courtiers and magistrates called the "ignorant, coarse, superstitious" nonsense of crude and
illiterate villagers. Other states with less well-developed levels of appellate
courts fell victim all the more easily to the fears and suspicions of rural
people. This was perhaps especially true of the many ecclesiastical territories of the Holy Roman Empire, in prince bishoprics such as those of Augsburg, Trier, and Cologne, or in imperial abbeys such as Fulda, or princely
prebendaries such as Ellwangen, but also in secular territories such as the
duchy of Lorraine or the kingdom of Scotland. Scholars have learned to
notice the importance of differences between the fears and imaginings of
the learned and those of ordinary villagers.[24]

In this model, one can recognize at once the remarkable progress that
has been made over the past thirty to forty years. Scholars now possess a
basis for research that allows for generalizations, and a thesis that can be
tested against new data. Perhaps we will refine a thesis that helps explain
why witch trials were severe in one place and not so severe in another; perhaps it will prove incapable of truly general extension. While the model
helps in understanding regional variation, it has not yet illuminated temporal patterns of witch-hunting: when and why witchcraft trials broke out
in specific places and then spread or stopped. But the contrast with the
uninformed and basically anticlerical explanations of the 1960s is obvious.

Meanwhile, scholars have also built up a better picture of witchcraft
trials as they expanded in the late Middle Ages. Here the researches of
Richard Kieckhefer and Norman Cohn have proved crucial. As mentioned
above, they were the first to debunk the supposed mass witchcraft trials of

---

[23]For Bavaria, see Behringer, *Hexenverfolgung in Bayern*. For the German southwest, see Lorenz
and Schmidt, *Wider alle Hexerei und Teufelswerk*. For England, see Sharpe, *Instruments of Darkness*.
For Scotland, see Larner, *Enemies of God*; and Goodare, *Scottish Witch-Hunt in Context*.
[24]Briggs, "By the Strength of Fancie."

the fourteenth century. It has become clear that the earliest real witchcraft trials (that is, trials in which suspects were accused of having a pact with the devil) were found not in the fourteenth century, but in the 1420s and 1430s. Secular judges and magistrates, such as Peter von Greyerz and Claude Tholosan, were involved in these trials from the start, and they were at least as much concerned with the physical ravages caused by harmful magic as they were with any supposed heresy.[25] A research team at the University of Lausanne has made major contributions to this area of research by locating hitherto unknown trial documents, and by paying close attention to the exact transitions or developments in the alpine understanding of heresy and witchcraft.[26] The new waves of persecution emerged not from inquisitorial proceedings against surviving Cathars, but (at least in part) from continuing efforts to eradicate Waldensian survivors. Interestingly, townsmen looked for heretics in their towns, but when townsmen pursued criminals in their outlying countryside, they looked for witches and rebels.[27] Witchcraft fears and beliefs of the 1430s were also connected to strivings for ecclesiastical and social reform associated with the Council of Basel (which ran from 1431 to 1449, although after 1439, it was declared schismatic and heretical).[28] This major church council brought together bishops, abbots, and other churchmen, who absorbed and spread the current alpine rumors of heretical witches whose crimes now ominously combined *maleficium*, flight to a sabbath, cannibalism, infanticide, and a pact with the devil. One of the most important writers on witchcraft during the 1430s, Johannes Nider, was a Dominican reformer actively involved in the Council of Basel, which has thus emerged as a crucible for the new and newly dangerous doctrine.[29] Another reformer active at about the same time in Italy was the Franciscan friar Bernardino of Siena (1380–1444), whose fervent devotions and intended reforms also blurred the lines between witchcraft, sodomy, and heresy. He triggered witchcraft trials and executions, and wanted more than he was able to achieve during the years 1426 through 1428.[30] Richard Kieckhefer has made the general point that

[25]Paravy, "A propos de la genèse médiévale des chasses aux sorcières"; and Blauert, *Frühe Hexenverfolgungen.*

[26]Modestin and Tremp, "Zur Spätmittelalterlichen Hexenverfolgung."

[27]Tremp, *Quellen zur Geschichte der Waldenser von Freiburg;* and idem, *Waldenser, Wiedergänger, Hexen und Rebellen.*

[28]Helmrath, *Das Basler Konzil;* and Sudmann, *Das Basler Konzil.*

[29]Bailey, *Battling Demons;* Tschacher, *Der Formicarius des Johannes Nider;* Anheim and Ostorero, *Le diable en Procès;* Ostorero, Bagliani, Tremp, and Chène, *L'imaginaire du sabbat;* and Behringer, "Detecting the Ultimate Conspiracy."

[30]Mormando, *Preacher's Demons,* 52–108, 219–34.

in the early fifteenth century the "vigorous drive for reform of the Church in head and members" may well have been the spark that sufficed to ignite a conflagration beginning in the 1420s.[31]

Just as importantly, however, scholars have now recognized (and are beginning to digest) the fact that the major demonologies of the fifteenth and sixteenth centuries seem rather to have followed the most virulent witchcraft trials rather than preceding and inspiring them. In other words, scholarly understandings of witchcraft usually emerged as an effort to understand what had already happened in judicial proceedings. This was as true for Johannes Nider's *Formicarius* (1437) and the *Malleus Maleficarum* (1486) as for Jean Bodin's *De la démonomanie des sorciers* (1580) and Nicholas Remy's *Daemonolatria* (1595).[32] We can no longer maintain, as scholars used to do, that a horrid book (or a whole library of horrid books) kicked off the European witch hunt.

In view of the burgeoning literature about the devil, magic, and witchcraft in early modern Europe, scholars have also become much more cautious about labeling such treatises and their authors as superstitious or mad. We have perhaps outgrown Baconian or Protestant objections to the darkest Scholasticism, and it can easily be shown that even the most progressive intellects of the early modern period lived in a different world of ideas. Notions of magic, mysterious influences, demons, and the devil did not only comport well with tradition; they had their own inner, rational coherence and helped early modern scholars understand such diverse fields of study as medicine, politics, law, psychology, natural philosophy, and theology. In the words of Stuart Clark, demons were not just "good to think," but virtually indispensable for a culture that believed in a fairly literal interpretation of the Bible.[33] A better question, therefore, has emerged: under what conditions did this demon-filled and magical worldview come to seem insufficient or worn out? Learning to ask this question is also a sign of the progress made over the past forty years.

Since 1960, scholars have developed a quantifying social historical and juridical model for research that has cast a flood of welcome light on conditions in early modern villages as well as on the world of officials and magistrates. The inquisitorial records held in Madrid, Venice, and Rome are slowly revealing their secrets, with the astonishing result that in precisely

---

[31]Kieckhefer, *Magic in the Middle Ages*, 199–200.
[32]Behringer, *Witches and Witch-Hunts*, 91–108, esp. 102.
[33]Clark, *Thinking with Demons*.

those courts where the Catholic Church could control judicial procedures most closely, inquisitors revealed an early and deep skepticism and such a deep juridical caution that, after about 1520, they allowed extremely few witches to be condemned.[34] These early results will surely prompt further investigations that will reveal more about the intellectual world, the prejudices, and the practice of these inquisitors. But it has become obvious that one can no longer speak one-sidedly of a misogynistic church bent on destroying witchcraft with any means available.[35]

The records of witchcraft trials from early modern Europe have illuminated much more than just legal history. Already in the great work of Keith Thomas, it was clear how much one could learn about social and cultural history from trial documents and witchcraft treatises.[36] And in Thomas's work, one cannot neglect the great influence of social and cultural anthropology on witchcraft studies. If the past is another country, then one might be well advised to prepare oneself for such a foreign country with theories and examples, so that we, as travelers, might learn to see more than the illusory mirror image of our own face in the train window. Thomas tried to teach his readers how to step out of the train of their own *Weltanschauung* in order, so to speak, to mix and converse with the foreign natives of the past. His book, *Religion and the Decline of Magic* (1971), pointed a whole generation of historians to problems and themes that could be better understood with the help of social and cultural anthropology. Unfortunately, his effort was not welcomed by many British and American anthropologists, so that the projected collaboration between these two disciplines too often ground to a halt. The works of Wolfgang Behringer, Rainer Walz, Bob Scribner, Alan Macfarlane, Eva Labouvie, and David Sabean have shown, however, how much historians stand to gain from the insights of anthropology.[37]

---

[34]Homza, *Religious Authority in the Spanish Renaissance*; Monter, *Frontiers of Heresy*; Gari Lacruz, *Brujería e Inquisición en el Alto Aragon*; Bethencourt, *O Imaginario da Magia*; Bethencourt, "Portugal"; del Río, *La Santa Inquisición*; Henningsen, *Salazar Documents*; Decker, *Die Päpste und die Hexen*; Milani, *Streghe e Diavoli*; Martin, *Witchcraft and the Inquisition in Venice*; Di Simplicio, *Inquisizione, Stregoneria, Medicina*; Foa, *Eretici*; and Schwerhoff, *Die Inquisition*, 114–26.

[35]See also Ostorero and Anheim, *Le diable en procès*; and Modestin, *Le diable chez l'évêque*.

[36]Thomas, *Religion and the Decline of Magic*.

[37]Macfarlane, *Witchcraft in Tudor and Stuart England*; Hutton, "Anthropological and Historical Approaches to Witchcraft"; Hsia and Scribner, *Problems in the Historical Anthropology of Early Modern Europe*; Barry, Hester, and Roberts, *Witchcraft in Early Modern Europe*; Behringer, *Hexenverfolgung in Bayern*; Labouvie, *Verbotene Künste*; Walz, *Hexenglaube und Magische Kommunikation*; Eiden, Voltmer, Franz, and Irsigler, *Hexenprozesse und Konzepte der Historischen Hexenforschung*; and Hutton, "Anthropological and Historical Approaches to Witchcraft."

Something similar could be said for insights coming from psychology. Forty years ago, the only efforts in this field were rather stiff and formulaic psychoanalytic attempts to explain witchcraft trials everywhere through a few easily identified traits or tendencies.[38] Because of the opposition of Johann Weyer (Wier) to witch trials, he was often celebrated as a father of modern psychiatry.[39] But over the last generation, a few scholars have succeeded in extracting careful analyses from a close reading of witchcraft trial records. Lyndal Roper is a good example (drawing on German evidence), but John Demos (using New England sources) provides another.[40] Such works have had the result that today, we are likely to find more valuable content in village accusations and in confessions, even if they were extracted by torture, than we used to when we saw them as nothing more than the crude application of force or the brutal impress of patriarchy. Roper has succeeded in using these difficult sources to illumine the lived world of mothers and postmenopausal women, a world in which other women and *not* men established the formative pressures of many gender expectations. Although one runs a risk in viewing the past through the psychological lenses of the present, careful work has brought real insights here.[41]

What else? In recent decades we have finally succeeded in freeing the history of demonic possession from the history of superstition. We now recognize the exemplary force of successful exorcisms. They formed a topos that actually began with the healing miracles of Jesus and that continues today.[42] It has also become clear that this history is not the same as that of witchcraft. They could flow together in such a way that possession cases might lead to accusations of witchcraft, but this connection was far from necessary. The notion of superstition, too, has come in for much

---

[38]Masters, *Eros and Evil*; Midelfort, "Charcot, Freud, and the Demons"; and Ferber, "Charcot's Demons."

[39]Zilboorg, *The Medical Man and the Witch during the Renaissance*.

[40]Roper, *Oedipus and the Devil*; Roper, *Witch Craze*; and Demos, *Entertaining Satan*.

[41]For a note of caution, see Midelfort, *History of Madness in Sixteenth-Century Germany*. Recent work has also shown that in many places men were frequently accused of witchcraft: Labouvie, "Männer im Hexenprozeß"; Schulte, *Hexenmeister*; and Apps and Gow, *Male Witches in Early Modern Europe*.

[42]Ernst, *Teufelsaustreibungen*; Walker, *Unclean Spirits*; Legué, Tourette, and de Certeau, *Soeur Jeanne des Anges*; Sands, *Demon Possession in Elizabethan England*; Sluhovsky, "Devil in the Convent"; Ferber, *Demonic Possession and Exorcism*; Caciola, *Discerning Spirits*; Sharpe, *Bewitching of Anne Gunter*; Midelfort, *Exorcism and Enlightenment*; and Waardt, Midelfort, Schmidt, Lorenz, and Bauer, *Dämonische Besessenheit*.

more searching analysis than ever before.[43] The best works on this topic were hardly imaginable thirty or forty years ago.

And finally, one must mention a series of comparative studies such as the exemplary work of Johannes Dillinger, who has systematically studied two separate territories (Swabian Austria in the German southwest and Electoral Trier in the west) in order to isolate common features along with sharp contrasts.[44] In addition to such works, we now also have a series of excellent local investigations, ranging from village studies to outbreaks in imperial cities, monasteries, and counties.[45] There is no space here to do more than refer to the tidal wave of German studies that began about twenty years ago and that continues to grow increasingly complex and subtle with every passing year.[46] Separate scholarly workshops and conference groups have formed over the past twenty years for the German southwest,[47] the region around Trier in the west,[48] and for the German north.[49] Dissertations have proliferated in the last generation in the fields of history, gender studies, anthropology, literature, folklore, and classics—works that reflect the current fascination with this topic. A new journal has even been founded to gather, channel, and evaluate the recent torrents of research.[50] Recently, the Internet has allowed scholars, especially in Germany, to keep track of the burgeoning literature on various aspects of witchcraft.[51]

[43]Harmening, *Superstitio*; Pott, *Aufklärung und Aberglaube*; Parish, *Religion and Superstition in Reformation Europe*; Armstrong, "Superstition and the Idols of the Mind"; Styers, *Making Magic*; Dym, "Divining Science"; and Bailey, *Magic and Superstition in Europe*.

[44]Dillinger, *Böse Leute*. ✓

[45]Gaskill, *Witchfinders*; Behringer, *Shaman of Oberstdorf*; de Certeau, *Possession at Loudun*; Rapley, *A Case of Witchcraft*; Eiden and Voltmer, *Hexenprozesse und Gerichtspraxis*; Rowlands, *Witchcraft Narratives in Germany*; and Morton and Dähms, *Trial of Tempel Anneke*.

[46]The best German monographs try diligently, with more or less success, to master the increasingly unruly and mountainous literature of the last two decades. The best of these works are at least implicitly, if not explicitly (like that of Dillinger), comparative.

[47]The *Arbeitskreis interdisziplinäre Hexenforschung* (*AKIH*), an interdisciplinary group that has been meeting since 1985, maintains a website at http://www.uni-tuebingen.de/IfGL/akih/akih.htm, and also sponsors conferences, exhibitions, and a series of monographs and conference volumes entitled *Hexenforschung* (11 volumes to date, 1995–2007).

[48]The Arbeitsgemeinschaft Hexenprozesse im Trierer Land has sponsored exhibitions, conferences, and a publication series: *Trierer Hexenprozesse—Quellen und Darstellungen* (7 volumes to date, 1996–2005). See the home page of the project: *Zauberei- und Hexenprozesse im Maas-Rhein-Mosel Raum, mit besonderer Berücksichtigung räumlicher Aspekte*, edited by Franz-Josef Knöchel und Rita Voltmer (http://www.uni-trier.de/hexen).

[49]For northern Germany, a separate group was formed in 2001 by Katrin Moeller of the Universität Halle-Wittenberg and Burghart Schmidt of the Universität Hamburg; *Arbeitskreis für Norddeutsche Hexen- und Kriminalitätsforschung*, http://www2.geschichte.uni-halle.de/hexen/hexproj.htm.

[50]*Magic, Ritual and Witchcraft* (founded in 2006 by Brian Copenhaver and Michael Bailey).

[51]See especially, Schwerhoff, *Dresdner Auswahlbibliographie zur Hexenforschung*; Graf, Edited

It is surely not too much to say that in the midst of all this scholarly effort witchcraft research has come of age, with thriving international websites, conferences, exhibitions, and publication series. We are a long way from 1960.

The Future of Witchcraft Research

So what should this mature research topic with its various methods undertake now? What is still lacking? We will of course continue to see more of what we have already noticed: research that evaluates the European, colonial, and global dimensions of witchcraft steadily filling in the shrinking blank spots on the map with bright, assertive colors or with the scholarly gray tones of imperfect knowledge. Studying the sociology or epidemiology of witchcraft trials is a procedure that at least implicitly examines every surviving witch trial and places it under the lenses of gender, legal, social, anthropological, and confessional history. In Britain and the German-speaking lands, this great project is nearing its end. As with any mature industry, this is not the sort of research from which one can reasonably expect large or rapid future gains. It is unlikely that the best work will follow the model of legal or social epidemiology. For one thing, witchcraft studies (like most other areas of history) have been affected by the linguistic turn, and many scholars are no longer persuaded that the sources make it possible to tell a referential story of what really happened. As Marion Gibson has pointed out, even narrative sources that seem relatively unproblematic deployed plot devices and authorial selves that impede any straightforward reading from text to event.[52]

And yet there will remain much to do, for certain deficits are already evident. Scholars will have to seek out specific episodes in which they can find overlapping and linked sources (not just trial records), but sources from which they can hope to reconstruct a more exact picture of the politics, economy, wealth relations, neighborhood tensions, and the church history of communities, rather than the one-dimensional picture obtained from even the densest judicial records. In most cases, a diverse array of sources is not available, or they survive only in fragments. A classic example of what this sort of research can achieve, however, can be found in the

---

discussion group, "Hexenforschung," on the history of witchcraft; Gersmann, *Das Lexikon zur Geschichte der europäischen Hexenverfolgung*; *La Chasse aux Sorcières (on French trials and sources)*; and *Salem Witchcraft Trials, 1692*.

[52]Gibson, *Reading Witchcraft*. See also Purkiss, *The Witch in History*.

notorious panic at Salem, Massachusetts, in 1692. There, the literate and zealous New Englanders preserved such exact tax, settlement, council, and probate records, such careful church memoranda and minutes, such complete accounts of judicial proceedings, such remarkable manuscript caches of letters, diaries, and sermons, along with so many helpful maps, that historians continue to make discoveries almost every year. In 1950, historians already knew what had happened at Salem, but since that date scholars have produced well over twenty substantial books that exploit the surviving wealth of records. These books do more than illustrate the various virtues of microhistory; they also display the progress that comes with the most diverse sets of questions.[53] Scholars can now study themes that the general history of witchcraft in Europe (including Britain) has only rarely examined. We can compare the relations of rich and poor in witchcraft accusations,[54] study the theological views of the Salem Village minister, Samuel Parris, both before and during the panic,[55] study the involvement of village leaders and estimate their various reasons for the views they expressed,[56] and examine the practice of medicine in Salem and see how and why physicians came to conclude that the afflicted girls were suffering from unnatural or supernatural assaults.[57] Scholars now know much more about the position of women and girls in Salem: which ones were more likely to become victims of the devil, which ones more likely the victims of their neighbors.[58] We can now better evaluate the tardy involvement of Governor Phips and the colonial Massachusetts magistracy in the affair.[59] Scholars have begun to learn more about the impact of Indian raids and frontier troubles upon the local fears in Salem,[60] and are approaching a better

---

[53]Using the amazingly rich colonial records, local studies of Salem, Massachusetts, and of New England witchcraft more generally, have mushroomed into a subspecialty of their own. Here and in the following notes are a sampling: Francis, *Judge Sewall's Apology*; Cooper, *Escaping Salem*; Norton, *In the Devil's Snare*; Hoffer, *Salem Witchcraft Trials*; Cooper and Minkema, *Sermon Notebook of Samuel Parris*; Boyer and Nissenbaum, *Salem-Village Witchcraft*; and Boyer and Nissenbaum, *Salem Possessed*.

[54]Boyer and Nissenbaum, *Salem Possessed*.

[55]Weisman, *Witchcraft, Magic, and Religion*; Gragg, *Quest for Security*; Cooper and Minkema, *Sermon Notebook of Samuel Parris*; and Godbeer, *Devil's Dominion*. Cf. Upton, *Devil and George Burroughs*.

[56]Boyer and Nissenbaum, *Salem Possessed*; Boyer and Nissenbaum, *Salem Witchcraft Papers*; and Boyer and Nissenbaum, *Salem-Village Witchcraft*.

[57]Fox, *Science and Justice*; and Carlson, *Fever in Salem*.

[58]Reis, *Damned Women*; and Karlsen, *Devil in the Shape of a Woman*.

[59]Gildrie, *Salem, Massachusetts, 1626–1683*; Demos, *Entertaining Satan*; Konig, *Law and Society in Puritan Massachusetts*; Hoffer, *Salem Witchcraft Trials*; and Ray, "New Discoveries of the Salem Witchcraft Trials."

[60]Norton, *In the Devil's Snare*.

understanding of racial problems in New England, starting from the important fact that a West Indian slave, Tituba, had practiced (and taught?) magic of a sort to the children in Samuel Parris's household, children who later claimed to be afflicted by witchcraft.[61] And scholars now know that the life histories of several of the actors in Salem were intertwined in ways that we never suspected a generation ago.[62] After some years of neglect, religious tensions in and around Salem are coming back into focus.[63]

This list of themes could be extended almost *ad libitum*, even without noting the remarkable outpouring of popular literature, readers, collections of essays, and children's books.[64] But one conclusion should be clear: with so many interlinked and overlapping sources, and with so many different scholars working through them, much more is known today than ever was before about the religious, family, economic, gender, racial, political, legal, medical, and military conditions that together shaped the witchcraft trials of colonial New England. No one historian could have achieved this result alone, and no team could have done so either. This richness was possible only because ambitious and competitive scholars have been eager to make their mark by disagreeing with much that they had read on their chosen topic. In a word, despite solid work done in the nineteenth and early twentieth centuries, the last generation has not remained content with the "definitive" works of yesterday's masters.

The moral of this little American tale would seem to be that we should perhaps place less emphasis upon composing final and exhaustive habilitation-worthy accounts of the trial records as we find them all over Europe. Instead, scholars should seek out especially favored caches of sources, where various points of view might find grist for their various mills. As an example, consider the records that survive for the ducal town of Calw in Württemberg, where a major outbreak of witchcraft panic was

---

[61]Breslaw, *Tituba, Reluctant Witch of Salem*; Hubbard, *Recovered Writers/Recovered Texts*; and Cox, *Postmodern Tales of Slavery in the Americas*. Cf. the novel by Maryse Condé, *Moi, Tituba Socière: Noire de Salem*.

[62]Hill, *Delusion of Satan*; Hoffer, *Devil's Disciples*; Roach, *Salem Witch Trials*; LeBeau, *Story of the Salem Witch Trials*; Robinson, *Salem Witchcraft and Hawthorne's House of the Seven Gables*; and especially the insightful close reading of Rosenthal, *Salem Story*.

[63]Francis, *Judge Sewall's Apology*; Latner, "Here Are No Newters"; Ray, "Satan's War Against the Covenant"; and see the special issue of the *William and Mary Quarterly* (forthcoming in 2008) devoted to revising Salem, which will include Ray, "Geography of Witchcraft Accusations in Salem Village, 1692."

[64]Recent works include Levack, *Witchcraft in Colonial America*; Herget, *Die Salemer Hexenverfolgungen*; Sebald, *Witch-Children*; Mappen, *Witches and Historians*; Geis, *Trial of Witches*; Hall, *Witch-Hunting in Seventeenth-Century New England*; and Breslaw, *Witches of the Atlantic World*.

narrowly avoided in 1684. Even knowing Calw had been a hotbed of proto-industry and early Pietism, I was simply overwhelmed on encountering this episode in the state archives of Stuttgart and Ludwigsburg.[65] If one stacked up the records on Calw alone, the pile would be over three meters in height. I struggled to tell a little story that I hoped would get the basic story straight, but it was clear that other sources such as the tax records, church accounts, and personal letters would certainly extend the primary source base in a manner that might illumine the history of much more than just the witchcraft trials. What if Calw (or other cases like it) could become another Salem?[66]

More intensive histories are needed, But also needed are legal studies that take more than witchcraft trials into account. Here the works of Gerd Schwerhoff and Andreas Blauert provide models,[67] but their approach is extended in the recent dissertation of Laura Stokes, who is considering the broad context of punishment for felonies in fifteenth-century Swiss and German towns.[68]

Concepts that defined witchcraft also need to be handled more carefully. It should not be assumed (as too many have done) that every magistrate and inquisitor had read everything that is available today on demonology. And there needs to be noted what might be called an epidemiology of the competing concepts of witchcraft in order to see, if possible, which ideas spread, and where, and when. Here, folklorists have already done good work, and Wolfgang Behringer made some use of their work in his little book, *Shaman of Oberstdorf.*[69] But generally, it is still not known where the chief ideas of the *Malleus Maleficarum* were deployed, and where one must rather suspect the influence of Peter Binsfeld, Jean Bodin, Johann Weyer (Wier), Martin Delrio, or others. Even if one read everything that had been published on witchcraft in the German southwest (a

---

[65]Lehmann, *Pietismus und Weltliche Ordnung*. This episode is also covered in Midelfort, *Witch Hunting in Southwestern Germany*.

[66]In 2008 Thomas W. Robisheaux will publish *The Miller's Wife: Sorcery and Witchcraft in a German Village*, a study of a densely documented witchcraft investigation in the Franconian village of Hürden (Hohenlohe).

[67]Blauert and Schwerhoff, *Kriminalitätsgeschichte*; Schreiner and Schwerhoff, *Verletzte Ehre*; Blauert and Schwerhoff, *Mit den Waffen der Justiz*; Schwerhoff, *Köln im Kreuzverhör*; Blauert, *Ketzer, Zauberer, Hexen*; Blauert, *Das Urfehdewesen im Deutschen Südwesten*; and Blauert and Wiebel, *Gauner- und Diebslisten*. See also Oestmann, *Hexenprozesse am Reichskammergericht*; and Eiden and Voltmer, *Hexenprozesse und Gerichtspraxis*.

[68]Stokes, "Demons of Urban Reform."

[69]Behringer, *Shaman of Oberstdorf.*

useful project in itself), this method is obviously inadequate to the task of seeing what ideas were available here or there at specific times.

In the future, more attention should be spent on the "small" witch-craft trials that were so common throughout northern Europe. So much effort has been poured into examining the worst cases, the massive chain reaction trials that sent hundreds of victims to the stake, that there is a risk of ignoring the far more common small-scale suspicions, resentments, and trials they provoked. The supposedly sharp distinction between trials for magic (sorcery) and trials for witchcraft (heresy) needs to be examined much more closely, or simply set aside, as Wolfgang Behringer does in his recent *Witches and Witch-Hunts*. The imperial legal code of 1532, called the *Carolina*, made no such distinction, choosing to punish harmful magic with death by fire, and harmless magic in some milder manner.

It is also time to discover what happened to those accused of witch-craft who were not executed. Some large number was exiled, for example, but there exists no good history of exiles in most parts of northern Europe. What did exile mean for a single woman or for an old man?[70] The sources for such a question may be unusually difficult because when a person was exiled, he or she usually disappeared from the local judicial records. Did such persons regularly resurface elsewhere as beggars or vagabonds?

It should also be recognized that cultural history does not always (or even usually) follow the lead or intentions of the cultural leaders or intellec-tuals. Important events often run directly counter to intent and expectation. Witchcraft historians have spent a lot of energy examining those figures who openly and explicitly opposed witchcraft trials: Johann Weyer (Wier), Reginald Scot, Cornelius Loos, Anton Praetorius, Friedrich Spee, Balthasar Bekker, and Christian Thomasius.[71] Scholars have also begun to appreciate even the lesser-known skeptics, such as Hermann Löher (author of the *Wehmütige Klage*, printed in 1676).[72] It has, however, turned out to be diffi-cult to find any direct influence of the skeptic upon actual witchcraft trials. More often, a wave of trials ended in exhaustion or in the chastened recog-nition that one no longer knew how exactly to eradicate witches. Judges and

---

[70]A few examples are Shaw, *Politics of Exile*; Starn, *Contrary Commonwealth*; and Grasmück, *Exi-lium*. But these studies treat mainly the problems of learned and elite exiles, not those of the poorer classes. Jason Coy has written a dissertation dealing with banishment as a punishment in Ulm; "In Punishment of Open Vice."

[71]For a survey of many of the major skeptics, see Lehmann and Ulbricht, *Vom Unfug der Hexen-prozesse*.

[72]Becker, "Die 'wehmütige Klage.'"

magistrates almost never condemned their own prosecutions as unfair, illegal, fanatic exercises, or as procedures that were essentially wrong or evil. But they did, often enough, recognize that waves of trials had succeeded mainly because procedural safeguards had been relaxed, leading to confusion and the acceptance of false testimony. And so, again and again, from place to place, witchcraft trials were locally stopped by men who still believed in witchcraft. That also helps explain why the statutes permitting witch trials were usually revised only long after actual trials had dried up.[73] There are deep ironies here that scholars will need to explore more fully in the future.

It is in this limited sense that one may welcome a recent book by Walter Stephens, who has concluded that the demonological writings of the late Middle Ages do not at all mean what we have thought. He has argued that when theologians and jurists emphasized that witches had real and fleshly intercourse with demons, when they assembled confessions of diabolical sex and looked for almost pornographic details of what demonic sex was like, it was because these thinkers were actually seeking physical evidence for the existence of the world of spirits.[74] According to Stephens, this quest stemmed from their anxiety and hidden doubts that the reciprocal relations of spirits and human beings could not be demonstrated, and that without proof crucial Christian doctrines might be vulnerable to critique. On these lines, the theorists of witchcraft were not deeply persuaded of their theories, but were, in truth, writhing in an agony of doubt. The more fanatic they seemed, the more anxious they must have been. The real struggle between the skeptic and the believer was, therefore, an inner one, and the witch hunt was fueled not by faith or credulity, but by doubt.[75] Stephens has not proven such a counterintuitive and postmodern claim, one that might suggest the even stranger thesis that those figures who have seemed to be the great early modern skeptics, such as Johann Weyer, were actually far more credulous than the desperate demonologists.[76] But he has at least read the fifteenth-century demonologists closely enough to suggest important revisions of how Kramer composed and altered his *Malleus*

[73]Levack, "Decline and End of Witchcraft Prosecutions."

[74]Stephens, *Demon Lovers.*

[75]Stephens, *Demon Lovers,* 364. Modern scholars seem to have difficulty believing that a true believer may truly believe what he says. Stephens's argument runs parallel to that of Richard Marius (*Thomas More: A Biography*), in which More's intense opposition to Lutheran heresy was interpreted as a symptom of unexpressed doubts.

[76]See the sharp rebuke of Wolfgang Behringer in his review of *Demon Lovers.* See also Clark, Review of *Demon Lovers.*

Maleficarum, and he has reminded us that history can be full of strange ironies.

Hans Peter Broedel has presented a related argument in his 2003 book on the *Malleus Maleficarum,* in which he argues that the extraordinary emphasis in that text upon female fleshly lusts as a source of witchcraft rested not upon male confidence in masculine superiority to women, but on an anxiety concerning the supposedly insatiable appetites and sexual energy of women.[77] How and why such an anxiety grew and under what circumstances will surely be an important question for the coming generation. The past decade has seen some good work on critical episodes of gender panic in the eighteenth, nineteenth, and twentieth centuries, but it may be that this concept needs to be extended back to the late Middle Ages in order to comprehend the gender anxieties of zealous demonologists.[78] There may turn out to be connections between the reforming impulse of fifteenth-century churchmen and the hitherto neglected anxieties of the later Middle Ages. In the recent work of Tamar Herzig, for example, Heinrich Kramer's views of witches have been compared with his newly discovered views of the female mystics of northern Italy, whom Kramer extravagantly admired and even envied. His attitude, in other words, cannot be simply summarized as one of misogyny.[79]

Scholars are just beginning to realize how deeply witchcraft was intertwined with more general questions regarding nature, miracles, and the supernatural. It is known that the devil and his demons were regularly conceived as fallen angels, and that as such they provided theologians with important evidence concerning the world of the spirit and of spirits. In the seventeenth century, Joseph Glanvill spoke for many of his contemporaries when he remarked that unbelief often took its first step as a denial of witchcraft and the physical reality of the devil. For that reason, he worked tirelessly in the years between 1660 and his death in 1680 to collect eyewitness accounts of demonic presence, pressing the new natural sciences into the service of his theological goals and investigating every rumor of poltergeists.[80]

---

[77]Broedel, *Malleus Maleficarum and the Construction of Witchcraft,* 180.

[78]See the examples of Wahrman, "Percy's Prologue"; Quinby, *Millennial Seduction;* Berlanstein, *Daughters of Eve;* Hirdman, "Importance of Gender in the Swedish Labor Movement"; McLaren, *Trials of Masculinity;* and Roberts, *Civilization without Sexes.*

[79]Herzig, "Witches, Saints, and Heretics."

[80]Glanvill, *Sadducismus Triumphatus;* Pauschert, *Joseph Glanvill und die Neue Wissenschaft;* Burns, *Great Debate on Miracles;* Talmor, *Glanvill;* and Hunter, "Witchcraft and the Decline of Belief."

That is also the reason that the biblical passages describing Jesus' encounters with unclean spirits and his exorcisms remained so controversial all the way to the end of the eighteenth century. Thomas Hobbes, Anton Van Dale, and Balthasar Bekker might declare that demons had no physical effects in this world and that priests had generally served to defraud the pious, but such a conclusion seemed to require a much more elaborate and well-argued hermeneutic before mainline Protestant theologians could overcome their suspicion that this sort of skepticism might undermine the whole Christian message.[81] It was not before the second half of the eighteenth century that Lutheran theologians began to recognize what this might involve.[82] Meanwhile, Methodists and Roman Catholics tended to maintain a more literal understanding of Christ's exorcisms, and with it a more physical understanding of the devil and witchcraft. These theological problems will need more attention as we realize just how thoroughly the devil and notions of magic infused the history of Christianity. Meanwhile, ordinary people held fast to notions of magic and witchcraft long after their fashionable social superiors had grown embarrassed over the topic. Good work has been done here, especially for England and the Netherlands, but much more needs to be done.[83]

The future of witchcraft research will not necessarily run along the lines adumbrated above, but it is safe to say that a wide variety of problems of various sorts will continue to haunt and stimulate scholarship. Even if scholars can manage to get the sociology of the great witch hunt straight, and can describe the conditions under which men, rather than women, were the favored suspects, or groups of deviants fell victim, as opposed to isolated members of a community, large questions of theory and interdisciplinary practice remain. It is only when a definitive history of witchcraft is finally achieved that it can be said that the field sadly no longer has any future at all.

---

[81]Hobbes, *Leviathan*, pt. 4, chap. 45; Bekker, *De Betoverde Weereld*; Attfield, "Balthasar Bekker and the Decline of the Witch-Craze"; Fix, *Fallen Angels*; and van Dale, *Dissertationes de origine ac progressu idololatriæ et superstitionum*.

[82]See Midelfort, *Exorcism and Enlightenment*, chap. 4. Cf. Aner, *Die Theologie der Lessingzeit*.

[83]Davies, *Witchcraft, Magic and Culture*; Davies, *Cunning-folk*; de Blécourt and Davies, *Beyond the Witch Trials*; Davies and de Blécourt, *Witchcraft Continued*; de Blécourt, Hutton, and La Fontaine, *Witchcraft and Magic in Europe*; and Gijswijt-Hofstra and Frijhoff, *Witchcraft in the Netherlands*.

Bibliography

This list includes works discussed or cited in the text and more recent scholarly works. For a much more extensive bibliography, see the list of electronic sources or Richard Golden's *Encyclopedia of Witchcraft*.

ELECTRONIC RESOURCES

Arbeitskreis für Norddeutsche Hexen- und Kriminalitätsforschung:
   http://www2.geschichte.uni-halle.de/hexen/hexproj.htm
Arbeitskreis interdisziplinäre Hexenforschung: http://www.uni-tuebingen.de
Behringer, Wolfgang. "Publications":
   http://www.uni-saarland.de/fak3/behringer/HP/index.html
La Chasse aux Sorcières (French trials and sources):
   http://membres.lycos.fr/chassesorcieres
Dresdner Auswahlbibliographie zur Hexenforschung (DABHEX):
   http://rcswww.urz.tu-dresden.de/~frnz/dabhex/haupt.html.
Gersmann, Gudrun. *Das Lexikon zur Geschichte der europäischen Hexenverfolgung*:
   http://www.sfn.uni-muenchen.de/hexenverfolgung/frame_lexikon.html
Geschichtswissenschaften im Internet, Hexenforschung Themen: http://www.historicum.net/
   themen/hexenforschung/thementexte/forschungsberichte
Graf, Klaus. *Archives of Hexenforschung [Witchcraft Research] Listserv*:
   http://www.listserv.dfn.de/archives/hexenforschung.html
Linder, Douglas. *Famous American Trials: Salem Witchcraft Trials, 1692*:
   http://www.law.umkc.edu/faculty/projects/ftrials/salem/SALEM.HTM.
Schwerhoff, Gerd. *Dresdner Auswahlbibliographie zur Hexenforschung*:
   http://rcswww.urz.tu-dresden.de/~frnz/dabhex/navigation.html
University of Edinburgh. *Survey of Scottish Witchcraft, 1563–1736*:
   http://www.arts.ed.ac.uk/witches/
University of Oxford. *Witch-craft and Witch-Hunting in Early Modern Europe, Bibliography*: www.history.ox.ac.uk/currentunder/bibliographies/prelims-os-witchcraft.pdf
University of Virginia. *Salem Witch Trials, Documental Archive and Transcription Project*:
   http://etext.virginia.edu/salem/witchcraft/home.html

PRINTED SOURCES

Adams, Gretchen A. "The Specter of Salem in American Culture." PhD diss., University of New Hampshire, 2001.
Allen, Richard M. "Crime and Punishment in Sixteenth-Century Reutlingen." PhD diss., University of Virginia, 1980.
Aner, Karl. *Die Theologie der Lessingzeit*. Halle: M. Niemeyer, 1929.
Anheim, Etienne, and Martine Ostorero. *Le diable en Procès: Démonologie et sorcellerie à la fin du Moyen Age*. Vincennes: Presses Universitaires de Vincennes, 2003.
Ankarloo, Bengt. *Att stilla herrevrede: Trolldomsdåden på Vegeholm, 1653–54*. Stockholm: Författarförlaget, 1988.
———, and Gustav Henningsen, eds. *Early Modern European Witchcraft: Centres and Peripheries*. Oxford: Clarendon Press, 1990.
Apps, Lara, and Andrew Gow. *Male Witches in Early Modern Europe*. Manchester, UK: Manchester University Press, 2003.

Armstrong, Sean. "Superstition and the Idols of the Mind: How the Witch Hunt Helped Shape the Scientific Revolution in England." PhD diss., York University (Canada), 2004.

Attfield, Robin. "Balthasar Bekker and the Decline of the Witch-Craze: The Old Demonology and the New Philosophy." *Annals of Science* 42 (1988): 383–95.

Bailey, Michael D. *Battling Demons: Witchcraft, Heresy, and Reform in the Late Middle Ages.* University Park: Pennsylvania State University Press, 2003.

————. *Historical Dictionary of Witchcraft.* Lanham, MD: Scarecrow Press, 2003.

————. *Magic and Superstition in Europe: A Concise History from Antiquity to the Present.* Lanham, MD: Rowman & Littlefield, 2007.

Barry, Jonathan. "Keith Thomas and the Problem of Witchcraft." In Barry, Hester, and Roberts, *Witchcraft in Early Modern Europe*, 1–48.

————, and Owen Davies, eds. *Palgrave Advances in Witchcraft Studies.* New York: Palgrave Macmillan, 2007.

————, Marianne Hester, and Gareth Roberts, eds. *Witchcraft in Early Modern Europe: Studies in Culture and Belief.* Cambridge: Cambridge University Press, 1996.

Becker, Thomas P. *Hexenverfolgung im Rheinland: Ergebnisse neuerer Lokal- und Regionalstudien.* Bensberger Protokolle 85. Bergisch Gladbach: Thomas-Morus-Akademie Bensberg, 1996.

————. "Die 'wehmütige Klage' des Hermann Löher. Ein Augenzeugenbericht über die Hexenverfolgung in einer rheinischen Kleinstadt." *Zeitenblicke* 1, no. 1 (7 August 2002). http://www.zeitenblicke.historicum.net/2002/01/becker/becker.html (accessed 2 April 2007). For the text itself, see Thomas P. Becker, Theresia Becker, Rainer Decker, and Hans de Waardt, eds. *Hochnötige Unterthanige Wemütige Klage der Frommen Unschültigen.* Amsterdam, 1676. Available online at http://www.sfn.uni-muenchen.de/loeher.

Becker-Cantarino, Barbara. "'Feminist Consciousness' and 'Wicked Witches': Recent Studies." *Signs* 20 (1994): 152–75.

Behringer, Wolfgang. "Detecting the Ultimate Conspiracy, or How Waldensians Became Witches." In *Conspiracies and Conspiracy Theory in Early Modern Europe. From the Waldensians to the French Revolution*, edited by Barry Coward and Julian Swann, 13–34. Aldershot: Ashgate, 2004.

————. "Erträge und Perspektiven der Hexenforschung." *Historische Zeitschrift* 249 (1988): 619–40.

————. "Geschichte der Hexenforschung." In *Wider alle Hexerei und Teufelswerk: Die europäische Hexenverfolgung und ihre Auswirkungen auf Südwestdeutschland*, edited by Sönke Lorenz and Jürgen Michael Schmidt, 485–668. Ostfildern: Jan Thorbeke, 2004.

————. *Hexenverfolgung in Bayern: Volksmagie, Glaubenseifer und Staatsräson in der Frühen Neuzeit.* Munich: R. Oldenbourg, 1987. Poorly translated and truncated by J. C. Grayson and David Lederer as *Witchcraft Persecutions in Bavaria: Popular Magic, Religious Zealotry and Reason of State in Early Modern Europe* (Cambridge: Cambridge University Press, 1997).

————. Review of *Demon Lovers: Witchcraft, Sex, and the Crisis of Belief*, by Walter Stephens. *American Historical Review* 108, no. 4 (2003): 1207–8. Available online at http://www.uni-saarland.de/fak3/behringer/HP/pdf_behringer/AHR.pdf (accessed 2 April 2007).

————. *Shaman of Oberstdorf: Chonrad Stoeckhlin and the Phantoms of the Night.* Translated by H. C. Erik Midelfort. Charlottesville: University Press of Virginia, 1998.

————. "Witchcraft Studies in Austria, Germany and Switzerland." In *Witchcraft in Early Modern Europe: Studies in Culture and Belief,* edited by Jonathan Barry, Marianne Hester, and Gareth Roberts, 64–95. Cambridge: Cambridge University, 1996.

————. *Witches and Witch-Hunts: A Global History.* Cambridge: Polity Press, 2004.

————, and Günter Jerouschek, eds. *Der Hexenhammer: Malleus maleficarum von Heinrich Institoris und Jakob Sprenger.* Translated by Werner Tschacher. München: Deutscher Taschenbuch Verlag, 2000.

Bekker, Balthasar. *De Betoverde Weereld,* 4 vols. Amsterdam: D. van den Dalen, 1691–93.

Bender-Wittmann, Ursula. "Hexenprozesse in Lemgo 1628–1637: Eine sozialgeschichtliche Analyse." In *Der Weserraum zwischen 1500 und 1650: Gesellschaft, Wirtschaft und Kultur in der frühen Neuzeit,* 235–66. Marburg: Jonas, 1993.

Berlanstein, Lenard R. *Daughters of Eve: A Cultural History of French Theater Women from the Old Regime to the Fin-de-Siècle.* Cambridge, MA: Harvard University Press, 2001.

Bertolin, Silvia. *La stregoneria nella Valle d'Aosta medievale.* Quart (AO): Musumeci, 2003.

Bertram, Benjamin Glenn. "Skepticism and Social Struggle in Early Modern England." PhD diss., University of California, San Diego, 1997.

Bethencourt, Francisco. *O Imaginario da Magia: Feiticeiras, Saludadores e Nigromantes no Século 16.* Lisbon: Universidade Nova, 1987.

————. "Portugal." In *Early Modern European Witchcraft: Centres and Peripheries,* edited by Bengt Ankarloo and Gustav Henningsen, 403–24. Oxford: Oxford University Press, 1990.

Bever, Edward W. M. "Witchcraft in Early Modern Württemberg (Germany)." PhD diss., Princeton University, 1983.

Biesel, Elisabeth. *Hexenjustiz, Volksmagie und soziale Konflikte im lothringischen Raum.* Trier: Spee, 1997.

Blauert, Andreas. *Das Urfehdewesen im Deutschen Südwesten im Spätmittelalter und in der Frühen Neuzeit.* Tübingen: Bibliotheca Academica, 2000.

————. *Frühe Hexenverfolgungen: Ketzer-, Zauberei- und Hexenprozesse des 15. Jahrhunderts.* Hamburg: Junius, 1989.

————, and Eva Wiebel. *Gauner- und Diebslisten: Registrieren, Identifizieren und Fahnden im 18: Jahrhundert.* Frankfurt am Main: Klostermann, 2001.

————, ed. *Ketzer, Zauberer, Hexen: Die Anfänge der Europäischen Hexenverfolgungen.* Frankfurt am Main: Suhrkamp, 1990.

————, and Gerd Schwerhoff, eds. *Kriminalitätsgeschichte: Beiträge zur Sozial- und Kulturgeschichte der Vormoderne.* Konstanz: Universitätsverlag Konstanz, 2000.

————, and Gerd Schwerhoff, eds. *Mit den Waffen der Justiz: Zur Kriminalitätsgeschichte des Spätmittelalters und der Frühen Neuzeit.* Frankfurt am Main: Fischer Taschenbuch Verlag, 1993.

Boyer, Paul S., and Stephen Nissenbaum, eds. *Salem Possessed: The Social Origins of Witchcraft.* Cambridge, MA: Harvard University Press, 1974.

————, eds. *Salem-Village Witchcraft: A Documentary Record of Local Conflict in Colonial New England.* Boston: Northeastern University Press, 1993.

————, eds. *The Salem Witchcraft Papers: Verbatim Transcripts of the Legal Documents of the Salem Witchcraft Outbreak of 1692.* New York: Da Capo Press, 1977.

Bremmer, Jan N. *The Metamorphosis of Magic from Late Antiquity to the Early Modern Period.* Leuven: Peeters, 2002.

Breslaw, Elaine G. *Witches of the Atlantic World: A Historical Reader & Primary Sourcebook.* New York: New York University Press, 2000.

———, ed. *Tituba, Reluctant Witch of Salem: Devilish Indians and Puritan Fantasies*. New York: New York University Press, 1996.

Briggs, Robin. "By the Strength of Fancie: Witchcraft and the Early Modern Imagination." *Folklore* 115 (2004): 259–72.

———. "Verteidigungsstrategien gegen Hexereibeschuldigungen: Der Fall Lothringen." In *Methoden und Konzepte der historischen Hexenforschung*, edited by Herbert Eiden, Rita Voltmer, Gunther Franz, and Franz Irsigler, 109–28. Trier: Spee, 1998.

———. *Witches and Neighbors: The Social and Cultural Context of European Witchcraft*. New York: Viking, 1996.

Broedel, Hans Peter. *The Malleus Maleficarum and the Construction of Witchcraft: Theology and Popular Belief*. Manchester, UK: Manchester University Press, 2003.

Brooke, Rosalind, and Christopher Brooke. *Popular Religion in the Middle Ages: Western Europe, 1000–1300*. London: Thames and Hudson, 1984.

Burghartz, Susanna. "Hexenverfolgung als Frauenverfolgung? Zur Gleichsetzung von Hexen und Frauen am Beispiel der Luzerner und Lausanner Hexenprozesse des 15. und 16. Jahrhunderts." In *Der Hexenstreit: Frauen in der frühneuzeitlichen Hexenverfolgung*, edited by Claudia Opitz and Ingrid Ahrendt-Schulte, 147–73. Freiburg im Breisgau: Herder, 1995.

Burke, Peter. "The Bishop's Questions and the People's Religion." In *The Historical Anthropology of Early Modern Italy: Essays on Perception and Communication*, edited by Peter Burke, 40–47. Cambridge: Cambridge University Press, 1987.

Burns, Robert M. *The Great Debate on Miracles: From Joseph Glanvill to David Hume*. Lewisburg, PA: Bucknell University Press, 1981.

Butler, Jon. "Witchcraft, Healing, and Historians' Crazes." *Journal of Social History* 18 (1984): 111–18.

Byloff, Fritz. *Hexenglaube und Hexenverfolgung in den österreichischen Alpenländern*. Berlin: de Gruyter, 1934.

Caciola, Nancy. *Discerning Spirits: Divine and Demonic Possession in the Middle Ages*. Ithaca, NY: Cornell University Press, 2003.

Calhoon, Cristina Gardino. "Livia the Poisoner: Genesis of an Historical Myth." PhD diss., University of California, Irvine, 1994.

Callan, Maeve Brigid. "'No such art in this land': Heresy and Witchcraft in Ireland, 1310–1360." PhD diss., Northwestern University, 2002.

Cameron, Euan. *The European Reformation*. Oxford: Clarendon Press, 1991.

Camus, Dominique. *Pouvoirs sorciers: Enquête sur les pratiques actuelles de sorcellerie*. Paris: Imago, 1988.

Carlson, Laurie M. *A Fever in Salem: A New Interpretation of the New England Witch Trials*. Chicago: I. R. Dee, 1999.

Castillo, Monica Del R. "Las brujas y la Inquisición en Cartagena de Indias: En busca de una identidad femenina." PhD diss., Arizona State University, 2001.

Choné, Paulette. "Strafe und Erbarmen: Hexenprozesse gegen Kinder in Lothringen, 1600–1630." In *Im Zeichen der Krise: Religiosität im Europa des 17. Jahrhunderts*, edited by Hartmut Lehmann and Anne-Charlott Trepp, 359–86. Göttingen: Vandenhoeck and Ruprecht, 1999.

Clack, Brian R. *Wittgenstein, Frazer, and Religion*. New York: St. Martin's Press, 1999.

Clark, Stuart. Review of *Demon Lovers*, by Walter Stephens. *Shakespeare Studies* 31 (2003): 296–309.

———. *Thinking with Demons: The Idea of Witchcraft in Early Modern Europe*. Oxford: Oxford University Press, 1997.

————. *Vanities of the Eye: Vision in Early Modern European Culture*. Oxford: Oxford University Press, 2007.

Clauser, Mark Douglas. "Lucan's Erictho and the Roman Witch Tradition." PhD diss., Ohio State University, 1993.

Cohn, Norman. *Europe's Inner Demons: An Inquiry Inspired by the Great Witch Hunt*. London: Chatto, 1975. Rev. ed. New York: Pimlico, 1993.

Condé, Maryse. *Moi, Tituba, Sorcière: Noire de Salem*. Paris: Mercure de France, 1986. Translated by Richard Philcox as *I, Tituba, Black Witch of Salem* (Charlottesville: University Press of Virginia, 1992).

Cooper, James F., Jr., and Kenneth P. Minkema, eds. *The Sermon Notebook of Samuel Parris, 1689–1694*. Charlottesville: University Press of Virginia, 1993.

Cooper, Richard. *Escaping Salem: The Other Witch Hunt of 1692*. New York: Oxford University Press, 2005.

Copenhaver, Brian P. *Symphorien Champier and the Reception of the Occultist Tradition in Renaissance France*. The Hague: Mouton, 1979.

————, ed. and trans. *Hermetica: The Greek Corpus Hermeticum and the Latin Asclepius in a New English Translation, with Notes and Introduction*. Cambridge: Cambridge University Press, 1992.

Coudert, Allison P. "The Myth of the Improved Status of Protestant Women: The Case of the Witchcraze." In *The Politics of Gender in Early Modern Europe*, edited by Jean R. Brink, Alison Coudert, and Maryanne Cline Horowitz, 61–90. Kirksville, MO: Sixteenth Century Journal Publishers, 1989.

Cox, Timothy J. *Postmodern Tales of Slavery in the Americas: From Alejo Carpentier to Charles Johnson*. New York: Garland, 2001.

Coy, Jason Philip. "In Punishment of Open Vice: Criminality and Authority in Sixteenth-Century Ulm." PhD diss., University of California at Los Angeles, 2001.

Crohns, Hjelmar. *Die Summa Theologica des Antonin von Florenz und die Schätzung des Weibes im Hexenhammer*. Helsingfors: Druckerei der Finnischen Litteratur-Gesellschaft, 1903.

Davidson, Jane P. *The Witch in Northern European Art, 1470–1750*. Freren: Luca Verlag, 1987.

Davies, Owen. *Cunning-Folk: Popular Magic in English History*. London: Hambledon, 2003.

————. *Witchcraft, Magic and Culture, 1736–1951*. Manchester, UK: Manchester University Press, 1999.

de Blécourt, Willem, and Owen Davies, eds. *Beyond the Witch Trials: Witchcraft and Magic in Enlightenment Europe*. Manchester, UK: Manchester University Press, 2004.

————, eds. *Witchcraft Continued: Popular Magic in Modern Europe*. Manchester, UK: Manchester University Press, 2004.

de Blécourt, Willem, Ronald Hutton, and Jean La Fontaine. *Witchcraft and Magic in Europe: The Twentieth Century*. London: Athlone, 1999.

de Certeau, Michel. *The Possession at Loudun*. Translated by Michael B. Smith. Chicago: University of Chicago, 2000.

Deal, Laura Kay. "Whores and Witches: The Language of Female Misbehavior in Early Modern England, 1560–1650." PhD diss., University of Colorado, 1996.

Decker, Rainer. "Die Haltung der römischen Inquisition gegenüber Hexenglauben und Exorzismus am Beispiel der Teufelsaustreibungen in Paderborn 1657." In *Das Ende der Hexenverfolgung*, edited by Sönke Lorenz, 97–115. Stuttgart: F. Steiner, 1995.

————. *Die Hexen und ihre Henker: Ein Fallbericht*. Freiburg im Breisgau: Herder, 1994.

———. *Die Päpste und die Hexen: Aus den Geheimen Akten der Inquisition.* Darmstadt: Primus, 2003.

Degn, Christian, Hartmut Lehmann, and Dagmar Unverhau. *Hexenprozesse: Deutsche und Skandinavische Beiträge.* Neumünster: K. Wachholtz, 1983.

Delcambre, Etienne. *Le concept de la sorcellerie dans le Duché de Lorraine au XVIe et au XVIIe siècle.* Nancy: Société d'Archéologie Lorraine, 1948.

del Río, Alfredo Gil. *La Santa Inquisición: Sus Principales Procesos contra la Brujería en España.* Madrid: Edimat Libros, 2002.

Demos, John. *Entertaining Satan: Witchcraft and the Culture of Early New England.* New York: Oxford University Press, 1982.

DeRosa, Robin. "Specters, Scholars, and Sightseers: The Salem Witch Trials and American Memory." PhD diss., Tufts University, 2002.

Desplat, Christian. *Sorcières et diables en Gascogne: Fin XIVe–début XIXe siècle.* Pau: Cairn, 2001.

Diedler, Jean-Claude. *Démons et sorcières en Lorraine: Le bien et le mal dans les communautés rurales de 1550 à 1660.* Paris: Éditions Messene, 1996.

Dienst, Heide. "Entwicklung, Stand und Probleme der Textaufnahme von österreichischen Zaubereiprozeßakten." In *Methoden und Konzepte der historischen Hexenforschung,* edited by Herbert Eiden, Rita Voltmer, Gunther Franz, and Franz Irsigler, 53–68. Trier: Spee, 1998.

Dillinger, Johannes. *Böse Leute: Hexenverfolgungen in Schwäbisch-Österreich und Kurtrier im Vergleich.* Trier: Spee, 1999.

———. "Hexenverfolgungen in Städten." In *Methoden und Konzepte der historischen Hexenforschung,* edited by Herbert Eiden, Rita Voltmer, Gunther Franz, and Franz Irsigler, 129–65. Trier: Spee, 1998.

———. "Richter als Angeklagte: Hexenprozesse gegen herrschaftliche Amtsträger in Kurtrier und Schwäbisch-Österreich." In *Vergleichende Perspektive—Perspektiven des Vergleichs: Studien zur europäischen Geschichte von der Spätantike bis ins 20. Jahrhundert,* edited by Helga Schanbel-Schüle and Werner Daum, 123–69. Mainz: P. van Zabern, 1998.

Dinzelbacher, Peter. *Handbuch der Religionsgeschichte im deutschsprachigen Raum.* Vol. 2, *Hoch- und Spätmittelalter.* Paderborn: Ferdinand Schöningh, 2000.

Di Simplicio, Oscar. *Autunno della stregoneria: Maleficio e magia nell'Italia moderna.* Bologna: Il mulino, 2005.

———. *Inquisizione, stregoneria, medicina: Siena e il suo stato (1580–1721).* Monteriggioni: Il leccio, 2000.

Duerr, Hans Peter, ed. *Der Wissenschaftler und das Irrationale,* 4 vols. Frankfurt am Main: Syndikat, 1985.

Dukes, Eugene D. "Magic and Witchcraft in the Writings of the Western Church Fathers." PhD diss., Kent State University, 1972.

Dusseau, Joëlle. *Le juge et la sorcière [Pierre de Lancre].* Bordeaux: Éditions Sud ouest, 2002.

Dym, Warren Alexander. "Divining Science: Treasure hunting and the Saxon mining industry, 1500–1800." PhD diss., University of California, Davis, 2005.

Eiden, Herbert, and Rita Voltmer, eds. *Hexenprozesse und Gerichtspraxis.* Trier: Spee, 2002.

Eiden, Herbert, Rita Voltmer, Gunther Franz, and Herbert Irsigler, eds. *Methoden und Konzepte der Historischen Hexenforschung.* Trier: Spee, 1998.

Eire, Carlos M. N. "'Bite this, Satan!': The Devil in Luther's "Table Talk." In *Piety and Family in Early Modern Europe: Essays in Honour of Steven Ozment*, edited by Marc R. Forster, 70–93. Aldershot: Ashgate, 2005.

Ernst, Cécile. *Teufelaustreibungen: Die Praxis der katholischen Kirche im 16.und 17. Jahrhundert.* Bern: H. Huber, 1972.

Estes, Leland. "Incarnation of Evil: Changing Perspectives on the European Witch Craze." *Clio* 13 (1984): 133–47.

———. "The Role of Medicine and Medical Theories in the Rise and Fall of the Witch Hunts in England." PhD diss., University of Chicago, 1985.

Ewen, C. L'Estrange, ed. *Witch Hunting and Witch Trial: The Indictments for Witchcraft from the Records of 1373 Assizes held for the Home Circuit A.D. 1559–1736.* London: K. Paul, Trench, Trubner, 1929.

Favret-Saada, Jeanne. *Deadly Words: Witchcraft in the Bocage.* Translated by Catherine Cullen. New York: Cambridge University Press, 1980.

Febvre, Lucien. *The Problem of Unbelief in the 16th Century: The Religion of Rabelais.* Translated by Beatrice Gottlieb. Cambridge, MA: Harvard University Press, 1982.

Ferber, Sarah. "Charcot's Demons: Retrospective Medicine and Historical Diagnosis in the Writings of the Salpêtrière School." In *Illness and Healing Alternatives in Western Europe*, edited by Marijke Gijswijt-Hofstra, Hilary Marland, and Hans de Waardt, 120–40. London: Routledge, 1997.

———. *Demonic Possession and Exorcism in Early Modern France.* London: Routledge, 2004.

Fisher, Anne Louise. "The Power of a 'Naughty Name': Performing Witchcraft in Early Modern England [1587–1621]." PhD diss., Pennsylvania State University, 2000.

Fix, Andrew. *Fallen Angels: Balthasar Bekker, Spirit Belief and Confessionalism in the Seventeenth-Century Dutch Republic.* Dordrecht: Kluwer, 1999.

Foa, Anna. *Eretici: Storie di Streghe, Ebrei e Convertiti.* Bologna: Mulino, 2004.

Fox, Sanford J. *Science and Justice: The Massachusetts Witchcraft Trials.* Baltimore, MD: Johns Hopkins Press, 1968.

Francis, Richard. *Judge Sewall's Apology: The Salem Witch Trials and the Forming of the American Conscience.* New York: Fourth Estate, 2005.

Franz, Gunther, Günter Gehl, and Franz Irsigler, eds. *Hexenprozesse und deren Gegner im trierisch-lothringischen Raum.* Weimar: Dadder, 1997.

Freytag, Nils. *Aberglauben im 19. Jahrhundert: Preussen und seine Rheinprovinz zwischen Tradition und Moderne (1815–1918).* Berlin: Duncker & Humblot, 2003.

———, and Benoît van den Bossche. "Aberglauben, Krankheit und das Böse: Exorzismus und Teufelsglaube im 18. und 19. Jahrhundert." *Rheinisch-westfälische Zeitschrift für Volkskunde* 44 (1999): 67–93.

Fritz, Thomas. "Hexenverfolgungen in der Reichsstadt Reutlingen." In *Zum Feuer verdammt: Die Hexenverfolgungen in der Grafschaft Hohenberg, der Reichsstadt Reutlingen und der Fürstpropstei Ellwangen*, edited by Thomas Fritz, Johannes Dillinger, and Wolfgang Mährle, 163–324. Stuttgart: F. Steiner, 1998.

Fuchs, Ralf-Peter. "'Von diesen unbesonnenen, ärgerlichen und gottlosen Hexen-Processen': Schlaglichter auf die Hexenverfolgungen in Herford zur Zeit des Dreißigjährigen Krieges." *Historisches Jahrbuch für den Kreis Herford* (1993): 17–52.

Gaboriau, Patrick. *La pensée ensorcelée: La sorcellerie actuelle en Anjou et en Vendée.* Les Sables-d'Olonne: Le Cercle d'or, 1987.

Gage, Matilda Joslyn. *Woman, Church and State: A Historical Account of the Status of Woman through the Christian Ages; With Reminiscences of the Matriarchate.* New York: Truth Seeker Co., 1893.

Gallucci, Mary Margaret. "The Erotics of Witchcraft and the Politics of Desire in Renaissance Florence." PhD diss., University of Connecticut, 1997.

Ganz, Peter, ed. *Das Buch als magisches und als Repräsentationsobjekt.* Wiesbaden: Harrossowitz, 1992.

Gari Lacruz, Angel. *Brujería e Inquisición en el Alto Aragón en la Primera Mitad del Siglo XVII.* Zaragoza: Diputación General de Aragón, 1991.

Garrett, Julia Milligan. "Community and Intimacy in English Witchcraft Discourse." PhD diss., University of California, Santa Barbara, 2004.

Gaskill, Malcolm. *Witchfinders: A Seventeenth-Century English Tragedy.* Cambridge, MA: Harvard University Press, 2005.

Gebhard, Horst. *Hexenprozesse im Kurfürstentum Mainz des 17. Jahrhunderts.* Aschaffenburg: Geschichts- und Kunstverein Aschaffenburg, 1989.

Geis, Gilbert. *A Trial of Witches: A Seventeenth-Century Witchcraft Prosecution.* London: Routledge, 1997.

Gersmann, Gudrun. "Die Hexe als Heimatheldin: Die Hexenverfolgungen der Frühen Neuzeit im Visier der Heimathistoriker." *Westfälische Forschungen* 45 (1995): 102–33.

———. "'Gehe hin und verthedige dich!': Injurienklagen als Mittel der Abwehr von Hexereiverdächtigungen; Ein Fallbeispiel aus dem Fürstbistum Münster." In *Ehrkonzepte in der Frühen Neuzeit: Identitäten und Abgrenzungen*, edited by Sybylle Backman and Ute Ecker-Offenhäusser, 239–69. Berlin: Akademie Verlag, 1998.

———. "Wasserproben und Hexenprozesse: Ansichten der Hexenverfolgung im Fürstbistum Münster." *Westfälische Forschungen* 48 (1998): 449–79.

Gibson, Marion. *Reading Witchcraft: Stories of Early English Witches.* London: Routledge, 1999.

Gijswijt-Hofstra, Marijke. "Recent Witchcraft Research in the Low Countries." In *Historical Research in the Low Countries*, edited by N. van Sas and Els Witte, 23–34. Den Haag: Nederlands Historisch Genootschap, 1992.

———, and Willem Frijhoff, eds. *Witchcraft in the Netherlands: From the Fourteenth to the Twentieth Century.* Translated by Rachel M. J. van der Wilden-Fall. Rotterdam: Universitaire Pers Rotterdam, 1991.

Gildrie, Richard P. *Salem, Massachusetts, 1626–1683: A Covenant Community.* Charlottesville: University Press of Virginia, 1975.

Ginzburg, Carlo. *Ecstasies: Deciphering the Witches' Sabbath.* Translated by Raymond Rosenthal. London: Hutchinson Radius, 1990.

———. *I benandanti: Stregoneria e culti agrari tra Cinquecento e Seicento.* Turin, 1966. Translated by John and Anne Tedeschi as *The Night Battles: Witchcraft & Agrarian Cults in the Sixteenth & Seventeenth Centuries.* London: Routledge & Kegan Paul, 1983.

Glanvill, Joseph. *Sadducismus Triumphatus: or, Full and Plain Evidence Regarding Witches and Apparitions.* London, 1681.

Gloger, Bruno, and Walter Zöllner, eds. *Teufelsglaube und Hexenwahn.* Wien: Böhlau, 1999.

Godbeer, Richard. *The Devil's Dominion: Magic and Religion in Early New England.* Cambridge: Cambridge University Press, 1992.

Golden, Richard, ed. *The Encyclopedia of Witchcraft: The Western Tradition.* 4 vols. Santa Barbara, CA: ABC-Clio, 2006.

Goodare, Julian, ed. *The Scottish Witch-Hunt in Context.* Manchester. UK: Manchester University Press, 2002.

Göttsch, Silke. "Hexenglauben und Schadenszauber: Zur Disziplinierung leibeigener Untertanen." *Kieler Blätter zur Volkskunde* 23 (1991): 55–65.

Graf, Klaus. "Carlo Ginzburg's Hexensabbat: Herausforderung an die Methodendiskussion der Geschichtswissenschaft." *Zeitschrift für Kulturwissenschaften* 5 (1993): 1–16.

Gragg, Larry Dale. *A Quest for Security: The Life of Samuel Parris, 1653–1720.* New York: Greenwood Press, 1990.

Graham, Michael F. *The Uses of Reform: "Godly Discipline" and Popular Behavior in Scotland and Beyond, 1560–1610.* Leiden: Brill, 1996.

Grasmück, Ernst Ludwig. *Exilium: Untersuchungen zur Verbannung in der Antike.* Paderborn: Schöningh, 1978.

Grinnell, Richard William. "English Demonology and Renaissance Drama: The Politics of Fear." PhD diss., University of Minnesota, 1992.

Hall, David D., ed. *Witch-Hunting in Seventeenth-Century New England: A Documentary History, 1638–1693.* Boston: Northeastern University Press, 1991.

Hansen, Joseph. *Quellen und Untersuchungen zur Geschichte des Hexenwahns und der Hexenverfolgung im Mittelalter.* Bonn: C. Georgi, 1901.

———. *Zauberwahn, Inquisition und Hexenprozess im Mittelalter und die Entstehung der grossen Hexenverfolgung.* Munich: Oldenbourg, 1900.

Harline, Craig. "Official Religion: Popular Religion in Recent Historiography of the Catholic Reformation." *Archiv für Reformationsgeschichte* 81 (1990): 239–62.

Harmening, Dieter. *Superstitio: Überlieferungs- und theoriegeschichtliche Untersuchungen zur kirchlich-theologischen Aberglaubensliteratur des Mittelalters.* Berlin: E. Schmidt, 1979.

———, and Andrea Rudolph, eds. *Hexenverfolgung in Mecklenburg: Regionale und überregionale Aspekte.* Dettelbach: Röll, 1997.

Hehl, Ulrich von. "Hexenprozesse und Geschichtswissenschaft." *Historisches Jahrbuch* 107 (1987): 349–75.

Helmrath, Johannes. *Das Basler Konzil 1431–1449: Forschungsstand und Probleme.* Cologne: Böhlau, 1978.

Henningsen, Gustav, ed. *The Salazar Documents: Inquisitor Alonso de Salazar Frías and Others on the Basque Witch Persecution.* Leiden: Brill, 2004.

———. *The Witches' Advocate: Basque Witchcraft and the Spanish Inquisition, 1609–1614.* Reno: University of Nevada Press, 1980.

———, and John A. Tedeschi, eds. *The Inquisition in Early Modern Europe: Studies on Sources and Methods.* Dekalb: Northern Illinois University Press, 1986.

Herget, Winfried, ed. *Die Salemer Hexenverfolgungen: Perspektiven, Kontexte, Repräsentationen.* Trier: Wissenschaftlicher Verlag Trier, 1994.

Herzig, Tamar. "Witches, Saints, and Heretics: Heinrich Kramer's Ties with Italian Female Mystics." *Magic, Ritual and Witchcraft* 1 (2006): 24–55.

Hess, Albert. "Hunting Witches: A Survey of Some Recent Literature."*Criminal Justice History* 3 (1982): 47–79.

Hill, Frances A. *Delusion of Satan: The Full Story of the Salem Witch Trials.* New York: Doubleday, 1995.

Hirdman, Yvonne. "The Importance of Gender in the Swedish Labor Movement. Or: A Swedish Dilemma." *Abetarrörelsens Arkiv och Bibliotek* (2002): 1–11.

Hobbes, Thomas. *Leviathan, or The Matter, Forme, & Power of a Common-wealth Ecclesiasticall and Civill.* London: Andrew Crooke, 1651.

Hoffer, Peter Charles. *The Devil's Disciples: Makers of the Salem Witchcraft Trials.* Baltimore, MD: Johns Hopkins University Press, 1996.

———. *The Salem Witchcraft Trials: A Legal History.* Lawrence: University Press of Kansas, 1997.

Homza, Lu Ann. *Religious Authority in the Spanish Renaissance.* Baltimore, MD: Johns Hopkins University Press, 2000.

Hsia, Ronnie Po-Chia, and Robert W. Scribner, eds. *Problems in the Historical Anthropology of Early Modern Europe.* Wiesbaden: Harrassowitz, 1997.

Hubbard, Dolan. *Recovered Writers/Recovered Texts: Race, Class, and Gender in Black Women's Literature.* Knoxville: University of Tennessee Press, 1997.

Hults, Linda C. *The Witch as Muse: Art, Gender, and Power in Early Modern Europe.* Philadelphia: University of Pennsylvania, 2005.

Hunter, Michael. "Witchcraft and the Decline of Belief." *Eighteenth-Century Life* 22 (1998): 139–47.

Hutton, Ronald. "Anthropological and Historical Approaches to Witchcraft: Potential for a New Collaboration?" *Historical Journal* 47 (2004): 413–34.

———. *The Triumph of the Moon: A History of Modern Pagan Witchcraft.* Oxford: Oxford University Press, 1999.

Jäger, Berthold. "Zur Geschichte der Hexenprozesse im Stift Fulda: Forschungsstand, Kritik, Perspektiven." *Fuldaer Geschichtsblätter* 73 (1997): 7–64.

Jerouschek, Günter. "Der Hexenprozeß als politisches Machtinstrument: Der mysteriöse Tod des Hexeninquisitors Daniel Hauff und das Ende der Hexenverfolgung in Esslingen nebst Überlegungen zur Psychohistorie der Hexenverfolgungen." In *Das Ende der Hexenverfolgung*, edited by Sönke Lorenz, Dieter R. Bauer, and Gerald Maier, 117–28. Stuttgart: F. Steiner, 1995.

Jochens, Jenny. "Hexerie Eller Blind Alarm: Recent Scandinavian Witchcraft Studies." *Scandinavian Studies* 65 (1993): 103–13.

Kamber, Peter. "La chasse aux sorciers et aux sorcières dans le Pays de Vaud: Aspects quantitatifs (1581–1620)." *Revue historique vaudoise* 90 (1982): 21–33.

Kamen, Henry. *The Spanish Inquisition.* London: Weidenfeld and Nicolson, 1965.

Karlsen, Carol F. *The Devil in the Shape of a Woman: Witchcraft in Colonial New England.* New York: Norton, 1987.

Kempf, Karl. "Hexenverfolgung in Rottenburg." In *Hexenverfolgung: Beiträge zur Forschung, unter besonderer Berücksichtigung des südwestdeutschen Raumes*, edited by Sönke Lorenz and Dieter R. Bauer, 159–202. Würzburg: Königshausen und Neumann, 1995.

Kern, Edmund Michael. "The Styrian Witch Trials: Secular Authority and Religious Orthodoxy in the Early Modern Period." PhD diss., University of Minnesota, 1995.

Kettel, Adolf. "Kleriker im Hexenprozeß: Beispiele aus den Manderscheider Territorien und dem Trierer Land." In *Methoden und Konzepte der historischen Hexenforschung*, edited by Eiden Herbert, Rita Voltmer, Gunther Franz, and Herbert Irsigler, 169–91. Trier: Spee, 1998.

Kidd, Paul McCarry. "King James VI and the Demonic Conspiracy: Witch-Hunting and Anti-Catholicism in 16 c. and early 17 c. Scotland." MPhil thesis, University of Glasgow, 2004. Available online at https://dspace.gla.ac.uk/retrieve/542/04kidd%5Fmphil.pdf

Kieckhefer, Richard. *European Witch Trials: Their Foundation in Popular and Learned Culture, 1300–1500.* Berkeley: University of California Press, 1976.

———. *Forbidden Rites: A Necromancer's Manual of the Fifteenth Century: Magic in History.* University Park: Pennsylvania State University Press, 1998

———. *Magic in the Middle Ages.* Cambridge: Cambridge University Press, 1989.

Kittredge, George Lyman. *Witchcraft in Old and New England.* Cambridge, MA: Harvard University Press, 1929.

Klaniczay, Gábor. *The Uses of Supernatural Power: The Transformation of Popular Religion in Medieval and Early-Modern Europe.* Translated by Susan Singerman. Cambridge: Polity, 1990.

Knutsen, Gunnar W. "The Decline and End of Witch Trials in Scandinavia." *Arv: Journal of Scandinavian Folklore* (2006): 143–64.

———. "Norwegian Witchcraft Trials: A Reassessment." *Continuity and Change* 18 (2003): 185–200.

———. *Servants of Satan and Masters of Demons.* Oslo: Unipub forlag, 2004.

———. "Trolldomsprosessenes opphør i Skandinavia." *Historisk Tidsskrift* 84, no. 4 (2005): 593–611.

Konig, David Thomas. *Law and Society in Puritan Massachusetts: Essex County, 1629–1692.* Chapel Hill: University of North Carolina Press, 1979.

Kors, Alan C., and Edward Peters, eds. *Witchcraft in Europe, 1100–1700: A Documentary History.* Philadelphia: University of Pennsylvania Press, 1972.

Labouvie, Eva. "Hexenforschung als Regionalgeschichte: Probleme, Grenzen und neue Perspektiven." In *Hexenverfolgung und Regionalgeschichte: Die Grafschaft Lippe im Vergleich*, edited by Gisela Wilbertz, Gerd Schwerhoff, and Jürgen Scheffler, 46–60. Bielefeld: Verlag für Regionalgeschichte, 1994.

———. "Männer im Hexenprozeß: Zur Sozialanthropologie eines 'männlichen' Verständnisses von Magie u. Hexerei." *Geschichte und Gesellschaft* 16 (1990): 56–78.

———. *Verbotene Künste: Volksmagie und ländlicher Aberglaube in den Dorfgemeinden des Saarraumes (16.–19. Jahrhundert).* St. Ingbert: Röhrig Verlag, 1992.

Lambrecht, Karen. *Hexenverfolgung und Zaubereiprozesse in den schlesischen Territorien.* Cologne: Böhlau, 1995.

Lancre, Pierre de. *On the Inconstancy of Witches: Pierre de Lancre's Tableau de l'inconstance des mauvais anges et demons (1612).* Translated by Harriet Stone and Gerhild Scholz Williams. Edited by Gerhild Scholz Williams, Michaela Giesenkirchen, and John Morris. Tempe: Arizona Center for Medieval and Renaissance Studies, 2006.

Langdon, Rande Eve. "Religion, Witchcraft, and the Supernatural in Elizabethan England." PhD diss., Harvard University, 1977.

Lange, Thomas, and Jürgen Rainer Wolf. "Hexenverfolgung in Hessen-Darmstadt zur Zeit Georgs I.: Mit einer Edition des Briefwechsels zwischen den Landgrafen Georg I. und Wilhelm IV. über Hexereifälle im Jahre 1582." *Archiv für hessische Geschichte u. Altertumskunde* 52 (1994): 139–58.

Lapoint, Elwyn. "Irish Immunity to Witch Hunting, 1534–1711." *Eire-Ireland* 27 (1992): 76–92.

Larner, Christina. *Enemies of God: The Witch-Hunt in Scotland.* London: Chatto and Windus, 1981.

———. *Witchcraft and Religion. The Politics of Popular Belief.* New York: Blackwell, 1984.

Latner, Richard. "'Here Are No Newters': Witchcraft and Religious Discord in Salem Village and Andover." *New England Quarterly* 79 (2006): 92–122.

Laulainen-Schein, Diana Lyn. "Comparative Counterpoints: Witchcraft Accusations in Early Modern Lancashire and the Chesapeake." PhD diss., University of Minnesota, 2004.

Lea, Henry Charles. *A History of the Inquisition of the Middle Ages*. 3 vols. New York: Harper & Brothers, 1888.

———. *Materials toward a History of Witchcraft*. Edited by Arthur C. Howland. Philadelphia: University of Pennsylvania Press, 1939.

LeBeau, Bryan F. *The Story of the Salem Witch Trials: "We walked in clouds and could not see our way."* Upper Saddle River, NJ: Prentice Hall, 1998.

Legué, Gabriel, Gilles de la Tourette, and Michel de Certeau, eds. *Sœur Jeanne des Anges*. Montbonnot: Jerome Millon, 1985.

Lehmann, Hartmut. *Pietismus und Weltliche Ordnung in Württemberg vom 17. bis zum 20. Jahrhundert*. Stuttgart: Kohlhammer, 1969.

———, and Otto Ulbricht, eds. *Vom Unfug der Hexenprozesse: Gegner der Hexenverfolgung von Johann Weyer bis Friedrich Spee*. Wiesbaden: O. Harrassowitz, 1992.

Leuschner, Kristin Jeanne. "Creating the 'Known True Story': Sixteenth- and Seventeenth-Century Murder and Witchcraft Pamphlets and Plays." PhD diss., University of California, Los Angeles, 1992.

Levack, Brian. "The Decline and End of Witchcraft Prosecutions." In *Witchcraft and Magic in Europe: The Eighteenth and Nineteenth Centuries*, edited by Bengt Ankarloo and Stuart Clark, 1–93. Philadelphia: University of Pennsylvania Press, 1999.

———. *The Witch-Hunt in Early Modern Europe*. London: Longman, 1987.

———, ed. *Witchcraft in Colonial America*. New York: Garland, 1992.

Logan, Rebecca L. "Witches and Poisoners in the Colonial Chesapeake." PhD diss., Union Institute, 2001.

Loi, Salvatore. *Inquisizione, magia e stregoneria in Sardegna*. Cagliari: AM & D, 2003.

Lorenz, Sönke. "Die Rechtsgutachten von Johann Fichard in Sachen Hexenprozeß." In *Hexenverfolgung: Beiträge zur Forschung, unter besonderer Berücksichtigung des südwestdeutschen Raumes*, edited by Sönke Lorenz and Dieter R. Bauer, 203–40. Würzburg: Königshausen und Neumann, 1995.

———, and Jürgen Michael Schmidt, eds. *Wider alle Hexerei und Teufelswerk: Die Europäische Hexenverfolgung und ihre Auswirkungen auf Südwestdeutschland*. Ostfildern: Thorbecke, 2004.

Lorey, Elmar M. "Das Werwolfstereotyp als instabile Variante im Hexenprozeß: 'Gefragt, wie oft er sich des Jahrß zu einem Wehr Wolff gemacht.'" *Nassauische Annalen* 112 (2001): 135–76.

Lo Scrudato, Vito. *La magara: Un processo di stregoneria nella Sicilia del Cinquecento*. Palermo: Sellerio, 2001.

Macdonald, Stuart. "Threats to a Godly Society: The Witch-Hunt in Fife, Scotland, 1560–1710." PhD diss., University of Guelph (Canada), 1998.

———. *The Witches of Fife: Witch-Hunting in a Scottish Shire, 1560–1710*. East Linton, UK: Tuckwell Press, 2002.

Macfarlane, Alan. *Witchcraft in Tudor and Stuart England: A Regional and Comparative Study*. London: Routledge and Kegan Paul, 1970.

Maltby, William S. *The Black Legend in England: The Development of Anti-Spanish Sentiment, 1558–1660*. Durham, NC: Duke University Press, 1971.

Mappen, Marc. *Witches & Historians: Interpretations of Salem*. Huntington, NY: Krieger, 1980.

Marcaccioli Castiglioni, Anna. *Streghe e roghi nel Ducato di Milano: Processi per stregoneria a Vengono superiore nel 1520*. Milan: Thélema Edizioni, 1999.

Martin, Lauren. "The Devil and the Domestic: Witchcraft, Women's Work and Marriage in Early Modern Scotland." PhD diss., New School University, 2004.

Martin, Ruth. *Witchcraft and the Inquisition in Venice, 1550-1650.* Oxford: Blackwell, 1989.

Masters, Robert E. L. *Eros and Evil: The Sexual Psychopathology of Witchcraft.* New York: Julian Press, 1962.

Maxwell-Stuart, P. G. *An Abundance of Witches: The Great Scottish Witch-Hunt.* Stroud: Tempus, 2005.

McGinnis, Timothy Scott. *George Gifford and the Reformation of the Common Sort: Puritan Priorities in Elizabethan Religious Life.* Sixteenth Century Essays and Studies 70. Kirksville, MO: Truman State University Press, 2004.

Mcguire, Linda Helen. "Witches in the Roman World: A Literary and Sociological Study." PhD diss., University of Edinburgh, 1994.

McLaren, Angus. *The Trials of Masculinity: Policing Sexual Boundaries, 1870-1930.* Chicago: University of Chicago Press, 1997.

McLoughlin, Nancy Ann. "*Universitas,* Secular-Mendicant Conflict and the Construction of Learned Male Authority in the Thought of John Gerson (1363-1429)." PhD diss., University of California, Santa Barbara, 2005.

Meier, Christine. "Die Anfänge der Hexenprozesse in Lemgo." In *Hexenverfolgung und Regionalgeschichte: Die Grafschaft Lippe im Vergleich,* edited by Gisela Wilbertz, Gerd Schwerhoff, and Jürgen Scheffler, 83-106. Bielefeld: Verlag für Regionalgeschichte, 1994.

Mercier, Franck. *La vauderie d'Arras: Une chasse aux sorcières à l'automne du Moyen-Âge.* Rennes: Presses universitaires de Rennes, 2006.

Michelet, Julles. *La Sorcière.* Paris: E. Dentu Libraire-Editeur, 1862.

Midelfort, H. C. Erik. "Charcot, Freud, and the Demons." In *Werewolves, Witches, and Wandering Spirits: Traditional Belief and Folklore in Early Modern Europe,* edited by Kathryn A. Edwards, 199-215. Sixteenth Century Essays and Studies 62. Kirksville, MO: Truman State University Press, 2002.

———. *Exorcism and Enlightenment: Johann Joseph Gassner and the Demons of Eighteenth-Century Germany.* New Haven, CT: Yale University Press, 2005.

———. *A History of Madness in Sixteenth-Century Germany.* Stanford, CA: Stanford University Press, 1999.

———. "Natur und Besessenheit: Natürliche Erklärungen für Besessenheit von der Melancholie bis zum Magnetismus." In *Dämonische Besessenheit [Demonic possession]: Zur Interpretation eines kulturhistorischen Phänomens,* edited by Hans de Waardt, et al., 73-87. Bielefeld: Verlag für Regionalgeschichte, 2005.

———. "The Night Battles." *Catholic Historical Review* 72 (1986): 648-50.

———. "Recent Witch Hunting Research, Or Where Do We Go From Here?" *Papers of the Bibliographical Society of America* 61 (1968): 373-420.

———. "The Renaissance of Witchcraft Research." *Journal of the History of the Behavioral Sciences* 13 (1977): 194-97.

———. "Witchcraft, Magic and the Occult." In *Reformation Europe: A Guide to Research,* edited by Steven Ozment, 183-210. St. Louis, MO: Center for Reformation Research, 1982.

———. *Witch Hunting in Southwestern Germany, 1562-1684: The Social and Intellectual Foundations.* Stanford, CA: Stanford University Press, 1972.

Milani, Marisa, ed. *Streghe e Diavoli nei Processi del S. Uffizio: Venezia, 1554-1587.* Bassano del Grappa: Ghedina & Tassotti, 1994.

Modestin, Georg. *Le diable chez l'évêque: Chasse aux sorciers dans le diocèse de Lausanne (vers 1460).* Lausanne: Université de Lausanne, 1999.

———, and Kathrin Utz Tremp. "Zur spätmittelalterlichen Hexenverfolgung in der heutigen Westschweiz: Ein Forschungsbericht." *Zeitenblicke* 1, no. 1 (7 August 2002). Available online at http://www.zeitenblicke.historicum.net/2002/01/modestin/ modestin.html (accessed 2 April 2007).

Moeller, Katrin. "Hexenprozesse in Mecklenburg: Eine quantitative Auswertung." In *Quantität und Struktur: Festschrift für Kersten Krüger zum 60: Geburtstag*, edited by Werner Buchholz, 283–99. Rostock: Universität Rost, 1999.

Molero, Valérie. *Magie et sorcellerie en Espagne au siècle des lumières: 1700–1820*. Paris: Harmattan, 2006.

Monter, E. William. *Frontiers of Heresy: The Spanish Inquisition from the Basque Lands to Sicily*. New York: Cambridge University Press, 1990.

———. "The Historiography of European Witchcraft: Progress and Prospects." *Journal of Interdisciplinary History* 2 (1972): 435–51.

———. "Re-contextualizing British Witchcraft." *Journal of Interdisciplinary History* 35 (2004): 105–11.

———. *Witchcraft in France and Switzerland: The Borderlands during the Reformation*. Ithaca, NY: Cornell University Press, 1976.

Mormando, Franco. *The Preacher's Demons: Bernardino of Siena and the Social Underworld of Early Renaissance Italy*. Chicago: University of Chicago, 1999.

Morton, Peter A., ed. *The Trial of Tempel Anneke: Records of a Witchcraft Trial in Brunswick, Germany, 1663*. Translated by Barbara Dähms. Peterborough, ON: Broadview, 2005.

Muchembled, Robert. *Sorcières: Justice et société aux 16e et 17e siècles*. Paris: Editions Imago, 1987.

———, and Martine Desmons. *Les derniers bûchers: Un village de Flandre et ses sorcières sous Louis XIV*. Paris: Ramsay, 1981.

Nagel, Petra. *Die Bedeutung der "Disquisitionum magicarum libri sex" von Martin Delrio für das Verfahren in Hexenprozessen*. Frankfurt am Main: Lang, 1995.

Nenonen, Marko. "Noituus, taikuus ja noitavainot Ala-Satakunnan, Pohjois-Pohjanmaan ja Viipurin Karjalan maaseudulla vuosina, 1620–1700. [Witchcraft, magic, and witch trials in rural lower Satakunta, northern Ostrobothnia and Viipuri Karelia (Finland), 1620–1700]." PhD diss., Tampereen Yliopisto (Finland), 1992.

Neureiter, Suzanne Finley. "Mapping Early Modern English Witchcraft: A Study of Pamphlet, Treatise, and Drama." PhD diss., University of Pennsylvania, 1995.

Norton, Mary Beth. *In the Devil's Snare: The Salem Witchcraft Crisis of 1692*. New York: Alfred A. Knopf, 2002.

Notestein, Wallace. *A History of Witchcraft in England from 1558 to 1718*. Washington, DC: American Historical Association, 1911.

Nugent, Donald. "Witchcraft Studies, 1959–1971: A Bibliographical Survey." *Journal of Popular Culture* 5 (1971): 710–25.

Oestmann, Peter. "Die Offenburger Hexenprozesse im Spannungsfeld zwischen Reichshofrat und Reichskammergericht." *Ortenau* 75:179–220.

———. *Hexenprozesse am Reichskammergericht*. Cologne: Böhlau, 1997.

Olbrys, Stephen Charles. "'More Weight': Social Evil, Civil Rights, and the Commodification of the Salem Witch Trials." PhD diss., Indiana University, 2003.

Ostling, Per-Anders. "Blåkulla, magi och trolldomsprocesser: En folkloristisk studie av folkliga trosforestallningar och av trolldomsprocesserna inom Svea Hovratts jurisdiktion, 1597–1720." PhD diss., Uppsala University, 2002.

Ostorero, Martine, and Étienne Anheim, eds. *Le diable en procès: Démonologie et sorcellerie à la fin du moyen âge*. Saint-Denis: Presses universitaires de Vincennes, 2003.

————, Agostino Paravicini Bagliani, Kathrin Utz Tremp, and Catherine Chène, eds. *L'imaginaire du sabbat: Édition critique des textes les plus anciens (1430 c.–1440 c.).* Lausanne: Université de Lausanne, 1999.

Paravy, Pierrette. "A propos de la genèse médiévale des chasses aux sorcières: Le traité de Claude Tholosan, juge Dauphinois (vers 1436): Mélanges de l'Ecole Française de Rome." *Moyen Age/Temps Modernes* 91 (1979): 332–79. Translated as "Zur Genesis der Hexenverfolgungen im Mittelalter: Der Traktat des Claude Tholosan, Richter in der Dauphiné (um 1436)." In *Ketzer, Zauberer, Hexen: Die europäischen Hexenverfolgungen,* edited by Andreas Blauert, 118–59 (Frankfurt am Main: Suhrkamp, 1990).

Parish, Helen L., ed. *Religion and Superstition in Reformation Europe.* Manchester, UK: Manchester University Press, 2002.

Parker, Geoffrey. "Some Recent Work on the Inquisition in Spain and Italy." *Journal of Modern History* 54 (1982): 519–32.

Pauschert, Uwe. *Joseph Glanvill und die Neue Wissenschaft des 17. Jahrhunderts.* Frankfurt am Main: P. Lang, 1994.

Pearl, Jonathan L. *The Crime of Crimes: Demonology and Politics in France, 1560–1620.* Waterloo, ON: Wilfrid Laurier University Press, 1999.

Perego, Natale. *Stregherie e malefici: Paure, superstizioni, fatti miracolosi a Lecco e nella Brianza del Cinque e Seicento.* Oggiono: Cattaneo, 2003.

Pinies, Jean-Pierre. *Figures de la sorcellerie languedocienne: Brèish, endevinaire, armièr.* Paris: Editions du CNRS, 1983.

Pizzinini, Meinrad. "Aspekte der neuen Hexen-Literatur." *Innsbrucker Historische Studien* 12–13 (1990): 581–601.

Pocs, Eva. *Between the Living & the Dead: A Perspective on Witches & Seers in the Early Modern Age.* Budapest: Central European University Press, 1999.

Pohl, Herbert. *Zauberglaube und Hexenangst im Kurfürstentum Mainz: Ein Beitrag zur Hexenfrage im 16. und beginnenden 17. Jahrhundert.* Stuttgart: Steiner, 1988.

Pollock, Adrian. "Regions of Evil: A Geography of Witchcraft and Social Change in Early Modern England." PhD diss., University of Michigan, 1977.

Portone, Paolo. *Il noce di Benevento: La stregoneria e l'Italia del Sud.* Milan: Xenia, 1990.

Pott, Martin. *Aufklärung und Aberglaube: Die deutsche Frühaufklärung im Spiegel ihrer Aberglaubenskritik.* Tübingen: Niemeyer, 1992.

Purkiss, Diane. *The Witch in History: Early Modern and Twentieth-Century Representations.* London: Routledge, 1996.

Quinby, Lee. *Millennial Seduction: A Skeptic Confronts Apocalyptic Culture.* Ithaca, NY: Cornell University Press, 1999.

Rabinowitz, Jacob David. "The Origin of the Witch in Classical Antiquity's Demonization of the Fertility Goddess." PhD diss., Brown University, 1994.

Raith, Anita. "Hexenprozesse beim württembergischen Oberrat." In *Hexenverfolgung: Beiträge zur Forschung, unter besonderer Berücksichtigung des südwestdeutschen Raumes,* edited by Sönke Lorenz, 101–21. Würzburg: Königshausen und Neumann, 1995.

Rampton, Martha. "The Gender of Magic in the Early Middle Ages." PhD diss., University of Virginia, 1998.

Rapley, Robert. *A Case of Witchcraft: The Trial of Urbain Grandier.* Montreal: McGill-Queen's University Press, 1998.

Rapp, Ludwig. *Die Hexenprozesse und ihre Gegner aus Tirol.* Innsbruck: Wagner, 1874.

Ray, Benjamin C. "The Geography of Witchcraft Accusations in Salem Village, 1692." *William and Mary Quarterly*, forthcoming.

———. "Satan's War against the Covenant in Salem Village, 1692." *New England Quarterly* 80 (2007): 1–27.

Reis, Elizabeth Sarah. *Damned Women: Sinners and Witches in Puritan New England*. Ithaca, NY: Cornell University Press, 1997.

Riezler, Sigmund. *Geschichte der Hexenprozesse in Bayern. Im Lichte der allgemeinen Entwicklung dargestellt.* Stuttgart: J. G. Cotta, 1896.

Roach, Marilynne K. *The Salem Witch Trials: A Day-by-Day Chronicle of a Community under Siege.* New York: Cooper Square Press, 2002.

Roberts, Mary Louise. *Civilization without Sexes: Reconstructing Gender in Postwar France, 1917–1927.* Chicago: University of Chicago Press, 1994.

Robinson, Enders A. *Salem Witchcraft and Hawthorne's House of the Seven Gables.* Bowie, MD: Heritage Books, 1992.

Robisheaux, Thomas W. *The Miller's Wife: Sorcery and Witchcraft in a German Village.* New York: W. W. Norton, forthcoming.

Rochelandet, Brigitte. *Sorcières, diables et bûchers en Franche-Comté aux XVIe et XVIIe siècles.* Besançon: Cêtre, 1997.

Rogge, Roswitha. "Schadenzauber, Hexerei und die Waffe der Justiz im frühneuzeitlichen Hamburg." In *Hexerei, Magie und Volksmedizin: Beiträge aus dem Hexenarchiv des Museums für Völkerkunde Hamburg*, edited by Bernd Schmelz, 149–72. Bonn: Holos Verlag, 1997.

Romeo, Giovanni. *Inquisitori, esorcisti e streghe nell'Italia della Controriforma.* Florence: Sansoni, 1990.

Roper, Lyndal. *Oedipus & the Devil: Witchcraft, Sexuality, & Religion in Early Modern Europe.* London: Routledge, 1994.

———. *Witch Craze: Terror and Fantasy in Baroque Germany.* New Haven, CT: Yale University Press, 2004.

Rosenthal, Bernard. *Salem Story: Reading the Witch Trials of 1692.* Cambridge: Cambridge University Press, 1993.

Rowlands, Alison. *Witchcraft Narratives in Germany: Rothenburg 1561–1652.* Manchester, UK: Manchester University Press, 2003.

Rummel, Walter. *Bauern, Herren und Hexen: Studien zur Sozialgeschichte Sponheimischer und Kurtrierischer Hexenprozesse 1574–1664.* Göttingen: Vandenhoeck & Ruprecht, 1991.

———. "'Der Krieg gegen die Hexen': Ein Krieg fanatischer Kirchenfürsten oder ein Angebot zur Realisierung sozialer Chancen? Sozialgeschichtliche Anmerkungen zu zwei neuen Büchern." *Rheinische Vierteljahrsblätter* 56 (1992): 311–24.

———. "'Weise' Frauen und 'weise' Männer im Kampf gegen Hexerei: Die Widerlegung einer modernen Fabel." In *Europäische Sozialgeschichte: Festschrift für Wolfgang Schieder*, edited by Christof Dipper, 353–76. Berlin: Duncker and Humblot, 2000.

Russell, Jeffrey B. *Witchcraft in the Middle Ages.* Ithaca, NY: Cornell University Press, 1972.

Sanchez, Franklyn D. "Witchcraft and Demonology in the Work of John Donne." PhD diss., New York University, 1994.

Sands, Kathleen R. *Demon Possession in Elizabethan England.* Westport, CT: Praeger, 2004.

Schatzmann, Niklaus. *Verdorrende Bäume und Brote wie Kuhfladen: Hexenprozesse in der Leventina 1431–1459 und die Anfänge der Hexenverfolgung auf der Alpensüdseite.* Zürich: Chronos Verlag, 2003.

Schleich, Johann. *Hexen, Zauberer und Teufelskult in Österreich.* Graz: Steirische Verlagsgesellschaft, 1999.

Schmidt, Jürgen Michael. "Das Hexereidelikt in den kursächsischen Konstitutionen von 1572." In *Benedict Carpzov: Neue Perspektiven zu einem umstrittenen sächsischen Juristen*, edited by Günter Jerouschek, 111–35. Tübingen: Edition Diskord, 2000.

———. *Glaube und Skepsis: Die Kurpfalz und die abendländische Hexenverfolgung 1446–1685.* Bielefeld: Verlag für Regionalgeschichte, 2000.

Schmidt, Leigh Eric. "From Demon Possession to Magic Show: Ventriloquism, Religion, and the Enlightenment." *Church History* 67 (1998): 274–304.

Schnyder, André. "'Opus nouum vero partium compilatione…: Die Ordnung der Rede über die Hexerei, ihre Autoren und ihre Adressaten im 'Malleus maleficarum' von Institoris und Sprenger." *Mittellateinisches Jahrbuch* 30 (1995): 99–121.

Scholz Williams, Gerhild. *Defining Dominion: The Discourses of Magic and Witchcraft in Early Modern France and Germany.* Ann Arbor: University of Michigan Press, 1995.

———. *Ways of Knowing in Early Modern Germany: Johannes Praetorius as a Witness to His Time.* Aldershot: Ashgate, 2006.

Schons, Melissa Jane. "Horror and the Characterization of the Witch from Horace to Lucan." PhD diss., University of California, Los Angeles, 1998.

Schormann, Gerhard. *Der Krieg gegen die Hexen: Das Ausrottungsprogramm des Kurfürsten von Köln.* Göttingen: Vandenhoeck & Ruprecht, 1991.

———. *Hexenprozesse in Deutschland.* Göttingen: Vandenhoeck & Ruprecht, 1981.

———. *Hexenprozesse in Nordwestdeutschland.* Hildesheim: Lax, 1977.

———. "Städtische Gesellschaft und Hexenprozeß." In *Stadt im Wandel: Kunst und Kultur des Bürgertums in Norddeutschland 1150–1650; Ausstellungskatalog*, edited by Cord Meckseper, 175–87. Stuttgart-Bad Canstatt: Cantz, 1985.

Schreiner, Klaus, and Gerd Schwerhoff, eds. *Verletzte Ehre: Ehrkonflikte in Gesellschaften des Mittelalters und der Frühen Neuzeit.* Cologne: Böhlau, 1995.

Schulte, Rolf. *Hexenmeister: Die Verfolgung von Männern im Rahmen der Hexenverfolgung von 1530–1730 im Alten Reich.* Frankfurt am Main: Lang, 2001.

Schwaiger, Georg. "Das Ende der Hexenprozesse im Zeitalter der Aufklärung." In *Teufelsglaube und Hexenprozesse*, edited by Georg Schwaiger, 150–79. Munich: C. H. Beck, 1999.

Schwerhoff, Gerd. "Aufgeklärter Traditionalismus—Christian Thomasius zu Hexenprozeß und Folter." *Zeitschrift der Savigny-Stiftung für Rechtsgeschichte, Germanistische Abteilung* 117 (1987): 247–60.

———. *Die Inquisition: Ketzerverfolgung in Mittelalter und Neuzeit.* München: Beck, 2004.

———. *Köln im Kreuzverhör: Kriminalität, Herrschaft und Gesellschaft in einer Frühneuzeitlichen Stadt.* Bonn: Bouvier, 1991.

———. "Vom Alltagsverdacht zur Massenverfolgung: Neuere deutsche Forschungen zum frühneuzeitlichen Hexenwesen." *Zeitschrift des Geschichte in Wissenschaft und Unterricht* 46 (1995): 359–80.

Schwillus, Harald. *Kleriker im Hexenprozeß: Geistliche als Opfer d. Hexenprozesse d. 16. u. 17. Jh. in Deutschland.* Würzburg: Echter, 1992.

Sebald, Hans. *Witch-Children: From Salem Witch-Hunts to Modern Courtrooms.* Buffalo, NY: Prometheus, 1993.

Seitz, Jonathan. "Natural or supernatural? Witchcraft, Inquisition and views of nature at the dawn of the Scientific Revolution." PhD diss., University of Wisconsin, 2006.

Semeraro, Martino. *Il tribunale del Santo Officio di Oria: Inediti processi di stregoneria per la storia dell'Inquisizione in età moderna.* Milan: A. Giuffrè, 2003.

Seymour, St. John D. *Irish Witchcraft and Demonology*. Baltimore, MD: Norman, Remington & Co., 1913.

Sharpe, James. *The Bewitching of Anne Gunter: A Horrible and True Story of Deception, Witchcraft, Murder, and the King of England*. New York: Routledge, 2000.

———. *Instruments of Darkness: Witchcraft in England, 1550–1750*. New York: Penguin, 1996.

Shaw, Christine. *The Politics of Exile in Renaissance Italy*. Cambridge: Cambridge University Press, 2000.

Sidky, H. *Witchcraft, Lycanthropy, Drugs and Disease: An Anthropological Study of the European Witch-Hunts*. New York: Lang, 1997.

Singer, Gordon Andreas. "'La Vauderie d'Arras,' 1459–1491: An Episode of Witchcraft in Later Medieval France." PhD diss., University of Maryland, 1974.

Sluhovsky, Moshe. "The Devil in the Convent." *American Historical Review* 107 (2002): 379–411.

Soldan, Wilhelm Gottlieb. *Geschichte der Hexenprozesse*. 2 vols. Edited by Max Bauer, 1843. Second edition edited by Heinrich Heppe, 1880. Third edition edited by G. Müller. Munich, 1912.

Soman, Alfred. *Sorcellerie et justice criminelle: Le Parlement de Paris, 16e–18e siècles*. Brookfield, VT: Variorum, 1992.

Sörlin, Per. "Trolldoms- och vidskepelseprocesserna i Gota hovratt, 1635–1754." PhD diss., Umea University (Sweden), 1993.

———. *Wicked Arts: Witchcraft and Magic Trials in Southern Sweden, 1635–1754*. Leiden: Brill, 1999.

Starn, Randolph. *Contrary Commonwealth: The Theme of Exile in Medieval and Renaissance Italy*. Berkeley: University of California Press, 1982.

Stephens, Walter. *Demon Lovers: Witchcraft, Sex, and the Crisis of Belief*. Chicago: University of Chicago, 2002.

Stokes, Laura P. "Demons of Urban Reform: The Rise of Witchcraft Prosecution in Basel, Lucerne and Nuremberg 1430–1530." PhD diss., University of Virginia, 2006.

Styers, Randall. *Making Magic: Religion, Magic and Science in the Modern World*. Oxford: Oxford University Press, 2004.

Sudmann, Stefan. *Das Basler Konzil: Synodale Praxis zwischen Routine und Revolution*. Tradition-Reform-Innovation, Studien zur Modernität des Mittelalters 8. Frankfurt am Main: Peter-Lang, 2005.

Swan, Claudia. *Art, Science, and Witchcraft in Early Modern Holland: Jacques de Gheyn II (1565–1629)*. Cambridge: Cambridge University Press, 2005.

Switzer, Richard. *Étienne-Léon de Lamothe-Langon et le Roman Populaire Français de 1800 à 1830*. Paris: E. Privat, 1962.

Tal, Guy. "Witches on Top: Magic, Power, and Imagination in the Art of Early Modern Italy." PhD diss., Indiana University, 2006.

Talmor, Sascha. *Glanvill: The Uses and Abuses of Scepticism*. Oxford: Pergamon Press, 1981.

Tambiah, Stanley Jerayaja. *Magic, Science, Religion, and the Scope of Rationality*. Cambridge: Cambridge University Press, 1990.

Taric Zumsteg, Fabienne. *Les sorciers à l'assaut du village: Gollion (1615–1631)*. Lausanne: Zebre, 2000.

Tausiet, María. *Los posesos de Tosos (1812–1814): Brujería y justicia popular en tiempos de revolución*. Zaragoza: Instituto Aragonés de Antropología, 2002.

———. *Ponzoña en los ojos: Brujeria y superstición en Aragón en el siglo XVI*. Saragossa: Institución Fernando el Católico, 2000.

Tedeschi, John. *The Prosecution of Heresy: Collected Studies on the Inquisition in Early Modern Italy.* Binghamton, NY: Center for Medieval and Early Renaissance Studies, 1991.

Tegler Jerselius, Kristina Emma T. *"Den stora häxdansen. Vidskepelse, väckelse och vetande i Gagnef 1858."* PhD diss., Uppsala University, 2003.

Thomas, Keith. *Religion and the Decline of Magic.* London: Weidenfeld and Nicholson, 1971.

Todd, Margo. *The Culture of Protestantism in Early Modern Scotland.* New Haven, CT: Yale University Press, 2002.

Tremp, Kathrin Utz. *Quellen zur Geschichte der Waldenser von Freiburg im Uechtland (1399–1439).* Hannover: Hahn, 2000.

———. *Waldenser, Wiedergänger, Hexen und Rebellen: Biographien zu den Waldenserprozessen von Freiburg im Uechtland (1399 und 1430).* Freiburg: Freiburger Geschichtsblätter, Sonderband, 1999.

Trevor-Roper, H. R. *Religion, the Reformation and Social Change, and Other Essays.* London: Macmillan, 1967.

Trusen, Winfried. "Vom Inquisitionsverfahren zum Ketzer- und Hexenprozeß: Fragen der Abgrenzung und Beeinflussung." In *Staat, Kirche, Wissenschaft in einer pluralistischen Gesellschaft: Festschrift zum 65. Geburtstag von Paul Mikat,* edited by Dieter Schwab, 435–59. Berlin: Duncker & Humblot, 1989.

Tschacher, Werner. *Der Formicarius des Johannes Nider von 1437/38: Studien zu den Anfängen der Europäischen Hexenverfolgungen im Spätmittelalter.* Aachen: Shaker Verlag, 2000.

Tschaikner, Manfred. *Damit das Böse ausgerottet werde: Hexenverfolgungen in Vorarlberg im 16. und 17. Jahrhundert.* Bregenz: Vorarlberger Autoren Gesellschaft, 1992.

———. *Hexenverfolgungen in Hohenems: Einschliesslich des Reichshofs Lustenau, sowie der österreichischen Herrschaften Feldkirch und Neuburg unter hohenemsischen Pfandherren und Vögten.* Konstanz: UVK Verlagsgesellschaft, 2004.

———. *Magie und Hexerei im südlichen Vorarlberg zu Beginn der Neuzeit.* Konstanz: UVK, Universitätsverlag Konstanz, 1997.

———. "'Der Teufel und die Hexen müssen aus dem Land...': Frühneuzeitliche Hexenverfolgungen in Liechtenstein." *Jahrbuch des Historischen Vereins für das Fürstentum Liechtenstein* 96 (1998): 1–210.

Upton, Gilbert. *The Devil and George Burroughs: A Study in Seventeenth-Century Justice.* London: Wordwright Pub., 1997.

Vance, Lash Keith, Jr. "Theorizing Space in the Early Modern Period." PhD diss., University of California, Riverside, 2000.

van Dale, Antonius. *Dissertationes de origine ac progressu idololatriæ et superstitionum, de vera ac falsa prophetia: Uti et de divinationibus idololatricis Judæorum.* Amsterdam: Boom, 1696.

Van Engen, John. "The Christian Middle Ages as an Historiographical Problem." *American Historical Review* 91 (1986): 519–52.

Vaupel, Ursula. *"Sie wollen die Hexen brennen": Hexenprozesse 1657 in Eschwege.* Kassel: Verein für hessische Geschichte und Landeskunde, 1997.

Vetere, Lisa M. "All the Rage at Salem: Witchcraft Tales and the Politics of Domestic Complaints in Early and Antebellum America." PhD diss., Lehigh University, 2003.

Vogel, Hubert. *Der große Schongauer Hexenprozeß und seine Opfer, 1589–1592: Berichte und Dokumente.* Schongau: Stadt Schongau, 1989.

Voltmer, Rita. "'Gott ist tot und der Teufel ist jetzt Meister!' Hexenverfolgungen und dörfliche Krisen im Trierer Land des 16. und 17. Jahrhunderts." *Kurtrierisches Jahrbuch* 39 (1999): 175–223.

Waardt, Hans de. *Mending Minds: A Cultural History of Dutch Academic Psychiatry*. Rotterdam: Erasmus, 2005.

———. *Toverij en samenleving: Holland 1500–1800*. Den Haag: Stickting Hollandse Historische Reeks, 1991.

———, H. C. Erik Midelfort, Jürgen Michael Schmidt, Sönke Lorenz, and Dieter R. Bauer., eds., *Dämonische Besessenheit: Zur Interpretation eines kulturhistorischen Phänomens* [Demonic Possession: Interpretations of a Historico-Cultural Phenomenon]. Hexenforschung 9. Bielefeld: Verlag vür Regionalsgeschichte, 2005.

———, Marijke Gijswijt-Hofstra, and Hilary Marland, eds. *Illness and Healing Alternatives in Western Europe*. London: Routledge, 1997.

Wahrman, Dror. "Percy's Prologue: Gender Panic and Cultural Change in late 18th-Century England." *Past and Present* 159 (1998): 113–60.

Walker, D. P. *Unclean Spirits: Possession and Exorcism in France and England in the late Sixteenth and Early Seventeenth Centuries*. Philadelphia: University of Pennsylvania Press, 1981.

Walz, Rainer. *Hexenglaube und Magische Kommunikation im Dorf der frühen Neuzeit: die Verfolgungen in der Grafschaft Lippe*. Paderborn: F. Schöningh, 1993.

———. "Kinder in Hexenprozessen: Die Grafsch. Lippe 1654–1663." In *Hexenverfolgung und Regionalgeschichte: Die Grafschaft Lippe im Vergleich*, edited by Gisela Wilbertz, Gerd Schwerhoff, and Jürgen Scheffler, 211–31. Bielefeld: Verlag für Regionalgeschichte, 1994.

Weber, Hartwig. *Kinderhexenprozesse*. Frankfurt am Main: Insel-Verlag, 1991.

Wehtje, Thomas Jefferson. "Out of Darkness, Light: The Theological Implications of (Dis)Belief in Witchcraft in Early Modern English Literature and Thought." PhD diss., State University of New York at Stony Brook, 2004.

Weisman, Richard. *Witchcraft, Magic, and Religion in 17th-Century Massachusetts*. Amherst: University of Massachusetts Press, 1984.

Wilbertz, Gisela, and Jürgen Scheffler, eds. *Biographieforschung und Stadtgeschichte: Lemgo in der Spätphase der Hexenverfolgung*. Bielefeld: Verlag für Regionalgeschichte, 2000.

Wilkin, Rebecca May. "Feminizing Imagination in France, 1563–1678." PhD diss., University of Michigan, 2000.

Williams, Sarah Frances. "'Now Rise Infernal Tones': The Representations of Early Modern English Witchcraft in Sound and Music." PhD diss., Northwestern University, 2006.

Wise, Paul. "Cotton Mather's 'Wonders of the Invisible World': An Authoritative Edition." PhD diss., Georgia State University, 2005.

Yavneh, Naomi. "The Threat of Sensuality: Tasso's Temptress and the Counter-Reformation." PhD diss., University of California, Berkeley, 1991.

Zanelli, Giuliana. *Diamantina e le altre: Streghe, fattucchiere e inquisitori in Romagna (XVI–XVII secolo)*. Imola: La Mandragora, 2001.

Zika, Charles. *Exorcising our Demons: Magic, Witchcraft and Visual Culture in Early Modern Europe*. Leiden: Brill, 2003.

———, ed. *No Gods Except Me: Orthodoxy and Religious Practice in Europe, 1200–1600*. Parkville, Victoria: University of Melbourne, 1991.

Zilboorg, Gregory, *The Medical Man and the Witch during the Renaissance*. Baltimore, MD: Johns Hopkins Press, 1935.

16

Society and the Sexes Revisited

Merry Wiesner-Hanks

Steven Ozment's 1982 *Reformation Europe: A Guide to Research*, now a quarter-century old, includes a chapter by Joyce Irwin titled "Society and the Sexes" that makes one almost nostalgic for the good old days. In a four-page bibliography, Irwin includes almost everything available in English that even touches on women, marriage, and the family, some of which was still in the form of unpublished conference papers. Ten years later, in *Reformation Europe: A Guide to Research* II (edited by William Maltby), the bibliography for my article covering similar topics was three times as long, and this did not include materials that had been covered in Kathryn Norberg's article on women in the Catholic Reformation that appeared in John O'Malley's 1987 *Catholicism in Early Modern History: A Guide to Research*. I began that article by noting that "perhaps no area of Reformation studies has seen more expansion than research on women and the family," but I had no idea of what was to come. If 1983 through 1992 saw an expansion, the 1990s and 2000s have seen an explosion. In 1994, a group of scholars from many disciplines formed the Society for the Study of Early Modern Women, which now sponsors book prizes, travel scholarships, sessions at various meetings, a listserv, triennial specialized conferences, and has just started a separate print journal.[1] In 1996 the University of Chicago Press began publishing a series of translations of works by (and a few about) women titled

---

[1] *Early Modern Women: An Interdisciplinary Journal* was first published in 2006 and appears annually. The Society for the Study of Early Modern Women's website is http://www.ssemw.org.

The Other Voice in Early Modern Europe, edited by Margaret King and Albert Rabil Jr. This series has published almost forty books, including more than ten on religious issues, and many more are on the way. In the same year, Marquette University Press began the Women of the Reformation Series, edited by Kenneth Hagen and Merry Wiesner-Hanks, which publishes parallel texts of original language and English translations of works by women. In 2001, with the sponsorship of Erika Gaffney, Ashgate Press began publishing the series Women and Gender in the Early Modern World, edited by Allyson Poska and Abby Zanger, and it now has more than thirty titles. Every major journal in the field has had special issues or thematic sections on women, gender, marriage, or sexuality, and sometimes on all four. Books on these topics are in every series that publishes in English on Reformation or early modern issues. It is now nearly impossible to even know about all the new scholarship, to say nothing of reading it. Thus, in an attempt to keep the bibliography for this article manageable, I have included only books that have appeared since 1991; a complete bibliography would have hundreds and hundreds of items.[2]

Though the bibliography in Irwin's article can make one yearn for the day when it was possible to read everything, the article itself makes one realize how far we have come. Irwin calls for study of "those women who remained Catholic, whether by choice or circumstance"; the many studies of convents and women religious have been one of the great strengths of recent research. She calls for work that "concentrates on analysis" rather than "polemical arguments" in which one side "paints a rosy picture of the Reformation's bringing about a better life for women, while others bemoan the reformers' elevation of married life." Recent research has certainly done this; indeed, few scholars working in the field today would answer the question, "Was the Reformation a good thing or a bad thing for women?" with anything other than "It depends" followed by a long discussion about differences in women's experience. Irwin ends her article with an appeal that has proved prophetic, calling on Reformation historians to "claim the decades between 1580 and 1630," because a "crucial chapter is missing when the story ends with an earlier date." The enormous amount of work on the later Reformation, particularly on confessionalization and social discipline, has certainly filled in much of this missing chapter, as has work

[2]Longer bibliographies can be found in Wiesner-Hanks, *Women and Gender in Early Modern Europe*; and Wiesner-Hanks, "Reflections on a Quarter-Century of Research on Women." Some of the material from that article is included in this article.

that has begun to analyze the Reformation in global terms as missionaries and settlers, male and female, took their faiths with them as they left Europe.

Convents and Women Religious

The great attention to women religious over the last several decades is in part a function of sources, for convents housed literate women, controlled property and people, and were often linked with powerful families, all of which means they frequently left extensive records. These records were often transferred as a body to some larger archives, but remain a manageable group of sources for a dissertation project. In Italy, Gabriella Zarri at the University of Bologna has directed teams of researchers exploring convents, holy women, and hagiographical texts, and sponsored regular conferences on these topics.[3]

In Germany, convents in areas becoming Protestant often fought the Reformation through letter writing, family influence, physical bravery, and what one might call sheer cussedness—stuffing wax in their ears so as not to hear Protestant sermons and refusing to leave their houses unless they were physically dragged out. In some cases, authorities finally gave up and the convents remained islands of Catholicism for centuries. Others supported the Protestant Reformation theologically on some issues, but ignored its message about the value of convent life and remade themselves into institutions that were acceptable to Protestant authorities, educating girls and providing an honorable place for women who could not, or chose not to follow the Protestant injunction to marry.[4]

Research on convents and religious women in Catholic Europe has also focused on those who challenged boundaries. Not surprisingly, Teresa of Avila has been explored from the most angles: her milieu, her political influence, her spirituality, her sense of authorship and of self.[5] These studies have been joined recently by several that focus on her predecessors and contemporaries. They make it clear that, though Teresa is unique, she also followed a pattern found in other Spanish and Italian women: close relationship with a confessor, physical manifestations of her piety, doubts about her own self-worth, and effective alliances with local (and sometimes

---

[3]Zarri provides editions of the proceedings of these conferences in her *Donna, disciplina, creanza cristiana*; and *Il monachesimo femminile in Italia*.

[4]Ranft, *Women and the Religious Life*; Woodford, *Nuns as Historians*; Strasser, *State of Virginity*; Winston-Allen, *Convent Chronicles*; and Leonard, *Nails in the Wall*.

[5]Slade, *Saint Teresa of Avila*; and Ahlgren, *Teresa of Avila*.

national) political leaders.[6] Some of these women were able to retain reputations as holy women—*beatas*—throughout their lives or even, like Teresa, make it somewhere on the ladder to sanctity. Others were judged to be false saints, accused of faking their stigmata or ability to live without food, and exerting malicious influence over their followers and confessors, ultimately ending up before an Inquisition or other type of religious court, which is how their stories became known.[7]

Along with Catholic women who walked the (narrow) boundary between sanctity and heresy, there were also those who challenged the boundaries between lay and religious life. Mary Ward (the eventual founder of the English Ladies), the Ursulines and Daughters of Charity in Italy and France, and other so-called Jesuitesses have all received scholarly attention in the last decade for their attempts to create an active religious vocation for women out in the world.[8] The older opinion about such efforts is that they were either a failure or insignificant—what are a few hospitals or a few schools for girls?—but there has been increasing recognition that their actions and those of women religious in Protestant areas disrupt standard narratives about the Reformations. It is difficult to make the claim that "the Reformation led to the closing of the convents in Protestant areas" (which is standard in textbooks and more specialized studies) when they survived in Saxony, Braunschweig, Strasbourg, and who knows yet where else. It is difficult to say that "convents in Catholic Europe after Trent were all enclosed" (another standard statement) when the convent walls were permeable in so many places. The activities of early modern women religious also disrupt standard narratives in women's history; it is difficult to say, for example, that "Florence Nightingale was the first female nurse," or even that "Florence Nightingale made nursing respectable for women," when completely respectable middle-class Frenchwomen had been nursing as Ursulines for several centuries.

Studies of women religious have not only examined those who broke boundaries, but have also broken boundaries themselves, particularly those between disciplines. Art historians have explored how convents acted as patrons of the visual arts, ordering paintings and sculpture with specific

[6]Harline, *Burdens of Sister Margaret*; Surtz, *Writing Women*; Velasco, *Demons, Nausea and Resistance*; Haliczer, *Sexuality in the Confessional*; and Haliczer, *Between Exaltation and Infamy*.

[7]Zarri, *Le sante vive*; Tomizza, *Heavenly Supper*; Fernández, *Beatas y santas neocastellanas*; and Schutte, *Aspiring Saints*.

[8]Rapley, *Dévotes*; Conrad, *Zwischen Kloster und Welt*; Zarri, *Recinti*; Rapley, *Social History of the Cloister*; Lux-Sterritt, *Redefining Female Religious Life*; and Dinan, *Women and Poor Relief*.

subjects and particular styles for their own buildings and those of the male religious institutions they supported, thus shaping the religious images seen by men as well as women. Music historians have shown how women sang, composed, and played musical instruments, with their sounds sometimes reaching far beyond convent walls. Religious historians have examined the ways in which women circumvented, subverted, opposed, and occasionally followed the wishes of church authorities. Social historians have explored the ways in which women behind convent walls shaped family dynamics and thus political life. More importantly, scholars in all these fields have thought about the ways their stories intersect, as art and music both shape devotional practices and are shaped by them, as family chapels and tombs—often built by women—represent and reinforce power hierarchies, as artistic, literary, political, and intellectual patronage relationships influence and are influenced by doctrinal and institutional changes in the church.[9] This scholarship has thus changed the narrative of the Catholic Reformation and also provided a good example of how problematic the notion of a clear public/private dichotomy can be in women's history. Even in post-Tridentine Europe, convents and their residents were very much part of the public realm of power politics and culture.

Many of the abbesses and other female religious wrote extensively, and their works are beginning to see modern editions and translations, or in some cases the first appearance of their words in print.[10] This scholarship parallels the explosion of editions and reprints of the works by early modern secular women, particularly women in England.[11] These texts

[9] For convent residents and the arts, see Monson, *Crannied Wall*; Monson, *Disembodied Voices*; Poutrin, *Le voile et la plume*; Wood, *Women, Art, and Spirituality*; Kendrick, *Celestial Sirens*; Matter and Coakley, *Creative Women*; Lawrence, *Women and Art*; Reiss and Wilkins, *Beyond Isabella*; Weaver, *Convent Theatre*; Lowe, *Nuns' Chronicles*; and Hills, *Invisible City*. For the economic and political patronage of religious women, see McNamara, *Sisters in Arms*; Hernández, *Patronato, regio y órdenes religiosas femeninas*; Sperling, *Convents and the Body Politic*; Baernstein, *Convent Tale*; Burschel and Conrad, *Vorbild, Inbild, Abbild*; Walker, *Gender and Politics*; Diefendorf, *From Penitence to Charity*; and Lehfeldt, *Religious Women*.

[10] Ferrazzi, *Autobiography of an Aspiring Saint*; Pulci, *Florentine Drama*; Wiesner-Hanks and Skocir, *Convents Confront the Reformation*; Rhodes, *"This Tight Embrace"*; Tornabuoni, *Sacred Narratives*; San José, *Book for the Hour of Recreation*; Pascal, *Rule for Children*; Coignard, *Spiritual Sonnets*; and Lierheimer, *Spiritual Autobiography*.

[11] There are now three series devoted to the reprinting or electronic dissemination of early modern Englishwomen's writing, including writing on religion: The Early Modern Englishwoman: A Facsimile Library of Essential Works, published by Ashgate and edited by Betty S. Travitsky and Patrick Cullen; Women Writers in English, 1350–1850, published by Oxford University Press and edited by Susanne Woods and Elizabeth H. Hageman; and the Brown University Women Writers Project, which offers more than two hundred texts from 1450 to 1830, and is available online (with some parts free

have deepened our understanding of convent life and female spirituality, for they contain plays that nuns wrote for their sisters to perform, as well as letters telling of attempts at converting Protestants in the street and of supporting Catholics in prison, along with polemics praising convent life for its richness and attacking it for its shallowness. These newly discovered or newly made available sources have provided excellent examples of women's religious opinions and spiritual creativity, and they have further increased the complexity of our analysis of the Catholic Reformation.

Laywomen's Experience

Though in sheer numbers, studies of religious women have been far more numerous than was their share of the female population, research into laywomen has also expanded. Historians have looked at Protestant pastors' wives creating a new ideal for women, and at other Protestant women preaching and participating in iconoclastic riots. They have looked at both Protestant and Catholic women defying their husbands in the name of their faith, converting their husbands or other household members, and writing and translating religious literature.[12] Research from many parts of Europe has made it clear that women's experience of the Reformation, as of any historical development, differed according to categories already set out based on male experience (social class, geographic location, rural or urban setting), but also categories that had previously not been taken into account, such as marital status, position in the family, and number of children. Statements about the impact of particular religious ideas on women have been replaced by more nuanced observations. Older scholarship on the radical Reformation, for example, often made generalizations, with some authors arguing that the radical groups offered women more opportunities, and others contending that they were more restrictive and patriarchal. More recent research has emphasized the differences among radical groups, thus fitting with the general stress on difference and diversity in women's history.[13]

and some by license) at http://www.wwp.brown.edu. For further references to the vast literature on English women writers, see Travitsky and Roberts, *English Women Writers, 1500–1640: A Reference Guide*. The Other Voice in Early Modern Europe series has published a number of translations of the writings of secular women from continental Europe, especially Italy.

[12]Crawford, *Women and Religion*; Westphal, *Frau und lutherische Konfessionalisierung*; Matheson, *Argula von Grumbach*; Watt, *Secretaries of God*; McKee, *Katharina Schütz Zell*; Wiesner, *Gender, Church and State*; Conrad, *"In Christo"*; Burschel and Conrad, *Vorbild, Inbild, Abbild*; Peters, *Patterns of Piety*; and Diefendorf, *From Penitence to Charity*.

[13]Kobelt-Groch, *Aufsässige Töchter Gottes*; Snyder and Hecht, *Profiles of Anabaptist Women*; and

This same attention to nuance has shaped studies of the ideas of male reformers about women. Though, like other early modern writers so often caught up in the debate about women, reformers often made categorical statements about women in the abstract, they also spoke specifically about certain individuals or groups of women—Mary, Old Testament matriarchs, Eve, nuns. Recent analyses have focused on these more specific comments, and they have also discussed the ideas of reformers other than Luther and Calvin.[14] Studies of reformers' ideas about men *as men* are still relatively few, though some of the many works on the construction of early modern masculinity include religious writings in their analyses.[15] Judging by the upsurge of interest in men's history, this will no doubt be a growth field in the future.[16]

Editing, analyzing, and translating women's religious writings have not been limited to convent residents. Though the names of a few Protestant women writers have been known for decades, only within the last several years have their whole works finally been made available. The model of such scholarship is Elsie McKee's magisterial two-volume work on Katharina Schütz Zell, a woman who used to be described as "the wife of the reformer Matthias Zell," but for whom a better description, following McKee, would be "a Strasbourg reformer."[17] Most of this work has so far concentrated on previously known works and figures, such as the German noblewoman Argula von Grumbach, the Genevan abbess Marie Dentière, or the English martyr Anne Askew, but the works of lesser-known writers, such as Dutch Anabaptist women who wrote hymns and letters, are beginning to see the light of day.[18]

While current work on the radicals reinforces the emphasis on difference and diversity, research on women in the English Reformation and

---

Umble and Schmidt, *Strangers at Home.*

[14]Thompson, *John Calvin and Daughters of Sarah*; and Thompson, *Writing the Wrongs*; Rummel, *Erasmus on Women*; Schnell, *Text and Geschlecht*; Selderhuis, *Marriage and Divorce*; Bast, *Honor Your Fathers*; Karant-Nunn and Wiesner-Hanks, *Luther on Women*; Kreitzer, *Reforming Mary*; Mattox, *Most Holy Matriarchs*; and Petry, *Gender, Kabbalah and the Reformation.*

[15]Scott Hendrix and Susan Karant-Nunn are currently editing a collection of essays on the Reformation and masculinity. Works that consider religious issues include Schnell, *Text und Geschlecht*; and Schnell, *Frauendiskurs*; Dinges, *Hausväter, Priester, Kastraten*; Tlusty, *Bacchus and Civic Order*; Martin, *Alcohol, Sex, and Gender*; Long, *High Anxiety*; Shepard, *Meanings of Manhood*; and Biberman, *Masculinity, Anti-Semitism.*

[16]In early 2005, I found more than thirty titles on the construction of masculinity in England, not including studies of masculinity in literature, which would add at least another thirty.

[17]McKee, *Reforming Popular Piety*; and idem, *Katharina Schütz Zell.*

[18]Matheson, *Argula von Grumbach*; and Joldersma and Grijp, *"Elisabeth's Manly Courage."*

English Puritanism fits with another strong theme in women's history: the questioning of periodization. Such questioning has led many women's historians to dump the Renaissance, the Enlightenment, and the golden age of Athens, or at least to put quotation marks around them when they use them in reference to women. In this instance, examination of the ideas of Christian humanists on such issues as marriage, spousal relations, and proper family life has led historians of England to question whether the Protestants or Puritans were saying anything new.[19] They might have emphasized spousal affection and the importance of stable families to the social order more loudly and at greater length than their predecessors, but these were hardly new ideas. More recently, Christine Peters finds continuities in patterns of Christocentric piety and ideals for women extending from the fifteenth through the seventeenth centuries.[20] Recent surveys of women or gender in early modern England similarly do not see the Reformation as changing very much.[21]

These same doubts about the novelty of the Protestant message also emerge in the work of Heide Wunder, though she looks to a different source for their ideas than do those who point to Christian humanism. She sees changes in family life and ideas about marriage as a result not of changes in religious ideology, but of social and economic changes that allowed a wider spectrum of the population to marry, and made the marital pair the basic production and consumption unit. This "familialization of work and life" happened, in her view, in the High Middle Ages, which means Reformation ideas about the family did not create the bourgeois family, but resulted from it.[22] Medieval historians, most prominently Judith Bennett, have similarly questioned the significance of this great divide; some have suggested that the twelfth century might be a better choice for a major turning point, whereas others have rejected the idea of significant transformations altogether in favor of a focus on continuity.[23]

These doubts about the significance of 1500, and the resulting premodern/modern dichotomy, have emerged at just the same time that this dichotomy has been reinforced in another exploding area of historical

---

[19]Todd, *Christian Humanism.*

[20]Peters, *Patterns of Piety.*

[21]Both Anthony Fletcher (*Gender, Sex, and Subordination in England 1500–1800*) and Sara Mendelson and Patricia Crawford (*Women in Early Modern England*) find little dramatic change.

[22]Wunder, *"Er ist die Sonn"*; and Wunder and Engel, *Geschlechterperspektiven.*

[23]Bennett, "Medieval Women, Modern Women"; and Bennett, "Confronting Continuities."

research, the history of sexuality. Because of the influence of Michel Foucault, or better said, because of the influence of a particular way of reading Foucault's work on sex, much research has explored the development of modern sexuality or simply taken modern sexuality as its topic. Foucault, in the first volume of *History of Sexuality*, locates the beginning of the transformation of sex into discourse with the practice of confession, and recognizes that this expanded after the Reformation as Catholics required more extensive and frequent confession, and Protestants substituted the personal examination of conscience for oral confession to a priest.[24] This discourse about sexuality was later taken over by medical, political, and educational authorities, and it is this point that most of Foucault's successors (and disciples) see as the beginning of what interests them, going on to explore the mechanisms that define and regulate sexuality, and investigating the ways in which individuals and groups described and understood their sexual lives. Even those who do look at earlier periods and who stress the socially constructed and historically variable nature of all things sexual tend to accept this notion of one clear break, terming their work the study of premodern sexuality.[25]

This notion of a decisive break sometime in the eighteenth century works fine for medievalists, whose era has always been before the break anyway. For Reformation scholars, however, this is more problematic; the Reformation has always been on *this* side of the great break, part of what made the early modern period modern. So how is it that the modern family emerged from the Reformation (or, following Heide Wunder, even earlier and then was strengthened by the Reformation), but modern sexuality did not develop until several centuries later?[26] If 1500 is dethroned and the break is moved later, does that make Reformation scholars all late medievalists? Or should the notion of a Middle Ages be junked entirely (as a few medievalists themselves are suggesting) as yet another piece of Renaissance intellectual baggage, so that those who study the thirteenth century are as much modernists as those who study the sixteenth?

---

[24]Foucault, *L'Histoire de la sexualité 1: La Volonté de savoir*.

[25]Murray and Eisenbichler, *Desire and Discipline*; Fradenburg and Freccero, *Premodern Sexualities*; and McLanan and Encarnación, *Material Culture of Sex, Procreation, and Marriage*.

[26]Lyndal Roper traces other problems with the "exaggerated significance [of] the late seventeenth and eighteenth centuries as the crucial period of change" on notions of sexuality and the body, in her review article of gender and the Reformation in *Archives for Reformation History* 92 (2001): 298–301, quote at 299.

Social Discipline and Colonial Christianity

The thought of dumping 1500 in favor of an earlier, a later, or no break is frightening (or perhaps better said, anathema) to many early modernists, as well as to textbook publishers and department chairs who would have to revamp their entire offerings. There are also two lines of research related to women and the Reformation that suggest that such a dethroning may be premature.

The first of these are studies of social discipline, the reform of popular culture, or the civilizing process (whatever term one uses) that recognize there were two sexes (or more, given the new scholarship on third sexes and transgendering). Early scholarship on these issues, though very aware of class and geographic differences, was largely blind to gender, which seems particularly odd given the fact that so much about social discipline is related to sex. That has changed for many scholars. Though most of this newer gendered scholarship on social discipline recognizes the medieval roots of such processes as the restriction of sexuality to marriage, the encouragement of moral discipline and sexual decorum, the glorification of heterosexual married love, and the establishing of institutions for regulating and regularizing behavior, it also emphasizes that all of these processes were strengthened in the sixteenth century, and that this had a different effect on women than on men. Laws regarding such issues as adultery, divorce, "lascivious carriage," enclosure of monastics, and interdenominational and interracial marriage were never gender neutral. The enforcement of such laws was even more discriminatory, of course, for though undisciplined sexuality and immoral behavior were portrayed from the pulpit or press as a threat to Christian order, it was women's lack of discipline that was most often punished. The newer scholarship on marriage, divorce, the family, and sexuality in the context of the Reformations makes clear that the roots of this strengthening are complex and include much more than theology; though most studies are not directly comparative, as a whole they suggest that these changes occurred in Catholic areas as well as Protestant, and that they involved church bodies such as the Inquisition, as well as secular courts and other institutions.[27]

[27]For examples of gendered scholarship on social discipline, see Watt, *Making of Modern Marriage*; Carlson, *Marriage and the English Reformation*; Harrington, *Reordering Marriage and Society*; Kingdon, *Adultery and Divorce*; Farr, *Authority and Sexuality*; Fernándes, *Espelhos, cartas e guias*; Adair, *Courtship, Illegitimacy and Marriage*; Graham, *Uses of Reform*; Dixon, *Reformation and Rural Society*; Bast, *Honor Your Fathers*; Karant-Nunn, *Reformation of Ritual*; Cressy, *Birth, Marriage and*

√ Differences in the timing and intensity of measures of social discipline have meant that most historians are unwilling to draw up grand schema and timetables—no one is currently setting dates for the rise of the restricted patriarchal nuclear family for example, as Lawrence Stone once did—but this scholarship does suggest that there was enough of a break with a pre-1500 past to retain this date as significant. It also underscores the fact that this break is a process that takes many decades or even centuries, but that it is just as significant as and also tightly interwoven with the more familiar early modern processes such as the rise of the nation-state and the growth of protoindustrial capitalism.

The second line of research is one that is only beginning to be related to the Reformation but will clearly be a key area of research in the coming decades—the expansion of Christianity beyond Europe with the first wave of colonialism. Viewing 1500 as a great gulf came not only from the chain of events that began in 1517, but also from the events that began in 1492. Were it reviewing recent and looming developments in early modern economic or cultural history, or English literature, this essay would certainly have started rather than ended with this. Viewing European women in the sixteenth century in a global context has begun, not surprisingly, for scholars of Iberia, who now regularly hold conferences, publish article collections, and carry out their own research from a transoceanic perspective.[28] This has been joined by research on French Catholic women in Canada, some of whom continued the fight for a noncloistered life on the other side of the Atlantic.[29]

This wider geographic perspective should not be limited to those countries that actually founded colonies in the early modern era, however. Many of the descriptions of the New World so favored by cultural analysts in their analyses of "othering" and "orientalizing" were printed in Germany, as were the maps both armchair and real travelers examined. Though America was named by an Italian, the name stuck because of the

---

Death; Burghartz, *Zeiten der Reinheit*; Wiesner-Hanks, *Christianity and Regulation of Sexuality*; Parish, *Clerical Marriage*; Black, *Perfect Wives, Other Women*; Boer, *Conquest of the Soul*; Puff, *Sodomy*; Barahona, *Sex Crimes, Honour, and the Law*; Hacke, *Women, Sex, and Marriage*; and Eisenach, *Husbands, Wives, and Concubines*.

[28]Conrad, *I Congreso*; Giles, *Women in the Inquisition*; Blackmore and Hutcheson, *Queer Iberia*; Burns, *Colonial Habits*; Ibsen, *Women's Spiritual Autobiography*; Black, *Creating the Cult of St. Joseph*; Myers, *Neither Saints nor Sinners*; Brewer, *Shamanism, Catholicism, and Gender Relations*; Jaffary, *Gender, Race, and Religion*.

[29]Davis, *Women on the Margins*; Simpson, *Marquerite Bourgeoys*; Dinan and Meyers, *Women and Religion*; Greer and Bilinkoff, *Colonial Saints*; and Greer, *Mohawk Saint*.

influence of the German mapmaker Martin Waldseemüller, who wrote, "I see no reason why, and by what right, this land of Amerigo should not be named America after that wise and ingenious man who discovered it, since both Europe and Asia had been allotted the names of women."[30] Ursulines and Jesuits from all over Europe thought the wider world needed their services, and reformers of all confessions were concerned about social, religious, ethnic, and racial mixing, whether it was Anabaptists marrying Lutherans, wives continuing their Jewish, Muslim, Catholic, Protestant, or pagan practices without their husbands' approval, or Catholic wet nurses suckling Calvinist babies. European men and women carried their notions of proper and godly gender roles, marriages, families, and sexual activities, as well as their plans for salvation, with them, whether they actually traveled or simply read about other lands. Studies of "society and the sexes"—Irwin's forward-looking title—have reshaped the way scholars view the origins and impact of the Protestant and Catholic Reformations in Europe over the last thirty years, and will no doubt be key to understanding the role of religion as Europeans established colonial empires in the centuries after Luther. Studies that explore the intersection of gender and empire have overwhelmingly focused on the later British experience, but it is clear that analysis of this intersection in the early modern period has much to offer both Reformation studies and wider world history.

Bibliography

BIBLIOGRAPHIC WORKS AND SPECIAL ISSUES

Diefendorf, Barbara. "Gender and the Family." In Mack P. Holt, ed., *Renaissance and Reformation France*, 99–118. Oxford: Oxford University Press, 2002.

Norberg, Katherine. "The Counter-Reformation and Women, Religious and Lay." In John O'Malley, ed., *Catholicism in Early Modern History: A Guide to Research*, 133–46. St. Louis, MO: Center for Reformation Research, 1988.

Special issue on gender and the Reformation with essays by Lyndal Roper, Heide Wunder, Susanna Peyronel Rambaldi, and Luisa Accati. *Archive for Reformation History* 92 (2001): 264–320.

Special issue on marriage. *Sixteenth Century Journal* 34/2 (2003).

Special issue on women. *Sixteenth Century Journal* 31/1 (2000).

Travitsky, Betty S., and Josephine A. Roberts. *English Women Writers, 1500–1640: A Reference Guide (1750–1996)*. New York: G. K. Hall, 1997.

Weber, Alison. "Women and Religion in Early Modern Spain." *Renaissance Quarterly* 52/1 (1999): 197–206.

[30]Waldseemüller's 1507 *Introduction to Cosmography* is translated in George Kish, *A Source Book in Geography* (Cambridge, MA: Harvard University Press, 1978).

Wiesner, Merry E. "Studies of Women, the Family and Gender." In William S. Maltby, ed., *Reformation Europe: A Guide to Research II*, 159–87. St. Louis, MO: Center for Reformation Research, 1992.

PRIMARY SOURCES (IN TRANSLATION)

Apostoles, Francisca de los. *Visions on Trial: The Inquisitional Trial of Francisca de los Apostoles*. Edited and translated by Gillian Ahlgren. Chicago: University of Chicago Press, 2005.

Coignard, Gabrielle de. *Spiritual Sonnets*. Edited and translated by Melanie Gregg. Chicago: University of Chicago Press, 2003.

Colonna, Vittoria, Chiara Matraini, and Lucrezia Marinella. *Marian Writings*. Edited and translated by Susan Haskins. Chicago: University of Chicago Press, forthcoming.

Dentière, Marie. *Epistles* [to Calvin]. Edited and translated by Mary McKinley. Chicago: University of Chicago Press, 2004.

Ferrazzi, Cecelia. *Autobiography of an Aspiring Saint*. Edited and translated by Anne Jacobson Schutte. Chicago: University of Chicago Press, 1996.

Joldersma, Hermina, and Louis Grijp, eds. and trans. *"Elisabeth's Manly Courage": Testimonials and Songs by and about Martyred Anabaptist Women*. Milwaukee, WI: Marquette University Press, 2001.

Karant-Nunn, Susan C., and Merry E. Wiesner-Hanks, eds. and trans. *Luther on Women: A Sourcebook*. Cambridge: Cambridge University Press, 2003.

Lierheimer, Linda, ed. and trans. *Spiritual Autobiography and the Construction of Self: The Mémoires of Antoinette Micolon*. Milwaukee, WI: Marquette University Press, 2004.

Matheson, Peter, ed. and trans. *Argula von Grumbach: A Woman's Voice in the Reformation*. Edinburgh: T. and T. Clark, 1995.

Pascal, Jacqueline. *A Rule for Children and Other Writings*. Edited and translated by John Conley. Chicago: University of Chicago Press, 2003.

Pulci, Antonia. *Florentine Drama for Convent and Festival*. Edited and translated by James Wyatt Cook and Barbara Collier Cook. Chicago: University of Chicago Press, 1996.

Rhodes, Elizabeth, ed. and trans. *"This Tight Embrace": Luise de Carvajal y Mendoza (1566–1614)*. Milwaukee, WI: Marquette University Press, 2000.

Rummel, Erika. *Erasmus on Women*. Toronto: University of Toronto Press, 1996.

San José, Maria de. *Book for the Hour of Recreation*. Edited and translated by Amanda Powell and Alison Weber. Chicago: University of Chicago Press, 2002.

———. *Word from New Spain: The Spiritual Autobiography of Madre María de San José (1656–1719)*. Edited and translated by Kathleen Ann Myers. Liverpool: Liverpool University Press, 1999.

Schurman, Anna Maria van. *Whether a Christian Woman Should Be Educated and Other Writings from Her Intellectual Circle*. Edited and translated by Joyce Irwin. Chicago: University of Chicago Press, 1998.

Tarabotti, Arcangela. *Paternal Tyranny*. Edited and translated by Letizia Panizza. Chicago: University of Chicago Press, 2004.

Tornabuoni, Lucrezia. *Sacred Narratives*. Edited and translated by Jane Tylus. Chicago: University of Chicago Press, 2001.

Wiesner-Hanks, Merry, and Joan Skocir, eds. and trans. *Convents Confront the Reformation: Catholic and Protestant Nuns in Germany*. Milwaukee, WI: Marquette University Press, 1996.

Zell, Katharina Schütz. *Church Mother: The Writings of a Protestant Reformer in Sixteenth-Century Germany.* Edited and translated by Elsie McKee. Chicago: University of Chicago Press, 2006.

SECONDARY SOURCES

Adair, Richard. *Courtship, Illegitimacy and Marriage in Early Modern England.* Manchester, UK: Manchester University Press, 1996.

Ahlgren, Gillian T. *Teresa of Avila and the Politics of Sanctity.* Ithaca, NY: Cornell University Press, 1996.

Baernstein, P. Renee. *A Convent Tale: A Century of Sisterhood in Spanish Milan.* New York: Routledge, 2002.

Barahona, Renato. *Sex Crimes, Honour, and the Law in Early Modern Spain: Vizcaya, 1500–1750.* Toronto: University of Toronto Press, 2003.

Bast, Robert James. *Honor Your Fathers: Catechisms and the Emergence of a Patriarchal Ideology in Germany, 1400–1600.* Leiden: Brill, 1997.

Bennett, Judith. "Confronting Continuities." *Journal of Women's History* 9 (1997): 73–94.

———. "Medieval Women, Modern Women: Across the Great Divide." In *Culture and History 1350–1600: Essays on English Communities, Identities and Writing,* edited by David Aers, 147–75. Detroit: Wayne State University Press, 1992.

Biberman, Matthew. *Masculinity, Anti-semitism and Early Modern English Literature: From the Satanic to the Effeminate Jew.* Aldershot: Ashgate, 2004.

Black, Charles Villaseñor. *Creating the Cult of St. Joseph: Art and Gender in the Spanish Empire.* Princeton, NJ: Princeton University Press, 2003.

Black, Georgina Dopico. *Perfect Wives, Other Women: Adultery and Inquisition in Early Modern Spain.* Durham, NC: Duke University Press, 2001.

Blackmore, Josiah, and Gregory S. Hutcheson, eds. *Queer Iberia: Sexualities, Cultures, and Crossings from the Middle Ages to the Renaissance.* Durham, NC: Duke University Press, 1999.

Boer, Wietse de. *The Conquest of the Soul: Confession, Discipline, and Public Order in Counter-Reformation Milan.* Leiden: Brill, 2001.

Breitenberg, Mark, ed. *Anxious Masculinity in Early Modern England.* Cambridge: Cambridge University Press, 1996.

Brewer, Carolyn. *Shamanism, Catholicism, and Gender Relations in Colonial Philippines, 1521–1685.* Aldershot: Ashgate, 2004.

Burghartz, Susanna. *Zeiten der Reinheit, Orte der Unzucht: Ehe und Sexualität in Basel während der Frühen Neuzeit.* Paderborn: Schoeningen, 1999.

Burns, Kathryn. *Colonial Habits: Convents and the Spiritual Economy of Cuzco, Peru.* Durham, NC: Duke University Press, 1999.

Burschel, Peter, and Anne Conrad, eds. *Vorbild, Inbild, Abbild: Religiöse Lebensmodelle in geschlechtergeschichtlicher Perspektive.* Freiburg im Breisgau: Rombach, 2003.

Carlson, Eric Josef. *Marriage and the English Reformation.* Oxford: Blackwell, 1994.

Carroll, Jane Louise, and Alison G. Stewart. *Saints, Sinners, and Sisters: Gender and Northern Art in Medieval and Early Modern Europe.* Aldershot: Ashgate, 2003.

Cavallo, Sandra, and Lyndan Warner, eds. *Widowhood in Medieval and Early Modern Europe.* London: Addison Wesley, 1999.

Conrad, Anne. *I Congreso Internacional del monacato femenino en España, Portugal y América, 1492–1992.* 2 vol. León: Ediciones Lancia, 1993.

————. _Zwischen Kloster und Welt: Ursulinen und Jesuitinnen in der Katholischen Reformbewegung des 16./17. Jahrhunderts._ Mainz: Zabern, 1991.

————, ed. _"In Christo ist weden man noch weyb": Frauen in der Zeit der Reformation und der katholischen Reform._ Münster: Aschendorff, 1999.

Crawford, Patricia. _Women and Religion in England, 1500–1750._ London: Routledge, 1993.

Cressy, David. _Birth, Marriage and Death: Ritual, Religion, and the Life-Cycle in Tudor and Stuart England._ Oxford: Oxford University Press, 1997.

Davis, Natalie Zemon. _Women on the Margins: Three Seventeenth-Century Lives._ Cambridge, MA: Harvard University Press, 1995.

Diefendorf, Barbara. _From Penitence to Charity: Pious Women and the Catholic Reformation in Paris._ Oxford: Oxford University Press, 2004.

Dinan, Susan E. _Women and Poor Relief in Seventeenth-Century France: The Early History of the Daughters of Charity._ Aldershot: Ashgate, 2006.

————, and Debra Meyers, eds. _Women and Religion in Old and New Worlds._ London: Routledge, 2001.

Dinges, Martin, ed. _Hausväter, Priester, Kastraten: Zur Konstruktion von Männlichkeit in Spätmittelalter und früher Neuzeit._ Göttingen: Vandenhoeck, 1999.

Dixon, C. Scott. _The Reformation and Rural Society: The Parishes of Brandenburg-Ansbach-Kulmbach, 1528–1603._ Cambridge: Cambridge University Press, 1996.

Eisenach, Emlyn. _Husbands, Wives, and Concubines: Marriage, Family, and Social Order in Sixteenth-Century Verona._ Kirksville, MO: Truman State University Press, 2004.

Farr, James R. _Authority and Sexuality in Early Modern Burgundy._ New York: Oxford University Press, 1995.

Fernándes, Maria de Lurdes Correia. _Espelhos, cartas e guias: Casamento e espiritualidade na Peninsula Iberica 1450–1700._ Porto: Instituto de Cultura Portuguesa, 1995.

Fernández, Angela Muñoz. _Beatas y santas neocastellanas: Ambivalencias de la religión y políticas correctoras del poder (ss. XIV–XVI)._ Madrid: Comunidad de Madrid, 1994.

Fletcher, Anthony. _Gender, Sex, and Subordination in England 1500–1800._ New Haven, CT: Yale University Press, 1995.

Forster, Marc R., and Benjamin J. Kaplan, eds. _Piety and Family in Early Modern Europe: Essays in Honor of Steven Ozment._ Aldershot: Ashgate, 2005.

Foucault, Michel. _L'Histoire de la sexualité 1: La Volonté de savoir._ Paris, 1976.

Foyster, Elizabeth A. _Manhood in Early Modern England: Honour, Sex and Marriage._ London: Longman, 1999.

Fradenburg, Louise, and Carla Freccero, eds., _Premodern Sexualities._ New York: Routledge, 1996.

Giles, Mary G., ed. _Women in the Inquisition: Spain and the New World._ Baltimore: Johns Hopkins University Press, 1998.

Graham, Michael Francis. _The Uses of Reform: "Godly Discipline" and Popular Behavior in Scotland and Beyond 1560–1610._ Leiden: Brill, 1996.

Greer, Alan. _Mohawk Saint: Catherine Tekakwitha and the Jesuits._ New York: Oxford University Press, 2004.

————, and Jodi Bilinkoff, eds. _Colonial Saints: Discovering the Holy in the Americas, 1500–1800._ New York: Routledge, 2003.

Hacke, Daniela. _Women, Sex, and Marriage in Early Modern Venice._ Aldershot: Ashgate, 2004.

Haliczer, Stephen. _Between Exaltation and Infamy: Female Mystics in the Golden Age of Spain._ New York: Oxford University Press, 2002.

——. *Sexuality in the Confessional: A Sacrament Profaned*. New York: Oxford University Press, 1996.

Harline, Craig. *The Burdens of Sister Margaret: Private Lives in a Seventeenth-Century Convent*. New York: Doubleday, 1994.

Harrington, Joel F. *Reordering Marriage and Society in Reformation Germany*. Cambridge: Cambridge University Press, 1995.

Hernández, María Leticia Sánchez. *Patronato, regio y órdenes religiosas femeninas en el Madrid de los Austrias*. Madrid: Fundación Universitaria Española, 1997.

Hills, Helen. *Invisible City: The Architecture of Devotion in Seventeenth-Century Neapolitan Convents*. Oxford: Oxford University Press, 2004.

——, ed. *Architecture and the Politics of Gender in Early Modern Europe*. Aldershot: Ashgate, 2003.

Ibsen, Kristine. *Women's Spiritual Autobiography in Colonial Spanish America*. Gainesville: University Press of Florida, 1999.

Jaffary, Nora E., ed. *Gender, Race, and Religion in the Colonization of the Americas*. Aldershot: Ashgate, 2007.

Karant-Nunn, Susan C. *The Reformation of Ritual: An Interpretation of Early Modern Germany*. London: Routledge, 1997.

Kendrick, Robert L. *Celestial Sirens: Nuns and Their Music in Early Modern Italy*. Oxford: Oxford University Press, 1996.

Kingdon, Robert. *Adultery and Divorce in Calvin's Geneva*. Cambridge, MA: Harvard University Press, 1995.

Kobelt-Groch, Marion. *Aufsässige Töchter Gottes: Frauen im Bauernkrieg und in den Taüferbewegungen*. Frankfurt: Campus, 1993.

Kreitzer, Beth. *Reforming Mary: Lutheran Preaching on the Virgin Mary in the Sixteenth Century*. Oxford: Oxford University Press, 2004.

Laven, Mary. *Virgins of Venice: Broken Vows and Cloistered Lives in the Renaissance Convent*. New York: Penguin/Viking, 2004.

Lawrence, Cynthia Miller., ed. *Women and Art in Early Modern Europe: Patrons, Collectors, and Connoisseurs*. University Park: Pennsylvania State University Press, 1997.

Lehfeldt, Elizabeth A. *Religious Women in Golden Age Spain: The Permeable Cloister*. Aldershot: Ashgate, 2005.

Leonard, Amy. *Nails in the Wall: Catholic Nuns in Reformation Germany*. Chicago: University of Chicago Press, 2005.

Long, Katherine, ed. *High Anxiety: Anxious Masculinity in Early Modern France*. Kirksville, MO: Truman State University Press, 2002.

Lowe, K. J. P. *Nuns' Chronicles and Convent Culture in Renaissance and Counter-Reformation Italy*. Cambridge: Cambridge University Press, 2003.

Lux-Sterritt, Laurence. *Redefining Female Religious Life: French Ursulines and English Ladies in Seventeenth-Century Catholicism*. Aldershot: Ashgate, 2006.

Martin, A. Lynn. *Alcohol, Sex, and Gender in Late Medieval and Early Modern Europe*. New York: Palgrave MacMillan, 2001.

Matter, E. Ann, and John Wayland Coakley, eds. *Creative Women in Medieval and Early Modern Italy*. Philadelphia: University of Pennsylvania Press, 1997.

Mattox, Mickey Leland. *Defender of the Most Holy Matriarchs: Martin Luther's Interpretation of the Women of Genesis in the* Enarrationes in Genesin, *1535–1545*. Leiden: Brill, 2004.

McIntosh, Marjorie Keniston. *Controlling Misbehavior in England, 1370–1600*. Cambridge: Cambridge University Press, 1998.

McKee, Elsie Anne. *Katharina Schütz Zell*. Vol. 1, *The Life and Thought of a Sixteenth-Century Reformer*. Vol. 2, *The Writings: A Critical Edition*. Leiden: Brill, 1999.

———. *Reforming Popular Piety in 16th Century Strasbourg: Katherine Schütz Zell and Her Hymnbook*. Studies in Reformed Theology and History. Princeton, NJ: Princeton Theological Seminary, 1994.

McLanan, Anne L., and Karen Rosoff Encarnación, eds. *The Material Culture of Sex, Procreation, and Marriage in Premodern Europe*. London: Palgrave Macmillan, 2002.

McNamara, Jo Ann. *Sisters in Arms: Catholic Nuns through Two Millennia*. Cambridge, MA: Harvard University Press, 1996.

Mendelson, Sara, and Patricia Crawford. *Women in Early Modern England*. Oxford: Oxford University Press, 1998.

Monson, Craig, ed. *The Crannied Wall: Women, Religion and the Arts in Early Modern Europe*. Ann Arbor: University of Michigan Press, 1992.

———. *Disembodied Voices: Music and Culture in an Early Modern Italian Convent*. Berkeley: University of California Press, 1995.

Murray, Jacqueline, and Konrad Eisenbichler, eds. *Desire and Discipline: Sex and Sexuality in the Premodern West*. Toronto: University of Toronto Press, 1996.

Myers, Kathleen Ann. *Neither Saints nor Sinners: Writing the Lives of Women in Spanish America*. Oxford: Oxford University Press, 2003.

Ozment, Steven E. *The Bürgermeister's Daughter: Scandal in a Sixteenth-Century German Town*. New York: St. Martin's Press, 1996.

Parish, Helen L. *Clerical Marriage and the English Reformation: Precedent, Policy and Practice*. Aldershot: Ashgate, 2000.

Peters, Christine. *Patterns of Piety: Women, Gender, and Religion in Late Medieval and Reformation England*. Cambridge: Cambridge University Press, 2003.

Petry, Yvonne. *Gender, Kabbalah and the Reformation: The Mystical Theology of Guillaume Postel (1510–1581)*. Leiden: Brill, 2004.

Poutrin, Isabelle. *Le voile et la plume: Autobiographie et sainteté féminine dans l'Espagne moderne*. Madrid: Casa de Velásquez, 1995.

Puff, Helmut. *Sodomy in Reformation Germany and Switzerland, 1400–1600*. Chicago: University of Chicago Press, 2003.

Rapley, Elizabeth. *The Dévotes: Women and Church in Seventeenth-Century France*. Montreal: McGill-Queen's University Press, 1990.

———. *A Social History of the Cloister: Daily Life in the Teaching Monasteries of the Old Regime*. Montreal: McGill-Queen's University Press, 2001.

Ranft, Patricia. *Women and the Religious Life in Premodern Europe*. New York: St. Martin's, 1996.

Reiss, Sheryl E., and David G. Wilkins, eds. *Beyond Isabella: Secular Women Patrons of the Arts in Renaissance Italy*. Kirksville, MO: Truman State University Press, 2001.

Roper, Lyndal. *Oedipus and the Devil: Witchcraft, Sexuality, and Religion in Early Modern Europe*. London: Routledge, 1994.

Scaraffia, Lucetta, and Gabriella Zarri, eds. *Women and Faith: Catholic Religious Life in Italy from Late Antiquity to the Present*. Cambridge, MA: Harvard University Press, 1999.

Schmidt, Heinrich Reinhard. *Dorf und Religion: Reformierte Sittenzucht in Berner Landgemeinde der Frühen Neuzeit*. Stuttgart: G. Fischer, 1995.

Schnell, Rüdiger, ed. *Text und Geschlecht: Mann und Frau in Eheschriften der frühen Neuzeit*. Frankfurt: Suhrkamp, 1997.

————. *Frauendiskurs, Männerdiskurs, Ehediskurs: Textsorten und Geschlechterkonzepte in Mittelalter und Früher Neuzeit.* Frankfurt: Campus, 1998.

Schutte, Anne Jacobson. *Aspiring Saints: Pretense of Holiness, Inquisition, and Gender in the Republic of Venice, 1618–1750.* Baltimore: Johns Hopkins University Press, 2001.

————, Thomas Kuehn, and Silvana Seidel Menchi, eds. *Time, Space and Women's Lives in Early Modern Europe.* Kirksville, MO: Truman State University Press, 2001.

Selderhuis, Herman Johan. *Marriage and Divorce in the Thought of Martin Bucer.* Kirksville, MO: Truman State University Press, 1998.

Shepard, Alexandra. *Meanings of Manhood in Early Modern England.* Oxford: Oxford University Press, 2003.

Sibeth, Uwe. *Eherecht und Staatsbildung: Ehegesetzgebung und Eherechtssprechung in der Landgrafschaft Hessen (-Kassel) in der frühen Neuzeit.* Darmstadt: Hessische Historische Kommission Darmstad, 1994.

Simpson, Patricia. *Marguerite Bourgeoys and Montreal.* Montreal: McGill-Queen's University Press, 1997.

Slade, Carole. *Saint Teresa of Avila: Author of a Heroic Life.* Berkeley: University of California Press, 1995.

Snyder, C. Arnold, and Linda A. Huebert Hecht, eds. *Profiles of Anabaptist Women: Sixteenth-Century Reforming Pioneers.* Waterloo, ON: Wilfrid Laurier University Press, 1996.

Sperling, Jutta Gisella. *Convents and the Body Politic in Renaissance Venice.* Chicago: University of Chicago Press, 2000.

Stephenson, Barbara. *The Power and Patronage of Marguerite de Navarre.* Aldershot: Ashgate, 2004.

Strasser, Ulrike. *State of Virginity: Gender, Religion, and Politics in an Early Modern Catholic State.* Ann Arbor: University of Michigan Press, 2004.

Surtz, Ronald E. *Writing Women in Late Medieval and Early Modern Spain: The Mothers of Saint Teresa of Avila.* Philadelphia: University of Pennsylvania Press, 1995.

Tatlock, Lynne, ed. *The Graph of Sex and the German Text: Gendered Culture in Early Modern Germany.* Chloe 19. Amsterdam: Rodopi, 1994.

Thompson, John Lee. *John Calvin and the Daughters of Sarah: Women in Regular and Exceptional Roles in the Exegesis of Calvin, His Predecessors and His Contemporaries.* Geneva: Droz, 1992.

————. *Writing the Wrongs: Women of the Old Testament in Biblical Commentators from Philo through the Reformation.* Oxford: Oxford University Press, 2001.

Tlusty, B. Ann. *Bacchus and Civic Order: The Culture of Drink in Early Modern Germany.* Charlottesville: University of Virginia Press, 2001.

Todd, Margo. *Christian Humanism and the Puritan Social Order.* Cambridge: Cambridge University Press, 1987.

Tomizza, Fulvio. *Heavenly Supper: The Story of Maria Janis.* Translated by Anne Jacobsen Schutte. Chicago: University of Chicago Press, 1993.

Umble, Diane Zimmerman, and Kimberley D. Schmidt, eds. *Strangers at Home: Amish and Mennonite Women in History.* Baltimore: Johns Hopkins University Press, 2002.

Velasco, Sherry M. *Demons, Nausea and Resistance in the Autobiography of Isabel de Jesús (1611–1682).* Albuquerque: University of New Mexico Press, 1996.

Walker, Claire. *Gender and Politics in Early Modern Europe: English Convents in France and the Low Countries.* London: Palgrave Macmillan, 2003.

Warren, Nancy Bradley. *Women of God and Arms: Female Spirituality and Political Conflict, 1380–1600.* Philadelphia: University of Pennsylvania Press, 2005.

Watt, Diane. *Secretaries of God: Women Prophets in Late Medieval and Early Modern England.* Rochester, NY: Bowdell and Brewer, 1997.

Watt, Jeffry R. *The Making of Modern Marriage: Matrimonial Control and the Rise of Sentiment in Neuchâtel, 1550–1800.* Ithaca, NY: Cornell University Press, 1992.

Weaver, Elissa. *Convent Theatre in Early Modern Italy: Spiritual Fun and Learning for Women.* Cambridge: Cambridge University Press, 2002.

Westphal, Siegrid. *Frau und lutherische Konfessionalisierung: Eine Untersuchung zum Fürstentum Pfalz-Neuburg, 1542–1614.* Frankfurt: Peter Lang, 1994.

Wiesner, Merry E. *Gender, Church and State in Early Modern Germany.* London: Longmans, 1998.

Wiesner-Hanks, Merry E. *Christianity and the Regulation of Sexuality in the Early Modern World: Regulating Desire, Reforming Practice.* London: Routledge, 2000.

Winston-Allen, Anne. *Convent Chronicles: Women Writing about Women and Reform in the Late Middle Ages.* University Park: Pennsylvania State University Press, 2004.

Wood, Jeryldene. *Women, Art, and Spirituality: The Poor Clares of Early Modern Italy.* Cambridge: Cambridge University Press, 1996.

Woodford, C. *Nuns as Historians in Early Modern Germany.* Oxford: Oxford University Press, 2003.

Wunder, Heide. *"Er ist die Sonn, sie ist der Mond": Frauen in der frühen Neuzeit.* Munich: C.H. Beck'sche, 1992. Translated by Thomas Dunlap as *He Is the Sun, She Is the Moon: Women in Early Modern Germany* (Cambridge, MA: Harvard University Press, 1998).

———, and Gisella Engel, eds. *Geschlechterperspektiven: Forschungen zur Frühen Neuzeit.* Königstein: Helmer, 1998.

Zarri, Gabriella. *Le sante vive: Profezie di corte e devozione femminile tra '400 e '500.* Turin: Rosenberg and Sellier, 1990.

———. *Recinti: Donne, clausura, e matrimonio nella prima età moderna.* Bologna: Il mulino, 2000.

———, ed. *Donna, disciplina, creanza cristiana dal XV al XVII secolo: Studi e testi a stampa.* Roma: Edizione de storia e letteratura, 1996.

———, ed. *Il monachesimo femminile in Italia dall'alto Medioevo al secolo XVII: A confronto con l'oggi,* Atti del VI Convegno del "Centro di studi farfensi," Santa Vittoria in Mantenano, 21–24 settembre 1995. Verona: San Pietro in Cariano, 1997.

17

Art History

Larry Silver

In current art history, both methodological self-consciousness and rich interdisciplinary dialogue prevail. These perspectives help dispel deep-seated modern biases of a museum culture toward named artists, usually painters. No longer does exclusive or uncritical attention embrace either Italian ideal figures or Flemish verisimilitude as progressive imagery foundational for the illusionism in art of the following four centuries. Today scholars attend more frequently to anonymous craftsmen and to diverse media, such as luxuriously illuminated manuscripts or tapestries, deluxe items that stem from the late medieval court world of Huizinga, which still persisted within wider Europe during the sixteenth century.[1] Greater attention also gets paid now to pictorial novelties other than paintings, especially printed books and independent prints.

Earlier, general neglect of German art, reinforced by the stigma attached to German culture by the justifiable biases of twentieth-century politics, is now being redressed. Even within Germany, other art centers besides Dürer's Nürnberg now include cities—Augsburg, Cologne, and the Rhineland up to Switzerland—as well as courts (notably those of Emperor Maximilian and the dukes of Saxony and Bavaria).[2] Major media of monumental sculpture are complemented with bronze medals to provide

---

[1] Belozerskaya, *Rethinking the Renaissance*.

[2] Kaufmann, *Court, Cloister, City*. On Augsburg, see Cuneo, *Art and Politics in Early Modern Germany*; Morrall *Jörg Breu the Elder*; and Bierende *Lucas Cranach d. Ä. Und der deutsche Humanismus*.

increased social engagement throughout the sixteenth century.[3] Today, Central Europe consists of more than German-speaking countries; specifically, Bohemian and Polish art no longer lie beyond a Cold War Iron Curtain, though they still carry a Slavic language barrier for most scholars. Modern geographical boundaries have been expanded, especially by Thomas Kaufmann, following earlier, more regional apologetics of Jan Bialostocki.

Moreover, French, Spanish, and English art no longer are considered backwaters relative to Flemish art. French art includes interpretive readings of visual works within an emerging national cultural identity, no longer confined to Fontainebleau.[4] Spanish art is no longer dominated by El Greco studies. Traditional Spanish religious art has been examined, including carved *retablos* and liturgical manuscripts, as well as monumental projects in Madrid and the Escorial.[5] Indeed, one great new frontier of art history is Spanish (and Portuguese Brazilian) colonial material, increasingly revisited as a site of tensions from the side of both the indigenous populations and the European settlers.[6] English connections of art to royal interests and imagery have always been central,[7] but now English art in all its diversity is receiving expanded attention.[8] Even Holbein studies now take account of archival sources and the traces of lost works in English visual culture.[9]

Perhaps no other part of Europe has expanded its boundaries and media and range of interests more than Italy. Other urban centers, particularly Siena, have joined the traditional triumvirate of Florence, Rome, and Venice. Vital contributions of courts—Sforza Milan, Este Ferrara, Gonzagan Mantua—finally have received their due.[10] And in no other region have expanded interests in other media played so great a role: manuscripts, tapestries, prints, and even neglected genres of panel painting, such as *cassoni*.[11]

---

[3]Smith, *German Sculpture of the Later Renaissance*; and Baxandall, *Limewood Sculptors of Renaissance Germany*.

[4]Zerner, *Renaissance Art in Florence*; and Zorach, *Blood, Milk, Ink, Gold*.

[5]Sobré, *Behind the Altar Table*; and Mulcahy *Decoration of the Royal Basilica of El Escorial*.

[6]Bailey, *Art of Colonial Latin America*.

[7]Hearn, *Dynasties*; Howarth, *Images of Rule*; and Starkey and Doran, *Elizabeth*.

[8]Marks and Williamson, *Gothic*; Erickson and Hulse, *Early Modern Visual Culture*; Fumerton *Cultural Aesthetics*; and Gent and Llewellyn, *Renaissance Bodies*.

[9]Foister, *Holbein and England*.

[10]Cole, *Virtue and Magnificence*; Welch, *Art and Authority in Renaissance Milan*; Chambers and Martineau, *Splendours of the Gonzaga*; and Campbell, *Artists at Court*.

[11]Campbell, *Tapestry in the Renaissance*; Lincoln, *Invention of the Renaissance Printmaker*;

Indeed, art historians now are increasingly likely to look at contacts linking different regions of Europe,[12] even the contact between Europe's art and other regions of the world after 1492—whether Spain with the New World, or else the Portuguese and then the Dutch with Africa and Asia. Such a broader vision already underlies one important anthology, appropriately entitled *Reframing the Renaissance*.[13] Groundbreaking exhibitions have devoted catalogues to America and Australia, and even to the entire world around the time of Columbus.[14] International collaborations by Jesuits, both within Europe and abroad, have recently been examined.[15] Reciprocal importance of foreign ventures impinges on Dutch visual culture, particularly in the form of maps and atlases.[16] A 2004 exhibition examined broader interactions of Europe with Asia from both points of view.[17] Such contacts have spurred increasing interest in what is termed cultural geography, recently reexamined by Thomas Kaufmann.[18] In addition, although visual specialists have ignored the profoundly visual world of cartographers, map scholars remind us of the continuity between later sixteenth-century mapmaking and the Dutch golden age, or between territories of Spanish colonies and their representation.[19] The recent volume on early modern maps organized by the late David Woodward will consolidate this important field for art historians as well as other scholars.[20]

Current art historical research does move into a more inclusive vision of what constellates visual culture in its historical period, permitting attention to objects, often anonymous, that were previously not even considered artworks at all. Jan van der Stock's close study of sixteenth-century Antwerp archives offers a newly inclusive range of all printed images, including wallpapers and anonymous, cheap religious images, within an encompassing production of visual publications.[21] Similarly, the basic survey book on

---

Alexander, *Painted Page*; and Baskins, *Cassone Painting, Humanism and Gender.*

[12]Aikema, Brown, and Sciré, *Renaissance Venice and the North*; Nuttall, *From Flanders to Florence*; and Levenson, *Encompassing the Globe.*

[13]Farago, *Reframing the Renaissance.*

[14]Vandenbroeck, *Bride of the Sun*; Eisler and Smith, *Terra Australis*; and Levenson, *Circa 1492.*

[15]Bailey, *Art on the Jesuit Missions in Asia and Latin America*; and O'Malley, *Jesuits.*

[16]Schmidt, *Innocence Abroad*; and Zandvliet, *Dutch Encounter with Asia.*

[17]Jackson and Jaffer, *Encounters.*

[18]Kaufmann, *Towards a Geography of Art.*

[19]Zandvliet, *Mapping for Money*; Mignolo, *Darker Side of the Renaissance*; and Kagan, *Urban Images of the Hispanic World.*

[20]Woodward, *Cartography in the European Renaissance.*

[21]Stock, *Printing Images in Antwerp.* On the incunabula of woodcuts, see Parshall and Schoch, *Origins of European Printmaking.*

Renaissance prints devotes attention to religious images, broadsheets, town plans, and maps, as well as what we would now call scientific illustrations, such as herbals.[22] "Counterfeit" images represent nature, especially via replicable printed images, whose verisimilitude made them major contributors to sixteenth-century taxonomy of the natural world.[23] Related contributions to art history have also come from sister disciplines, focusing on fruitful overlaps of interest between imagery and knowledge.[24] But in return, art historians have also contributed to understanding scientific knowledge through its visual codification: exhibitions on humors and palmistry.[25]

Traditional Renaissance emphasis on knowledge of antiquity receives ongoing attention, notably by Leonard Barkan, building on the standard reference by Bober and Rubinstein.[26] Pagan mythology retains its scholarly interest.[27] This field has expanded to encompass a complementary Venetian fascination with the Levant.[28]

Concerning religious experience, art has become an ever more important component, including studies of Reformation iconoclasm against the "power of the image."[29] Late medieval spirituality has benefited richly from studies of the use of images, particularly in female piety, and considerations of the altarpiece and icon have become staples of period discussion.[30] Pictorial details have been analyzed tellingly for their role in participatory devotion: Passion imagery in relation to contemporary practices of public corporal punishment for criminals, details in landscapes, even fruits and flowers in concert with other senses.[31] Italian religious art has been reconsidered in terms of its spiritual effectiveness.[32] Visual rhetoric as

[22]Landau and Parshall, *Renaissance Print.*

[23]Parshall, "Imago contrafacta." On curiosity, see Parshall, *Origins of European Printmaking*; and Kenseth, *Age of the Marvelous.*

[24]Daston and Park, *Wonders and the Order of Nature*; Smith, *Sensuous Worship*; and Smith, *Body of the Artisan.*

[25]Filipczak, *Hot Dry Men, Cold Wet Women*; and Richter Sherman, *Writing on Hands.*

[26]Barkan, *Unearthing the Past*; Bober and Rubinstein, *Renaissance Artists and Antique Sculpture*; Rowland, *Culture of the High Renaissance*; Brown, *Venice and Antiquity*; and Campbell, *Artists at Court.*

[27]Bull, *Mirror of the Gods*; Freedman, *Revival of the Olympian Gods in Renaissance Art*; and Dempsey, *Portrayal of Love.*

[28]Howard, *Venice and the East*; and Carboni, *Venice and the Islamic World.*

[29]Freedberg, *Power of Images*; Michalski, *Reformation and the Visual Arts*; and Parshall, *Art and the Reformation.*

[30]Duffy, *Stripping of the Altars*; Belting, *Likeness and Presence*; Hamburger, *Visual and the Visionary*; and Wolf, *Schleier und Spiegel.*

[31]Merback, *The Thief, the Cross, and the Wheel*; Falkenburg, *Joachim Patinir*; and Falkenburg, *Fruit of Devotion.*

[32]Nagel, *Michelangelo and the Reform of Art*; Holmes, *Fra Filippo Lippi, the Carmelite Painter*;

an instrument of devotion has received general treatment,[33] and has also been applied to Lutheran imagery (including prints),[34] Jesuit imagery,[35] and even Calvinist visuality.[36]

Wider consideration of visual rhetoric has led to a focus on the dialogue of art with Renaissance verbal rhetoric and visual art, including Netherlandish art.[37] Formative texts have always served as a mainstay of art in Italy,[38] and abetted the learning of artists,[39] including the formative art author Vasari[40] and his counterpart in the Netherlands, Karel van Mander.[41] The rhetoric of the framed image itself, in isolation and within images of collections, has also been examined.[42]

Art history has also made contributions to social history and the interpretation of values, especially through the popular medium of prints, which often incorporate accompanying texts. This has been particularly true for images of warfare, especially in Germany and Italy.[43] Social groups, especially outsiders, appear in Netherlandish genre images.[44] Family history has become a topical issue, both in respect to the relations between the sexes and the rearing of children,[45] complementing feminist interests in sex and gender.[46] Artistic images of witchcraft, especially in

Hood, *Fra Angelico at San Marco*; Verdon and Henderson, *Christianity and the Renaissance*; and Humfrey and Kemp, *Altarpiece in the Renaissance*.

[33]Shearman, *Only Connect*; Lavin, *Bernini and the Unity of the Arts*; Stoichita, *Visionary Experience in the Gold Age of Spanish Art*; and Krüger, *Das Bild als Schleier des Unsichtbaren*.

[34]Scribner, *For the Sake of Simple Folk*; Koerner, *Reformation of the Image*; and Noble, "'A work in which the angels are wont to rejoice.'"

[35]Smith, *Sensuous Worship*; and Levy, *Propaganda and the Jesuit Baroque*.

[36]Finney, *Seeing Through the Word*.

[37]Meadow, *Pieter Bruegel the Elder's Netherlandish Proverbs and the Practice of Rhetoric*; and Hulse, *Rule of Art*.

[38]Baxandall, *Giotto and the Orators*; Baxandall, *Painting and Experience in Fifteenth Century Italy*; Kemp, *Behind the Picture*; and Ames-Lewis, *Intellectual Life of the Early Renaissance Artist*.

[39]Cole and Pardo, *Inventions of the Studio*.

[40]Rubin, *Giorgio Vasari*; Barolsky, *Michelangelo's Nose*; idem, *Why Mona Lisa Smiles and Other Tales by Vasari*; and idem, *Giotto's Father and the Family of Vasari's Lives*.

[41]Melion, *Shaping the Netherlandish Canon*; and Miedema, *Karel van Mander*.

[42]Stoichita, *Self-Aware Image*.

[43]Moxey, *Peasants, Warriors, and Wives*; Hale, *Artists and Warfare in the Renaissance*; Cuneo, *Artful Armies, Beautiful Battles*; Kunzle, *From Criminal to Courtier*; and Clifton, *Plains of Mars*.

[44]Vandenbroeck, *Beeld van der andere, vertoog over zichzelf*; and Jongh and Luijten, *Mirror of Everyday Life*.

[45]Bedaux and Ekkart, *Pride and Joy*; and Musacchio, *Art and Ritual of Childbirth in Renaissance Italy*.

[46]Bleyerveld, *Hoe bedreichelijck dat die vrouwen zijn*; Grössinger, *Picturing Women in Late Medieval and Renaissance Art*; Franits, *Paragons of Virtue*; and Salomon, *Shifting Priorities*.

Germany and the Low Countries, have received sensitive analysis.[47]
Images of rape and of eros—straight and gay—also found their most
explicit representation during the early modern period.[48] The significance
of clothing has been explicated by literary historians.[49]

Patronage has been a dominant art historical topic, especially for
Italy, where city centers,[50] individuals (e.g., Cosimo de' Medici or popes),[51]
courts,[52] and corporate confraternities supported the arts.[53] The social role
of female patrons is enjoying a revival, particularly for sixteenth-century
female regents/rulers: Margaret of Austria (Dagmar Eichberger), Catherine
de' Medici (Sheila ffolliott), and Elizabeth I of England (Roy Strong, David
Starkey, Louis Montrose).[54] Moreover, women artists have received new
attention, chiefly in Italy.[55] Portraits combine the emphasis on patronage
with the role of the artist, even more closely in the case of self-portraits.[56]

Another social issue that has been garnering increased attention in
recent decades is the economics of art history. Research has chiefly focused
on the Netherlands, revealing both the market institutions and personal
side of art sales through dealer networks.[57] The work of Montias and De
Marchi-Van Miegroet also extends well into the seventeenth century. Considering the implications of the art market for objects, other scholars have
analyzed the effects of the money economy, whether in the choice of mon-
etary themes for images, or else new production processes to satisfy a

[47]Schade, *Schadenzauber und die Magie des Körpers*; Roper, *Oedipus and the Devil*; Zika, *Exorcising Our Demons*; and Hults, *Witch as Muse*.

[48]Wolfthal, *Images of Rape*; Talvacchia, *Taking Positions*; Saslow, *Ganymede in the Renaissance*;
Barkan, *Transuming Passion*; and Randolph, *Engaging Symbols*.

[49]Jones and Stallybrass, *Renaissance Clothing and the Materials of Memory*.

[50]Kempers, *Painting, Power, and Patronage*; Norman, *Siena, Florence, and Padua*; Starn and
Partridge, *Arts of Power*; and Rosand, *Myths of Venice*.

[51]Kent, *Cosimo de' Medici and the Florentine Renaissance*. For popes, see *Hochrenaissance im
Vatikan*.

[52]Campbell, *Artists at Court*; and Fliegel, Jugie, and Barthélémy, *Art from the Court of Burgundy
1364–1419*.

[53]Wisch and Ahl, *Confraternities and the Visual Arts in Renaissance Italy*; and Brown, *Venetian
Narrative Painting in the Age of Carpaccio*.

[54]See also Lawrence, *Women and Art in Early Modern Europe*; and Reiss and Wilkins, *Beyond
Isabella*.

[55]Jacobs, *Defining the Renaissance Virtuosa*. On early women artists from Italy, see Perlingieri,
Sofonisba Anguissola; and Murphy, *Lavinia Fontana*.

[56]Campbell, *Renaissance Portraits*; Dülberg, *Privatporträts*; Woods-Marsden, *Renaissance Self-
Portraiture*; Cranston, *Poetics of Portraiture in the Italian Renaissance*; and Adams, *Public Faces and
Private Identities*.

[57]Vermeylen, *Painting for the Market*; Montias, "Socio-Economic Aspects of Netherlandish Art";
De Marchi and Van Miegroet, "Exploring Markets for Netherlandish Paintings"; and De Marchi and
Van Miegroet, "Rules Versus Play in Early Modern Markets."

growing consumer culture.[58] One intriguing, wide-ranging recent anthology, *Merchants and Marvels*, even brings together art collecting, science, and commerce.[59]

What really characterizes current art history is this kind of strong social or cultural orientation, where groups and their values link research much more closely to historical concerns. As a result the dialogue between art history and sister disciplines in the humanities—religion, literature, history of all kinds—has never been stronger, to the mutual benefit of all scholars. The citations here of contributions by scholars from other academic fields offer testimony that art history has become part of the concern of colleagues, while also offering them new insights for their home disciplines. At the same time, the drive towards interdisciplinary research and to what Clifford Geertz called "local knowledge" has resulted in increasingly specific topics and publications, rather than earlier syntheses. That kind of command of the larger period, combined with the older restriction of interest to painting (sometimes also sculpture or architecture), used to make the Renaissance a period essentially defined by art (especially for Italy), as codified first by Vasari, then for the modern university by Burckhardt. Consequently, there are few reliable, let alone up-to-date, art history references about the Renaissance period today. Even the benchmark art history series by Yale Pelican continues to add titles about other parts of the world, but still lacks credible volumes for this period, either north or south, fifteenth or sixteenth century. But, in rewarding compensation, the increased range of regions and media, and the expanded roster of questions and historical investigations have made art history into an engaged participant within the wider humanities—as together they reconstitute this marvelous era of transition from medieval to modern, now with important, new visual evidence.

Bibliography

Adams, Ann Jensen. *Public Faces and Private Identities in Seventeenth-Century Holland.* Cambridge: Cambridge University Press, 2007.

Aikema, Bernard, Beverly Brown, and Giovanna Nepi Sciré, eds. *Renaissance Venice and the North: Crosscurrents in the Time of Bellini, Dürer, and Titian.* Exhibition catalogue. New York: Rizzoli, 2000. Originally published as *Il Rinascimento a Venezia: E la pittura del Nord ai tempi di Bellini, Dürer, Tiziano* (Milan: Bompiani, 1999).

---

[58]Yamey, *Art and Accounting*; Jacobs, *Early Netherlandish Carved Altarpieces*; Wilson, *Painting in Bruges at the Close of the Middle Ages*; Honig, *Painting and the Market in Early Modern Antwerp*; Stock, *Printing Images in Antwerp*; and Silver, *Peasant Scenes and Landscapes*.

[59]Smith and Findlen, *Merchants and Marvels*.

Alexander, Jonathan. *The Painted Page: Italian Renaissance Book Illumination, 1450–1550.* New York: Prestel, 1994.

Ames-Lewis, Francis. *Intellectual Life of the Early Renaissance Artist.* New Haven, CT: Yale University Press, 2000.

Bailey, Gauvin. *Art of Colonial Latin America.* London: Phaidon, 2005.

———. *Art on the Jesuit Missions in Asia and Latin America, 1542–1773.* Toronto: University of Toronto Press, 1999.

Barkan, Leonard. *Unearthing the Past: Archaeology and Aesthetics in the Making of Renaissance Culture.* New Haven, CT: Yale University Press, 1999.

Barolsky, Paul. *Giotto's Father and the Family of Vasari's Lives.* University Park: Pennsylvania State University Press, 1992.

———. *Michelangelo's Nose: A Myth and Its Maker.* University Park: Pennsylvania State University Press, 1990.

———. *Why Mona Lisa Smiles and Other Tales by Vasari.* University Park: Pennsylvania State University Press, 1991.

Baskins, Christelle. *Cassone Painting, Humanism and Gender in Early Modern Italy.* Cambridge: Cambridge University Press, 1998.

Baxandall, Michael. *Giotto and the Orators, Humanist Observers of Painting in Italy and the Discovery of Pictorial Composition, 1350–1450.* Oxford: Clarendon, 1971.

———. *The Limewood Sculptors of Renaissance Germany.* New Haven, CT: Yale University Press, 1980.

———. *Painting and Experience in Fifteenth Century Italy: A Primer in the Social History of Pictorial Style.* Oxford: Oxford University Press, 1988.

Bedaux, Jan Baptist, and Rudi Ekkart, eds. *Pride and Joy: Children's Portraits in the Netherlands 1500–1700.* Ghent: Ludion, 2000.

Belozerskaya, Marina. *Rethinking the Renaissance.* Cambridge: Cambridge University Press, 2002.

Belting, Hans. *Likeness and Presence: A History of the Image before the Era of Art.* Chicago: University of Chicago Press, 1994.

Bierende, Edgar. *Lucas Cranach d. Ä. und der deutsche Humanismus: Tafelmalerei im Kontext von Rhetorik, Chroniken und Fürstenspiegeln.* Munich: Deutscher Kunstverlag, 2002.

Bleyerveld, Yvonne. *Hoe bedriechelijck dat die vrouwen zijn: Vrouwenlisten in de beeldende kunst in de Nederlanden circa 1350–1650.* Leiden: Primavera, 2000.

Bober, Phyllis, and Ruth Rubinstein. *Renaissance Artists and Antique Sculpture: A Handbook of Sources.* Oxford: Oxford University Press, 1986.

Brown, Paricia Fortini. *Venetian Narrative Painting in the Age of Carpaccio.* New Haven, CT: Yale University Press, 1998.

———. *Venice and Antiquity: The Venetian Sense of the Past.* New Haven, CT: Yale University Press, 1996.

Bull, Malcolm. *Mirror of the Gods.* Oxford: Oxford University Press, 2005

Campbell, Lorne. *Renaissance Portraits: European Portrait-Painting in the 14th, 15th, and 16th Centuries.* New Haven, CT: Yale University Press, 1990.

Campbell, Stephen, ed. *Artists at Court: Image-Making and Identity, 1300–1550.* Boston: Isabella Stuart Gardner Museum, 2004.

Campbell, Thomas. *Tapestry in the Renaissance.* New York: Metropolitan Museum of Art, 2002.

Carboni, Stefano, ed. *Venice and the Islamic World 828–1797.* New York: Metropolian Museum of Art, 2007.

Chambers, David, and Jane Martineau, eds. *Splendours of the Gonzaga*. London: The Museum, 1982.

Clifton, James. *The Plains of Mars: European War Prints, 1500–1825*. Exhibition catalog. Houston: Museum of Fine Arts, forthcoming.

Cole, Alison. *Virtue and Magnificence: Art of the Italian Renaissance Courts*. New York: H. N. Abrams, 1995.

Cole, Michael, and Mary Pardo, eds. *Inventions of the Studio: Renaissance to Romanticism*. Chapel Hill: University of North Carolina Press, 2005.

Cranston, Jodi. *The Poetics of Portraiture in the Italian Renaissance*. Cambridge: Cambridge University Press, 2000.

Cuneo, Pia. *Art and Politics in Early Modern Germany*. Leiden: Brill, 1998.

———, ed. *Artful Armies, Beautiful Battles: Art and Warfare in Early Modern Europe*. Leiden: Brill, 2002.

Daston, Lorraine, and Katherine Park. *Wonders and the Order of Nature 1150–1750*. Cambridge, MA: MIT Press, 1998.

De Marchi, Neil, and Hans Van Miegroet. "Exploring Markets for Netherlandish Paintings in Spain and Nueva España." *Nederlands Kunsthistorisch Jaarboek* 50 (1999): 81–111.

———. "Rules versus Play in Early Modern Markets." *Recherches Economiques de Louvain* 66 (2000): 145–65.

Dempsey, Charles. *Portrayal of Love: Botticelli's Primavera and Humanist Culture of the Time of Lorenzo the Magnificent*. Princeton: Princeton University Press, 1992.

Duffy, Eamon. *Stripping of the Altars: Traditional Religion in England c. 1400–c. 1580*. 2nd ed. New Haven, CT: Yale University Press, 2005.

Dülberg, Angelica. *Privatporträts: Geschichte und Ikonologie einer Gattung im 15. und 16. Jahrhundert*. Berlin: Mann, 1990.

Eisler, William, and Bernard Smith. *Terra Australis: The Furthest Shore*. Sydney: International Cultural Corporation of Australia, 1988.

Erickson, Peter, and Clark Hulse, eds. *Early Modern Visual Culture: Representation, Race, Empire in Renaissance England*. Philadelphia: University of Pennsylvania Press, 2000.

Falkenburg, Reindert, *Fruit of Devotion: Mysticism and the Imagery of Love in Flemish Paintings of the Virgin and Child, 1450–1550*. Amsterdam: Benjamins, 1994.

———. *Joachim Patinir: Landscape as an Image of the Pilgrimage of Life*. Amsterdam: Benjamins, 1988.

Farago, Claire, ed. *Reframing the Renaissance: Visual Culture in Europe and Latin America 1450–1650*. New Haven, CT: Yale University Press, 1995.

Filipczak, Zirka. *Hot Dry Men, Cold Wet Women: The Theory of Humors in Western European Art, 1575–1700*. New York: American Federation of Arts, 1997.

Finney, Paul Corby, ed. *Seeing Through the Word: Visual Arts and the Calvinist Tradition*. Grand Rapids, MI: Eerdmans, 1999.

Foister, Susan. *Holbein and England*. New Haven, CT: Yale University Press, 2004.

Franits, Wayne. *Paragons of Virtue: Women and Domesticity in Seventeenth-Century Dutch Art*. Cambridge: Cambridge University Press, 1993.

Freedberg, David. *Power of Images: Studies in the History and Theory of Response*. Chicago: University of Chicago Press, 1991.

Freedman, Luba. *Revival of the Olympian Gods in Renaissance Art*. Cambridge: Cambridge University Press, 2003

Fumerton, Patricia. *Cultural Aesthetics: Renaissance Literature and the Practice of Social Ornament*. Chicago: University of Chicago Press, 1991.

Gent, Lucy, and Nigel Llewellyn, eds. *Renaissance Bodies: The Human Figure in English Culture, 1540–1660*. London: Reaktion Books, 1990.

Grössinger, Chrisa. *Picturing Women in Late Medieval and Renaissance Art*. Manchester: Manchester University Press, 1997.

Hale, J. R. *Artists and Warfare in the Renaissance*. New Haven: Yale University Press, 1990.

Hamburger, Jeffrey. *Visual and the Visionary: Art and Female Spirituality in Late Medieval Germany*. New York: Zone, 1998.

——, and Anne-Marie Bouché, eds. *Mind's Eye: Art and Theological Argument in the Middle Ages*. Princeton: Princeton University Press, 2006.

Hearn, Karen, ed. *Dynasties: Painting in Tudor and Jacobean England, 1530–1630*. London: Tate Publications, 1995.

Holmes, Megan. *Fra Filippo Lippi, the Carmelite Painter*. New Haven: Yale University Press, 1999.

Honig, Elizabeth. *Painting and the Market in Early Modern Antwerp*. New Haven, CT: Yale University Press, 1998.

Hood, William. *Fra Angelico at San Marco*. New Haven: Yale University Press, 1993.

Howard, Deborah. *Venice and the East: The Impact of the Islamic World on Venetian Architecture 1100–1500*. New Haven: Yale University Press, 2000.

Howarth, David. *Images of Rule: Art and Politics in Renaissance England, 1485–1649*. Berkeley: University of California Press, 1997.

Hulse, Clark. *Rule of Art: Literature and Painting in the Renaissance*. Chicago: University of Chicago Press, 1990.

Hults, Linda. *Witch as Muse: Art, Gender, and Power in Early Modern Europe*. Philadelphia: University of Pennsylvania Press, 2005.

Humfrey, Peter, and Martin Kemp, eds. *Altarpiece in the Renaissance*. Cambridge: Cambridge University Press, 1990.

Jackson, Anna, and Amin Jaffer, eds. *Encounters: The Meeting of Asia and Europe, 1500–1800*. London: V & A, 2004.

Jacobs, Fredrika. *Defining the Renaissance Virtuosa: Women Artists and the Language of Art History and Criticism*. Cambridge: Cambridge University Press, 1997.

Jacobs, Lynn. *Early Netherlandish Carved Altarpieces, 1380–1550: Medieval Tastes and Mass Marketing*. Cambridge: Cambridge University Press, 1998.

Jones, Ann Rosalind, and Peter Stallybrass, *Renaissance Clothing and the Materials of Memory*. Cambridge: Cambridge University Press, 2000.

Jongh, Edy de, and Ger Luijten, eds., *Mirror of Everyday Life: Genre Prints in the Netherlands, 1550–1700*. Exhibition catalog. Amsterdam: Rijksmuseum, 1997.

Kagan, Richard. *Urban Images of the Hispanic World, 1493–1793*. New Haven, CT: Yale University Press, 2000.

Kaufmann, Thomas Dacosta. *Court, Cloister, City: The Art and Culture of Central Europe, 1450–1800*. Chicago: University of Chicago Press, 1995.

——. *Towards a Geography of Art*. Chicago: University of Chicago Press, 2004.

Kemp, Martin. *Behind the Picture: Art and Evidence in the Italian Renaissance*. New Haven, CT: Yale University Press, 1997.

Kempers, Bram. *Painting, Power, and Patronage: The Rise of the Professional Artist in the Italian Renaissance*. New York: Penguin, 1992.

Kenseth, Joy, ed. *The Age of the Marvelous*. Hanover, NH: Hood Museum of Art, 1991.

Kent, D. W. *Cosimo de' Medici and the Florentine Renaissance: The Patron's Oeuvre*. New Haven, CT: Yale University Press, 2000.

Koerner, Joseph. *Reformation of the Image*. London: Reaktion, 2004.

Krüger, Klaus. *Das Bild als Schleier des Unsichtbaren: Aesthetische Illusion in der Kunst der frühen Neuzeit.* Munich: Fink, 2001.

Kunzle, David. *From Criminal to Courtier: The Soldier in Netherlandish Art, 1550–1672.* Leiden: Brill, 2002.

Landau, David, and Peter Parshall. *The Renaissance Print, 1470–1550.* New Haven, CT: Yale University Press, 1994.

Lavin, Irving. *Bernini and the Unity of the Arts.* New York: Morgan Library, 1980.

Lawrence, Cynthia. *Women and Art in Early Modern Europe: Patrons, Collectors, and Connoisseurs.* University Park: Pennsylvania State University Press, 1997.

Levenson, Jay. *Encompassing the Globe: Portugal and the World in the 16th and 17th Centuries.* Exhibition catalog. Washington: Smithsonian Institution, 2007.

———, ed. *Circa 1492: Art in the Age of Exploration.* Washington, DC: National Gallery of Art, 1991.

Levy, Evonne. *Propaganda and the Jesuit Baroque.* Berkeley: University of California Press, 2004.

Lincoln, Evelyn. *The Invention of the Renaissance Printmaker.* New Haven, CT: Yale University Press, 2000.

Marks, Richard, and Paul Williamson, eds. *Gothic: Art for England 1400–1547.* London: V & A, 2003.

Meadow, Mark. *Pieter Bruegel the Elder's Netherlandish Proverbs and the Practice of Rhetoric.* Zwolle: Waanders, 2002.

Melion, Walter. *Shaping the Netherlandish Canon: Karel van Mander's Schilder-Boeck.* Chicago: University of Chicago Press, 1991.

Merback, Mitchell. *The Thief, the Cross, and the Wheel: Pain and the Spectacle of Punishment in Medieval and Renaissance Europe.* Chicago: University of Chicago Press, 1999.

Michalski, Sergiusz. *Reformation and the Visual Arts: The Protestant Image Question in Western and Eastern Europe.* London: Routledge, 1993.

Miedema, Hessel, ed. *Karel van Mander, the Lives of the Illustrious Netherlandish and German Painters, from the First Edition of the Schilder-Boeck (1603–1604).* Doornspijk: Davaco, 1994–99.

Mignolo, Walter. *The Darker Side of the Renaissance: Literacy, Territoriality, and Colonization.* Ann Arbor: University of Michigan Press, 1998.

Montias, John Michael. "Socio-Economic Aspects of Netherlandish Art from the Fifteenth to the Seventeenth Century: A Survey." *Art Bulletin* 72, no. 3 (Sept. 1990): 358–73.

Montrose, Louis. *The Subject of Elizabeth: Authority, Gender, and Representation.* Chicago: University of Chicago Press, 2006.

Morrall, Andrew. *Jörg Breu the Elder: Art, Culture, and Belief in Reformation Augsburg.* Aldershot, UK: Ashgate, 2001.

Moxey, Keith. *Peasants, Warriors, and Wives: Popular Imagery in the Reformation.* Chicago: University of Chicago Press, 1989.

Mulcahy, Rosemarie. *The Decoration of the Royal Basilica of El Escorial.* Cambridge: Cambridge University Press, 1994.

Murphy, Caroline. *Lavinia Fontana: A Painter and Her Patrons in Sixteenth-Century Bologna.* New Haven, CT: Yale University Press, 2003.

Musacchio, Jacqueline. *The Art and Ritual of Childbirth in Renaissance Italy.* New Haven, CT: Yale University Press, 1999.

Nagel, Alexander. *Michelangelo and the Reform of Art.* Cambridge: Cambridge University Press, 2000.

Noble, Bonnie J. "'A work in which the angels are wont to rejoice': Lucas Cranach's Schneeberg Altarpiece." *Sixteenth Century Journal* 34 (2003): 1011–37.

Norman, Diana, ed.. *Siena, Florence, and Padua: Art, Society, and Religion 1280–1400*. New Haven, CT: Yale University Press, 1995.

Nuttall, Paula. *From Flanders to Florence: The Impact of Netherlandish Painting, 1400–1500*. New Haven, CT: Yale University Press, 2004.

O'Malley, John, Gauvin Alexander Bailey, T. Frank Kennedy, eds. *The Jesuits: Cultures, Sciences, and the Arts, 1540–1773*. Toronto: University of Toronto Press, 1999.

Parshall, Peter. "*Imago contrafacta*: Images and Facts in the Northern Renaissance." *Art History* 16 (1993): 554–79.

——, and Rainer Schoch. *Origins of European Printmaking: Fifteenth-Century Woodcuts and Their Public*. Washington, DC: National Gallery of Art, 2005.

Parshall, Peter and Linda. *Art and the Reformation: An Annotated Bibliography*. Boston: G. K. Hall, 1986.

Perlingieri, Ilya. *Sofonisba Anguissola: The First Great Woman Artist of the Renaissance*. New York: Rizzoli, 1992.

Randolph, Adrian. *Engaging Symbols: Gender, Politis, and Public Art in Fifteenth-Century Florence*. New Haven, CT: Yale University Press, 2002.

Reiss, Sheryl, and David Wilkins, eds. *Beyond Isabella: Secular Women Patrons of Art in Renaissance Italy*. Kirksville, MO: Truman State University Press, 2001.

Richter Sherman, Claire. *Writing on Hands: Memory and Knowledge in Early Modern Europe*. Carlisle, PA: Trout Gallery, Dickinson College, 2000.

Roper, Lyndal. *Oedipus and the Devil: Witchcraft, Sexuality, and Religion in Early Modern Europe*. New York: Routledge, 1994.

Rosand, David. *Myths of Venice: The Figuration of State*. Chapel Hill: University of North Carolina Press, 2001.

Rosen, Jochai. "The Dutch Guardroom Scene in the Golden Age: A Definition." *Artibus et Historiae* 53 (2006): 151–74.

Rowland, Ingrid. *The Culture of the High Renaissance: Ancients and Moderns in Sixteenth-Century Rome*. Cambridge: Cambridge University Press, 1998.

Rubin, Patricia. *Giorgio Vasari: Art and History*. New Haven, CT: Yale University Press, 1995.

Salomon, Nanette. *Shifting Priorities: Gender and Genre in Seventeenth-Century Dutch Painting*. Stanford: Stanford University Press, 2004.

Saslow, James. *Ganymede in the Renaissance: Homosexuality in Art and Society*. New Haven, CT: Yale University Press, 1986.

Schade, Sigrid. *Schadenzauber und die Magie des Körpers: Hexenbilder der frühen Neuzeit*. Worms: Werner, 1983.

Schmidt, Benjamin. *Innocence Abroad: The Dutch Imagination and the New World, 1570–1670*. Cambridge: Cambridge University Press, 2001.

Scribner, Robert. *For the Sake of Simple Folk: Popular Propaganda of the German Reformation*. Oxford: Oxford University Press, 1994.

Shearman, John. *Only Connect: Art and the Spectator in the Italian Renaissance*. Princeton: Princeton University Press, 1992.

Silver, Larry. *Peasant Scenes and Landscapes: The Rise of Pictorial Genres in the Antwerp Art Market*. Philadelphia: University of Pennsylvania Press, 2006.

Smith, Jeffrey Chipps. *German Sculpture of the Later Renaissance c. 1520–1580*. Princeton, NJ: Princeton University Press, 1994.

——. *Sensuous Worship: Jesuits and the Art of the Early Catholic Reformation in Germany*. Princeton, NJ: Princeton University Press, 2002.

Smith, Pamela. *The Body of the Artisan: Art and Experience in the Scientific Revolution.* Chicago: University of Chicago Press, 2004.

———, and Paula Findlen, eds. *Merchants and Marvels: Commerce, Science, and Art in Early Modern Europe.* New York: Routledge, 2002.

Sobré, Judith Berg. *Behind the Altar Table: The Development of the Painted Retable in Spain, 1350–1500.* Columbia: University of Missouri Press, 1989.

Starkey, David, and Susan Doran. *Elizabeth: The Exhibition at the National Maritime Museum.* London: Chatto and Windus, 2003.

Starn, Randolph and Loren Patridge. *Arts of Power: Three Halls of State in Italy, 1300–1600.* Berkeley: University of California Press, 1992.

Stock, Jan van der. *Printing Images in Antwerp, Fifteenth Century to 1585.* Rotterdam: Sound and Vision Interactive, 1998.

Stoichita, Victor. *Self-Aware Image: An Insight into Early Modern Meta-Painting.* Cambridge: Cambridge University Press, 1997.

———. *Visionary Experience in the Golden Age of Spanish Art.* London: Reaktion, 1995.

Talvacchia, Bette. *Taking Positions: On the Erotic in Renaissance Culture.* Princeton, NJ: Princeton University Press, 1999.

Vandenbroeck, Paul. *Beeld van de andere, vertoog over zichzelf.* Exhibition catalog. Antwerp: Koninklijk Museum, 1987.

———. *Bride of the Sun.* Antwerp: Royal National Museum, 1992.

Verdon, Timothy, and John Henderson, eds. *Christianity and the Renaissance: Image and Religious Imagination in the Quattrocento.* Syracuse: Syracuse University Press, 1990.

Vermeylen, Filip. *Painting for the Market: Commercialization of Art in Antwerp's Golden Age.* Turnhout: Brepols, 2003.

Welch, Evelyn. *Art and Authority in Renaissance Milan.* New Haven, CT: Yale University Press, 1995.

Wilson, Jean. *Painting in Bruges at the Close of the Middle Ages: Studies in Society and Visual Culture.* University Park: Pennsylvania State University Press, 1998.

Wisch, Barbara, and Diane Ahl, eds. *Confraternities and the Visual Arts in Renaissance Italy: Ritual, Spectacle, Image.* Cambridge: Cambridge University Press, 2000.

Wolf, Gerhard. *Schleier und Spiegel: Tradition des Christusbildes und die Bildkonzepte der Renaissance.* Munich: Fink, 2002.

Wolfthal, Diane. *Images of Rape: The 'Heroic Tradition and Its Alternatives.* Cambridge: Cambridge University Press, 1999.

Woods-Marsden, Joanna. *Renaissance Self-Portraiture: The Visual Construction of Identity and the Social Status of the Artist.* New Haven, CT: Yale University Press, 1998.

Woodward, David. *Cartogaphy in the European Renaissance.* Vol. 3 of *The History of Cartography.* Chicago: University of Chicago Press, 2007.

Yamey, Basil. *Art and Accounting.* New Haven, CT: Yale University Press, 1989.

Zandvliet, Kees. *The Dutch Encounter with Asia 1600–1950.* Amsterdam: Rijksmuseum, 2003.

———. *Mapping for Money: Maps, Plans, and Topographic Paintings and Their Role in Dutch Overseas Expansion during the 16th and 17th Centuries.* Amsterdam: Batavian Lion International, 1998.

Zerner, Henri. *Renaissance Art in France.* Translated by Deke Dusinberre, Scott Wilson, and Rachel Zerner. Paris: Flammarion, 2003.

Zika, Charles. *Exorcising Our Demons: Magic, Witchcraft, and Visual Culture in Early Modern Europe.* Leiden: Brill, 2003.

Zorach, Rebecca. *Blood, Milk, Ink, Gold: Abundance and Excess in the French Renaissance.* Chicago: University of Chicago Press, 2005.

18

Books and Printing

Andrew Pettegree

The printed book has always been—and no doubt always will be—a cornerstone of research on the Reformation. This is true in more than the obvious sense that sixteenth-century books provide one of the most important windows into the religious changes of the period. Books also represent a cornerstone for understanding the early modern period. For those brought up with an essentially progress-oriented view of the Renaissance, the printing press is firmly established as one of the critical technologies that justify the sense of fundamental change. Print was an essential component of the surge toward modernity. This view, most eloquently articulated for the English-speaking world in the work of Elizabeth Eisenstein, in fact underpins most of the general studies of the origins and growth of printing.[1] Print was (and still to a large extent is) seen as a crucial stage in the process of intellectual enlightenment and political empowerment.

Printing is also widely seen as having a particular affinity with the new movements of evangelical change. Certainly Martin Luther himself promoted the power of the book as energetically as he seized on the new medium to promote his own theological agenda. For Luther, print was a gift of a beneficent God, a view shared and repeatedly articulated by other Protestant preachers and spokesmen. In Luther's words, printing was God's highest and most extreme act of grace, whereby the business of the gospel is driven forward. For John Foxe, author of the famous martyrology, it was

---

[1] Eisenstein, *Printing Press as an Agent of Change.*

printing that made the Reformation possible: "The Lord began to work for his church not with sword and target to subdue his exalted adversary, but with printing, writing and reading...so that either the pope must abolish knowledge and printing or printing must at length root him out."[2] This sense of the power of print had also the beneficent result that from the first years of the Reformation, Protestant books were systematically preserved and collected—even the sort of short ephemeral pamphlets, or single-sheet broadsheets, that might otherwise have been expected to have been destroyed were carefully gathered up. Thus books are not only an indispensable window on the culture of the Reformation—they are also a sturdy and dependable source. Rates of survival are generally good, and especially so for Protestant books.

That said, it is as well to understand the limitations of available knowledge of this crucial communication medium. Much less work has been done on what one might call the contextual history of Reformation print—the place of the book in the broader information culture of the period. Nor has there been the same interest shown in the way in which the book industry functioned commercially, either in specialized local markets for vernacular print, or in a persuasive explanation of the pan-European market in Latin works. Study of the place of print and print culture in the Reformation has, as with much else, started with Martin Luther and his transformation of theological writing in the 1520s; how long this can stand as a metaphor for the wider impact of print has not yet been fully explored.

In the first decade of the Reformation, the impact of the book was both profound and to many contemporaries deeply shocking. Early critics within the church were first scandalized and then alarmed by Luther's blatant courting of a broad public through printed tracts and sermons. Contemporaries were well aware that in harnessing the previously rather formal, stolid world of the book to serve these ends, Evangelical critics of the Catholic Church had achieved something fundamentally new. A new form of book, the *Flugschriften*, short pamphlets in quarto format, came rapidly to dominate the output of German print shops. Demand for books expanded very rapidly after 1517, as religious debate engaged the interest of a new, largely nonclerical audience. An exceptionally high proportion of these books addressed the new controversies, and in Luther, a writer of

[2]Eisenstein, *Printing Press as an Agent of Change*, 150–51.

genius and extraordinary facility, Germany's publishers had found their ideal partner. Luther could write with phenomenal speed and quickly developed an extraordinary range, from the homiletic sermon, through excoriating satire, to careful, systematic exposition of complex theological issues.

The impact of the book in these years has been extensively explored in a range of bibliographic and analytic studies reaching back to Josef Benzing's milestone bibliography of Luther's works, published in 1966.[3] The wider context of Luther's writing has also been explored with the fundamental work of the Tübingen Flugschriften project, which over a space of years collected and quantified a vast mass of the writings published by Luther and others sympathetic to the Reformation.[4] Mark Edwards draws heavily on this material for his *Printing, Propaganda and Martin Luther*, a fine and perceptive survey of the impact of Reformation literature.[5] Further statistical analysis is provided in articles by Richard Crofts and by the work of Miriam Usher Chrisman on Strasburg.[6] Meanwhile, the late Robert Scribner offered in his highly influential monograph, *For the Sake of Simple Folk*, a vision of how the Reformation message might resonate with a larger, mostly nonliterate public.[7] For the repertoire of illustrated books and broadsheets that figure largely in this project, he was able to draw both on his own research and on a four-volume collection dedicated to *The German Single Leaf Woodcut*, a publication that both brought a new appreciation for the exquisite quality of much German woodcut art, and helped fix the association of the reform movement with exploitation of the visual media.[8] From this range of studies, and sense of the vibrancy of the book in the service of the German Reformation, has developed a dominant view of the role that the printed media played in the process of Reformation. This model, what one might call the German paradigm, consists of several elements. First, and most importantly, it has engendered a clear sense of the Evangelical dominance of print. It is also understood that the Reformation achieved its impact partly through the rapid spread of print to multiple printing centers, as popular texts were spread by local reprints. This was accentuated by

---

[3]Benzing, *Lutherbibliographie.*

[4]On the Tübingen Flugschriften project, see Köhler, *Flugschriften als Massenmedium.*

[5]Edwards, *Printing, Propaganda and Martin Luther*; and Edwards, "Statistics on Sixteenth-Century Printing."

[6]Crofts, "Books, Reform and Reformation"; Crofts, "Printing, Reform and the Catholic Reformation"; and Chrisman, *Conflicting Visions of Reform.*

[7]Scribner, *For the Sake of Simple Folk.*

[8]Geisberg, *German Single-Leaf Woodcut*; Strauss, *German Single-Leaf Woodcut*; and Anderson, *German Single-Leaf Woodcut.*

the difficulty authorities faced in controlling the spread of dissident ideas, especially in Germany. Lastly, historians view the Reformation as a critical phase in the victory of the vernacular over Latin in European intellectual culture and affirm the importance of illustration in spreading the Reformation message to those who could not read for themselves.

It is important to recognize for what follows the extent to which this paradigm has been developed essentially from the German model of the first evangelical generation and how little it has been tested against the experience of other European cultures where the Reformation enjoyed more halting progress, where the medium of print was often used effectively by the defenders of the old order, or where the Reformation sometimes succeeded before the development of an indigenous print culture.[9] The fact is that the German paradigm has been allowed to stand as normative partly because historians have lacked the basic data for other national cultures to subject it to systematic, skeptical analysis. There was, until recently, no equivalent to the Tübingen Flugschriften project for other parts of Europe. This deficiency is now being addressed, not least through the general ongoing transformation of the resource base through major national bibliographic projects and the availability of major online resources (not least library catalogs). These make possible not only a new generation of analytic studies, sketched below, but also a more general refinement of an understanding of the relationship between the book and the Reformation. This can be characterized in three main developments: a more complete sense of how the Reformation served (or failed) Protestantism outside Germany, a developing understanding of how the book was also successfully exploited by the defenders of traditional religion, and an understanding that the overwhelming domination of print by Evangelicals suggested by a knowledge of Germany in the 1520s does not mean that this situation was typical over the whole Reformation century and in all countries.

Given that so much attention has been given to the power of the printed word, it is perhaps surprising that a knowledge of the global world of sixteenth-century print has rested on such insecure foundations. Many studies have focused on the origins of print and the great innovative publishers of the first generations, but attempts to map the expanding world of print (such as that attempted by Febvre and Martin for their seminal text,

---

[9]Pettegree and Hall, "Reformation and the Book."

The Coming of the Book) have rested on remarkably shaky statistical foundations.[10] In the 1960s an attempt was made to address this deficiency with the *Index Aureliensis*, a project that was to publish a list of all books published in the century, organized by author.[11] Progress with this massive enterprise was inevitably slow, and even now the project has progressed only as far as volume 15, on the letter *D*. The repertoire of information was based, particularly in the earliest volumes, on the largest collections (such as London and Paris) for which printed catalogs already existed; the project has now in large measure been overwhelmed and superseded by the vast quantity of data available through online catalogs, and it cannot be expected ever to be concluded.

The insufficiency of the global bibliographic data has to some extent been disguised for students of the English Reformation by the exceptionally high quality of bibliographic resources for English-language printing. For almost one hundred years now, students of the book in England have disposed of a complete listing of books published in England and in English abroad in Pollard and Redgrave's *Short Title Catalogue (STC)*, a model for all subsequent ventures of this type.[12] We owe this good fortune to particular circumstances, not least the fact that the English book world was in absolute terms relatively small and heavily concentrated in one well-regulated center of production (London)—this was not the normative case for other European language zones. The accident of collecting, with especially rich concentrations of books in only three centers—Oxford, Cambridge, and London—also assisted Pollard and Redgrave in their labors. Books in collections further afield, particularly in the United States, were then incorporated into a second edition, completed under the direction of Kathleen Pantzer at Harvard and Paul Newman in Oxford and published in three volumes between 1976 and 1991, a work that also incorporated the fruits of much specialist bibliographic work accomplished in the intervening half century. This resource has been further developed with the production of the whole *STC* on microfilm, a boon for those working at a distance from any but the largest research libraries. The onward march of technology has produced, in recent years, an online searchable version of the *STC*. The OSTC (Online Short Title Catalog) can be searched by *STC* number, title, author, or printer. In many research university libraries, it is

---

[10]Febvre and Martin, *Coming of the Book.*
[11]*Index Aureliensis.*
[12]Pollard and Redgrave, *Short Title Catalogue of Books.*

also cross-referenced to EEBO (Early English Books Online). There are two different editions of EEBO currently available. The first-generation EEBO allows one to search in the exact same manner as in the OSTC and then download the desired item as a PDF file. The PDF is not searchable and is picture based, rather than text based. The second generation of EEBO is the result of the EEBO Text Creation Partnership (TCP). The partnership is transcribing all the works in EEBO. Currently, approximately ten thousand works have been transcribed, with the other fifteen thousand still to come. The EEBO TCP is currently available only on the campuses that are participating in the work of transcription. However, one can now search entire texts for exact phrases, use Boolean searching, and so on.[13]

New books unknown to the compilers of the *STC* continue to surface, such as a broadsheet summary of the essentials of the Protestant faith discovered in the binding of a book purchased by the Scheide Library in Princeton and two French-language London imprints recently discovered in Halle.[14] But in the main, students of the English Reformation are quite exceptionally well served by this fundamental resource base.

The situation is very different for France, where a truly comprehensive listing of sixteenth-century publications is still lacking. This situation reflects both the greater complexity of the task and the very different tradition of French bibliographic research. France was, from the beginning, one of the largest centers of European book production, based largely in the precocious book metropolis of Paris, with Lyon as a second major center of production. During the course of the sixteenth century, book publication also became established in over one hundred provincial towns. Patterns of collecting have also been very different. While most students of sixteenth-century French culture rely mostly on the great collections in Paris, the confiscations of the property of the religious houses during the French Revolution also brought enormous numbers of books into the possession of the French Bibliothèques Municipales—where they remain to this day. The enormous task of charting the history of Paris printing was undertaken by two great bibliographers, Brigitte Moreau and Philippe Renouard.

---

[13]The OSTC is available free online at The British Library's website, http://estc.bl.uk. Early English Books Online is available at http://eebo.chadwyck.com/home.

[14]*L'Epistre du roy d'angleterre aux princes & peuple chrestien touchant le concile à venire* (London: Thomas Berthelet, 1539); and *La protestation et advis du roy d'Angleterre touchant le Concile qui se debuoit tenir à Mantue* (London: Thomas Berthelet, 1539). Both books are located in Halle Universitäts- und Landesbibliothek (ULB): AB 154113 (15 & 16).

Neither completed their work. Moreau, working on a chronological survey of Paris printing in the post-incunabula age, had, at the time of her death, reached only 1535, when the history of the French book was only beginning to be transformed by contemporary events.[15] Renouard adopted a different approach, embarking on a printer-by-printer survey of each publishing house. Published volumes cover only printers whose names begin with the first two letters of the alphabet, although Renouard's card fiche catalogs, deposited in the Réserve of the Bibliothèque Nationale, are made available to researchers on a generous basis.[16] Lyon print was surveyed at the beginning of the century in twelve volumes, again arranged by printer, by H.-L. and J. Baudrier.[17] The Baudriers based their studies on their own substantial private collection of local imprints and on the holdings of the libraries of Lyon, Aix, and Grenoble; an attempt to rework and complete this work, this time on a chronological basis, is ongoing.[18] The work of the Baudriers inaugurated a tradition of local bibliographic scholarship continued in the *Répertoire Bibliographique du livre du seizième siècle*, a town-by-town listing of all the books published in each locality, consigned to the responsibility of a local specialist.[19] The volumes are of varying quality, many based only on inspections of local collections, collated with the major collections in Paris; all inevitably miss dispersed items located in other parts of France or in libraries abroad. The lack of a global survey of French vernacular print, so essential to a real understanding of the impact of the Reformation, is presently being addressed by the St. Andrews French Vernacular Book Project (first volumes published in fall 2007).[20] The St. Andrews team will then continue their work to document the production of Latin literature in France. This will be published as a separate annex to the French Vernacular Book Project in 2011.

For Germany the listing and analysis of the pamphlet literature of the Reformation proceeded largely in advance of systematic bibliographic research. As was the case with French-language publication in France,

---

[15]Moreau, *Inventaire Chronologique.*

[16]Renouard, *Imprimeurs et libraires Parisiens.*

[17]Baudrier, Baudrier, and Tricou, *Bibliographie lyonnaise.*

[18]Gültingen, *Bibliographie des livres imprimés.* Thus far, this covers Lyon print between 1500 and around 1540.

[19]Desgraves, *Répertoire Bibliographique.*

[20]Information on the current state of the project and libraries surveyed is available online on the project website: http://www.st-andrews.ac.uk/reformation/book/. See also Pettegree, Walsby, and Wilkinson, *French Vernacular Books.*

German-language publication suffered from the problem of fragmentation, with no single dominant center of production. In the case of Germany, this problem was exacerbated by the dispersal and destruction of major collections of printed books during the wars of the twentieth century. The twentieth-century division of Germany, with many of the largest libraries located in the Communist German Democrat Republic, also posed a major obstacle to a systematic study of all books published in the German-speaking lands. In the 1980s, an attempt was made to address this deficiency with the *Verzeichnis der im deutschen Sprachbereich erschienenen Drucke des XVI. Jahrhunderts*, normally abbreviated as *VD16*, a global survey of all sixteenth-century German print. This project based its published volumes on the two largest collections then available to book specialists, at Munich and Wolfenbüttel, and since its completion in 2000 has been an indispensable research tool. Inevitably the use of only two main libraries, however vast, resulted in the omission of large numbers of editions, a problem exacerbated by the decision, now somewhat perplexing, to omit all single-sheet publication (e.g., broadsheets). The *VD16* is now available as an online resource that incorporates many thousands of new items unearthed in other libraries; all told it now offers data on some one hundred thousand bibliographically distinct items.[21]

The holdings of the foundation collections of the VD16, Munich and Wolfenbüttel, are also now included in the online *Handpress Book Database*, a major resource created by CERL (Consortium of European Research Libraries), available to all users of subscribing libraries. The *Handpress Book Database* is composed of data offered by particulating libraries, mostly members of CERL. This offers the obvious advantage of being able to search many different databases at a single time, but also results in numerous duplications that must be carefully examined. The database is really a conglomeration of databases and therefore cannot determine that two "items" are actually the same publication and that catalogers entered them differently.[22]

The religious controversies raised by Luther made an immediate impact in the Netherlands, stimulating a wave of local Dutch publications of his works and an immediate hostile response from church authorities.

---

[21] *VD16* is available online at http://www.vd16.de.

[22] For example, if one cataloger in one library transcribed Wittenberg as it actually appears on many sixteenth-century publications as *VVittenberg*, while another updated it by using the *W* instead of two *Vs*, the HPBD will produce two hits.

The bibliographic footprint of these conflicts, and the great outpouring of print that accompanied the later events of the Dutch Revolt, may now be followed in three major works. The three volumes of the *Nederlandsche Bibliographie* of Kronenberg and Nijhoff (NK) document the publication of books in the Low Countries until 1540, encompassing the great outpouring of religious print of the first generation after Luther.[23] This work can be supplemented from the catalog of the great Knuttel collection of pamphlets in the Royal Library, The Hague, now also available in its entirety on microfilm.[24] But it is only recently that the work of NK has been continued through to the end of the century, in two separate projects, one, the *Belgica Typographica*, dealing with books published in present-day Belgium, the other, the *Typographia Batava*, covering books published in the present-day Netherlands.[25] Leaving aside the complications that arise from a division based on modern national boundaries that have no basis in sixteenth-century reality, both projects are in their own way problematic. The *Belgica Typographica* is a three-volume work, the first registering the holdings of the Royal Library in Brussels, with the holdings of other Belgian libraries covered in two further volumes. Books published in the southern Netherlands that survive in libraries elsewhere are not surveyed. The *Typographia Batava* has cast its net wider to identify books published in the northern Netherlands (a much smaller number), but it is essentially the work of a single bibliographer, Paul Valkema Blouw, and reflects his own specific interests. Thus, while a huge amount of scholarly work is embedded in the project, particularly in the identification of printers responsible for works published anonymously, the *Typographia Batava* lacks information normally regarded as standard in a work of this sort (such as formats). Students of the religious book culture of the Netherlands are badly in need of an initiative that would consolidate and harmonize this diverse bibliographic material.

For Italy, there is a national bibliographic project known as *Edit 16*, which began as a hard copy publication but has now raced ahead as an online resource.[26] *Edit 16* comprises over sixty thousand records, provided by a huge number of participating libraries. This breadth of coverage is

---

[23]Nijhoff and Kronenberg, *Nederlandsche Bibliographie*.

[24]*Dutch Pamphlets, 1486–1853*, commonly known as The Knuttel Collection.

[25]Cockx-Indestege and Glorieux, *Belgica typographica*; and Blouw, *Typographia Batava*. These two, with the NK, log some twenty-one thousand editions of books published in Belgium or the Netherlands during the sixteenth century.

[26]*Edit 16, Censimento delle edizioni italiane del XVI secolo*.

both a great virtue of the project and a practical necessity, because, rather like in France, the cultural heritage of Italy is spread around a very large number of libraries. *Edit 16* is also notable for the quality of its editorial work. It is the only major sixteenth-century bibliographic project to make use of fingerprinting, a technique for providing a unique identifying signature for a book devised in the British rare book librarianship community but now largely abandoned there.[27] Non-Italian titles in Italian libraries can also be investigated through the ICCU, another substantial online resource.[28]

For Spain, the nearest equivalent to the *Short Title Catalogue* is the *Catálogo colectivo del patrimonio bibliográfico espagñol*.[29] This does not of course take into account the large number of Spanish titles that may survive exclusively in libraries outside Spain; the task of integrating this material has now been undertaken by a major new bibliographic project to be managed by Dr. Alexander Wilkinson at University College, Dublin.

These six major markets—France, Germany, Italy, Spain, the Netherlands, and England—were responsible, together with the international market in Latin publishing, for over 95 percent of all books published in the sixteenth century. Outlying markets, such as Scandinavia, Poland, and Scotland, were small and have been the subject of mostly local investigations. The current and recently published bibliographic projects surveyed above present the possibility of a much more complete and integrated understanding of the European book world, along the lines of what is already available for the fifteenth century (albeit with much smaller global numbers) with the ISTC (the British Library's Incunabula Short Title Catalog).[30] However, pan-European bibliographic analysis will be possible only if different national bibliographic resources are brought together and made mutually searchable. This is the purpose of a new project begun at the University of St. Andrews in 2007, aimed at creating a composite resource, the Universal Short Title Catalogue (USTC). This will develop technology to

[27]Harris, "Tribal Lays."

[28]Istituto Centrale per il Catálogo Unico delle Biblioteche Italiane e per le Informazioni Bibliografiche: http://www.iccu.sbn.it.

[29]http://www.mcu.es/ccpb/ccpb-eng.html.

[30]http://picarta.pica.nl/login/DB=3.29/LNG=EN/. The I-STC records more than twenty-five thousand editions published before 1501, including around fifteen hundred items of single-sheet printing. The expectation is that the total will eventually settle at around twenty-eight thousand editions. Full information about the project is available online at http://www.bl.uk/collections/hoinc.html. See also Hellinga and Goldfinch, "Ten Years of the Incunabula Short-Title Catalogue"; and Hellinga and Goldfinch, *Bibliography and the Study of 15th Century Civilization*.

permit the searching of all the major national bibliographic catalogs through a shared interface. For the first time, information on all books published in the sixteenth century throughout Europe will be available in one place. The USTC will also make provision to attach full-text digital copies to allow major research collections to be accessed remotely. Historians of the Reformation already have many reasons to be grateful for commercial publishers of major microfilm and fiche series, such as the Dutch company IDC, which has made available a large number of sixteenth-century books in thematically organized collections.[31] The tendency of libraries to catalog individual items without distinguishing sufficiently clearly from sixteenth-century originals presents a hazard for bibliography; for scholars, however, the multiplication of available texts is an enormous boon. Irritatingly, one must also note that many libraries do not catalog items within a specific IDC fiche collection separately, and so one should search not only by the title of the work being sought, but also by the IDC collection's title. This is especially true in the United States and should be noted when searching on WorldCat (http://www.worldcat.org). Despite these cataloging pitfalls, the enormous progress made in recent years in creating more complete bibliographic resources has helped to stimulate a new wave of scholarship on the Reformation and the book, though, as described later, this scholarship has advanced more rapidly in some areas than in others.

In Germany scholars of the Reformation have long been in possession of an unrivaled range of high-quality resources, from complete editions of the works of Luther in both German and English to a huge range of German Reformation *Flugschriften* in the published microfiche version of the Tübingen project.[32] The groundbreaking bibliographic work of Benzing has been enhanced by the patient surveys of dispersed collections of German Reformation pamphlets by the British bibliographer Michael Pegg.[33] Given the quality of these resources and the very high rate of survival of Luther's works, it is all the more astonishing that there has been so little work on the print industry of Wittenberg, a subject that still awaits

[31]IDC: http://www.idc.nl/.

[32]*Sixteenth Century Pamphlets: Flugschriften des 16. Jahrhunderts.* Part I (1500–1530) contains five thousand German and Latin pamphlets. Part II (1531–1600), still in progress, contains between three thousand five hundred and five thousand pamphlets.

[33]For British and French libraries, see Pegg, *Bibliotheca Lindesiana.* For Swiss libraries, see Pegg, *Catalogue of German Reformation Pamphlets in Swiss Libraries.* For Swedish libraries, see Pegg, *Catalogue of German Reformation Pamphlets in Swedish Libraries.*

systematic study. Specialist monographs (based on exhibition catalogs) have now been devoted to illustrated title-page design in Wittenberg and to the Luther Bible.[34] There is also a fine reproduction edition of the early catalog of Wittenberg University Library.[35] Strasbourg, the second city of Protestant publishing in the empire, has fared better, thanks largely to Miriam Usher Chrisman's pioneering study of Strasbourg imprints and subsequent monograph treatment of the same subject.[36] But there is no comparative study of Nuremberg, Augsburg, or Protestant print in the Low German language zone of northern Germany. The role of music in the dissemination of the Reformation is explored in two important monographs by Rebecca Wagner Oettinger and Alexander Fisher.[37] This apart, much of the most original and groundbreaking work has been devoted to the previously ignored subject of Luther's Catholic opponents, who, while undoubtedly cautious of the implications of public debate, did engage the polemical debate with a vigor not always recognized. To the work of David Bagchi on Luther's Catholic opponents must now be added important monographs by Frank Aurich and Christoph Volkmar.[38] The importance of print to traditional religion, before but also during the Reformation, is the subject of work on a published sermon epitome by Anne Thayer.[39] Attention has also turned to the provision of published literature for the Lutheran peoples of Europe in the second half of the sixteenth century. Pending the publication of an important monograph study of the pamphlet literature of the Magdeburg resistance movement to Charles V,[40] much of this work is embedded in major ongoing collaborative research projects, such as the *Database Sources Confessionalization, 1548–1577/80,* of the University of Mainz.[41] The radical Reformation is also well represented in bibliographic projects, not least in the series *Bibliotheca Dissidentium.*[42]

In the Swiss Confederation, Zurich strangely never developed a print culture commensurate with the towering status of its two major Reformers, Ulrich Zwingli and Heinrich Bullinger. Bullinger's influence was felt largely

---

[34]Strehle, *Cranach im Detail*; and Reinitzer, *Biblia deutsch.*

[35]Kusokawa, *Wittenberg University Library Catalogue.*

[36]Chrisman, *Bibliography of Strasbourg Imprints*; and Chrisman, *Conflicting Visions of Reform.*

[37]Oettinger, *Music as Propaganda*; and Fisher, *Music and Religious Identity.*

[38]Bagchi, *Luther's Earliest Opponents*; Aurich, *Die Anfänge des Buchdrucks*; and Volkmar, *Die Heiligenerhebung Bennos von Meissen.*

[39]Thayer, *Penitence, Preaching and the Coming of the Reformation.*

[40]Rein, *Chancery of God.*

[41]http://www.litdb.evtheol.uni-mainz.de/databank/index.php.

[42]*Bibliotheca Dissidentium.*

through his correspondence, but also in his printed works, the subject of a fine and painstaking bibliography by Staedtke. These works formed the mainstay of the published editions of Zurich's preeminent (and for much of the time, only) publishing house, Froschover's, analyzed in a recent article by Urs Lau.[43] There is also a serviceable bibliography of Zurich publications.[44] Urs Lau has also recently published a painstaking reconstruction of Bullinger's private library. That Zurich publishing did not develop beyond these limits may partly be attributed to the established position of Basle in the international publishing world, a subject that badly requires a modern study.[45]

In the Francophone world, one should first of all treat the particular case of Geneva. Geneva has always been especially well served by its bibliographers, who have charted the blossoming from exceptionally modest beginnings of one of Europe's major publishing centers, fueled by the international popularity of the works of John Calvin and of the French Protestant Bible. The bibliography of Genevan print published by Chaix, Dufour, and Moekli is now being replaced by the work of Jean-François Gilmont, already responsible for the fine bibliography of the works of Jean Calvin, published in three volumes between 1991 and 2000.[46] Gilmont has currently accumulated information on over four thousand Genevan imprints, in French and Latin. This work will also substantially replace Gardy's venerable bibliography of Theodore de Bèze, at least for works published in Geneva; for Bèze, the St. Andrews French Vernacular Book Project has also contributed a large number of previously unknown editions published in France at the beginning of the French Wars of Religion.[47] This fundamental bibliographic work is the basis of a body of interpretative scholarship, including Gilmont's own *Calvin et le livre imprimé* and an important collection of essays.[48] The economics of the Genevan book industry are considered in two older monographs and in the more recent work of Ingeborg Jostock.[49]

Looking beyond Geneva, knowledge of French Protestant printing has been transformed, particularly for the early decades of the sixteenth

[43]Lau, "Die Zürcher Buch- und Lesekultur."
[44]Vischer, *Bibliographie des Zürcher Druckschriften*; and Vischer, *Zürcher Einblattdrucke*.
[45]Bietenholz, *Basle and France in the Sixteenth Century*.
[46]Chaix, *Les Livres imprimés*; and Gilmont and Rodolphe, *Bibliotheca Calviniana*.
[47]Gardy, *Bibliographie des oeuvres théologiques*.
[48]Gilmont, *Jean Calvin*; and Gilmont, *Le livre et ses secrets*.
[49]Jostock, "La censure au quotidien."

century, by the work of Francis Higman. His discoveries of previously unknown French translations of Luther's works are set out in a series of essays now available in a collected volume, *Lire et découvrir*.[50] For French Bibles, the standard work remains Bettye Chambers's *Bibliography of French Bibles*, reinforced by a specialist study of the maps and diagrams developed for these iconic publications.[51] There is also an ongoing project to establish a parallel bibliography of the French Protestant Psalter, perhaps the archetypal book of militant French Protestantism. For the period of the religious wars, earlier bibliographic studies of printing at La Rochelle and Orléans can be supplemented by new work on the Orléans press of Eloy Gibier by Jean-François Gilmont, and on Protestant printing in Caen and Lyon by Andrew Pettegree.[52] Important French Protestant authors such as Simon Goulart, Philippe du Plessis Mornay, Jean de l'Espine, and Antoine de La Roche Chandieu are also the subject of recent and ongoing studies.

In France, Protestant domination of the printing press was never uncontested, yet the skill with which Catholic authors exploited the press has been slow to be recognized. An older tradition of scholarship, in which the robust polemical style of these Catholic authors was widely deprecated, is represented by Frank Giese's study of Artus Désiré, who was in fact a subtle and effective defender of traditional values.[53] A more sensitive evaluation of the skill shown by Catholic authors (often doctors of the Sorbonne, writing away from their natural medium of Latin) is provided in recent monograph studies by Christopher Elwood and Luc Racaut.[54]

In the Netherlands, the standard work on Luther remains Vischer's *Luthers geschriften in de Nederlanden*, sadly never translated into English. More recent discoveries of German Protestant influences are explored by Andrew Johnston. Early Dutch Bibles have also been the subject of systematic study.[55] The emergence of Calvinism in the Netherlands is charted in

[50]Higman, "Luther et la piété de l'église gallicane"; Higman, "Theology for the Layman"; and Higman, *Lire et découvrir*.

[51]Chambers, *Bibliography of French Bibles*; and Delano-Smith and Morley Ingram, *Maps in Bibles*.

[52]Droz, *L'imprimerie à La Rochelle*, vol. 3, *La veuve Berton*; Droz, *L'imprimerie à La Rochelle*, vol. 1, *Barthélémy Berton*; Desgraves, *L'imprimerie à La Rochelle*, vol. 2, *Les Haultin*; Desgraves, *Eloi Gibier*; Pettegree, "Protestantism, Publication and the French Wars of Religion"; Pettegree, "Protestant Printing"; and Gilmont, "La première diffusion."

[53]Giese, *Artus Désiré*.

[54]Elwood, *Body Broken*; and Racaut, *Hatred in Print*.

[55]Rosier, *Bible in Print*; and Den Hollander, *De Nederlandse Bijbelvertalingen*.

the bibliographic investigations of Willem Heijting (on catechisms and confessions of faith) and Andrew Pettegree (on the exile printing center Emden, the northern Geneva).[56] But the most fundamental work is that of Paul Valkema Blouw, who succeeded, in a series of intricate bibliographic case studies pursued in parallel with his work on the *Typographia Batavae*, in establishing the corpus of works published by a series of largely obscure or even wholly unknown printers. These men often published in conditions of great secrecy in relatively obscure corners of the Netherlands away from the main centers of population—their rediscovery represents bibliographic detective work at its most masterly. These articles, translated by Alastair Hamilton, are mostly to be found in the Dutch bibliographic journal *Quaerendo*. Hamilton has made his own significant contribution to the field through editions of the major works of Dutch dissident thinkers such as Hendrik Nikaes.[57] In this way, the enduring Anabaptist strand of Dutch dissent has not been neglected. For the period of the Dutch Revolt, considerable attention has also been devoted to satirical prints and woodcuts that spread like a virus through the cities of Flanders and Holland, pouring scorn and opprobrium on the Spanish ruling power. Here are found both valuable collections of the prints (often in exhibition catalogs) and the beginnings of analytic work, represented most accessibly in recent articles published by Alastair Duke.

In Scandinavia, the introduction of a state-sponsored Lutheran Reformation did not stimulate a robust vernacular print culture. The limited output of the Danish and Scandinavian presses is reviewed by Anne Rijsing and Remi Kick in the articles in the accessible and valuable collection *The Reformation and the Book*.[58] Scotland was another place where a successful Protestant Reformation largely preceded the establishment of an indigenous publishing industry. Even in the later stages of the century, a close, largely dependent relationship with printers in London and continental Europe could not entirely be avoided. In the case of Italy, the cause of Evangelical reform inevitably became tangled with the larger conflicts over authority in the Roman church and the debate, conducted at the highest levels of the hierarchy, over how the Catholic Church should respond theologically to the challenge of the Reformation. Interest in the Evangelical doctrines found its echo in a tentative attempt to make the works of the

---

[56]Heijting, *De catechisme en confessies*; and Pettegree, *Emden and the Dutch Revolt*.
[57]Hamilton, *Documenta anabaptistica Neerlandica*.
[58]Rijsing, "Book and the Reformation."

northern Reformers known through vernacular Italian editions. These works were published under the auspices, sometimes even disguised as their work, of the group of reform-minded writers and churchmen known as the *spirituali*. These rare and interesting editions are surveyed in the article contributed by Ugo Rozzo and Silvana Seidel Menchi to Jean-François Gilmont's collection *The Reformation and the Book*.[59]

Charting the difficult and dangerous work of bringing the Evangelical gospel to Spain was the life work of Gordon Kinder, pursued through a series of bibliographic and biographical studies of the major figures of Spanish Evangelism.[60] In truth, the perils of the enterprise were such that Evangelical publishing made only a limited impact on the Iberian Peninsula. Despite the difficult working conditions, many print workers from northern lands (particularly France) still sought to make a living in Spain, where their skills were much in demand. Some inevitably ran afoul of the authorities. The meticulous files kept by the Inquisition reveal a great deal about print shop practice and about the itinerant lifestyle of print shop workers.[61] Most Spanish dissidents made their most substantial contribution to the Evangelical movement while abroad, in the cities of the Swiss Confederation, in the Netherlands, or in England.[62]

The role of print in the English Reformation had not been a leading feature of the debates that have consumed scholars since the concept of the rapid and largely painless triumph of Protestantism was first subjected to sustained criticism some thirty years ago. In this context, the descent into the archives stimulated by the attempt to chart the slow progress of Protestant penetration in English county communities led to a different type of monograph study. It is possible too that the early success of the *Short Title Catalogue* in establishing the corpus of English print has meant that the absence of a sense of fundamental discovery had led to a comparative lack of interest in the role of English print. This relative neglect may now be in the process of being corrected. The dependence of English Protestantism on continental imports in the first generation of reform had been remarked, as had the extraordinary transformation of the London printing industry under Edward VI, though this still awaits systematic study. The recognition of the importance of the publications of the Marian exiles in

[59]Rozzo and Seidel, "Book and the Reformation."
[60]Kinder, *Spanish Protestants and Reformers.*
[61]Griffin, *Journeymen-Printers, Heresy, and the Inquisition.*
[62]Kinder, *Casiodoro De Reina*; and Kinder, *Confessión de fe Christiana.*

keeping the Protestant faith alive has not been matched by a similarly systematic exploration of Catholic printing in England during the same years. The raw materials for such a study certainly exist, not just in the ESTC and EEBO but also in the numerous individual printer biographies embedded in the new *Dictionary of National Biography*[63] and in the systematic mapping of book collecting in the successive volumes of the English Renaissance Libraries series.

In bibliographic terms, the second half of the sixteenth century has fared rather better. The debate over the English Reformation concentrated attention on the reign of Elizabeth, when historians now believe Protestantism established a real resonance with a substantial mass of the population. The role of the printed book in this process has received a substantial amount of attention, not least in Ian Green's monumental (and ongoing) three-volume study of English Protestant book culture.[64] The role of cheap print in disseminating the principles of Protestantism among the broader population is one subject of a monograph by Tessa Watt; Adam Fox has offered a sensitive exploration of the interface between print, manuscript, and oral culture.[65] At the other end of the theological spectrum, the influence of Calvin's writings in England (and in English) is analyzed in articles by Francis Higman and Andrew Pettegree; full details of the editions can be found in Jean-François Gilmont's exhaustive bibliography.[66] The impact of different continental authors on English readership can also be gauged in the inventories of books compiled from Cambridge inventories by Elizabeth Leedham-Green.[67]

The organization of the London print industry can be followed in the eighty individual contributions contained in the two relevant volumes of the *Cambridge History of the Book in Britain*.[68] One of the editors of this project, David McKitterick, has also charted the uncertain fortunes of academic publishing in England in his history of the Cambridge University Press.[69] Other specialist aspects of the book trade in England are studied in

---

[63]The dictionary is also available online through monthly, quarterly, or yearly subscription to individuals or through institutions: http://www.oxforddnb.com/.

[64]Green, *Christian's ABC*; and Green, *Print and Protestantism*.

[65]Watt, *Cheap Print and Popular Piety*; and Fox, *Oral and Literate Culture*.

[66]Higman, "Calvin's Works in Translation"; and Pettegree, "Reception of Calvinism in Britain."

[67]Leedham-Green, *Books in Cambridge Inventories*.

[68]Hellinga and Trapp, *Cambridge History of the Book in Britain*, vol. 3, *1400–1557*; and Barnard and Mckenzie, *Cambridge History of the Book in Britain*, vol. 4, *1557–1695*.

[69]McKitterick, *History of Cambridge University Press*, vol. 1, *Printing and the Book Trade in Cambridge*.

Krummel's monograph on music printing and in various articles on the publication history of Foxe's book of martyrs scattered through the serial volumes of essays sponsored by the British Academy John Foxe project.[70] Finally, the early halting beginnings of the book in Colonial America are the subject of a fine volume edited by Hugh Amory and David D. Hall, the first volume of the *Cambridge History of the Book in America*.[71]

For the Reformation, the book was always a potent instrument; for that reason the dissemination of the word in print was never without strict controls. For the most part—and this is a point that needs emphasis—these controls were developed and maintained by the industry itself. The publication of almost any book in the sixteenth century involved an element of financial risk (to this the early publications of Luther in the 1520s were almost certainly a shining exception, which is why they were so popular with printers). So the publisher of religious works, whether these were a lucrative catechism or a stately Latin biblical commentary, required a guarantee that their market would not be spoiled by an opportunist competitor. For this reason, all of Europe's book markets developed systems of privilege to protect the interests of publishers—in the established book markets, these systems were generally in place before the Reformation.[72]

The competition of ideas with the dawn of Protestantism brought a new edge to this desire to control markets, where not only economic rivals, but also dissident theologies were seen to threaten social harmony. In Germany, the very dispersed nature of political power made the circulation of books especially hard to control; elsewhere, the governing powers could build naturally on existing mechanisms of control to impose strict censorship. The pioneer in this regard was the regime of Charles V in the Netherlands, but France soon followed suit, and soon an *Index of Prohibited Books* was a standard feature of all European Catholic cultures.[73] Protestant regimes also developed systems of regulation to ensure that only works in harmony with the prevailing local confession could be published. This prior inspection of texts was especially firmly enforced in Geneva.[74] In England, the establishment of the Stationers' Company brought together the twin goals of industry regulation and intellectual control. The records

---

[70]Krummel, *English Music Printing*; and Smith, *Thomas East and Music Publishing*.

[71]Amory and Hall, *History of the Book in America*, vol. 1, *The Colonial Book*.

[72]Armstrong, *Before Copyright*.

[73]Reusch, *Der Index der verboten Bücher*; Putnam, *Censorship of the Church of Rome*; and Grendler, *Roman Inquisition and the Venetian Press*.

[74]Chaix, *Recherches sur l'imprimerie*.

generated by these two forms of regulation—prior control and prohibition of books already on the market—in fact form a valuable source of information for books that may have existed but now appear to be lost.[75] Other sources of information on such lost books are the early encyclopedic bibliographic projects of Antoine du Verdier or Du Croix du Maine, and the early booksellers' catalogs, such as those produced for the Frankfurt Fair.[76] It is, for historians, one of the great scholarly conundrums to come to a realistic estimate of how large a proportion of the books published in the Reformation era may now be totally lost. The best approach may be to postulate highly differentiated rates of survival. It is likely that almost all editions of works by a man as famous as Luther survive in at least one copy, because they would have been preserved as highly collectible—such was Luther's renown, even in his own lifetime. Large-scale books, such as folio Bibles and Latin commentaries, are also unlikely to have disappeared entirely. But small books by anonymous authors have probably survived far less well. At the end of the nineteenth century a small cache of Dutch Evangelical books was unearthed in a castle in the Netherlands. Of the seven books in the cache, only two were previously known through a surviving library copy. Only a few years ago, a second discovery, this time in the rafter of a house being renovated, produced a further three previously unknown editions (of five books in the bundle). It is an enticing thought what new discoveries may await historians of the Reformation as the systematic logging of books in large and small libraries around the world increases the corpus of information at the historian's disposal.

Bibliography

ELECTRONIC RESOURCES

The British Library, Incunabula Collections: http://www.bl.uk/collections/hoinc.html.
Catálogo colectivo del patrimonio bibliográfico español:
  http://www.mcu.es/ccpb/ccpb-eng.html
Database Sources Confessionalization, 1548–1577/80, University of Mainz:
  http://www.litdb.evtheol.uni-mainz.de/databank/index_front.php
Early English Books Online: http://eebo.chadwyck.com/home
Edit 16. *Censimento delle edizioni italiane del XVI secolo.* http://edit16.iccu.sbn.it/
Electronic Short Title Catalog, British Library: http://estc.bl.uk
IDC: http://www.idc.nl/.
Incunabula Short Title Catalog: http://picarta.pica.nl/login/DB=3.29/LNG=EN/.

[75]Bujanda, *Index des livres interdits.*
[76]*La bibliothèque d'Antoine dv Verdier* (Lyon: Honorati, 1585); and *Premier volume de la bibliothèque de la Croix du Maine* (Paris: Langelier, 1584).

Istituto Centrale per il Catálogo Unico delle Biblioteche Italiane e per le Informazioni Bibliografiche: http://www.iccu.sbn.it

Oxford Dictionary of National Biography: http://www.oxforddnb.com/

St. Andrews French Vernacular Book Project: http://www.st-andrews.ac.uk/reformation/book/

VD16: http://www.vd16.de

PRINTED SOURCES

Amory, Hugh, and David D. Hall. *A History of the Book in America.* Vol. 1, *The Colonial Book in the Atlantic World.* Cambridge: Cambridge University Press, 2000.

Anderson, Dorothy, in collaboration with Walter L. Strauss. *The German Single-Leaf Woodcut, 1600–1700: A Pictorial Catalogue.* 2 vols. New York: Abaris, 1977.

Armstrong, Elizabeth A. *Before Copyright: The French Book-Privilege System 1498–1526.* Cambridge: Cambridge University Press, 1990.

Aurich, Frank. *Die Anfänge des Buchdrucks in Dresden: Die Emserpresse, 1524–1526.* Dresden: Sächsische Landesbibliothek, 2000.

Bagchi, David V. N. *Luther's Earliest Opponents: Catholic Controversialists, 1518–1525.* Minneapolis, MN: Fortress, 1991.

Barnard, John, and D. F. Mckenzie. *The Cambridge History of the Book in Britain.* Vol. 4, *1557–1695.* Cambridge: Cambridge University Press, 2002.

Baudrier, Henri-Louis, Julien Baudrier, and Georges Tricou. *Bibliographie lyonnaise: Recherches sur les imprimeurs, libraires, relieurs et fondeurs de lettres de Lyon au XVIe siècle.* 12 vols. Lyon: Librairie ancienne d'Auguste Brun, 1895–1921.

Benzing, Josef. *Lutherbibliographie.* Baden-Baden: Heitz, 1966.

Bibliotheca Dissidentium: Répertoire des non-conformistes religieux des seizième et dix-septième siècles. 23 vols. Baden-Baden: Koerner, 1980–2004.

Bietenholz, Peter G. *Basle and France in the Sixteenth Century: The Basle Humanists and Printers in Their Contacts with Francophone Culture.* Toronto: University of Toronto Press, 1971.

Blouw, Paul Valkema. *Typographia Batava, 1541–1600.* Nieuwkoop: de Graaf, 1998.

Bujanda, Jesús Martínez de, ed. *Index des livres interdits.* 10 vols. Geneva: Droz, 1984–96.

Chaix, Paul. *Recherches sur l'imprimerie à Genève de 1550 à 1564: Etude bibliographique, économique et littéraire.* Geneva: Droz, 1954.

——, Alain Dufour, and Gustave Moeckli. *Les Livres imprimés à Genève de 1550 à 1600.* Geneva: Droz, 1966.

Chambers, Bettye Thomas. *Bibliography of French Bibles: Fifteenth- and Sixteenth-Century French-Language Editions of the Scriptures.* Geneva: Droz, 1983.

Chrisman, Miriam. *Bibliography of Strasbourg Imprints, 1480–1599.* New Haven, CT: Yale University Press, 1982.

——. *Conflicting Visions of Reform: German Lay Propaganda Pamphlets, 1519–1530.* Atlantic Highlands, NJ: Humanities Press, 1996.

Cockx-Indestege, Elly, and Geneviève Glorieux. *Belgica typographica 1541–1600: Catalogus librorum impressorum ab anno MDXLI ad annum MDC in regionibus quae nunc Regni Belgarum partes sunt.* Nieuwkoop: de Graaf, 1968–94.

Crofts, Richard A. "Books, Reform and Reformation." *Archiv für Reformationsgechichte* 71 (1980): 21–36.

——. "Printing, Reform and the Catholic Reformation in Germany (1521–1545)." *Sixteenth Century Journal* 16 (1985): 369–81.

Delano-Smith, Catherine, and Elizabeth Morley Ingram. *Maps in Bibles, 1500–1600: An Illustrated Catalogue.* Geneva: Droz, 1991.

Den Hollander, Arie Nicolaas Jan. *De Nederlandse Bijbelvertalingen 1522–1545.* Nieuwkoop: de Graaf, 1997.

Desgraves, Louis. *Eloi Gibier imprimeur à Orléans (1536–1588).* Geneva: Droz, 1966.

———. *L'imprimerie à La Rochelle.* Vol. 2, *Les Haultin, 1571–1623.* Geneva: Droz, 1960.

———. *Répertoire bibliographique des livres imprimés en France au seizième siècle.* Baden-Baden: Heitz, 1968–80.

Droz, Eugénie. *L'imprimerie à La Rochelle.* Vol. 1, *Barthélémy Berton, 1563–1573.* Geneva: Droz, 1960.

———. *L'imprimerie à La Rochelle.* Vol. 3, *La veuve Berton et Jean Portau, 1573–1589.* Geneva: Droz, 1960.

Dutch Pamphlets, 1486–1853. Microfiche edition of the collection of pamphlets in the Royal Library in the Hague cataloged by W. P. C. Knuttel. Zug: IDC, 1972–82. Commonly known as the Knuttel Collection.

Edwards, Mark. *Printing, Propaganda and Martin Luther.* Berkeley: University of California Press, 1994.

———. "Statistics on Sixteenth-Century Printing." In *The Process of Change in Early Modern Europe,* edited by P. Bebb and S. Marshall, 149–63. Athens: Ohio University Press, 1988.

Eisenstein, Elizabeth. *The Printing Press as an Agent of Change.* Cambridge: Cambridge University Press, 1982.

Elwood, Christopher. *The Body Broken: The Calvinist Doctrine of the Eucharist and the Symbolization of Power in Sixteenth-Century France.* Oxford: Oxford University Press, 1999.

Febvre, Lucien, and Henri Martin. *The Coming of the Book: The Impact of Printing, 1450–1800.* London: NLB, 1976.

Fisher, Alexander J. *Music and Religious Identity in Counter-Reformation Augsburg, 1580–1630.* St. Andrews Studies in Reformation History. Aldershot: Ashgate, 2004.

Fox, Adam. *Oral and Literate Culture in England, 1500–1700.* Oxford: Oxford University Press, 2000.

Gardy, Frederic, ed. *Bibliographie des oeuvres théologiques, littéraires, historiques et juridiques de Théodore de Bèze.* Geneva: Droz, 1960.

Geisberg, Max. *The German Single-Leaf Woodcut, 1500–1550.* 4 vols. Revised and edited by Walter L. Strauss. New York: Hacker Art Books, 1974.

Giese, Frank S. *Artus Désiré: Priest and Pamphleteer of the Sixteenth Century.* Chapel Hill: University of North Carolina Press, 1973.

Gilmont, Jean-François. *Jean Calvin et le livre imprimé.* Geneva: Droz, 1997.

———. "La première diffusion des *Mémoires de Condé* par Éloi Gibier en 1562–1563." In *Le livre dans l'Europe de la Renaissance: Actes du XXVIIIe Colloque international d'études humanistes de Tours,* edited by P. Aquilon and H.-J. Martin, 58–70. Paris: Promodis, 1988. A revised and updated version of this article also appears in a recent volume of Gilmont's collected papers, *Le livre et ses secrets,* 191–212.

———. *Le livre et ses secrets.* Geneva: Droz, 2003.

———, and Peter Rodolphe. *Bibliotheca Calviniana: Les oeuvres de Jean Calvin publiés au XVIe siècle.* 3 vols. Geneva: Droz, 1991–2000.

Green, Ian. *The Christian's ABC: Catechisms and Catechizing in England, c. 1530–1740.* Oxford: Clarendon Press, 1996.

———. *Print and Protestantism in Early Modern England*. Oxford: Oxford University Press, 2000.

Grendler, Paul. *The Roman Inquisition and the Venetian Press, 1540–1605*. Princeton, NJ: Princeton University Press, 1977.

Griffin, Clive. *Journeymen-Printers, Heresy, and the Inquisition in Sixteenth-Century Spain*. Oxford: Oxford University Press, 2005.

Gültingen, Sybille von. *Bibliographie des livres imprimés à Lyon au seizième siècle*. 4 vols. Baden-Baden: Koerner, 1992–96.

Hamilton, Alastair, ed. *Documenta anabaptistica Neerlandica*. Leiden: Brill, 1988.

Harris, Neil. "Tribal Lays and the History of the Fingerprint." In *Many into One: Problems and Opportunities in Creating Shared Catalogues of Older Books*, edited by David Shaw, 21–72. London: Consortium of European Research Libraries, 2006.

Heijting, W. *De catechisme en confessies in de Nederlandse Reformatie tot 1585*. 2 vols. Nieuwkoop: de Graaf, 1989.

Hellinga, Lotte, and John Goldfinch. *Bibliography and the Study of 15th Century Civilization*. London: British Library, 1987.

———. "Ten Years of the Incunabula Short-Title Catalogue (ISTC)." *Bulletin du Bibliophile* (1990): 125–31.

Hellinga, Lotte, and Joseph Burney Trapp. *The Cambridge History of the Book in Britain*. Vol. 3, *1400–1557*. Cambridge: Cambridge University Press, 1999.

Higman, Francis. "Calvin's Works in Translation." In *Calvinism in Europe, 1540–1620*, edited by Andrew Pettegree, A. C. Duke, and Gillian Lewis, 82–99. Cambridge: Cambridge University Press, 1994.

———. *Lire et découvrir: La circulation des idées au temps de la Réforme*. Geneva: Droz, 1998.

———. "Luther et la piété de léglise gallicane: Le Livre de vraye et parfaicte oraison." *Revue d'Histoire et de philosophie religieuses* 63 (1983): 91–111.

———. "Theology for the Layman in the French Reformation." *The Library* 6 (1987): 105–27.

Index Aureliensis: Catalogus Librorum Sedecimo Saeculo Impressorum. 13 vols. Baden-Baden: Koerner, 1965–2003.

Jostock, I. "La censure au quotidien: Le contrôle de l'imprimerie à Genève, 1560–1600." In *The Sixteenth-Century French Religious Book*, edited by Andrew Pettegree, Paul Neave Nelles, and Philip Connor, 210–38. St. Andrews Studies in Reformation History. Aldershot: Ashgate, 2001.

Kick, R. "The Book and the Reformation in the Kingdom of Sweden." In *The Reformation and the Book*, edited by Jean-François Gilmont and translated by Karin Maag. St. Andrews Studies in Reformation History. Aldershot: Ashgate, 1998.

Kinder, Arthur Gordon. *Casiodoro De Reina: Spanish Reformer of the Sixteenth Century*. London: Tamesis, 1975.

———. *Spanish Protestants and Reformers in the Sixteenth Century: A Bibliography*. London: Grant & Culter, 1983.

Köhler, Hans-Joachim, ed. *Flugschriften als Massenmedium der Reformationszeit: Beiträge zum Tübinger Symposion 1980*. Stuttgart: Klett-Cotta, 1981.

Krummel, Donald W. *English Music Printing, 1553–1700*. London: Bibliographical Society, 1975.

Kusokawa, Sachiko. *A Wittenberg University Library Catalogue of 1536*. Binghamton, NY: Medieval and Renaissance Texts and Studies, 1995.

Leedham-Green, Elizabeth S. *Books in Cambridge Inventories: Book-Lists from Vice-Chancellor's Court Probate Inventories in the Tudor and Stuart Periods.* Cambridge: Cambridge University Press, 1986.

Lau Urs B. "Die Zürcher Buch- und Lesekultur, 1520–1575." In *Heinrich Bullinger und seine Zeit*, edited by Emidio Campi, 61–90. Zurich: Theologischer Verlag, 2003.

McKitterick, David. *A History of Cambridge University Press.* Vol. 1, *Printing and the Book Trade in Cambridge, 1534–1698.* Cambridge: Cambridge University Press, 1992.

Moreau, Brigitte. *Inventaire Chronologique des éditions parisiennes du XVIe siècle.* 5 vols. Paris: Service des travaux historiques de la ville de Paris, 1972–2004.

Nijhoff, Wouter, and Maria Elizabeth Kronenberg. *Nederlandsche Bibliographie van 1500 tot 1540.* 3 vols. The Hague: S'Gravenhage, Nijhoff, 1923–61.

Oettinger, Rebecca Wagner. *Music as Propaganda in the German Reformation.* St. Andrews Studies in Reformation History. Aldershot: Ashgate, 2001.

Pegg, Michael A. *Bibliotheca Lindesiana, and Other Collections of German Sixteenth-Century Pamphlets in Libraries of Britain and France.* Baden-Baden: Koerner, 1977.

———. *A Catalogue of German Reformation Pamphlets (1516–1550) in Swedish Libraries.* Baden-Baden: Koerner, 1995.

———. *Catalogue of German Reformation Pamphlets (1516–1550) in Swiss Libraries.* Baden-Baden: Koerner, 1983.

Pettegree, Andrew. *Emden and the Dutch Revolt: Exile and the Development of Reformed Protestantism.* Oxford: Oxford University Press, 1992.

———. *The French Book and the European Book World.* Leiden: Brill, 2007.

———. "Protestantism, Publication and the French Wars of Religion: The Case of Caen." In *Continuity and Change: The Harvest of Late-Mediaeval and Reformation History*, edited by Robert Bast and Andrew Gow, 109–32. Leiden: Brill, 2000.

———. "Protestant Printing during the French Wars of Religion: The Lyon Press of Jean Saugrain." In *Essays Presented to Heiko Oberman on His Seventieth Birthday*, edited by Thomas Brady Jr. and James Tracy, 163–82. Leiden: Brill, 2003.

———. "The Reception of Calvinism in Britain." In *Calvinus Sincerioris Religionis Vindex: Calvin as Protector of the Purer Religion*, edited by Wilhelm H. Neuser and Brian G. Armstrong, 267–89. Kirksville, MO: Truman State University Press, 1997.

———, and Matthew Hall. "The Reformation and the Book: A Reconsideration." *Historical Journal* 47 (2004): 785–808.

———, Malcolm Walsby, and Alexander Wilkinson, eds. *French Vernacular Books: Books Published in the French Language before 1601.* Leiden: Brill, 2007.

Pollard, Alfred W., and Gilbert Richard Redgrave. *A Short Title Catalogue of Books Printed in England, Scotland and Ireland, and of English Books Printed Abroad, 1475–1640.* 3 vols. London: Bibliographical Society, 1926. London: Bibliographical Society, 1976–91.

Putnam, George Palmer. *The Censorship of the Church of Rome.* 2 vols. London: Putnam Sons, 1906.

Racaut, Luc. *Hatred in Print: Catholic Propaganda and Protestant Identity during the French Wars of Religion.* St. Andrews Studies in Reformation History. Aldershot: Ashgate, 2002.

Rein, Nathan. *The Chancery of God: Protestant Propaganda against the Empire, Magdeburg 1546–1551.* St. Andrews Studies in Reformation History. Aldershot: Ashgate, 2007.

Reina, Casiodoro de. *Confesión de fe Christiana = The Spanish Protestant Confession of Faith: London, 1560/61.* Edited from the sole surviving copy of the bilingual edition by Arthur Gordon Kinder. Exeter: University of Exeter Press, 1988.

Reinitzer, Heimo, ed. *Biblia deutsch: Luthers Bibelübersetzung und ihre Tradition.* Wolfenbüttel: Herzog August Bibliothek, 1983.

Renouard, Pierre. *Imprimeurs et libraires Parisiens du XVe siècle.* 5 vols. Paris: Service des travaux historiques de la ville de Paris, 1964–91.

Reusch, Franz Heinrich. *Der Index der verboten Bücher; ein Beitrag zur Kirchen- und Literaturgeschichte.* 2 vols. Bonn: Cohen & Sohn, 1883–85.

Rijsing, A. "The Book and the Reformation in Denmark and Norway, 1523–1540." In *The Reformation and the Book,* edited by Jean-François Gilmont and translated by Karin Maag. St. Andrews Studies in Reformation History. Aldershot: Ashgate, 1998.

Rosier, Bart A. *The Bible in Print: Netherlandish Bible Illustrations in the Sixteenth Century.* 2 vols. Leiden: Brill, 1997.

Rozzo, U., and S. Seidel. "The Book and the Reformation in Italy." In *The Reformation and the Book,* edited by Jean-François Gilmont and translated by Karin Maag. St. Andrews Studies in Reformation History. Aldershot: Ashgate, 1998.

Scribner, Robert. *For the Sake of Simple Folk: Popular Propaganda for the German Reformation.* Cambridge: Cambridge University Press, 1981.

Sixteenth Century Pamphlets = Flugschriften des 16. Jahrhunderts. Microfiche collection cataloged by Hans-Joachim Köhler, Hildegard Hebenstreit-Wilfert, and Christoph Weismann. Leiden, IDC, 1978–.

Smith, Jeremy L. *Thomas East and Music Publishing in Renaissance England.* Oxford: Oxford University Press, 2003.

Strauss, Walter. *The German Single-Leaf Woodcut, 1550–1600: A Pictorial Catalogue.* 3 vols. New York: Abaris, 1975.

Strehle, Jutta. *Cranach im Detail: Buchschmuck Lucas Cranachs des Älteren und seiner Werkstatt.* Ausstellung Lutherhalle Wittenberg, 1994.

Thayer, Anne T. *Penitence, Preaching and the Coming of the Reformation.* St. Andrews Studies in Reformation History. Ashgate: Aldershot, 2002.

Verzeichnis der im deutschen Sprachbereich erschienenen Drucke des XVI. Jahrhunderts 25 vols. Stuttgart: Hiersemann, 1983–2000. Commonly known as *VD16.*

Vischer, Manfred. *Bibliographie des Zürcher Druckschriften des 15. und 16. Jahrhunderts.* Baden-Baden: Koerner, 1991.

———. *Zürcher Einblattdrucke des 16. Jahrhunderts.* Baden-Baden: Koerner, 2001.

Volkmar, Christoph. *Die Heiligenerhebung Bennos von Meissen (1523–1524): Spätmittelalterliche Frömmigkeit, landesherrliche Kirchenpolitik und reformatorische Kritik im albertinischen Sachsen in der frühen Reformationszeit.* Münster: Aschendorff, 2002.

Watt, Tessa. *Cheap Print and Popular Piety, 1550–1640.* Cambridge: Cambridge University Press, 1991.

Contributors

ROBERT BIRELEY, SJ, is professor of history at Loyola University, Chicago. He is the author most recently of *The Refashioning of Catholicism, 1450–1700: A Reassessment of the Counter Reformation* (1999) and *The Jesuits and the Thirty Years' War: Kings, Courts and Confessors* (2003), and is working on a biography of Emperor Ferdinand II. He will serve as president of the American Catholic Historical Association in 2008.

AMY NELSON BURNETT is professor of history at the University of Nebraska–Lincoln. She is the author of *Teaching the Reformation: Ministers and Their Message in Basel, 1529–1629* (2006) and *The Yoke of Christ: Martin Bucer and Church Discipline* (1994), as well as several articles and essays on the Reformation in south Germany and Switzerland. She is currently working on a cross-confessional study of sermons printed in Germany between 1518 and 1650.

BARBARA B. DIEFENDORF is professor of history at Boston University. She is the author of *From Penitence to Charity: Pious Women and the Catholic Reformation in France* (2004), *Beneath the Cross: Catholics and Huguenots in Sixteenth-Century Paris* (1991), *Paris City Councillors in the Sixteenth Century: The Politics of Patrimony* (1983), and a number of articles on the social and religious history of early modern France. She is currently working on study of Catholic activism in sixteenth- and seventeenth-century France.

KATHRYN A. EDWARDS is associate professor of history at the University of South Carolina. She is the author of *Families and Frontiers: Re-creating Communities and Boundaries in the Early Modern Burgundies* (2002) and

453

editor of *Werewolves, Witches, and Wandering Spirits: Folklore and Traditional Belief in Early Modern Europe* (2002). She is currently working on a history of European beliefs about ghosts, *Living with Ghosts: The Dead in European Society from the Black Death to the Enlightenment.*

MATT GOLDISH is Samuel M. and Esther Melton Professor of Jewish History and director of the Melton Center for Jewish Studies at the Ohio State University. His books include *Judaism in the Theology of Sir Isaac Newton* (1998) and *The Sabbatean Prophets* (2004).

BRUCE GORDON is professor of modern history at the University of St. Andrews. From 2008, he will be professor of Reformation history at the Yale Divinity School. He is the author of *Clerical Discipline and the Rural Reformation* (1992) and the *Swiss Reformation* (2002). He is writing a biography of John Calvin to appear in 2009 and is leading a research project on the Protestant Latin Bibles of the Sixteenth Century funded by the Arts and Humanities Council in the United Kingdom.

HOWARD HOTSON is fellow and tutor in modern history at St. Anne's College, Oxford. His interests range over the intellectual history of early modern Europe, with a particular focus on Reformed Germany. His recent monograph, *Commonplace Learning: Ramism and Its German Ramifications, 1542–1630* (2007), will be followed by a study of the diaspora of Reformed intellectuals from central Europe during the Thirty Years' War.

CHRISTINE KOOI is associate professor of history at Louisiana State University. She is the author of *Liberty and Religion: Church and State in Leiden's Reformation, 1572–1620* (2000), as well as numerous articles on the Reformation in the Low Countries. She is currently at work on a study of relations between Catholics and Calvinists in the Dutch Republic during the Golden Age.

UTE LOTZ-HEUMANN is an assistant professor at Humboldt University, Berlin. She is the author of *Die doppelte Konfessionalisierung in Irland: Konflikt und Koexistenz im 16. und in der ersten Hälfte des 17. Jahrhunderts* (2000). She has also coauthored (with Stefan Ehrenpreis) an introduction to Reformation historiography for advanced students, *Reformation und konfessionelles Zeitalter, Kontroversen um die Geschichte* (2002). She is currently working on the eighteenth century with a research project on the cultural and social history of spas in Germany.

PETER MARSHALL is professor of early modern religious history at the University of Warwick. His books include *Reformation England 1480–1642* (2003) and *Mother Leakey and the Bishop: A Ghost Story* (2007). He is currently writing a short introduction to the Reformation for Oxford University Press.

R. EMMET MCLAUGHLIN is professor of early modern history at Villanova University. He is the author of *Caspar Schwenckfeld, Reluctant Radical* (1986) and *The Freedom of the Spirit, Social Privilege, and Religious Dissent: Caspar Schwenckfeld and the Schwenckfelders (1996)*, as well as articles on the Radical Reformation and the history of the clergy. His current project is a study of the concept of "Spirit" in early modern Europe.

H. C. ERIK MIDELFORT is the C. Julian Bishko Professor of History and Religious Studies at the University of Virginia. He is the author of books on the history of witchcraft, madness, and demonic possession as well as several translations of books on early modern German history. His most recent book is *Exorcism and Enlightenment: Johann Joseph Gassner and the Demons of Eighteenth-Century Germany* (2005).

ANDREW PETTEGREE is professor of modern history at the University of St. Andrews. He is the author of a number of works including *Europe in the Sixteenth Century* (2002) and *Reformation and the Culture of Persuasion* (2005). He is the founding director of the St. Andrews Reformation Studies Institute and director of the St. Andrews French Book Project.

ALLYSON POSKA is a professor of history at the University of Mary Washington. She is the author of *Regulating the People: The Catholic Reformation in Seventeenth-Century Spain* (1998) and *Women and Authority in Early Modern Spain: The Peasants of Galicia* (2006), which won the 2006 Bainton Prize. Her scholarly work has earned her a 2007–08 American Council of Learned Societies/SSRC/NEH International and Area Studies Fellowship.

LARRY SILVER is the Farquhar Professor of Art History at the University of Pennsylvania. A specialist in painting and graphics of Northern Europe, he has recently authored several books on Netherlandish and German art including *Peasant Scenes and Landscapes* (2006), *Bosch* (2006), and *Marketing Maximilian: The Visual Ideology of a Holy Roman Emperor* (in press).

NICHOLAS TERPSTRA is professor of history at the University of Toronto. He is the author of *Abandoned Children of the Italian Renaissance* (2005) and *Lay Confraternities and Civic Religion in Renaissance Bologna* (1995), and has edited a number of essay collections, including *The Politics of Ritual Kinship: Confraternities and Social Order in Early Modern Italy* (2000). He is currently working on *The Art of Executing Well: Rituals of Execution in Renaissance Italy* and a study of the network of social and financial agencies developed in Renaissance Bologna to aid women in need.

DAVID WHITFORD is associate professor of the history of Christianity at United Theological Seminary. He is the author of *Tyranny and Resistance: The Lutheran Tradition and the Magdeburg Confession* (2001) as well as a number of articles on Martin Luther. He is the associate editor of the *Sixteenth Century Journal*. His book, *Luther: A Guide for the Perplexed,* is forthcoming in 2009.

MERRY WIESNER-HANKS is UWM Distinguished Professor in the Department of History at the University of Wisconsin–Milwaukee. She is the co-editor of the *Sixteenth Century Journal* and the author or editor of many books and articles that have appeared in English, German, Italian, Spanish and Chinese. These include *Early Modern Europe 1450–1789* (2006); *Women and Gender in Early Modern Europe* (2nd ed., 2000), and *Gender in History* (2001).